IFIP Advances in Information
and Communication Technology 297

IFIP – The International Federation for Information Processing

IFIP was founded in 1960 under the auspices of UNESCO, following the First World Computer Congress held in Paris the previous year. An umbrella organization for societies working in information processing, IFIP's aim is two-fold: to support information processing within its member countries and to encourage technology transfer to developing nations. As its mission statement clearly states,

> *IFIP's mission is to be the leading, truly international, apolitical organization which encourages and assists in the development, exploitation and application of information technology for the benefit of all people.*

IFIP is a non-profitmaking organization, run almost solely by 2500 volunteers. It operates through a number of technical committees, which organize events and publications. IFIP's events range from an international congress to local seminars, but the most important are:

- The IFIP World Computer Congress, held every second year;
- Open conferences;
- Working conferences.

The flagship event is the IFIP World Computer Congress, at which both invited and contributed papers are presented. Contributed papers are rigorously refereed and the rejection rate is high.

As with the Congress, participation in the open conferences is open to all and papers may be invited or submitted. Again, submitted papers are stringently refereed.

The working conferences are structured differently. They are usually run by a working group and attendance is small and by invitation only. Their purpose is to create an atmosphere conducive to innovation and development. Refereeing is less rigorous and papers are subjected to extensive group discussion.

Publications arising from IFIP events vary. The papers presented at the IFIP World Computer Congress and at open conferences are published as conference proceedings, while the results of the working conferences are often published as collections of selected and edited papers.

Any national society whose primary activity is in information may apply to become a full member of IFIP, although full membership is restricted to one society per country. Full members are entitled to vote at the annual General Assembly, National societies preferring a less committed involvement may apply for associate or corresponding membership. Associate members enjoy the same benefits as full members, but without voting rights. Corresponding members are not represented in IFIP bodies. Affiliated membership is open to non-national societies, and individual and honorary membership schemes are also offered.

Dimitris Gritzalis   Javier Lopez (Eds.)

Emerging Challenges for Security, Privacy and Trust

24th IFIP TC 11 International Information
Security Conference, SEC 2009
Pafos, Cyprus, May 18–20, 2009
Proceedings

 Springer

Volume Editors

Dimitris Gritzalis
Athens University of Economics and Business, Department of Informatics
Information Security and Infrastructure Protection Research Group
76 Patission Ave., 10434 Athens, Greece
E-mail: dgrit@aueb.gr

Javier Lopez
University of Malaga, Computer Science Department
E.T.S.I. Informatica
Campus Teatinos, 29071 Malaga, Spain
E-mail: jlm@lcc.uma.es

Library of Congress Control Number: Applied for

CR Subject Classification (1998): C.2, D.4.6, H.2.0, H.2.7, K.4.4, K.6.5

ISSN   1868-4238

ISBN-13   978-3-642-10176-2   e-ISBN-13   978-3-642-01244-0

springer.com

© International Federation for Information Processing 2010
Printed in Germany

Printed on acid-free paper   6/3180   5 4 3 2 1 0

Preface

It was an honor and a privilege to chair the 24th IFIP International Information Security Conference (SEC 2009), a 24-year-old event that has become a tradition for information security professionals around the world. SEC 2009 was organized by the Technical Committee 11 (TC-11) of IFIP, and took place in Pafos, Cyprus, during May 18–20, 2009.

It is an indication of good fortune for a Chair to serve a conference that takes place in a country with the natural beauty of Cyprus, an island where the hospitality and friendliness of the people have been going together, hand-in-hand, with its long history.

This volume contains the papers selected for presentation at SEC 2009. In response to the call for papers, 176 papers were submitted to the conference. All of them were evaluated on the basis of their novelty and technical quality, and reviewed by at least two members of the conference Program Committee.

Of the papers submitted, 39 were selected for presentation at the conference; the acceptance rate was as low as 22%, thus making the conference a highly competitive forum.

It is the commitment of several people that makes international conferences possible. That also holds true for SEC 2009. The list of people who volunteered their time and energy to help is really long.

We would like to express our sincere appreciation to the members of the Program Committee, to the external reviewers, and to the authors who trusted their work in our hands. Many thanks go, also, to all conference attendees.

We thank our distinguished keynote speakers, namely, Bart Preneel (Katholieke Universiteit Leuven) and Christos Ellinides (European Commission/DIGIT) for accepting our invitation and for honoring the conference with their presence and their inspired talks.

Last, but by no means least, we thank the local organizers and hosts, first among them being Philippos Peleties and Panikos Masouras, who took care of every detail, so that SEC 2009 would be a successful and memorable event.

Finally, let us express a short personal note. We would like to thank all TC-11 members for giving us the opportunity to serve the SEC 2009 in a PC Chair's capacity.

It was the first time such an opportunity was given to Javier Lopez, the national representative of Spain. It was the third time (SEC 1996/Samos, SEC 2003/Athens, SEC 2009/Pafos) this opportunity was given to Dimitris Gritzalis, the national representative of Greece, who has, thus, already become a kind of …dinosaur in the long history of the SEC conferences.

Dimitris Gritzalis
Javier Lopez

Organization

General Chairs

Philippos Peleties   Cyprus Computer Society, Cyprus
Panikos Masouras   Cyprus Computer Society, Cyprus

Program Chairs

Dimitris Gritzalis   Athens University of Economics and Business, Greece
Javier Lopez   University of Malaga, Spain

Program Committee

Vijay Atluri	Rutgers University, USA
Lujo Bauer	Carnegie Mellon University, USA
Joachim Biskup	Technical University of Dortmund, Germany
Jan Camenisch	IBM Research, Switzerland
Bart de Decker	Katholieke Universiteit Leuven, Belgium
Yves Deswarte	LAAS-CNRS, France
Ed Dawson	Queensland University of Technology, Australia
Jan Eloff	University of Pretoria, South Africa
Simone Fischer-Huebner	Karlstad University, Sweden
Debora Frincke	Pacific Northwest National Laboratory, USA
Steven Furnell	University of Plymouth, UK
Sushil Jajodia	George Mason University, USA
Lech Janczewski	University of Auckland, New Zealand
Sokratis Katsikas	University of Piraeus, Greece
Costas Lambrinoudakis	University of the Aegean, Greece
Fabio Martinelli	National Research Council, Italy
Natalia Miloslavskaya	MEPHI, Russia
Refic Molva	Institut Eurecom, France
Kostas Moulinos	ENISA, European Union
Yuko Murayama	Iwate Prefectural University, Japan
Eiji Okamoto	University of Tsukuba, Japan
Rolf Oppliger	eSecurity, Switzerland
George Pangalos	Aristotle University of Thessaloniki, Greece
Jong-Hyuk Park	Kyungnam University, South Korea
Gunther Pernul	University of Regensburg, Germany
Bart Preneel	Katholieke Universiteit Leuven, Belgium

Sihan Qing	Chinese Academy of Sciences, China
Kai Rannenberg	Goethe University Frankfurt, Germany
Rodrigo Roman	University of Malaga, Spain
Pierangela Samarati	University of Milan (Bicocca), Italy
Sujeet Shenoi	University of Tulsa, USA
Miguel Soriano	Technical University of Catalonia, Spain
Willy Susilo	University of Wollongong, Australia
Stefanie Teufel	University of Freiburg, Switzerland
Bill Tsoumas	Ernst & Young, Greece
Gene Tsudik	University of California (Irvine), USA
Rossouw von Solms	Nelson Mandela Metropolitan University, South Africa
Tatjana Welzer	University of Maribor, Slovenia
Stephen Wolthusen	Gjovik University College, Norway
Louise Yngstrom	University of Stockholm, Sweden
Jianying Zhou	I2R, Singapore

Local Organizing Committee

Yiannos Aletraris	Cyprus Computer Society
Michalis Georgiou	Cyprus Computer Society
George Beitis	Cyprus Computer Society
Elena Stylianou	Cyprus Computer Society

Additonal Reviewers

Albers, Andreas	Fritsch, Lothar
Ardagna, Claudio	Fucks, Ludwig
Balopoulos, Theodoros	Fujihara, Yasuhiro
Belsis, Petros	Gambs, Sebastien
Blass, Erik-Oliver	Geneiatakis, Dimitris
Broser, Christian	Gerber, Mariana
Cutillo, Leucio Antonio	Gmelch, Oliver
Davidson, Alan	Goovaerts, Tom
De Capitani Di Vimercati, Sabrina	Holbl, Marko
De Cock, Danny	Indesteege, Sebastiaan
De Cristofaro, Emiliano	Ji, Qingguang
Desmet, Lieven	Jia, Limin
Diaz, Claudia	Kahl, Christian
Doerbeck, Stefan	Kahr, Caroline
El Defrawy, Karim	Kantzavelou, Ioanna
El Kalam, Anas Abou	Karopoulos, Giorgos
Foresti, Sara	Kim, Jihye
Fritsch, Christoph	Koschinat, Sascha

Li, Gai Cheng
Liesebach, Katja
Lochner, Jan-Hendrik
Ma, Di
Maliga, Daniel
Mallios, Ioannis
Martucci, Leonardo
Matteucci, Ilaria
Meier, Michael
Merten, Patrick
Michailidis, Manos
Munoz-Tapia, Jose Luis
Naessens, Vincent
Netter, Michael
Nigusse, Girma
Norman, Ulrika
Papagiannakopoulos, Panagiotis
Popov, Oliver
Radmacher, Mike
Rekleitis, Evaggelos
Roudier, Yves
Royer, Denis

Schillinger, Rolf
Schluter, Jan
Shafiq, Basit
Shen, Qingni
Simpson, Leonie
Smith, Jason
Solis, John
Soriente, Claudio
Spathoulas, Georgios
Stotzer, Martin
Strufe, Thorsten
Thompson, Kerry-Lyn
Tomas-Buliart, Joan
Troncoso, Carmela
Tschersich, Markus
Tsochou, Aggeliki
Uzun, Ersin
Van Nierk, Johan
Weng, Li
Win, Khin Tan
Zhang, Ge
Zibuschka, Jan

Table of Contents

Identification and Authentication I

Flexible and Transparent User Authentication for Mobile Devices 1
  Nathan Clarke, Sevasti Karatzouni, and Steven Furnell

Combining Authentication, Reputation and Classification to Make
Phishing Unprofitable 13
  Amir Herzberg

Audio CAPTCHA for SIP-Based VoIP 25
  Yannis Soupionis, George Tountas, and Dimitris Gritzalis

Threats and Attacks

Roving Bugnet: Distributed Surveillance Threat and Mitigation 39
  Ryan Farley and Xinyuan Wang

On Robust Covert Channels Inside DNS 51
  Lucas Nussbaum, Pierre Neyron, and Olivier Richard

Discovering Application-Level Insider Attacks Using Symbolic
Execution 63
  *Karthik Pattabiraman, Nithin Nakka, Zbigniew Kalbarczyk, and
  Ravishankar Iyer*

Identification and Authentication II

Custom JPEG Quantization for Improved Iris Recognition Accuracy ... 76
  Gerald Stefan Kostmajer, Herbert Stögner, and Andreas Uhl

On the IPP Properties of Reed-Solomon Codes 87
  *Marcel Fernandez, Josep Cotrina, Miguel Soriano, and
  Neus Domingo*

A Generic Authentication LoA Derivation Model..................... 98
  Li Yao and Ning Zhang

Applications of Cryptography and Information Hiding

Media-Break Resistant eSignatures in eGovernment: An Austrian
Experience 109
  Herbert Leitold, Reinhard Posch, and Thomas Rössler

How to Bootstrap Security for Ad-Hoc Network: Revisited 119
  Wook Shin, Carl A. Gunter, Shinsaku Kiyomoto,
  Kazuhide Fukushima, and Toshiaki Tanaka

Steganalysis of Hydan 132
  Jorge Blasco, Julio C. Hernandez-Castro, Juan M.E. Tapiador,
  Arturo Ribagorda, and Miguel A. Orellana-Quiros

Trusted Computing

On the Impossibility of Detecting Virtual Machine Monitors 143
  Shay Gueron and Jean-Pierre Seifert

Implementation of a Trusted Ticket System 152
  Andreas Leicher, Nicolai Kuntze, and Andreas U. Schmidt

Security Policies

A Policy Based Approach for the Management of Web Browser
Resources to Prevent Anonymity Attacks in Tor 164
  Guillermo Navarro-Arribas and Joaquin Garcia-Alfaro

A Policy Language for Modelling Recommendations 176
  Anas Abou El Kalam and Philippe Balbiani

Validation, Verification, Evaluation

On the Security Validation of Integrated Security Solutions 190
  Andreas Fuchs, Sigrid Gürgens, and Carsten Rudolph

Verification of Security Policy Enforcement in Enterprise Systems 202
  Puneet Gupta and Scott D. Stoller

Optimization of the Controlled Evaluation of Closed Relational
Queries 214
  Joachim Biskup, Jan-Hendrik Lochner, and Sebastian Sonntag

Privacy Protection - Security Assessment

Collaborative Privacy – A Community-Based Privacy Infrastructure 226
  Jan Kolter, Thomas Kernchen, and Günther Pernul

Security and Privacy Improvements for the Belgian eID Technology 237
  Pieter Verhaeghe, Jorn Lapon, Bart De Decker,
  Vincent Naessens, and Kristof Verslype

A Structured Security Assessment Methodology for Manufacturers of
Critical Infrastructure Components 248
Thomas Brandstetter, Konstantin Knorr, and Ute Rosenbaum

Role Mining and Content Protection

Mining Stable Roles in RBAC 259
*Alessandro Colantonio, Roberto Di Pietro, Alberto Ocello, and
Nino Vincenzo Verde*

Privacy-Preserving Content-Based Publish/Subscribe Networks 270
Abdullatif Shikfa, Melek Önen, and Refik Molva

Broadcast Encryption for Differently Privileged 283
Hongxia Jin and Jeffery Lotspiech

Ontology-Based Secure XML Content Distribution 294
*Mohammad Ashiqur Rahaman, Yves Roudier, Philip Miseldine, and
Andreas Schaad*

Security Protocols

NGBPA Next Generation BotNet Protocol Analysis 307
Felix S. Leder and Peter Martini

Non-repudiation Analysis with LySa 318
Mayla Brusò and Agostino Cortesi

A Provably Secure Secret Handshake with Dynamic Controlled
Matching 330
Alessandro Sorniotti and Refik Molva

Towards a Theory of White-Box Security 342
Amir Herzberg, Haya Shulman, Amitabh Saxena, and Bruno Crispo

Access Control

On a Taxonomy of Delegation 353
Quan Pham, Jason Reid, Adrian McCullagh, and Ed Dawson

Efficient Key Management for Enforcing Access Control in Outsourced
Scenarios 364
*Carlo Blundo, Stelvio Cimato, Sabrina De Capitani di Vimercati,
Alfredo De Santis, Sara Foresti, Stefano Paraboschi, and
Pierangela Samarati*

A Probabilistic Bound on the Basic Role Mining Problem and Its
Applications 376
   Alessandro Colantonio, Roberto Di Pietro, Alberto Ocello, and
   Nino Vincenzo Verde

Automating Access Control Logics in Simple Type Theory with
LEO-II 387
   Christoph Benzmüller

Internet and Web Applications Security

In Law We Trust? Trusted Computing and Legal Responsibility for
Internet Security 399
   Yianna Danidou and Burkhard Schafer

Persona: Network Layer Anonymity and Accountability for Next
Generation Internet 410
   Yannis Mallios, Sudeep Modi, Aditya Agarwala, and Christina Johns

Jason: A Scalable Reputation System for the Semantic Web 421
   Sandra Steinbrecher, Stephan Groß, and Markus Meichau

Which Web Browsers Process SSL Certificates in a Standardized
Way? 432
   Ahmad Samer Wazan, Romain Laborde, David W. Chadwick,
   François Barrere, and AbdelMalek Benzekri

Author Index 443

Flexible and Transparent User Authentication for Mobile Devices

Nathan Clarke, Sevasti Karatzouni, and Steven Furnell

Centre for Information Security & Network Research, University of Plymouth,
Plymouth, PL4 8AA, United Kingdom
info@cisnr.org
http://www.cisnr.org

Abstract. The mobile device has become a ubiquitous technology that is capable of supporting an increasingly large array of services, applications and information. Given their increasing importance, it is imperative to ensure that such devices are not misused or abused. Unfortunately, a key enabling control to prevent this, user authentication, has not kept up with the advances in device technology. This paper presents the outcomes of a 2 year study that proposes the use of transparent and continuous biometric authentication of the user: providing more comprehensive identity verification; minimizing user inconvenience; and providing security throughout the period of use. A Non-Intrusive and Continuous Authentication (NICA) system is described that maintains a continuous measure of confidence in the identity of the user, removing access to sensitive services and information with low confidence levels and providing automatic access with higher confidence levels. An evaluation of the framework is undertaken from an end-user perspective via a trial involving 27 participants. Whilst the findings raise concerns over education, privacy and intrusiveness, overall 92% of users felt the system offered a more secure environment when compared to existing forms of authentication.

1 Introduction

Recent years have witnessed a considerable increase in the power and capabilities of mobile devices, with the users of today's smartphones and PDAs having access to a far richer range of features and functionality than they enjoyed a few years ago. Although offering a number of clear benefits, this transition poses serious security considerations for mobile users. With the ability to access and store a wide variety of more sensitive information, the need to ensure this information is not misused or abused is imperative. Whereas the replacement cost arising from loss or theft might previously have been the principal risk associated with mobile devices, unauthorized access to its data could now be a far more significant problem (introducing threats ranging from personal identity theft through to serious corporate loss and increasingly liability).

Given the changing nature of the mobile device and network, it is necessary to consider whether the current authentication on mobile handsets is capable of providing the level of security that is necessary to meet the changing requirements. Even with increasingly large amounts of literature suggesting that secret-knowledge techniques are

D. Gritzalis and J. Lopez (Eds.): SEC 2009, IFIP AICT 297, pp. 1–12, 2009.
© IFIP International Federation for Information Processing 2009

ineffective [5,8], the Personal Identification Number (PIN) is still the most widely used approach on mobile devices. The increasing requirement for protection is evidenced by a survey of 230 business professionals, which found that 81% considered the information on their PDA was either somewhat or extremely valuable. As a result, 70% were interested in having a security system for their PDA [10].

Looking beyond secret-knowledge, two other forms of authentication are available, namely tokens and biometrics. However, only the latter are able to realistically provide more secure mechanisms for user authentication. Tokens rarely authenticate the user, but rather authenticate the presence of the token; with the assumption being the legitimate user is in possession of the token. Moreover, its application within a mobile device context would require a user to remember both the device and token or more commonly simply leave the token in situ within the device (e.g. the use of the SIM card). However, given the evolving nature of mobile devices, simply replacing one authentication mechanism with another is arguably not sufficient. Rather, only through an analysis of the requirements can an effective solution be proposed.

This paper presents the results from a two-year study investigating and proposing a new user authentication approach for mobile devices. The paper begins by presenting the research undertaken to develop and understand the requirements in order to derive the objectives of the system. Section 3 then broadly describes the proposed framework; in particular, focusing upon the key processes that enable security and usability. Section 4 presents the end-user trial of the system, with the final section describing the conclusions and future work.

2   Analysis of Stakeholder Requirements

In order to establish an understanding of stakeholder requirements, a qualitative and quantitative research methodology was undertaken. Stakeholders were largely divided into two groups: end-users of mobile devices and managers of mobile devices/networks (e.g. network operators, system administrators). It was determined that the end-user group, representing the principle stakeholder group, it would be assessed both quantitatively through a survey and qualitatively through a focus-group. It was felt, due to the specialist nature of the other group of stakeholders and getting sufficient access to them, a qualitative focus-group based methodology would be most appropriate. To this end, two activities were undertaken:

1. A survey of end-user attitudes and opinions towards current and future forms of user authentication technologies. A total of 297 participants took part in the survey and complete published results can be found in [1].
2. A focus group activity involving all stakeholders. A total of 12 participants took part and a series of questions were put forward regarding current authentication and the security requirements of current and future services. In order to maximise the usefulness of the focus group, this activity was devised based upon the analysis and findings of the survey. Detailed information on the focus group and its outcomes can be found in [6].

In summary, the survey found that 34% of the 297 respondents did not use any PIN security. In addition, even for those respondents who did use the PIN at switch-on only, 85% would leave their handset on for more than 10 hours a day, thereby undermining any security the PIN might provide. Interestingly, however, it would appear that users do have an appreciation of security, with 85% of respondents in favour of additional security for their device.

Within the focus group these findings were not so evident, with the end-user group finding it difficult to understand why such protection was required. Whilst this was somewhat expected given current usage (with most end-users simply using their device for telephony or texting); the few enterprise-level users of devices (using advanced features such as email and corporate network access) that participated in the focus group understood and agreed with the need for better protection. Moreover, once the possible future uses of the mobile devices were explained to end-users (for instance micro-payments and accessing back accounts), they also understood the need for better security. From the other stakeholder groups, it became evident that existing controls were not sufficient, with system administrators particularly concerned regarding the increasing integration of mobile devices within their organisations network and the effective control and management of them.

When taking the feedback into consideration and reflecting upon all the other requirements, such as: varying hardware configurations and processing capabilities of mobile devices; network versus device centric operation; an enormous end-user population of approximately 2.7 billion [7]; privacy of end-user data (particular biometric based); it became evident that a flexible authentication scheme would be preferable. As no single authentication technique would be suitable for all situations it would be far more appropriate to provide a suite of authentication techniques within an appropriate framework that could provide an overall authentication approach for mobile devices.

From the analysis of stakeholder requirements, it is envisaged that a successful authentication mechanism for mobile devices must address a number of requirements:

- to increase the authentication security beyond secret-knowledge based approaches;
- to provide transparent authentication of the user (within limits) to remove the inconvenience factor from authentication;
- to provide continuous or periodic authentication of the user, so that the confidence in the identity of the user can be maintained throughout the life of the device;
- to link security to service provision, so that for instance the risk associated with sending a text message and accessing a bank account can be understood and be incorporated with the decision making process;
- to provide an architecture that would function (to one extent or another) across the complete range of mobile devices, taking into account the differing hardware configurations, processing capabilities and network connectivity.

From these requirements a Non-Intrusive and Continuous Authentication (NICA) system was devised.

3   Non-Intrusive and Continuous Authentication (NICA) for Mobile Devices

NICA operates by utilising a combination of secret knowledge and biometric techniques within a flexible framework. The framework operates by initially establishing a baseline level of security, using secret knowledge approaches, which progressively increases as the user interacts with their device and biometric samples are captured. Although user authentication will begin rather intrusively (e.g. when the device is switched on for the first time), with the user having to re-authenticate periodically, the system will quickly adapt, and as it does so the reliance upon secret knowledge techniques is replaced by a reliance upon biometrics – where the user will be continuously and non-intrusively authenticated. The result is a highly modular framework that can utilise a wide-range of standardised biometrics, and which is able to take advantage of the different hardware configurations of mobile devices – where a combination of cameras, microphones, keypads etc can be found.

3.1   Proposed Framework

Architecturally this system could take many forms, but it is proposed that a number of key components would be required, such as an ability to capture and authenticate biometric samples, an intelligent controller, administrative capabilities and storage of the biometric profiles and authentication algorithms. Although principally conceived around a client-server topology, the system also has the flexibility of operating in an autonomous mode to ensure security is maintained even during periods with limited or no network connectivity. Figure 1 outlines the functional components of the architecture.

The client-side includes all of the components illustrated in figure 1 and the server-side architecture includes all but the input and output components (the Data Collection engine, Security Status and Intrusion Interface). The implementation of the architecture will differ depending upon the context that a device is being used within. For instance, in a standalone implementation the device has no use for the Communications Engine – as no network exists to which it can connect. Meanwhile, in a client-server topology the components required will vary depending upon the processing split between the server and client. There are numerous reasons why a network administrator may wish to split the processing and control of NICA differently, such as network bandwidth and availability, centralised storage and processing of the biometric templates, and memory requirements of the mobile device. For example, in order to minimise network traffic, the network administrator may require the host device to authenticate user samples locally, or conversely, the administrator may wish the device to only perform pre-processing of input samples and allow the server to perform the authentication, thus removing the majority of the computational overhead from the device, but still reducing the sample size before transmitting across the network.

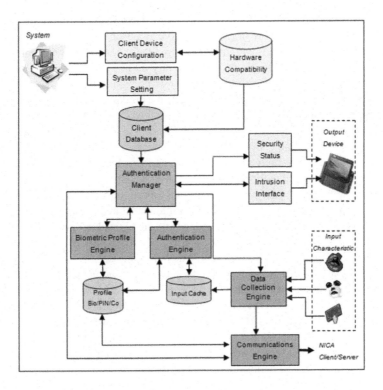

Fig. 1. NICA Architecture

3.2 Security and Usability Processes

The principal objective of the system is to maintain the level of security required commensurate with the services being provided by the device and to achieve this in a user friendly and convenient fashion. To this end, two key processes operate to ensure this:

● Authentication Confidence Level   ● Alert Level

The Authentication Confidence Level (AuCL) process assists in ensuring security through maintaining a continuous level of confidence in the identity of the user. It is a sliding numerical value between -5 and +5 (these values are merely suggestions rather than definitive values), with -5 indicating low security, 0 a normal 'device switch-on' level, and +5 indicating a high security level. The confidence level is modified depending upon the result of authentication requests and the time that has elapsed between them. The magnitude to which the AuCL is modified is dependent upon the authentication technique – recognising that a difference exists between strong biometrics such as face and fingerprints and weaker biometrics such as keystroke analysis. A protection mechanism also exists to ensure a user utilising a weaker biometric is unable to achieve high levels of confidence. This confidence level is then associated with the services and information the device is capable of providing, so that a user who already has sufficient confidence to access a service is automatically provided access. However, should a user request access to a service for which they currently do not have sufficient confidence for, a subsequent intrusive authentication request will be made.

The Alert Level is the second of the key security processes working at the core of this framework. Its purpose is to ensure continuous identity verification of the user in a transparent and therefore convenient fashion. There are six levels (depicted in table 1) with the level of authentication security being increased until the device is locked (requiring an administrative password or PUK code from a cellular network provider). The number of stages was determined by a compromise between requiring a good level of user convenience and better security. Through mixing transparent and intrusive authentication requests into a single algorithm it is intended that the majority of authorised users will only experience the transparent stages of the algorithm. The intrusive stages of the algorithm are required to ensure the validity of the user by utilising the stronger authentication tools before finally locking the device from use.

The Alert Level algorithm is inherently biased toward the authorised user, as they are given three non-intrusive chances to authenticate correctly, with two subsequent additional intrusive chances. This enables the system to minimise inconvenience from the authorised user perspective. However, due to the trade-off between the error rates, this has a detrimental effect on the false acceptance rate, increasing the probability of wrongfully accepting an impostor every time an authentication request is sent. With this in mind, for an impostor to be locked out of the device they must have their authentication request rejected a maximum of 5 consecutive times. However, this is where the companion process, the AuCL, has a significant role. The probability of an impostor continually being accepted by the framework becomes very small as the number of authentication requests increase. This would indicate that the impostor will be identified correctly more often than not (even if not consecutively as required by the Alert Level), reducing the AuCL value to a level where the majority if not all of the services and file access permissions have been removed – essentially locking the device from any practical use. In a practical situation, it is likely an impostor will be able to undertake tasks with a low risk, such as, a telephone call or sending a text message, for a short period of time before the system locks down. However, all of the key sensitive and expensive services will be locked out of use. By permitting this limited misuse of the device , it is possible to achieve a much higher level of user convenience at minimal expense to the security.

3.3   NICA Prototype

A proof-of-concept prototype was developed in order to assess the effectiveness of the proposed framework. The prototype, based upon the client-server model, comprised of four software systems:

1. Authentication Manager – providing the entire server-side operational functionality, including, biometric profiling, authentication and data synchronization.
2. Administrative Console – containing all the administrative and system settings, and providing a visualisation of active devices and their operational status.

Table 1. Escalation of the alert level

Alert Level	NICA Authentication action
1	Perform transparent authentication using the most recent data in input cache.
2	Perform transparent authentication using remaining data in input cache.
3	Perform transparent authentication using the next available user input.
4	Issue an intrusive authentication request using a high-confidence method.
5	Issue a further intrusive authentication request using a high-confidence method.
6	Successive authentication failure invokes a system lock.

3. Client-Side Interface – providing the simulated mobile handset functionality, data capture and intrusion control.
4. Databases – an SQL server containing all the server-side databases.

The hardware utilised for the prototype included a Samsung Q45 that acted as the Authentication Manager, Console Manager and contained the databases. The nature of these components meant they could be deployed in separate systems. The clients were deployed on a Sony Vaio UX1 and HP Mini-Note 2133 running Microsoft Vista and XP platforms respectively. Whilst these client devices are classed as mobile devices, they do not represent the traditional mobile handset that the framework was devised for. The decision to utilise these platforms over mobile handsets was largely due to development constraints within the timeframe of the funded project, as mobile platform development would have had to been undertaken using unmanaged code in C++, rather than rapid prototyping languages such as Visual Basic.

Having undertaken a thorough examination of biometric technologies and the commercial products that were available, it was determined that few suitable commercial biometric solutions existed for integration within NICA. The principal reason for this was the lack of available Software Development Kits (SDKs), with vendors preferring to design bespoke solutions for customers rather than license their biometric solutions for development. The project therefore identified some facial and voice verification algorithms developed in MatLab and sought to modify these for use within NICA [9]. These were accompanied by keystroke analysis algorithms previously created by the authors [2]. It was considered that these biometric approaches would provide the appropriate variety of transparent and intrusive authentication required for the proof-of-concept.

4 End-User Trial of NICA

In order to evaluate the approach, a user trial was conducted that ultimately involved 27 participants. The trial activity was split to two phases:

- **Enrolment Phase:** The participants used the prototype to provide face, voice and keystroke biometric samples that would be subsequently used to create their biometric profiles and also define two cognitive questions. A simple to use and intuitive interface was used to capture the samples. 8 samples for face, 9 for voice and 15 for each cognitive response they gave (which they were asked to provide 2) from which keystroke information was extracted. The enrolment process took no more that 15 minutes per person and at the end the participants were asked to complete the first questionnaire that looked to assess their experience.

- **Usability Phase:** Each participant was asked to follow a series of steps that would force an interaction with the device while the authentication prototype was running on the background. This would enable for biometric samples to be captured transparently as well as force access to services set to be of high security in order to test the operation of the alert level algorithm and the authentication mechanism in general. In order to ensure that the participants would have something to do during the 'usability' phase of the trial, and to ensure that contexts would occur in which different aspects of the prototype could be utilised, each user was asked to work through a given set of tasks such as using Instant Messenger, Microsoft Word, Microsoft Excel and an Internet Browser. The length of this phase varies as each user took different periods of time to interact with the device and complete the tasks. The average time of this phase was 45 minutes and on average over 60 biometric samples were captured from each participant during the usability phase of the trial. After completion of the scenario, the user was asked to fill in a questionnaire assessing their experience and the system. After that, the participants were asked to play the role of an impostor on the same device using the profile of another person and through using the same steps see how quickly the system would recognise that they were not the legitimate users.

The results from the evaluation overall demonstrated a positive opinion of the authentication system, with 92% of the users considering that it offered a more secure environment in comparison to traditional forms of authentication. The participants were also asked to evaluate how convenient the system was in a scale of 1 to 5, the results of which appear in figure 2. Although the responses were mixed, a slight skew towards the system being convenient exists on average. It is worth noting that through observation of the evaluation, participants' opinions were affected by the delays that occurred on the system while trying to manage all the processing. These occurred in some cases where applications might have been initialising concurrently and thus giving extra overhead to the system with NICA running in the background. This was a function of the prototype and a real system would not have such significant delays.

Furthermore the above views were also affected by the transparency of the system which was not always ideal. The lack of robust biometric algorithms caused a lot of transparent authentication requests to fail, prompting some of the users to experience more intrusive requests that they would normally get. Unfortunately the biometric techniques being utilised were largely developed in-house due to a lack of availability of commercial algorithms. In order to mitigate the errors a manual trimming of the threshold was taking place during the experiment in order not to allow the lack of accuracy from the biometric algorithms to affect the performance of the actual system. Nevertheless, what also happened in the experiment was that the scenario included access to a number of protected services in a small amount of time causing even more intrusive requests to occur but not necessarily having the chance to build the required confidence in the user while authenticating them transparently. Unfortunately, it was not possible

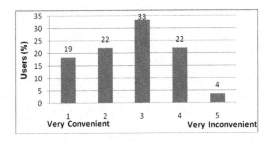

Fig. 2. Perceived convenience of the NICA prototype

to have the participants use the system for a prolonged period of days, so therefore the experimental study had to artificially include a number of steps to fully evaluate the prototype. It is likely this artificial environment resulted in a more negative attitude towards the system than what would have occurred in practice. The responses of the participants with regards to the transparency of the system are illustrated in figure 3.

With regard to the individual techniques that were utilised, there was a slight preference towards voice verification and keystroke analysis. From verbal feedback from participants there was a strong preference to techniques that did not require much explicit user interaction and were not very time consuming. As such, cognitive responses as an intrusive means of authentication were not very popular. The same occurred with face recognition as the algorithm utilised in the prototype required more time than other techniques to perform the authentication and the user also had to keep facing the camera until a sample was captured. At the same time voice verification (in its intrusive form) appeared to be more preferable as the user only had to repeat a small phrase with a subsequent quick response from the NICA server. Although many of the above were affected by the robustness of the algorithms utilised it still provides an insight that users prefer to have a higher level of security with the least overhead in their interaction. Usability and convenience were stronger preferences than security.

Regardless of the aforementioned problems regarding the convenience of the system, the majority of the users (70%) registered a preference to the use of transparent and continuous authentication as a protection mechanism. Although many of the participants suggested that the requests were too frequent the idea of being constantly protected and

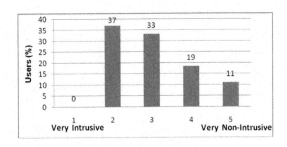

Fig. 3. Perceived intrusiveness of the new authentication system

specifically having extra security for highly sensitive information was very appealing to them. As such, 81% of the users said that they would use such system in practice as they would feel more protected than using traditional means of authentication. Although the remaining 19% stated they would not use it, their justification was that although they believed the system would offer higher security they do not perceive that their current use of their mobile device actually required a higher level of protection as they do not store or access personal information. This was actually an opinion that had arisen on a number of occasions during discussions with stakeholders. A body of users exist for which the mobile device is only (and will remain only) a telephony-based device. They have no desire to use it for any other purpose and as such do not perceive the need for additional security.

When the evaluation came to the participants acting as impostors it must be noted that although a number of users were not very positive when acting as the authorised user, their opinion became more positive when they saw the performance of the system reacting to an impostor. When the participants were asked whether the system managed to detect them and locked them out in a timely manner, 81% said yes. When the users where asked on how secure the system was their answers were very positive with 86% leaning to being secure or very secure.

5   Conclusions and Further Work

The research has resulted in the development of an operational proof-of-concept prototype, which is not dependent upon specific hardware and is functional across Windows XP and Vista platforms. It is able to operate in both client-server and standalone modes, and has successfully integrated three biometric techniques.

The evaluation of NICA clearly demonstrates the strengths and weaknesses of the proposed system. It is evident from the findings that such a transparent and continuous system has real merit and a large proportion of the participants felt it would provide the additional security they desire for their mobile devices. Unfortunately, with almost half of the world's population having a mobile device, it is difficult to establish an approach that satisfies all users. NICA has specifically considered this and developed a flexible approach that can utilise a variety of biometric and other authentication techniques and through a series of operational settings that can vary the level of security both transparent and intrusive being provided. Through this flexibility it is hoped the majority of users will be able to find a suitable mixture of settings and techniques they prefer and desire.

Whilst the prototype and subsequent evaluation has illustrated a number of key findings, it is important to highlight that if the system was operating within specification (i.e. the performance of the biometric techniques was good and the operational performance of the server was managed rather than everything operating for a single server) the nature of the transparency would mean few users would ever experience intrusive authentication. During the evaluation, however, the framework was configured to perform authentication on a more frequent basis than normal in order to ensure that sufficient judgments were made during the trial session. This was done in order to ensure that participants would see the full extent of the system in operation, but the consequence was that they also encountered more intrusive authentication requests than would normally be expected. In some trial sessions, these requests were too frequent and time consuming, and participants therefore formed a more negative impression of the prototype.

The study has accomplished its overall aims of developing a next generation user authentication system. It has taken into account stakeholder considerations of usability, flexibility and convenience and provided a system that can improve the level of security in a continuous and transparent fashion – moving beyond traditional point-of-entry authentication. Whilst the prototype has a number of operational shortcomings, it is not anticipated that any of these would actually prevent a NICA-type approach from being operationally viable in the future. The project has also identified a host of additional avenues that require further consideration and research. In particular future work will focus upon three aspects:

1. Transparency of biometric techniques – Developing biometric approaches that will not only operate in point-of-entry mode but in a transparent fashion with varying environmental factors.
2. Privacy of biometric samples – the importance of this data is paramount and large adoption of any biometric system will only occur when such issues can be resolved to the satisfaction of all stakeholders.
3. Developing a risk assessment and management strategy for mobile devices. Given the wide-stakeholder group, varying responsibilities from general users to network operators and system administrators, it is imperative that an approach is designed so that the level of risk associated with a particular service request can be better understood and therefore protected.

The authors have already begun to consider the issue of transparency with respect to facial recognition, signature recognition and keystroke analysis [2,3,4] and will continue to address other key biometric approaches.

Acknowledgement. This research was support by a two year grant from the Eduserv Foundation.

References

1. Clarke, N.L., Furnell, S.M.: Authentication of Users on Mobile Telephones - A Survey of Attitudes and Practices. Computers & Security 24(7), 519–527 (2005)
2. Clarke, N.L., Furnell, S.M.: Authenticating Mobile Phone Users Using Keystroke Analysis. International Journal of Information Security, 1–14 (2006)
3. Clarke, N.L., Mekala, A.R.: Transparent Handwriting Verification for Mobile Devices. In: Proceedings of the Sixth International Network Conference (INC 2006), Plymouth, UK, 11-14 July, pp. 277–288 (2006)
4. Clarke, N.L., Karatzouni, S., Furnell, S.M.: Transparent Facial Recognition for Mobile Devices. In: Proceedings of the 7th Security Conference, Las Vegas, June 2-3 (2008)
5. Denning, D.: Information Warfare & Security. ACM Press, US (1999)

6. Karatzouni, S., Furnell, S.M., Clarke, N.L., Botha, R.A.: Perceptions of User Authentication on Mobile Devices. In: Proceedings of the ISOneWorld Conference, Las Vegas, CD-Proceedings (0-9772107-6-6) (2007)

7. GSM World GSM Subscriber Statistics. GSMWorld.Com (2002),
   http://www.gsmworld.com

8. Lemos, R.: Passwords: The Weakest Link? Hackers can crack most in less than a minute. CNET News.Com (2002),
   http://news.com.com/2009-1001-916719.html

9. Rosa, L.: Biometric Source Code. Advanced Source Code (2008),
   http://www.advancedsourcecode.com

10. Shaw, K.: Data on PDAs mostly unprotected. Network World Fusion (2004),
    http://www.nwfusion.com

Combining Authentication, Reputation and Classification to Make Phishing Unprofitable

Amir Herzberg

Bar Ilan University, Computer Science Department, Ramat Gan, 52900, Israel
herzbea@cs.biu.ac.il

Abstract. We present and analyze a design of an filtering system to block email phishing messages, combining reputation, authentication and classification mechanisms. We present simple economical model and analysis, showing sufficient conditions on the precision of the content-classifier, to make phishing unprofitable.

1 Introduction

Phishing is a common social-engineering attack on computer users, causing significant losses to individuals and society. In a phishing attack, Phil, the 'phisherman', sends email (or other message) to Vic, the victim (user). The email lures Vic into exposing herself to further attacks. Phishing is based on deception; Vic is led to believe that the email is from a trustworthy source, such as her bank, e.g. VIC-Bank.com. In a typical attack, Vic follows a hyperlink in the message, which causes her browser to open a *spoofed website*, e.g. a clone of the login page of VIC-Bank.com. If Vic does not detect that the site is spoofed, she may enter her credential, thereby allowing Phil control over Vic's account.

Phishing emails are one of the most harmful categories of spam. There are many products, services and proposals to allow mail servers and readers to block phishing (and spam) emails. Many of these mechanisms fall into the following three classes:

Reputation mechanisms, e.g. blacklists: These systems map the identity of the sender, to some measure of his reputation as a mail sender. The simplest reputation systems, which are also most common, are *blacklists* (and *whitelists*), which simply list known phisherman/spammers (or, respectively, trustworthy senders known not be phishermen/spammers). More elaborate reputation systems may return a measure of the reputation of the sender. Notice that many blacklists are not sufficiently reliable, and may suffer from many false positives. It is often advisable for organizations to use two blacklists, a 'short' blacklist (often maintained locally), where false positives are very rare, and a 'long' blacklist, which contains many more suspected senders (and more false positives). Most blacklists use the IP address of the sending mail server as the identifier, allowing for highly efficient lookups (using DNS).

D. Gritzalis and J. Lopez (Eds.): SEC 2009, IFIP AICT 297, pp. 13–24, 2009.

Authentication mechanisms: These mechanisms authenticate the identity of the sender, or of the sending domain. There are several authentication mechanisms for email, mostly based on the security of routing and DNS, and/or on cryptographic authentication such as using digital signatures. We discuss the predominant mechanisms: SPF [14] and SenderID (SIDF) [11], based on security of routing and DNS, and DKIM [2,10], based on security of digital signatures.

Content classifiers: These mechanisms classify emails based on their contents, typically to suspect email (spam or phishing) vs. 'good' email (sometimes referred to as 'ham').

Many email systems, employ some combination of reputation, authentication and classification mechanisms. A high-level design of an email filtering system is shown in Figure 1. In this design, we use four steps: step two is sender authentication, step four is classification, and steps one and three (either 3a or 3b) use reputation (a 'short' blacklist in step one, a domain-name sender reputation lookup in step 3a, or a 'long' blacklist in step 3b). We next give a brief description of these steps; for more details on this design, see Section 2.

In the first step, we confirm that the sending mail server is not listed in a blacklist of servers suspected of frequently sending spam/phishing emails. This step is very efficient, esp. since blacklists are usually kept as DNS records, and hence retrieved and cached efficiently. Unfortunately, most phishing messages are sent from legitimate domains, see e.g. [5]. Hence, often the sender of the phishing email will not have bad reputation (e.g. not be in the blacklist), and will only be detected by the following steps.

In the second step, we authenticate the sender identity (name), if an appropriate authentication mechanism is available. Such authentication mechanisms include validating a digital signature (e.g. using DKIM) and/or checking that the sending server is listed in a 'email sending policy' DNS record controlled by the sender (e.g. using SPF or SIDF). If no authentication data is available, we cannot identify the sender (by name), and proceed using only the IP address of the sending server (in step 3b). If authentication data exists but the validation fails, then we reject the email, and optionally add the sending server's IP address to the 'short blacklist' (so future emails from this server are blocked immediately and efficiently by the IP-based 'short' blacklist, in step 1).

If the authentication validates correctly the identity of the sender and/or of the sending mail server, then we use this identity (or identities) in step 3a, to check the reputation of the sender. In this case, we can block the email if the sender is a known spammer/phishermen, or display it if the sender is known to be trustworthy.

If the email is not authenticated at all, then we may check if the sender (or sending mail server) is listed in the 'long' blacklist (step 3b). The 'long' blacklist is applied only for unauthenticated senders, since it is less reliable than other mechanisms (contains many false positives). In addition, the 'long' blacklist is often located as a remote server, therefore querying it involves delay and overhead. If the sender appears in the 'long' blacklist then the email is blocked; optionally, the sender is also added to the 'short' blacklist, for improved efficiency of additional messages from that sender.

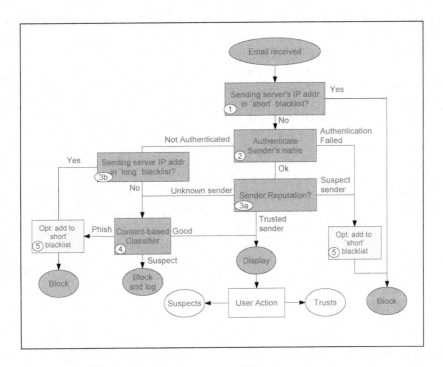

Fig. 1. High level design of an email filtering system, using four steps. Steps 1 and 3 use reputation (by blacklist of IP addresses, and by a reputation database for senders). Step 2 authenticates the sender, and step 4 classify the email (based on its contents).

If the sender is not authenticated, yet not blacklisted, or authenticated by without sufficient (positive or negative) reputation, then we must invoke the last and most computationally-consuming step (4): content-based classification. The content classification system determines whether the email is good (to display) or bad (to block, and possibly to log). Notice that content classification systems are both computationally expensive and never fully reliable, therefore it makes sense to apply them only if the more efficient authentication and reputation mechanisms failed to produce a conclusive determination. The classification system may also use results from the previous mechanisms; in particular, often it may consider the (inconclusive) reputation as part of its input.

Finally, once the mail reader displays the email to the user, then the user makes the final determination: to trust the email or to suspect it (in which case, the user may simply discard it, or may report this, e.g. to a blacklist. The user's decision may be (partially) based on sender identifiers presented by the mail reader, e.g. the sender's address, usually from the FROM email message header [12]; these email identifiers may be authenticated, e.g. with Sender-ID and/or DKIM. However, practical experience, as well as usability experiments [4], show that users often trust phishing email based on its contents, even when it has the wrong 'from' address, especially when using similar characters, e.g. accts@VIC-Bank.com vs. accts@VIC-Bank.com (it may indeed be difficult to see, that the second address uses (lower case) *l* instead of (upper case) *I*).

Combinations of reputation, authentication and classification mechanisms, similar to the design outlined above, are often deployed by email systems, to block phishing and other spam emails; see also [9]. In this paper, we describe and analyze the details of this design. We also explain the relevant adversary models, with brief background on relevant Internet protocols (IP, DNS and SMTP).

Furthermore, we present a simple modeling of the economics of phishing. Our analysis shows sufficient conditions under which a phishing-defense system following the design in Figure 1, can ensure that phishing is not profitable. These conditions are derived under reasonable simplifying assumptions.

Our analysis is especially meaningful for the design of the content classification mechanisms. First, the conditions we identify for making phishing unprofitable, imply required level of precision for content classification. Second, the analysis shows that it may suffice to ensure that phishing messages are either classified (as 'suspect'), or simply suspected (or ignored) by the user.

This motivates us to recommend that sensitive senders, e.g. banks, use email authentication mechanisms (e.g. DKIM and SPF), and in addition adopt a standard form for their emails, allowing easy classification of emails with similar form and ensuring that users will suspect (and ignore) emails which claim to be from the bank but have different form. When senders use this combination of authentication and easy-to-classify form, the content classifier can identify emails which use the bank form; any such email which is not properly authenticated, is probably phishing email. Such high-precision detection of phishing emails allows the use of automated means to detect and punish the phishermen, making phishing less lucrative or unprofitable. Details within.

Email authentication is a central element in our phishing-detection design, as shown in Figure 1. Currently, there are several proposals for email authentication. We describe and evaluate the three predominant proposals: the Sender Policy Framework (SPF) [14], the Domain-Keys Identified Mail (DKIM) design [2,10] and the Sender-ID Framework (SDIF) [11]. We make several recommendation as to best method to use (and combine) these mechanisms, and explain their security properties, clearing up some possible misconceptions and unjustified expectations.

To summarize, we believe this paper has the following contributions. First, we present a detailed design combining authentication, reputation and classification mechanisms, to filter phishing and spam messages; our design includes some new insights, such as improving the classification by identifying emails which may appear to the user to come from specific senders. Second, we present economic analysis, showing sufficient conditions for phishing to be unprofitable. Third, we present and compare the three predominant email authentication mechanisms (SPF, Sender-ID and DKIM), describing their correct usage and limitations, and map them to the corresponding adversary models.

2   Design of an Integrated Email Filtering System

In this section, we present and discuss a high-level design for an email filtering system, incorporating reputation, authentication and classification mechanisms. As illustrated in Figure 1, the design incorporates four steps; these steps are denoted by the rectangles with gray background, numbered 1-4. Notice that not all recipients will use exactly these steps or exactly this order of steps.

In the first step, the filter looks up a blacklist containing IP addresses suspected to be in use, or to be available for use, by phishermen and spammers. Such lookup is very efficient, in particular since it is usually done by an DNS query, and the results are cached. The IP address to be used here should be of the last untrusted MTA which sent (relayed) the message; if this IP address appears in the blacklist, the message is blocked. This step can be skipped if it was already performed by some trusted MTA along the route (after which the mail passed only via trusted agents), e.g. by the incoming border MTA of the recipient's organization or ISP. Some recipients may also block email when the IP address used by sending MTAs has not been used in the (reasonably recent but not immediate) past to send email. This can block many 'bad' servers (albeit also few legitimate but new servers), since these newly-used addresses may not yet appear in blacklists, yet much of the spam and phishing email arrive from such 'new' IP addresses [5].

In the second step, the filter tries to authenticate the sender, using IP-based authentication (e.g. SPF) and/or cryptographic authentication (e.g. DKIM). If the authentication fails, i.e. the email is signed but the signature is invalid (for DKIM) or the SPF record last untrusted MTA which sent (relayed) the message, then the email is blocked. If authentication is successful, namely the email sender or sending domain is authenticated, then this identity is passed to the next step, to check the reputation of the sender (or sending domain). If there is no authentication data, then we skip the next step (cannot check reputation for unidentified senders) and move to the following step (content classification).

The third step is reached only if the sender of the email, or the sending domain, was successfully authenticated in the previous step. In this case, we can now consult reputation database, using the identity of the sender (or sending domain) as keys. If the reputation data for this sender is conclusive, we block the email (for a suspected sender) or display it to the user (for a trusted sender). If there is no conclusive reputation data for this sender, we pass whatever reputation data we obtained to the next and final step of content classification.

The fourth (and last) step is content-based classification, based on heuristic rules, machine learning and/or other approaches. Unfortunately, all content classification mechanisms are both computationally intensive, as well as not fully reliable. Therefore, we execute this step only when all previous steps failed to provide an conclusive decision; furthermore, at this step, we may use the outputs of the previous steps, such sender identity (if identified) and reputation (if some, non-conclusive, reputation data was found). We make additional recommendations about this step below.

Identification of phishing email is challenging, since phishing messages are designed to mimic legitimate messages from a specific, trusted sender (e.g. VIC-Bank.com), in order to trick Vic into believing the message came from VIC-Bank.com. This may make classification of messages to phishing vs. non-phishing more challenging, compared to classification of 'regular' spam messages.

In spite of this challenge, classifiers have been shown to achieve good precision in identifying phishing messages, over collections containing typical phishing messages

[6,3,1], using features which are often unnoticed by (human) victims, e.g. hyperlinks to suspect websites in the email. In existing email filtering systems, there is usually a 'classification engine' which applies heuristic or machine learning rules, to classify directly to undesirable (spam/phishing) vs. legitimate ('ham'). Alternatively, the classification engine may output a 'grade', which is combined with 'grades' from the reputation steps, to determine if to accept or block the email.

However, it is hard to predict whether automated classifiers would be able to maintain such good precision in the long run, after being widely adopted, since at that point phishermen are likely to try to adapt their messages to try to avoid detection (via phishing-related features). This motivates our different, possibly complementing, approach, namely to use classifiers to identify *PhishOrReal* emails, i.e. messages which *appear* to come from VIC-Bank.com (regardless of whether they really come from VIC-Bank.com, or are phishing). Since phishermen try to mislead Vic into believing their phishing email is really from VIC-Bank.com, the identification of *PhishOrReal* emails should be easier, than classifying emails as phishing. Furthermore, it should not be too difficult to generate and collect a large corpus of *PhishOrReal* messages, to use to train, test and/or fine-tune the classifying engine.

Therefore, we suggest to use a 'classification engine' (using heuristics, machine learning, etc.), to classify incoming emails to *three* groups: messages directly identified as spam or phishing; *PhishOrReal* messages; and other messages. Since our design invokes the classification engine only at step 4, and, assuming VIC-Bank.com emails are properly authenticated, then they were already been identified and displayed (in step 3). Therefore, email classified as *PhishOrReal* at step four, is almost certain to be phishing email, and can be blocked. Furthermore, since this identification is automated and with high confidence, the system can respond to it in ways that will penalize the phishermen, e.g. alert blacklists and other reputation mechanism, or traceback and punish the phisherman; we later model this by a relatively high cost c_f to the phishermen from such 'step 4 blocking'. This simple design for the classification phase is illustrated in Figure 2.

Notice that trustworthy senders, e.g. VIC-Bank.com, often use distinctive visual identification such as company name, trademarks, and logos; we refer to such visual identifiers as the bank's *letterhead*. We believe that users can be educated to look for the bank's letterhead and to suspect emails containing variants of it; when users suspect the email, we can try to detect this (possibly by user signaling, e.g. 'spam' button), and then penalize the phisherman; however we expect the penalty (cost) c_u to the attacker due to a user suspecting the email, to be much smaller than the cost c_f when the email is filtered by the classifier (step 4), i.e. $c_u << c_f$.

To avoid detection by the user, thereby losing c_u as well as any potential gain from phishing message, the phishermen will have to try to clone VIC-Bank.com's letterhead in phishing messages, which will make it easier to classify these messages as *PhishOrReal* emails. This places the phishermen in a dilemma: if he sends messages that are more likely to mislead the user, then these messages are also more likely to be *PhishOrReal*-classified; and on the other hand, messages that are less likely to be *PhishOrReal*-classified, are also less likely to mislead the user. In addition, the phisherman will be wary of using 'evasion techniques' designed to avoid classification as

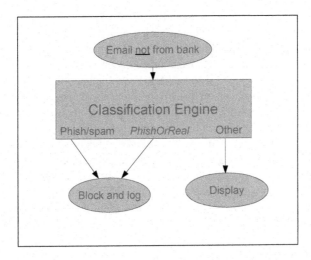

Fig. 2. Design of the classifier phase, using arbitrary classifying engine

PhishOrReal, since the classifier may detect these technique and directly classify the email as 'phishing'.

We model this trade-off by assuming that the attacker can select the probability of the message being *PhishOrReal*-classified, p_f, and the probability of the user ignoring the message, p_u, but only *as long as their sum* is below some threshold x, i.e. $p_u + p_f \leq x$. Notice that this dilemma holds only if the phishermen are not able to send messages that pass the authentication (otherwise, these messages will be delivered even if they are *PhishOrReal*-classified).

It is desirable to evaluate the ability of users to detect phishing emails when a company uses (different types of) letterheads. Furthermore, it would be interesting to evaluate the ability of phishermen to create letterheads, that users will consider as legitimate email from VIC-Bank.com, yet would not be classified as *PhishOrReal* (or as spam/phishing) by the content classifier. Such evaluation is challenging and requires careful, long-term usability studies, to ensure reliable results and to maintain ethical standards, and is therefore beyond the scope of this paper; see e.g. [8,13,7]. Notice that there may be significant impact to the design and consistency of using the letterhead, on the ability of the classifiers and the users to detect *PhishOrReal* and suspect emails, and on the ability of the phishermen to trick both classifier (to consider message as 'other' - neither phish not *PhishOrReal*) and user (to consider the message as valid message from bank). For example, intuitively, we may expect an advantage to simple textual letterheads, compared to more elaborate letterheads involving graphics and (dynamic) HTML; of course, this intuition should be validated experimentally.

3   Analysis of Effectiveness

In this section we present a simple economical model, and use it to analyze the effectiveness of an email anti-phishing filtering system. Our analysis focuses on the design we presented in the previous section (and in Figure 1), but it is applicable to many practical email filtering systems. The goal of our analysis is to identify sufficient conditions, under which the phishermen is likely to lose more, in average, per phishing message (due to costs due to detection), than the average profit he hopes to make from the message (due to profits when it succeeds in reaching and misleading the user). Our analysis is focused on the utility for the phishermen; we do not consider the expected utility to the user, which is mostly impacted by the false positives and false negative ratios, and the costs associated with the filtering mechanism.

Figure 3 illustrates the processing upon receipt of a phishing message by the filtering system. The filter first applies the authentication and repudiation mechanisms, which filter out messages from reputable, known senders such as VIC-Bank.com, as well as messages from known spammers and phishermen. The probability of filtering in these steps appear unrelated to the probability of filtering by the classifier and of trust by the user, and related to expenses for the phisherman (e.g. to use many IP addresses). Therefore, for simplicity, we ignore this probability, i.e. our analysis is for a phishing email that is *not* filtered by the authentication and reputation mechanisms (steps 1-3).

Phishing email is often classified as 'phishing' or *PhishOrReal* in both cases, it is 'suspected' and therefore blocked, and since this is automated, high-confidence detection, this result in significant penalty (cost) c_f to the adversary. We assume that the phisherman can determine the probability of classification as 'phishing' or *PhishOrReal* by the classifier, by appropriate selection of the contents of the email. Namely, we assume that the classifier suspects the email with probability p_f, controlled by the phishermen.

Email which is *not* suspected by the filter, is displayed to the user Vic. With probability p_u, the user will suspect the phishing email. In this case, the user may report this phishing email, or the system may detect that the email is phishing by user's reaction to it; this may impact the phishermen, e.g. by reduction of reputation (or entering the phisherman's IP address to a blacklist). We denote the amortized cost to the phisherman due to each time the user suspects the email, by c_u. We expect c_u to be non-negligible, yet much smaller than the penalty due to the (higher-confidence, automated) detection by the classifier, i.e. $c_u \ll c_f$.

The phisherman may try to find and send messages that minimize p_u and p_f, and in fact, finding a message that minimizes only one of the two is usually easy. However, the challenge to the phisherman is to minimize both p_u and p_f. We model this constraint of the adversary, by assuming that the phisherman can only find messages s.t. $p_u + p_f \geq x$, where x is some bound on the ability to minimize both probabilities. Clearly $0 < x < 2$; and based on typical detection rates in usability testing and on typical precision of classifiers, it seems reasonable to expect that typically $0.5 < x < 1.5$. Since we assumed that x is fixed, the attacker can only select p_u (and then use $p_f = x - p_u$).

The attacker gains only if the email is displayed to the user, which then does not suspect it. This happens with probability $(1 - p_f)(1 - p_u)$. Let g denote the amortized gain to the phisherman from each such successfully displayed phishing email.

While a more detailed analysis can be done, we will show that two simple conditions, s.t. if one of them holds, phishing is not profitable. Specifically, the two sufficient conditions are:

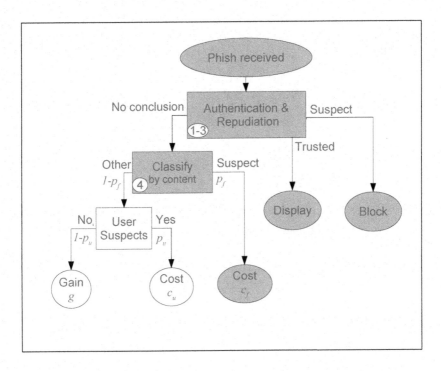

Fig. 3. Processing an incoming phishing email. We assume phishing email never authenticates successfully (as legitimate bank email). With probability p_f, it is detected as 'Phish' by the classifier, with cost c_f to the phisherman. Otherwise, it is displayed to Vic. With probability p_u, Vic suspects the email (and either ignores it or reports it), with average cost c_u to the phisherman. With probability $1 - p_u$, Vic trusts the email, with average gain g to the phisherman.

$$(g \le c_f - 2c_u) \wedge \left(g < \frac{c_u \cdot x}{1 - x} \right) \wedge (x < 1) \tag{1}$$

$$(g \le c_f - 2c_u) \wedge (x \ge 1) \tag{2}$$

We believe that these conditions are reasonable. In particular, the common condition of $g \le c_f - 2c_u$ should hold, provided there is rapid, decisive response to confirmed detection of phishing emails (increasing c_f), together with the use of web-based phishing and other defenses, which can reduce significantly the amortized gain g to the phisherman from a displayed phishing message. In particular, $x \ge 1$ seems a reasonable goal for content classification systems.

Theorem 1 (Sufficient conditions for phishing to be unprofitable). *The maximal amortized utility of the phisherman $U^*_{g,c_u,c_f,x}$ for a phishing message received by the process in Figure 3 is non-positive, if $c_f > c_u$, and at least one of the two conditions 1, 2 above hold.*

Proof: The phisherman's amortized utility for a message received, U, is the following function of the 'fixed' parameters g, c_u, c_f, x and of the user detection probability p_u ($0 \leq p_u \leq \min(1, x)$):

$$U_{g, c_u, c_f, x}(p_u) = -p_f \cdot c_f + (1 - p_f)(-p_u \cdot c_u + (1 - p_u)g)$$
$$= (p_u - x) \cdot c_f + (1 - x + p_u)(-p_u \cdot c_u + (1 - p_u)g)$$

Which gives:

$$U_{g, c_u, c_f, x}(p_u) = -(g + c_u)p_u^2 + (c_f + (x-1)c_u + x \cdot g) \cdot p_u + (1-x)g - x \cdot c_f \qquad (3)$$

Let $\hat{p}_u = \arg\max_{p_u}\left(U_{g, c_u, c_f, x}(p_u)\right)$, i.e. the value of p_u bringing phisherman's utility U to maximum, ignoring the restriction $0 \leq p_u \leq \min(1, x)$. Since the utility in Eq. 3 is simply a parabola, $\hat{p}_u$ is given easily as:

$$\hat{p}_u = \frac{c_f - c_u}{2(g + c_u)} + \frac{x}{2} \qquad (4)$$

Since in both conditions 1 and 2 holds $g \leq c_f - 2c_u$, we have:

$$\hat{p}_u \geq \frac{1}{2} + \frac{x}{2} \geq \min\{x, 1\} \qquad (5)$$

Let $p_u^* = \arg\max_{0 \leq p_u \leq \min(1, x)}\left(U_{g, c_u, c_f, x}(p_u)\right)$, i.e. the value of p_u bringing phisherman's utility U to maximum, *considering* the restriction $0 \leq p_u \leq \min(1, x)$. The maximal utility for the phisherman is $U_{g, c_u, c_f, x}^* = \max_{0 \leq p_u \leq \min(1, x)}\left(U_{g, c_u, c_f, x}(p_u)\right)$, i.e. $U_{g, c_u, c_f, x}^* = U_{g, c_u, c_f, x}(p_u^*)$. We next analyze the following cases:

1. $1 \leq x$ and $1 \leq \hat{p}_u$, i.e. $g \leq \frac{c_f - c_u}{2 - x} - c_u$. In this case, $p_u^* = 1$, hence trivially phisherman's utility for message received is negative.
2. $x \leq 1$ and $x \leq \hat{p}_u$. Since $x \leq 1$, condition 2 definitely does not hold; hence we can assume that condition 1 holds, and in particular that $g \leq \frac{c_u x}{1 - x}$.
3. $\hat{p}_u < 0$. In this case, $p_u^* = 0$. This happens if and only if $c_f \leq c_u(1 - x) - xg$. However, this contradicts our assumption that $c_f > c_u$. Therefore, this case never holds.
4. Otherwise, i.e. $0 \leq \hat{p}_u \leq \min\{1, x\}$. In this case, $p_u^* = \hat{p}_u$. However, from Eq. 5, it follows that this case cannot hold (if either condition 1 or condition 2 hold).

It remains to analyze case 2, i.e. $x \leq 1$ and $x \leq \hat{p}_u$. Since $\hat{p}_u = \frac{c_f - c_u}{2(g + c_u)} + \frac{x}{2} \geq x$, we have $c_f \geq c_u(1 + x) + g \cdot x$, or equivalently $g \leq \frac{c_f - c_u}{x} - c_u$.

Since the parabola is monotonously increasing, the phisherman uses $p_u^* = x$, and his utility is at most:

$$U_{g, c_u, c_f, x}^* = U_{g, c_u, c_f, x}(x)$$
$$= -(g + c_u)x^2 + (c_f + (x - 1)c_u + x \cdot g) \cdot x + (1 - x)g - x \cdot c_f$$
$$= (1 - x)g - x \cdot c_u$$

However, since we know that condition 1 holds here, and in particular that $g \leq \frac{c_u \cdot x}{1-x}$, we see that the utility cannot be positive, i.e. also in this case phishing is not profitable.   □

Acknowledgement. Many thanks to Jim Fenton and Nathaniel (Nathan) Borenstein for their extremely detailed and helpful feedback, and to Ahmad Jbara, who participated in early discussions about this research. Thanks also to Haya Shulman for her assistance.

This work was supported by Israeli Science Foundation grant ISF 1014/07.

References

1. Abu-Nimeh, S., Nappa, D., Wang, X., Nair, S.: A comparison of machine learning techniques for phishing detection. In: Cranor, L.F. (ed.) Proceedings of the Anti-Phishing Working Groups 2nd Annual eCrime Researchers Summit 2007, Pittsburgh, Pennsylvania, USA. ACM International Conference Proceeding Series, vol. 269, pp. 60–69. ACM, New York (2007),
   http://doi.acm.org/10.1145/1299015.1299021
2. Allman, E., Callas, J., Delany, M., Libbey, M., Fenton, J., Thomas, M.: DomainKeys Identified Mail (DKIM) signatures. Internet Request for Comment RFC 4871, Internet Engineering Task Force (2007), http://tools.ietf.org/html/4871
3. del Castillo, M.D., Iglesias, Á., Serrano, J.I.: An integrated approach to filtering phishing E-mails. In: Moreno Díaz, R., Pichler, F., Quesada Arencibia, A. (eds.) EUROCAST 2007. LNCS, vol. 4739, pp. 321–328. Springer, Heidelberg (2007),
   http://dx.doi.org/10.1007/978-3-540-75867-9_41
4. Dhamija, R., Tygar, D., Hearst, M.: Why phishing works. In: Proceedings of the Conference on Human Factors in Computing Systems (CHI 2006), Montreal, Quebec, Canada, pp. 581–590 (2006)
5. Duan, Z., Gopalan, K., Yuan, X.: Behavioral characteristics of spammers and their network reachability properties. In: Proc. of the International Conference on Communications (ICC), Glasgow, UK (June 2007)
6. Fette, I., Sadeh, N.M., Tomasic, A.: In: Williamson, C.L., Zurko, M.E., Patel-Schneider, P.F., Shenoy, P.J. (eds.) Proceedings of the 16th International Conference on World Wide Web, WWW 2007, Banff, Alberta, Canada, May 8-12, pp. 649–656. ACM, New York (2007),
   http://doi.acm.org/10.1145/1242572.1242660
7. Herzberg, A., Jbara, A.: Security and identification indicators for browsers against spoofing and phishing attacks. IEEE Transactions on Internet Technology (2008)
8. Jakobsson, M., Ratkiewicz, J.: Designing ethical phishing experiments: a study of (rot13) ronl query features. In: WWW 2006: Proceedings of the 15th international conference on World Wide Web, pp. 513–522. ACM Press, New York (2006),
   http://doi.acm.org/10.1145/1135777.1135853
9. Leiba, B., Borenstein, N.S.: A multifaceted approach to spam reduction. In: CEAS 2004 - First Conference on Email and Anti-Spam (2004)
10. Lieba, B., Fenton, J.: DomainKeys Identified Mail (DKIM): Using digital signatures for domain verification. In: CEAS 2007: The Third Conference on Email and Anti-Spam (2007)
11. Lyon, J., Wong, M.W.: Sender ID: Authenticating E-mail. Internet Request for Comment RFC 4406, Internet Engineering Task Force (2006)

12. Resnick, P.: Internet message format. Request for comments 2822 (2001)
13. Sheng, S., Magnien, B., Kumaraguru, P., Acquisti, A., Cranor, L.F., Hong, J.I., Nunge, E.: Anti-phishing phil: the design and evaluation of a game that teaches people not to fall for phish. In: Cranor, L.F. (ed.) Proceedings of the 3rd Symposium on Usable Privacy and Security, SOUPS, Pittsburgh, Pennsylvania, USA. ACM International Conference Proceeding Series, vol. 229, pp. 88–99. ACM, New York (2007),
http://doi.acm.org/10.1145/1280680.1280692
14. Wong, M., Schlitt, W.: Sender Policy Framework (SPF) for authorizing use of domains in E-mail, version 1. Internet Request for Comment RFC 4871, Internet Engineering Task Force (2006), http://tools.ietf.org/html/4408

Audio CAPTCHA for SIP-Based VoIP

Yannis Soupionis, George Tountas, and Dimitris Gritzalis

Information Security and Critical Infrastructure Protection Research Group
Dept. of Informatics, Athens University of Economics & Business, Greece
jsoup@aueb.gr, gtountas@aueb.gr, dgrit@aueb.gr

Abstract. Voice over IP (VoIP) introduces new ways of communication, while utilizing existing data networks to provide inexpensive voice communications worldwide as a promising alternative to the traditional PSTN telephony. SPam over Internet Telephony (SPIT) is one potential source of future annoyance in VoIP. A common way to launch a SPIT attack is the use of an automated procedure (bot), which generates calls and produces audio advertisements. In this paper, our goal is to design appropriate CAPTCHA to fight such bots. We focus on and develop audio CAPTCHA, as the audio format is more suitable for VoIP environments and we implement it in a SIP-based VoIP environment. Furthermore, we suggest and evaluate the specific attributes that audio CAPTCHA should incorporate in order to be effective, and test it against an open source bot implementation.

1 Introduction

A serious obstacle when trying to prevent Spam over Internet Telephony (SPIT) is identifying VoIP communications which originate from software robots (bots). Alan Turing's Turing Test" paper [1] discusses the special case of a human tester who attempts to distinguish humans from artificial intelligence (AI) computer programs. The research interest in this subject has spurred a number of proposals for CAPTCHA (Completely Automated Public Tests to tell Computers and Humans Apart) [2,3,4,5]. Commercial examples include major stakeholders in the field, such as Google and MSN, which require CAPTCHA (visual or audio), in order to provide services to users. However, more advanced computer programs can break a number of CAPTCHA that have been proposed to date.

In this paper, we develop an audio CAPTCHA suitable for use in VoIP infrastructures, which are based on the Session Initiation Protocol (SIP). We first illustrate some of the SIP-based SPIT characteristics and present background work. We then explain how a CAPTCHA can be utilized in a VoIP infrastructure. In section 3, we propose a classification of the characteristics/attributes of audio CAPTCHA. In section 4 we briefly introduce a bot that is currently publicly available and will be used for testing purposes. We also present an example of how this bot solves CAPTCHA. In section 5 we implement a new audio CAPTCHA, which is based on the attributes shown in section 3. Finally, we present the results of the tests performed to order to evaluate its performance.

D. Gritzalis and J. Lopez (Eds.): SEC 2009, IFIP AICT 297, pp. 25–38, 2009.

2 Background

SPIT constitutes a new, emerging type of threat in VoIP environments. It illustrates several similarities to email spam. Both spammers and spitters use the Internet to target a group of users to initiate bulk and unsolicited messages and calls, respectively. Compared to traditional telephony, IP telephony provides a more effective channel, since messages are sent in bulk, and at a low cost. Marketers can use spam-bots to harvest VoIP addresses. Furthermore, since call-route tracing over IP is more difficult, the potential for fraud is considerably greater.

A method that is widely used to uphold automated SPAM attacks is CAPTCHA. The same technique can be used in order to mitigate SPIT. Each time a callee receives a call from an unknown caller, an automated reverse Turing test would be triggered, which the spit-bot needs to solve in order to complete its attack. Integrating such a technique into a VoIP infrastructure raises two issues. Firstly, the CAPTCHA module should be combined with other anti-SPIT controls, i.e. not every call should pass through the CAPTCHA challenge, since each audio CAPTCHA requires considerable computational resources. A simultaneous triggering of numerous CAPTCHA challenges may eventually lead to denial of service. Challenges would also cause annoyance to users, if they had to solve one for every single call they make. Moreover, the CAPTCHA needs to be designed in a friendly way to humans and also remain solvable by them.

2.1 CAPTCHA

A CAPTCHA challenge is a test that most humans should be able to pass, but current computer programs should not. Such a test is often based on hard, open AI problems, e.g. automatic recognition of distorted text, or of human speech against a noisy background. Differing from the original Turing test, CAPTCHA challenges are automatically generated and graded by a computer. Since only humans are able to return a sensible response, an automated Turing test embedded in the above protocol can verify whether there is a human or a bot behind the challenged computer. Although the original Turing test was designed as a measure of progress for AI, CAPTCHA is a human-nature-authentication mechanism. In this paper, we focus on audio CAPTCHA. These were initially created to enable people that are visually impaired to register or make use of a service that requires solving of a CAPTCHA. Nowadays, an audio CAPTCHA would also be useful to defend against automated audio VoIP messages, as visual CAPTCHA are hard to apply in VoIP environments due to the limitations of end-user devices (e.g. IP phones). If an adequate CAPTCHA is used, it should be hard for a spit-bot to respond correctly and, thus, manage to initiate a call. Audio CAPTCHA also seem attractive, as text-based CAPTCHA have been proven to be breakable [7,8,9,10,11]. We validate our results with user tests and with a bot that was configured in order to solve difficult audio CAPTCHA. The proposed CAPTCHA must be: (a). Easy for humans to solve, (b). Easy for a tester machine to generate and grade, (c). Hard for a software bot to solve.

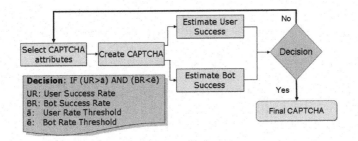

Fig. 1. A generic CAPTCHA development process

The first requirement implies that user studies are necessary in order to evaluate the effectiveness of CAPTCHA. The latter ones imply that a test with a new property is required: the test must be easy to generate, but intractable to pass without special knowledge available to humans and not computers. Audio recognition seems to fit in the category. Humans can easily identify words in a noisy environment, but this is not true for computers. Specification-wise, CAPTCHA do not need to be 100% effective at identifying software bots. A design goal for a CAPTCHA could be to prevent bots from having a success rate greater than 0.01% [6]. Since CAPTCHA use increases the cost of a software robot, the CAPTCHA can still be effective, as long as this increased cost remains higher than the cost of using a human. In order to develop a new audio CAPTCHA, we followed an iterative approach: (a) we selected a set of attributes appropriate for audio CAPTCHA, (b) we developed a CAPTCHA that is based on these attributes, and (c) we evaluated the CAPTCHA by calculating the success rates of a bot and a number of users until the results were satisfying and the attributes did not require further adjustment (see Fig 1).

3   CAPTCHA Attributes

High success rates by users is a key factor in deciding whether the CAPTCHA is effective or not. This is particularly important in the case of audio CAPTCHA, as it does not only refer to VoIP callers, but also to visually impaired users of a VoIP service. Equally important is the success rate of a bot, which should be kept to a minimum. Both factors depend on several attributes, which we classified into four categories (Fig. 2): (a). *vocabulary*, (b). *background noise*, (c). *time*, and (d). *audio production*.

Vocabulary attributes: CAPTCHA can vary based on the vocabulary used, by the following attributes:

1. *Adequate data field*: A data field (called alphabet) is used as a pool for selecting the characters to be included in an audio CAPTCHA. For the development of our CAPTCHA we used an alphabet of ten one-digit numbers, i.e. 0,,9. Such a choice allows the use of the DTMF method for answering the audio CAPTCHA. Other examples of audio CAPTCHA that use only digits are the MSN and the Google ones. A limited alphabet may make an audio method quite vulnerable to attacks.

Therefore, in order to make the CAPTCHA solution harder for a bot, a means that we adopted, is to use a number of different human speakers for each digit of the alphabet.

2. *Spoken characters variation*: Another drawback is the use of a fixed number of characters. Having a non variable number of characters in combination with a limited alphabet can make a CAPTCHA particularly vulnerable to attacks. For example, if only 3-digit CAPTCA are used and a bot can successfully recognize 2 of the digits, then it would easily reach 10% success.

3. *Language requirements*: Another important factor is the mother tongue of the users, as it plays a major role in achieving a high success rate by human users. This is particularly important in the case of audio methods, where there is a greater difficulty in identifying spoken characters when the mother tongue differs from that of the user. As a result, the language used should meet the scope of the specific CAPTCA application. As a good practice, the spoken characters should be few. The CAPTCHA we proposed can be adjusted for non English users, as the CAPTCHA are created dynamically and different characters can be added easily.

Background noise attributes: The background noise is another important attribute of an audio CAPTCHA, as it increases the difficulty for an automated procedure to solve it [12]. The main noise attributes are the following:

1. *Noise patterns*: The noise, which can be added during the production of a voice message, can make CAPTCHA particularly resistant to attacks by automated bots. Application of background noise requires a great variety of such noises to be available. These noises should be rotated in an erratic manner. In our proposal, instead of developing a repository with noises, we chose to proceed with a dynamic production of noises, which are distorted in a random manner. The way various noises are produced should prevent the easy elimination of them by automated programs that use learning techniques. An example of an audio CAPTCHA which is vulnerable to attacks, because of the static nature of the added noise is the MSN audio CAPTCHA (violated by the J. van der Vorms bot, success rate of 75%) [13]. The Google audio CAPTCHA, with a noise production different than the MSN and with different announcers for each character, appears to be harder for the same bot (33%) [13]. In any case, the final version of the audio message, resulting from the combined use of different distortion techniques and added noise, should be such that the majority of users can recognize it as easily as possible.

2. *Sound distortion techniques*: Sound distortion techniques may prevent an automated program to isolate the spoken characters from a voice message correctly. One needs to select the scale in which a distortion method will be applied to the spoken characters, the background noise added, or both. The deformation can last for the entire duration of the voice message, or it can be applied only when characters are announced, or even appear at random time intervals. In our CAPTCHA the distortion is applied between the characters, as there appears to be no effective method for evaluating how people understand digits with distortion.

Time attributes: During the production of an audio snapshot, a set of variables should be defined. These variables refer to the length of the audio message, which depends on: (a). the number of characters spoken, (b). the characters chosen, and (c). the time required for each character to be announced, which depends on the announcer of each character. The beginning and the end of each character spoken should also be defined. This depends on the duration of each character, as well as to the duration of the pause between the spoken characters, which could vary for each CAPTCHA. If the above time parameters follow specific patterns, then the resistance of the audio CAPTCHA to an automated program will decrease. In our CAPTCHA, we tried to eliminate such time-related patterns.

Audio production attributes: An audio CAPTCHA production procedure should be automated. An acceptable human interference refers only to the adjustment of various thresholds.

1. *Automated production process*: The automation of the CAPTCHA production process is a desirable but hard to achieve property. The various elements that compose an audio CAPTCHA, such as the number of characters of a message, the different announcers of each character, the different background sound, the timing and the distortion of the message, make the process time-costly and demanding of hardware resources. Our choice is to produce audio CAPTCHA periodically in order: (a) not to produce them in real-time, and (b) not to produce identical snapshots for extended time periods.

2. *Audio CAPTCHA reappearance*: An audio CAPTCHA should reappear rarely. In any case, especially with short alphabets, every CAPTCHA is expected to reappear after a while. Due to the attributes of the voice messages (e.g., technical distortion, added noise, language, speakers, etc.), as well as to the context of the user (e.g., noisy environment, etc.), a voice message may not be identified by the user on the first attempt. Therefore, a second chance may be given. In this case, a different CAPTCHA should be used.

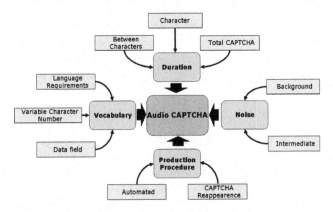

Fig. 2. Audio CAPTCHA attributes

4   CAPTCHA Bot

Frequency and energy pick detection bots
There are various methods/tools to recognize the words spoken in an audio file, such as the HTK toolkit [16] and the Sphinx [17]. These methods are demanding in hardware and time resources, because they use combinations of speech recognition methods. Moreover, they do not focus on how quick they reach a result but on how correct the result is. Therefore, we selected a bot category which employs frequency and energy peak detection methods and can be used to solve audio CAPTCHA for the following reasons:

- *Such bots have been proven effective*: Demonstrative (though perhaps not thorough enough) tests of such bots against popular audio CAPTCHA implementations have been successful [13,14,15] (e.g., SPIT prevention infrastructures, registrations for visually impaired people, etc.)
- *Such bots are easy to implement*: Frequency and energy peak detection bots are comparatively easy to implement using open-source software.
- *Such bots require limited time to solve a CAPTCHA*: Fast CAPTCHA solving is required because most services leave a small time frame for their users to solve the tests (5-15 sec), especially if VoIP services are considered. The CAPTCHA solving bot must analyze and reform the solution to the desired form (SIP message, DTMF, etc.), in a limited time frame.
- *Such bots occupy a small amount of system recourses*: An automated spam attack is selected when its cost is lower than employing humans. Also, a spitter performs multiple attacks simultaneously (e.g. the goal is to initiate SIP calls or messages in parallel). Thus, a bot must be inexpensive in terms of system recourses, which will allow the spammer/spitter to run several instances of the bot at the same time. Regarding time constraints, frequency and energy peak detection processes are less demanding than other approaches, which use different methods such as Hidden Markov Models (HMM) [16].

On the other hand, there are drawbacks when using these bots, mainly due to the fact that they require a training session. In this session a human identifies a number of selected CAPTCHA. The human recognizes the announced characters and records them in a file, from which the bot receives the data to solve the CAPTCHA. The set of training audio CAPTCHA might be extensive if the CAPTCHA data field (alphabet) is long. However, in the VoIP domain, the available alphabet is relatively small as it contains only digits (0-9), which increases the applicability of the mechanism.

The bot used
For the purpose of this paper we used the bot developed by J. van der Vorm [13]. This bot uses frequency analysis and energy peak detection, in order to segment and solve an audio CAPTCHA. The bot works as follows: it first reads the audio file. It skips as many starting bytes as the user has predefined (to avoid the starting bells that many services have, e.g. Google). Then, the samples are treated with a hamming window defined by the user. Each block is transformed into the frequency domain using Discrete Fourier

Transformation. Then, the frequencies are put in a predefined number of bins (the bins are not equally wide, the higher the frequency, the larger the band). After that, the bot looks at the highest frequency bin. Every block that has more energy in a window than the predefined threshold energy is considered a peak (see Fig. 3). These peaks are used to segment the audio file in the different spoken digits. Then the bot looks for a number of windows around the peaks and prints all the frequency bins. This is the profile of the digit. The profiles of the digits are then compared with the ones in the training file, and the closest match is chosen as a possible guess for each digit.

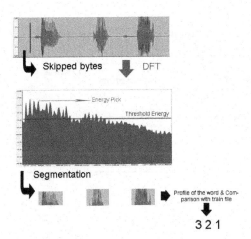

Fig. 3. Audio analysis of the bot

During the training session of the bot, the user gives as input to the bot an audio CAPTCHA. Then, for each profile of the digit that the bot chooses, the user enters which digit it actually was (this procedure can be automated if the user names the audio files accordingly, i.e., if an audio CAPTCHA file includes the digits 3, 2 and 1, the file name can be 321.wav). Obviously, the larger the number of audio CAPTCHA in the training set is, the higher the success ratio of the bot would be.

Bot applicability to SIP-based VoIP
In order to implement the bot in a SIP-based VoIP environment and examine its applicability, it was decided that the implementation procedure should consist of three stages. The procedure and the exchanged SIP messages between the participating entities are presented in Fig. 4.

Stage 0: It is dominated by the administrator of the callees domain (Domain2). When the callees domain receives a SIP INVITE message, there are three possible distinct outcomes: (a) forward the message to the caller, (b) reject the message, and (c) send a CAPTCHA to the caller (UA1).

Stage 1: An audio CAPTCHA is sent (in the form of a 182 message) to the caller (UA1). In the proposed implementation, the caller is replaced by a bot. It must record the audio CAPTCHA, reform it to an appropriate audio format (wav, 8000Hz, 16 bit), and identify the announced digits. The procedure depends mainly on the time needed to reform the message. Moreover, the particular bot needs approximately 0.10 sec to identify a 3-digit CAPTCHA and 0.15 sec to identify a 4-digit one.

Stage 2: When the bot has generated an answer, it forms a SIP message by using SIPp [14], which includes the DTMF answer. This answer is sent as a reply of the CAPTCHA puzzle. If the caller does not receive a 200 OK message, a new CAPTCHA is sent and the bot starts to record again (Stage 1).

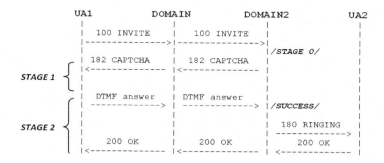

Fig. 4. SIP message exchange for CAPTCHA

The procedure above should be completed within a specific time frame. This time slot opens when the audio file is received by the caller and closes when the timeout of the users input expires (defined by the service CAPTCHA provider). The duration of the CAPTCHA playback does not affect the time frame because the waiting time for an answer starts when the playback is complete. If an answer arrives before the timeout, then it is validated by CAPTCHA service (and if it is correct the call is established), otherwise the bot has another try. In our proposal, the bot is given 6 sec to respond to the CAPTCHA, whereas the maximum number of attempts is set to three (3).

Table 1 illustrates the time required by the various stages in the proposed implementation. The selected bot is able to answer properly to CAPTCHA puzzle in much less time than the proposed time frame. Since a CAPTCHA is desired to be easy for humans, we suggest that the time frame, in which the caller should answer the CAPTCHA puzzle, should not be less than 3 sec. That is because many groups of users, such as physically impaired or elderly people, may not be able to respond promptly.

5   Audio CAPTCHA Implementation

Selected Attributes
In order to develop an effective audio CAPTCHA, we decided upon the following attributes:

Different announcers: The announcer of each and every digit is selected randomly.

Table 1. Stage duration

Stage	Step	Duration (sec)
1	Reform audio	~1.00
	Identify digits	~ 0.15
2	Create SIPp message	~0.40
	Send SIPp message	~0.00
Total (sec)		~1.55

Random positioning of each digit in the CAPTCHA: The digits of the CAPTCHA are physically distributed randomly in the available space.

Background noise of each digit: Background noise, randomly selected, is added to each and every digit of the audio CAPTCHA. The audio noise files are segments (from 1 to 3 seconds) of randomly selected music files and not auto-generated by other methods (e.g. creation of white noise). We wanted to ensure that they will be less annoying for the user to listen to. The automatic generation of background and intermediate noises would require statistical analysis. Moreover, the volume level of the noise is lower than the level of the digits so that they remain audible to humans.

Loud noise between digits: Loud noise is introduced between the digits (the noise is not very loud, to minimize the discomfort of the user).

Different duration and file size: Each audio CAPTCHA file has different duration and different size.

Vocabulary:The vocabulary was limited to digits 0,,9, since the audio CAPTCHA was designed for a SIP-based VoIP infrastructure, where DTMF signals need to be sent.

CAPTCHA development

The audio CAPTCHA development was carried out in five incremental Stages (Stage 1 to Stage 5), in terms of the number of attributes adopted. Each development stage was tested and evaluated upon its efficiency according to the success rate of the bot and the success rate of human users. The audio CAPTCHA produced in Stage 1 were pronounced by one sole announcer without including additional features. Furthermore, the first digit of every word started at the exact same point as the other ones, and the time difference between each digit was equal. The waveforms of the resulting 3- and 4-digit CAPTCHA appear in Fig. 5(a) and 5(e). In such a simple audio CAPTCHA, a bot can use a detection method, such as energy peak detection, and easily segment and recognize the digits. An important factor in this process is the number of audio CAPTCHA that were used during the training of the bot. If a small number was used, then there is a high chance that not all digits are given as an input in the training process; thus, the bot may have a low success rate. That is the case with the 4-digit CAPTCHA (Fig. 5(e)). The random training sequence did not involve many instances of some digits (such us 8 and 9), therefore, the bot resulted in a relatively low (69%) success rate.

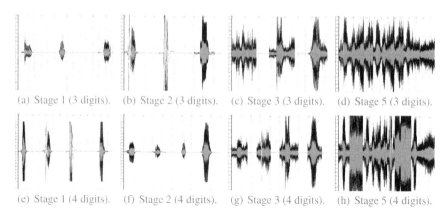

(a) Stage 1 (3 digits).   (b) Stage 2 (3 digits).   (c) Stage 3 (3 digits).   (d) Stage 5 (3 digits).

(e) Stage 1 (4 digits).   (f) Stage 2 (4 digits).   (g) Stage 3 (4 digits).   (h) Stage 5 (4 digits).

Fig. 5. Audio files' waveforms in implementation stages

During Stage 2, the audio CAPTCHA were produced by using 7 different announcers. Each digit was pronounced by a randomly selected announcer. This modification affected the success of the bot, but it mainly depended on the training set. When a larger training set was provided in the case of 4-digit audio CAPTCHA, the bot was able to maintain a relatively high success rate. However, when the same number of audio files, as in the 3-digit CAPTCHA process, was provided, the success rate decreased slightly. Moreover, we should mention that 4-digit CAPTCHA offer more digits to the training procedure. For example, if we use 100 3-digit CAPTCHA for training, we have 300 digits recorded, whereas with the same number of 4-digit CAPTCHA we get 400 digits. Figs. 5(b) and 5(f) show the waveforms of the produced digits.

In Stage 3 background noise was added against each digit. This way we managed to suppress the success rate of the bot, but it still remained relatively high (30% for the 3-digit CAPTCHA and 55% for the 4-digit ones). Figs. 5(c) and 5(g) show the waveforms of the produced digits with the background noise. The high success rate is due to the ability of the bot to cut off the low energy sounds (i.e., the noise) by checking above a certain threshold energy. The difference between the success of 3- and 4-digit CAPTCHA is due to the difference in the training sets. In this case we allowed a training of 50 audio CAPTCHA for the 3-digit ones and 150 for the 4-digit ones. As a result, the available digits taking part in the training process were 150 and 600, respectively.

In Stage 4 we raised the volume of the background noise of each digit. Although the bot success rate fell noticeably (10-15% success), the produced audio CAPTCHA were too difficult to solve for humans, as the loud background noise made it hard for the users to distinguish the digits spoken.

In Stage 5 we introduced loud noise between the digits (intermediate noise) (Fig. 5(d), 5(h)). This resulted in the bot being unable to segment the audio file correctly. This happened because there were more energy peaks than the digits spoken. The loud intermediate noises were recognized as additional digits, because they produce high energy peaks as well, when transformed with the Discrete Fourier Transformation. As a consequence, the bot could not be trained, as it failed to recognize successfully any digits.

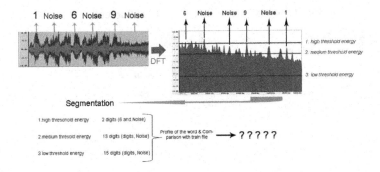

Fig. 6. Demonstration of a bot failing to solve a CAPTCHA

Stage 5 is described, in more detail in Fig. 6. When the bot transforms such an audio into the frequency domain, the energy peaks that can be found are both digits and noise. Therefore, the bot recognizes more digits than those which are actually included in the file. One possible solution for the bot would be to raise or lower the threshold of the energy. In that case (see Fig 6), the bot would still fail. If the threshold energy is very high, then the bot would not recognize some of the digits in the CAPTCHA, while at the same time it would recognize some intermediate noise as digits. On the other hand, if the threshold energy is lowered, then the bot would recognize all digits, but at the same time all intermediate noises would also be considered digits, as well. As a result, the bot would assume that there were 12 or 15 digits in the CAPTCHA.

CAPTCHA testing
User and bot success rates are the main factors that form the decision of whether a CAPTCHA is efficient or not. The corresponding success rates, regarding the CAPTCHA we described in section 5.2, appear on Fig. 7. Each attribute added efficiency to the CAPTCHA and directly affected the user and bot success rates.

The CAPTCHA developed in Stage 5 had an average user success rate of 83%, with an average bot success rate less than 1%.[1]

CAPTCHA implementation
During the implementation of the proposed audio CAPTCHA, the audio files had the following attributes:

1. They were created automatically; therefore they can be updated at random time-periods, without human intervention. The overall process for creating a full set of 3-digit CAPTCHA took 8 sec, whereas for creating a full set of 4-digit CAPTCHA it took 107 sec. Thus, the reproduction of the whole set of CAPTCHA does not

---

[1] The users who were invited to solve the CAPTCHA (sample) were 22 in number and mainly between 20-30 years old. Most of them were university students. All CAPTCHA were in english, which was not the mother tongue of any of the participants (there was a requirment for them to speak english).

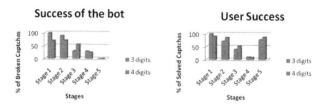

Fig. 7. Bot's and users' success rates

cause significant overhead to our VoIP infrastructure (the VoIP server was a 2GHz Core2Duo, with 2GB RAM).

2. All constituting parts of the audio CAPTCHA, such as the digits and the noise, lay in different folders. Moreover, each time a set of CAPTCHA is produced, the program selects randomly each digit from a different announcer, as well as a random background noise.
3. The noise between the digits is random and has different volume and energy.
4. The pronounced digits and the noise have random duration, which results in a random duration of each audio CAPTCHA.

6   Conclusions, Limitations and Future Plans

CAPTCHA are expected to play a key role for preventing email spam and voice spam (SPIT) in the near future. In order for them to be effective, they must be easy to solve for humans, while at the same time very hard for bots to pass. The CAPTCHA we proposed incorporated several attributes, such us different digit announcers, background noise against each digit, noise between digits and all of them in a random1 and automated way. We produced audio CAPTCHA, which are regularly refreshed, with a limited chance of creating the same instance of an audio CAPTCHA more than once. The production of the CAPTCHA was done in five discrete stages. Each time the CAPTCHA were tested both with a frequency and energy peak detection bot, as well as by a number of users. The bot managed to achieve a high success rate during the first four stages (up to 98%), but that rate dropped dramatically at the last one (less than 2%).

Additionally, we determined an appropriate level of background noise of each digit, in order for them to solvable by humans and difficult to break by bots. However, each attribute alone is not enough for making CAPTCHA robust; it is the combination of the features that make the CAPTCHA resistant. Needless to say, every CAPTCHA is efficient, as long as there is a high rate of success for humans and a low one for bots.

A limitation of the proposed CAPTCHA is that there has been no evaluation of its effectivenss and its attributes by audio/speech recognition tools, such as HTK which uses Hidden Markov Model (HHM). Most audio recognition systems are based on identifing conversations, where each word should have a connection with other words. However, an extensive research with an Automated Speech Recognition (ASR) system could support a more reliable evaluation of our implementation Also it would be interesting to compare our CAPTCHA with other audio CAPTCHA implementations [18], that have not been tested with the particular bot yet.

Another possible extension is to consider different populations of users and take into consideration the specific requirements of each set. This could be done if a major SIP provider can provide personalized services to its clients and, as a result, provide various CAPTCHA types for each specific user.

Acknowledgement. This work has been performed within the SPIDER (COOP-32720) Project, which is partly funded by the European Commission. The authors would like to acknowledge the contribution of our colleagues from Athens University of Economics & Business (GR), Fokus (D), Eleven (D), Voztelecom (E), Telio (NO) and IPTEGO (D).

References

1. Turing, A.: Computing machinery and intelligence. Mind LIX(236), 433–460 (1950)
2. Blum, M., von Ahn, L., Langford, J., Hopper, N.: The CAPTCHA Project (November 2000)
3. von Ahn, L., Blum, M., Hopper, N., Langford, J.: CAPTCHA: Using hard AI problems for security. In: Biham, E. (ed.) EUROCRYPT 2003. LNCS, vol. 2656, pp. 294–311. Springer, Heidelberg (2003)
4. von Ahn, L., Blum, M., Langford, J.: Telling Humans and Computer Apart Automatically. Com. of the ACM 47(2), 57–60 (2004)
5. von Ahn, L., Maurer, B., McMillen, C., Abraham, D., Blum, M.: CAPTCHA: human-based character recognition via Web security. Science 321(5895), 1465–1468 (2008)
6. Chellapilla, K., Larson, K., Simard, P., Czerwinski, M.: Building Segmentation Based Human Friendly Human Interaction proofs. In: Proc. of the SIGCHI conference on Human Factors in Computing Systems, pp. 711–720. ACM Press, New York (2005)
7. Chew, M., Baird, H.: Baffletext: A Human Interactive Proof. In: Proc. of the 10th SPIE/IS&T Document Recognition & Retrieval Conference, USA, pp. 305–316 (January 2003)
8. Mori, G., Malik, J.: Recognizing objects in adversarial clutter: Breaking a visual CAPTCHA. In: Proc. of the Computer Vision and Pattern Recognition Conference, pp. 134–141. IEEE Press, Los Alamitos (2003)
9. Defeated CAPTCHA (retrieved May 18, 2008),
   http://libcaca.zoy.org/wiki/PWNtcha
10. Yan, J., El Ahmad, A.: Breaking Visual CAPTCHA with Naive Pattern Recognition Algorithms. In: Samarati, P., et al. (eds.)Proc. of the 23rd Annual Computer Security Applications Conference (ACSAC 2007), pp. 279–291. IEEE Computer Society, Los Alamitos (2007)
11. Yan, J.: A El Ahmad, A Low-cost attack on a Microsoft CAPTCHA, Technical Report, School of Computer Science, Newcastle University, United Kingdom (February 2008)
12. Jurafsky, D., Martin, J.: Speech and Language Processing: An Introduction to Natural Language Processing, Computational Linguistics and Speech Recognition, 2nd edn. Prentice-Hall, Englewood Cliffs (2008)
13. Defeating Audio (Voice) CAPTCHA (retrieved October 10, 2008),
   http://vorm.net/captchas/

14. SIPP Traffic Generator for the SIP Protocol (retrieved September 30, 2008),
    http://sipp.sourceforge.net/
15. Breaking Gmails Audio CAPTCHA (retrieved October 10, 2008),
    http://blog.wintercore.com/?p=11
16. HTK: Hidden Markov Model Toolkit (retrieved October 10, 2008),
    http://htk.eng.cam.ac.uk/
17. SPHINX: The CMU Sphinx Group Open Source Speech Recognition Engines (retrieved
    January 2, 2009),
    http://cmusphinx.sourceforge.net/html/cmusphinx.php
18. Tam, J., Simsa, J., Huggins-Daines, D., von Ahn, L., Blum, M.: Improving Audio
    CAPTCHA. In: Proc. of the Symposium on Usable Privacy and Security (SOUPS 2008),
    USA (2008)

Roving Bugnet: Distributed Surveillance Threat and Mitigation

Ryan Farley and Xinyuan Wang

George Mason University, Department of Computer Science, Fairfax, Virginia, USA
rfarley3@gmu.edu, xwangc@gmu.edu

Abstract. Advanced mobile devices such as laptops and smartphones make convenient hiding places for surveillance spyware. They commonly have a microphone and camera built-in, are increasingly network accessible, frequently within close proximity of their users, and almost always lack mechanisms designed to prevent unauthorized microphone or camera access.

In order to explore surveillance intrusion and detection methods, we present a modernized version of a microphone hijacker for Windows and Mac OS X. This attack can be executed as soon as the target connects to the Internet from anywhere in the world without requiring interaction from victimized users. As the attacker compromises additional machines they are organized into a botnet so the attacker can maintain stealthy control of the systems and launch later surveillance attacks.

We then present a mechanism to detect the threat on Windows, as well as a novel method to deceive an attacker in order to permit traceback. As a result of the detection mechanism we address a missing segment of resource control, decreasing the complexity of privacy concerns as exploitable devices become more pervasive.

1 Introduction

The capabilities of spyware have expanded as always-on Internet connections have become increasingly frequent [11,30]. It's not only data stored on the compromised machine that is at risk. Variants of spyware that provide audio and video surveillance through peripherals such as microphones and web-cams have been around for over ten years. This may all sound like old news, but that is deceivingly wrong.

There are a few factors why well structured surveillance attacks are only a recently growing concern and an increasingly unchecked threat reaching critical potential. Primarily, consumers are realizing that a smartphone with an unlimited data plan is almost as vulnerable as a desktop on broadband at home [19]. Also laptops, which have long had built-in microphones and Internet accessibility, are recently also being sold with built-in web-cams. Protection is even more of a concern in the modern computing environment where new regulations are constantly driving up the accountability of organizations for the loss of private data.

It is important to point out that we are not implying that surveillance spyware will be as widespread as other malware. A microphone in every house with Internet access is of

D. Gritzalis and J. Lopez (Eds.): SEC 2009, IFIP AICT 297, pp. 39–50, 2009.

little use to the average attacker and surveillance attacks will probably involve specific victims known to the attacker. This does not diminish how universal of a threat this is, after all, potentially anyone is capable of gaining an unwanted stalker, jealous spouse, or generally becoming the target of espionage [20].

The most plausible use of surveillance spyware across a set of devices is to provide a roving bug. This is a term used for audio surveillance that follows a particular victim regardless of which device they are using. If the attacker has compromised a victim's home computer, work laptop, and smartphone, then the attacker would have a greater capacity to continuously monitor the victim.

To investigate feasible methods for surveillance threats, we have implemented a complete remote attack and control package called the *roving bugnet* that approximates observed distributed control systems. The bugnet consists of a scalable number of compromised devices called *bugbots* which can stream live microphone data to a remote attacker either continuously or for a set time. To modernize older surveillance programs, our prototype can automatically compromise a vulnerable Windows (95–Vista) or Mac OS X laptop and stealthily seize control of its microphone without any action by the victim as soon as the laptop connects to the Internet.

It appears that no existing malware defense provides a generic intrusion detection mechanism against the bugbot attack. To resolve this we present a preliminary mitigation mechanism that is designed to be compatible with most Windows platforms. It can detect a process that is actively using the microphone and allow the user to set access controls. This mechanism includes a novel method to deceive a remote attacker after detection by transparently replacing the microphone input with arbitrary and realistic decoy audio. The process would trick the attacker into believing that the bug is working, yet prevent any confidential information leakage and provide time to trace the connection back to its source in order to discover the attacker.

The rest of this paper contains implementation and testing scenarios as well as design challenges and considerations. In section 2, we discuss the design and implementation of the bugnet surveillance system. A demonstration of the system is presented in section 3. Then in section 4 we introduce the prototype detection and defense mechanism as well as detail the experiments performed to test its effectiveness. We discuss related work in section 5, and conclude in section 6 with the implications and open work for this low-cost high-reward threat.

2 Roving Bugnet Design

In order to remotely monitor a target with a distributed surveillance system there needs to be two functional components: one that accomplishes a microphone hijacking, and another that maintains stealthy remote control of a compromised system. Both the outdated trojans BackOrifice and SubSeven provide remote access and microphone recording plugins, but cannot stream live data. A modern trojan, Poison Ivy includes live streaming, but requires the victim to be actively connected in order to start and stop the microphone recording. Also, since these are all trojans, by definition they are designed to require victim interaction to infect a vulnerable host.

```
 1 start data handling thread          1 if using file open output file
 2 open UDP server for UI              2 if using network create socket
 3 fill in WinAPI structures           3 while WinAPI GetMessage
 4 WinAPI waveInOpen                    4   if MM_WIM_DATA
 5 WinAPI waveInAddBuffer               5     if using network
 6 WinAPI waveInStart                   6       send data to destination
 7 while listen for control input      7     if using file
 8   if input is stop recording        8       write data to file
 9     WinAPI waveInStop                9   WinAPI waveInAddBuffer
10     cleanup and exit
```

(a) Control thread for main loop and receiv-   (b) Data handling thread for receiving mes-
ing user control input.   sages from the sound card driver.

Fig. 1. Code overview of each waveIn recording application thread

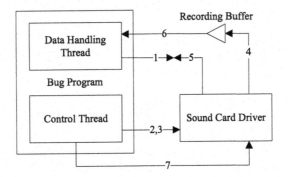

Fig. 2. Visualization of the bug program control flow. 1) Data handling thread waits for messages. 2) Control thread sets recording parameters and 3) initiates recording. 4) Sound card writes to buffers and 5) sends a message when each is full so that 6) the bug can access the recorded data. 7) Control thread stops recording when finished.

In this section we will introduce an updated remote surveillance package that can infect Internet connected hosts without victim interaction and provide persistent management access. The attacker can instruct hosts to turn on the bug at an arbitrary time or at particular system conditions and record for either an indefinite or specified duration. This roving bugnet design is presented in two layers: the prototype microphone surveillance program in section 2.1; and, the remote management botnet in section 2.2. The layered approach of this design allows a single generic cross-platform bot to employ OS specific microphone recording executables. In fact, while this paper only details Windows XP, we have already tested the versatility of this design by successfully implementing bugbots on Mac OS X as well.

2.1 Bugbot: Microphone Access

To develop the bugbot program we used the Microsoft Platform SDK, a free Windows application programming interface (WinAPI) that can be used for multimedia application development. Of the WinAPI functions, the waveIn set was selected since it has greater flexibility and the widest compatibility for Windows versions (from 95 to Vista) and existing hardware.

Figures 1 and 2 illustrate how the program is divided into two threads. It is worth noting that Mac OS X microphone recorders use this two thread approach as well. The primary thread, figure 1(a), acts as a control and the secondary, figure 1(b), handles the data returned from the sound card.

In figure 1(a) the control input handled at line 7 is from an UDP server. This allows interactive remote control such as starting and stopping a recording. It also controls switching between using a network socket for a live data feed, writing to a file for later retrieval, or both. Line 3 sets a data structure which contains the recording parameters for the raw data that will be returned from the sound card and is set by the call in line 4. Line 5 allows for a continuous stream of data by initializing a cyclical set of buffers. Finally, the sound card is instructed to begin and end the recording through the functions in lines 6 and 9 respectively.

When a buffer is filled by the sound card driver, a MM_WIM_DATA message is sent to the bugbot process. The data handling thread, as seen in figure 1(b) loops at line 3 on a blocking function which waits for messages. MM_WIM_DATA messages contain the recently filled buffer's location in memory and the size of the data stored in the buffer, allowing the process to access and output the data. Line 9 replenishes the cyclical buffers initially set by line 5 of the control thread.

As an added advantage the program can detect if the network connection dies and act appropriately. If the system call to send socket data fails, then a network accessibility test is run. If that test fails, then the application will output to a file until the network connection is restored. The attacker would wait for the machine to return onto the network, and then transfer the file for local playback.

This is just one piece of the overall puzzle. While the bugbot program is fully functional for microphone surveillance, it lacks a way to install itself on the victim's host, start itself to begin with, and easily manage multiple nodes. To accomplish a complete distributed surveillance system there needs to be a remote access framework, such as the method described in the next section.

2.2 Bugnet: Remote Control

An Internet Relay Chat (IRC) bot is a program or collection of scripts that acts on behalf of an user client. The goals of IRC bots vary widely, such as automatically kicking other users off or more nefarious things like spamming other IRC users. In this paper, a free standing IRC bot is presented that monitors an IRC channel for commands from a particular user and responds accordingly.

A botnet is a collection of bots, usually under the control of a botherder, or botmaster, using a communication method, such as IRC, to execute actions in proxy on the bots [23]. The overall structure resembles figure 3(a). Plausible purposes of botnets are click-fraud, DoS attacks, and distributed processing. The general motivation of the botmaster is to acquire as many machines as desired and maintain control for either resale or some ulterior purpose [15].

While there are many preexisting IRC bots freely available online that could be adapted for this threat, for simplicity and greater control we developed our own from

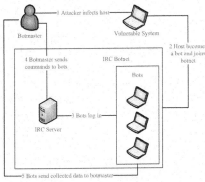

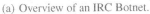

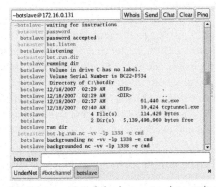

(a) Overview of an IRC Botnet.

(b) An example of the botmaster interacting with a bot.

Fig. 3. Botnet overview and sample control session

the ground up. The Windows version is written in C, and the OS X version is written in Perl to support both PPC and Intel platforms.

Our IRC bot has a limited set of procedures relating to controlling who can give the bot commands, obtaining the bot's status, and running arbitrary commands on the infected host at specified times. Only once a password and the botmaster's username are approved can the botmaster issue commands. For additional functionality, the IRC bot accepts any file transfers from the botmaster username using the Direct Client to Client (DCC) protocol and stores them into the working directory for later access. To facilitate self installation, when first executed the bot copies its executable into a hidden directory and establishes itself as a service to be started on each boot-up.

The following subset of the commands we have implemented on the bugbot represents a suggested minimum for bot development: <password>, authenticates nick as the botmaster if the password is correct; bot.listen, start to accept commands; bot.stats, report system status and details; bot.die, kill self; bot.[un]install, run the install or uninstall routine manually; and, bot.[bg.]run.[at<time>.], execute an arbitrary command, optionally in the background or at specified time.

Deciding on an infection vector to get the bot onto the target machine would need to vary by specific target; it should be noted however, that with a properly configured rootkit, the bot should remain undiscoverable on the victim's system [38].

3   Threat Demonstration

One goal of this paper is to present a viable example of a roving bugnet by means of a prototype demonstration. In this section we show each step of the entire life cycle of an example attack that can be adapted for other platforms. First, in section 3.1 we describe a method to remotely infect a Windows PC with an IRC bot. Second, in section 3.2 we show how the bot gains control of the microphone by installing the recording program and becomes the bugbot.

3.1   Infection Vector

It is possible for the attacker to use a variety of methods to get the spyware onto a victim's machine. Since advanced infection methods are beyond the scope of this paper we selected Metasploit's command line interface and the upload and execute shellcode as the payload. In order to use a familiar exploit, a default installation of Windows XP SP1 is exploited using the MS06_040 vulnerability module. All an attacker needs to do at this point is specify the bot executable as the local file that will be uploaded to the target and executed on it.

Once the bugbot is installed, it will attempt to join the botnet. At this point an IRC server is needed where the bot is programmed to look. The bot will then log in, join the predetermined channel, and post a message showing that it is ready to accept commands from the botmaster and that it can control the microphone.

3.2   Controlling the Microphone

After the bot has joined the IRC channel, the botmaster can interact with it using the commands listed in section 2.2. A basic session would resemble figure 3(b). When the attacker wishes to gain microphone control, the bug executable needs to be transfered to the compromised machine. For this implementation the attacker transfers the file to the victim using IRC DCC. Alternatively, it could be included in the original uploaded installation routine or downloaded with TFTP or FTP, both of which are included in default installs of Windows XP and Mac OS X.

With this level of remote control on each node within the bugnet, the attacker can now easily execute the surveillance program and activate the bug on any of the compromised systems. At a minimum, the attacker would need to specify how long to record as well as file storage and network transmission options. In our implementation the attacker can specify: the UDP server listening port number; how long to record for; whether to use a file, network stream, or both; the output filename; and, the network broadcast stream destination host IP address and port number. For run time controls, the attacker can send commands to the bug program through its UDP server.

4   Detection and Mitigation

Limiting microphone access can be done either in hardware, such as with a physical kill switch or cover, or in software like other resource controls such as application firewalls that monitor network access. Physical switches would be a difficult after-market option, and unlike application firewalls which have large market acceptance there appears to be no existing generic software based protection against microphone surveillance attacks.

There are particular reasons why monitoring microphone access should be a low burden to the user. First, unlike network access requests or prompts for privilege escalation the average low-tech user is capable of understanding the purpose of the microphone and when it should be turned on or off. Second, the frequency of microphone access requests should be much lower than other resources making it easier to track which applications should be permitted. This also prevents illegitimate access requests from hiding in a cluster of legitimate requests.

In this section we present a preliminary detection and mitigation mechanism for threats similar to bugbot. Our application can can detect if a Windows process is actively using the microphone and allow the user to set access controls similar to antivirus suites and application firewalls based on API call monitoring. This type of specification based intrusion detection [16] is accomplished by injecting target processes with a custom dynamic-linked library (DLL) that sets wrappers, known as hooks, for Windows API (WinAPI) calls.

When the monitored process calls a hooked function the injected DLL's version of the function is used instead. This then provides the DLL with transparent access to all arguments and the ability to return arbitrary values. For this paper, we used a free Microsoft Research package titled Detours [14] that provides tools and a simplified API for coding wrapper DLLs.

In section 4.1 we detail how to completely deny suspect processes. While this provides a solution that protects the true audio, it reduces the chances of tracing the source of the attack. In section 4.2 we present a solution to this problem by demonstrating how the victim can deceive the attacker by providing a decoy sound. The final product is tested section 4.3 where we present several scenarios and results.

4.1 Deploying the Protection Mechanism

As described in section 2.1, this demonstration uses the waveIn WinAPI and details are in terms of those functions. It should be noted that if other WinAPI functions are used, the same concept could be executed but with different functions detoured. In the bug program there are two pertinent function calls that are candidates for hooking into. A detour of `waveInOpen` would interfere with passing initialization data to the sound card driver, but a more direct way to intervene would be to hook into `waveInStart`. Once the DLL has detoured the bug's call it has the option to prevent the bug process from calling the true `waveInStart` function and return a failure value instead. This is an optimal place to insert an allow-or-deny behavior since a denied bug would simply fail to reach a state capable of gathering data.

Automating the decision of whether a process should be trusted or untrusted is a difficult problem. A simple and reliable technique, as we have implemented, is for the monitoring DLL to prompt the user to approve microphone requests on a case to case basis. It is safe to assume that while allow or deny decisions for frequently requested resources such as outbound network access can easily confuse untrained users, most know when they are or are not using their microphone. However, since a denied bug would be obvious to the attacker, a more effective response may be through misinformation, as we present in the next section.

4.2 Deception by Decoy Audio

In cases where it is necessary to have an audit trail, or there is a desire to fully trace an attack, it is advisable to create as much time between detecting an intrusion and the remote attacker leaving the system. One way is to deceive the attacker by feeding the

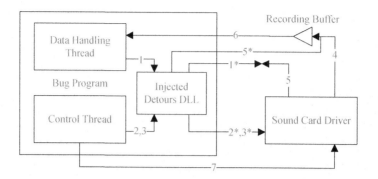

Fig. 4. Visualization of the bug program control flow using the deception method. Numbers refer to same steps as figure 2. 1*, 2*, and 3* are 1, 2, and 3 after DLL interception. 5*) After the DLL receives a "full buffer" message, it replaces the recording buffer with decoy audio and then passes the message to the data handling thread.

bug application crafted data. This method maintains viability even if a future surveillance program uses a yet undiscovered covert channel for exporting the data. This decoy sound should be believable and unpredictable so as to remain undiscovered in the hopes of buying enough time to permit a better trace to the source of the attack. For example, randomized keyboard clacking or indiscernible background mumble would be good candidates.

While the complete traceback of the remote attacker is still an open research problem, this technique is a building block toward such a goal. With properly crafted decoy audio, such as timed silence between predictable sounds, it is possible to introduce distinguishable elements into the transmitted data stream. Similar traceback methods have been used for other applications [33]. This could even hold in the case of compression or encryption, as recent research [25,36] has illustrated strong correlations between such streams and their original content.

To accomplish the deception method transparently, the Detours DLL should inject the crafted audio by replacing filled buffers, that the sound card returns, before the bug can read them. As illustrated in figure 4, if the DLL hooks into the WinAPI GetMessage call (1), then it could intercept (1*) the message from sound card driver (5) indicating a filled buffer. Inside of this message is a pointer to the buffer and the size of the data stored in the buffer. If the DLL also detoured the waveInOpen call (2), then it would know the format of the raw data in the buffer in order to match the decoy audio with it. This avoids deciphering the bug application's internal data structures and formats for storing the data. At this point the DLL could swap (5*) the buffer for an equal length snip from the decoy audio.

4.3   Test Scenarios

In order to observe the viability of injected DLLs that monitor processes for microphone requests we implemented the defense as a single DLL. When the monitor catches a request it prompts the user to either allow, deny, or deceive, by means of decoy audio, the process in question. In order to establish a reliable testing environment we ran two instances of the bugbot program, one to represent the untrusted bugbot process and the other to represent an arbitrary trusted processes.

We initially examined baseline tests with the bugbot and trusted application running separately. When either was not monitored, or monitored but allowed by the user, it had access to the true audio. When either was monitored and denied, or deceived, then neither could access the microphone's audio.

In the next tests we concurrently executed monitored instances of the applications to demonstrate that a monitor in deception mode would not interfere with legitimate recordings. We ran two sets of tests, in one the bugbot attempted to record before the trusted application initialized the microphone and in the other the bugbot attempted to record after. In both cases, when the user chose to deceive the bugbot our mitigation technique transparently replaced the audio from the microphone with a specified recording loop. As a result, the attacker heard the decoy sound while the trusted application continued using the true microphone input.

5   Related Works

Malware detection has been an area of active research, and there are many methods proposed to detect or mitigate malware [7,8,9,12,13,27,32,35]. StackGuard [6], Stack-Ghost [10], RAD [4] and Windows vaccination [21] prevent stack based overflow by protecting the return address from being modified by the malware. However, they are not effective against other attack vectors such as heap based overflow [5].

Another method, packet vaccine [34], seeks to detect malware exploit packets by randomizing address-like stings in the packet payloads. Similar to other randomization based approaches [1,2,17,18,24], which protect applications and systems via randomizing the instruction set or address layout, packet vaccine will cause the vulnerable applications to crash when they are exploited by malware.

Taint analysis aims to detect illegal information flow by tracking the taint, and it has been widely used for analyzing malware [3,22,26,28,29,31,37]. As pointed out by Saxena et al. [26], taint tracking usually incurs high performance overhead. This makes it difficult to be used for detecting malware in real-time.

To the best of our knowledge, no existing malware defense approach has been shown to be effective in detecting the bugbot we have presented.

6   Conclusion

Remote surveillance is a significantly invasive threat, arguably even more so than identity theft. As it stands now, most vulnerable devices do not have the protection necessary to distinctly address microphone or camera hijacks. As a growing number of mobile devices with exploitable operation systems gain more reliable Internet access, this long standing problem is reaching a critical potential.

The risk of surveillance attacks is increased on systems shared with untrusted users. Since multiple users can open the microphone simultaneously, regardless of who is physically at the system, any user of a system can be compromised even if just one user of that system is not protected. Imagine a spouse that exploits this weakness on purpose to spy on his or her partner through a shared computer. This leads to questioning how to properly handle the lack of control over shared resources as more people adopt true multi-user environments.

To demonstrate the viability of a surveillance intrusion, we developed a modern interpretation of a stealthy microphone hijack threat. The features of the bugnet closely match in-the-wild exploits. It uses a botnet framework and is able to exploit a system as soon as the target connects to the Internet.

We then investigated ways to mitigate the threat. Physical protection is an option, such as a cover or on-off switch, but most devices do not have this built-in, leaving software as the only answer for a vast majority of the vulnerable systems. Given the infrequency of microphone access by the average user, adding a way to monitor and interactively control recording access should be unobtrusive. As a solution we developed a mitigation mechanism that can be broadly applied to detect and prevent surveillance exploits. This methodology employs API hooks to monitor processes and uses extensible permissions testing to provide an allow-or-deny behavior.

To facilitate forensic analysis, our bugbot mitigation technique additionally involves using a decoy audio loop that consists of well crafted believable noise, such as background keyboard clacking or indiscernible talking to retain the remote attacker's network connection while keeping the true audio recording confidential. The additional time created could then be used to trace the source of the attacker's connection, or at minimum, gathering as much audit information as possible.

Currently most devices with network access and microphones, such as laptops and smartphones, are vulnerable to this type of attack. Yet there is still no widely accepted way for users to protect themselves. As awareness of this problem increases, the potential threat to privacy may lead consumers and businesses to lessen their dependence on such devices.

References

1. Barrantes, E., Ackley, D., Forrest, S., Palmer, T., Stefanovic, D., Zovi, D.: Randomized instruction set emulation to disrupt binary code injection attacks. In: Proc. of the 10th ACM Conf. on Computer and Communications Security (CCS 2003), pp. 281–289. ACM, New York (2003)
2. Bhatkar, S., DuVarney, D.C., Sekar, R.: Address obfuscation: An efficient approach to combat a broad range of memory error exploits. In: Proc. of the 12th USENIX Security Sym. (2003)
3. Chen, S., Xu, J., Nakka, N., Kalbarczyk, Z., Iyer, R.K.: Defeating memory corruption attacks via pointer taintedness detection. In: Proc. of the 2005 International Conf. on Dependable Systems and Networks (DSN 2005). IEEE, Los Alamitos (2005)
4. Chiueh, T., Hsu, F.H.: RAD: A compile-time solution to buffer overflow attacks. In: Proc. of the 21st International Conf. on Distributed Computing Systems (ICDCS 2001), pp. 409–417. IEEE, Los Alamitos (2001)
5. Conover, M.: w00w00 on heap overflows (1999),
   http://www.w00w00.org/files/articles/heaptut.txt

6. Cowan, C., Pu, C., Maier, D., Hinton, H., Walpole, J., Bakke, P., Beattie, S., Grier, A., Wagle, P., Zhang, Q.: StackGuard: Automatic adaptive detection and prevention of buffer-overflow attacks. In: Proc. of the 7th USENIX Security Sym., pp. 63–78 (1998)
7. Feng, H.H., Giffin, J.T., Huang, Y., Jha, S., Lee, W., Miller, B.P.: Formalizing sensitivity in static analysis for intrusion detection. In: Proc. of the 2004 IEEE Sym. on Security and Privacy (S&P 2004) (2004)
8. Feng, H.H., Kolesnikov, O.M., Fogla, P., Lee, W., Gong, W.: Anomaly detection using call stack information. In: Proc. of the 2003 IEEE Sym. on Security and Privacy (S&P 2003) (2003)
9. Forrest, S., Hofmeyr, S.A., Somayaji, A., Longstaff, T.A.: A sense of self for unix processes. In: Proc. of the 1996 IEEE Sym. on Security and Privacy (S&P 1996). IEEE, Los Alamitos (1996)
10. Frantzen, M., Shuey, M.: StackGhost: Hardware facilitated stack protection. In: Proc. of the 10th USENIX Security Sym., pp. 55–66 (2001)
11. Gibson, S.: Spyware was inevitable. Commun. ACM 48(8), 37–39 (2005)
12. Giffin, J.T., Dagon, D., Jha, S., Lee, W., Miller, B.P.: Environment-sensitive intrusion detection. In: Valdes, A., Zamboni, D. (eds.) RAID 2005. LNCS, vol. 3858, pp. 185–206. Springer, Heidelberg (2006)
13. Giffin, J.T., Jha, S., Miller, B.P.: Efficient context-sensitive intrusion detection. In: Proc. of the 11th Network and Distributed System Security Sym (NDSS 2004) (2004)
14. Hunt, G., Brubacher, D.: Detours: Binary interception of Win32 functions. In: Proc. of the 3rd USENIX Windows NT Sym., pp. 135–143 (1999)
15. Ianelli, N., Hackworth, A.: Botnets as a vehicle for online crime. Tech. rep., CERT (2005)
16. Idika, N., Mathur, A.P.: A survey of malware detection techniques. Tech. rep., SERC, SERC-TR-286 (2007)
17. Jun Xu, Z.K., Iyer, R.K.: Transparent runtime randomization for security. In: Proc. of the 22nd Sym. on Reliable and Distributed Systems (SRDS 2003). IEEE, Los Alamitos (2003)
18. Kc, G.S., Keromytis, A.D., Prevelakis, V.: Countering code-injection attacks with instruction-set randomization. In: Proc. of the 10th ACM Conf. on Computer and Communications Security (CCS 2003), pp. 272–280. ACM, New York (2003)
19. Leavitt, N.: Mobile phones: the next frontier for hackers? IEEE Computer 38(4), 20–23 (2005), doi:10.1109/MC.2005.134
20. McCullagh, D.: FBI taps cell phone mic as eavesdropping tool. ZDNet News (2006)
21. Nebenzahl, D., Sagiv, M., Wool, A.: Install-time vaccination of Windows executables to defend against stack smashing attacks. IEEE Transactions on Dependable and Secure Computing (TDSC) 3(1), 78–90 (2006)
22. Newsome, J., Song, D.: Dynamic taint analysis for automatic detection, analysis, and signature generation of exploits on commodity software. In: Proc. of the 12th Network and Distributed System Security Sym. (NDSS 2005) (2005)
23. Rajab, M.A., Zarfoss, J., Monrose, F., Terzis, A.: A multifaceted approach to understanding the botnet phenomenon. In: IMC 2006: Proc. of the 6th ACM SIGCOMM Conf. on Internet Measurement, pp. 41–52 (2006)
24. Sandeep Bhatkar, R.S., DuVarney, D.C.: Efficient techniques for comprehensive protection from memory error exploits. In: Proc. of the 14th USENIX Security Sym. (2005)
25. Saponas, S.T., Lester, J., Hartung, C., Agarwal, S., Kohno, T.: Devices that tell on you: Privacy trends in consumer ubiquitous computing. In: Proc. of the 16th USENIX Security Sym., pp. 55–70 (2007)
26. Saxena, P., Sekar, R., Puranik, V.: Efficient fine-grained binary instrumentation with applications to taint-tracking. In: Proc. of the 2008 International Sym. on Code Generation and Optimization (CGO 2008) (2008)

27. Sekar, R., Bendre, M., Bollineni, P.: A fast automaton-based method for detecting anomalous program behaviors. In: Proc. of the 2001 IEEE Sym. on Security and Privacy (S&P 2001) (2001)

28. Shankar, U., Talwar, K., Foster, J.S., Wagner, D.: Detecting format string vulnerabilities with type qualifiers. In: Proc. of the 10th USENIX Security Sym. (2001)

29. Su, Z., Wassermann, G.: The essence of command injection attacks in web applications. In: Proc. of the 33rd ACM Sym. on Principles of Programming Languages (POPL 2006) (2006)

30. Trilling, S., Nachenberg, C.: The future of malware. In: EICAR 1999 best paper proceedings (1999)

31. Vogt, P., Nentwich, F., Jovanovic, N., Kirda, E., Kruegel, C., Vigna, G.: Cross site scripting prevention with dynamic data tainting and static analysis. In: Proc. of the 14th Network and Distributed System Security Sym. (NDSS 2007) (2007)

32. Wagner, D., Dean, D.: Intrusion detection via static analysis. In: Proc. of the 2001 IEEE Sym. on Security and Privacy (S&P 2001) (2001)

33. Wang, X., Chen, S., Jajodia, S.: Tracking anonymous peer-to-peer VoIP calls on the internet. In: Proc. of the 12th ACM Conf. on Computer Communications Security (2005)

34. Wang, X., Li, Z., Xu, J., Reiter, M.K., Kil, C., Choi, J.Y.: Packet vaccine: Black-box exploit detection and signature generation. In: Proc. of the 13th ACM Conf. on Computer and Communications Security (CCS 2006). ACM, New York (2006)

35. Warrender, C., Forrest, S., Pearlmutter, B.: Detecting intrusions using system calls: Alternative data models. In: Proc. of the 1999 IEEE Sym. on Security and Privacy (S&P 1999), pp. 133–145 (1999)

36. Wright, C.V., Ballard, L., Monrose, F., Masson, G.M.: Language identification of encrypted VoIP traffic: Alejandra y Roberto or Alice and Bob? In: Proc. of the 16th USENIX Security Sym. (2007)

37. Xu, W., Bhatkar, S., Sekar, R.: Taint-enhanced policy enforcement: A practical approach to defeat a wide range of attacks. In: Proc. of the 15th USENIX Security Sym. (2006)

38. Zaystev, O.: Rootkits, Spyware/Adware, Keyloggers and Backdoors: Detection and Neutralization. A-List Publishing (2006)

On Robust Covert Channels Inside DNS

Lucas Nussbaum[1], Pierre Neyron[2], and Olivier Richard[3]

[1] LIP, ENS Lyon
lucas.nussbaum@ens-lyon.fr
[2] INRIA
pierre.neyron@imag.fr
[3] Laboratoire d'Informatique de Grenoble
olivier.richard@imag.fr

Abstract. Covert channels inside DNS allow evasion of networks which only provide a restricted access to the Internet. By encapsulating data inside DNS requests and replies exchanged with a server located outside the restricted network, several existing implementations provide either an IP over DNS tunnel, or a socket-like service (TCP over DNS). This paper contributes a detailed overview of the challenges faced by the design of such tunnels, and describes the existing implementations. Then, it introduces TUNS, our prototype of an IP over DNS tunnel, focused on simplicity and protocol compliance. Comparison of TUNS and the other implementations showed that this approach is successful: TUNS works on all the networks we tested, and provides reasonable performance despite its use of less efficient encapsulation techniques, especially when facing degraded network conditions.

1 Introduction

Nowadays, more and more networks only allow limited access to the Internet (intranets of companies, wireless networks in hotels, censored Internet access in some countries ...). As a result, many people have tried to leverage an unfiltered protocol to get a full access to the Internet, by establishing a communication channel to another system on the Internet. It has been shown that it is possible to hide data into IP and TCP headers [12], but also using protocols such as ICMP [11], HTTP and HTTPS [8,13], or even IPv6 [9], for example.

In this article, we focus on covert channels using DNS. The DNS protocol is interesting for covert channels, because of its omnipresence: it is indeed difficult to provide an Internet access without providing access to a DNS service (one case is however possible, with configurations providing Web access only and where DNS resolution can then only be required on the HTTP proxy machine, but not on the end-clients). Furthermore, on networks where authentication or payment is required for users to get granted an access to Internet (usually using a *captive portal* [10]), DNS servers cannot return incorrect results until the user authenticates: if the DNS servers would return incorrect results to the users, the users' applications (web browser, for example) could cache the wrong result, and re-use it after authentication, preventing the user from connecting to some hosts even after authentication. As a result, networks that only allow Internet access after authentication on a captive portal, like those found in airports or hotels, allow full DNS access even before the user has logged in or paid the connection fee.

D. Gritzalis and J. Lopez (Eds.): SEC 2009, IFIP AICT 297, pp. 51–62, 2009.

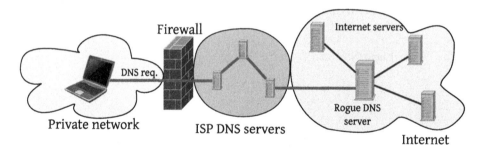

Fig. 1. General principle of covert channels inside DNS

But encapsulating information in DNS packets raises a number of interesting challenges, since the DNS protocol entails a lot of restrictions. It restricts the size of packets and DNS records, leading the existing implementations of DNS tunnels to make compromises between protocol compliance and performance, making most of them easily detectable and then filtered. Those compromises are difficult to choose, because experiments need to happen on a lot of real networks to confirm that a given choice doesn't break the tunnel on some networks.

In the remainder of this article, we present an overview of IP over DNS tunnels (Section 2), and describe the existing implementations (Section 3). Then, we introduce TUNS, our implementation of an IP over DNS tunnel (Section 4), and evaluate it together with the other existing implementations (Section 5).

2   Overview

Figure 1 describes the general principle of covert channels inside DNS tunnels. The client is located in a network where communications to the outside world are going through a firewall. To communicate with servers on the Internet, the client encapsulates data in DNS queries related to the domain delegated to a rogue DNS server located on the Internet. Those queries are sent to the local network's DNS server (direct communication to other DNS servers is usually firewalled), then travel through the ISP's DNS infrastructure, and finally reach the rogue DNS server. Once there, the rogue DNS server decodes the data, and sends it to its target destination, as if it originated from the rogue server itself.

The return path works in a similar way: since the data was sent from the rogue DNS server, replies from target servers return back to the rogue server, which then encapsulates the data in DNS replies sent back to the initial client. However, since those DNS replies can only be sent in reply to DNS queries sent by the client, the client must keep polling the server for data.

Since DNS queries and replies travel through the ISP's DNS infrastructure, they must not differ too much from normal DNS packets. If they are not RFC-compliant or too easy to detect, they will be filtered. For example, data sent from the client to the server is usually encoded in the name being queried, using Base32 (5 bits of information per character) or Base64 (6 bits per character) encodings. But DNS only allows 63 different characters ([a-z] [A-Z] [0-9] -), forcing implementations that choose to use Base64 to add a non-compliant character to this set. Another problem is that Base64 is case-sensitive, while DNS allows servers to change the queries' case (RFC 1035 [5], section 2.3.3: *When data enters the domain system, its original case should be preserved whenever possible.*).

To deal with those constraints, the existing implementations make various compromises, which we describe in the following section.

3   Existing Implementations

There are several existing implementations of covert channels using DNS, which can be divided into two categories:

- covert channels that provide an IP over DNS tunnel (that allow to transmit IP packets through the communication channel) ;
- covert channels that provide a single TCP-like communication channel, allowing to establish an SSH connection (or any other kind of TCP connection) through it.

3.1   IP over DNS Tunnels

IP over DNS tunnels generally use a tun (level 3) or tap (level 2) device, allowing the user to route packets to that interface. Their use is transparent for applications.

NSTX [3] is the older of such implementations. To encode data into queries, it uses a non-compliant Base64 encoding (using "_" in addition to the 63 characters allowed by the DNS RFC). Replies are encoded into TXT records.

Iodine [2] is a more recent project. It uses either Base32 or a non-compliant Base64 encoding to encode the data (chosen via a configuration option). Replies are sent using NULL records. NULL records are described in RFC 1035 [5] section 3.3.10 as a container for any data, up to 65535 bytes long. It is used as a placeholder in some experimental DNS extensions.

Additionally, Iodine uses EDNS0 [6], a DNS extension that allows to use DNS packets longer than the 512-byte limit initially chosen in RFC 1035.

Both NSTX and Iodine split IP packets into several DNS packets, send them separately, then reassemble the IP packets at the other endpoint (in a way similar to IP fragmentation).

3.2   TCP over DNS Tunnels

The second category of tunnels only provides a single TCP connection. The user generally establishes an SSH connection, then uses SSH's *port forwarding* and *SOCKS proxy* features.

The main drawback of those solutions is that they must provide a reliable communication channel over an unreliable protocol, and thus deal with losses, retransmissions, reordering and duplication of DNS packets.

OzymanDNS [4] is the most known implementation. It uses Base32 to encode queries, TXT records for replies, and the EDNS0 extension. During our tests, it proved unstable, crashing frequently.

dns2tcp [1] is a more recent implementation. It uses TXT records, and a non-compliant Base64 encoding (use of '/' in addition to the 63 characters allowed in DNS).

3.3 Conclusion

We tested those four implementations on a dozen of different DNS infrastructures (various french DSL providers, academic networks, public hotspots in hotels, airports, train stations, ...). The four implementations we tested failed to work on a majority of networks. This was expected, since:

- NSTX and dns2tcp can be blocked by forbidding non-compliant names in queries (both of them use DNS names with additional characters).
- All the implementations can be blocked by not serving queries for rarely used DNS records (TXT, NULL) or extensions (EDNS0). This is not an option on most networks, because it would break existing protocols (TXT records are used by the SPF anti-spam system, for example). But it is an acceptable option for commercial hotspots, where the user is less likely to expect a complete access to all Internet features.

4   TUNS

Since the four existing implementations failed to work on a majority of networks, we wrote our own prototype, named TUNS. We aimed at using only standard and widely used features of DNS, so TUNS' packets would be harder to filter in firewalls.

TUNS is an IP over DNS tunnel, written in Ruby, and available under the GNU GPL[1]. Contrary to other solutions, which use TXT or NULL records, rarely used for legitimate reasons, TUNS only uses CNAME records. It encodes the IP packets using a Base32 encoding (Figure 2). Unlike NSTX and Iodine, TUNS doesn't split IP packets into several smaller DNS packets: instead, the MTU of the tunnel's interface is reduced to a much smaller value (140 bytes by default), and the operating system is responsible for splitting IP packets using IP fragmentation. This removes the need to implement a state-machine to retransmit lost DNS packets, and increases the reliability of the tunnel in case of packet loss, but reduces the amount of useful information that can be transmitted, since the IP headers are repeated in each DNS packet.

When there is data to transmit on the client side, they are immediately encapsulated into a DNS query, and sent to the server. To receive data from the server, the client polls it on a regular basis with short DNS queries. If the server has data that must be sent to the client, it answers the client's query immediately. If it doesn't have data to send to the client, it waits for a small amount of time before sending an empty reply. If data to be transmitted arrives during this waiting delay, it is transmitted immediately.

---

[1] TUNS can be downloaded from http://www-id.imag.fr/~nussbaum/tuns.php

The client sends a data packet to the server:

```
Domain Name System (query)
  dIUAAAVAAABAAAQABJ5K4BKBVAHAKQNICBAAAOS5TD4ASKPSQIJEM7VABAAEASC.
  MRTGQ2TMNY0.domain.tld: type CNAME, class IN
```

The client sends a short query that the server will use to send a reply:

```
Domain Name System (query)
  r882.domain.tld: type CNAME, class IN
```

The server acknowledges the data that was sent. In its reply, it indicates the size of the server-side queue (l4.domain.tld, so 4 packets), so the client can send more requests for data:

```
Domain Name System (response)
  Queries
  dIUAAAVAAABAAAQABJ5K4BKBVAHAKQNICBAAAOS5TD4ASKPSQIJEM7VABAAEASC.
  MRTGQ2TMNY0.domain.tld: type CNAME, class IN
  Answers
  dIUA[..]0.domain.tld: type CNAME, class IN, cname 14.domain.tld
```

The server sends a reply containing data to the client:

```
Domain Name System (response)
  Queries
  r882.domain.tld: type CNAME, class IN
  Answers
  r882.domain.tld: type CNAME, class IN, cname dIUAAAVCWIUAAAQABH
  VCY2DMO2HQ7EAQSEIZEEUTCOKBJFIVSYLJOF4YDC.MRTGQ2TMNY0.domain.tld
```

Later, to another request for data, the server replies that it doesn't have any data to send:

```
Domain Name System (response)
  Queries
  r993.domain.tld: type CNAME, class IN
  Answers
  r993.domain.tld: type CNAME, class IN, cname dzero.domain.tld
```

Fig. 2. Content of DNS packets exchanged between a TUNS client and server, as seen with the wireshark network analyzer. Some packets have been shortened for space reasons.

This allows to reduce latency in interactive communications (such as SSH sessions for instance).

Another problem that is addressed in TUNS is the fact that DNS infrastructures sometimes send duplicated queries (probably, in a selfish way, to increase their chances to get a reply despite packet loss): a single query from a client can be duplicated by an intermediate server, and the final server will receive that query twice. In that case, the DNS server must return the same reply to both queries, otherwise an IP packet will be lost. A cache was added in TUNS to allow that.

We tested TUNS on a wide range of networks (including those where we previously tested the other implementations), and TUNS always worked properly.

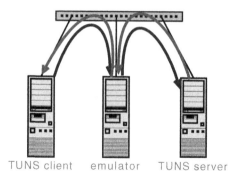

TUNS client   emulator   TUNS server

Fig. 3. Experimental setup

5   Performance Evaluation

We evaluated the performance of NSTX 1.1 beta6, Iodine 0.4.1 and TUNS 0.9.2. To
be able to compare them using a wide range of network conditions, we used network
emulation (our experimental setup is described in figure 3). The experiments were performed on 3 nodes of the Grid'5000 platform (quad-Opteron 2.2 GHz, 4 GB of RAM,
connected to Gigabit Ethernet). The nodes are running Linux 2.6.22 compiled for x86,
not x86-64, to allow network emulation to benefit from the support for high-frequency
timers, which didn't exist for x86-64 in Linux 2.6.22. Emulation settings are applied
using the TC (Traffic Control) subsystem of Linux when the packets exit the emulator
node, both when travelling from the client to the server, and on their way back from
the server. Latency measurements were performed using `ping`, with one measurement
per second. Bandwidth measurements were done using `iperf`. For all experiments, the
network bandwidth was limited to 1 Mbps, to reproduce conditions found on slow wireless networks. This bandwidth limitation was confirmed to be realistic by measuring the
available bandwidth on a few wireless networks.

5.1   Influence of Latency

Our first set of experiments focus on determining how the various solutions react to
high-latency situations. Such situations are frequent with such tools, for example when
the client connects to a server located overseas. Figure 4 shows the perceived latency,
when the underlying network latency between the client and server ranges from 0 ms to
100 ms (so the maximum Round Trip Time is 200 ms). All solutions perform in similar
ways in that case, but TUNS and Iodine exhibit a small, constant overhead compared to
NSTX.

Figure 5 shows the measured upload bandwidth. Iodine gives the best results, while
NSTX is slower than Iodine, especially when the latency is relatively low. TUNS is
significantly slower than the other implementations. There are several reasons for this:

- TUNS uses Base32 encoding, while NSTX and Iodine use Base64, which is more
  efficient, but not RFC-compliant.

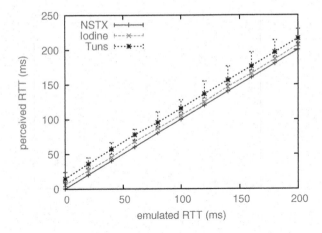

Fig. 4. Perceived latency using *pings* initiated on the client side. Vertical bars indicate the minimum and maximum values over 20 measurements.

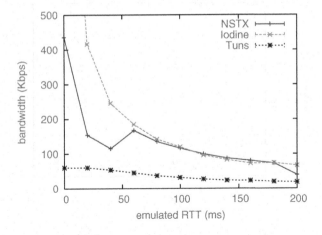

Fig. 5. Upload bandwidth (client to server)

- NSTX and Iodine split IP packets, while TUNS relies on IP fragmentation. This causes the IP headers to be encoded in each packet, leaving less space for the rest of the data.
- NSTX and Iodine are written in C, while TUNS is written in Ruby. The use of an interpreted scripting language clearly increases the processing overhead. After discovering the performance problems of our implementation, we profiled TUNS using Ruby's profiler, and the Ruby DNS library we used proved to be a major bottleneck. The development version of Ruby (Ruby 1.9) improves performance slightly.

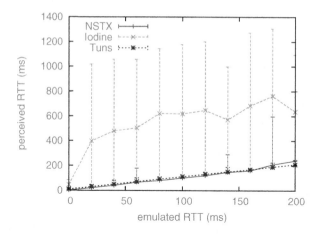

Fig. 6. Perceived latency using *pings* initiated on the server side

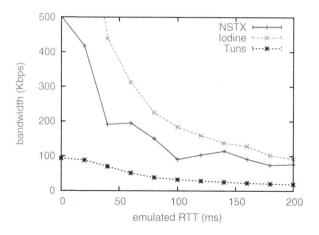

Fig. 7. Download bandwidth (server to client)

Figure 6 describes the tunnel latency using *pings* initiated from the server. It shows the efficiency of the polling method used by the tunnel. While NSTX and TUNS provide similar performance, Iodine's performance is much lower. Further investigations show that Iodine responds immediately to polling requests, even if it doesn't have anything to send. Instead, in that case, NSTX and TUNS wait for a while. If data to be sent to the client arrives during that waiting period, it can then be sent immediately. This optimization has a drawback: if the server takes too much time to reply, an intermediate DNS server (part of the ISP's infrastructure, for instance) might report a failure. In TUNS, the duration which the server is allowed to wait is configurable from the client-side, to adjust to different DNS infrastructures.

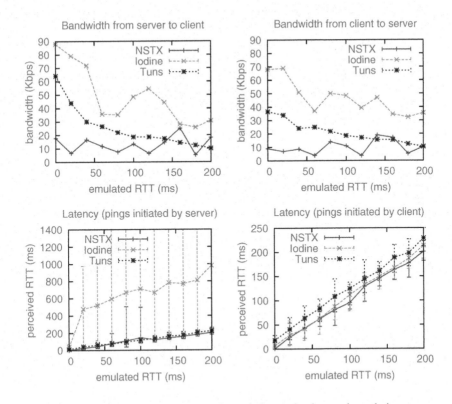

Fig. 8. Measurements on a network emulating packet loss and reordering

As seen in figure 7, the download bandwidth (server to client) is similar to the upload bandwidth (Figure 5). During all our bandwidth measurements, NSTX provided more variable performance than TUNS and Iodine.

5.2   Influence of Degraded Network Conditions

After this first set of measurements, we focused on how the various implementations would perform in degraded network conditions. We emulated a network with 5% of packet loss (uniformly distributed), and latency varied of 10 ms around the value we defined (following normal distribution), causing packets reordering.

Results (Figure 8) show that, while the latency is mostly unaffected, the bandwidth is clearly penalized by such conditions. While TUNS was clearly the slowest implementation in *perfect* network conditions, it now outperforms NSTX.

This is very likely to be caused by the fact that Iodine and NSTX split the IP packets into several DNS packets: when a DNS packet is lost, Iodine and NSTX must take care of retransmitting it, or must discard the other DNS packets split from the same IP packet, and wait for that IP packet to be retransmitted.

6   Changing Tunnel Parameters

While TUNS makes a compromise with efficiency to be able to function properly on more networks than the other implementations, there are cases where this compromise is not necessary. It is interesting to be able to adjust the tunnel's parameters, to match what the network will tolerate. However, this configuration change must be done remotely, from the client-side: the user might lock himself out while trying different parameters if that's not possible.

In TUNS, the client can send special DNS requests to change the configuration of the server. Currently, the following parameters can be changed:

- MTU of the tunnel interface: some DNS infrastructure allow to send larger DNS packets (more than 512 bytes). That allows to increase the length of the IP packets going through the tunnel, thus increasing the efficiency of the tunnel.
- Delay during which the server can keep a request before answering it: as explained in section 5.1, this affects the efficiency of the polling mechanism.

In the future, TUNS could be modified to allow other parameters to be changed as well:

- Encoding used for queries and replies (allow to switch from Base32 to Base64 if the network allows it);
- Type of requests used (switch from CNAME to TXT or NULL);
- Allow to enable EDNS0, and DNS queries over TCP.

7   Future Work

In addition to the change of other tunnel parameters, several other improvements could be investigated for TUNS.

First, it would be interesting if TUNS could automatically adapt to a network: it could infer the optimal polling frequency for a path, and detect which countermeasures/filtering a network does to choose the optimal settings for encoding.

To increase the bandwidth of the tunnel, focus should be put on increasing the amount of useful data transferred in each DNS packet. Mechanisms like headers compression [7] could be use to decrease the overhead of using short IP packets. However, to be able to reduce the number of DNS packets, and not only the size of independent DNS packets, such mechanisms should be used before IP fragmentation happens, so it would have to be done in the kernel. A simple way to reach this goal could be to use PPP, instead of simply encapsulating IP packets.

Working on the encoding scheme could also bring interesting results. While the original DNS RFC doesn't allow the "_" character, this character is used in several DNS extensions (for example, it's commonly used in DNS SRV records). During our experiments, we encountered both networks that dropped queries containing the "_", and networks that allowed queries containing "_" for all records (not only SRV). Allowing Base64 using "_" as an option is a fairly conservative choice.

Another option is to add an escape mechanism to do Base64 using only the 63 valid characters. The problem with this is that it will cause the packet length to vary. In our experiments with changing the tunnel's MTU (which causes the DNS packets to increase or decrease size), we discovered that many DNS infrastructures were very strict on the packet length they allowed, which could cause some IP packets to never be transmitted through the tunnel, causing some connections (e.g TCP connections) to hang. A workaround could be to allow several escape mechanisms to co-exist and be chosen on a per-packet basis: the implementation could then choose the escape scheme that produces the shortest DNS packet, for each IP packet it tries to transmit.

8 Conclusion

The number of existing implementations proves it: the idea of using IP over DNS tunnels is not new. However, the number of existing implementations also shows that none of the implementations bring a definitive answer to this problem, due to the number of challenges that such tunnels need to overcome. This paper provides a detailed exploration of those challenges.

Specifically, TUNS proposes interesting solutions to address those challenges. It favors a simple design, and stays within the boundaries fixed by the DNS protocol specification. This proved successful: TUNS is the only tunnel that worked on all the real networks we could try. TUNS also achieves reasonable performance compared to the other solutions, especially when facing bad network conditions, which are frequent with wireless hotspots.

Finally, TUNS demonstrates that it is possible to achieve reasonable performance without resorting to obscure DNS features or non-compliant behaviour. From a network administrator point of view, it seems difficult to block TUNS without also blocking legitimate traffic: the only solution left is to reduce the bandwidth of the covert channel by using traffic shaping techniques (to rate-limit the DNS queries), thus making the channel mostly useless.

References

1. Dns2tcp, http://hsc.fr/ressources/outils/dns2tcp/
2. Iodine, http://code.kryo.se/iodine/
3. Nstx, http://thomer.com/howtos/nstx.html
4. Ozymandns, http://www.doxpara.com/
5. RFC 1035: Domain names - implementation and specification
6. RFC 2671: Extension mechanisms for DNS (EDNS0)
7. RFC 3095: ROHC framework and four profiles: RTP, UDP, ESP, and uncompressed
8. Llamas, D., Allison, C., Miller, A.: Covert channels in internet protocols: A survey. In: 6th Annual Postgraduate Symposium about the Convergence of Telecommunications, Networking and Broadcasting (2005)
9. Lucena, N., Lewandowski, G., Chapin, S.: Covert channels in iPv6. In: Danezis, G., Martin, D. (eds.) PET 2005. LNCS, vol. 3856, pp. 147–166. Springer, Heidelberg (2006)

10. Mejia-Nogales, J.L., Vidal-Beltran, S., Lopez-Bonilla, J.L.: Design and implementation of a secure access system to information resources for ieee 802.11 wireless networks. In: CERMA 2006: Proceedings of the Electronics, Robotics and Automotive Mechanics Conference (CERMA 2006) (2006)
11. Ray, B., Mishra, S.: Secure and reliable covert channel. In: CSIIRW 2008: Proceedings of the 4th annual workshop on Cyber security and informaiton intelligence research (2008)
12. Rowland, C.H.: Covert channels in the TCP/IP protocol suite. First Monday 2(5) (1997)
13. Zander, S., Armitage, G., Branch, P.: Covert channels and countermeasures in computer network protocols. IEEE Communications Magazines 45(12) (2007)

Discovering Application-Level Insider Attacks Using Symbolic Execution

Karthik Pattabiraman, Nithin Nakka, Zbigniew Kalbarczyk, and Ravishankar Iyer

Center for Reliable and High-Performance Computing (CRHC),
University of Illinois at Urbana-Champaign (UIUC), Urbana, IL
{pattabir,nakka,kalbarcz,rkiyer}@uiuc.edu

Abstract. This paper presents a technique to systematically discover insider attacks in applications. An attack model where the insider is in the same address space as the process and can corrupt arbitrary data is assumed. A formal technique based on symbolic execution and model-checking is developed to comprehensively enumerate all possible insider attacks corresponding to a given attack goal. The main advantage of the technique is that it operates directly on the program code in assembly language and no manual effort is necessary to translate the program into a formal model. We apply the technique to security-critical segments of the OpenSSH application.

1 Introduction

Insider threats have gained prominence as an emerging and important class of security threats [1, 2]. An insider is a person who is part of the organization and either steals secrets or subverts the working of the organization by exploiting hidden system flaws for malicious purposes. For example, a web browser may have a malicious plugin that overwrites the address bar with the address of a phishing website. Or a disgruntled programmer may plant a logical flaw in a banking application that allows an external user to fraudulently withdraw money. Both are examples of how a trusted insider can compromise an application and subvert it for malicious purposes.

This paper considers *application-level* insider attacks. We define an application-level insider attack as one in which a malicious insider attempts to overwrite one or more data items in the application, in order to achieve a specific attack goal. The overwriting may be carried out by exploiting existing vulnerabilities in the application (e.g. buffer overflows), by introducing logical flaws in the application code or through malicious third-party libraries. It is also possible (though not required) to launch insider attacks from a malicious operating system or higher-privileged process. Application-level insider attacks are particularly insidious because, (1) by attacking the application an insider can evade detection by mimicking its normal behavior (from the point of view of the system), and (2) to attack the application, it is enough for the insider to have the same privilege as that of the application (assuming a flat address space where all modules have equal privileges), whereas attacking the network or operating system may require super-user privileges.

Before defending against insider attacks, we need a model for reasoning about insiders. Previous work has modeled insider attacks at the network and operating system (OS) levels using higher-level formalisms such as attack graphs [3] and process calculi [4]. However, modeling application-level insider attacks requires analysis of the application's code as an insider has access to the application and can hence launch attacks on the application's implementation. Higher-level models are too coarse grained to enable reasoning about attacks that can be launched at the application code level. Further, higher-level models typically require application vulnerabilities to be identified up-front in order to reason about insider attacks.

This paper introduces a technique to formally model application-level insider attacks on the application code (expressed in assembly language). The advantage of modeling at the assembly level is that the assembly code includes the program, libraries, and any state added by the compiler (e.g. stack pointer and return addresses), and enables accurate reasoning about all *software-based* insider attacks.

The proposed technique uses a combination of symbolic execution and model checking to systematically enumerate *all* possible insider attacks in a given application corresponding to an attack goal. The technique can be automatically deployed on the application's code and no formal specifications need to be provided other than generic specifications about the attacker's end goal(s).

The value of the analysis performed by the proposed technique is that it can expose non-intuitive cases of insider attacks that may be missed by manual code inspection. This is because the technique exhaustively considers corruptions of data items used in the application (under a given input), and enumerates all corruptions that lead to a successful attack (based on the specified attack goal). The results of the analysis can be used to guide the development of defense mechanisms (e.g. assertions).

We have implemented the proposed technique as a tool, *SymPLAID*, which directly analyzes MIPS-based assembly code. The tool identifies for each attack, (1) The program point at which the attack must be launched, (2) The data item that must be overwritten by the attacker, and (3) The value that must be used for overwriting the data item in order to carry out the attack.

SymPLAID builds on our earlier tool, SymPLFIED [5], used to evaluate the effect of transient errors on the application. SymPLFIED groups individual errors into a single abstract class (*err*), and considers the effect of the entire class of errors on the program. This is because in the case of randomly occurring errors, we are more interested in the propagation of the error rather than the precise set of circumstances that caused the error. In contrast, security attacks are launched by an intelligent adversary and hence it is important to know precisely what values are corrupted by the attacker in order to design efficient defense mechanisms against the attack(s). Therefore, SymPLAID was built from the ground up to emphasize precision in terms of identifying the specific conditions for an attack. Thus, rather than abstracting the attacker's behavior into a single class, the effect of each value corruption is considered individually, and its propagation is tracked in the program. The key contributions of the paper are:

1. Introduces a formal model for reasoning about application-level insider attacks at the assembly-code level,
2. Shows how application-level insiders may be able to subvert the execution of the application for malicious purposes,
3. Describes a technique to automatically discover *all* possible insider attacks in an application using symbolic execution and model checking,
4. Demonstrates the proposed techniques using a case-study drawn from the authentication module of the OpenSSH application [6].

2   Insider Attack Model

This section describes the attack model for insider attacks and an example scenario for an insider attack.

2.1   Characterization of Insider

Capabilities: The insider is a part of the application and has unfettered access to the program's address space. This includes the ability to both read and write the program's memory and registers. However, we assume that the insider cannot modify the program's code, which is reasonable since in most programs the code segment is marked read-only after the program is loaded. An attacker may get into the application (and become an insider) in one or more of the following ways:

1. By a logical loophole in the application planted by a disgruntled or malicious programmer,
2. Through a malicious (or buggy) third-party library loaded into the address space of the application,
3. By exploiting known security loopholes such as buffer overflow attacks and planting the attack code,
4. By overwriting the process's registers or memory from another process (with higher privilege) or debugger,
5. Through a security vulnerability in the operating system or virtual machine (if present)

In each of the above scenarios, the insider can corrupt the values of either memory locations or registers while the application is executing. The first three scenarios only require the insider to have the same privileges as the applications, while the last two require higher privileges.

Goal: The attacker's goal is to subvert the application to perform malicious functions on behalf of the attacker. However, the attacker wants to elude detection or culpability (as far as possible), so the attacker's code may not directly carry out the attack, but may instead overwrite elements of the program's data or control in order to achieve the attacker's aims. From an external perspective, it will appear as though the attack originated due to an application malfunction, and hence the attack code will not be blamed. Therefore, the attacker can execute code to overwrite crucial elements of the program's data or control elements.

It is assumed that the attacker does not want to crash the application, but wants to subvert its execution for some malicious purpose. The attack is typically launched only under a specific set of inputs to the program (known to the attacker), and the input sequence that launches the attack is indistinguishable from a legitimate input for the program. Even if the insider is unable to launch the attack by himself/herself, he/she may have a colluding user who supplies the required inputs to launch the attack.

2.2   Attack Scenario

Figure 1 shows an example attack scenario where the insider has planted a "logic bomb" in the application which is triggered under a specific set of inputs. Normal users are unlikely to accidentally supply the trigger sequence and will be able to use the application without any problems. However, a colluding user knows about the time-bomb and supplies the trigger sequence as input. Perimeter based protection techniques such as firewalls will not notice anything unusual as the trigger sequence is indistinguishable from a regular input for all practical purposes. However, the input will trigger the time-bomb in the application thereby launching the security attack on behalf of the insider.

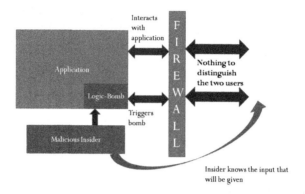

Fig. 1. Attack scenario of an insider attack

2.3 Problem Definition

The problem of attack generation from the insider's point of view may be summed up as follows: "If the input sequence to trigger the attack is known (AND) the attacker's code is executed at specific points in the program, what data items in the program should be corrupted and in what way to achieve the attack goal?"

This paper develops a technique to automatically discover conditions for insider attacks in an application given (i) the inputs to trigger the attack (e.g. a specific user-name as input), (ii) the attacker's objective stated in terms of the final state of the application (e.g. to allow a particular user to log in with the wrong password) and (iii) the attacker's capabilities in terms of the points from which the attack can be launched (e.g. within a specific function). The analysis identifies both the target data to be corrupted and what value it should be replaced with to achieve the attacker's goal. To facilitate the analysis, the following assumptions are made about the attacker by the technique. (1) Only one value can be corrupted, but the corrupted value can be any valid value. This assumption ensures that the footprint of the attack is kept small which makes it easier to evade detection (from a defense technique) and (2) Corruption is only allowed at fixed program points. This assumption reflects the fact that an insider may be able launch their attacks only at fixed program points – for example, where the untrusted library function is called.

3 Example Code and Attacks

This section considers an example code fragment to illustrate the attack scenario in Section 2.2. The example is motivated by the OpenSSH program [6], but is not the actual code extract (we consider the real OpenSSH application in Section 5).

```
int authenticate(void* src, void* dst, void* temp, int len){
  1: readSystemPassword(temp);
  2: strncpy(src, temp, len)
  3: readUserPassword(temp);
  4: strncpy(dst, temp, len);
  5: if (! strncmp(dst, src, len) ) return 1;
  return 0;
}
```

Fig. 2. Code of the authenticate function

Figure 2 shows an example code fragment containing the *authenticate* function. The *authenticate* function reads the values of the system password and the user password into the *tmp* buffer. It copies the value of the system password into the *src* buffer and the value of the user password into the *dst* buffer. It then compares the values in the *src* and *dst* buffers and if they match, it returns the value 1 (authenticated). Otherwise it returns the value 0 (unauthenticated) to the caller.

We take the attacker's perspective in coming up with insider attacks on the code in Figure 2. The attacker's goal is to allow a colluding user (who may be the same person as the attacker) to be validated even if he/she has entered the wrong password. The following assumptions are made in this example, for simplicity of explanation:

1. The attack can be invoked only within the body of the *authenticate* function.
2. The attacker can overwrite the value of registers and local variables, but not global variables and heap buffers (due to practical limitations such as not knowing the exact address of global variables and dynamic memory objects).
3. The attack points are immediately before the function calls within the *authenticate* function, i.e., the arguments to any of the functions called by the *authenticate* function may be overwritten prior to the function call.

Table 1. Insider attacks on the authenticate function

Program Point	Variable to be corrupted	Corrupted value of variable	Comments/Explanation
strncmp point (line 5)	dst	src buf	The *src* buffer is compared with itself
	src	dst buf	The *dst* buffer is compared with itself
	src	temp buf	The *dst* buffer is compared with the *temp* buffer which contains the same string
	len	<= 0	The strncmp function terminates early and returns 0 (the strings are identical)
strncpy point (line 4)	temp	src buf	This copies the string in the *src* buffer to the *dst* buffer, thereby ensuring that the strings match
	dst	srcBuf – strlen(buf)	This writes a '\0' character in the *src* buffer, effectively converting it to a empty string. The *dst* buffer is also empty as it is not initialized (assuming it is initially set to all zeroes), and hence the strings match.
readUser Password point (line 3)	temp	dst buf	The temp buffer originally contains the system password.
	temp	Any unused location in memory	Due to the attack, the value in the *temp* buffer is not replaced with the user password. Therefore, the system password is copied to the *dst* buffer, which matches the contents of the *src* buffer i.e., the system password.

Table 1 shows the set of all possible attacks the attacker could launch in the above function. A particularly interesting attack found is presented in row 6 of Table 1, where the *dst* argument of the *strncpy* function was set to overlay the *src* string in memory. This replaces the first character of the *src* string with '\0', effectively converting it to a NULL string. The *dst* string also becomes NULL as the *dst* buffer is not filled by the *strncpy* function (we assume that it has initially been filled with all zeroes). The two strings will match when compared and the *authenticate* function will return '1'. This allows the colluding user to be authenticated.

As Table 1 shows, discovering all possible insider attacks manually (by inspection) is cumbersome and non-trivial even for the modestly sized piece of code that is considered in Figure 2. Therefore, we have developed a tool, SymPLAID, to automatically generate insider attacks scenarios. The attacks in Table 1 were discovered by SymPLAID. Although the tool works on assembly language programs, we have shown the program as C-language code in Figure 2 for simplicity. We have validated the attacks shown in Table 1 using the GNU debugger (*gdb*) to corrupt the values of chosen variables in the application on an AMD machine running the Linux operating system. All the attacks in Table 1 were found to be successful i.e. they led to the user being authenticated in spite of providing the wrong password.

The attacks in Table 1 contain both "obvious attacks" as well as surprising corner cases. It can be argued that finding obvious attacks is not very useful as they are likely to be revealed by manual inspection of the code. However, the power of the proposed technique is that it can reveal *all* such attacks on the code, whereas a human operator may miss one or more attacks. This is especially important from the developer's perspective, as *all* the security holes in the application need to be plugged before it can be claimed that the application is secure (as all the attacker needs to exploit is a single vulnerability). Moreover, the ability to discover corner-case attacks is the real benefit of using an automated approach.

The attacks discovered by SymPLAID can be used to guide the development of defense mechanisms. For example, for the attacks discovered in Table 1, we insert runtime checks at the following points:

1. Before the call to the *strncmp* function to ensure that the *src* and *dst* buffers of the *strncmp* function do not overlap with each other or with the *temp* buffer in terms of physical locations. This prevents attacks in rows 1 to 4 of Table 1.
2. After the call to the *readUserPassword* function in line 3 to ensure that the *temp* buffer is non-empty. This prevents attacks in the rows 7 and 8 of Table 1.
3. Before the call to the *strncpy* function to ensure that neither the *temp* buffer nor the *dst* buffer overlap with the *src* buffer. This prevents attacks in the rows 5 and 6 of Table 1.

Figure 3 shows the code in Figure 2 with the checks inserted as *assert* statements. It is assumed that the checks are themselves immune to attack from an insider.

```
int authenticate(void* src, void* dst, void* temp, int len){
   1: readSystemPassword(temp);
   2: strncpy(src, temp, len)
   3: readuserPassword(temp);
   assert( isNotEmpty(temp) );  assert( noOverlap(temp, src) and noOverlap(temp, dst) )
   4: strncpy(dst, temp, len);
   assert( noOverlap(src, dst) and noOverlap(src, temp) );  assert( len > 0 );
   5: if (! strncmp(dst, src, len) ) return 1;
   return 0;
}
```

Fig. 3. Code of authenticate function with assertions

4 Technique and Tool

This section describes the key techniques used in the automation and the design of a tool to automatically discover insider attacks in an application.

4.1 Symbolic Execution Technique

We represent an insider attack as a corruption of data values at specific points in the program's execution i.e. attack points. The attack points are chosen by the program developer based on knowledge of where an insider can attack the application. For example, all the places where the application calls an untrusted third-party library are attack points as an insider can launch an attack from these points. In the worst-case, every instruction in the application can be an attack point.

The program is executed with a known (concrete) input, and when one of the specified execution points is reached, a single variable[1] is chosen from the set of all variables in the program and assigned a symbolic value (i.e. not a concrete value). The program's execution is continued with the symbolic value for the chosen variable. All other variables in the program are unchanged. The above procedure is repeated exhaustively for each data value in the program at each of the specified attack points. This allows enumeration of all insider attacks on a given program.

The key technique used to comprehensively enumerate insider attacks is *symbolic execution-based model checking*. This means that the program is executed with a combination of concrete values and symbolic values, and model-checking is used to "fill-in" the symbolic values as and when needed. Symbolic values are treated similar to concrete values in arithmetic and logical computations performed in the system. The main difference is in how branches and memory accesses based on expressions involving symbolic values are handled. When a memory access is performed with a symbolic expression as the address operand, the execution of the program is forked and the symbolic expression is equated to a different memory address in each fork. The value stored at the address is read or written in the corresponding fork and the program's execution is continued. Once the symbolic value has been assigned to an address, all expressions involving the symbolic value in the state are concretized.

---

[1] We use the generic term variable to refer to both registers and memory locations in the program.

Similarly, in the case of branches involving symbolic expressions, the program execution is forked at the branch point. The branch condition is added as a constraint to the first fork, while the negation of the condition is added as a constraint to the second fork. For each program fork encountered above, the model checker checks whether (1) The fork is a viable one, based on the past constraints of the symbolic expressions, and (2) whether the fork leads to a desired outcome (of the attacker). If these two conditions are satisfied, the model checker will print the state of the program corresponding to the fork i.e. attack state.

As in most model-checking approaches, the number of states explored can be exponential in the size of the program and its address space. However, very few of the states explored by the model-checker will satisfy the attacker's goal(s). Hence, the model-checker can prune branches of the search tree once it is clear that the branch will not lead to a state satisfying the goal. This is the key to the scalability of the approach, and underlies the importance of specifying an attack goal for the insider.

4.2 SymPLAID Tool

The symbolic execution technique described in the previous section has been implemented in an automated tool – SymPLAID (*Symbolic Program Level Attack Injection and Detection*). This is based on our earlier tool, SymPLFIED, used to study the effect of transient errors on programs [5].

SymPLAID accepts the following inputs: (1) an assembly language program along with libraries (if any), (2) a set of pre-defined inputs for the program, (3) a specification of the desired goal of the attacker (expressed as a formula in first-order logic) and (4) a set of attack points in the application. It generates a comprehensive set of insider attacks that lead to the goal state. For each attack, SymPLAID generates both the location (memory or register) to be corrupted as well as the value that must be written to the location by the attacker.

SymPLAID directly parses and interprets assembly language programs written for a MIPS processor. The current implementation supports the entire range of MIPS instructions, including (1) arithmetic/logical instructions, (2) memory accesses (both aligned and unaligned) and (3) branches (both direct and indirect). However, it does not support system calls. The lack of system call support is compensated for by the provision of native support for input/output operations. Floating point operations are also not considered by SymPLAID. This is not a bottleneck as floating-point operations are typically not used by security-critical code in applications.

SymPLAID is implemented using Maude, a high-performance language and system that supports specification and programming in rewriting logic [7]. SymPLAID models the execution semantics of an assembly language program using both equations and rewriting rules. Equations are used to model the concrete semantics of the machine, while rewriting rules are used for introducing non-determinism due to symbolic evaluation. SymPLAID maintains precise dependencies both in terms of arithmetic and logical constraints and solves the constraints without incurring false-positives. This is the biggest difference between SymPLAID and SymPLFIED [5], which aggregates symbolic values into a single class and hence incurs false-positives.

5   Case Study: OpenSSH Authentication Module

To evaluate the SymPLAID tool on a real application, we considered a reduced version of the OpenSSH application [6] involving only the user-authentication part. This is because SymPLAID does not support all the features used in the complete SSH application, e.g. system calls. We retain the core functions in the authentication part of OpenSSH with little or no modifications, and replace the more complex ones with stub versions – i.e. simplified functions that approximate the behavior of their original versions. We also replace the system calls with stubs. The reduced version, the *authentication module*, consists of about 250 lines of C code and emulates the behavior of the SSH application starting from the point after the user enters his/her username and password to the point that he/she is authenticated or denied authentication by the system (we consider only password-based authentication).

We ran SymPLAID on the authentication module after compiling it to MIPS assembly using the *gcc* compiler. As before, the goal is to find insider attacks that will allow the user to be authenticated. It is assumed that the insider can overwrite the value of any register prior to executing any instruction within the authentication module. The input to the authentication module is the username and password. The username may or may not be a valid username in the system, and the password may or may not be correct. These lead to four possible categories of inputs.

SymPLAID discovered attacks corresponding to the categories where an invalid username is supplied with a valid password (for the application) and where a valid user-name is supplied with an incorrect password. An example of an attack where the invalid username is supplied is considered. Due to space constraints, the other attacks are not described and may be found in the technical report [8].

5.1   Example Attack: Invalid User-Name

The authentication part of SSH works as follows: when the user enters his/her name, the program first checks the user-name against a list of users who are allowed to log into the system. If the user is allowed to log into the system, the user record is assigned to a data-structure called an *authctxt* and the user details are stored into the *authctxt* structure. If the name is not found on the list, the record is assigned to a special data-structure in memory called as *fake*. *fake* is also an *authctxt* structure, except that it holds a dummy username and password. This ensures that there is no observable difference in the time it takes to process legitimate and illegitimate users (which may enable attackers to learn if a username is valid by repeated attempts).

In order to prevent potential attackers from logging on by providing this dummy password, the *authctxt* structure has an additional field called *valid*. This field is set to *true* only for legitimate *authctxt* records i.e. those for which the username is in the list of valid users for the system. The *fake* structure has the *valid* field set to *false* by default. In order for the authentication to succeed, the encrypted value of the user password must match the (encrypted) system password, *and* the valid flag of the *authctxt* record must be set to 1. Figure 4 shows the *auth_password* function that performs the above checks. The function first calls the *sys_auth_passwd* to check if the passwords match, and then checks if the *valid* flag is set in the *authctxt* record. Only if both conditions are true will the function return 1 (authenticated) to its caller.

```
int sys_auth_passwd(Authctxt *authctxt, const char *password) {
1:      struct passwd *pw = authctxt->pw;
2:      char *encrypted_password;
3:      char *pw_password = authctxt->valid ?
4:                          shadow_pw(pw) : pw->pw_passwd;
5:      if (strcmp(pw_password, "") == 0 &&
6:              strcmp(password, "") == 0)
7:              return (1);
8:      encrypted_password = xcrypt(password,
9:              (pw_password[0] && pw_password[1]) ?
10:             pw_password : "xx");
11:   return (strcmp(encrypted_password, pw_password) == 0);
}


int auth_password(Authctxt *authctxt, const char *password) {
12:             int permit_empty_passwd = 0;
13:     struct passwd * pw = authctxt->pw;
14:     int result, ok = authctxt->valid;
15:     if (*password == '\0' && permit_empty_passwd == 0)
16:             return 0;
17:     result = sys_auth_passwd(authctxt, password);
18:     if (authctxt->force_pwchange)
19:             disable_forwarding();
20:     return (result && ok);
}
```

Fig. 4. SSH code fragment corresponding to the attack

An insider can launch an attack by setting the *valid* flag to true for the *fake* authctxt structure. This will authenticate a user who enters an invalid user name, but enters the password stored in the *fake* structure. The password in the *fake* structure is a string that is hardcoded into the program. To mimic this attack, we supply an invalid user-name and a password that matches the *fake* (dummy) password. We expected SymPLAID to find the attack where the insider overwrites the valid flag of the *fake* structure. Sym-PLAID found this attack, but it also found other interesting attacks.

We consider an example of an attack found by SymPLAID. The attack occurs in the *sys_auth_password* function, at line 11 before the call to the *strcmp* function (in Figure 4). At this point, the insider corrupts the value of the stack pointer (stored in register $30 in the MIPS architecture) to point within the stack frame of the caller function, namely *auth_password*. When the *strcmp* function is called, it pushes the current frame pointer onto the stack, increments the stack pointer and sets its frame pointer to be equal to the value of the stack pointer (corrupted by the attacker).

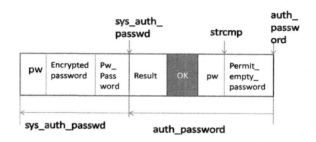

Fig. 5. Stack layout when strcmp() is called

Figure 5 shows the stack layout when the function is called (only the variables relevant to the attack are shown). The top-row of Figure 5 shows the frame-pointers of the functions on the stack due to the attack. Observe that the attack causes the stack frame of the *strcmp* function to overlap with that of the *auth_password* function. The *strcmp* function is invoked with the addresses of the *encrypted_pasword* and the *pw_password* buffers in registers *$3* and *$4* (function arguments are passed in registers on MIPS processors). The function copies the contents of these registers to locations within its stack frame at offsets of 4 and 8 respectively from its frame pointer. This overwrites the value of the local variable *ok* in the *auth_password* function with a non-zero value (since both buffers are at non-zero addresses). When the *strcmp* function returns, the value of $30 is restored to the frame pointer of *sys_auth_passwd*, which in turn returns to the *auth_password* function. The *auth_password* function checks if the result returned from *sys_auth_password* is non-zero and if the *ok* flag is non-zero. Both conditions are satisfied, so it returns the value 1 to its caller, and the user is authenticated successfully by the system.

5.2 Performance Results

The model-checking task is highly parallelizable and can be broken into independent sub-tasks, with each sub-task considering attacks in a different code region of the application. The authentication module consists of about 500 assembly language instructions, and the task was broken up into 50 parallel sub-tasks each of which analyzes 10 instructions in the program. We executed the sub-tasks on a parallel cluster consisting of dual-processor AMD Opteron nodes, each of which has 2 GB RAM. The maximum time allowed for each task was capped at 48 hours (2 days).

The total time taken to execute all sub-tasks is at most 36 days. However, the task finished in less than 2 days due to the highly parallel nature of the search task. While the running time seems high, it is not a concern as the goal is to discover all potential insider attacks (in a reasonable time) and to find protection mechanisms against them.

6 Related Work

Insider attacks have traditionally been modeled at the network level. Philips and Swiler [9] introduced the attack graph model to represent the set of all possible attacks that can be launched in a network. Ammann et al. [10] introduce a model-checking based technique to automatically find attacks starting from a known goal state of the attacker. Sheyner et al. generalize this technique to generate all possible attack paths, thereby generating the entire attack graph [11]. Chinchani et al. [3] present a variant of attack graphs called key-challenge graphs to represent insider attacks, and use model-checking to generate all possible insider attacks in a network.

Insider attacks have been modeled at the operating system level by Probst et al. [4]. In this model, applications are represented as sets of processes that can access sets of resources in the system. An insider is modeled as a malicious process in the system.

Attack-graphs and process graphs are too coarse grained for representing application-level attacks, and hence we directly analyze the application's code. Further, we do not require the developer to provide a formal description of the system being analyzed, which can require significant effort. Since we analyze the application's code directly, we can model attacks both in the design and implementation of the application. This is important as an insider typically has access to the application's source code, and can launch low-level attacks on its implementation.

Symbolic execution is a well-explored technique to find program errors [12]. Recently, it has also been used to find security vulnerabilities in applications [13-16]. Symbolic techniques are typically concerned with generating application inputs to exploit known or unknown vulnerabilities. In contrast, our technique attempts to generate attacks under a given input, assuming that the attacker is already present in the application. Further, the attacks found using our technique do not require the application to have an exploitable vulnerability (e.g. buffer overflows), but can be launched by a malicious insider in the system.

Fault-injection is an experimental technique to assess the vulnerability of computer systems to random events or faults [17]. Fault-injection has also been used to expose security vulnerabilities in applications. Fault-injection studies [18, 19] into commonly used cryptographic systems have shown that transient faults can weaken the guarantees provided by these systems. The main difference between these studies and ours is that our technique can be applied for any general security-critical system, and not just crypto-systems. Xu et al. [20] consider the effect of transient errors (single-bit flips) in instructions on application security. Govindavajhala and Appel [21] explore the effects of transient errors on the security of the Java virtual machine, assuming the attacker can execute a specially crafted application. The main difference between these techniques and our technique is that we consider all possible attacks on the application, and are not restricted to injecting single bit-flips. Further, we do not require the attacker to execute specially crafted programs as assumed by [21].

7 Conclusions

This paper presented a novel approach to discover insider attacks in applications. An automated technique to find all possible insider attacks on application code is presented. The technique uses a combination of symbolic execution and model-checking to systematically enumerate insider attacks for a given goal of the attacker. We have implemented the technique in the SymPLAID tool, and demonstrate it using the code segments corresponding to the authentication part of the OpenSSH program.

Acknowledgments. This work was supported in part by NSF grants CNS-0406351 (Next-generation Software), CNS-05-24695, CNS-05-51665, the Gigascale Systems Research Center (GSRC/MARCO), and Boeing Corporation as part of Boeing Trusted Software Center at the Information Trust Institute.

References

1. Randazzo, M.R., et al.: Insider Threat Study: Illicit Cyber Activity in the Banking and Finance Sector, p. 25. ERT Coordination Center/Software Engineering Institute, Philadelphia, PA (2004)
2. Keeney, M.M., Kowalski, E.F.: Insider Threat Study: Computer System Sabotage in Critical Infrastructure Sectors. CERT/CC, Philadelphia, PA (2005)

3. Chinchani, R., et al.: Towards a Theory of Insider Threat Assessment. In: Proceedings of the 2005 International Conference on Dependable Systems and Networks. IEEE Computer Society, Los Alamitos (2005)
4. Probst, C.W., Hansen, R.R., Nielson, F.: Where Can an Insider Attack? In: Dimitrakos, T., Martinelli, F., Ryan, P.Y.A., Schneider, S. (eds.) FAST 2006. LNCS, vol. 4691, pp. 127–142. Springer, Heidelberg (2007)
5. Pattabiraman, K., Nakka, N., Kalbarczyk, Z.: SymPLFIED: Symbolic Program Level Fault-Injection and Error-Detection Framework. In: International Conference on Dependable Systems and Networks (DSN) (2008)
6. OpenSSH Development Team., OpenSSH 4.21 (2004)
7. Clavel, M., et al.: The Maude 2.0 System. In: Rewriting Technologies and Applications. Springer, Heidelberg (2001)
8. Pattabiraman, K., et al.: Discovering Application-level Insider Attacks using Symbolic Execution, CRHC Technical Report, UIUC, Champaign, IL (2008)
9. Phillips, C., Swiler, L.P.: A graph-based system for network-vulnerability analysis. In: Proceedings of the 1998 workshop on New security paradigms. ACM, Charlottesville (1998)
10. Ammann, P., Wijesekera, D., Kaushik, S.: Scalable, graph-based network vulnerability analysis. In: Proceedings of the 9th ACM conference on Computer and communications security. ACM, Washington (2002)
11. Sheyner, O., et al.: Automated Generation and Analysis of Attack Graphs. In: Proceedings of the 2002 IEEE Symposium on Security and Privacy. IEEE Computer Society, Los Alamitos (2002)
12. King, J.C.: Symbolic execution and program testing. Commun. ACM 19(7), 385–394 (1976)
13. Costa, M., et al.: Bouncer: securing software by blocking bad input. In: Proceedings of twenty-first ACM SIGOPS symposium on Operating systems principles. ACM, Stevenson (2007)
14. Kruegel, C., et al.: Automating mimicry attacks using static binary analysis. In: Proceedings of the 14th conference on USENIX Security Symposium, vol. 14. USENIX, Baltimore (2005)
15. Molnar, D.A., Wagner, D.: Catchconv: Symbolic execution and run-time type inference for integer conversion errors, EECS Department, University of California, Berkeley (2007)
16. Cadar, C., et al.: EXE: automatically generating inputs of death. In: Proceedings of the 13th ACM conference on Computer and communications security. ACM, Virginia (2006)
17. Hsueh, M.-C., Tsai, T.K., Iyer, R.K.: Fault Injection Techniques and Tools. IEEE Computer 30(4), 75–82 (1997)
18. Boneh, D., DeMillo, R., Lipton, R.J.: On the importance of checking cryptographic protocols for faults. In: Fumy, W. (ed.) EUROCRYPT 1997. LNCS, vol. 1233, pp. 37–51. Springer, Heidelberg (1997)
19. Kocher, P.C., Jaffe, J., Jun, B.: Differential Power Analysis. In: Wiener, M. (ed.) CRYPTO 1999. LNCS, vol. 1666, p. 388. Springer, Heidelberg (1999)
20. Xu, J., et al.: An Experimental Study of Security Vulnerabilities Caused by Errors. In: Proceedings of International Conference on Dependable Systems and Networks (DSN) (2001)
21. Govindavajhala, S., Appel, A.W.: Using Memory Errors to Attack a Virtual Machine. In: Proceedings of the 2003 IEEE Symposium on Security and Privacy. IEEE, Los Alamitos (2003)

Custom JPEG Quantization for Improved Iris Recognition Accuracy

Gerald Stefan Kostmajer[1], Herbert Stögner[1], and Andreas Uhl[2]

[1] School of Communication Engineering for IT, Carinthia Tech Institute, Austria
[2] Department of Computer Sciences, University of Salzburg, Austria
uhl@cosy.sbg.ac.at

Abstract. Custom JPEG quantization matrices are proposed to be used in the context of compression within iris recognition. Superior matching results in terms of average Hamming distance and improved ROC is found as compared to the use of the default quantization table especially for low FAR. This leads to improved user convenience in case high security is required.

1 Introduction

With the increasing usage of biometric systems the question arises naturally how to store and handle the acquired sensor data. In this context, the compression of these data may become imperative under certain circumstances due to the large amounts of data involved. Among other possibilities (e.g. like template storage on IC cards), compression technology may be used in two stages of the processing chain in classical biometric recognition:

1. **Transmission of sample data after sensor data acquisition:** In distributed biometric systems, the data acquisition stage is often dislocated from the feature extraction and matching stage (this is true for the enrollment phase as well as for authentication). In such environments the sensor data have to be transferred via a network link to the respective location, often over wireless channels with low bandwidth and high latency. Therefore, a minimization of the amount of data to be transferred is highly desirable, which is achieved by compressing the data before transmission. An alternative solution would be to extract the features before transmission and to transfer feature data only – in many cases, feature extraction is more demanding as compared to compression which generates additional workload for the often mobile and low power acquisition devices.
2. **Storage of reference data:** In most template databases (where the reference data of the enrolled individuals is stored) only the extracted features required for the matching step are stored as opposed to retaining the originally acquired sensor data. However, in case the features should be replaced for some reason (e.g. when a superior or license-free matching technique involving a different feature set becomes available), having stored only extracted features implies the requirement for all legitimate users for a re-enrollment, which can be expensive and is highly undesired since user-acceptance of the entire biometric system will suffer. Storing the original

D. Gritzalis and J. Lopez (Eds.): SEC 2009, IFIP AICT 297, pp. 76–86, 2009.
© IFIP International Federation for Information Processing 2009

sensor data in addition to the features required for the current matching technique solves this problem. Of course, these data need to be stored in compressed (to save storage space) and encrypted (to protect privacy) form.

Having found that compression of the raw sensor data can be advantageous in certain applications, we have to identify techniques suited to accomplish this task in an optimal manner. In order to maximize the benefit in terms of data reduction, lossy compression techniques have to be applied. However, the distortions introduced by compression artifacts usually interfere with subsequent feature extraction and may degrade the matching results. In particular, FRR or FNMR will increase (since features of the data of legitimate users are extracted less accurately from compressed data) which in turn affects user convenience and general acceptance of the biometric system. In extreme cases, even FAR or FMR might be affected.

In this work, we will focus on the lossy compression of iris images using the JPEG standard. We discuss the use of custom quantization matrices in order to reflect the specific properties of iris imagery. Contrasting to the overwhelming majority of literature and studies in the field of compressing biometric sample data, we will not rely on assessing the resulting objective and subjective image quality after compression, but we will apply a biometric iris recognition systems to the compressed sensor data to evaluate the effects of compression on recognition accuracy, in particular on the matching results of legitimate and illegitimate users.

In Section 2, we will review and discuss the available literature on biometric sample data compression with focus on iris data storage. Section 3 is the main part of this work where we discuss properties of iris imagery and present several variants of custom JPEG quantization matrices (designed in order to hopefully improve recognition accuracy). In section 4 we first describe the employed iris recognition system and the data this algorithm are applied to. Subsequently we discuss our experimental results with respect to the observed improvements of recognition accuracy.

2   Iris Image Compression

Iris recognition is claimed to be the most secure biometric modality exhibiting practically 0% FAR and low FRR. An interesting fact is that the iris recognition market is strongly dominated by Iridian Inc. based technology which is based on algorithms of J. Daugman [2]. The certainly most relevant standard for compressing iris image data is the recent ISO/IEC 19794-6 standard on Biometric Data Interchange Formats.

While the data formats specified by the ISO/IEC 19794 standard are fixed at present state, their customized use tailored to a specific target modality and the corresponding impact on recognition accuracy as compared to the default settings has not been investigated. This is the scope of the current paper.

ISO/IEC 19794-6 allows iris image data to be stored in lossy manner in the JPEG and JPEG2000 formats. Two types of iris image data are considered: rectilinear images (i.e. images of the entire eye) and polar images (which are basically the result of iris detection and segmentation), the latter much smaller in terms of storage requirement (e.g. 2kB vs. 25-30kB for rectilinear images). It is important to note that with this standardization it might become more attractive for companies to investigate alternatives to Iridian products due to the available common data format iris recognition systems can rely on.

Only recently, first results and techniques are available on iris image compression and its impact on recognition performance. Ives et al. [5,6] apply JPEG2000 up to a compression rate of 20 to rectilinear image data (the CASIA database and a proprietary image collection is used) and investigate the effects on FAR and FRR of a 1-D version of the Daugman algorithm (the same system which is used in this study). Rakshit and Monro [11] again use JPEG2000 to compress polar iris images up to a compression rate of 80 and study the impact on verification accuracy of three iris recognition systems (including the Daugman algorithm, the CASIA database is used). Daugman and Downing [3] apply JPEG and JPEG2000 to rectilinear image data (the NIST ICE database is used) and remove image background (i.e. parts of the image not being part of the eye like eye-lids are replaced by constant average gray) before compression is applied. A more compact way of representing the Daugman IrisCode is discussed in [12], however, these results refer to template compression and are only valid for the techniques related to Iridian products. In previous work [9,7], we have compared five general purpose compression algorithms (including JPEG and JPEG2000) with respect to their impact on iris recognition accuracy of three different recognition schemes (the CASIA database has been used). In accordance to [3] superior compression performance of JPEG2000 over JPEG is found especially for low bitrates, however, for high and medium quality JPEG is still an option to consider. So far, compression algorithms have been applied to iris imagery with their respective standard settings.

In the subsequent study we apply JPEG as covered by ISO/IEC 19794-6 to rectilinear iris images and propose to use custom quantization matrices adapted to properties of iris imagery. Contrasting to the optimization of the JPEG quantization matrix with respect to human perception as done for the development of the standard matrix, rate/distortion criteria have also been used successfully for the design of this matrix (see e.g. [4]). In [1] compression algorithms tuned for application in the pattern recognition context are proposed, which are based on the modification of the standard compression algorithms: this is done by emphasizing middle and high frequencies and discarding low frequencies (the standard JPEG quantization matrix is rotated by 180 degrees). JPEG quantization matrix optimization has already been considered in biometrics – [8] employ a rate/distortion criterion in the context of face recognition and achieve superior recognition performance as compared to the standard matrix.

3   Custom JPEG Quantization

The JPEG still image compression standard [10] allows to use custom quantization tables (Q-tables) in case image material with special properties is subject to compression. These tables are signalled in the header information. The default quantization matrices have been designed with respect to psychovisual optimality employing large scale experimentation involving a high number of test subjects. There are two reasons which suggest to use different Q-tables as the default configuration: First, iris imagery might have different properties as compared to common arbitrary images, and second, a pleasant viewing experience as being the aim in designing the default tables, might not deliver optimal matching results in the context of biometric recognition (e.g. sharp edges required for exact matching could appear appealing to human observers).

Therefore, as a first stage, we have investigated iris imagery in more detail. 8x8 pixel blocks have been subjected to DCT transform and the resulting coefficients are averaged for a large number of blocks (i.e. 2000, 525, and 44160 blocks for the three types of imagery, respectively). As a first class of blocks, we have used arbitrary images and blocks are extracted randomly. The second class of blocks is extracted iris texture taken left and right of the pupil while the third class is taken from polar iris images generated by the employed matching algorithm (see below). Fig. 1 displays the result of all three classes where the DC and the largest AC coefficient are set to white, zero is set to black and the remaining values are scaled in between (note that the logarithm is applied to the magnitude of all coefficients before this scaling operation).

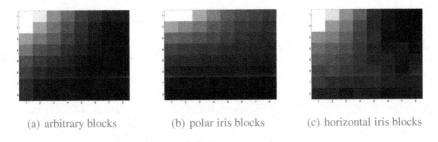

(a) arbitrary blocks   (b) polar iris blocks   (c) horizontal iris blocks

Fig. 1. Averaged 8x8 DCT blocks

The arbitrary blocks (Fig. 1.a) show the typical expected behaviour with decreasing coefficient magnitude for increasing frequency and symmetry with respect to the coordinate axes. Fig. 1.b reveals that in polar iris images there is more energy in the higher frequencies in horizontal direction as compared to vertical direction. This is to be expected since luminance fluctuations in iris texture are more pronounced in radial direction as compared to perpendicular direction. Finally, Fig. 1.c confirms this expectation showing more energy in the higher frequencies in vertical direction.

While we cannot exploit the direction bias of iris texture in compression since we are dealing with rectangular iris images, we conjecture that the highest and medium

(a) Q-table 12

16	11	10	16	24	40	255	255
12	12	14	19	26	255	255	255
14	13	16	24	255	255	255	255
14	17	22	255	255	255	255	255
18	22	255	255	255	255	255	255
24	255	255	255	255	255	255	255
255	255	255	255	255	255	255	255
255	255	255	255	255	255	255	255

(b) Q-table 13

16	11	10	16	24	255	255	255
12	12	14	19	255	255	255	255
14	13	16	255	255	255	255	255
14	17	255	255	255	255	255	255
18	255	255	255	255	255	255	255
255	255	255	255	255	255	255	255
255	255	255	255	255	255	255	255
255	255	255	255	255	255	255	255

(c) Q-table 15

16	11	10	16	255	255	255	255
12	12	14	255	255	255	255	255
14	13	255	255	255	255	255	255
14	255	255	255	255	255	255	255
255	255	255	255	255	255	255	255
255	255	255	255	255	255	255	255
255	255	255	255	255	255	255	255
255	255	255	255	255	255	255	255

(d) Q-table 16

16	11	10	255	255	255	255	255
12	12	255	255	255	255	255	255
14	255	255	255	255	255	255	255
255	255	255	255	255	255	255	255
255	255	255	255	255	255	255	255
255	255	255	255	255	255	255	255
255	255	255	255	255	255	255	255
255	255	255	255	255	255	255	255

Fig. 2. JPEG Quantization tables

frequencies might not be required for he matching stage due to the coarse quantization used for template generation while at least medium frequencies are required for pleasant viewing. Fig. 2 displays the Q-tables used in our experiments.

From left to right, an increasing amount of high frequencies is suppressed following the zig-zag scan known from JPEG bitstream generation (by dividing the coefficients by 255), coefficients not affected are quantized as defined in the default Q-table. For the rightmost Q-table 16, only the 6 leading coefficients are quantized in the regular manner, the rest is severely quantized. The rationale behind the selection of these matrices is to investigate the importance of medium frequency information in iris recognition (high frequency information is assumed to be not useful in any case).

4   Experimental Study

4.1   Setting and Methods

4.1.1   Iris Recognition System

The employed iris recognition system is Libor Masek's Matlab implementation[1] of a 1-D version of the Daugman iris recognition algorithm. First, this algorithm segments the eye image into the iris and the remainder of the image. Iris image texture is mapped to polar coordinates resulting in a rectangular patch which is denoted "polar image". After extracting the features if the iris (which are strongly quantized phase responses of complex 1-D Gabor filters in this case), considering translation, rotations and disturbed regions in the iris (a noise mask is generated), the algorithm outputs the similarity score by giving the hamming distance between two extracted templates. The range of the hamming distance reaches from zero (ideal matching of two iris images of the same person) to 0.5 (ideal mismatch between two iris images of different persons).

4.1.2   Sample Data

For all our experiments we considered 320x280 pixel images with 8-bit grayscale information per pixel from the CASIA[2] 1.0 iris image database. For rectilinear iris images, we applied the experimental calculations on the images of 100 persons using 3 images for each eye (i.e. 600 images). Note that it makes an important difference if compression is applied to rectangular or polar iris images which has an important implication on the performance of the entire system. Whereas in the case of compressing polar iris images [11] only the iris texture information is affected, in the case of compressing rectangular image data also the iris detection and determination of the noise mask is potentially affected in addition to degrading texture information. Figure 3 shows an example of a JPEG2000 compressed (compression rate 96) iris image of one person, together with the extracted iris template data and the noise masks (template and noise mask have been scaled in y-direction by a factor of 4 for proper display). The noise mask is hardly affected by the compression, whereas in the two templates differences resulting from compression artifacts are clearly observable.

---

[1] http://www.csse.uwa.edu.au/~pk/studentprojects/libor/
sourcecode.html

[2] http://www.sinobiometrics.com

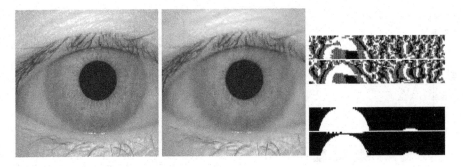

Fig. 3. Comparison of uncompressed/compressed iris image and the corresponding iris templates and noise masks

Compression can be used in various stages of the matching process. Either the stored reference data may be in compressed form, or the sample data acquired for verification may be compressed (e.g. for efficient transfer), or both. Therefore, we use two settings in our experiments: either both images are compressed and matched against each other or only one image is compressed in the matching stage. For investigating correct matches (matches from legitimate users enrolled in the database), we rely on 12000 generated images (i.e. for each of the 100 persons, we have 3 images for each eye resulting in 3! possible correct matches for each eye; for 200 eyes, this totals in 1200 images per compression rate; considering the 10 different compression rates we finally result in 12000 overall images considered). This is only true in the scenario with only 1 compressed image, for 2 compressed images this number is half-ed due to symmetry reasons. For investigating matches between different persons (imposter matches), far more data is available of course.

4.2   Experimental Results

Figure 4.a shows the averaged rate distortion comparison of the different compression algorithms applied to all iris images considered for three Q-tables. It is clearly displayed that employment of the default Q-table results in the best PSNR across the entire range of bitrates considered. Therefore, a corresponding matching behaviour (best results for the default Q-table) could be expected in the context of iris recognition.

In the following, we investigate the impact of compression on the matching score (i.e. obtained hamming distance (HD)). The interval of $0.26 \leq HD \leq 0.35$ is discussed as the border between match and mismatch in iris recognition [2] – based on recommendations for the specific technique [5] used and results shown subsequently we suggest to choose $HD = 0.34$ as decision criterion between match and mismatch.

Fig. 4.b shows the plot of the HD after applying the iris recognition algorithm to both JPEG compressed iris images in the case of imposter matches (i.e. irises of different persons / eyes are matched against each other). The x-axis shows the compression rates, whereas the y-axis shows the averaged hamming distance. For reference, we have included the average HD for the case of uncompressed images as horizontal dotted line in light gray (labelled UC).

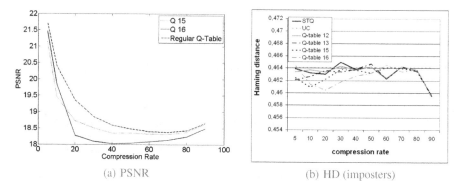

(a) PSNR   (b) HD (imposters)

Fig. 4. Impact of varying compression rate

For the case of imposters the HD remains above 0.46 across the whole range of compression rates for all sensible compression rates. This means that JPEG compression does not introduce any false positive matches on average no matter how severe compression is applied. Of course, this does not exclude the possibility of the existence of statistical outliers of course. There are no significant differences among the different Q-tables since the fluctuations occur in a negligible range. The same behaviour is observed in case only one image is compressed (not shown).

In the case of genuine users (see Fig. 5), the mean value of the HD in the uncompressed case is approximately 0.31. First we consider the standard Q-table (labelled STQ). For increasing compression rate the HD stays constant at approximately 0.305 until the compression rate exceeds 10 and increases subsequently. A further increase of the compression rate leads to a steady increase of HD and crosses the suggested matching threshold of 0.34 between compression rates 30 and 40. Note that the reported numbers refer to averaged HD values which implies the occurrence of a significant number of false negative matches at this compression rate. In the case of both images being compressed, HD is lower on average up to a compression rate of 20.

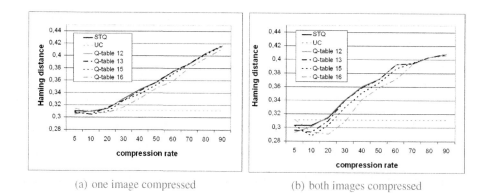

(a) one image compressed   (b) both images compressed

Fig. 5. Impact of varying compression rate on HD of genuine users' matches

When comparing these results to those obtained with different Q-tables, we notice that Q-tables 15 and 16 clearly improve on the results of STQ from compression rate 20 upwards where Q-table 16 does so in a more pronounced manner. For compression rate 10 all other Q-tables improve slightly on STQ and for compression rate 5, Q-tables 12 and 13 are superior to STQ in terms of average HD. In the case of two images being compressed, the observed behaviour is more significant but similar in principle.

These results indicate that PSNR is indeed **NOT** a good predictor for matching performance with compressed iris images in terms of average Hamming distance. The claim that compression up to a rate of 16 even improves the matching scores of not compressed images [11] can be supported at least for the 2 compressed images case and the STQ, for "better" Q-tables this is correct even up to compression rate 20 and higher.

In order to consider the hidden statistical outliers in the comparisons and to use a quantity often employed in the assessment of biometric system performance, we will focus on the receiver operating characteristic (ROC) by computing and plotting the false rejection rate (FRR) against the false acceptance rate (FAR) for different compression rates:

$$FRR = \frac{\text{Number of (false) negative matches}}{\text{Number of legitimate users' matches}} . \tag{1}$$

$$FAR = \frac{\text{Number of (false) positive matches}}{\text{Number of imposter matches}} . \tag{2}$$

Figs. 6 to 8 compare the ROC of different Q-tables for compression rates 5, 10, and 20 since it is not realistic to operate the iris recognition system at a higher compression rate. Again, the two compressed image scenario is compared to the case where only one image is compressed.

For compression rate 5, our proposed Q-tables are not really able to substantially improve ROC. While for one compressed image (Fig. 6.b) only Q-table 15 improves STQ slightly (and only starting from $FRR > 0.08$), significant improvements are seen for Q-tables 15, 16, and 13 (Fig. 6.a). However, only Q-table 15 starts improving at a reasonable low $FRR > 0.04$.

In the case of compression rate 10, the situation changes drastically. Again, Q-table 15 shows the most significant improvements. For two compressed images (Fig. 7.a), at FAR 0.028, Q-table delivers a FRR of almost 0 whereas STQ exhibits an FRR of 0.15. Also the other proposed Q-tables improve on STQ in the interesting lower FRR range.

In the case of only one compressed image we still find improvements, but far less pronounced (Fig. 7.b): For an FAR of 0.041, again Q-table 15 gives FRR almost 0 whereas STQ is almost at FRR 0.9. Again, also Q-tables 13 and 16 improve on STQ.

Finally, when turning to compression rate 20 the situation is different (Fig. 8): now Q-table 16 shows the most significant improvements in the two compressed images case and shows behaviour similar to Q-table 15 also for one compressed image. The most noticeable improvement is found in the latter case at a FAR of 0.035 where Q-table 15 exhibits FRR close to 0 and STQ has an FRR of 1.2.

There is one more interesting thing to note: at least for compression rate 20 it is entirely clear that it is **NOT** advantageous to compress both images involved in matching–

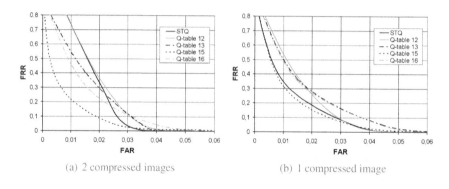

(a) 2 compressed images   (b) 1 compressed image

Fig. 6. Compression rate 5

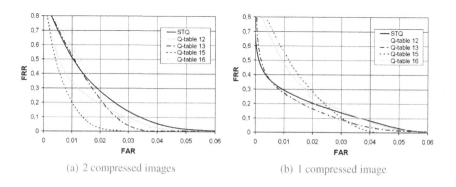

(a) 2 compressed images   (b) 1 compressed image

Fig. 7. Compression rate 10

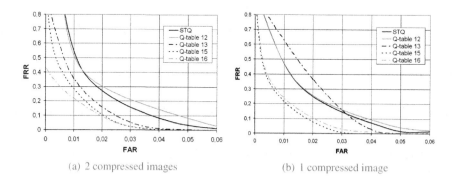

(a) 2 compressed images   (b) 1 compressed image

Fig. 8. Compression rate 20

in terms of ROC, clearly the case of one compressed image is superior here. For compression rates 5 and 10 the better choice highly depends on the target FAR/FRR and the Q-table in use.

5   Conclusion and Future Work

We have found that custom designed quantization tables in JPEG can improve matching results in terms of average HD and ROC behaviour. This is especially true for compression rates of 10 and higher where improvements are seen especially for low FAR. In this case, FRR can be limited much more effective as compared to the default quantization table. In addition to that we have found PSNR to be not at all suited to predict the recognition performance in iris recognition systems. The advantage of compressing both images involved in the matching process cannot be confirmed, in contrary, evidence for the opposite is found for higher compression rates.

In future work we will consider additional alternative iris recognition algorithms in order to identify possible interference between compression technique and iris recognition system. Furthermore we will employ optimization techniques (e.g. GAs) in order to design even more customized quantization tables for this application scenario.

Acknowledgements

Most of the work described in this paper has been done in the scope of the ILV "Compression Technologies and Data Formats" (winter term 2007/2008) in the master program on "Communication Engineering for IT" at Carinthia Tech Institute. The artificial name Gerald Stefan Kostmajer represents the following group of students working on this project: Eigner Raimund, Fischelschweiger Erik, Gernig Stefan, Jereb Martin, Kampusch Andreas, Konrad Mario, Lenzhofer Michael, Mataln Martin, Rabl Manuel, Schlögl Daniel, and Theuermann Klaus. This work has been partially supported by the Austrian Science Fund, project no. L554-N15.

References

1. Chen, M., Zhang, S., Karim, M.: Modification of standard image compression methods for correlation-based pattern recognition. Optical Engineering 43(8), 1723–1730 (2004)
2. Daugman, J.: How iris recognition works. IEEE Transactions on Circuits and Systems for Video Technology 14(1), 21–30 (2004)
3. Daugman, J., Downing, C.: Effect of severe image compression on iris recognition performance. IEEE Transactions on Information Forensics and Security 3(1), 52–61 (2008)
4. Fong, W., Chan, S., Ho, K.: Designing JPEG quantization matrix using rate-distortion approachand human visual system model. In: Proceedings of the IEEE International Conference on Communications (ICC 1997), vol. 3, pp. 1659–1663 (1997)
5. Ives, R., Bonney, B., Etter, D.: Effect of image compression on iris recognition. In: IMTC 2005 – Instrumentation and Measurement Technology Conference (2005)
6. Ives, R.W., Broussard, R.P., Kennell, L.R., Soldan, D.L.: Effects of image compression on iris recognition system performance. Journal of Electronic Imaging 17, 011, 015 (2008), doi:10.1117/1.2891
7. Jenisch, S., Lukesch, S., Uhl, A.: Comparison of compression algorithms' impact on iris recognition accuracy II: revisiting JPEG. In: Proceedings of SPIE, Security, Forensics, Steganography, and Watermarking of Multimedia Contents X, vol. 6819, p. 68190M ff, San Jose, CA, USA (2008)

8. Jeong, G.M., Kim, C., Ahn, H.S., Ahn, B.J.: JPEG quantization table design for face images and its application to face recognition. IEICE Transactions on Fundamentals of Electronics, Communications and Computer Science E69-A(11), 2990–2993 (2006)

9. Matschitsch, S., Tschinder, M., Uhl, A.: Comparison of compression algorithms' impact on iris recognition accuracy. In: Lee, S.-W., Li, S.Z. (eds.) ICB 2007. LNCS, vol. 4642, pp. 232–241. Springer, Heidelberg (2007)

10. Pennebaker, W., Mitchell, J.: JPEG – Still image compression standard. Van Nostrand Reinhold, New York (1993)

11. Rakshit, S., Monro, D.: Effects of sampling and compression on human iris verification. In: Proceedings of the IEEE International Conference on Acustics, Speech, and Signal Processing (ICASSP 2006), Tolouse, France, pp. II–337–II–340 (2006)

12. von Seelen, U.: IrisCode template compression and its effects on authentication performance. In: Biometrics Consortium Conference 2003 (2003)

On the IPP Properties of Reed-Solomon Codes[*]

Marcel Fernandez[1], Josep Cotrina[1], Miguel Soriano[1,2], and Neus Domingo[3]

[1] Technical University of Catalonia, Department of Telematic Engineering
[2] CTTC. Centre Tecnologic de Telecomunicacions de Catalunya, Barcelona, Spain
[3] I.E.S. J.V Foix. Rubi. Barcelona, Spain

Abstract. Codes with traceability properties are used in schemes where the identification of users that illegally redistribute content is required. For any code with traceability properties, the Identifiable Parent Property (c-IPP) seems to be less restrictive than the Traceability (c-TA) property. In this paper, we show that for Reed-Solomon codes both properties are in many cases equivalent. More precisely, we show that for an $[n,k,d]$ Reed-Solomon code, defined over a field that contains the $n - d$ roots of unity, both properties are equivalent. This answers a question posted by Silverberg et al. in [10,11], for a large family of Reed-Solomon codes.

1 Introduction

The concept of traitor tracing was coined in [5] as a method to discourage piracy. Traitor tracing schemes are useful in scenarios where the distributed content may only be accessible to authorized users, like decrypting broadcast messages, software installation and distribution of multimedia content.

This paper discusses the characteristics of the *identifiable parent property* (IPP) of Reed-Solomon codes used in traitor tracing and fingerprinting schemes. However, before we get into technical matters, we give an intuitive overview. By doing this at the beginning of the paper, we try to separate the concepts from where our work emanates from the intrinsic mathematical development and also hopefully provide the reader an extra motivation for going deep into our results.

The scenario we will deal with is the following one. A distributor D, that sells digital content, wishes to discourage illegal redistribution of its products. To this end, he embeds a *unique* set of symbols to each copy of the content before it is delivered. This makes each copy unique and therefore if a dishonest user illegally redistributes his copy, he can be unambiguously identified by simply extracting the set of symbols.

A weakness to this scheme can be spotted by noting that a coalition of two or more dishonest users can get together and by comparing their copies they perform a *collusion attack*. This attack consists in detecting the positions in which their copies differ and with this knowledge, they create a new copy that in every detected position contains a

---

[*] This work has been supported in part by the Spanish Research Council (CICYT) Project TSI2005-07293-C02-01 (SECONNET), by CICYT Project TEC2006-04504, TEC2008-06663-C03-0 P2PSEC and by CONSOLIDER CSD2007-00004 "ARES", funded by the Spanish Ministry of Science and Education.

D. Gritzalis and J. Lopez (Eds.): SEC 2009, IFIP AICT 297, pp. 87–97, 2009.

symbol of one of the members of the coalition. This new copy is a pirate copy that tries to disguise the identity of the guilty users and is the one they redistribute.

More precisely, the distributor assigns a codeword from a q-ary fingerprinting code to each user. To embed the codeword into each users object, the object is first divided into blocks. The distributor then picks a set of these blocks at random. This set of blocks is kept secret and will be the same for all users. Then using a watermarking algorithm a mark of the fingerprint codeword is embedded in each block. Note that a given user will have one of the q versions of the block. The colluding traitors compare their copies, detect the blocks where their copies differ and with this information at hand, they construct a pirate copy where each block belongs to the corresponding block of one of the traitors. Since each mark is embedded using a different random sequence, and these sequences are unknown to the traitors, they cannot create a version of the block that they do not have.

With the above scenario in mind, it is clear that the distributor D, has to embed sets of symbols that are secure against collusion attacks. One way to obtain such sets is by using codes with the *Identifiable Parent Property* (c-IPP).

1.1   Previous Work

Codes with the IPP were introduced in [8]. Informally, and using the traitor tracing scenario described above, a code has the c-IPP property if given a pirate copy, all coalitions of at most c traitors that can generate this pirate copy have a non-empty intersection.

The IPP has received considerable attention in the recent years, having been studied by several authors [3,4,13,9,14,1,2,7].

A stronger property is the Traceability (c-TA) property. In this case given a pirate copy, one of the traitors involved in its creation is the closest one in terms of the Hamming metric.

In [12], sufficient conditions for a linear error correcting code to be a c-TA code are given. Efficient algorithms for the identification of traitors in schemes using c-TA codes are discussed in [10,11].

In [10,11] it is stated that tracing for TA codes is an $O(N)$ process, with N the number of users, whereas for IPP codes tracing is more expensive since it is an $O(\binom{N}{c})$ process. Since the TA property is stronger than the IPP, and tracing is far more expensive for the IPP, it seems natural to expect that by relaxing the TA requirements one could still have a code that, even though in no longer c-TA, still possesses IPP. However in [11] some examples using truncated Reed-Solomon codes lead toward the opposite, that is, if a Reed-Solomon code does not have the TA property then it does not have the IPP one either.

1.2   Our Contribution

In this paper we answer a question posted by Silverberg et al. in [10,11]. The results we present hopefully give way to a total understanding of the IPP property in Reed-Solomon codes.

In [12, Lemma 1.3] authors prove that a c-TA code is a c-IPP code. However as seen before, the TA property is stronger than IPP, taking this into account Silverberg et al. in [10,11] asked the following question:

Question 11 [11]: It is the case that all c-IPP Reed-Solomon codes are c-TA codes?

Below, and as a result of expressing the IPP in an algebraic manner, we give an affirmative answer to this question for a large family of Reed-Solomon codes. Surprisingly enough, the answer is positive for codes defined over a field that contains the $n - d$ roots of unity. Note that our results imply that for this family of Reed-Solomon codes, failing to be c-TA also involves failing to be c-IPP.

For a more precise statement of the Question 11 [11], see Section 2.1 below.

1.3   Organization of the Paper

The paper is organized as follows. In Section 2, we provide the necessary background in coding theory, traceability and IPP. In Section 3 we start our discussion by defining a set of polynomials that allow us to express the IPP algebraically. The main result of the paper is presented in Section 4, and comes in the form of a theorem giving the necessary and sufficient conditions for Reed-Solomon codes to be c-IPP codes. A complete example to clarify our results is given in Section 5. We draw our conclusions in Section 6.

2   Definitions and Previous Results

We define a *code* as a set of n-tuples of elements from a set of scalars. The set of scalars is called the *code alphabet*. An n-tuple in the code is called a *word* and the elements of the code are called *code words*. If the code alphabet is a finite field $\mathbb{F}_q$, then a code C is a *linear code* if it forms a vectorial subspace. The dimension of the code is defined as the dimension of the vectorial subspace.

Let $\mathbf{a}, \mathbf{b} \in \mathbb{F}_q^n$ be two words, then the *Hamming distance* $d(\mathbf{a}, \mathbf{b})$ between $\mathbf{a}$ and $\mathbf{b}$ is the number of positions where $\mathbf{a}$ and $\mathbf{b}$ differ. Let C be a code, the *minimum distance* of C, $d(C)$, is defined as the smallest distance between two different codewords.

A linear code with length n, dimension k and minimum distance d is denoted as a $[n, k, d]$-code, or simply as an (n, d) code.

A well known class of linear codes are Reed-Solomon codes, that can be defined as follows:

Let $\mathbb{F}_q[x]$ be the ring of polynomials defined over $\mathbb{F}_q$. Consider the set of polynomials of degree less than k, $\mathbb{F}_q[x]_k \subset \mathbb{F}_q[x]$. Let γ be a primitive element of $\mathbb{F}_q$, and $\lambda_1, \ldots, \lambda_n \in \mathbb{F}_q - \{0\}$.

Definition 1. *We define a generalized Reed-Solomon, $RS[n, k]_q$, code as the vectorial subspace of $\mathbb{F}_q^n$ determined by the vectors of the form*

$$\mathbf{v} = (\lambda_1 f(\gamma^1), \ldots, \lambda_n f(\gamma^{d-1}))$$

where $f \in \mathbb{F}_q[x]_k$. Note that $n = q - 1$.

2.1   Background and Previous Results on c-IPP Traceability Codes

Given a code $C(n,d)$ defined over the finite field of q elements, $\mathbb{F}_q$, where n denotes the code length and d the minimum distance of the code, the *set of descendants* (false fingerprint) of any subset $T = \{\mathbf{t}^1,\ldots,\mathbf{t}^c\} \subseteq C$, where $\mathbf{t}^i = (t_1^i,\ldots,t_n^i)$, denoted $desc(T)$, is defined as

$$desc(T) = \left\{\mathbf{y} = (y_1,\ldots,y_n) \in \mathbb{F}_q^n | y_i \in \{t_i^j | \mathbf{t}^j \in T\}, 1 \le i \le n\right\}.$$

Definition 2. *A code C is a c-traceability code (denoted c-TA), for $c > 0$, if for all subsets (coalitions) $T \subseteq C$ of at most c code words, if $\mathbf{y} \in desc(T)$, then there exists a $\mathbf{t} \in T$ such that $d(\mathbf{y},\mathbf{t}) < d(\mathbf{y},\mathbf{w})$ for all $\mathbf{w} \in C - T$.*

Definition 3. *A code $C(n,d)$, defined over $\mathbb{F}_q$, is a c-identifiable parent property code (denoted c-IPP), $c > 0$, if for all $\mathbf{y} \in \mathbb{F}_q^n$ and all the coalitions $T \subseteq C$ of at most c code words, we have $\mathbf{y} \notin \bigcup_T desc(T)$ or*

$$\bigcap_{\mathbf{y} \in desc(T)} T \neq \emptyset.$$

In [12, Lemma 1.3] it is shown that that a c-TA code is a c-IPP code. In [5][6][12, Theorem 4.4] it is proved that any $C(n,d)$ code with $d > n - n/c^2$ is a c-TA code. Moreover, if $C(n,d)$ is a code defined over $\mathbb{F}_q$, in [12, Lemma 1.6] authors show that if $|C| > c \ge q$ then C is not a c-IPP code.

Given a code $C(n,d)$, authors in [11, Section IV], construct unordered sets from the ordered sets that constitute the code as follows: to a codeword $\mathbf{x} = (x_1,\ldots,x_n) \in C$ they associate the set $x' = \{(1,x_1),\ldots,(n,x_n)\}$. Then they define TA set systems (as opposed to TA codes) in the natural way, with the noteworthy difference that a pirate unordered set (unordered fingerprint) consist of n elements such that each element is a member of some coalition member's set. In [11, Theorem 7], authors prove that if $C(n,d)$ is a Reed-Solomon code with minimum distance $d \le n - n/c^2$ then the set system corresponding to C is not a c-TA system. Note that this result does not implies that $d > n - n/c^2$ is a necessary condition for RS codes to be c-TA.

Moreover in [11, Theorem 8] authors construct a family of truncated ($n < q - 1$) $RS[n,k]_q$ codes that fail to be c-IPP if $c^2 > n/(n-d)$.

Then in [11, Question 11] the authors ask if it is always true that the c-IPP fails if $c^2 > n/(n-d)$.

In this paper we give another partial positive answer of this question, showing that there are other families of Reed-Solomon codes that fail to be c-IPP if $c^2 > n/(n-d)$. Obviously this does not close the problem, but we think that it gives some hints that may hopefully be useful in finding the final response.

3   The IPP Condition for Reed-Solomon Codes

In this section we set the ground for the discussion of our main results. Informally, we define a set of polynomials (denoted $h_{ij}(x)$), that help us construct an algebraic representation of the IPP. Using these polynomials, we set up a system of equations for which the existence of a solution implies that the code is not c-IPP. In Section 4, we will show how to solve this equation system for a large number of Reed-Solomon codes.

Let $0 < c_1 \leq c_2$ be two integer numbers. We say that a code C is not a (c_1, c_2)-IPP code if there exist coalitions T_1 of c_1 code words and T_2 of c_2 codewords, such that

$$desc(T_1) \bigcap desc(T_2) \neq \emptyset \text{ and } T_1 \bigcap T_2 = \emptyset.$$

Obviously, from Definition 3 the code C is not c_2-IPP.

Therefore, if a $RS[n,k]_q$ code fails to be (c_1, c_2)-IPP this means that there exist two disjoint coalitions, with c_1 and c_2 distinct code words respectively, $T_1 = \{f_0(x), \ldots, f_{c_1-1}(x)\}$, $T_2 = \{g_0(x), \ldots g_{c_2-1}(x)\}$ (where $f_i(x), g_j(x) \in \mathbb{F}_q[x]_k$, but with an abuse of notation they also represent vectors of the form

$$\mathbf{f_i} = (\lambda_1 f_i(\gamma^1), \ldots, \lambda_n f_i(\gamma^n)),$$

with $T_1 \cap T_2 = \emptyset$ and that can generate the same descendant (false fingerprint) $\mathbf{y}$.

We can always assume that code word $\mathbf{0}$ is a code word of coalition T_1, otherwise consider coalitions $T_1 - \mathbf{f_0} = \{\mathbf{f_0} - \mathbf{f_0}, \ldots, \mathbf{f_{c_1-1}} - \mathbf{f_0}\}$ and $T_2 - \mathbf{f_0} = \{\mathbf{g_0} - \mathbf{f_0}, \ldots, \mathbf{g_{c_2-1}} - \mathbf{f_0}\}$. Then it is not difficult to verify that $(T_1 - \mathbf{f_0}) \cap (T_2 - \mathbf{f_0}) = \emptyset$ and they both can generate the fingerprint $\mathbf{y} - \mathbf{f_0}$. Thus, in what follows, we will assume that $\mathbf{f_0} = \mathbf{0}$.

We define polynomials

$$h_{ij}(x) \triangleq f_i(x) - g_j(x) = \beta_{ij} \prod_{k=1}^{s_{ij}} (x - \alpha_k^{ij}) \tag{1}$$

for $i = 0, \ldots, c_1 - 1$ and $j = 0, \ldots, c_2 - 1$.

The polynomials $h_{ij}(x)$ will be a key tool in all the subsequent work. In a sense, they allow us to have an algebraic representation of the IPP .

Note that the polynomials $h_{ij}(x)$ have at most $n - d = k - 1$ roots, thus $s_{ij} \leq n - d$, otherwise two distinct code words in the code would agree in more than $n - d$ coordinates, and this is not possible.

We will make an extensive use of the following result:

Lemma 4. *If a $RS[n,k]_q$ code fails to be (c_1, c_2)-IPP, (T_1 and T_2 can generate the same descendant), then the set of roots of the set of polynomials $\{h_{ij}(x)\}$ is $\mathbb{F}_q - \{0\}$. Therefore, $\sum_{ij} s_{ij} \geq n$, $x^n - 1 | \prod_{ij} h_{ij}(x)$ and $c_1 c_2 (n - d) \geq n$.*

Proof. The proof is straight forward from the definition of the polynomials $h_{ij}(x)$ and the definition of the (c_1, c_2)-IPP. □

In the previous reasoning we have seen that we always can take $f_0(x) = 0$, therefore

$$g_j(x) = f_0(x) - h_{0j}(x) = -\beta_{0j} \prod_{k=1}^{s_{0j}} (x - \alpha_k^{0j}) \quad j = 0, \ldots, c_2 - 1$$

Since $f_i(x) = \sum_{k=0}^{n-d} f_i^k x^k$ for $i = 1, \ldots, c_1 - 1$ then we can write down the following equation system(with an abuse of notation, because we are assuming that $s_{ij} = n - d$ for all i, j, that in fact is the worst case situation):

$$\left.\begin{aligned}
f_i^0 &= \beta_{ij}\prod\left(-\alpha_k^{ij}\right) - \beta_{0j}\prod\left(-\alpha_k^{0j}\right)\\
\cdots\\
f_i^{n-d-1} &= -\beta_{ij}\left(\sum\alpha_k^{ij}\right) + \beta_{0j}\left(\sum\alpha_k^{0j}\right)\\
f_i^{n-d} &= \beta_{ij} - \beta_{0j}
\end{aligned}\right\} \tag{2}$$

where $i = 1,\ldots,c_1 - 1$ and $j = 0,\ldots,c_2 - 1$.

Note that if this equation system has a solution then the associated Reed-Solomon is not (c_1,c_2)-IPP.

When finding a solution for (2), we observe that the equation system has $(c_1 - 1)c_2(n - d + 1)$ equations, and $(c_1 - 1)(n - d + 1) + c_1c_2 + n$, degrees of freedom. However, there is an important restriction due to Lemma 4, that is, the values of the α_k^{ij} ($i = 0,\ldots,c_1 - 1$ and $j = 0,\ldots,c_2 - 1$) must take distinct n values in $\mathbb{F}_q$, and this reduces the chance to find a solution. Note that if we assume that the values of α_k^{ij} are arbitrarily assigned then we only have $(c_1 - 1)(n - d + 1) + c_1c_2$ degrees of freedom.

Below, in Section 4, we will show how a solution can be found for a large family of Reed-Solomon codes.

Before concluding this section, we review some trivial results on non IPP conditions.

Lemma 5. *Here we consider* $[n,k,d]$ *Reed-Solomon codes and assume that the code length n is fixed.*

1. *For a fixed value d, if the code is not $(c_1,c_2) - IPP$ then it is not (c_1',c_2')-IPP, for any pair of values $c_1' \geq c_1, c_2' \geq c_2$.*
2. *If the code is not $(c_1,c_2) - IPP$ for some value of d, then it is not (c_1,c_2)-IPP for any value $d' \leq d$.*

4   Main Result on IPP Reed-Solomon Codes

In this section we discuss the main result in this paper that gives an answer to the question posed in [11] ([Question 11]) asking whether if it is always true that c-IPP property fails if $c^2 > n/(n-d)$.

In Theorem 6 below, we show that in fact is true that c-IPP property fails if $c^2 > n/(n-d)$, for all Reed-Solomon codes defined over a field that contains the $n - d$ roots of unity.

Intuitively, our strategy is as follows. From Lemma 4 and the subsequent reasoning, it is clear that, if for a given code the equation system (2) has a solution then the code is not (c_1,c_2)-IPP. Since (2) has more equations (although may of the equations might be redundant) than degrees of freedom it is necessary to invert this situation. We accomplish this by finding a suitable set of polynomials $h_{ij}(x)$.

Theorem 6. *Let $RS[n,k]_q$ be a Reed-Solomon code. Consider two integer numbers $c_1 \leq c_2$. If $c_1c_2 < n/(n-d)$ the code is (c_1,c_2)-IPP. Moreover, if $n - d$ divides $q - 1$, then the code is (c_1,c_2)-IPP if and only if $c_1c_2 < n/(n-d)$.*

Proof. The sufficient part it is already known, but we prove again it for completeness. If we consider a coalition T_1 of at most c_1 code words that can produce a descendant (false fingerprint) $\mathbf{y}$, we can ensure that one of the c_1 code words in the coalition agrees with $\mathbf{y}$ in at least $n/c_1 > (n-d)c_2$ of the coordinates. But any member $\mathbf{v}$ of any coalition T_2 of at most c_2 code words, with $T_2 \cap T_1 = \emptyset$, can only agree with $\mathbf{y}$ in at most $(n-d)c_1$ coordinates, otherwise $\mathbf{v}$ shall coincide in more than $n-d$ coordinates with a code word in T_1, and this is not possible because of the definition of minimum distance of a code. Thus the code words in coalition T_2 can generate at most $(n-d)c_1c_2 < n$ coordinates of $\mathbf{y}$, that is, they can not generate the descendant $\mathbf{y}$.

For the necessary condition, in virtue of Lemma 5 we can assume that $c_1c_2 = \lceil n/(n-d) \rceil$.

If $n-d$ divides $q-1$, we have that the $(n-d)$-roots of the unity belong to $\mathbb{F}_q$. Let $s = (q-1)/(n-d)$, then we can express the $(n-d)$-roots of the unity as α^{sk}, where α is a primitive element of $\mathbb{F}_q$.

We define the polynomial

$$P(x) \triangleq \prod_{k=1}^{n-d} (x - \alpha^{ks}) = x^{n-d} - 1.$$

now we can express the polynomials $h_{ij}(x)$ as

$$h_{ij}(x) \triangleq \beta_{ij} P(\alpha^{ic_2+j}x) = \beta_{ij}\alpha^{(ic_2+j)(n-d)} \prod_{k=1}^{n-d} \left(x - \alpha^{ks-ic_2-j}\right) =$$

$$= \beta_{ij}\alpha^{(ic_2+j)(n-d)}x^{n-d} - \beta_{ij},$$

for $i = 0,\ldots,c_1 - 1, j = 0,\ldots c_2 - 1$, where $c_1c_2 \geq s$. Clearly the α^{ks-ic_2-j}'s take as value all the elements in $\mathbb{F}_q - \{0\}$ for $i = 0,\ldots,c_1 - 1, \ j = 0,\ldots c_2 - 1$ and $k = 1,\ldots,n - d$.

Now, the equation system (2) can be re-expressed as

$$\left.\begin{array}{l} f_i^0 = -\beta_{ij} + \beta_{0j} \\ f_i^{n-d} = \beta_{ij}\alpha^{(ic_2+j)(n-d)} - \beta_{0j}\alpha^{j(n-d)} \end{array}\right\} \tag{3}$$

To solve this system we first will take $f_i^{n-d} = 0$ (in other words, we take the $f_i(x)$ polynomials as constant). We have that

$$\begin{array}{l} f_i^{n-d} = 0 \\ \beta_{ij} = \beta_{0j}\alpha^{-ic_2(n-d)} \end{array} \tag{4}$$

and by taking $\beta_{0j} = 1$, it follows that

$$\begin{array}{l} \beta_{0j} = 1 \\ f_i^0 = -\alpha^{-ic_2(n-d)} + 1 \end{array} \tag{5}$$

It is clear that (5) solves the equation system (2), and the theorem is proved. However, before we finish the proof perhaps some observations are in order.

First note that if $f_i^0 = 0$ for some i, then we would have more than a single zero polynomial, however since we are assuming that $c_1c_2 = \lceil n/(n-d) \rceil$ this can not happen.

Also, note that the equation system (2) is simplified since the coefficients of degree $s \neq 0, n - d$ of $h_{ij}(x)$ and of $g_j(x) = h_{0j}(x)$ are 0, and so the equations are of the form "f_i^s equals 0", for all j, and therefore are satisfied trivially by simply taking $f_i^s = 0$.

Finally, observe that if $\alpha^{j(n-d)} = -1 = \alpha^{n/2}$ then $2c_2 > \lceil n/(n-d) \rceil$, thus $c_1 \leq 1$, and $c_2 = \lceil n/(n-d) \rceil$. But this directly implies that the code is not (c_1, c_2)-IPP.   □

5   Example

In this section we present an example of the above results.

We take a Reed-Solomon code over $\mathbb{F}_{13}$ (q=13). We denote the elements of $\mathbb{F}_{13}$ as $\{0, 1, 2, 3, 4, 5, 6, 7, 8, 9, 10, 11, 12\}$. Since we wish to prove that if $d < n - \frac{n}{c^2}$ then the code is not c-IPP then we take the code with parameters $[n = 12, k = 4, d = 9]$ and $c = 2$. Note that $n - d$ divides $q - 1$ ($\mathbb{F}_{13}$ contains the $n - d = 3$ roots of unity).

With the above reasoning in mind, we need to find polynomials $f_0(x), f_1(x), g_0(x), g_1(x)$ such that when grouped into two disjoint coalitions the corresponding code words can generate the same descendant (false fingerprint). In other words, we wish to find (disjoint) Coalition 1 $\{f_0(x) = 0, f_1(x)\}$ and Coalition 2 $\{g_0(x), g_1(x)\}$ such that their corresponding code words $\{\mathbf{f_0}, \mathbf{f_1}\}$ and $\{\mathbf{g_0}, \mathbf{g_1}\}$ can generate the same exact descendant (false fingerprint).

First of all, we define the h_{ij} polynomials.

$$
\begin{aligned}
h_{00} &= f_0 - g_0 = \beta_{00}(x - \alpha_1^{00})(x - \alpha_2^{00})(x - \alpha_3^{00}) \\
h_{01} &= f_0 - g_1 = \beta_{01}(x - \alpha_1^{01})(x - \alpha_2^{01})(x - \alpha_3^{01}) \\
h_{10} &= f_1 - g_0 = \beta_{10}(x - \alpha_1^{10})(x - \alpha_2^{10})(x - \alpha_3^{10}) \\
h_{11} &= f_1 - g_1 = \beta_{11}(x - \alpha_1^{11})(x - \alpha_2^{11})(x - \alpha_3^{11})
\end{aligned}
\tag{6}
$$

where the α_l^{ij} take *all* of the non-zero values of $\mathbb{F}_{13}$.

Taking into account that $f_0(x) = 0$, we have that:

$$
\begin{aligned}
g_0 &= -h_{00} &&= -\beta_{00}(x - \alpha_1^{00})(x - \alpha_2^{00})(x - \alpha_3^{00}) \\
g_1 &= -h_{01} &&= -\beta_{01}(x - \alpha_1^{01})(x - \alpha_2^{01})(x - \alpha_3^{01}) \\
f_1 &= h_{10} + g_0 &&= \beta_{10}(x - \alpha_1^{10})(x - \alpha_2^{10})(x - \alpha_3^{10}) \\
&&&\quad - \beta_{00}(x - \alpha_1^{00})(x - \alpha_2^{00})(x - \alpha_3^{00}) \\
f_1 &= h_{11} + g_1 &&= \beta_{11}(x - \alpha_1^{11})(x - \alpha_2^{11})(x - \alpha_3^{11}) \\
&&&\quad - \beta_{01}(x - \alpha_1^{01})(x - \alpha_2^{01})(x - \alpha_3^{01})
\end{aligned}
\tag{7}
$$

and since $f_1(x) = f_1^0 + f_1^1 x + f_1^2 x^2 + f_1^3 x^3$ (because $k - 1 = n - d = 3$), it follows that the system to be solved is

$$
\left.
\begin{aligned}
f_1^0 &= -\beta_{10}\alpha_1^{10}\alpha_2^{10}\alpha_3^{10} + \beta_{00}\alpha_1^{00}\alpha_2^{00}\alpha_3^{00} \\
f_1^1 &= \beta_{10}(\alpha_1^{10}\alpha_2^{10} + \alpha_1^{10}\alpha_3^{10} + \alpha_2^{10}\alpha_3^{10}) - \beta_{00}(\alpha_1^{00}\alpha_2^{00} + \alpha_1^{00}\alpha_3^{00} + \alpha_2^{00}\alpha_3^{00}) \\
f_1^2 &= -\beta_{10}(\alpha_1^{10} + \alpha_2^{10} + \alpha_3^{10}) + \beta_{00}(\alpha_1^{00} + \alpha_2^{00} + \alpha_3^{00}) \\
f_1^3 &= \beta_{10} - \beta_{00} \\
\\
f_1^0 &= -\beta_{11}\alpha_1^{11}\alpha_2^{11}\alpha_3^{11} + \beta_{01}\alpha_1^{01}\alpha_2^{01}\alpha_3^{01} \\
f_1^1 &= \beta_{11}(\alpha_1^{11}\alpha_2^{11} + \alpha_1^{11}\alpha_3^{11} + \alpha_2^{11}\alpha_3^{11}) - \beta_{01}(\alpha_1^{01}\alpha_2^{01} + \alpha_1^{01}\alpha_3^{01} + \alpha_2^{01}\alpha_3^{01}) \\
f_1^2 &= -\beta_{11}(\alpha_1^{11} + \alpha_2^{11} + \alpha_3^{11}) + \beta_{01}(\alpha_1^{01} + \alpha_2^{01} + \alpha_3^{01}) \\
f_1^3 &= \beta_{11} - \beta_{01}
\end{aligned}
\right\}
\tag{8}
$$

Next, we define the $h_{ij}(x)$ polynomials as

$$h_{ij}(x) = \beta_{ij}\alpha^{(ic+j)(n-d)}x^{n-d} - \beta_{ij} \tag{9}$$

with $i = \{0,1\}$, $j = \{0,1\}$ the integer value $c = 2$ and $\alpha = 2$ a primitive element of $\mathbb{F}_{13}$, so

$$h_{ij}(x) = \beta_{ij}2^{(i2+j)(n-d)}x^{n-d} - \beta_{ij} \tag{10}$$

Now by plugging (10) in (7), the equation system (8) becomes:

$$(i=1, j=0) \qquad \left.\begin{array}{l} f_1^0 = -\beta_{10} + \beta_{00} \\ f_1^3 = 2^6\beta_{10} - \beta_{00} \end{array}\right\} \tag{11}$$

$$(i=1, j=1) \qquad \left.\begin{array}{l} f_1^0 = -\beta_{11} + \beta_{01} \\ f_1^3 = 2^9\beta_{11} - 2^3\beta_{01} \end{array}\right\} \tag{12}$$

We take for instance (11) (taking (12) leads to the same result). As seen in (4), we have that:

$$f_3^0 = 0$$

now taking $\beta_{00} = 1$ and using (5), yields

$$(i=1, j=0) \qquad \left.\begin{array}{l} f_1^3 = 0 \\ \beta_{00} = 1 \\ \beta_{10} = 12 \\ f_1^0 = -12 + 1 = 2 \end{array}\right\} \tag{13}$$

Therefore,

$$\begin{array}{l} f_0(x) = 0 \\ f_1(x) = 2 \end{array} \tag{14}$$

Using these values in (12):

$$(i=1, j=1) \qquad \left.\begin{array}{l} 2 = -\beta_{11} + \beta_{01} \\ 0 = 2^9\beta_{11} - 2^3\beta_{01} \end{array}\right\} \tag{15}$$

solving, we have that

$$\beta_{01} = 1 \quad \text{and} \quad \beta_{11} = 12 \tag{16}$$

Which yields

$$\begin{array}{llll} h_{00}(x) = x^3 - 1 & = x^3 + 12 \\ h_{01}(x) = 2^3x^3 - 1 & = 8x^3 + 12 \\ h_{10}(x) = 12 \cdot 2^6x^3 - 12 = x^3 + 1 \\ h_{11}(x) = 12 \cdot 2^9x^3 - 12 = 8x^3 + 1 \end{array} \tag{17}$$

Finally, using (7) we have

$$\begin{array}{l} g_0(x) = 12x^3 + 1 \\ g_1(x) = 5x^3 + 1 \end{array} \tag{18}$$

We have arrived at Coalition 1: $f_0(x) = 0, f_1(x) = 2$ and Coalition 2: $g_0(x) = 12x^3 + 1, g_1(x) = 5x^3 + 1$.

Encoding these polynomials, we have that for Coalition 1:

$$\mathbf{f_0} = (0,0,0,0,0,0,0,0,0,0,0,0)$$
$$\mathbf{f_1} = (2,2,2,2,2,2,2,2,2,2,2,2)$$

and for Coalition 2:

$$\mathbf{g_0} = (0,6,0,2,6,6,9,9,0,2,9,2)$$
$$\mathbf{g_1} = (6,2,6,9,2,2,0,0,6,9,0,9)$$

It is clear that both coalitions can create the same descendant (false fingerprint):

$$(0,2,0,2,2,2,0,0,0,2,0,2)$$

6   Conclusions

In this paper we have discussed the IPP in Reed-Solomon codes. The goal of our work was to answer a question by Silverberg et al. in [10,11] inquiring whether all c-IPP Reed-Solomon codes are also c-TA codes. By expressing the IPP algebraically through the definition of a suitable set of polynomials, we have shown that for a large family of Reed-Solomon codes this is in fact true. That is, all $[n,k,d]$ Reed-Solomon codes defined over a field that contains the $n - d$ roots of unity are IPP codes if and only if they are also TA codes.

It is surprising that from our results it seems that the IPP characteristics of a Reed-Solomon code lie solely in the field over which the code is defined. To devise the exact extension of this dependence will be a subject of further research.

References

1. Alon, N., Fischer, E., Szegedy, M.: Parent-identifying codes. J. Comb. Theory, Ser. A 95(2), 349–359 (2001)
2. Alon, N., Stav, U.: New bounds on parent-identifying codes: The case of multiple parents. Combinatorics, Probability & Computing 37(6), 795–807 (2004)
3. Barg, A., Cohen, G., Encheva, S., Kabatiansky, G., Zémor, G.: A hypergraph approach to the identifying parent property: the case of multiple parents. Tech. rep., DIMACS 2000-20 (2000)
4. Barg, A., Kabatiansky, G.A.: A class of i.p.p. codes with efficient identification. J. Complexity 20(2-3), 137–147 (2004)
5. Chor, B., Fiat, A., Naor, M.: Tracing traitors. In: Desmedt, Y.G. (ed.) CRYPTO 1994. LNCS, vol. 839, pp. 480–491. Springer, Heidelberg (1994)
6. Chor, B., Fiat, A., Naor, M., Pinkas, B.: Tracing traitors. IEEE Trans. Inform. Theory 46, 893–910 (2000)
7. Fernandez, M., Soriano, M.: Algorithm to decode identifiable parent property codes. Electronics Letters 38(12), 552–553 (2002)
8. Hollmann, H.D.L., van Lint, J.H., Linnartz, J.P., Tolhuizen, L.M.G.M.: On codes with the Identifiable Parent Property. J. Combinatorial Theory 82(2), 121–133 (1998)
9. Sarkar, P., Stinson, D.R.: Frameproof and IPP codes. In: Pandu Rangan, C., Ding, C. (eds.) INDOCRYPT 2001. LNCS, vol. 2247, pp. 117–127. Springer, Heidelberg (2001), citeseer.ist.psu.edu/486714.html

10. Silverberg, A., Staddon, J., Walker, J.: Efficient traitor tracing algorithms using list decoding. In: Boyd, C. (ed.) ASIACRYPT 2001. LNCS, vol. 2248, p. 175. Springer, Heidelberg (2001)
11. Silverberg, A., Staddon, J., Walker, J.L.: Applications of list decoding to tracing traitors. IEEE Transactions on Information Theory 49(5), 1312–1318 (2003)
12. Staddon, J.N., Stinson, D.R., Wei, R.: Combinatorial properties of frameproof and traceability codes. IEEE Trans. Inform. Theory 47(3), 1042–1049 (2001)
13. Tô, V.D., Safavi-Naini, R.: On the maximal codes of length 3 with the 2-identifiable parent property. SIAM J. Discrete Math. 17(4), 548–570 (2004)
14. van Trung, T., Martirosyan, S.: New constructions for ipp codes. Des. Codes Cryptography 35(2), 227–239 (2005)

A Generic Authentication LoA Derivation Model

Li Yao and Ning Zhang

School of Computer Science, University of Manchester
yaol@cs.man.ac.uk, zhangn@cs.man.ac.uk

Abstract. One way of achieving a more fine-grained access control is to link an authentication level of assurance (LoA) derived from a requester's authentication instance to the authorisation decision made to the requester. To realise this vision, there is a need for designing a LoA derivation model that supports the use and quantification of multiple LoA-effecting attributes, and analyse their composite effect on a given authentication instance. This paper reports the design of such a model, namely a generic LoA derivation model (GEA- LoADM). GEA-LoADM takes into account of multiple authentication attributes along with their relationships, abstracts the composite effect by the multiple attributes into a generic value, authentication LoA, and provides algorithms for the run-time derivation of LoA. The algorithms are tailored to reflect the relationships among the attributes involved in an authentication instance. The model has a number of valuable properties, including flexibility and extensibility; it can be applied to different application contexts and support easy addition of new attributes and removal of obsolete ones.

1 Introduction

In a virtual organisational (VO) environment, services and data are provided and shared among organisations from different administrative domains and protected with dissimilar security policies and mechanisms. These services and data (collectively called resources hereafter) may have varying levels of sensitivity, thus requiring a more fine-grained access control solution. One way of achieving this is to link an authentication level of assurance (LoA) derived from a requester's authentication instance to the authorisation decision made to the requester.

Electronic authentication (e-authentication) is an electronic process by which a remote user can be identified. Different authentication methods and processes provide different levels of assurance (LoA) in identifying a remote user. As defined by NIST [2], LoA reflects the degree of confidence in an authentication process used to establish the identity of an entity (an individual or a software component) to whom a credential was issued, and the degree of confidence that the entity using the credential is indeed the entity that the credential was issued to. In other words, LoA is an indicator of the strength of an authentication process. It is influenced by all the factors directly or indirectly associated to the process, including the method used for identity proofing, the authentication protocol/method used by the underlying authentication service and the environment under which the authentication is performed [2,10,13]. The extent to

D. Gritzalis and J. Lopez (Eds.): SEC 2009, IFIP AICT 297, pp. 98–108, 2009.

which an authentication event is coupled to an authorisation event should also be taken into account when LoA is established.

In a VO, or a large-scale distributed resource sharing environment, resources are likely to be more diversified and have varying levels of sensitivity. The existing approach to access control is a binary approach. A grant or deny authorisation decision is made merely based upon the verification outcome of the requester's identity credential. It is well-known that identity verification cannot always produce a perfect and reliable outcome. This approach to access control, disregarding the quality of authentication in authorisation decision making, cannot satisfy the need for effective and cost-efficient security provision in diversified resource sharing environments. To overcome this limitation, there is a need for the design and development of an adaptive authentication solution that allows the selection of different authentication methods with varying levels of assurance as matched with resource sensitivity levels at run-time.

This paper describes the design of an authentication model, called the generic e-authentication LoA derivation model (GEA-LoADM), to materialise our vision depicted above. The model supports the use and quantification of multiple LoA- effecting attributes in an authentication instance and derives an aggregate LoA for the given set of attributes at run-time. By grouping LoA attributes, analysing their mutual relationships and the composite effect on an authentication outcome, the authentication model is robust and more flexible than the existing binary authentication model. The major novel contributions of this paper include the identification and classification of LoA-effecting attributes (i.e. authentication factors) used in various e-authentication scenarios, the analysis of the mutual relationships and composite effect of these attributes, and the design of LoA derivation algorithms that derives an aggregate LoA for a given set of LoA attributes along with their respective LoA contributions and the mutual relationships.

The rest of this paper is organised as follows. Section 2 discusses related works and efforts on defining and using authentication assurance levels. Section 3 describes, in detail, the design of GEA-LoADM, including its architecture and architectural components. Section 4 presents aggregate authentication LoA derivation algorithms. Section 5 concludes the paper and outlines our future work.

2   Related Works

The concept of authentication LoA has been around since 2000 when the UK Office of the e-Envoy (now the CabinetOffice e-Government Unit) first initiated the effort on defining authentication LoA and on issuing guidance on using some specific types of identification and authentication methods to achieve appropriate levels of assurance so as to ensure that on-line government services are protected properly. This initial effort was then followed up by the US Office of Management and Budget (OMB) that defined e-Authentication guidance for federal agencies [10]. In this guidance, four authentication assurance levels, Levels 1 through to 4, are defined in terms of the consequences of authentication errors and misuse of credentials. The lowest, Level 1, denotes little or no confidence in the validity of an asserted identity, and the highest, Level 4, denotes very high confidence in the asserted identity's validity. While this OMB guidance specifies criteria for determining the authentication assurance levels required for specific on-line services and transactions based upon the risks in each service and transaction category, NIST (US National Institute of Standards and Technology) further defined technical requirements for implementing these four assurance levels in its Special Publication 800-63 [2]. Similar efforts have also been made by the Japanese Government [6], the Australian Government [1], and the Canadian Government [3] as part of their e-government initiatives. These efforts either use, or adopt a similar specification as, the OMB/NIST guidelines mentioned above.

It is worth emphasising that all the LoA guidelines and efforts discussed above are centred on the user-to-system authentication use case scenarios. They do not consider machine-to-machine nor software-to-software authentication scenarios. Nor do they address the authentication of a person via a physical authentication mechanism, e.g. location-based or biometrics based services. In addition, issues related to how LoA may be fed into the authorisation process are also outside the scope of these efforts. There is also a lack of solutions to link LoA to authorisation decision making at run-time. Most of the existing authentication LoA efforts, such as the one recommended by the OMB/NIST, uses an off-line approach to LoA compliance. With this approach, LoA definitions are given as guidelines and the parties concerned are required to comply with these guidelines by conducting a risk assessment of the underlying system, mapping identified risks to an applicable assurance level, selecting appropriate authentication methods and technologies based upon the technical guidelines, and validating the implemented systems to make sure that it has achieved the required assurance level. This off-line approach to authentication assurance level conformance may be adequate for a static and homogeneous environment where resources and their sensitivity levels are pre-defined prior to run-time and the services are provided by a single service provider, such as the case in e- Government scenarios. This approach is certainly not sufficient for Grid computing or large-scale distributed resource sharing environments environments in which both service consumers and service providers are expected to be diversified and dynamic in nature.

The first and the only effort so far (to the authors best knowledge) on linking authentication LoA to authorisation decision making at run-time was made by the FAME-PERMIS (Flexible Authentication Middleware Extensions to the PERMIS) project team [www.fame-permis.org]. The project developed a software component that derives a LoA value based upon a user's authentication token presented to the authentication service, and asserts the value to a role-based access control decision engine run at the SP (Service Provider) side thus achieving LoA lined access control [9,15]. However, the software is in a very basic form; it only implements the LoA definition versus token types as defined by the NIST guideline [2]. It does not consider the impacts of other LoA- effecting factors such as authentication models and credentials used in Grid applications. Nor does it consider the composite effect by multiple LoA- effecting attributes.

Some works [4,5] on the estimation of trustworthiness of a user done in the ubiquitous computing community may be relevant to our work described here. However, the algorithms given are largely for the context of a ubiquitous computing environment. For example, [4] proposes a model to calculate the trustworthiness of a user's pervasive device, and [5] describes a parameterised authentication model for calculating the authentication reliability of authentication sensors in a sensor based networks. Both of these works are centred at a broad level of trust in a ubiquitous environment, whereas our work focuses on identifying authentication attributes in large-scale and dynamic distributed resource sharing environments such as Data Grids, analysing and quantifying the composite effect of these attributes on user identification and authentication assurance level and linking it to authorisation decision making at run-time. In our problem context, the design issues of flexibility and extensibility are more acute.

3   GEA-LoADM Model

3.1   Architecture Overview

As shown in Figure 1, the GEA-LoADM model has a number of architectural components, which can largely be classified into the following groups, an off-line component, a real-time component and a global LoA- effecting attributes policy database (GLoA-APDB). The output of the model is consumed by a replying party (i.e. a service provider) that can be a shibboleth attribute authority [14], or an authorisation decision engine.

The off-line component, called a Global LoA-effecting Attributes Policy Manager (GLoA-APM), is responsible for identifying LoA-effecting attributes and calculating the weightings among additive attributes. It comprises two further functional modules, the Global LoA-effecting Attributes Hierarchical Structure (GLoA-AHS), and the Global LoA-effecting Attributes Weightings Allocation Module (GLoA-AWAM). GLoA-AHS is responsible for identifying all the LoA-effecting attributes in a given authentication context/environment, constructing a hierarchical LoA-effecting attributes structure (such as the one shown in Figure 2), and categorising the attributes into different groups and levels based on their mutual relationships. These tasks are expected to be undertaken manually by an authentication administrator or access policy decision maker based on their security policies and access control requirements. GLoA-AWAM is responsible for calculating LoA weightings for additive attributes (additive LoA attributes refer to those LoA attributes that are in an elevating relationship, i.e. the

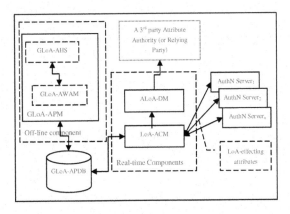

Fig. 1. GEA-LoADM architecture

aggregated LoA value measuring the composite effect of a set of additive LoA attributes on authentication assurance level is not lower than any of the individual component LoA values in the attribute set). The weightings, along with other related information, including the attributes hierarchical structure, the indicators of the relationships among different attributes, component LoA values are all stored in GLoA-APDB. The working mechanisms of, and the methodology used in the design of these functional modules are detailed in Sections 3.2.

The real-time component has two functional modules, a LoA-effecting Attributes Collection Module (LoA-ACM), and an Authentication LoA Derivation Module (ALoA- DM). The LoA-ACM module first receives a notification of the set of contributing LoA-effecting attributes involved in an authentication event/instance from authentication services. It then fetches the component LoA values corresponding to each of the attributes in the attribute set, along with their respective weightings, from GLoA-APDB. Next, LoA-ACM sends the contributing attributes names along with their relationships, component LoA values and weightings to ALoA-DM. Once these parameter values are obtained, ALoA-DM calculates an aggregated LoA using a LoA derivation algorithm corresponding to the settings of this authentication instance. The design details of LoA-ACM and ALoA-DM are described in section 3.4 and 3.5, and the LoA derivation algorithms are discussed in section 4.

GLoA-APDB is a database storing all the LoA-effecting attributes identified by GLoA-AHS, their relationships, component LoA values and additive LoA attributes weightings. The technical details of this module is described in section 3.3. In the following subsections, we further describe the designs of the architectural components and how they interact with one another.

3.2   Global LoA-Effecting Attributes Policy Manager (GLoA-APM)

GLoA-APM has two functional modules, each performing some well defined tasks. The first module, GLoA-AHS, identifies and classifies LoA effecting attributes and organises them into a hierarchical structure based upon their mutual relationships. The second module, GLoA-AWAM, provides the algorithms that can systematically and scientifically assess and calculate the weightings of additive LoA-effecting attributes for a given authentication model.

Performing these tasks requires a thorough analysis and evaluation of the underlying authentication context/environment and access control policies, which can be a time-consuming process. Therefore, GLoA-APM is also termed as an offline component, meaning that its functional tasks should be performed prior to the execution of authentication procedures.

3.2.1   Global LoA-Effecting Attributes Hierarchical Structure (GLoA-AHS)

As mentioned, the GLoA-AHS module is responsible for:

- managing (i.e. adding, deleting and classifying) LoA-effecting attributes;
- assigning component (or attribute) LoA values to each of the attributes; and
- constructing the attributes into a hierarchical structure based on their mutual relationships.

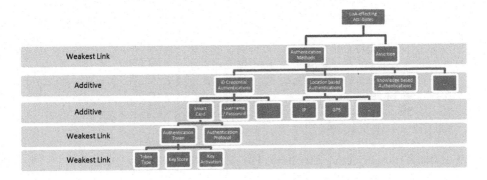

Fig. 2. An exemplar GLoA-AHS structure

The first two tasks are authentication context dependent. They are also dependent on access policies that are, in turn, influenced by factors such as asset values and the underlying risks in the access environment. We have examined and extended the attributes identified by NIST [2] and OASIS [13], and produced a generic set of LoA-effecting attributes. In addition, we have examined the mutual relationships among these attributes and organised them into a hierarchical structure, as shown in Figure 2. From the figure, it can be seen that the structure highlight the mutual relationship among the group of attributes located at the same level. This structured approach to LoA-effecting attributes' identification, classification, and organisation is an essential step towards the determination of their respective weightings on, and the derivation of, the overall confidence level for an authentication instance, in a scientific manner. This structure has a number of additional merits. For example, it is flexible and extensible. Any emerging LoA-effecting attributes can be easily added into the structure, and any obsolete ones can be removed from it without affecting other levels in the hierarchy. Also, once constructed, a GLoA-AHS instance for a given authentication setting will only need to be revised when there is any change in the authentication attributes at any level.

3.2.2   LoA-Effecting Attributes Weighting Allocation Module (LoA-AWAM)

When calculating an aggregate LoA for a group of attributes that are in an additive relationship, their respective weightings should be determined first. The GLoA-AWAM module uses AHP pair-wise comparison technique [11] to calculate the relative weightings of the attributes. For a group of n additive attributes in the same level, $X = x_1$, $x_2,...,x_n$, at a given level in a GLoA-AHS structure, the LoA-AWAM module works as follows [12,7]:

1. Based on the fundamental scale (developed by [11], and is used to represent the intensity of importance among the attributes), the decision maker inputs the comparison values $a_{ij}=x_i/x_j$; i,j $\subseteq$ [1...n], where x_i and x_j are the ith and j^{th} attributes in the set, and the algorithm constructs matrix:

$$A = (a_{ij})_{n \times n} = \begin{pmatrix} a_{11} & a_{12} & ... & a_{1n} \\ a_{21} & a_{22} & ... & a_{2n} \\ ... & ... & ... & ... \\ a_{n1} & a_{n2} & ... & a_{nn} \end{pmatrix}.$$

2. Compute the principle eigenvalue λ_{max} and the corresponding eigenvector W = $[w_1, w_2, ..., w_n]$.
3. Check for consistency.
4. If matrix A is consistent or acceptably consistent, the algorithm derives the normalised eigenvector W'$=[w'_1, w'_2, ..., w'_n]$ from W, and W' is the normalised weight for the set of attributes X.
5. Repeat steps (1)-(4) above for every attribute groups located at additive levels in the GLoA-AHS hierarchy.

3.3   Global LoA-Effecting Attributes Policy Database (GLoA-APDB)

GLoA-APDB is a database containing three tables, storing, respectively, the GLoA-AHS data structure, the LoA-effecting attributes along with their component LoA values and weightings (for additive attributes), and aggregate LoA values and the corresponding information in the case of successful LoA derivation for an authentication event. The table for storing the GLoA-AHS data is called the Hierarchy Table. The second table, called the Attribute Table, stores AttributeNames, ComponentLoAValues, Weightings and RelationshipTypes of the LoA effecting attributes. These two tables store all the information required by the GLoA-APM module. The third table is named as the Aggregated LoA Table and it is for logging LoA information related to authentication events. That is, if an authentication event is successful, the Table stores the aggregated LoA value calculated for the event along with the corresponding contributing LoA-effecting attributes.

3.4   LoA-Effecting Attributes Collection Module (LoA-ACM)

The LoA-ACM module performs three tasks. Firstly, it interacts with all the authentication services involved in an authentication event to identify contributing LoA-effecting attributes. Secondly, it queries GLoA-APDB to obtain the component LoA values and weightings of the attributes. Thirdly, it sends all the data fetched from GLoA-APDB to ALoA-DM that then derives the aggregated authentication LoA value for the event.

3.5   Authentication LoA Derivation Module (ALoA-DM)

ALoA-DM receives a set of LoA-effecting attributes along with their component LoA values and weightings for an authentication event from LoA-ACM and derives an aggregated authentication LoA value for the event. The derivation is done by using either of the two algorithms detailed in Section 4. Once the aggregated LoA value is calculated, the LoA-effecting attributes along with the aggregated LoA value will be stored in GLoA-APDB for auditing purposes and for future references. Optionally, these data may be stored in a third party attribute directory or an attribute authority for consumptions by other relying parties. For example, the data may be sent to the attribute authority in the Shibboleth system for attribute assertion [14,15], or to the attribute authority for creating and assigning an attribute certificate.

4   Estimating the Composite Effect of Multiple LoA-Effecting Attributes

4.1   The Method Overview

As discussed in section 3, for any given authentication system, there will be a set of multiple LoA-effecting attributes, and the attributes can be organised into a GLoA-AHS structure. Using the structure, we can estimate the composite effect (i.e. aggregated LoA) of these attributes. This is done in a bottom-up manner. Assuming that there are m levels (levels 1, ..., m) in the structure. From the bottom level m, based upon the relationship (the weakest link, or the additive) of the attributes at the level, an aggregated LoA derivation algorithm (corresponding to the relationship) is used to calculate the aggregated LoA for this level. This aggregated LoA value is then used as the component LoA of the connected attribute at the level immediately above, i.e. Level $(m-1)$. This process continues until the top level, i.e. Level 1, of the structure is reached, and the aggregated LoA value at Level 1 is the overall confidence level, i.e. the aggregated LoA, for the entire authentication event.

Obviously, for different relationships among multiple attributes, different LoA derivation algorithms should be used. The following two subsections discuss the weakest link relationship algorithm and additive relationship algorithm respectively.

4.2   The $ALoA_{WL}$ Algorithm

The $ALoA_{WL}$ (Aggregated LoA for the Weakest Link relationship) algorithm discussed in this section is designed for estimating an aggregated LoA value given a set of attributes that are in the weakest link relationship. Assume that there is a group of attributes $\{a_1, a_2, ..., a_n\}$ at level k and their respective component LoA values are $\{LoA_{a1}, LoA_{a2}, ..., LoA_{an}\}$, and that these attributes are in the weakest link relationship. The composite effect of these attributes on the authentication assurance level should be the lowest component LoA value in the set. Mathematically, this can be expressed as:

$$ALOA_{(WL.level-k)} = min(LoA_{a1}, LoA_{a2}, ..., LoA_{an});, \tag{1}$$

where min is the minimum function, and $ALOA_{(WL.level-k)}$ is the aggregated LoA value for level k with attributes in the weakest link relationship.

From this discussion, it can be seen that the derivation of an aggregated LoA value for a group of attributes that are in the weakest link relationship only requires the attributes component LoA values.

4.3   The $ALoA_{AD}$ Algorithm

The design of the $ALoA_{AD}$ (Aggregated LoA for the additive relationship) algorithm that is required for estimating an aggregated LoA value given a set of attributes that are in an additive relationship is not as straightforward as the case for $ALoA_{WL}$. A scientific method that can take into account of the attributes' component LoA values as well as their respective weightings is required. Subjective Logic [8], defined to mathematically describe and quantify subjective beliefs, consists of a belief model named opinion model and set of operations for combining opinions. It can be used to define various operations for processing multiple opinions such as conjunction, disjunction, negation, consensus, recommendation and ordering. The $ALoA_{AD}$ algorithm employs the subjective logic opinion (SLO) model and its consensus operation to derive the aggregated LoA [8].

Using the SLO model, each of the additive attributes is transformed into an 'opinion' in the opinion model. For example, an attribute x's opinion about the aggregated authentication assurance level can be expressed as,

$$\pi_p^x = b + d + u = 1, b, d, u \subseteq [0,1] \tag{2}$$

Where π is the opinion function, p is the proposition which π has opinion to (in this case, p refers to the aggregated LoA), x is the attribute, and b, d, and u represent belief, disbelief and uncertainty, respectively.

We now need to determine the values for tuple $< b, d, u >$. Belief b refers to the level of trust in attribute x's opinion. It is set to a value in the range [0,1], where 0 stands for no certainty and 1 stands for absolute certainty. The level of trust in an authentication outcome (i.e. the meaning of b) obviously has a similar meaning as the component LoA (which refers to the level of confidence in an authentication outcome). However, as LoA values are scoped between 1 to 4, and b in the subjective logic uses a scale from 0 to 1, we need a transform method to transform LoA values from the scale of [1, 4] to values in the scale of [0, 1]. This scale transformation is done using the following mapping, $b(0.25) = LoA_x(1)$, $b(0.5) = LoA_x(2)$, $b(0.75) = LoA_x(3)$, and $b(1) = LoA_x(4)$.

Disbelief d refers to the level of accuracy in attribute x's opinion. It is usually used to measure the accuracy of some hardware-based authentication attributes such as the case in biometric authentication and hardware sensor- based authentication [5]. Unlike hardware-based authentication attributes, credential-based authentication attributes only have belief and uncertainty values, but not accuracy value. This is because, for credential based authentication, if the authentication outcome is successful, then the level of accuracy is taken as 100% (i.e. d = 0).

Based upon these considerations, for credential-based authentication attributes, we can define the opinion for attribute x as follows:

$$\pi_p^x = \{b + d + u\} = \begin{cases} b = LoA_x \\ d = 0 \\ u = 1 - LoA_x \end{cases}$$

The opinion definitions for cases where disbelief is not zero, such as the case of sensor or location based authentication method, will be addressed in our future work. Once the opinions of all the attributes involved are defined, we can calculate a combined opinion by using the consensus operation defined in [8].

This consensus operation assumes that the contributions (i.e. the weightings) by each opinion are the same. However, for different authentication events and in different access environments, the weightings of different additive LoA- effecting attributes are likely to be different, and these differences may influence the final LoA derivation result significantly. For example, consider the case where a smartcard authentication attribute with a component LoA value 3, and an IP authentication attribute with a component

LoA value 1, are both used in an authentication event. If the ratio of their authentication impact/weighting is (1:1), then the calculated combined opinion will be {b=0.77, d=0, u=0.33}. However, if the ratio is (3:1), then the combined opinion will be different and b is expected to be higher than 0.77. Therefore, there is a need for a method to integrate the influence of various weightings into the algorithm. We do this by integrating the weighting of an attribute into its component LoA. The following describes this method.

Assume that w_i is the weighting, LoA_i is the original component LoA value, and LoA_{ai} is the adjusted LoA value, of attribute a_i. In other words, the effect of a_i's weighting on the final aggregated LoA is embedded into the adjusted component LoA value of attribute a_i, LoA_{ai}. It is worth noting that the sum of the weightings by all the attributes is always 1. Assume there are n attributes, if we take that the assumed contributions (or assumed weightings) by each of the attributes are always the same, and that each such weighting equals to 1/n, then the adjusted weighting for attribute a_i will be the difference between the real weighting, w_i, and the assumed weighting, 1/n. That is, the adjusted component LoA value for attribute a_i is

$$LoA_{ai} = LoA_i \times (1 + (w_i - 1/n)) \tag{3}$$

By integrating attributes' weightings into their respective component LoA values, the adjusted component LoA values can capture the effects of the attributes on the overall authentication assurance level of an authentication event in a more accurate manner. Then the consensus operation mentioned earlier can be used to derive the final aggregated LoA value.

5   Conclusion and Future Work

This paper has discussed the concept of authentication level of assurance and the potential benefits in using it to achieve more fine grained access control. However, owing to the number, the variety and the complexity of the attributes concerned, quantifying their composite effect and deriving an aggregate assurance level given multiple authentication attributes for an authentication event is a very challenging research issue.

The paper has made some novel contributions in addressing this research issue by proposing a framework, by which an authentication assurance level as influenced by multiple attributes can be systematically estimated. This framework includes a Global LoA-effecting Attributes Hierarchical Structure (GLoA-AHS) by which a large number of LoA- effecting attributes can be organised into a hierarchical structure with distinctive mutual relationships. Two aggregated LoA derivation algorithms are designed to accommodate the identified relationships. With the use of these algorithms, along with the GLoA-AHS structure and additional architectural component, the framework is able to automatically derive a composite LoA value given a set of LoA-effecting attributes. The major advantage of this model is its ability to accommodate a complex set of attributes, and to provide a quantitative measure for authentication assurance levels in the face of the complex attributes. Our ongoing work includes prototyping and evaluating the framework, and extending it to accommodate more complex Grid authentication scenarios. The consequent data privacy protection is another research issue and how to safely employ users authentication information without misuse will be included in our future work.

References

1. Australian e-Government & Information Management (cited October 10, 2008), `http://www.finance.gov.au/e-government/index.html`
2. Burr, W. E., et al.: Electronic Authentication Guideline. In: NIST Special Publication 800-63. NIST (cited October 15, 2008), `http://csrc.nist.gov/publications/PubsSPs.html`
3. Canadian e-authenticaiton (2004) (cited October 10, 2008), `http://www.ic.gc.ca/epic/site/ecic-ceac.nsf/en/h_gv00090e.html`
4. Creese, S., et al.: Authentication for Pervasive Computing. In: Hutter, D., Müller, G., Stephan, W., Ullmann, M. (eds.) Security in Pervasive Computing. LNCS, vol. 2802, pp. 116–129. Springer, Heidelberg (2004)
5. Covington, J., et al.: Parameterized Authentication. In: Samarati, P., Ryan, P.Y.A., Gollmann, D., Molva, R. (eds.) ESORICS 2004. LNCS, vol. 3193, pp. 276–292. Springer, Heidelberg (2004)
6. Japan, An overview of International Initiatives in the field of Electronic Authentication (2005) (cited October 10, 2008), `http://www.japanpkiforum.jp/shiryou/e-auth_policy/overview_e-auth_v07.pdf`
7. Johnson, H., et al.: A Decision System for Adequate Authentication. p. 185, doi:10.1109/ICNICONSMCL.2006.9
8. Josang, A., et al.: Legal Reasoning with Subjective Logic. Artificial Intelligence and Law 8(4), 289–315 (2000)
9. Nenadic, A., et al.: Fame: Adding Multi-Level Authentication to Shibboleth. In: IEEE Conference of E-Science and Grid Computing, Amsterdam, Holland, p. 157 (2006)
10. OMB Memorandum M-04-04, E-Authentication Guidance for Federal agencies. OMB (cited October 10, 2008), `http://www.whitehouse.gov/OMB/memoranda/fy04/m04-04.pdf`
11. Saaty, T.L.: Scaling method for priorities in hierarchical structures. Journal of Mathematical Psychology 15(3), 234–281 (1977)
12. Saaty, T.L.: How to make a decision: The analytic hierarchy process. European Journal of Operational Research IC/1990/48, 9–26 (1990)
13. SAML 2.0 Authentication Context specification. OASIS (cited October 10, 2008), `http://docs.oasis-open.org/security/saml/v2.0/saml-authn-context-2.0-os.pdf`
14. Shibboleth Architecture technical overview (2005), `http://shibboleth.internet2.edu/docs/draft-mace-shibboleth-tech-overview-latest.pdf`
15. Zhang, N., Yao, L., et al.: doi: 10.1002/cpe.v19:9

Media-Break Resistant eSignatures in eGovernment: An Austrian Experience

Herbert Leitold[1], Reinhard Posch[2], and Thomas Rössler[3]

[1] Secure Information Technology Center – Austria (A-SIT)
Herbert.Leitold@a-sit.at
[2] Federal Chief Information Officer Austria
Reinhard.Posch@cio.gv.at
[3] IAIK, Graz University of Technology
Thomas.Roessler@iaik.tugraz.at

Abstract. Governments and public administrations produce documents – laws, orders, permits, notifications, etc. With the transition from traditional paper-based administration to eGovernment that we have seen in the last decade, authentic electronic documents gain importance. Electronic signatures promise to be a tool of choice. However, given the choice of access channels – electronic or conventional – public administrations offer, eDocuments will have to co-exist with traditional paper documents for several years, if not for decades. In this paper we discuss the Austrian practical experience gained with eSignatures and eDocuments in eGovernment.

1 Introduction

Electronic government (eGovernment) is increasingly supplementing or even replacing traditional means of carrying out public administration. 7 x 24 availability, efficiency, accessibility, reduced red tape, better services for citizens and businesses, reduced costs, or accessibility are the promises. These promises are made for citizen to administration (C2A), business to administration (B2A), and intra-government (administration to administration A2A) communication. Cross-border eGovernment bridging different legislations increasingly gets on the agenda: In the EU policy initiatives such as within eEurope2005 [1] i2010 [2] showed impact and EU Member States–in addition to their existing national eGovernment programs–committed themselves to improve their services towards such cross-border services.

Austria has introduced electronic signature in eGovernment early, such as for official notifications or in 2003 even for official promulgation of laws [3]. The achievements made in Austria have been confirmed by an annual eGovernment benchmark carried out by the European Commission [4] reporting for Austria 100% online-availability of the twenty services that have been benchmarked.

In such an environment where sensitive personal data are processed or where misuse of data may severely impact citizens' or businesses' rights, information security and privacy is a clear must. Research has shown that privacy is among the main concerns in eGovernment, such as shown by an Oxford Internet Institute (et al.) research

D. Gritzalis and J. Lopez (Eds.): SEC 2009, IFIP AICT 297, pp. 109–118, 2009.

that has included lack of trust and inadequate security and privacy safeguards in seven key barriers to eGovernment [5]. Citizens need to have certainty that their data is well protected. Public administrations need certainty that they are dealing with the citizen or the business claiming to have filed an application. Both citizens/businesses and public administrations need assurance that data are authentic. Last not least, the pro- bative value of eDocuments as evidence in court proceedings needs to be ensured.

A number of technologies and tools are needed and are employed to support in- formation security in eGovernment. In this paper we limit our-selves to the role of electronic signatures in eGovernment, i.e. to data-origin authentication. We refer to qualified electronic signatures as electronic signatures that yield legal equivalence to manual ones, i.e. "satisfy the legal requirements of a signature in relation to data in electronic form in the same manner as a handwritten signature satisfies those re- quirements in relation to paper-based data". This legal definition has been taken from in the EU Signature Directive [6]. The national implementations are domestic signa- ture laws such as the Austrian Signature Act [7].

The technologies backing electronic signatures exist for a while, i.e. digital signa- ture and public key infrastructure (PKI). While these technologies are widely de- ployed in commodity products such as email clients, or document viewers, deploying the technologies in eGovernment for nationwide or cross-border use may lead to some additional requirements.

We discuss such requirements, roads followed, solutions developed, and practical experiences in the Austrian case in the remainder of this paper: In section 2 chal- lenges to eDocuments in eGovernment are discussed. While some of the challenges are found in other environments such as in the private sector, others may be consid- ered specific to the public sector. An example of such specific situations are fairly long transition periods from paper to electronic processes that are caused due to the many actors on national, regional, and local level. In section 3 we discuss electronic signatures created by citizens, i.e. signing applications. While this seems to be easy at first sight, the relatively low frequency of a few government contacts per year asks for open solutions that search for synergies with private sector applications in order to in- crease take up and to make infrastructure investments economic. We continue in sec- tion 3 with discussing electronic signatures created by public administrations. The problem addressed here is that co-existence of conventional paper-based documents and electronic documents shall not lead to a duplication of infrastructure. This shall serve as an outlook how the experience made in Austria may serve as best practice. Finally, conclusions are given.

2   Challenges to eDocuments in eGovernment

Documents are the fundamental vehicles of public administration – we are used to show birth certificates as birth date confirmation and legal presence documents, we fill forms to apply for a driver license; we receive building permits from the authority, or show a proof of citizenship when applying for a passport.

Taking a birth certificate as an example, basic characteristics are that the document is needed for many years and it is used in many different processes with a variety of different authorities. Assume that birth certificates are issued as electronic documents where an electronic signature ensures authenticity: We than can state two desired properties: (1) From a government's perspective, the signed eDocument should also be usable by authorities or in processes that are not yet online and not yet electronic. Thus, paper copies should be possible so that the citizen can print the electronic birth certificate and use it as an attachment to a conventional, paper-based application. This of course raises the question of how authenticity of the printed document can be ensured and how one can verify that the document has been created by an authority. (2) The second requirement stems from a citizen's perspective: If an official document is delivered electronically the citizen may not want to be burdened with keeping a reliable electronic archive for decades – think e.g. of the birth certificate example. Even though today computers are found in almost any household, life-situations may change or computers may break which shall not render essential official documents inaccessible. Again printing important documents on paper may be seen as a proven durable backup media.

The considerations made so far lead to the requirement that when migrating to official eDocuments printouts should remain a genuine representation. Authenticity of eDocuments should be ensured in a way that tolerates media breaks. To state a more stringent requirement, printouts of official eDocuments shall have legal probative value and the assumption of genuineness should apply to printed eDocuments – two requirements that have been included in the Austrian eGovernment Act [8]. We will describe in section 4 how this has been implemented technically in Austrian eGovernment based on electronic signatures.

3   Citizens' Signatures – The Mass-Deployment Challenge

An initiative to employ smartcards to facilitate citizens' access to public services has been launched in an Austrian Cabinet Council in 2000. In early stages of this citizen card project it became obvious, that two major challenges need to be solved [9]:

- The relatively low frequency of citizen contacts with public administrations asks for solutions that are not limited to the public sector, but search for synergies with the private sector. This applies to both government-issued citizen cards used in private sector applications needing adequate security levels (e.g. Internet banking) and enabling the private sector to issue own tokens (e.g. bank cards) as citizen cards that can be used as official electronic identities (eID) in eGovernment.
- Applications usually need to be signed by the applicant. Qualified electronic signatures give the legal basis to sign electronic forms [6] [7]. eGovernment user interfaces of choice – Web browsers – however give no standardized vendor-independent and platform-independent way to sign forms. Integration of smartcards is usually limited to client authentication using SSL/TLS [10].

To address these challenges, Austria has chosen to develop an open specification "Security Layer" between the Web browser and the citizen card [11]. The interface is based on the hypertext transport protocol (HTTP) and thus is accessible via any Web browser using standardized methods. The implementation of the interface is a middleware called "citizen card environment". Aside de-coupling the citizen card from the browser, the middleware integrates the different tokens, as various smartcards can be used. The concepts, the identity management model, and the security architecture of the citizen card are described in detail in [12].

The process of signing electronic data using the middleware bases on a simple XML based request-response protocol. To sign a document, an XML command "CreateXMLSignatureRequest" selecting the key pair and certificate for a qualified signature is sent by the application to the middleware. The data to be signed is referred by a so called "DataObjectInfo"-element. The result is an XMLDSIG signature [13] which is returned by the middleware as corresponding "CreateXMLSignatureResponse". Using complex requests the data to be signed can be almost arbitrary XML data, can include transformations, or can contain supplements. As an alternative signature format cryptographic message syntax (CMS) [14] is supported.

4   Administrations' Signatures – The Media-Break Challenge

In this section we discuss electronic signatures created by public authorities, such as on official notifications. We refer to such signatures as "official signatures". We first describe the underlying concepts and then give two case studies of actual implementations in sub-sections 4.1 and 4.2.

With reference to the challenges for authentic eDocuments that have been discussed in section 2, the two underlying objectives to be addressed by official signatures are:

- Verifiability that the signer was a public authority or a public official
- Authenticity robust against media-breaks

To meet the goal of identifying a public authority an attribute to the signature certificate has been specified. An object identifier (OID) has been defined as an extension to the X.509 certificate and has been registered as "Austrian eGovernment OID". Using OIDs to define attributes in certificates is a common approach in PKI [15]. It however requires that verification software interprets the OID and informs the relying party. For a domestic administration that e.g. receives an eDocument containing an official signature it is an easy task to identify the official signature, as the national OID is known. For citizens or foreign administrations the problem arises that standard signature verification software can verify the signature, but usually is not aware of an Austrian eGovernment OID. The problem however turns out minor as the eGovernment Act [8] asks the authority (i.e. the signer) to provide a link to information on how to validate an eDocument it issues. This is usually a validation service that does the signature validation and makes an attestation that the document has been issued by the authority based on the eGovernment OID.

The tricky problem is how the media breaks can be overcome. The chosen solution was to apply an electronic signature to the (electronic) document and to construct the eDocument in a way that all information needed to validate the electronic signature is visible on the document – thus printable and also visible on the printout. We define the following conditions:

1. Relevant information needs to be text based. The limitation is however minor for official documents that usually are text documents (for official signatures including images and other binary data, see the binary mode in section 4.2)
2. Text information that can lead to ambiguity on printouts, such as different hyphens, multiple blank spaces or tabs, or diacritics, need to be normalized to an unmistakable representation

3. All elements in the electronic signature are appended as visible text elements to the document as a visible signature block

XMLDSIG [13] has been chosen as signature format being a text-based format meeting condition (1) above. A normalization algorithm has been specified to meet (2). Figure 1 illustrates a signature block (3).

Signature Value		K5EY07ClXqArMBUv/ACqWlZy8dk5fGFYMdMOR6A06nudhDtqIkiv7EU2KYQ5ImWJ
(logo: SIGNATURINFORMATIONEN)	Signatory	T=Dipl. Ing.,serialNumber=865438804219,givenName=Herbert,SN=Leitold,CN=Herbert Leitold,C=AT
	Date/Time-UTC	2009-01-18T16:39:58Z
	Issuer-Certificate	CN=a-sign-Premium-Sig-02,OU=a-sign-Premium-Sig-02,O=A-Trust Ges. f. Sicherheitssysteme im elektr. Datenverkehr GmbH,C=AT
	Serial-No.	92575
	Method	urn:pdfsigfilter:bka.gv.at:text:v1.1.0
	Parameter	etsi-bka-1.0@1232296799-64918006@23101-9724-0-2175-20711
Verification		Validation service: https://www.buergerkarte.at/signature-verification/

Fig. 1. Visual signature block over this paper

The signature block shown in figure 1 is a qualified electronic signature over this contribution to SEC2009 that you are currently reading. It is created in a "text-mode" using the PDF official signature tools described in sub-section 4.2. The electronic signature can be verified using the verification link either based on the electronic file (if available) or based on the typed text if just the printout is available (admittedly, the length of the paper makes typing without allowing a single typo troublesome. Compare however to the little amount of relevant data on your birth certificate which easily can be typed).

The signature block needed to validate the signature contains the following elements:

- A *logo*: The logo has no security value, but is used to allow citizens to visually identify an authority's official signature.
- The *signature value*: That is the cryptographic result of the XMLDSIG [13] signature in base-64 encoding.
- *Signatory* is the person who signed the document. Either the distinguished name (DN) taken from the signature certificate is shown or a friendly name that can be freely chosen.
- *Date-Time/UTC*: The time when the signature has been created in coordinated universal time.
- *Issuer-Certificate* and *Serial-No.*: The issuer-field and the certificate serial number uniquely identify the certificate and, for qualified certificates or other sufficiently reliable CAs, the signatory. Provided that certificates are published in a directory service (e.g. LDAP [16]), the certificate can be retrieved using this data. This eliminates the need to include all certificate content in the signature block.
- *Method* refers to the text extraction, normalization and representation method used. This also identifies the form used. The form can be a single text block, or arbitrary complex XML structures. An example of official signatures used with complex forms is given in section 4.1.

- *Parameter:* Additional parameters used in the XMLDSIG signature-creation process are encoded in this string.
- *Verification* is a reference to the signature validation service that can be used to verify the document. In the example in figure 1 the URL of such a service provided by the official citizen card web page is given.

Validating the electronic signature using the electronic version of the eDocument has no difference with conventional XMLDSIG signature validation, as all data including the signature certificate is given in the eDocument. When reconstructing and verifying authenticity a few preparatory steps are needed: Let's assume that the relying party has used optical character recognition (OCR) to convert the printout to a text-stream. The next step is to carry out a text analysis to identify the signature block(s) that can be at arbitrary positions in the text stream. The next step is to identify the *method*, i.e. which document format has been used to convert XML. The XML form is retrieved and filled with the text from the OCR-stream. Finally, the certificate is retrieved from the CA's directory service. The result is an XMLDSIG structure and the signature can be verified.

The considerations made so far on official signatures are independent from the document format. Tools have been developed to sign raw text, complex XML structures, portable document format (PDF) documents, OpenOffice documents, or Microsoft Office Word 2007 documents. Taking two examples from this list, the following sub-sections describe how official signatures are used with XML data and PDF.

4.1   Case Study: XML Plus Stylesheet

The first case study of signed eDocuments is structured XML data. Having read the validation process from printouts described above, the reader might have wondered whether this actually will work in practice, such as typing long text from paper with conversion errors that still are frequent with OCR systems. Any mistyped character would render the electronic signature invalid and may be hard to find. Two aspects are however to be considered: On the one hand, reconstruction from paper is the scarce case – usually validation is done using the electronic version as an attachment to an application and even with paper the assumption of genuineness is challenged just in doubt. On the other hand, most official documents (forms) are highly regular and have just a few dynamic elements such as a reference number, the citizen's name, or a date as variable elements. Significant portions are static – permits or other content is often made of known text blocks with little variables. This allows to provide a Web-form that gives the look-and-feel of the paper-document. By filling a few dynamic elements the electronic original is reconstructed.

To give an example of how verifying authenticity of printed official signatures is used in practice, we use the criminal record certificate showing convictions of the applicant. Such certificates are frequently used, as in public procurement a fresh criminal record is to be provided by the bidder. In the majority of cases the certificate shows no convictions. Thus, a limited amount of data is dynamic. Figure 2 below is the Web form to validate a printed criminal record certificate. It requests for entering few data only.

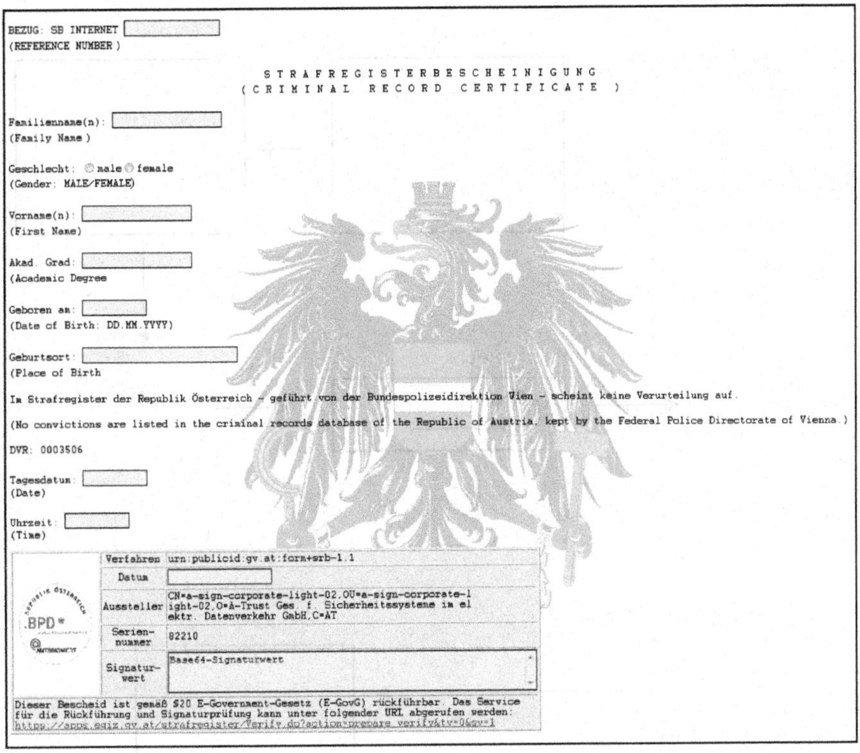

Fig. 2. Reconstruction-form for signature validation from printouts

4.2   Case Study: Official Signatures and PDF

PDF is a desirable document format for official signatures, as it is frequently used and PCs are often shipped with PDF readers as pre-installed standard software. Even though PDF has electronic signature features since its version 1.6 [17], the official signature requirement to allow for reconstruction from the printout could not be fulfilled. Thus, separate tools have been developed in Austria. Two signature-modes are supported:

- A *binary mode* where the PDF document is considered a binary stream that is signed. That allows signing arbitrary data including images, but bit-identical reconstruction from printouts is not possible.
- A *text mode* where the raw visible text is signed. This mode does not include images or other binary data into the signed data, but allows for validating the signature from printouts [8].

Binary signatures on PDF documents are similar to PDF signatures defined in [17]. The main difference is that a visible signature block with data shown in figure 1 is created – which gives additional information compared to PDF signatures as known from Acrobat® products.

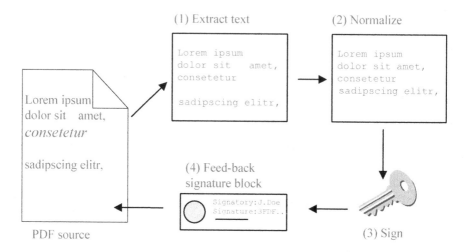

Fig. 3. Text mode signature-creation for PDF documents

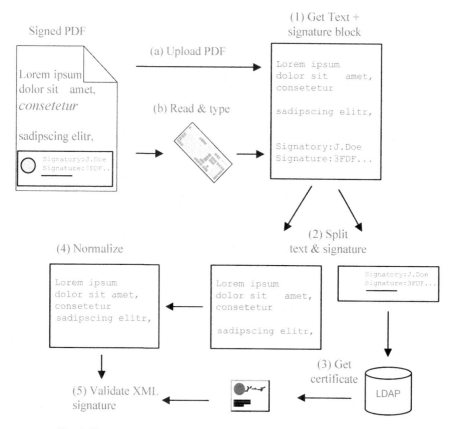

Fig. 4. Signature validation from the electronic document (a) or a printout (b)

We therefore focus on text mode signatures that allow validation from printouts. The tools carry out four steps during signature-creation, as illustrated in figure 3: (1) First the raw visible text is extracted from the PDF document as UTF-8 encoded stream. Formatting is ignored. A critical issue is that the text extraction needs to exactly represent the reading order "top left to bottom right". This is needed for reconstructing the text from printouts in the same order. It turned out that most PDF tools perform well on extracting from standard text documents, but depending on the PDF creation tools used for the document to be signed tables, headers, footers, and footnotes can result in reading order errors. (2) The second step is a normalization step to eliminate ambiguous characters or text representations on printouts. The normalization specification defines how to handle characters that can be mistaken with similar characters, such as similar hyphens, dashes, or diacritics. Moreover multiple spaces and tabs need to be eliminated. (3) The third step is to sign the normalized text. XMLDSIG [13] is used. (4) Finally, the signature block as shown in figure 1 is created and fed back into to PDF document.

If using the validation link in the signature block and the PDF version of the paper, signature validation follows five successive steps, as illustrated in figure 4: (1) the original text together with the text of the signature block is extracted and converted to a UTF-8 stream. This is either done by (a) uploading the electronic version and employing PDF text extraction tools or (b) by reading the printout and manually typing the text, using OCR tools, respectively. (2) The signature block – or signature blocks in case of multiple signatures – is separated. As the signature-block is well defined, that is done by rather simple text analysis. (3) The certificate issuer and the certificate serial number are taken from the signature block to identify the CA and the certificate. In case the certificate is not embedded into the electronic PDF, it is retrieved from the CA's directory service. (4) The text is normalized using the same algorithm as during signature creation. The methods used are identified by the *method* field in the signature block (cf. figure 1). (5) Conventional signature validation is done.

A set of tools has been developed to allow for creating and validating such *text mode* or *binary mode* PDF signatures using either the citizen card or server-based signature-creation devices for high volume operations. Among the most convenient ones is a plug-in for Acrobat® Standard or Acrobat® Professional. The signatory uses the plug-in to position the signature block using the mouse within the PDF document.

5 Conclusions

The paper has introduced Austrian electronic signature initiatives in eGovernment. Austria has started in 2001 with a comprehensive eGovernment program where electronic signatures play an important role as a security tool. Electronic signatures are however no end in itself, but the means to achieve authenticity with electronic documents. Thus, the main topic of the paper is how to achieve authentic eDocuments using electronic signatures as the vehicle to provide genuineness.

eDocuments can either be created by the citizen such as filling a form, or can be issued by the public authority as the electronic substitute of paper documents. On the former – applications of the citizens – the paper has briefly described the Austrian citizen card concept as the citizen's tool to electronically sign forms. On the latter – official documents created by an authority – the paper has described the concept of official signatures. Official signatures are electronic signatures created in a way that the relying party can verify that an eDocument origins from a public authority. A specific feature developed by Austria is that official signatures are robust against media breaks. That is that an electronic signature created using the concepts discussed can be validated even if printed on paper. This facilitates the introduction of eGovernment as the media preference or capabilities of the final receiver of a document – either the citizen or an authority receiving the document as an attachment – no longer determines on which media a document is issued.

References

1. European Commission, eEurope 2005: an Information Society for all, COM (2002)
2. European Commission, i2010 – A European Information Society for growth and employment, SEC (2005) 717
3. Republic of Austria, Austrian Federal Act on the Federal Law Gazette 2004 (Promulgation Act), Federal Law Gazette, part I, Nr. 100/2003 (2003)
4. CapGemini, The User Challenge Benchmarking The Supply Of Online Public Services, 7th measurement, Prepared by: Capgemini, For: European Commission Directorate General for Information Society and Media (2007)
5. Oxford Internet Institute, Breaking Barriers to eGovernment, MODINIS contract 29172, Deliverable 2, Prepared by: Oxford Internet Institute (and others) For: European Commission Directorate General for Information Society and Media (2007)
6. European Union, Directive 1999/93/EC of the European Parliament and of the Council of 13. December 1999 on a community framework for electronic signatures (1999)
7. Republic of Austria, Austrian Federal Act on Electronic Signatures, Federal Law Gazette, part I, Nr. 137/2000, last amended by Nr. 59/2008 (2000)
8. Republic of Austria, Austrian Federal Act on Provisions Facilitating Electronic Communications with Public Bodies; Federal Law Gazette, part I, Nr. 10/2004, last amended by Nr. 59/2008 (2004)
9. Posch, R., Leitold, H.: Weissbuch Bürgerkarte, Austrian Federal Ministry for Public Services and Sports, Federal IT-Coordination (2001) (in German)
10. Dierks, T., Rescorla, E.: The Transport Layer Security (TLS) Protocol, Version 1.1, IETF Request For Comment RFC 4346 (2006)
11. Hollosi, A., Karlinger, G.: The Austrian Citizen Card – Security Layer Application Interface, Version 1.2.2, Federal Staff Unit for ICT Strategy, Technology and Standards (2005)
12. Leitold, H., Hollosi, A., Posch, R.: Security Architecture of the Austrian Citizen Card Concept. In: Proceedings of 18th Annual Computer Security Applications Conference (ACSAC 2002), Las Vegas (2002)
13. Eastlake, D., Reagle, J., Solo, D.: XML-Signature Syntax and Processing, W3C Recommendation, 2002; RFC 3275 (2002)
14. Hously, R.: Cryptographic Message Syntax (CMS), IETF Request For Comment RFC 3852 (2004)
15. ITU-T, Information Technology – Open Systems Interconnection – Systems Management Overview – Procedures for the Operation of OSI Registration Authorities: General Procedures, ITU-T Recommendation X.660 (1992), ISO/IEC 9834-1 (1993)
16. Zeilenga, K.: Lightweight Directory Access Protocol version 2 (LDAPv2), RFC 3494 (2003)
17. Adobe Corporation, PDF Reference, fifth edition - Adobe Portable Document Format version 1.6 (2006)

How to Bootstrap Security for Ad-Hoc Network: Revisited

Wook Shin[1], Carl A. Gunter[2], Shinsaku Kiyomoto[1], Kazuhide Fukushima[1], and Toshiaki Tanaka[1]

[1] KDDI R&D Laboratories, Inc., 2-1-15 Ohara Fujimino-shi Saitama 356-8502, Japan
{wookshin,kiyomoto,ka-fukushima,toshi}@kddilabs.jp
[2] Dept. of Computer Science, University of Illinois at Urbana-Champaign, IL 61801, USA
http://seclab.uiuc.edu

Abstract. There are various network-enabled and embedded computers deployed around us. Although we can get enormous conveniences by connecting them together, it is difficult to securely associate them in an ad-hoc manner. The difficulties originate from authentication and key distribution problems among devices that are strangers to each other. In this paper, we review the existing ways of initiating secure communication for ad-hoc network devices, and propose another solution. Exploiting Pairing-based cryptography and the notion of location-limited channel, the proposed solution bootstraps security conveniently and efficiently. Further, it supports ownership enforcement and key-escrow.

1 Introduction

The number of computer-embedded intelligent devices deployed around us keeps increasing as the technology evolves. The devices are sometimes network-enabled to give even more benefits. Although the advantages can be augmented when a user can connect the devices together on demand, it is being obstructed by security and privacy threats. The communications over the intelligent and networked devices (called as "embedded devices" or just "devices", hereinafter) can be protected cryptographically, but bootstrapping security is not easy.

Security bootstrapping that includes key generation/distribution and authentication tends to impose configuration burdens upon users. For example, users need to follow a series of instruction steps for WPA2-PSK (WiFi Protected Access 2, Pre-shared key) configuration, even though the pre-shared key mode is the simplest option for using WPA. Establishing security among devices becomes more complicated in an ad-hoc network since there is no trusted entity always available online.

In this paper, we look over the related existing technologies and propose a rather intuitive and useful way of bootstrapping security for networked devices. Taking advantage of Pairing-based cryptography and the notion of location-limited channel, the proposed method provides an easy, secure, and efficient way of creating private communication channels over devices. A user does not have to follow intricate commands, but just brings a special device close to other devices to create a secure channel. Besides, users can acquire privileged ownership and key escrow support on their own channels. Only a channel owner can manage membership of the owned channel and reveal any

D. Gritzalis and J. Lopez (Eds.): SEC 2009, IFIP AICT 297, pp. 119–131, 2009.

secret over the channel. Our method also can be applied to other forms of networks (e.g., home Wi-Fi networks), not only to ad-hoc networks.

2 Background

Stajano and Anderson[26] addressed security bootstrapping difficulties in an ad-hoc network, which are caused by the absence of an online trusted entity. To tackle the problem, the authors suggested using a side channel approach, instead of relying on public key infrastructures that require online servers to confirm the validity of signed certificates, or traditional symmetric key-based ticket solutions[21,15,23] that need a ticket granting server.

In their scheme, devices exchange authentication information via an out-of-band channel, and then authenticate each other online based on the exchanged information.

Balfanz et al.[6] extended the idea by Stajano and Anderson and clarified the notion of *preauthentication* information that is exchanged in *location-limited side channel*. They listed the characteristics of the side channel as *demonstrative identification*, *authenticity*, and *secrecy*. The communication media of the side channel need to have special physical characteristics (e.g., a very short communication range and directed propagation) so that users visually identify to whom they are talking. In another study [4], the authors demonstrated an alternative peer authentication using an IrDA implemented location limited channel. When a user brings a computer to a wireless access point (AP), the two devices exchange pre-authentication information via IrDA ports, and then contact each other over an 802.11 network to execute further handshake protocols. Mccune et al.[19] used two dimensional (2D) barcodes and camera phones. In this study, a camera phone is used to authenticate devices. A device displays 2D barcodes that contain authentication digests of the device, and then a camera phone reads the barcodes and authenticates the device online based on the digest. A variety of out-of-band communication mediums[12,17,18] have been proposed to deliver secret information as well, such as sound, gestures, and laser lights.

Although the above approaches have utilized diverse communication mediums, there is still room for improvement in the usability and security aspects. Some require a user to bring a device to the other device, but it is not very practical when devices are heavy and physically apart from each other. Some require a user to perform delicate tasks. In the laser light approach, a user must hold the light emitter stably to complete the information transmission, but it can be difficult for seniors, especially persons experiencing hand tremors. Some need special equipment. The 2D barcode scheme requires a device to have a display screen, which could increase costs for a small device like a finger oximeter. Instead of having a display, a device can have printed barcodes on its surface, but the printed information could be missing or replaced by something else. Audio and gesture signals can be observed by an attacker, so it is not useful in public places (e.g., an airport or a station).

Cryptographic techniques in previous efforts need to be reconsidered as well. Conventional public key cryptography (e.g., RSA) could impose a high computational load and power demand for small devices. Symmetric key schemes impose key management overhead as the number of devices increases, and threaten the security of others by exposing shared secrets if one of devices were compromised or if a malicious device were accidentally connected.

Additionally, users need administrative authority to give or deprive membership on the secure channel they create over multiple devices. Private devices would allow only authorized users to have the authority. Public devices may be open to anyone for channel creation, but each channel should be distinguished and managed by its creator. The enforcement of ownership is useful when devices are invited into an administrative domain (e.g., a home, hospital, or company network). The owner or administrator of the domain would allow invited devices to use and interact with other network resources for a limited period. Channel owners should also be able to investigate communication history and decrypt messages on owned channels. The key escrow is useful for auditing and tracing anomalies in institutions and enterprises. Such ownership representation and key escrow need to be supported cryptographically but have not been considered adequately in previous approaches.

Although it is not a necessary requirement of the security bootstrapping in general, we try to support protected broadcast. Sometimes, one-way and non-critical notifications need be broadcast to participants on a channel. For example, in a home automation environment, a sensor on the main door could wake up all devices in a room from sleep mode when the master entered.

3   Requirements and Our Approaches

We try to provide an easy method of bootstrapping security, so that anyone can securely create and manage private communication channels over embedded devices. Some embedded system applications are designed for even non-computer literate seniors[16]. After reviewing the existing technologies in ad-hoc security bootstrapping, we can list the requirements that our system has to meet: 1) *user-friendly way of establishing security*, 2) *ownership representation and key escrow support*, 3) *low overhead performance, power, and key management*, and 4) *protected unicast and broadcast*.

In order to compose a solution addressing the purpose, we take the following approaches to exploit existing technologies.

How to intermediate: A USB flash drive is often used as a mediator of security establishment between Wi-Fi network devices, by delivering certificates or pre-shared keys. This kind of small mediator is rather handy for exchanging secret information between devices than direct contact of devices (cf. the IrDA approach[4]). Moreover, the intermediary could provide a user-friendly UI, store the configuration of created channels, and substantiate user ownership. It can also deliver security policies as the notion of "universal controller"[26], but policy enforcement is not the concern of this paper. For convenience, we call the intermediary AID (authentication intermediary device), hereinafter.

Communication media: Although a variety of communication mediums could be utilized to implement a location limited channel, a few wireless solutions seem to be plausible considering usability. RF is one possible medium. Bluetooth, a popular RF technology, could be employed, but it has a long working range where we cannot identify hidden participants. Some RFID techniques can be empowered within a short range, like within a few centimeters. However, RFID tags only return stored information or static series of information. Some have achieved selective responses to unauthorized reading of RFID tags, but the tags can be duplicated. Moreover, the tags are not highly programmable and do not have sufficient computational power yet for our purpose.

A high-speed infrared solution like Giga-IR[2] could be useful. It uses a directed wave, so devices need to be aligned along the line-of-sight, although usability would be improved with accessories helping alignment (e.g., docks or clips). The virtue of this technology is it provides secure and high-speed transmission at low cost (the module costs about 20 cents).

Recent efforts in very short range wireless communications are also noticeable. Transfer Jet[3] is a promising technology. Although based on omni-directional electromagnetic waves, its working range is only 3 centimeters, which is fairly shorter than that of general Near Field Communication, so that a user can identify all participants to the established communication. This helps to fulfill the *authenticity* and *demonstrative identity*. We expect our scheme to be embodied in very short-range wireless communication, but it is not tied to a specific medium. Any wireless communication is applicable if it has a short working range sufficient for users to identify communication participants.

Cryptography: On the one hand, we want to take advantage of asymmetric key-based cryptography (e.g., key management and signing and non-repudiation functionalities). On the other hand, we cannot impose the burdens of computation and high demand of power upon the devices. Envisioning a small embedded device in a personal network, it is reasonable to have hardware constraints similar to the typical wireless sensor networks (WSN), that is, 8-bit microprocessors with several hundred kilobytes of RAM and ROM.

Additionally, we need to support privileged administration of the created communication channels, which means only the channel owner can administrate security parameters and channel membership. Moreover, *key escrow* needs to be supported so that users can decrypt all messages and investigate stored information over their own channels as needed. We also need to protect messages that are transferred between two devices and protect messages that are broadcast to all devices of a channel.

Pairing-based cryptography (or PBC) is very suitable for our purpose. Although it is not as light as Elliptic Curve Cryptography, PBC imposes very little performance and power overheads comparing to RSA[14,27]. Moreover, it allow us to provide such useful functionalities with practical security as key escrow, ownership enforcement, and message unicast and broadcast.

4   System Description

Although the functions of AID can be implemented on top of a variety of handheld devices, a cell phone might be the most plausible device for AID embodiment because cell phones are widely deployed and empowered to perform cryptographic computations. An overview of creating a secure channel in our system can be depicted with a simple example scenario; *a user found a public photo printer in a library and wants to print pictures stored in a digital camera. The user chooses a menu on her cell phone, and then brings the phone close to the photo printer and the digital camera one after the other. As a result, the two devices will share a paired secret, so that the user can send the pictures to the printer safely.*

4.1 Identifiers

Based on the properties of PBC, two devices in our system will have mutually shared secrets derived from the IDs of the devices. There could be some consideration on how to generate and distribute IDs. Some identity-based encryption (IBE) applications use self-explanatory identifiers that can be uniquely inferred from some known properties of devices, such as the address or the network topology where the devices reside. Therefore, when a device wants to communicate, the former can easily acquire contact or the identifier of the latter if the former has one of either sets of information.

However, we do not use inferable identifiers since devices can have multiple IDs. The number of IDs for a device depends on how many channels associated with the device. IDs are generated and distributed by an AID, and there are two possible ways of ID generation: 1) The AID generates a set of IDs in advance for a given number of initial participants, and 2) generates an ID as the occasion demands. We use both methods. When a user generates a channel, the first is used, and when a new member is joining over the initial number of members, the second is used.

When a device wants to securely communicate with the other device, the former has to figure out how to make contact and what the ID is of the latter. On the other hand, the property of PBC builds a shared secret between pairs of IDs, even though the ID owners have not yet met. Authentication includes discovering the relationship between the contact and the ID of the peer, based on the shared secret. Contrary to the typical IBE applications, IDs are not inferable in our system. Therefore, devices acquire the information from an AID, otherwise they have to resolve it by themselves. These processes are discussed in Sect. 4.3.

4.2 Pairing Based Cryptography

The PBC bases on pairings that map a pair of elliptic curve points to an element of the multiplicative group of the finite field[1]. Bilinear pairings are special type of pairings defined as follows; G is an abelian group written in additive notation with identity element 0, and G_T is a cyclic group of order q written in multiplicative notation with identity element 1. We carefully select an elliptic curve $E(\mathbb{F}_q)$, and construct a Non-Interactive Key Distribution Scheme (NIKDS) as Boneh[7] and Sakai[24] proposed, by obtaining a map $\hat{e}$ that is derived from a Tate or Weil pairing on an elliptic curve, $\hat{e}: G \times G \rightarrow G_T$, which satisfies the following properties:

- Bilinearity: $\forall P, P', Q, Q' \in G$ we have $\hat{e}(P + P', Q) = \hat{e}(P, Q)\hat{e}(P', Q)$ and $\hat{e}(P, Q + Q') = \hat{e}(P, Q)\hat{e}(P, Q')$.
- Non-degeneracy: $\hat{e}(P, P) \neq 1$.

---

[1] The descriptions of the pairings refer to articles in Galbraith and Pattersons' book[25] (Chapter IX and X, respectively), and an introduction of Menezes[20]. Details can be found in the references.

- Symmetry: $\forall P, Q \in G$, $\hat{e}(P, Q) = \hat{e}(Q, P)$.
- Computability: $\hat{e}$ can be efficiently computed.
- Security: it is hard to compute the bilinear Diffie-Hellman problem and the decision-bilinear Diffie-Hellman problem.

The parameters $\langle G, G_T, \hat{e} \rangle$ are along with a cryptographic hash function, $\phi : \{0, 1\}^* \to G$, that map arbitrary length binary strings onto elements of G.

When a channel c is created, an AID selects a channel secret $CS^c \in \mathbb{Z}_r^*$. The AID can get a public/private key pair of device i by computing $Pub_i^c = \phi(ID_i)$ and $Priv_i^c = [CS^c]Pub_i^c$, respectively. The AID should implement the following functions:

- PROC_INIT_CHN: when a user requests to create a secure channel c, the AID generates the following initial security parameters with a given number of initial participants n:
  1) CS^c, ϕ^c for the channel c
  2) ID_i^c for the participating devices ($i = 1...n$), ID_M^c for the AID, ID_N^c for the channel network. ID_M^c and ID_N^c are used to derive the key pair of the AID and broadcast, respectively.
  3) private keys of devices, $Priv_i^c = [CS^c]\phi(ID_i^c)$. Note that, $\phi(ID_i^c)$ is the public key of i. The AID can optionally give the calculated public keys to devices to reduce the computational burden.
  4) a public/private key pair of the AID, $(Pub_M^c, Priv_M^c)$.
  5) a public/private key pair of the channel network, $(Pub_N^c, Priv_N^c)$.
- MSG_CHN_CNFRM: when the user brings the AID to device i, the AID asks if the channel (c, Pub_M^c) is already created on i.
- PROC_STORE_CHN: if the channel c has not been created yet on i, the AID sends ID_i^c and other security parameters (cf. MSG_DVC_PRMTR). The AID may store the contact of the device (e.g., address) for an administrative purposes.
- MSG_DVC_PRMTR: the AID sends $(ID_i^c, Priv_i^c, \{ID_j^c\}, \phi^c, ID_M^c, ID_N^c, Priv_N^c)$ (where $i \neq j$) to i.

An embedded device needs to implement the following functions:

- PROC_CHN_CNFRM: receiving MSG_CHN_CNFRM, a device checks whether a channel c is created with the name of Pub_M^c, and returns yes or no confirmation.
- MSG_CHN_CNFRM_ACK: answers with the contact information.
- PROC_DVC_PRMTR: Receiving MSG_DVC_PRMTR, the device stores the security parameters.

After the AID distributes security parameters to devices, two devices will share a pairwise secret $K_{i,j}$ as $\hat{e}(Priv_i^c, Pub_j^c) = \hat{e}(Pub_i^c, Pub_j^c)^{CS^c} = \hat{e}(Priv_j^c, Pub_i^c)$ by the bilinearity and the symmetry.

4.3   Session Key Establishments

A device could be in the following status according to whether it knows the contact or the ID of its communication peer: *Stat1*: the device recognizes the other and knows how to initiate contact, but does not know the ID of the other yet. *Stat2*: the device knows the peer's ID, but does not know how to initiate contact, or *Stat3*: the device knows both of these pieces of information. The session key establishment can be processed differently depending on the states of the devices[2]:

- Handshake1: it is the session key establishment between a device A in *Stat3*, and the other device B in any other state. Since A knows the ID and the address of B, A can sends a session key establishment request to B using the shared secret between them. A session key is derived as the below handshake case 1 below shows. An intruder cannot impersonate A nor B without knowing one of their private keys.
- Handshake2: the session key establishment between a device A in *Stat2*, and the other device B in *Stat2* or *Stat1*. Although A knows B's ID, A has to resolve B's address. It is same as the Handshake1, except that the first message is broadcast to every device on the channel. Despite every device receiving the message, only B can acknowledge correctly.

Handshake1 (Handshake2):

1. $A \to B \ (\underline{ALL})$: $c, ID_A^c, n_A, H[c, \hat{e}(Priv_A^c, Pub_B^c), n_A, 0]$
2. $B \to A$: $n_B, H[c, \hat{e}(Priv_A^c, Pub_B^c), n_A + 1, n_B, 1]$
(Key established as $H[c, \hat{e}(Priv_B^c, Pub_A^c), n_A + 2, n_B + 1]$)

- Handshake3: the session key establishment between two devices that are in *Stat1*. The devices need to exchange their ID and authenticate each other based on the shared information. Balfanz et al.[5] proposed a handshake protocol using pairing-based cryptography. We use a simplified version of the protocol. See the operation Mode3 below.

Handshake3:

1. $A \to B$: c, ID_A^c, n_A
2. $B \to A$: $ID_B^c, n_B, H[c, \hat{e}(Priv_B^c, Pub_A^c), n_A + 1, n_B, 2]$
3. $A \to B$: $H[c, \hat{e}(Priv_A^c, Pub_B^c), n_A + 1, n_B + 1, 3]$
(Key established as $H[c, \hat{e}(Priv_B^c, Pub_A^c), n_A + 2, n_B + 2]$)

Devices can negotiate a session key with slightly fewer messages and steps in the case of Handshake1. Hence, in order to maximize the number of nodes in *Stat3*, we assume that an AID generates and distributes IDs in the following **accumulative way**:

1. Create a channel: a user creates a channel with k initial participants. The AID generates k number of IDs and private keysalong with other channel security parameters.
2. Distribute security parameters: when the AID touches a new device, an unassigned ID is associated with the contact (e.g., address) of the device. Therefore, on $n(\leq k)$th touch, the AID can pass $n - 1$ associations to the new member. At this moment, everyone has k IDs, so that *Stat2* is always guaranteed with whomever they want to communicate. Also, nth one is in *Stat3* to $n - 1$ old members.

---

[2] a) $H[x]$ is the hashed value of x, $\{x\}_K$ is an encrypted message x with a key K, and n_A is a nonce generated by A. b) session key expiration is not represented and addressed in handshake protocols. The negotiation of session key expiration can be done after the entities confirm mutual secret, according to security policy of each device.

3. Over the initial number: the number of members could grow over the expected k. Assume that l members joined and exceeded k, then the total number of members are $t = (k + l)$. When mth member joins ($k < m < t$), the member is in $Stat3$ to $m - 1$ old members by receiving the accumulated associations, whereas the old members are in $Stat1$ to this since the member's ID is newly created. Also, the mth member is in $Stat1$ to $t - m$ members who joined after.

Two other ways of ID distribution could be **Method1:** do not generate the initial set of IDs, but hand over the accumulated association to a new member, and **Method2:** do not generate the initial IDs nor pass the accumulated information. In the Method2, every device is in $Stat1$ to everyone. In the Method1, every mth joined member is in $Stat1$ to $(t - m)$ members who joined later (where t is the total number of members). If the proposed method is used in this paper, mth member is in $Stat1$ to $(t - m)$ only when $m > k$, since k members are guaranteed to be in $Stat2$ with each other. Considering the complete possible combinations of communication initialization, $t(t - 1)$ connections might be initialized by devices in $Stat1$ to the other with Method2, $\sum_{i=1}^{t} t - i = t(t - 1)/2$ in $Stat1$ with Method1, and $kl + \sum_{i=1}^{l-1} i = \{t(t - 1) - k(k - 1)\}/2$ (, where $l = t - k$) in $Stat1$ with the accumulative way.

4.4 Broadcast in a Channel

Although novel approaches of pairing-based group key agreement protocols have been proposed[7,11,10], they do not provide sufficient security under certain conditions and impose even more of a performance burden on senders than receivers[9]. The asymmetric overhead can be exploited by an inside attacker for denial of service attacks.

We just take a very simple approach of using the pair of channel network keys $Priv_N{}^c$ and $Pub_N{}^c$. A can send a message using $\hat{e}(Priv_A{}^c, Pub_N{}^c)$, then others decrypt the message using $\hat{e}(Pub_A{}^c, Priv_N{}^c)$. Since only channel participants have $Priv_N{}^c$, outsiders cannot send or receive a broadcast message correctly. In this way, the computational burdens of sender and receiver are not very different. Consequently, an inside attacker needs to pay as much power and computation costs as the victims.

5 Analysis

The security of Handshake1 and Handshake2 is based on the shared secret between A and B, which again depends on the security of PBC. In Handshake3, devices exchange the ID and other information to authenticate each other, and an insider intruder might be able to intervene in the communication. In this section, we try to check if a middleman can acquire a session key while two other devices execute the Handshake3 protocol. We model the protocol using Coloured Petri Nets (CP-Nets)[13] which has known to compactly model concurrent behaviors by allowing the net elements to have value, type, and supporting functional expressions.

The Fig.1(A) and (B) show the behaviors of A and B in Handshake3 protocol. The two entities communicate via three types of messages that draw from the first to third messages of the Handshake3. When A issues an initial message (MSG_JOIN in the graphs) to establish a session key using a channel number, own ID, and nonce, the message will be passed to B so that B can return a message (MSG_TEST_EC) based on their

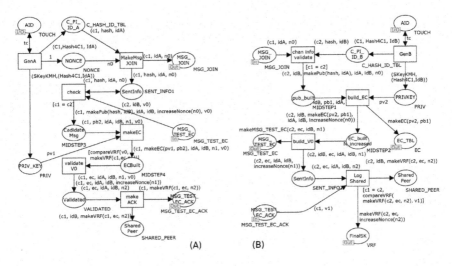

Fig. 1. The behavior of A (A) and B (B)

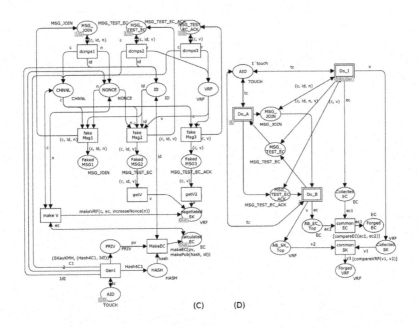

Fig. 2. The behavior of Intruder (C) and the top level diagram (D)

shared secret. A validates the digested message in the returned message, and confirm the message attaching a new digest(MSG_TEST_EC_ACK). Finally, they agree upon on a same session key. While the fourth message transmission of the protocol is omitted in the graphs to reduce the state space, we can confirm the agreement investigating tokens in the place, SharedPeer.

Additionally, we introduce an intruder to the model. The Fig.2(C) delineates the behavior of an intruder. As an insider, the intruder has the same security parameters as A and B except the private keys, takes messages, decomposes the messages into parts, constructs new messages using the collections, and puts the synthesized messages into the communication. The Fig.2(D) shows a top level diagram where A, B, and Intruder interact. The intruder aims at agreed session keys between A and B. If the intruder succeeded a token is placed on the ForgedVRF. Also, the ForgedEC place stores shared secrets that the intruder have forged and collected.

CP-Nets provides an automatic analysis tool, CPNTools[1]. As a result of state space analysis and token game simulation in our model, we received the only one dead transition commonSK and 0-bound with ForgedVRF (See Fig.2(D)), which means there is no session key exposed to the intruder. The intruder had tokens on 'ForgedEC', but only legal shared secrets between the intruder and B.

6   An Application: Zigbee Protocol

Zigbee[28] is a set of specification built upon IEEE 802.15.4 for wireless communications in a low-cost and low-power environment, which has similar target applications to this paper. The security service specification of Zigbee is based on Advanced Encryption Standard (AES). Communications among Zigbee devices are protected by link keys and network keys which are 128 bit keys for secure unicast and broadcast. The keys are obtained by pre-installation and key-transport. The link key is also established using a master key. The security between devices depends on how they initialize and install those keys. A special device that has a trust center role distributes keys and manages network and configuration.

There are some efforts to introduce public key cryptography to Zigbee security seeking for advantages in key management and additional functionalities such as signing and non-repudiation. Moreover, Nguyen and Rong[22] proposed using ID-based encryption for setting up the master key and the link key. In their system, a device provides its self-explanatory identifier to the trust center, then the trust center authenticates the device and gives the private key for the device.

Similarly, our system can be applied to Zigbee by establishing the three types of keys as follows:

1. The master key corresponds to the shared secret among devices. An AID can act as an offline trust center or domain controller, but the role can be delegated to an online entity by passing over security parameters if it is needed.
2. The link keys can be established via handshakes.
3. The network key corresponds to the broadcast key which the AID provides.

The expected advantages of using AID are support for multiple channels on top of Zigbee protocol, broadcast, and user-friendly interface, which are not included in the previous IBE scheme.

7   Discussions

The PBC has several advantages: it does not require an online trusted authority and imposes less overhead than the conventional public key cryptography. However, application of PBC is restricted because initial security parameters need to be generated by a trusted public key generator (PKG) and to be securely transplanted to devices. WSN applications overcome the restriction by having a base station perform the role of PKG and deliver the security parameters to sensor nodes before the nodes are deployed. Similarly in our system, the AID acts as the trusted entity and deliver security parameters using the out-of-band channel. Moreover, it enforces user ownership and support key escrow. Since security parameters of a channel are generated and distributed by an AID, only the user who has the AID can add or remove a channel member. After a channel is created, the channel participants also can authenticate the owner online relying on the public/private key pair of the AID.

We addressed ways to generate and distribute identifiers to save communication overhead. With an expected number of participating members k, we may expect reduce communication overhead by eliminating the $O(k^2)$ possible handshake overhead. The benefit increases as k moves closer to the total number of actual participants t (See Sect 4.3).

When users connect their private devices together, they may need to decide which AID they will use. It depends on participants' security policy that who will create and own a secure channel. For example, if a user wants to use her own electronic reminder when she is in a hospital, she may need to ask a nurse to connect the reminder to the hospital network. It is different from the example scenario of Sect. 4. Security policy negotiation needs to be investigated further for connecting devices that have different security policy.

Since the AID functionalities are expected to be embodied with a handheld and user-friendly device like a cellphone or portable game player, other fancy techniques could be combined as well as a simple PIN-based protection. For example, such biometrics as gesture, voice, fingerprint, and finger vein recognition could be merged to attract users and expand usability. A user can cast "Abracadabra" and draw a spell mark in the air before creating a secure channel. We cannot guarantee that these technologies will strengthen security, but we presume a successful design.

The security of our system depends not only on the property of PBC, but also on the location limited channel. Communication media should be carefully chosen to avoid eavesdropping threats[8]. Key revocation and broadcast issues of PBC need to be considered further as well. In our scheme, an inside attacker can send a broadcast message impersonating another (e.g., use $Pub_A{}^c$ and $Priv_N{}^c$ to pose as A). We assume that broadcast messages are used to deliver non-critical notifications. Also, we assume the key revocation and membership changes are done by a user manually, expecting network size is manageable by the user.

8   Conclusions

We proposed a way of creating secure communication channels over ad-hoc network devices using an easy-to-use intermediary. We employed several concepts and technologies to mobile networks and wireless sensor networks, such as pairing-based cryptography, the notion of location limited channel, and the very short range wireless communication media.

We described and specified the steps of security bootstrapping. We also demonstrated the security of the proposed protocols using a model checking approach equipped with an automatic analysis tool.

Owing to the property of pairng-based cryptography, users can acquire security with low overhead and enforce their ownership over secure communication channels that are dynamically created over networked devices. Users can create multiple channels for their own purposes. Channel owners are identified using security parameters, and they can reveal any secret on their private channels as needed. Since the security parameters are generated and managed by a handheld device, users can create the security channels on-the-fly in an ad-hoc environment.

Our approach can be generally applied to any network where dynamic secure channel creation and ownership representation are required, such as home networks, medical sensor networks, and so on. As an example, we showed how our method could be applied to the Zigbee security service.

As our further study, we are going to implement the scheme using a cell phone and a high speed IrDA[2]. Key revocation and broadcast will be reinforced later.

References

1. Cpn tools, http://wiki.daimi.au.dk/cpntools
2. Giga-ir,   http://techon.nikkeibp.co.jp/english/NEWS_EN/20080725/155461/
3. Transfer jet, http://www.transferjet.org/en/
4. Balfanz, D., et al.: Network-in-a-box: how to set up a secure wireless network in under a minute. In: Proc. of the 13th conference on USENIX Security Symposium, p. 15 (2004)
5. Balfanz, D., et al.: Secret handshakes from pairing-based key agreements. In: IEEE Symposium on Security and Privacy, pp. 180–196 (2003)
6. Balfanz, D., Smetters, D.K., Stewart, P., Wong, H.C.: Talking to strangers: Authentication in ad-hoc wireless networks. In: Proc. 2002 Network and Distributed Systems Security Symposium (NDSS), pp. 23–35 (2002)
7. Boneh, D., Franklin, M.K.: Identity-based encryption from the weil pairing. In: Kilian, J. (ed.) CRYPTO 2001. LNCS, vol. 2139, pp. 213–229. Springer, Heidelberg (2001)
8. Cheung, H.: How to: Building a bluesniper rifle. Tom's guide (2005), http://www.tomsguide.com/us/how-to-bluesniper-pt1,review-408.html
9. Chien, H.Y.: Comments on an efficient id-based broadcast encryption scheme. IEEE Transactions on Broadcasting 53(4), 809–810 (2007)
10. Choi, K.Y., Hwang, J.Y., Lee, D.H.: Id-based authenticated group key agreement secure against insider attacks. IEICE Transactions on Fundamentals of Electronics, Communcations and Computer Sciences E91-A, 1828–1830 (2008)
11. Du, X., Wang, Y., Ge, J., Wang, Y.: An id-based broadcast encryption scheme for key distribution. IEEE Transactions on Broadcasting 51, 264–266 (2005)
12. Goodrich, M.T., et al.: Loud and clear: Human-verifiable authentication based on audio. In: Proc. ICDCS 2006: 26th Conf. on Distributed Computing Systems, p. 10. IEEE, Los Alamitos (2006)
13. Jensen, K.: Coloured Petri nets: basic concepts, analysis methods and practical use, vol. 1, 2. Springer, London (1995)
14. Khalili, A., Katz, J., Arbaugh, W.A.: Toward secure key distribution in truly ad-hoc networks. In: Proc. of Symposium on Applications and the Internet Workshops, pp. 342–346 (2003)

15. Kohl, J.T., Neuman, B.C., Ts'o, T.Y.: The evolution of the Kerberos authentication service. IEEE Computer Soceity Press. Los Alamitos (1994)
16. May, M.J., Shin, W., Gunter, C.A., Lee, I.: Securing the drop-box architecture for assisted living. In: Formal Methods in Software Engineering (FMSE 2006). ACM, New York (2006)
17. Mayrhofer, R., Gellersen, H.: Shake well before use: Authentication based on accelerometer data. In: LaMarca, A., Langheinrich, M., Truong, K.N. (eds.) Pervasive 2007. LNCS, vol. 4480, pp. 144–161. Springer, Heidelberg (2007)
18. Mayrhofer, R., Welch, M.: A human-verifiable authentication protocol using visible laser light. In: Proc. of the Second International Conference on Availability, Reliability and Security, pp. 1143–1148 (2007)
19. Mccune, J.M., Perrig, A., Reiter, M.K.: Seeing-is-believing: Using camera phones for human-verifiable authentication. In: IEEE Symposium on Security and Privacy, pp. 110–124 (2005)
20. Menezes, A.: An introduction to pairing-based cryptography. notes from lectures given in (2005), http://www.math.uwaterloo.ca/~ajmeneze/publications/pairings.pdf
21. Needham, R.M., Schroeder, M.D.: Using encryption for authentication in large networks of computers. Communnication of the ACM 21(12), 993–999 (1978)
22. Nguyen, S.T., Rong, C.: Zigbee security using identity-based cryptography. In: Xiao, B., Yang, L.T., Ma, J., Muller-Schloer, C., Hua, Y. (eds.) ATC 2007. LNCS, vol. 4610, pp. 3–12. Springer, Heidelberg (2007)
23. Otway, D., Rees, O.: Efficient and timely mutual authentication. SIGOPS Oper. Syst. Rev. 21(1), 8–10 (1987)
24. Sakai, R., Ohgishi, K., Kasahara, M.: Cryptosystems based on pairing. In: Proc. of Symposium on Cryptography and Information Security (2000)
25. Smart, N.P., et al.: Advances in Elliptic Curve Cryptography. London Mathematical Society Lecture Note Series, vol. 317. Cambridge University Press, Cambridge (2005)
26. Stajano, F., Anderson, R.: The resurrecting duckling: Security issues for ad-hoc wireless networks. In: Okamoto, T. (ed.) ASIACRYPT 2000. LNCS, vol. 1976, pp. 172–194. Springer, Heidelberg (2000)
27. Szczechowiak, P., et al.: Testing the limits of elliptic curve cryptography in sensor networks. In: European conference on Wireless Sensor Networks (EWSN 2008), pp. 305–320 (2008)
28. ZigBee Alliance: Zigbee specification. ZigBee Document 053474r17 (2008)

Steganalysis of Hydan

Jorge Blasco[1], Julio C. Hernandez-Castro[1], Juan M.E. Tapiador[1], Arturo Ribagorda[1], and Miguel A. Orellana-Quiros[2]

[1] Carlos III University of Madrid, Av. de la Universidad 30, 28911 Leganés
jbalis@inf.uc3m.es, jcesar@inf.uc3m.es, jestevez@inf.uc3m.es,
arturo@inf.uc3m.es
[2] Ministry of Economy, Cl. Alcala,5, 28071 Madrid
mangel.orellana@meh.es

Abstract. *Hydan* is a steganographic tool which can be used to hide any kind of information inside executable files. In this work, we present an efficient distinguisher for it: We have developed a system that is able to detect executable files with embedded information through *Hydan*. Our system uses statistical analysis of instruction set distribution to distinguish between files with no hidden information and files that have been modified with *Hydan*. We have tested our algorithm against a mix of *clean* and stego-executable files. The proposed distinguisher is able to tell apart these files with a 0 ratio of false positives and negatives, thus detecting all files with hidden information through *Hydan*.

1 Introduction

Steganography is the art and science that tries to hide the existence of messages [4]. The objectives of steganography are not the same that those of cryptography, which main aim is to conceal the message contents by performing different transformations so only authorized persons can read it. At first, one may think that cryptography is enough to ensure the security of the communications between two parties, but there are scenarios where the knowledge of the existence of a communication between two parties may be critical. These scenarios all have something in common with that described by Simmons and known as *the Prisoners problem* [12]. In this, two prisoners (Alice and Bob) want to plot an escape plan. As they are not in the same cell they must communicate through a warden (Willie). If Willie ever suspects that Alice and Bob are planning to escape or are engaging in any kind of secret communication he will put them into isolation cells. In this scenario, Alice and Bob can not simply use cryptography because Willie will recognize encrypted messages and infer they are communicating secretly, so he will stop this channel. Alice and Bob should hide their messages into seemingly innocuous ones, so Willie will not notice the covert communication. Additionally, Willie can behave in different ways: If Willie just checks the messages and forwards them to its recipient, then Willie is a *passive warden*. On the other hand, if Willie has high suspicions of Alice and Bob planning an escape, but he does not have a proof, it is possible that he will modify slightly the message contents trying to perturb any hidden information. In this case, Willie is an *active warden*. Both possible scenarios must be considered when designing stego-systems, so the quality of a stego-system can be measured (in addittion

D. Gritzalis and J. Lopez (Eds.): SEC 2009, IFIP AICT 297, pp. 132–142, 2009.

to other properties) by means of the difficulty to detect its content and the possibility that hidden information is not lost even if the stego-object suffers some modifications.

The first documented use of steganography [5] was made by *Demaratus*, who wanted to warn the Greeks about a Persian invasion leaded by *Xerxes*. *Demaratus* sent a message written on a wooden table covered by wax, so it could pass all the guard controls and arrive to Sparta.

Since those days, steganography has developed as a science, and many different approaches have been used to cover contents of any kind [9]. Image Steganography [4] is one of the most used techniques. Covering contents into images can be done in many different ways. Most simple techniques hide information on the least significant bits (LSB) of each pixel. Other techniques use image compression algorithms. For example, the JPEG image compression algorithm is based on the parameters of the discrete cosine transform (DCT). Using different parameters in the DCT calculation allows hiding information in the image file. Another widely used cover are digital audio files. Audio steganography also includes techniques such as LSB (similar to image LSB steganography).

Changing the last significant bit on each audio sample produces slight modifications on audio files that can not generally be distinguished by humans, specially if the redundancy ratio is high. Audio steganography can be performed also in compressed audio files like MP3s. Some tools like MP3Stego [10] can hide information during the *inner loop* step, by modifying the DCT values. Much more steganographic techniques can be found in the literature such as subliminal channels [12], SMS [11], TCP/IP [6] and games [3].

All security requirements for cryptographic systems are usually (or should be) applied to steganographic systems. This means that the security of a steganographic algorithm should not rely itself on the secrecy of the algorithm, which should be public, but on the knowledge of the key. In steganography, it should not be possible to distinguish a *clean* object from a stego-object if the key is unknown. In this work, we prove that it is possible to distinguish a *clean* executable file from a stego-object created through *Hydan* without the possession of the key. The remainder of this document is structured as follows. Section 2 introduces previous work done in executable files steganography. Section 3 describes the basics of *Hydan* and how it works. Section 4 shows the steganalysis performed on *Hydan* and the resulting distinguisher. This section also performs a discussion on possible ways to overcome the steganalysis presented. Section 6 presents the gathered conclusions and possible lines of future work.

2 Previous Work

Hydan [2] is the first documented tool and scheme that uses directly executable files as a cover. During years, other techniques have been used to insert hidden information into source files, but for copyright protection purposes only. These involve access to source code, where programmers insert copyright marks and integrity checks right inside their code. Information inserted in this way can be used to prove the integrity and authorship of the program [13]. Outside *Hydan*, other authors [1] have later described different techniques to introduce information in executable files. Authors describe four different techniques. *Instruction Selection* replaces some of the instructions in the executable file for others with the same functionality. *Register Allocation* encodes embedded information in changes on the registers used by some instructions. *Instruction Scheduling* changes the order of non-dependant instructions. Finally, *Code Layout* uses the order of big blocks.

Authors have implemented all the proposed techniques in a more advanced tool called *Stilo*. A steganalysis of *Stilo* is proposed in the same paper based on a concept named *Code Transformation Signature*, which is defined as the set of characteristics that can be used to detect the presence of hidden information into *Stilo* executable files. Authors describe the *Code Transformation Signatures* for *Stilo* and propose a group of countermeasures to avoid them. Authors also mention *Hydan*, but they do not perform any steganalysis nor reveal the corresponding *Code Transformation Signatures* for *Hydan*. Apart from this work, no other techniques have been proposed to hide information on executable files. In this paper we describe the main properties (its *Code Transformation Signatures*) that can be used to detect executable-files with hidden information through *Hydan*. Based on those properties, a very efficient distinguisher is proposed.

3   Hydan

Hydan is a steganographic tool which covers messages in executable files. It does not change the functionality of the executable neither the size of it. A detailed description on how *Hydan* works can be found on [2].

Hydan uses the "redundancy" on the instructions sets of executable files to introduce hidden information. Specifically, *Hydan* uses the concept of *functionality-equivalent instructions*. A set of *functionality-equivalent instructions* is a group of instructions in which any instruction of the group can be replaced for other without loss of functionality. For example, to add a certain amount to a specific register it is possible to use *add, r1, 8* or , equivalently, use *sub, r1, -8*. In this case, the *add* instruction could encode the bit value 0, and the *sub* instruction may encode the bit value 1. Depending on the size of the *functionality-equivalent instructions* sets it is possible to encode more than one bit with one instruction. A set of four *functionality-equivalent instructions* would allow codifying 2 bits (00, 01, 10 and 11). Generally, with a set of n equivalent instructions it would be possible to encode $\lfloor \log_2(n) \rfloor$ bits. Table 1 describes the *functionality-equivalent instructions* groups and number of instructions in each of the groups for the *x86* set, which is the most common and the one used by *Hydan*.

Embedding process of *Hydan* is done in two steps. First step encrypts the message to be hidden using *AES* or *Blowfish* with the password given by the user. In the second step, the encrypted message is embedded into the executable file. Specifically, *Hydan* works as follows: Once the message has been encrypted, *Hydan* searches for possible places to introduce information. Then, *Hydan* generates a random number seeded with the password entered by the user. This number is used to select which of the selected places of the executable file will be used to hide the information. With this mechanism, the password will be needed to recover the data and different passwords will lead to different placements of the embedded information. Recovery process first extracts the encrypted message from the executable file. Then, the message is decrypted using the provided password.

Table 1. Groups of *functionality-equivalent instructions* used in *Hydan*

Group	Inst.	Group	Inst.	Group	Inst.
toac8	5	toac32	5	rrcmp8	2
rrcmp32	2	toasxc8	7	toasxc32	6
addsub8	2	addsub8-2	2	addsub32-1	2
addsub32-2	2	addsub32-3	2	xorsub8	4
xorsub32	4	add8	2	add32	2
adc8	2	adc32	2	and8	2
cmp8	2	cmp32	2	mov8	2
mov32	2	or8	2	or32	2
sbb8	2	sbb32	2	sub8	2
sub32	2	xor8	2	xor32	2
and32	2				

With *Hydan*, it is possible to embed (on average) 1 bit of information per 110 bits of executable code. In fact, it is possible to embed different ratios of information, but El-Khalil proposed the specified one as the better trade-off between security and capacity [2].

Hydan changes perceptibly the content of the executable files with hidden information. Therefore, if these changes lead to a specific signature, it is possible to build a system that is able to distinguish a *Hydan* executable file from any other executable file. This signature may show in many different ways. Next section discusses the possible methods to detect a *Hydan* modified executable and proposes a very efficient distinguisher to detect a *Hydan* covert-channel.

4   Steganalysis of Hydan

Changes introduced by *Hydan* into assembler code can modify different properties of the original executable file. *Hydan* does not change the size of the stego-object, but it changes the code itself. If the original program is available it will be possible to check through integrity checks (CRCs [8], hash functions [7], etc.) if the executable file has been modified, but these are not proof of embedded information. Other properties such as execution time, flag activation and copyright marks checks, can prove that executable code has been modified, but will not be proof of embedded information.

Most compilers often produce similar sets of instructions. Thus, if a compiler has to select between two instructions with the same functionality it will usually select the same instruction. This property of most compilers allows building a profile of *clean* applications based on the probability distribution of instructions inside *clean* programs. Changes made by *Hydan* may lead to another probability distribution of instructions. If these changes can be profiled and generalized, it would be possible to detect if an executable file has hidden information. Steganalysis performed on this paper is based on this approach.

We have built a distinguisher that is able to detect executable files with embedded information through *Hydan*. To construct this distinguisher, first we have built a

statistical model of *clean* executable files. Then, we have performed different concealment operations in a variety of executable files. We have analyzed the main differences
between the set of *clean* executables and the set of *Hydan* modified executables. In this
paper, we also describe possible countermeasures and the maximum capacity of *Hydan*
steganographic files to overcome this steganalysis.

4.1   Statistical Analysis of Clean Executable Files

The distinguisher proposed is based on the presence of unusual sets of instructions
on executable files. We have performed a statistical analysis of a set of 1261 *clean*
executable files retrieved from */usr/bin* and */usr/sbin* of an *Ubuntu x86* distribution.
Figure 1 shows the frequency distribution of the *functionality-equivalent instructions*
sets for our set of files. This distribution tells the probability that a random instruction
belongs to a *functionality-equivalent instruction* set. Depending on this distribution,
the bandwidth of the covert channel offered by an executable may differ a lot. The
bigger is the proportion of instructions belonging to a big set of *functionality-equivalent
instructions*, the bigger will be the information *Hydan* is able to hide.

Our analysis has shown that all the *functionality-equivalent sets* of instructions are
present in our test files. Nevertheless, most of the instructions found on the analyzed
files belong to a small group of *functionality-equivalent instructions* sets. Therefore,
the capacity of the covert channel depends on the capacity of these commonly used
sets (Fig. 1). In order to build our statistical model, we have analyzed distribution of
instructions inside each of the most frequent *functionality-equivalent instructions* sets.

One of the most used *functionality-equivalent instructions* sets is *toac32*. This set
includes five different instructions. Thus, it can encode $\lfloor \log_2(5) \rfloor = \lfloor 2.32 \rfloor = 2$ bits.
Frequency distribution of instructions inside the set is shown in Fig. 2.

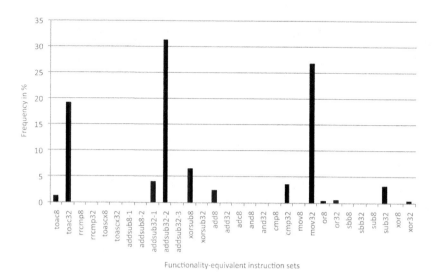

Fig. 1. Frequency distribution of *functionality-equivalent instructions* sets

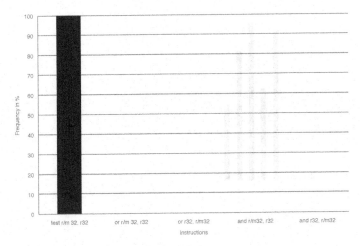

Fig. 2. Frequency distribution of instructions on *toac32* set

Results obtained in the frequency analysis of this instruction set have been gathered in Table 2.

Table 2. Frequency distribution of instructions on *toac32* set

Instruction	Frequency
test r/m32, r32	100.0%
or r/m32, r32	0.0%
or r32, r/m32	0.0%
and r/m32, r32	0.0%
and r32, r/m32	0.0%

In all analyzed files, only one instruction of this set was used. In this case, a variation of the distribution of instructions within this set would be detected easily.

For each of the remaining sets of equivalent functions, we have computed the frequency distribution of its instructions based on our set of executable files, as in the *toac32* set. Once we have constructed a frequency distribution model for each of the sets, we have also computed the proportion of instructions per set in each of the executable files. Each of the proportions computed for each file and *functionality-equivalent instructions* set has been compared using a chi-square statistic (χ^2) against the frequency distribution of that *functionality-equivalent instructions* set calculated for all the files. For each of the *functionality-equivalent instructions* sets we have calculated the average χ^2 statistic (Equation 1).

$$Average_{set_j} = \sum_{i=0}^{n} \frac{\chi^2_{file_i}}{n} \tag{1}$$

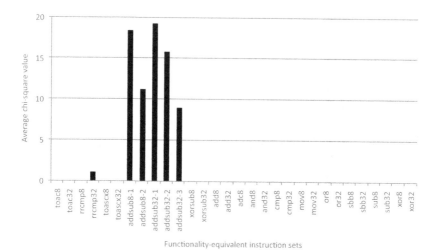

Fig. 3. Average chi-square statistic for each of the *functionality-equivalent instructions* sets

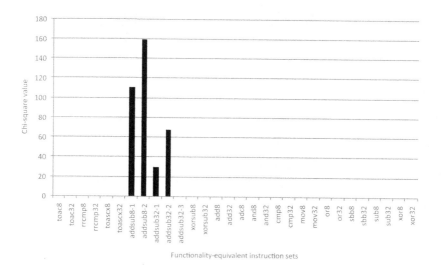

Fig. 4. Chi-square statistics for each of the equivalent instructions sets in *apt-get*

Where set_j is a *functionality-equivalent instructions* set, and $file_i$ is the *ith* file on our set of files. Figure 3 shows the average χ^2 for all the *functionality-equivalent instructions* sets. For most of the equivalent instructions sets, the distribution of its instructions has remained constant in all the executable files. Thus, its averaged chi-square is 0. *Functionality-equivalent instructions* sets with higher average value indicate that the frequency distribution of that sets has more variability between executable files. Figure 3 shows how six of the *functionality-equivalent instructions* sets suffer lots of variability on the distribution of its instructions depending on the executable file.

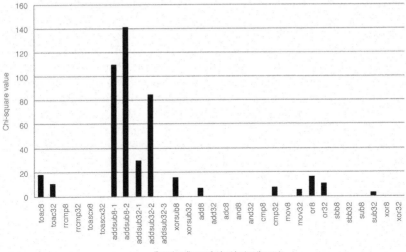

Functionality-equivalent instruction sets

Fig. 5. Chi-square values for each of the equivalent instruction sets in *apt-get* with hidden information

Differences introduced by *Hydan* will change the frequency distribution of instructions inside each of the *functionality-equivalent instructions* sets. Comparing the new instruction distributions obtained against the reference distributions for each of the *functionality-equivalent instructions* sets will allow to determine if information has been embedded into the executable file.

This can be easily seen through an example. Figure 4 represents the differences, in terms of a χ^2 statistic, on the frequency distribution of each *functionality-equivalent instruction* set of the *apt-get* executable file with no embedded information. Differences obtained are consistent with the average shown on Fig.3.

Inserting information into this executable file will modify the frequency distribution of instructions inside some of the sets of equivalent instructions. Figure 5 represents differences, in terms of a χ^2 statistic, on the distribution of instructions inside each of the equivalent instructions sets of the *apt-get* executable with embedded information.

Frequency distribution of instructions inside the highly variable functionality equivalent instruction sets has also offered high chi-square values, as in the reference (Fig. 3) and clean file comparison (Fig. 4). Nevertheless, distributions of some *functionality-equivalent instructions* sets have changed and its chi-square has increased comparing it with the reference comparison (Fig. 3) and the previous chi-square value (Fig. 4), which was 0.

The same procedure has been performed with all the executable files, obtaining for each set a model of the frequency distribution of that set. This has allowed us to establish which distributions of instructions inside *functionality-equivalent* instruction sets remain constant between different *clean* executable files.

These results have been used to build our distinguisher which is explained in the next section.

5   Distinguisher Design

The proposed distinguisher measures the changes on the distribution of instructions inside a selection of *functionality-equivalent instructions* sets. These measures have been made in terms of a χ^2 statistic against the reference distribution for each of the selected *functionality-equivalent instructions* sets. *Functionality-equivalent instructions* sets with high variability of instruction distribution between *clean* files have not been selected in the calculations of our distinguisher value. High variability may elevate the result offered by the distinguisher, marking some *clean* files as stego-objects. Our distinguisher only uses the *functionality-equivalent instructions* sets which its average chi-square value is 0, as calculated in 1. Therefore, 8 sets of *functionality-equivalent instructions* are not used: *toac8, rrcmp32, addsub8, addsub8-2, addsub32-1, addsub32-2, addsub32-3* and *xorsub8*. Mathematically, the value obtained with our distinguisher is expressed as follows:

$$D(file) = \sum_{i=0}^{n} \chi^2_{instruction\ set_i} \qquad (2)$$

Where n is the number of sets of *functionality-equivalent instructions* whose average chi-square value is 0. To obtain the threshold of our distinguisher we have calculated all the results the distinguisher offers from three set files: a set of clean files, a set of files with embedded information using a 40 % of its capacity and a set of files with embedded information using an 80 % of its capacity. We have calculated the mean and standard deviation of values obtained by the distinguisher for the three sets. Results obtained are shown in Table 3.

Table 3. Distinguisher results for different sets of executable files

Distinguisher	Clean	Hidden at 40%	Hidden at 80%
Mean	0.000604	151.254608	299.039886
Standard Deviation	0.024571	12.298561	17.292770

We have selected the threshold of our distinguisher as the addition of the mean and the standard deviation of the clean files set. When a file offers a value above the expected mean and typical deviation it is marked as a stego-object. Threshold of our distinguisher is described be as follows.

$$T = Mean_{clean} + T.Deviation_{clean} = 0.000604 + 0.24571 = 0.025175 \qquad (3)$$

5.1   Results

With the selected threshold we have performed a test over three sets of files, each having 1063 files. The first set of files is a selection of *clean* files from the *Ubuntu 8.10 x86* distribution. Second set of files is the set of *clean* files with embedded information up to 40% of the capacity of each file. Last set is composed by the first set of files with embedded information up to an 80% of the capacity of each file. Distinguisher values obtained for each of the files are shown in Fig. 6.

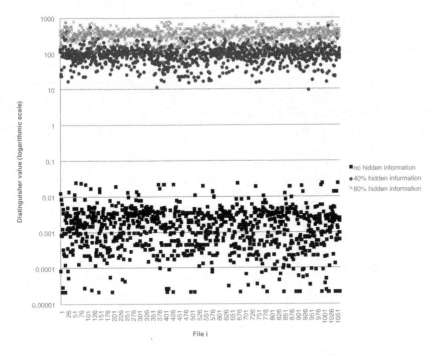

Fig. 6. Distinguisher results for sets of executable files

Values obtained by our distinguisher for the clean files are separated from the ones offered by files with embedded information. Some results offered by embedded information files are low, but higher than the values returned by any of the clean files. In fact, our distinguisher has classified all the executables correctly (Table 4).

Table 4. Distinguisher classification results for different sets of executable files

	Expected clean executables	Expected embedded exec.
Predicted clean executables	1063	0
Predicted embedded exec.	0	2126

In order to produce executable files that are not detected by our tool some changes should be done to *Hydan*. Our analysis have shown that replacement of *functionality-equivalent instructions* is not secure if the frequency distribution of instructions inside a *functionality-equivalent instruction* set is constant. A first approach to secure Hydan would be to use only the functionality-equivalent instruction sets not used by our distinguisher. This would reduce the capacity of hidden information up to a 35% of the original capacity. Stego-files generated this way would not be detected by the distinguiser, producing false negatives.

6   Conclusions and Future Work

Steganalysis techniques are needed in order to ensure and improve the security of stego-systems in the same way cryptanalysis is needed to foster the security of cryptography techniques. With this work, we have developed a distinguisher that is able to recognize executable files with hidden information through *Hydan*. To create our distinguisher we have built a statistical model of *clean* executable files. In our tests, the proposed distinguisher classified correctly all executable files in different proportions of concealment (0%, 40% and 80%). We have also described how to overcome this steganalysis. Research on steganography of executable files is not extensive at the moment, but improvements to secure *Hydan* and other related steganographic tools [1] could only be achieved through extensive research in the field. We have advanced in this direction, and plan to further advance by refining the steganalytic methods proposed in [1] against *Stilo*.

References

1. Anckaert, B., De Sutter, B., Chanet, D., De Bosschere, K.: Steganography for executables and code transformation signatures. In: Park, C.-s., Chee, S. (eds.) ICISC 2004. LNCS, vol. 3506, pp. 425–439. Springer, Heidelberg (2005)
2. El-Khalil, R.: Hydan: Hiding information in program binaries. In: López, J., Qing, S., Okamoto, E. (eds.) ICICS 2004. LNCS, vol. 3269, pp. 187–199. Springer, Heidelberg (2004)
3. Hernandez-Castro, J.C., Lopez, I.B., Tapiador, J.M.E., Ribagorda, A.: Steganography in Games. Computers and Security 25(1), 64–71 (2006)
4. Johnson, N.F., Jajodia, S.: Exploring steganography: Seeing the unseen. Computer 31(2), 26–34 (1998)
5. Kipper, G.: Investigator's Guide to Steganography. CRC Press, Boca Raton (2004)
6. Murdoch, S.J., Lewis, S.: Embedding Covert Channels into TCP/IP. In: Barni, M., Herrera-Joancomartí, J., Katzenbeisser, S., Pérez-González, F. (eds.) IH 2005. LNCS, vol. 3727, pp. 247–261. Springer, Heidelberg (2005)
7. Naor, M., Yung, M.: Universal One-Way Hash Functions and Their Cryptographic Applications. In: Proceedings of the twenty-first annual ACM symposium on Theory of computing, pp. 33–43. ACM, New York (1989)
8. Peterson, W., Brown, D.: Cyclic Codes for Error Detection. Proceedings of the IRE 49(1), 228–235 (1961)
9. Petitcolas, F.A.P., Anderson, R.J., Kuhn, M.G.: Information Hiding:A Survey. Proceedings of the IEEE 87(7), 1062–1078 (1999)
10. Petitcolas, F.A.P.: MP3Stego (2006) (Cited October 20, 2008), http://www.petitcolas.net/fabien/steganography
11. Shirali-Shahreza, M., Shirali-Shahreza, M.H.: Text Steganography In SMS. In: Int. Conference on Convergence Information Technology, pp. 2260–2265 (2007)
12. Simmons, G.J.: The History of Subliminal Channels. IEEE Journal on Selected Areas in Communications 16(4), 452–462 (1998)
13. Zhu, W., Thomborson, C.: Recognition in Software Watermarking. In: Proceedings of the 4th ACM international workshop on Contents protection and security, pp. 29–36. ACM, New York (2006)

On the Impossibility of Detecting Virtual Machine Monitors

Shay Gueron[1] and Jean-Pierre Seifert[2]

[1] Department of Mathematics, Faculty of Science, University of Haifa, Haifa 31905, Israel and
Intel Corporation, Israel Development Center, Haifa, Israel
shay@math.haifa.ac.il

[2] Technische Universität Berlin and Deutsche Telekom Laboratories, 10587 Berlin, Germany
jeanpierreseifert@yahoo.com

Abstract. Virtualization based upon Virtual Machines is a central building block of Trusted Computing, and it is believed to offer isolation and confinement of privileged instructions among other security benefits. However, it is not necessarily bullet-proof — some recent publications have shown that Virtual Machine technology could potentially allow the installation of undetectable malware root kits. As a result, it was suggested that such virtualization attacks could be mitigated by checking if a threatened system runs in a virtualized or in a native environment. This naturally raises the following problem: *Can a program determine whether it is running in a virtualized environment, or in a native machine environment?* We prove here that, under a classical VM model, this problem is not decidable. Further, although our result seems to be quite theoretic, we also show that it has practical implications on related virtualization problems.

1   Introduction

The concept of Virtual Machines (VM) has been closely coupled with Trusted Computing from its early days, cf. [20,2,31,4,36,40,43]. Clearly, isolation through a robust Virtual Machine Monitor implementation provides a very powerful security ingredient. This concept has already been extensively used for security reasons in past computer generations cf. [25,26,36]. Furthermore, recent mass-market oriented Trusted Computing efforts (driven by the Trusted Computing Group (TCG) [44,34]) also capitalize on this excellent domain isolation concept provided by Virtual Machines, cf. [1,6,10,23].

Along with the TCG efforts, a vibrant academic research community has addressed to solve numerous computer security problems through Virtualization. We mention here only a small sample from the many publications on this topic. The early influential works of [17,18] offer a broad view of various security applications enabled by the concept of Virtualization, such as Digital Rights Management (RDM) systems and the Rootkit installation problem. An excellent overview is given by [28].

However, even more recently, some interesting publications [39,27,46] have shown how the VM technology could be misused for allowing the installation of undetectable Rootkits. Finally, [19] described even a simple and convincing method for circumventing DRM schemes along the idea of misusing the Virtualization concept. To mitigate such "virtualization attacks", it is obvious to simply check whether or not a threatened

D. Gritzalis and J. Lopez (Eds.): SEC 2009, IFIP AICT 297, pp. 143–151, 2009.

application runs in a virtualized environment. Consequently, the following theoretical problem arises very naturally:

Can a program distinguish whether it is running in a virtualized environment or in a native machine environment?

This problem and its derivatives are the focus of our paper. We formally prove that, under a classical VM model, it is impossible to design an algorithm that would allow a program to determine whether it is running in a virtualized environment or in a native machine environment. Note that it makes no sense at all to ask the question of detecting "virtualization" for a specific fixed Virtual Machine Monitor and a specific fixed native machine.

Although our results seem theoretical at first sight, they bear practical security ramifications as pointed out by Microsoft and Intel. Our results especially show that Bill Gates' requirement, cf. [15], that "Microsoft must be careful that the VM does not become a security weakness through which an attacker could insert a VM under the operating system, negating Windows security protections" is a fundamental key issue. In light of our results it seems quite reasonable that Microsoft recommended in its public analysis of these rootkit issues, cf. [32], some strongly protected default settings for the Enabling/Disabling of the new hardware Virtualization extensions offered by AMD and Intel. Also Pat Gelsinger from Intel explained that there are gaps to be plugged around virtual security. "As virtual machine migrations become popular, they become vulnerable," he said, warning that a "whole new set" of attacks will emerge focused on VMs, cf. [38].

One may argue, cf. [5,12,14,13,11,16,18,21,37], that there may always be ways to discover whether or not the execution is taking place in a virtualized environment, and that these methods are not considered in our purely theoretical impossibility result that is offered here.

However, later in this paper we will explain why we expect that for security reasons, the reality would converge to our ideal model of virtualization. This assumed convergence of ideal virtualization is also nicely explained in [14], describing it there as a VMM detection arms race. And recent concerns, cf. [8], about the "Risk of Virtualization" fit very well into Microsoft's and Intel's concerns.

We also want to mention here that the appearance of our impossibility results is quite similar to the early theoretical work of Cohen on Computer Virus Detection, cf. [7]. It tackles a real-world computer security problem within a theoretical model, and derives an impossibility result which looks at first sight simple and not very relevant from the practical point of view. Nevertheless, it is the definitive and undisputable answer from the theory of computation aspect and confirms the VMM detection arms race of [14] which describe that there is a chance that VMMs eventually and successfully evade detection.

The paper is organized as follows. Section 2 gives a high-level introduction to the concepts Virtual Machine, Virtual Machine Monitor and even Virtualization, and develops the tools that allow a formalized proof of our main Theorem. This Theorem along with some important implications is presented in Section 3. In Section 4 we discuss the relevance of our theoretical result to the proposed heuristic methods to detect

Virtualization environments. Finally, Section 5 presents our conclusions and further directions of interesting research topics.

2   Definitions and Preliminaries

In this paper, we follow the classical formalism of Popek and Goldberg [37] to define the concepts of Virtualization, Virtual Machine, and Virtual Machine Monitor, and will use the following definitions.

Definition 1. A *Virtual Machine Monitor (VMM)* is any control program that satisfies the three properties: efficiency, resource control, and equivalence.

Definition 2. The functional environment that any program experiences when running with a VMM present is called a *Virtual Machine (VM)*. The VM consists of the original machine and the VMM.

Intuitively, a VM is an efficient, isolated duplicate of the real machine. A VMM is a piece of software that

1. Provides an environment for other programs, which is essentially identical to the environment provided by the original machine. Programs that run in this environment show, at most, a minor decrease in their running speed.
2. Has complete control of the system's resources. Here, "essentially identical" implies that only minor exceptions in the availability of system resources and only minor timing differences are tolerated.

Under this view, a classical Operating System that provides quasi-parallel execution of different processes is not considered as a VMM. "Efficient" requires that a statistically significant part of the machine's instructions are executed directly on the original machine, with no VMM intervention. Under this view, emulators and software interpreters are also not considered as a VMM. "Complete control" implies that programs

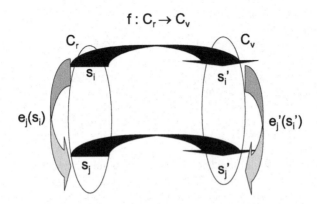

Fig. 1. The Virtual Machine map

running under a VMM control cannot gain system resources that were not explicitly assigned to them. However, on the other hand, under certain circumstances, a VMM itself can regain control of resources that have been already allocated.

The equivalence property can be defined in terms of a homomorphism on the possible machine states. To this end, we partition the set $\mathcal{C}$ of all possible states of the native machine into $\mathcal{C} = \mathcal{C}_r \cup \mathcal{C}_v$ where $\mathcal{C}_v$ contains the states for which the VMM is present in memory, and $\mathcal{C}_r$ consists of the remaining states. Each instruction i in the native machine can be viewed as a unitary operator $i : s_j \mapsto s_k$ operating on $\mathcal{C}$. Similarly, each sequence $i_1 \circ \cdots \circ i_n(s_1) = e_n(s_1) = s_2$ of n successive instructions can be viewed as an unitary operator operating on $\mathcal{C}$. Let the set of all sequences of instructions having a finite length be $\mathcal{I}$. We define a *Virtual Machine map* (VM map) $f : \mathcal{C}_r \to \mathcal{C}_v$ as a one-one homomorphism with respect to all of the operators e_i in $\mathcal{I}$. That is (see Figure 1), for any state $s_i \in \mathcal{C}_r$ and any instruction sequence e_i, there exists an instruction sequence e_i' such that $f(e_i(s_i))) = e_i'(f(s_i))$. We also require that f is one-one (i.e., it has a left inverse) and that for each e_i there is a way to find the appropriate e_i' and to execute it. We can now define "equivalence" and "essentially identical" as follows:

Definition 3. Let $\mathcal{M}$ be a real machine and $\mathcal{V}$ a virtual machine defined via the Virtual Machine map $f : \mathcal{C}_r \to \mathcal{C}_v$. Let s_1 be any starting state leading to a halting state s_2 of the real machine $\mathcal{M}$, where $f(s_1) = s_1'$. Suppose thet the starting state s_1' leads to a halting state s_2' in $\mathcal{V}$. The corresponding VMM is said to have the equivalence property, if $f(s_2) = s_2'$.

As mentioned above, the equivalence property [37] allows for two possible minor exceptions in timing and resource availability.

Timing

Due to occasional intervention of the control program, certain instructions of an executed program may take longer than expected. Thus, one cannot make assumptions about exact execution times. In our model, we first ignore such timing differences, and later comment on how this assumption could be ensured in certain hardware-supported virtualization environments.

Resources Availability

Note that, resources-wise, an actually constructed VM can be smaller than the real mother machine (a smaller version of the real machine, but logically still the same hardware). Thus, we require the equivalence to be guaranteed between the artificially smaller VM and the smaller version of the real machine

3   The Main Theorem

Unlike [12,14,13] we do not try check if another remotely-connected machine is a virtual machine or a native machine. The problem that we tackle here is whether some algorithm can distinguish between a native and a virtualized environment during its run-time, while it is running on this potentially "hostile" environment (about which it has to decide). In other words, the distinguishing algorithm cannot use any "trusted" or reliable external help like an oracle. For this environment, we prove the following result.

Theorem 1. *There exists no algorithm that can decide, for every real machine and for every VMM, whether it is running under control of a VMM or on a real machine without a VMM present.*

Proof. Consider real machines virtualizable along the above definitions from [37]. Assume by contradiction that there exists an algorithm A which for every real machine $\mathcal{M}$ and for every virtual machine $\mathcal{V}$ given by its virtual machine map $f : \mathcal{C}_r \to \mathcal{C}_v$ satisfies the following:

- When A is executed on a real machine $\mathcal{M}$, it leads $\mathcal{M}$ to a halting state $s_{\text{no VMM present}}$.
- When A is executed on a virtual machine $\mathcal{V}$ controlled by its corresponding VMM, it results in a halting state $s'_{\text{VMM present}}$ of $\mathcal{V}$.
- $f(s_{\text{no VMM present}}) = s'_{\text{VMM present}}$ with $s'_{\text{VMM present}} \neq s_{\text{no VMM present}}$, to have a unique distinction between the two cases.

Now, fix one real machine $\mathcal{M}$ and one virtual machine $\mathcal{V}$ for this fixed real machine. We define a new machine $\hat{\mathcal{M}}$, state-wise, to be identical to $\mathcal{V}$, where the VMM is hidden inside its finite state control thus being invisible for programs running on $\hat{\mathcal{M}}$. Intuitively, $\hat{\mathcal{M}}$ can be viewed as the process of moving the effects of the VMM (and especially the VMM program itself) directly into the finite state control of $\hat{\mathcal{M}}$. This process can be seen as realizing $\mathcal{V}$ "directly in hardware" where the effects of the VMM and its control behaviour are still present in $\hat{\mathcal{M}}$, but now without explicitly having the VMM present in memory any more.

By our assumption, algorithm A works for all real machines, i.e., in particular also on $\hat{\mathcal{M}}$. Since $\hat{\mathcal{M}}$ is defined to follow, state-wise, the actions of $\mathcal{V}$, the execution of A on $\hat{\mathcal{M}}$ must lead $\hat{\mathcal{M}}$ into the halting state

$$s'_{\text{VMM present}}. \tag{1}$$

However, on the other hand, executing A on $\hat{\mathcal{M}}$ is essentially equivalent to following the steps of the machine $\mathcal{M}$ without having the corresponding VMM present in memory. Thus, algorithm A executed on $\hat{\mathcal{M}}$ must end in the halting state

$$s_{\text{no VMM present}}. \tag{2}$$

The contradiction between the halting states (1) and (2) for executing A on $\hat{\mathcal{M}}$ shows that no universal distinguishing algorithm can exist.   □

3.1 Remark

Although the above proof looks simple or almost trivial, we would like to mention that the core of the above proof implicitly rests upon the ideas of the so called *S-m-n* Theorem and the *Recursion* Theorem of Kleene, (cf. [24]), which are among the two deepest theorems in the "Theory of Computing". However, following the advice from one of the most respected theoretical computer science theorist, cf. [22], that *"the very simple facts and the basic approaches are the ones that have most impact,"* we chose a simple and basic approach for our proof and explicitly avoided the former two heavy approaches.

3.2   Consequences of the Main Theorem

Here, we address the more practical question of constructing an algorithm for detecting a Virtualization attack when a specific machine and an arbitrary VMM for that machine are given. The following corollary states the result.

Corollary 1. *Suppose that a specific machine $\mathcal{M}$ and an arbitrary VMM for that machine are given. There exists no algorithm that is able to determine whether it is running on $\mathcal{M}$ under control of a VMM or on $\mathcal{M}$ without a VMM present in memory.*

Proof. First, we have to assume here that the given machine $\mathcal{M}$ is indeed virtualizable. We follow the proof of Theorem 1 for the given machine $\mathcal{M}$, constructing the new machine $\hat{\mathcal{M}}$ for an arbitrary but fixed virtual machine map f. By definition of the equivalence property (which of course holds for the map f) we get that $\hat{\mathcal{M}}$ and $\mathcal{M}$ are functionally equivalent. Thus, we are not changing the fixed and specific machine functionality implied by $\mathcal{M}$. Thus, when considering $\hat{\mathcal{M}}$ or $\mathcal{M}$ we still have the same fixed machine "functionality", we can simply follow the above proof and conclude the corollary.   □

4   Practical Detection of Virtualization

We comment here on the relation between our theoretical impossibility result and the common perception that in practice, there might be always methods to discover whether execution is happening in a virtualized or in a native environment (e.g., [5,12,14,13,11,16,18,21,37]). In this context, Lauradoux [30] suggested that a so called "hard-clock" and the cache timing behavior of the machine could be used for detecting whether an execution environment is virtualized or not. Similar artifacts of the underlying CPU microarchitecture were also subsequently used in [12,14,13]. Also, we would like to stress that the distinguishing algorithms of [12,14,13] rely on an external "trusted clock" which is not part of our model. Thus, their practical "remote detection" scenario doesn't compare at all with our classical detection problem which allows no external help. Indeed, [14] agree that this "trusted clock" is easy to circumvent by a malicious VMM by just disabling or masking the TCP timestamps, thus leaving the distinguisher in the dark. Moreover, [14] also briefly discuss getting rid off their "trusted external clock" but conclude that this an open and difficult question.

Timing artifacts which presumably provide a VMM detection mechanism, rely on the possibility to precisely measure the execution time, a task which is known to be a technical challenge for a full and secure virtualization (cf. [41,42]). Particularly, such precise timing is based on the non-privileged Read Time Stamp Counter (RDTSC for the x86 architecture) instruction being a critical instructions.

The recent Intel initiative to provide full secure Virtualization support using the IA-32 architecture (cf. [45]) followed the path outlined in [41]. Here, all instructions are classified as either critical or non-critical instructions, where the functionality of the critical instructions (including RDTSC) is "somehow" confined to a VMM level class, so the VMM itself has the freedom to decide how to handle the functionality of those critical instructions. The emerging problem in this case is that a VMM could give the programs running under its control the "precise timing illusion" of a real machine, by simply subtracting the extra cycles spent inside the VMM, from the Time Stamp Counter. Thus, as pointed out in [14], having the possibility to let the VMM directly control sensitive machine instructions like RDTSC complicates heuristic VMM detection algorithms relying on the discovery of timing artifacts, cf. [39,46].

5   Conclusions

We showed here that under the classical VM model, it is impossible to design an algorithm that would allow a program to decide whether it is running in a virtualized environment or in a native machine environment. We also proved here a stronger and more practical impossibility result. This result states that is even for specific and fixed machine type impossible to design an VMM detection algorithm.

This theoretical result has also practical implications. Noting Lampson [29] and some recent publications [3,33,35] that illustrate the security threats of indirect information leaks caused by imperfect isolation, we expect that closing all potential information leaks (including timing) would become a necessary requirement for future hardware virtualization technologies like [45]. Thus, we expect the reality converging (for security reasons) in the future to our ideal model of virtualization. On the other side, closing these holes may pose a serious challenge for heuristic virtualization detection mechanisms, cf. [5,11,30]. This confirms again the hypothesis of [14] that there is an VMM detection arms race which might result in that VMMs eventually and successfully evade detection.

As assumed by [15] and [38] this conflict hints that hardware-assisted Virtualization could become a double-edge sword, especially when considering the recent VM attacks from [39,27,46] and [19]. Thus, similarly to the topic considered in [9], the following new research vector naturally arises: *What kind of cryptographic protection against the VM adversary can we achieve by new constructions, if we have to assume running under the control of a potentially malicious VMM which has full control of what we are doing?*

References

1. Advanced Micro Devices, Pacifica — AMD Secure Virtual Machine Architecture Reference Manual, AMD (2005)
2. Attanasio, C.R.: Virtual Machines and Data Security. In: Proceedings of the Workshop on Virtual Computer Systems, pp. 206–209 (1973)
3. Bernstein, D.J.: Cache-timing attacks on AES, 37 pages (2005), http://cr.yp.to/papers.html/cachetiming

4. Bishop, M.: Computer Security: Art and Science. Addison Wesley Professional, Reading (2003)
5. Carpenter, M., Liston, T., Skoudis. E.: Hiding Virtualization from Attackers and Malware. IEEE Security and Privacy 5(3), 62–65 (2007)
6. Chen, Y., England, P., Peinado, M., Willman, B.: High Assurance Computing on Open Hardware Architectures, Microsoft Technical Report, MSR-TR-2003-20 (March 2003)
7. Cohen, F.B.: Computer Viruses: Theory and Experiments. Computers and Security 6, 22–35 (1987)
8. Dignan, L.: Virtualization: What are the security risks? ZDNet.com (January 22, 2008)
9. Dinda, P.A.: Addressing the trust asymmetry problem in grid computing with encrypted computation. In: Proceedings of the 7th Workshop on Languages, Compilers, and Run-time support for scalable systems, pp. 1–7 (2004)
10. England, P., Lampson, B., Manferdelli, J., Peinado, M., Willman, B.: A Trusted Open Platform. IEEE Computer 36(7), 55–62 (2003)
11. Ferrie, P.: Attacks on Virtual Machine Emulators. In: AVAR 2006, Auckland, New Zealand, December 3-5 (2006)
12. Franklin, J., Luk, M., McCune, J., Seshadri, A., Perrig, A., van Doorn, L.: Remote Virtual Machine Monitor Detection. In: ARO-DARPA-DHS Special Workshop on Botnets, Arlington, VA (June 2006)
13. Franklin, J., Luk, M., McCune, J., Seshadri, A., Perrig, A., van Doorn, L.: Remote Detection of Virtual Machine Monitors with Fuzzy Benchmarking. ACM SIGOPS Operating System Review (Special Issue on Computer Forensics) (April 2008)
14. Franklin, J., Luk, M., McCune, J., Seshadri, A., Perrig, A., van Doorn, L.: Towards Sound Detection of Virtual Machines. In: Lee, W., Wang, C., Dagon, D. (eds.) Botnet Detection: Countering the Largest Security Threat, November 2007. Springer, Heidelberg (2007)
15. Galli, P.: Microsoft puts IE enhancements of fast track. Interview with Bill Gates in *eWeek* 22(18) (2006)
16. Garfinkel, T., Adams, K., Warfield, A., Franklin, J.: Compatibility is Not Transparency: VMM Detection Myths and Realities. In: Proceedings of the 11th Workshop on Hot Topics in Operating Systems (HotOS-XI), (May 2007)
17. Garfinkel, T., Pfaff, B., Chow, J., Rosenblum, M., Boneh, D.: Terra: a virtual machine-based platform for trusted computing. In: Proceedings of the 19th ACM Symposium on Operating Systems Principles (2003)
18. Garfinkel, T., Rosenblum, M.: A virtual machine introspection-based architecture for intrusion detection. In: Proceedings of the 2003 Network and Distributed Systems Symposium (NDSS 2003) (2003)
19. Ghodke, N., Figueiredo, R.J.: On the Implications of Machine Virtualization for DRM and Fair Use: A Case Study of a Virtual Audio Device Driver. In: Proceedings of 4th ACM DRM Workshop (2004)
20. Goldberg, R.P.: Architecture of virtual machines. In: Proceedings of the Workshop on Virtual Computer Systems, pp. 74–112 (1973)
21. Goldberg, R.P.: Survey of virtual machine research. IEEE Computer Magazine 7, 34–45 (1974)
22. Goldreich, O., Rosenberg, A.L., Selman, A.L. (eds.): Theoretical Computer Science. LNCS, vol. 3895. Springer, Heidelberg (2006)
23. Grawrock, D.: The Intel Safer Computing Initiative: Building Blocks for Trusted Computing. Intel Press (2006)
24. Hopcroft, J.E., Ullman, J.D.: Introduction to Automata Theory, Languages, and Computation. Addison-Wesley Publishing Company, Reading (1979)

25. Karger, P., Zurko, M.E., Bonin, D.W., Mason, A.H., Kahn, C.E.: A VMM security kernel for the VAX architecture. In: Proceedings of the 1990 IEEE Symposium on Security and Privacy, pp. 2–19 (1990)
26. Karger, P., Zurko, M.E., Bonin, D.W., Mason, A.H., Kahn, C.E.: A Retrospective on the VAX VMM Security Kernel. IEEE Transactions on Software Engineering 17(11), 1147–1165 (1991)
27. King, S.T., Chen, P.M., Wang, Y.-M., Verbowski, C., Wang, H.J., Lorch, J.R.: SubVirt: Implementing malware with virtual machines. In: Proceedings of the 2006 IEEE Symposium on Security and Privacy (2006)
28. King, S.T., Smith, S.W.: Virtualization and Security: Back to the Future. IEEE Security & Privacy 6(5), 15 (2008)
29. Lampson, B.W.: A note on the confinement problem. Communications of the ACM 16(10), 613–615 (1973)
30. Lauraoux, C.: Detecting virtual machines (manuscript), cedric.lauradoux@inria.fr
31. Madnick, S.E., Donovan, J.J.: Application and analysis of the virtual machine approach to information system security and isolation. In: Proceedings of the Workshop on Virtual Computer Systems, pp. 210–224 (1973)
32. Microsoft, CPU Virtualization Extensions: Analysis of Rootkit Issues (October 2006), http://www.microsoft.com/whdc/system/platform/virtual/CPUVirtExt.mspx
33. Osvik, D.A., Shamir, A., Tromer, E.: Cache attacks and Countermeasures: the Case of AES, Cryptology ePrint Archive, Report 2005/271 (2005)
34. Pearson, S.: Trusted Computing Platforms: TCPA Technology in Context. Prentice Hall PTR, Englewood Cliffs (2002)
35. Percival, C.: Cache missing for fun and profit. In: Proc. of BSDCan 2005, Ottawa (manuscript, 2005), http://www.daemonology.net
36. Pfleeger, C.P., Lawrence Pfleeger, S.: Security in Computing, 3rd edn. Prentice Hall PTR, Englewood Cliffs (2002)
37. Popek, G., Goldberg, R.: Formal Requirements for Virtualizable Third Generation Architectures. Communications of the ACM 17(7), 412–421
38. Rogers, J.: Virtualization Is Key to Disaster Recovery, Byte and Switch News (September 11, 2007)
39. Rutkowska, J.: Subverting VistaTM Kernel For Fun And Profit. In: SyScan 2006, July 21st, Singapore, and Black Hat Briefings, August 3rd, Las Vegas (2006)
40. Silberschatz, A., Gagne, G., Galvin, P.B.: Operating system concepts, 7th edn. John Wiley and Sons, Chichester (2005)
41. Robin, J.S., Irvine, C.E.: Analysis of the Intel Pentium's Ability to Support a Secure Virtual Machine Monito. In: Proceedings of the 9th Usenix Security Symposium, pp. 129–144 (2000)
42. Sibert, O., Porras, P.A., Lindell, R.: The Intel 80x86 Processor Architecture: Pitfalls for Secure Systems. In: 1995 IEEE Symposium on Security and Privacy, pp. 211–223 (1995)
43. Smith, J., Nair, R.: Virtual Machines: Versatile Platforms for Systems and Proccesses. Elsevier Press, Amsterdam (2005)
44. Trusted Computing Group, http://www.trustedcomputinggroup.org
45. Uhlig, R., Neiger, G., Rodgers, D., Santoni, A.L., Martins, F.C.M., Anderson, A.V., Bennett, S.M., Kagi, A., Leung, F.H., Smith, L.: Intel Virtualization Technology. Computer 38(5), 48–56 (2005)
46. Dai Zovi, D.A.: Hardware Virtualization Rootkits. In: Black Hat Briefings 2006, Las Vegas, August 3 (2006)

Implementation of a Trusted Ticket System

Andreas Leicher[1], Nicolai Kuntze[2], and Andreas U. Schmidt[3]

[1] Johann Wolfgang Goethe-Universität, Frankfurt am Main, Germany
`leicher@cs.uni-frankfurt.de`
[2] Fraunhofer–Institute for Secure Information Technology, Rheinstraße 75, 64295 Darmstadt, Germany
`nicolai.kuntze@sit.fraunhofer.de`
[3] CREATE-NET Research Center, Via alla Cascata 56/D, 38100 Trento, Italy
`andreas.schmidt@create-net.org`

Abstract. Trusted Computing is a security technology which enables the establishment of trust between multiple parties. Previous work showed that Trusted Computing technology can be used to build tickets, a core concept of Identity Management Systems. Relying solely on the Trusted Platform Module we will demonstrate how this technology can be used in the context of Kerberos for an implementation variant of Identity Management.

1 Introduction

Trusted Computing (TC) as defined by the Trusted Computing Group (TCG) is usually seen as a protection technology centred on single devices. Yet, viewed as a platform-neutral security infrastructure, TC offers ways to establish trust between entities that are otherwise separated by technical boundaries, e.g., different access technologies and access control structures. Not surprisingly, some concepts of TC are rather similar to Identity management (IDM) and federation.

In previous work we have presented a concept for how to use TC within ticket systems such as Kerberos [1], and have also shown that identity federation between different provider domains can be supported by TC [9]. The present paper reports on the progress in this field, in particular a concrete realisation and integration in an existing authentication system, namely Kerberos. The combination of attestation of a client system's trustworthiness with user authentication and authorisation is a key issue. We show that this combination is efficient in a generic demonstration environment for TC-based applications. Part of this work is done within the EU FP7 project NanoDataCenters as a base for trust in distributed environments.

Section 2 provides some essential background on TC technology. Section 3 describes the demonstration environment we put together building on and combining available open source projects. Section 4 details the concepts for a TC-enabled ticket system architecture and describes the most important use cases, while Section 5 sketches the concrete integration into the Kerberos framework. We conclude with Section 6.

D. Gritzalis and J. Lopez (Eds.): SEC 2009, IFIP AICT 297, pp. 152–163, 2009.

2   Trusted Computing Essentials

The idea of building security into open, connected systems by using computing platforms enhanced by security-relevant functionality in protected places has a long history, rooted in the study by the Rand Corporation [13].

The TCG is the main industrial effort to standardise TC technology. Trust as defined by the TCG means that an entity always behaves in the expected manner for the intended purpose. The trust anchor, called Trusted Platform Module (TPM), offers various functions related to security. Each TPM is bound to a certain environment and together they form a trusted platform (TP) from which the TPM cannot be removed.

To prove trustworthiness of a TP to an external party, or verifier, processes called (remote) attestation and according protocols have been envisaged. They transport measurement values and data necessary to retrace the system state from them, so called measurement logs, to the verifier. The data is uniquely and verifiable bound to a particular platform, e.g. by a digital signature. Remote attestation can be supported by a PKI structure for instance to protect a platform owner's privacy by revealing the platform identity only to a trusted third party. The following technical details are taken from [17]. More can also be found in [14].

For the TPM to issue an assertion about the system state, two attestation protocols are available. As the uniqueness of every TPM leads to privacy concerns, they provide pseudonymity, resp., anonymity. Both protocols rest on Attestation Identity Keys (AIKs) which are placeholders for the EK. An AIK is a 1024 bit RSA key whose private portion is sealed inside the TPM. The simpler protocol Remote Attestation (RA) offers pseudonymity employing a trusted third party, the Privacy CA (PCA), which issues a credential stating that the respective AIK is generated by a sound TPM within a valid platform. The system state is measured by a reporting process with the TPM as central reporting authority receiving measurement values and calculating a unique representation of the state using hash values. For this, the TPM has several Platform Configuration Registers (PCR). Beginning with the system boot each component reports a measurement value, e.g., a hash value over the BIOS, to the TPM and stores it in a log file. During RA the communication partner acting as verifier receives this log file and the corresponding PCR value. The verifier can then decide if the device is in a configuration which is trustworthy from his perspective. Apart from RA, the TCG has defined Direct Anonymous Attestation. This involved protocol is based on a zero knowledge proof but due to certain constraints of the hardware it is not implemented in current TPMs.

AIKs are crucial for applications since they can not only be used, according to TCG standards, to attest the origin and authenticity of a trust measurement, but also to authenticate other keys and data generated by the TPM. Before an AIK can testify the authenticity of any data, a PCA has to issue a credential for it. This credential together with the AIK can therefore be used as an identity for this platform. Using the AIK as a signing key for arbitrary data is not directly possible but we have shown elsewhere how to circumvent this limitation [14,12].

3   Trusted Demonstration Environment

In order to develop and test various ideas and concepts of TC, we set up a Trusted Demonstration Environment. The goal was to design a system in which it is possible, without the need of a physical TPM, to access all desired TPM functions. In order to emulate a TPM in software, we used the TPM emulator from [5]. To simulate a complete system we decided to build upon Virtualisation. Therefore we established a connection between the emulated TPM and QEMU [3], thus enabling virtual machines to execute TPM applications and commands.

The **TPM emulator** enables to access and review the internal operations in the TPM, which made it a very powerful tool for analysis, testing and debugging. The emulator consists of three parts: an implementation of the TPM Device Driver Library (TDDL), a kernel module (tpmd_dev) and the TPM emulator daemon. As specified by the TCG, TDDL provides a convenient way to access the TPM from applications. By substituting this library, applications that use the TDDL are forced to use the TPM emulator instead of a hardware TPM. For those applications and libraries that access the TPM directly, the kernel module tpmd_dev simulates a hardware TPM by forwarding all messages directly to the TPM emulator daemon, which is the main component of the emulator. The tpmd listens on a Unix socket and waits for incoming commands. At current, most of the commands specified by the TCG are supported by the emulator. The installation of the TPM emulator is quite straightforward, compiling from source version 0.5.1. To prevent that QEMU gets disconnected from the emulator before the guest OS is up, as long as no TPM commands are issued during the boot process, we decided to change TPM_COMMAND_TIMEOUT in tpmd.c to a higher value (3000, default: 30).

To establish the connection between the tpmd and QEMU to gain a **virtualised client environment** we used a patch from [4]. We modified the patch to work with the current QEMU source version 0.9.1 [2]. The patch allows QEMU to connect to the Unix socket created by tpmd via command line option, and registers a new IO port inside QEMU and forwards all commands to the socket and thus to the TPM emulator.

We set up a virtual machine in QEMU using a standard debian distribution (etch). To communicate with the TPM the kernel (version 2.6.24-3) was recompiled, adding the IMA patch from IBM [6]. We configured the kernel to support TPMs In addition we enabled IMA.

IMA stands for Integrated Measurement Architecture and enables measurement and logging of every file that the kernel loads. Measurement is done in two steps: before execution, the SHA-1 hash of every file and library is measured and written to PCR 10 of the TPM using "extend" as in equation 1. Additionally the measured file and its SHA-1 hash gets logged in the /sys/kernel/security/ima/ascii_runtime_measurements file.

$$PCR10 = SHA\text{-}1\,(PCR10\|SHA\text{-}1\,(file)) \tag{1}$$

As a main concept of authenticated boot, measurement through IMA allows for a later attestation to a remote system. It should be noted that every file gets measured only once, upon first execution. While the measurement list contains all files that executed since the system boot, it is not a list of the current running configuration of the system. Thus IMA cannot implement an actual run-time measurement. Using emulation of both, the TPM and the machine connecting to it, enabled us to set up on a single host multiple clients each of them with its own TPM. Integrated in this framework is QEMU's capability to connect the clients to a virtual network and thus enabling a complete client/server infrastructure.

In order to access the TPM inside the client, we developed several applications in Java, based on the framework TPM/J from [7] implementing a **client-server infrastructure**. Around various little tools for creating and storing keys for later use, we implemented the complete process of Remote Attestation. In particular our environment can create an arbitrary number of AIKs and, by connecting to our PCA, realised as a single module written in Java, we can certify our AIKs.

The process of AIK certification is shown in figure 1. First, the client creates a new AIK using the TPM_MakeIdentity command. This creates the key and the TPM_IDENTITY_CONTENTS structure which contains the public AIK. This structure is then signed with the AIK and sent to the PCA together with the public EK and its certificate.

Our realisation of the PCA creates a random nonce and encrypts both, the public AIK and the nonce with the EK. The client then has to load the AIK into the TPM, decrypt the nonce using TPM_ActivateIdentity, and finally checks if the decrypted public AIK corresponds to the loaded AIK. Then the decrypted random nonce is sent back to the PCA. This is used as a handshake operation — extending the TCG's specification of this protocol — to ensure that the PCA communicates with the TPM that generated the AIK. The corresponding security weakness in the TCG's specified protocol was noted in [8], and we followed the solution proposed there. The handshake operation generates a reliable link between the EK (stored in the TPM) and the AIK. Omitting the handshake poses several risks. If an attacker can get hold of a public EK and the credentials, he can request PCA credentials for arbitrary RSA keys. These keys are not necessarily bound to the TPM and can be created without a TPM. Thus, one can imagine DoS attacks on the PCA. If a policy enables the PCA to issue only a limited amount of certificates for a certain TPM, or users are charged for the issuance of the certificates, this leads to further attacks. Note that the attacker will not be able to decrypt the credentials for the given AIK, as they can only be decrypted by the private EK which will not leave the TPM.

The PCA then verifies the correctness of the EK certificate and validates the AIK signature on the TPM_IDENTITY_CONTENTS. After generating the AIK certificate cert(AIK,PCA$_{cert}$), the PCA encrypts it using a symmetric key K. To ensure that only the requesting client can access the certificate, the key K, together with the hash of the public AIK is encrypted with the public EK in the TPM_EK_BLOB structure. The encrypted certificate and the encrypted TPM_EK_BLOB are then sent back to the client. The client's TPM can

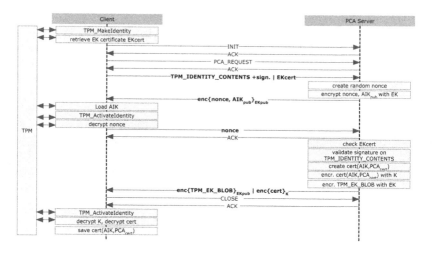

Fig. 1. Flow of the AIK certification protocol

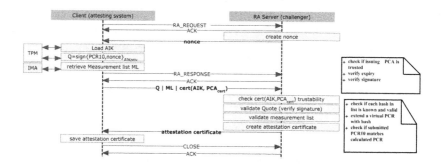

Fig. 2. Flow of the RA protocol

decrypt the symmetric key K using the TPM_ActivateIdentity command and can thus decrypt the cert(AIK,PCA$_{cert}$) which is stored for further use. With these certified AIKs it is possible to connect to our Remote Attestation (RA) server. The client sends the IMA measurement list together with the current value of PCR 10 signed with the AIK to the server. The RA server then checks if the AIK certificate is valid and issued by a trusted PCA. The RA server validates the measurement list in the following way: first, every entry in the measurement list is checked if it is contained in a database of known hash-values for programs defined as trusted. If the client executes a program that is considered untrusted, the hash will not be found in the database or in case of a virus/malware modifying a trusted program, the hash will be different. In this case, the client is considered untrusted and the attestation fails. If the hash value matches the known (trusted) value, a virtual PCR is extended as described in equation 1. After examining all entries in the measurement list, the RA server checks if the virtual PCR matches the submitted value from client's TPM. This procedure ensures that the submitted measurement list has not been tampered with. The client receives a certificate from the RA server with a timestamp. This certificate can then be used in a following connection to a service provider. The RA process is shown in figure 2. In the current demonstration environment we are not yet able to access the TPM emulator through the QEMU BIOS, preventing a measurement of the boot process. A patched version of the boot loader GRUB [10] exists and is installed in the client. As soon as a working patch for the QEMU BIOS exists, we will be able to establish a chain of trust starting at boot time of the virtual machine.

4 Usage Concepts

Our goal is to integrate the TC concepts in an **IDM** Environment. IDM is concerned with the management of user credentials and the means by which users use them to access different (online) services. A real life person's identity is formed of all attributes that belong to the individual such as name, address, hobbies, banking accounts. The identity can be split into partial identities which consist only of a subset of information, e.g. a drivers license contains name, date of birth, a picture and the type of vehicle a person is entitled to drive, whereas a credit card account contains name, account number and a list of last purchases. Internet usage increases the number of identities, represented by, e.g., different accounts for mail, online-shops, auctions and so on. Every identity contains different types of information about the subject.

One goal is the establishment of trust domains where participants can trust each other. In traditional scenarios trust is based on the fact that the participants know each other, e.g., because they belong to the same company. As the customer-business relation shifts from physical to electronic means it is necessary to develop and establish new ways of trust relationships between enterprises and their customers.

In general, IDM covers several aspects: (i) **Trust** is linked to a set of identity credentials, allowing an individual to be part of a trust domain. (ii) **Anonymity** and **pseudonymity** play an important role in IDM. The level of identity needed for a relationship in a trusted domain has to be considered. (iii) **Authentication** is needed to prove that a claimed identity really belongs to the agent. Examples are passwords, biometric devices or smartcards. (iv) **Authorisation** describes the process of either granting or denying access to a certain service or resource. (v) **Integrity** ensures that a message cannot be changed once it has been sent. (vi) **Non-repudiation** means the evidence for the existence of a certain message can be provided.

Several use cases of IDM can be imagined and are currently being widely promoted. In most web based services, the user needs to sign in for an account in order to access the service. This implies the need for an account management on behalf of the service provider. In an IDM scenario, the provider only has to care about authorisation and has to establish a trust relationship to an identity provider. The client only has to retrieve a ticket incorporating his identity from the identity provider. He then uses the obtained ticket and presents it to the provider without the need of an additional registration. This lowers entry barriers for users that want to access the service.

In existing IDM solutions one security concern is the phishing of the login information needed to sign up with the identity provider. Once this information gets stolen, all login information to services will be exposed. With our solution, the tickets will be build on the client's hardware TPM. As the tickets get bound to the user's device, an interception of login information is rendered useless. In addition, the spread of different, somehow loosely linked partial information leads to certain risks. As users tend to use same login information when registering with different services, gathering and linking informations contained in different identities can lead to a complete profile of an individual. This poses huge privacy concerns potentially enables further attacks such as identity theft where an attacker obtains enough key pieces of personal information to impersonate someone else [15].

We take an approach of trust, such that by transmitting authentication data, an agent enters the domain of trust of a principal. Within authentication, the trustworthiness of the agent can be attested, thus making a statement about the agent's identity and its state. The token used for authentication and attestation is called credential. In existing IDM solutions such as Kerberos, these credentials are embodied in (software) tickets. Using TC concepts we will build trust credentials that rely on the agent's TPM. By the means of mutual agreements trust can be established across different domains. In such an architecture every domain consists of (at least one) identity provider and multiple service providers. An acquired ticket can only be used inside the particular domain. In order to enable ticket usage across multiple domains, either cross certification (one CA signing the public key of the other CA) or a spanning CA can be used. This leads to a high technical overhead if many domains are involved. With the approach of using TC architecture we are be able to establish trust between different domains.

We build our trusted ticket system upon the identities embodied in the AIKs certified by a PCA. The tickets are generated locally on the user's device and the process of ticket acquisition and redemption is bound to the user's hardware TPM chip. The tickets are only be usable from the user's device, and thus prevent attacks that rely on copying the ticket (e.g. phishing). We establish an access control scheme allowing the user to access multiple services by maintaining non-repudiation (by the chain of trust), accountability (by the PCA) and pseudonymity (by the separation of duties), see [12,11].

As described in [14] we create the trusted tickets using an indirection. We use the notation cert(*entity, certificate*) for the **credential of the certified entity**. It is the union of the entity signed with the certificate's private key and the public key *certificate$_{pub}$*. The credential is verified by checking the signature.

First, the AIK representing a certain identity is certified by a PCA, yielding the AIK certificate cert(AIK,PCA$_{cert}$). As AIKs cannot be used to sign arbitrary data, we create a new RSA key pair in the TPM using

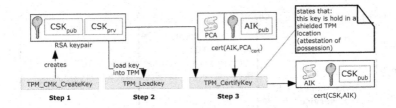

Fig. 3. Creation of the Certified Signing Key (CSK)

the TPM_CMK_CreateKey command. The resulting key pair is loaded into the TPM via the TPM_LoadKey command and then certified by the TPM_CertifyKey command. Using this indirection we are able to create for each AIK a certified key. This so called certified signing key (CSK) can then be used to sign arbitrary data. In order to access a service, a service request R is signed with the CSK and cert(R,CSK) is obtained. The service request R, together with cert(R,CSK), cert(CSK,AIK) and cert(AIK,PCA$_{cert}$) build the credential chain which is transferred to the Service Provider. This data embodies the ticket. By verifying the chain an authorisation decision can be made and access to the service can be granted. The process of CSK generation is detailed in [14] and sketched in Figure 3.

5   Trusted Tickets in Kerberos

This section exhibits how the CSKs can be generated in a Kerberos IDM environment and how the obtained tickets can be integrated into Kerberos.

The **Kerberos** authentication consists of three phases. First, the client requests a ticket granting ticket (TGT) from the Authentication Server (AS). The AS sends the TGT together with an encrypted session key back to the client. Only the client can decrypt the session key with his password. In the next phase, the client uses the TGT to request a service ticket (ST) from the Ticket Granting Server (TGS). The response contains the ST together with a second session key encrypted with the first session key. Finally the client uses the ST to access an application server providing the service. The whole process is shown in Figure 4.

The Kerberos protocol provides the *authorization-data* field which can be used to embed authorisation information into a Kerberos ticket. Referring to [16, p. 57], the usage of the *authorization-data* field is optional. We take advantage of this field and use it to include the information needed to build the trusted ticket. The type of this field is set to AD-IF-RELEVANT, so that servers, that don't understand the embedded information will be able to ignore the included data.

In our design, the AS takes the PCA functionality of signing and thus certifying AIKs. Therefore the client initiates the session by sending the request including authorisation data, the public part of the AIK, the EKC and the cert(AIK,EK) to the AS. By including the cert(AIK,EK) the client states that the AIK has been generated by the TPM hardware the EKC belongs to. The

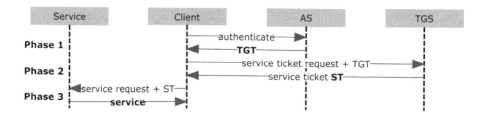

Fig. 4. Flow of the Kerberos protocol

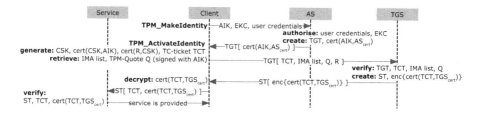

Fig. 5. Protocol of a TC enabled Kerberos Infrastructure

AS then checks the authorisation data provided by the client. By verifying the EKC, the AS verifies that the TPM is implemented by a trustworthy (at least known) manufacturer. Further, by checking the cert(AIK,EK) it can be verified that the AIK belongs to that single TPM. Upon success, the AS issues a certificate cert(AIK,AS$_{cert}$), binding the AIK to the respective identity. The certificate is encapsulated in the *authorization data* field of the TGT. When the client receives the TGT, he can extract the cert(AIK,AS$_{cert}$) from the ticket. By using the AIK certificate, the client is able to create a CSK belonging to this AIK by using the process described in Section 4.

When the client wants to access a certain service, he requests an ST. The client signs the request message R with the CSK and can thus build the credential chain cert(R,CSK), cert(CSK,AIK), cert(AIK,AS$_{cert}$). This credential chain is called TC-Ticket (TCT). Verifying the TCT means to check if the chain resolves to a trustworthy issuer (which is in our case the AS). In order to make a statement about the platform configuration, the client retrieves the IMA measurement list and a TPM quote of the PCR-10, signed with the AIK. The client then sends the service request R, the TCT, the IMA list and the quote enclosed in the TGT to the Ticket Granting Server.

Upon receipt, the TGS first verifies the TGT. If it is issued by a trustworthy AS, the TGS verifies the TCT. Therefore policies for authorisation and agreements on trust have to be established between AS and TGS in advance. Then the TGS will go on with the process of remote attestation as detailed in 3. The TGS can then create the certificate cert(TCT,TGS$_{cert}$), stating that the TCT comes from a valid client in a trustworthy state. Note that the certificate has to be equipped with a timestamp, making it valid only for a short period of time.

Otherwise, the system state could change in a significant way. In order to render eavesdropping useless, the TGS will encrypt the certificate with the public part of the CSK via the Tspi_Data_Bind Operation. Only the client that is in possession of the CSK (and the TPM it was created with) can then decrypt the certificate via the Tspi_Data_Unbind method.

In the case of a successful verification, the TGS issues the ST in which the encrypted cert(TCT,TGS$_{cert}$) is included. The TGS can resolve the credential chain to a single AIK that is certified by the AS. This allows for anonymity of the person using the TGS, as the identity is only known by and revealed to the AS. Only AS is able to de-anonymise users as the platform credentials provide the necessary information. In case of misbehaving users, AS could reveal the personal identity to the TGS.

After decrypting the received certificate from the TGS, the client is able to use the obtained ST together with its own created TCT and the newly received cert(TCT,TGS$_{cert}$) to access a service. The service provider has to verify if (i) the ST is issued by a trustworthy TGS, (ii) the TCT resolves to a trustworthy issuer and (iii) the cert(TCT,TGS$_{cert}$) belongs to the TCT and comes from a trustworthy TGS. The service is then provided to the client.

Note that the cert(TCT,TGS$_{cert}$) contains the signed service request as well as a timestamp. This also allows for protection against double spending of the ticket. The service provider therefore has to keep track of redeemed tickets. As they do not contain any data about the personal identity of the client, only a limited amount of information can be gathered. The client is able to generate a new AIK for every identity he wants to use.

6   Conclusions

We have shown how to integrate the concept of trusted tickets in the Kerberos protocol as an existing IDM solution. The complete process, from authentication over ticket generation to ticket redemption at the service provider is shown. A proof of concept integration into the Kerberos protocol is given. By integrating PCA functionality into the Kerberos AS and remote attestation done by the TGS, we are able to issue tickets bound to the client platform. By the separation between AS and TGS we showed how pseudonymity for the client can be achieved. In some scenarios it might be required to charge the client for accessing a certain service. As mentioned in [14], an additional charging for the use of certain services could easily be implemented by extending the protocol on the part of the AS and TGS entities. Upon issuing a ST for a certain service, the TGS then requests a charging for this ticket at the AS. The AS in turn can then initiate the charging for this ticket at a third party charging service. Upon charging, the charging provider must be able to identify the user by credit card account or similar means. Data protection laws can prevent the charging provider from disclosing identity related information. While this offers a protection for several identity based attacks, such as profiling, identity theft, phishing attacks, TC-based tickets additionally enable a binding of the tickets to the client's hardware. This is an important key in providing security against eavesdropping. The tickets are completely built on the TPM's basic functions. As in other TC applications like Digital Rights Management (DRM), the usage of a certain service is bound to the TPM. If the client's TPM fails, the tickets are no longer be valid. Thus there is no (financial) loss on the side of the service provider. In contrary to DRM where protected content is rendered unprotected and can cause monetary loss to the owner.

Our concept allows to implement multiple service access using one identity (AIK) to retrieve multiple STs. Every instance in the protocol is able to verify the chain of trust upwards to a trustworthy issuer. This concept maintains non-repudiation throughout the whole protocol. In order to enable usage of the tickets in different identity domains there have to be agreements on trust between the service providers and the respective AS and TGS servers. In this usage scenario, protection against multiple spending has to be implemented. Further usage of TC concepts could include an adaption of the attestation protocol which allows service providers to report their status to the clients. Such usage could prevent malicious service providers from stealing customer data, further increasing the security of online transactions.

References

1. Kerberos: The Network Authentication Protocol, http://web.mit.edu/Kerberos/
2. Nanodatacenters / Results / Security Experimentation Environment, http://nanodatacenters.eu/
3. QEMU, http://bellard.org/qemu/
4. [Qemu-devel] [PATCH] Add TPM support. http://www.mail-archive.com/qemu-devel@nongnu.org/msg13408.html
5. Software-based TPM Emulator, http://tpm-emulator.berlios.de/
6. SourceForge.net: Integrity Measurement Architecture (IMA), http://sourceforge.net/projects/linux-ima
7. TPM/J Java-based API for the Trusted Platform Module (TPM), http://projects.csail.mit.edu/tc/tpmj/
8. Gürgens, S., Rudolph, C.: AIK Certification. Technical report, Fraunhofer SIT / BSI. 13 (April 2006) (unpublished)
9. Trusted Computing Group: Home, https://www.trustedcomputinggroup.org/home
10. Trusted GRUB, http://trousers.sourceforge.net/grub.html
11. Fichtinger, B.: Trusted infrastructures for identities. Master's thesis, Fachhochschule Hagenberg, Austria (May 2007)
12. Fichtinger, B., Herrmann, E., Kuntze, N., Schmidt, A.U.: Trusted infrastructures for identities. In: Grimm, R., Hass, B. (eds.) Proc. 5th Internat. Workshop Virtual Goods, Koblenz, Hauppauge, New York, October 11-13, 2007. Nova Publishers (2008)
13. Gasser, M., Goldstein, A., Kaufman, C., Lampson, B.: The Digital Distributed System Security Architecture. In: Proc. 12th NIST-NCSC National Computer Security Conference, pp. 305–319 (1989)

14. Kuntze, N., Mähler, D., Schmidt, A.U.: Employing Trusted Computing for the forward pricing of pseudonyms in reputation systems. In: Proc. Axmedis 2006, Atti del Convegno, pp. 145–149. Firenze University Press (2006)
15. Liberty Alliance. Whitepaper: Identity Theft Primer (December 2005)
16. Neuman, C., Yu, T., Hartman, S., Raeburn, K.: The Kerberos Network Authentication Service (V5). RFC 4120, updated by RFCs 4537, 5021
17. TCG. TCG TPM Specification Version 1.2 Revision 103. Technical report, tcg (2007), Trusted Computing Group (retrieved February 29, 2008), https://www.trustedcomputinggroup.org/groups/tpm/

A Policy Based Approach for the Management of Web Browser Resources to Prevent Anonymity Attacks in Tor

Guillermo Navarro-Arribas[1] and Joaquin Garcia-Alfaro[2]

[1] IIIA – Artificial Intelligence Research Institute, CSIC – Spanish Council for
Scientic Research, Campus UAB s/n, 08193 Bellaterra, Catalonia, Spain
guille@iiia.csic.es
[2] UOC – Universitat Oberta de Catalunya, Rambla Poble Nou 156,
08018 Barcelona, Catalonia, Spain
joaquin.garcia-alfaro@acm.org

Abstract. Web browsers are becoming the universal interface to reach applications and services related with these systems. Different browsing contexts may be required in order to reach them, e.g., use of VPN tunnels, corporate proxies, anonymisers, etc. By browsing *context* we mean how the user browsers the Web, including mainly the concrete configuration of its browser. When the context of the browser changes, its security requirements also change. In this work, we present the use of authorisation policies to automatise the process of controlling the resources of a Web browser when its context changes. The objective of our proposal is oriented towards easing the adaptation to the security requirements of the new context and enforce them in the browser without the need for user intervention. We present a concrete application of our work as a *plug-in* for the adaption of security requirements in Mozilla/Firefox browser when a context of anonymous navigation through the Tor network is enabled.

1 Introduction

The Web is increasingly becoming a universal interface for the development of all kinds of applications: from traditional electronic banking and electronic mail, to text processors or even elaborated social networks. As the Web is evolving, the surrounding and supporting technologies are becoming more complex. This is specially relevant in applications that enable the interaction with the Web from the client side: the Web browsers. The current complexity of the Web has a direct impact on the security of such applications and more precisely in the treatment of its resources. Attacks against Web browsers can compromise the security and privacy of its users. This can have serious consequences given the pervasive presence of this piece of software in, for instance, important critical systems in industries such as health care, banking, government administration, and so on. Let us mention, for instance, the case of H.D. Moore, the lead developer of the Metasploit Project [12]. One of his projects is based on the exploitation of browser misconfiguration, such as permission of Java and JavaScript code when browsing anonymously through the *The second generation Onion Router* (Tor) network [5], with the objective of catching digital pirates and child pornographers [9]. Even if we agree in the legitimacy of these techniques for the discovery of criminals, these same

D. Gritzalis and J. Lopez (Eds.): SEC 2009, IFIP AICT 297, pp. 164–175, 2009.

techniques can lead to violations of fair users. For instance, similar techniques were used by Dan Egerstad in November 2007 [10], for capturing sensible information from legitimate Tor users. As a result of these experiments, several government, embassy, NGO, and other corporate user accounts and passwords were reported and disclosed.

We are currently working on the implementation of a contextual XACML [7] policy manager for Web browsers. The main objective of our work is to be able to automatise the management of resources associated with the browser in a dynamic and flexible way. The use and enforcement of different security contexts will also help in adapting the browsers to the security needs of the working environment of a given user. Such an automatism aims to lead to an error-free process in which non-expert users are protected about security and privacy weaknesses due to browser misconfiguration. We present in this article a concrete application of our proposal to adapt the browser security requirements when an anonymous navigation context is in use. By browsing *context* we mean how the user browsers the Web, including mainly the concrete configuration of its browser. We also describe in this work the current development of our proposal as a *plug-in* for the Mozilla/Firefox family of Web browsers. We consider that our approach must be seen as a design recommendation for future applications dealing with the Web paradigm.

2   Overview of the Proposal and Plan of the Paper

The article is organised as follows. In this Sec. 2 we introduce the XACML language, and the development of our proposal as a *plug-in* for Mozilla/Firefox browsers. In Sec. 3 we show a concrete application of our proposal to adapt the security requirements of Mozilla/Firefox to anonymous Web browsing through the Tor project infrastructure. We conclude the article in Sec. 4.

2.1   XACML

XACML (*eXtensible Access Control Markup Language*) is an XML based standard language [7], which provides the ability to specify both the access control policy and the request/response messages.

In XACML, an access control policy presents an specific format, having as the main element the *rule*. Each rule has an associated *target*, which determines to what (or who) the rule is applied, an *effect*, which is normally *permit* or *deny*, and a condition. If the condition is evaluated in a favourable manner, the result of the evaluation of the rule is the one determined by its effect. One or more rules are associated to a *policy*, which also can specify a target and *obligations*. Such obligations specify actions to be performed by the policy verifier when the policy is applied [16] (normally, these actions will be performed by a Policy Enforcement Point, e.g., a web browser enforcement agent). Finally, one or more policies are included in a *policy set* which can also have an associated target and obligations.

In XACML, the combination of the results of evaluating the rules included in the same policy and the evaluation of the policies included in the same policy set, is given by the combining algorithms. Such algorithms are not only used for the combination of rules and policies, but also for conflict resolution, because they are used when more than one rule or policy is applicable to the same *target*. There is a set of standard algorithms applied both to the combination of rules and the combination of policies. Among them, we remark the following ones:

- *deny-overrides*: an evaluation with *deny* effect takes precedence over the rest.
- *permit-overrides*: an evaluation with *permit* effect takes precedence over the rest.

In our case, in a very summarised way, by using XACML, we can specify the traditional tuple 'subject-resource-action' adapted to our concrete problem and context. That is, specify if a given script (subject) is allowed or not to access and/or modify (action) a given browser resource (object). In Sec. 3.3 we show with more detail how are the policies of our proposal defined.

2.2   The Plug-In for Mozilla/Firefox of Our Proposal

The specific implementation of our authorisation proposal, from now on XAPO (*XAcml Policy Officer*), is based on the Mozilla development framework for the implementation of browser extensions (plug-ins) in the Mozilla/Firefox Web browser. The development of XAPO is mainly based on Java, JavaScript, and XUL (*XML User Interface Language*) [6]. The plug-in is executed in the browser through the *chrome* interface used by the Mozilla applications [11]. From this interface, XAPO, as any other code executed in *chrome* mode, can perform the actions required by our proposal such as access to configuration options, storage and reading preferences, or activate and deactivate browser components (i.e Java, JavaScript, or Shockwave/Flash, etc.). This is done through the XPCOM interface of the Mozilla/Firefox browser. This option is only available in version 3 of the browser. For the implementation of the XACML components we have used *SunXACML* [18], an open source implementation of the XACML standard in Java. Such implementation, is executed inside XAPO by making use of the *LiveConnect* interface provided by Mozilla. The installation of all the set of components of XAPO is done with a single *xpi* package. The current version of XAPO is available under demand. In the following section we present the use of XAPO to adapt the security requirements of the Mozilla/Firefox browser when an anonymous browsing context is activated.

3   Preventing Attacks on a Context of Anonymous Browsing

We present in this section a specific application of our proposal. It allows us to adapt the security requirements of a browser when a context of anonymity is enabled on it. Our example scenario is based on the anonymous infrastructure of the Tor project. We introduce in the following subsection some characteristics of Tor, as well as the specific attack which is going to be addressed by our proposal.

3.1   The Anonymity Infrastructure of Tor

Several anonymity designs have been proposed in the literature with the objective of hiding senders identities for privacy purposes. From simple proxies to complex systems, anonymity networks can offer either strong anonymity for high latency services (e.g., email and Usenet messages) or weak anonymity for low-latency services (e.g., Web browsing). The most widely-used of the latter solutions is based on anonymous mixes and onion routing [15]. It is distributed as a free software implementation known as *The second generation Onion Router* (*Tor*) [5]. It can be installed as an end-user application on a wide range of operating systems to redirect the traffic of low-latency services with a very acceptable overhead.

The Tor objective is the protection of the anonymity of a sender as well as the contents of its messages. To do so, it transforms cryptographically those messages and mixes them via a circuit of routers. Through this circuit, routers transport the original message in an unpredictable way. The content of each message is moreover re-encrypted within each router with the objective of achieving anonymous communication even if a set of routers are compromised by an attacker. As soon as a router receives a new message, it decrypts its corresponding encryption layer with its private key to obtain the following hop and the encryption key of the following router in the path. This path is initially defined at the beginning of the process. Only the entity that creates the circuit — and which remains at the sender's side during all the process — knows the complete path to deliver a given message. The last router of the path, the *exit* node, decrypts the last layer and delivers an unencrypted version of the message to its target.

The maturity of the project and its low impact to the performance of on-line services make the infrastructure of Tor a promising solution to anonymously browse on Internet. To obtain this low impact over the performance of the services tunnelled by Tor, it relies on a very pragmatic threat model. Such a model assumes that adversaries can compromise some fraction of the onion routers in the network. If so, adversaries can not only observe but also manipulate some fraction of the network traffic of Tor. A first implication of this assumption is that the exit node has a complete view of the sender's messages. Therefore, without other countermeasures, it could perform a *Man-in-the-Middle* attack to forge answers. As a result, a malicious onion router acting as the exit router could try to redirect the client to malicious services or to perform denial of service. A second implication of the threat model of Tor is the possibility of suffering traffic analysis attacks with the objective of tracing back the sender's origin or to degrade Tor's anonymity. Several traffic analysis attacks against Tor have been reported in the literature, such as [2,13,19].

A third problem raises when the configuration of a browser is not handled properly. Beyond the proper installation and configuration of the software downloaded from the Tor project, some aspects of the browser must be adapted. Anonymous browsing with Tor requires not only different habits, but also reconfiguration of some resources. It is necessary to disable, for example, the execution of JavaScript and Java code, as well as plug-ins like Flash, ActiveX, etc. The use of cookies associated with previous visited sites, on the other hand, must also be taken into account. It might be relatively simple for an attacker to manipulate these components in order to obtain the identity or location of the user (e.g., by obtaining a public IP address associated with the user). We show in the following subsection a practical example that shows how to obtain the IP address of a browser configured to browse through the Tor network. The attack exploits a misconfigured browser that allows the execution of Java code.

3.2 Bypassing Tor via Attacks Targeting Web Browsers

In order to browse through the network of Tor, users should first configure their browsers to redirect its requests and responses via an HTTP proxy, such as Privoxy [14]. In fact, not only HTTP traffic must be redirected by the proxy. Any other traffic, such as DNS requests and responses, must be redirected. Privoxy and Tor allow these later redirections through the use of the SOCKS protocol [8]. There are many other resources on the browser that could leak information if they are not redirected by the proxy. The large amount of options on current browsers leads to an error prone process. The activation and execution of code by plug-ins, such as Flash, Java, ActiveX, etc., increases the dynamism of Web services, but also increases the number of potential targets to exploit. If these resources are not properly managed, an attacker can get control of them and violate user's anonymity via covered channels.

In [1], Abbott et al. describe the use of this kind of attacks, executed within Web browsers, in order to bypass the anonymity of Tor. Forcing the user to visit a specific Web site, e.g., using social engineering, phishing, or *Man-in-the-Middle* attacks, a malicious code embedded within the pages of such service opens a secret channel between the user and the attacker's Web domain. Later, performing an analysis of the traffic exchanged with each victim, the attacker collects and stores data related with the resources of each browser (e.g., IP addresses, operating system, browser characteristics, etc.). It is important to note that the collection of this information is not indeed an attack against Tor's infrastructure (cf. Fig. 1). The attack relies on the exploitation of tools and browser runtime components. More specifically, the attack is exploiting browser misconfiguration to bypass its proxy settings.

In [4], Christensen et al. extend this previous attack in order to compromise the identity of Tor users without the necessity of controlling end services (i.e., the visited Web service). The attacker only needs to control exit nodes of Tor. From these nodes, and modifying HTTP traffic, the attacker can successfully execute a *Man-in-the-Middle* attack to reveal user and hidden service identities. The modification of HTTP traffic aims at marking the traffic. For example, the use of HTML elements of type *iframe*, can allow the attacker to include unique references leading to malicious Web sites, as well as to associate a specific *cookie* to collect user data. This reference can force the browser to download malicious code, such as Java or Flash code. If the plug-in that is required by such code is enabled, the code can manage to steal user information and direct the output towards the attacker. Similarly to the attack shown in Fig. 1, the attacker can post-process the information in order to perform an analysis of traffic trying to reveal

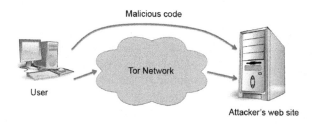

Fig. 1. Example of a Web attack to bypass the anonymity of Tor

the identity and activities of the set of victim users. Abbot et al. show in [1] how this and other similar attacks can be extended in order to increase the chance of discovery of Tor users and hidden services.

3.3   Using XAPO and XACML Policies to Prevent the Attack

To prevent attacks against the anonymity provided by Tor as the one described in Sec. 3.2, we use a concrete type of policy, which allows not only to prevent such attacks but also to introduce enough flexibility and fine-grained specification to be adapted to several contexts and degrees of anonymity.

The XACML policy used is divided in two specific policies. On one hand there is a general policy, which explicitly determines the browser resources that have to be protected: Java, JavaScript, . . . and on the other hand there is a *whitelist*-like policy that provides a fine-grained control of the trusted domains for which the activation and/or access to concrete resources is allowed.

The first policy is the *generic-tor-policy*. It is composed of a *policy* element containing a rule for each browser resource to be protected. The effect of such rules is always *deny*, indicating that such resource cannot be accessed when the policy is enforced (c.f. Fig. 2).

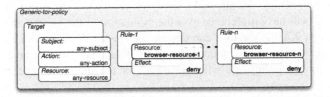

Fig. 2. Generic-tor-policy

The main purpose of the *generic-tor-policy* is to globally avoid problems such as the one described in Sec. 3.2. To that end, the access to all sensitive resources is explicitly denied when Tor is in use. Some important resources that need to be protected are [1]:

- Browser plug-ins such as: Java, Flash, ActiveX, RealPlayer, Quicktime, Adobe PDF, ... One can specify in the policy plug-ins one by one or use the special resource *all-plugins*. With this last reference, XAPO looks all the plug-ins currently installed in the browsers and turns them off.
- Cookies: it is important to protect the access to cookies, which could have been created previously to the activation of the Tor navigation.

As it can be appreciated, this policy is very restrictive and can limit the functionality of the applications accessed by the user. In order to improve the user experience, we consider it important to provide a *whitelist*-like policy to allow the definition of trusted domains, which are allowed to access some browser resources. This avoids the common scenario where a user is using two different browsers, one with Tor activated and with

---

[1] The policy may include other needed resources a part from plug-ins and cookies.

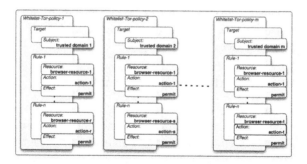

Fig. 3. Tor whitelist policy

a minimal functionality and another one without Tor and with a compete or extended functionality. That is, the user can determine some trusted applications and allow them to access given resources without giving up the anonymity measures provided by Tor and XAPO in the other domains.

The *tor-whitelist-policy* defines the domains which are allowed to access concrete browser resources. For each trusted domain, there is an specific policy, which has rules to describe which actions are allowed over which resources. The effect of these rules is *permit* and it will have preference over the evaluation of the *generic-tor-policy* (c.f. Fig. 3). Through XAPO, the user can choose the trusted domains and enable all the desired browser options and resources for them. This changes are stored in the corresponding whitelist policy and will take effect for the successive executions of the browser.

Both the generic policy and the whitelist policy are combined in an XACML policy set by the *permit-overrides* policy combining algorithm (c.f. Sec. 2.1). This makes the whitelist policy to take precedence over the generic one. Or in other words, the whitelist policy expresses *exceptions* of the generic policy.

3.4   Example of XAPO Policies for Tor

In this section we will show a simple example of XAPO policies for Tor in order to ensure an additional enforcement level and to prevent attacks against the anonymity of users even when they are browsing with Tor enabled. The description of the policies has been simplified to improve its legibility. At the same time, the example is quite simple, but it shows clearly and concisely, the way these policies work.

In the following listing (Listing 1) we show an example of a *generic-tor-policy*. The policy includes three rules: *java-plugin, javascript-plugin, cookies*. The first one makes XAPO to disable the Java plug-in, the second ones disables the JavaScript interpreter, and the third one prevents the reading of cookies for all domains.

Following the example, the user may want to activate the JavaScript interpreter and the Java plug-in but just for a concrete trusted email Web application (mail. trusted.domain.org), which is accessed through HTTPS. Instead of having to change or disable the Tor generic policy or initiate a new session without Tor, the user

```xml
<Policy PolicyId="tor-generic:default-tor-firefox"
        RuleCombiningAlgId="deny-overrides">
  <Target> ... </Target>
  <Rule RuleId="java-plugin" Effect="Deny">
    <Target>
      ...
      <Resources>
        <Resource>
          <ResourceMatch
              MatchId="function:anyURI-equal">
            <AttributeValue DataType="XMLSchema ∩
                #anyURI">urn:browser:plugin:java
  <Resources>
    <Resource>
      <ResourceMatch MatchId="function:∩
                      anyURI-equal">
        <AttributeValue DataType="XMLSchema∩
                        #anyURI">
          urn:browser:plugin:javascript
        </AttributeValue>
        <ResourceAttributeDesignator
            DataType="XMLSchema#anyURI"
            AttributeId ="resource:resource-id"/>
      </ResourceMatch>
    </Resource>
  </Resources>
    </Target>
  </Rule>
  <Rule RuleId="cookies" Effect="Deny">
    <Target>
      <Subjects><AnySubject/></Subjects>
      <Actions>
        <Attribute AttributeId ="action:action-id"
                   DataType="XMLSchema#string">
          <AttributeValue>read</AttributeValue>
```
```xml
        </AttributeValue>
        <ResourceAttributeDesignator
            DataType="XMLSchema#anyURI"
            AttributeId ="resource:resource-id"/>
      </ResourceMatch>
    </Resource>
  </Resources>
    </Target>
  </Rule>
  <Rule RuleId="javascrip-plugin" Effect="Deny">
    <Target>
      ...
      </Attribute>
      </Actions>
      <Resources>
        <Resource>
          <ResourceMatch
              MatchId="function:anyURI-equal">
            <AttributeValue
                DataType="XMLSchema#anyURI">
              urn:browser:document.cookie
            </AttributeValue>
            <ResourceAttributeDesignator
                DataType="XMLSchema#anyURI"
                AttributeId ="resource:resource-id"/>
          </ResourceMatch>
        </Resource>
      </Resources>
    </Target>
  </Rule>
</Policy>
```

Listing 1. Generic policy for Tor

```xml
<Policy PolicyId="tor-whitelist:mail "
        RuleCombiningAlgId="permit-overrides">
  <Target>
    <Subjects>
      <Attribute AttributeId ="subject:subject-id"
                 DataType="XMLSchema#anyURI">
        <AttributeValue>
          https: // mail. trusted .domain.org
        </AttributeValue>
      </Attribute>
    </Subjects>
    ...
  </Target>
  <Rule RuleId="java-rule" Effect="Permit">
    <Target>
      ...
      <Resources>
        <Resource>
          <ResourceMatch
              MatchId="function:anyURI-equal">
            <AttributeValue DataType="XMLSchema∩
                #anyURI">urn:browser:plugin:java
            </AttributeValue>
            <ResourceAttributeDesignator
                DataType="XMLSchema#anyURI"
                AttributeId ="resource:resource-id"/>
          </ResourceMatch>
```
```xml
        </Resource>
      </Resources>
    </Target>
  </Rule>
  <Rule RuleId="javascrip-rule" Effect="Permit">
    <Target>
      ...
      <Resources>
        <Resource>
          <ResourceMatch
              MatchId="function:anyURI-equal">
            <AttributeValue DataType="XMLSchema∩
                #anyURI">urn:browser:plugin:javascript
            </AttributeValue>
            <ResourceAttributeDesignator
                DataType="XMLSchema#anyURI"
                AttributeId ="resource:resource-id"/>
          </ResourceMatch>
        </Resource>
      </Resources>
    </Target>
  </Rule>
</Policy>
```

Listing 2. Tor-whitelist policy for the domain trusted.domain.org can include a whitelist policy to make XAPO allow the execution of JavaScript code from the trusted domain. The following listing (Listing 2) shows a policy to apply the corresponding domain with two rules, one to activate the Java plug-in and another for JavaScript.

Finally, in the following listing we show another whitelist policy (Listing 3), which tells XAPO to enable JavaScript only for the domain `trusted-bank.org`.

```
<Policy PolicyId="tor-whitelist:bank"                      MatchId="function:anyURI-equal">
        RuleCombiningAlgId="permit-overrides">                <AttributeValue
    <Target>                                                      DataType="XMLSchema#anyURI">
        <Subjects>                                                browser:plugin:javascript
            <Attribute AttributeId ="subject:subject-id"      </AttributeValue>
                    DataType="XMLSchema#anyURI">              <ResourceAttributeDesignator
                <AttributeValue>trusted-bank.org</AttributeValue>      DataType="XMLSchema#anyURI"
            </Attribute>                                              AttributeId ="resource:resource-id"/>
        </Subjects>                                           </ResourceMatch>
        ...                                                 </Resource>
    </Target>                                             </Resources>
    <Rule RuleId="javascrip-rule" Effect="Permit">        </Target>
        <Target>                                          </Rule>
            <Subjects><AnySubject/></Subjects>          </Policy>
            <Actions><AnyAction/></Actions>
            <Resources>
                <Resource>
                    <ResourceMatch
```

Listing 3. Tor-whitelist policy for the domain trusted-bank.org

As it can be seen, the policy allows the activation of the JavaScript interpreter for the concrete domain through the corresponding rule.

The three policies we have seen in the example, are combined in a policy set. A simplified example of such policy set can be seen in the following listing (Listing 4).

```
<PolicySet PolicySetId="xapo:tor-policyset"        </PolicyIdReference>
        PolicyCombiningAlgId="permit-overrides">    <PolicyIdReference>
    <Target />                                        tor-whitelist:bank
    <PolicyIdReference>                             </PolicyIdReference>
        tor-generic:default-tor-firefox            </PolicySet>
    </PolicyIdReference>
    <PolicyIdReference>
        tor-whitelist:mail
```

Listing 4. Policy set example for Tor

To conclude this section, we show with the practical example presented in Figs. 4(a) and 4(b), the way the activation of XAPO prevents the attacks seen in Sec. 3.2. The browser used is the Mozilla/Firefox 3 Beta 1, configured with XAPO and the Torbutton extension [17] (used for the automatic configuration of Privoxy in the browsing preferences of Mozilla/Firefox). As it has already been discussed, the elevated number of configuration options present in a Mozilla/Firefox browser make it possible, without the proper measures, to third parties to violate the anonymous channels provided by Tor and retrieve without problems the identity of the browser. The attack shown

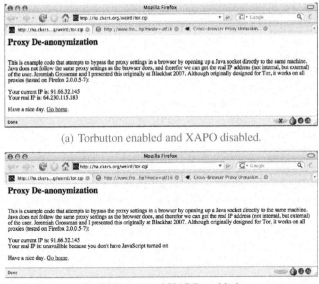

(a) Torbutton enabled and XAPO disabled.

(b) Torbutton and XAPO enabled.

Fig. 4. (a): Example of an attack to bypass the configuration of Privoxy in a Mozilla/Firefox browser with the Torbutton extension enabled and the XAPO extension disabled. The attack opens an addition channel between the execution environment of the browser and the attacker and, through this channel, it extracts the information associated with the browser; (b): Prevention of the attack by enabling the XAPO extension.

exploits the use of a Java code executed from JavaScript in order to open a socket through *LiveConnect*. This code makes an HTTP request to the server hosting the web page (http://ha.ckers.org/weird/tor.cgi). Given that the request does not go through the nodes of the Tor network, after a simple analysis of the received request, and automatically, the attacker of the visited web site gets to know and shows in the screen information associated to the user, such as the IP address. Fig. 4(b) shows how the activation of XAPO and thus the protections of resources associated with the XAPO policies, prevents the creation of the channel between the attacker and the victim browser.

4 Conclusions

In this article we have presented a proposal to apply security policies in a Web browser. More precisely, we have presented a Mozilla/Firefox extension, which allows the use of policies expressed in the XACML standard language to protect the resources of the browser. Furthermore, we have shown how this extension, named XAPO, can be used to enhance the anonymity of the users as a complement to the network infrastructure of the Tor project.

Tor suffers some security problems, since there are already known attacks, which can violate the anonymity of its users. By using a malicious code based on, for example Java or Flash animations, an attacker can set up a direct connection with Web servers under its control and the browser, jeopardising the anonymity of the user. Although the attack is actually exploiting the tools and the external environment of the Tor network, there are attacks in the literature (see, for instance, [1]) showing how to extend this and other similar attacks with the aim of augmenting the probabilities of an attacker to violate the anonymity of the users and services hided behind the network of the Tor project.

Our proposal allows to prevent such attacks by defining an enhanced security policy oriented to Tor, which guarantees to the user a better protection of his identity and sensitive information. To that end, the policy allows the definition of the browser resources that have to be protected as an additional measure to the protection already provided by Tor. Such policy is flexible enough to be adapted to all the browsing habits of the user. For example, while it provides a complete protection, it also allows the definition of a *whitelist* of trusted domains, which are allowed to use some given resources, improving the browsing experience of the user

Currently, the prototype of the proposal is being developed as an extension of the Mozilla/Firefox browser, but we are working on the development of equivalent extension for other browser such as Safari, or Internet Explorer. The use of an standard language such as XACML, allows to easily reuse and interchange the policies between different browsers.

Acknowledgement. Partial support by the Spanish MEC (projects eAEGIS TSI2007-65406-C03-02, and ARES - CONSOLIDER INGENIO 2010 CSD2007-00004) is acknowledged.

References

1. Abbott, T., Lai, K., Lieberman, M., Price, E.: Browser-Based Attacks on Tor. In: Borisov, N., Golle, P. (eds.) PET 2007. LNCS, vol. 4776, pp. 184–199. Springer, Heidelberg (2007)
2. Bauer, K., McCoy, D., Grunwald, D., Kohno, T., Sicker, D.: Low-resource routing attacks against Tor. In: ACM workshop on Privacy in electronic society, pp. 11–20 (2007)
3. Chaum, D.: Untraceable electronic mail, return addresses, and digital pseudonyms. Communications of the ACM 24(2), 84–88 (1981)
4. Christensen, A., et al.: Practical Onion Hacking. FortConsult (October 2006)
5. Dingledine, R., Mathewson, N., Syverson, P.F.: Tor: The second-generation Onion Router. In: 13th conference on USENIX Security Symposium (2004)
6. Ginda, R.: Writing a Mozilla Application with XUL and Javascript. O'Reilly, USA (2000)
7. Godik, S., et al.: eXtensible Access Control Markup Language (XACML) Version 2. Standard, OASIS (February 2005)
8. Leech, M., et al.: SOCKS Protocol Version 5. RFC1928 (March 1996)
9. Lemos, R.: Tor hack proposed to catch criminals. SecurityFocus (March 2007), http://www.securityfocus.com/news/11447
10. Lemos, R.: Embassy leaks highlight pitfalls of Tor. SecurityFocus (September 2007), http://www.securityfocus.com/news/11486
11. Mcfarlane, N.: Rapid Application Development with Mozilla. Prentice Hall PTR, Englewood Cliffs (2004)
12. Moore, H.D., et al.: The Metasploit Project, http://www.metasploit.com/
13. Murdoch, S.J., Danezis, G.: Low-cost traffic analysis of Tor. In: IEEE Symposium on Security and Privacy, pp. 183–195 (2005)

14. Privoxy - Home Page, http://www.privoxy.org/
15. Reed, M.G., Syverson, P.F., Goldschlag, D.M.: Anonymous connections and onion routing. IEEE Journal on Selected Areas in Communications 16(4), 482–494 (1998)
16. Sloman, M.: Policy Driven Management for Distributed Systems. Journal of Network and Systems Management 2, part 4 (1994)
17. Perry, M., Squires, S.: Torbutton, https://www.torproject.org/torbutton/
18. Sun Microsystems SunXACML, http://sunxacml.sourceforge.net
19. Wright, M.K., Adler, M., Levine, B.N., Shields, C.: Passive-Logging Attacks Against Anonymous Communications Systems. ACM Transactions on Information and System Security (TISSEC) 11(2), Article 7, 1–33 (2008)
20. Yavatkar, R., Pendarakis, D., Guerin, R.: A Framework for Policy-based Admission Control RFC 2753. The Internet Society (January 2000)

A Policy Language for Modelling Recommendations*

Anas Abou El Kalam and Philippe Balbiani

Université de Toulouse, IRIT
firstname.lastname@irit.fr

Abstract. While current and emergent applications become more and more complex, most of existing security policies and models only consider a yes/no response to the access requests. Consequently, modelling, formalizing and implementing permissions, obligations and prohibitions do not cover the richness of all the possible scenarios. In fact, several applications have access rules with the recommendation access modality. In this paper we focus on the problem of formalizing security policies with recommendation needs. The aim is to provide a generic domain-independent formal system for modelling not only permissions, prohibitions and obligations, but also recommendations. In this respect, we present our logic-based language, the semantics, the truth conditions, our axiomatic as well as inference rules. We also give a representative use case with our specification of recommendation requirements. Finally, we explain how our logical framework could be used to query the security policy and to check its consistency.

1 Problem Statement

Authorization aims at allowing legitimate actions: it forbids non-authorized users to carry out actions and forbids internal users to carry out non-authorized actions. Basically, in order to define authorized actions, we should establish a security policy. The Common Criteria define an *"organizational security policy"* as: *a set of security rules, procedures, or guidelines imposed by an actual or hypothetical organization in the operational environment* [1]. Such an organizational security policy usually relies on an *access control policy* [2]. The latter is generally specified through: (1) the security objectives that must be satisfied, e.g., *"classified information must remain secret"*; and (2) the rules expressing how the system may evolve in a secure way, e.g., *"the owner of an information is allowed to grant a read access right on the information to other users"*. An access control model is often used to rigorously specify and reason on the access control policy (e.g., to verify its consistency).

Unfortunately, while security models play an important role in any system, most researches on this topic are based on limited concepts, and do not capture all the richness of current and emergent applications. In particular, most of traditional policies are static and only make yes/no decisions in response to user requests.

Recently, several works was intended to model obligations [3] [4] [5] [6]. However, up to our knowledge, there is no existing work on recommendations, while this notion became extremely important in real applications. If we take health care systems as an example, most of the current regulations are in fact recommendations or guidelines: recommendations of the General Assembly of United Nations [7], Recommendations of the Council of Europe [8] [9], Guidelines of the European Parliament [10], etc.

---

* This work is supported by the ADCN Airbus contract and by the European NoE NewCom+.

D. Gritzalis and J. Lopez (Eds.): SEC 2009, IFIP AICT 297, pp. 176–189, 2009.

Similarly, in the critical infrastructures area, organizations such as the European Councils [11], the International Risk Governance Council (IGRC) [12], the North American Electric Reliability Council (NERC), etc. state several recommendations to protect these infrastructures (e.g., Electrical power grid) [13]. In these legislation and documents, we find rules such as: *"it is recommended that ..."*, *"it is inadvisable that ..."*.

However, while security policies should translate these recommendations to security rules, there is no logical framework that helps to adequately formalize this task. Basically, when building systems, we need firstly to precisely specify the underlying requirements (e.g., recommendations); and secondly, we need axioms, methods and tools for reasoning on these concepts. To date, these problems have not been really addressed. Dealing whit these issues, this paper is organized as follow. In Section 2, we discuss the security requirements already handled by classical security policies and models. After that, Section 3 defines the new recommendation access control modality. Then, Section 4 presents our new logical-based framework for modelling recommendations. In particular, we will define our new Recommendation language (RL), the related semantics, truth conditions and axiomatic. Then, Section 5 describes some ideas to query the security policy and to verify its consistency / coherence. Finally, Section 6 draws conclusions an perspectives.

2 Traditional Security Policies and Models

A security policy specifies, usually in a textual form, who has access to what, when and in which conditions? Nevertheless, the security policy does not guarantee a secure and correct functioning of the system. The security policy can indeed be badly designed or intentionally / accidentally violated. Consequently, it is important to associate a model to it; this kind of "precise statement" helps to: abstract the policy and handle its complexity; represent the secure states of a system (i.e., states that satisfies the security objectives) as well as the way in which the system may evolve (the possible executions of the system); verify the coherence of the security policy and detect possible conflicting situations (e.g., situation where a certain user has the recommendation (or the permission) and the prohibition to carry out a certain action on the same object); guarantee that all the security objectives are covered by the security mechanisms implementing the policy; etc.

We can assert that, until now, it is not possible to explicitly specify recommendations in existing access control models (e.g., discretionary "DAC" [14] [15], mandatory access control "MAC" [16] and Role-based Access Control "RBAC" [17]). For instance, the HRU model [15] represents with a matrix $M(s, o)$ the actions that a subject s is allowed to carry out on an object o. Similarly, in Role Based-Access Control (RBAC) roles are assigned to users, permissions are assigned to roles and users acquire permissions by playing roles [17].

Besides that, some works have addressed the notion of explicit prohibitions and obligations. For example, in the OrBAC model [18], security rules have the form *AccessModality (org; r; v; a; c)*; while *AccessModality* is a Permission, Obligation or a Prohibition. This rule means: in the context *c*, organization *org* grants role *r* the permission or the obligation or the prohibition to perform activity *a* on view *v*.

In XACML [19], obligations are a set of operations that must be fulfilled in conjunction with an authorization decision (permit or deny).

Bettini *et al.* distinguish between *provisions* and *obligations* [3]. Provisions are conditions that need to be satisfied or actions that must be performed before a decision is rendered, while obligations are actions that must be fulfilled by either the users or the system after the decision.

Hilty *et al.* Define the OSL, an Obligation Specification Language that allows formulating a wide range of usage control requirements [6]. They differentiate between usage and obligational formulae. Usage is concerned with operations (e.g., processing, rendering, execution, management, or distribution) on data that must be protected; while obligational formulae are conditions on the usage of data, e.g., "delete document D within 30 days". An obligational formula becomes an obligation once a data consumer is obliged to satisfy it, i.e., once the data consumer has received the data and committed to the condition.

3   The Recommendation Access Modality

By modelling permissions, obligations and prohibitions, traditional access control policies and models control who can (permission), must (obligation) and cannot (prohibition) access to data respectively. However, these access modalities do not deal with situations where the system interact with the user by advising him (not obliging him) to do something, and if the user does not follow this advise, he/she accepts the consequences of his/her action. In this respect, it seems interesting to consider an access modality that is stronger than permissions but not as restricting as obligations. This new modality is actually a *recommendation*.

For example, the law [20] gives patients the right to access their medical files, but it recommends that this access be done through the attending physician (because certain notions in the medical file could be badly understood by the patient, while the physician can understand and explain correctly the situation). The same law stipulates that if in addition the patient is minor or suffers from psychological disorders, it is *recommended* that he/she be accompanied with his/her tutor.

In fact, we see that this access is stronger than permissions (as the patient accepts the consequences if he/she does not respect the recommendation) but not as restricting as obligations (as he/she is not obliged to respect the recommendation, i.e., he/she can access his/her medical file).

Let us take another example, the Council of Europe Recommendation No. R (97) 5 "*on the Protection of Medical Data*" [9]. This legislation recommends that medical data shall be obtained from the data subject. It is not an obligation, as medical data can be obtained from other sources in certain situations (e.g., in particular if the data subject is not in a position to provide the required data). And in the same time, this access is stronger than a permission, as the data subject could ask for explanation / justification if the recommendation is not respected, and in certain situations he/she can contest before the judge.

In the same sense, some organizations (e.g., the Computer Emergency Readiness Team "CERT", the World Wide Web Consortium "W3C") and constructors (e.g., CISCO) regularly publish recommendations [21] [22] [23]. Moreover, in the Internet field for example, the IETF associate the "*Should*" verb to a "*recommendation requirement*" in the specification of standard track documents [24]. More precisely, the RFC

2119 states that: *"must"*, *"required"* or *"shall"* mean that the definition is an absolute requirement of the specification; *"must not"* or *"shall not"* mean that the definition is an absolute prohibition; *"should"* or the adjective ***"recommended"*** mean that there may exist valid reasons in particular circumstances to ignore a particular item, but the full implications must be understood and carefully weighed before choosing a different course; *"should not"* or ***"not recommended"*** mean that there may exist valid reasons in particular circumstances when the particular behavior is acceptable or even useful, but the full implications should be understood and the case carefully weighed before implementing any behavior described with this label. We can give several other examples, but due to space limitation we can conclude that security policies in many applications became more and more complex, and there is a great need to find mechanisms to handle the concept of recommendation. This is a big challenge that has never been addressed.

In this paper, we believe that the recommendation notion is halfway between permissions and obligations (i.e., recommendations are stronger than permissions but not as restricting as obligations); in the same way, inadvisabilities seem halfway between prohibited and elective (cf. next Section) actions (i.e., inadvisabilities are weaker than prohibitions but stronger than elective actions). The purpose of the two next sections is to present a logical framework that provides a means of specifying and reasoning about permissions, prohibitions, obligations, recommendations (e.g., should) and inadvisabilities (e.g., should not ...) in a given universe of entities.

4   Modelling Recommendations

Roughly speaking, the choice of a formal language for specifying a security policy is based, on one hand, on the expressive power of this language and, on the other hand, on the requirements of the targeted applications. Moreover, in order to specify the security policies that interest us in this paper, we need first to express norms, i.e. rules which say what *must* be the case, *must not* be the case, *may be* the case or *may not be* the case. Actually, this kind of notions (may, must, ...) was already addressed by several logical models such as deontic logic. The latter can be seen as an extension of modal logic that considers modal operators such as obligations, permissions and prohibitions. Note that researches in deontic reasoning within a modal logic point of view has already been done by several works such as by Aqvist [25] and Prior [26]. Moreover, within the context of computer security, several authors like Bieber and Cuppens [27], Glasgow et al. [28], Prakken and Sergot [29], etc. have used deontic logic.

In the rest of the following sub-sections, we progressively extend the modal logic in order to model the notions of "recommendation" and "inadvisabilities".

4.1   Syntax

Let *PV* be a countable set of propositional variables, with typical members denoted p, q, etc. By means of the Boolean operators $\neg$ ("not ...") and $\vee$ ("... or ...") of classical logic and the modal operator $\mathbf{O}$ ("it is obligatory that ...") of modal logic, we combine these variables so as to build up the set of formulas of deontic logic given by the rule:

- $\phi ::= p \mid \neg\phi \mid (\phi \vee \phi) \mid \mathbf{O}\phi.$

We make use of the standard abbreviations for the other Boolean operators. We supplement the language by the modal operators $\mathbf{F}$, $\mathbf{P}$, and $\mathbf{E}$ expressing "*it is forbidden that ...*", "*it is permitted that ...*", and "*it is elective that ...*": $\mathbf{F}\phi = \mathbf{O}\neg\phi$, $\mathbf{P}\phi = \neg\mathbf{O}\neg\phi$, $\mathbf{E}\phi = \neg\mathbf{O}\phi$. Basically, the specific characteristic of a norm is the consistency of the set of all obligations that make it up. This characteristic corresponds to the formula $\neg(\mathbf{O}\phi \wedge \mathbf{O}\neg\phi)$. Seeing that the "obligatory that" is the "forbidden that not" and the "forbidden that" is the "obligatory that not"; this characteristic also corresponds to the formulas $\neg(\mathbf{F}\phi \wedge \mathbf{F}\neg\phi)$ and $\neg(\mathbf{O}\phi \wedge \mathbf{F}\phi)$.

Furthermore, using the equivalences $\neg\mathbf{O}\neg\phi \leftrightarrow \mathbf{E}\neg\phi$ and $\neg\mathbf{F}\neg\phi \leftrightarrow \mathbf{P}\neg\phi$, we can deduce that $\mathbf{O}\phi \to \mathbf{E}\neg\phi$ and $\mathbf{F}\phi \to \mathbf{P}\neg\phi$. The modal operators $\mathbf{P}$ ("*it is permitted that ...*") and $\mathbf{E}$ ("*it is elective that ...*") keep up similar relations: the "permission that" is the "elective that not" and the "elective that" is the "permission that not". Hence, we can deduce the following formulas $\mathbf{O}\phi \to \mathbf{P}\phi$ and $\mathbf{F}\phi \to \mathbf{E}\phi$.

However, none of the previous modalities is able to directly capture the notion of "*recommendation*". Subsequently, we introduce the modal operator $\mathbf{R}$ ("*it is recommended that ...*") and we use it to extend the previous set of deontic logic formulas. In fact, let us now consider the set of formulas given by the rule:

- $\phi ::= p \mid \neg\phi \mid (\phi \vee \phi) \mid \mathbf{O}\phi \mid \mathbf{R}\phi$.

Let us take a simple example. If we assume that (Read, Bob, UserGuide) is a formula expressing the fact that Bob read the user guide, in our language we can express formulas such as $\mathbf{R}$(Read, Bob, UserGuide); meaning that: it is recommended that Bob read the user guide.

Moreover, to be able to express rules / sentences such as "*it is inadvisable that ...*", we supplement the language by the modal operator $\mathbf{I}$: $\mathbf{I}\phi = \mathbf{R}\neg\phi$. E.g., the formula $\mathbf{I}$(Execute, Bob, OldVersion) means that executing the old version of the program is inadvisable; i.e., it is recommended to not execute the old version.

In this respect, our new set of formulas allows us to give an account of the *consistency* of a set of recommendations by means of the formula $\neg(\mathbf{R}\phi \wedge \mathbf{R}\neg\phi)$. In fact, seeing that the "recommended that" is the "inadvisable that not" and the "inadvisable that" is the "recommended that not", this formula corresponds to the following formulas $\neg(\mathbf{I}\phi \wedge \mathbf{I}\neg\phi)$ and $\neg(\mathbf{R}\phi \wedge \mathbf{I}\phi)$: it is not possible that something being both recommended and inadvisable. The question that arises now is: what are the relations between the "obligatory that", the "recommended that" and the "permitted that" on one hand, and the "forbidden that", the "inadvisable that" and the "elective that" , on the other hand. The semantics and the axiomatics of the two next subsections will allow us to show, among others, that the formulas $\mathbf{O}\phi \to \mathbf{R}\phi$, $\mathbf{R}\phi \to \mathbf{P}\phi$, $\mathbf{F}\phi \to \mathbf{I}\phi$ and $\mathbf{I}\phi \to \mathbf{E}\phi$ express indisputable obvious deontic facts.

4.2   Semantics

The most elementary model of obligations is composed of a non-empty set W of states and a relation $\mathfrak{R}$ on W. Therefore, a *deontic frame* will be an ordered pair:

- $\mathscr{F} = (W, \mathfrak{R})$

where W is a nonempty set of states and $\Re$ is a binary relation on W called accessibility relation: for all states x, the states y such that $x\Re y$ are those states in which *all* the obligations in x are satisfied. For this reason, we may also consider that for all states x, the set $\Re(x) = \{y: x\Re y\}$ characterizes the set of all permissions in x.

Actually, the formulas of deontic logic are valued at states. The valuation of the formula $\mathbf{O}\phi$ at state x depends on the valuation of ϕ at states y such that $x\Re y$.

In this respect, a *deontic model* is an ordered triple:

- $\mathcal{M} = (W, \Re, V)$

where $\mathcal{F} = (W, \Re)$ is a deontic frame and V is a valuation on W, i.e. a function assigning to each state x in W a subset $V(x)$ of the set PV of all propositional variables. $V(x)$ can thus be considered as the set of propositional variables that x verifies.

Subsequently, in the deontic model $\mathcal{M}$, the function V can be extended to the function $\bar{V}$ defined as follows:

- $p \in \bar{V}(x)$ iff $p \in V(x)$; and $\neg\phi \in \bar{V}(x)$ iff $\phi \notin \bar{V}(x)$;
- $\phi \vee \psi \in \bar{V}(x)$ iff $\phi \in \bar{V}(x)$ or $\psi \in \bar{V}(x)$;
- $\mathbf{O}\phi \in \bar{V}(x)$ iff for all states y such that $x\Re y$, $\phi \in \bar{V}(y)$.

Furthermore, according to the relationships between obligations, permissions, prohibitions (*cf.* Section 4.1), it is a simple matter to check that:

- $\mathbf{F}\phi \in \bar{V}(x)$ iff for all states y such that $x\Re y$, $\phi \notin \bar{V}(y)$,
- $\mathbf{P}\phi \in \bar{V}(x)$ iff for some state y with $x\Re y$, $\phi \in \bar{V}(y)$,
- $\mathbf{E}\phi \in \bar{V}(x)$ iff for some state y with $x\Re y$, $\phi \notin \bar{V}(y)$.

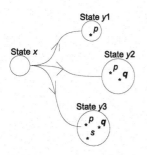

Fig. 1. A model with recommendations

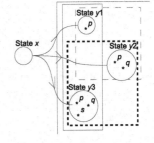

Fig. 2. Exemple of a large subset

In the model given in Fig. 1, p is obligatory at state x, whereas q and s are only permitted.

Let us now define the notions of "satisfiability" and "validity" in our model. Let ϕ be any formula. We say that ϕ is *valid* in the model $\mathcal{M} = (W, \Re, V)$ iff $\phi \in \bar{V}(x)$ for all states x; whereas ϕ is said to be valid in the frame $\mathcal{F} = (W, \Re)$ iff ϕ is valid in every model $\mathcal{M} = (W, \Re, V)$ based on $\mathcal{F}$.

Furthermore, we say that ϕ is *satisfiable* in $\mathcal{M} = (W, \Re, V)$ iff $\neg\phi$ is *not valid* in $\mathcal{M} = (W, \Re, V)$; whereas ϕ is said to be satisfiable in frame $\mathcal{F} = (W, \Re)$ iff ϕ is satisfiable in some model $\mathcal{M} = (W, \Re, V)$ based on $\mathcal{F}$.

Actually, the definitions of satisfiability and validity come from the semantics for modal logic. Correspondence theory in modal logic teaches us the ways the validity of the modal formulas $\neg(\mathbf{O}\phi \wedge \mathbf{O}\neg\phi)$, $\neg(\mathbf{F}\phi \wedge \mathbf{F}\neg\phi)$ and $\neg(\mathbf{O}\phi \wedge \mathbf{F}\phi)$ considered above is related to the condition of seriality saying that for all states x, there exists a state y such that $x\Re y$. For this reason, in the sequel, we will always consider that frames are fitted out with a serial relation.

Let us now focus on the modal operators $\mathbf{O}$ and $\mathbf{P}$. The reader may easily verify that in all models $\mathscr{M} = (W, \Re, V)$:

- $\mathbf{O}\phi \in \bar{V}(x)$ iff $\Re(x) \cap \{y\colon \phi \in \bar{V}(y)\} = \Re(x)$, i.e. $\{y\colon \phi \in \bar{V}(y)\}$ *entirely covers* $\Re(x)$,
- $\mathbf{P}\phi \in \bar{V}(x)$ iff $\Re(x) \cap \{y\colon \phi \in \bar{V}(y)\} \neq \emptyset$, i.e. $\{y\colon \phi \in \bar{V}(y)\}$ *partially covers* $\Re(x)$.

Seeing that we would like the formulas $\mathbf{O}\phi \to \mathbf{R}\phi$ and $\mathbf{R}\phi \to \mathbf{P}\phi$ to be valid, the interpretation of the recommendation modal operator $\mathbf{R}$ in a model $\mathscr{M} = (W, \Re, V)$ should actually be halfway between the interpretations of $\mathbf{O}$ and $\mathbf{P}$ (*cf.* Section 3), i.e. it should correspond to the following interpretation:

- $\mathbf{R}\phi \in \bar{V}(x)$ iff $\{y\colon \phi \in \bar{V}(y)\}$ *covers a large part of* $\Re(x)$.

In this respect, the interpretation of $\mathbf{I}$ in $\mathscr{M} = (W, \Re, V)$ should correspond to $\mathbf{I}\phi \in \bar{V}(x)$ iff $\{y\colon \phi \in \bar{V}(y)\}$ *covers a small part of* $\Re(x)$.

Note that the notions "*entirely cover* (obligations), *partially cover* (permissions) and *cover a large part* (recommendations) perfectly reflect that recommendations are stronger than permissions but not as restricting as obligations (cf. Section 3).

Following our reasoning, we consider that a frame for recommendation is an ordered triple:

- $\mathscr{F} = (W, \Re, \mathscr{N})$

where $(W, \Re)$ is a deontic frame and $\mathscr{N}$ is a neighborhood function on W, i.e. a function assigning to each state x in W a set $\mathscr{N}(x)$ of subsets of $\Re(x)$. For all states x, we will think of $\mathscr{N}(x)$ as the set of large subsets of $\Re(x)$. Such large subsets will characterize the set of all recommendations in x.

Now, with the recommendation notion, our model is an ordered 4-tuple:

- $\mathscr{M} = (W, \Re, \mathscr{N}, V)$

where $\mathscr{F} = (W, \Re, \mathscr{N})$ is a frame for recommendation and V is a valuation on W. In this respect, the function V can be extended (in $\mathscr{M}$) to the function $\bar{V}$ as follows:

- $\mathbf{R}\phi \in \bar{V}(x)$ iff $\Re(x) \cap \{y\colon \phi \in \bar{V}(y)\} \in \mathscr{N}(x)$.

For example, let us consider the model $\mathscr{M} = (W, \Re, \mathscr{N}, V)$ given in Fig. 2 and obtained from Fig. 1 by defining $\mathscr{N}(x) = \{\{y1, y2\}, \{y2, y3\}, \{y1, y3\}, \{y1, y2, y3\}\}$ (Fig. 2). As the subset $\{\{y2, y3\}$ is considered as a large surset of $\Re(x)$, $\{\{y2, y2\} \in \mathscr{N}(x)$. Hence, q is recommended at state x. Note that q is not obligatory at x and that s is not recommended at x.

The reader may easily verify that the validity of the modal formulas $\mathbf{O}\phi \to \mathbf{R}\phi$, $\mathbf{R}\phi \to \mathbf{P}\phi$ considered above is related to the condition saying that for all states x, $\Re(x) \in \mathscr{N}(x)$ and $\emptyset \notin \mathscr{N}(x)$.

Seeing that we would like the formulas $\mathbf{O}\phi \to \mathbf{R}\phi$ and $\mathbf{R}\phi \to \mathbf{P}\phi$ to be *valid*; in the sequel, we always consider that frames of recommendation are fitted out with a neighborhood function $\mathcal{N}$ such that for all states x, $\mathfrak{R}(x) \in \mathcal{N}(x)$ and $\emptyset \notin \mathcal{N}(x)$. Note that in such frames, since $\mathbf{F}\phi = \mathbf{O}\neg\phi$, $\mathbf{E}\phi = \mathbf{P}\neg\phi$ and $\mathbf{I}\phi = \mathbf{R}\neg\phi$, then the formulas $\mathbf{F}\phi \to \mathbf{I}\phi$ and $\mathbf{I}\phi \to \mathbf{E}\phi$ are also valid.

4.3 Axiomatization/Completeness

The previous section presents the semantics of our specification and representation language for obligations and recommendations. This is certainly a first step in building a global and robust logical framework; but it remains not sufficient as we need a mean to derive new informations and to reason (e.g. by verification) on our language. Moreover, it seems necessary to give axioms and rules that define the relationships between the different access modalities (obligations, recommendations and permissions). To achieve these tasks and, thus, to complete our logical framework, we define in this section the axiomatic system *LR* of our Logic of Recommendation. In addition to the classical axioms of propositional logic, we define the following axioms of *LR*:

- $\mathbf{O}(\phi \to \psi) \to (\mathbf{O}\phi \to \mathbf{O}\psi)$,
- $\mathbf{O}\phi \to \mathbf{P}\phi$,
- $\mathbf{O}(\phi \leftrightarrow \psi) \to (\mathbf{R}\phi \leftrightarrow \mathbf{R}\psi)$,
- $\mathbf{O}\phi \to \mathbf{R}\phi$,
- $\mathbf{R}\phi \to \mathbf{P}\phi$.

The axiom $\mathbf{O}(\phi \to \psi) \to (\mathbf{O}\phi \to \mathbf{O}\psi)$ is called axiom (K). It corresponds to the fact that the modal operator $\mathbf{O}$ is interpreted in models by means of a binary relation.

The axiom $\mathbf{O}\phi \to \mathbf{P}\phi$ (axiom D) corresponds to the fact that in every frame $\mathscr{F} = (W, \mathfrak{R}, \mathcal{N})$, $\mathfrak{R}$ is such that for all states x, there exists a state y such that $x\mathfrak{R}y$.

Furthermore, the axiom $\mathbf{O}(\phi \leftrightarrow \psi) \to (\mathbf{R}\phi \leftrightarrow \mathbf{R}\psi)$ is new and has never been considered before within the context of deontic logic. It corresponds to the fact that the modal operator $\mathbf{R}$ is interpreted in models by means of a neighborhood function. This axiom can be easily analysed as follows: if its antecedent $\mathbf{O}(\phi \leftrightarrow \psi)$ -which says that ϕ and ψ are true in the same accessible words- is true, then the set of accessible ϕ-worlds and the set of accessible ψ-worlds are equal. In this case, its conclusion $\mathbf{O}\phi \to \mathbf{O}\psi$ must be true. Moreover, as for $\mathbf{O}\phi \to \mathbf{R}\phi$ and $\mathbf{R}\phi \to \mathbf{P}\phi$, we have seen that these axioms are related to the fact that in every frame $\mathscr{F} = (W, \mathfrak{R}, \mathcal{N})$, $\mathcal{N}$ is such that for all states x, $\mathfrak{R}(x) \in \mathcal{N}(x)$ and $\emptyset \notin \mathcal{N}(x)$.

Besides that, in addition to the classical inference rules of propositional logic, the inference rules of *LR* are: "from ϕ, infer $\mathbf{O}\phi$". It can be proved that all the formulas of the following forms are derivable from the axioms and inference rules of *LR*:

- $\mathbf{O}\phi \wedge \mathbf{O}\psi \to \mathbf{O}(\phi \wedge \psi)$,
- $\mathbf{O}\phi \wedge \mathbf{R}\psi \to \mathbf{R}(\phi \wedge \psi)$,
- $\mathbf{O}\phi \wedge \mathbf{P}\psi \to \mathbf{P}(\phi \wedge \psi)$.

These formulas obviously correspond to our intuitive notions of obligations, recommendations and permissions. The truth of the matter is that:

Proposition 1. *All formulas derivable from the axioms and inference rules of LR are valid in all frames.*

Proof. The proof can be done by induction on the length of the derivation of ϕ in LR that if ϕ is derivable in LR then ϕ is valid in all frames.

Proposition 2. *All formulas valid in all frames are derivable from the axioms and inference rules of LR.*

Proof. The proof is done by means of a canonical model construction. Let $\mathcal{M} = (W, \mathcal{R}, \mathcal{N}, V)$ be the model defined as follows:

- W is the set of all maximal LR-consistent sets of formulas,
- $\mathcal{R}$ is the binary relation on W such that for all x, y in W, $x\mathcal{R}y$ iff $\{\phi: O\phi \in x\} \subseteq y$,
- $\mathcal{N}$ is the neighborhood function such that for all x in W and for all subsets S of $\mathcal{R}(x)$, S is in $\mathcal{N}(x)$ iff there exists a formula ϕ such that $R\phi \in x$ and $S = \{y \in W: x\mathcal{R}y$ and $\phi \in y\}$,
- V is the valuation function such that for all x in W, $V(x) = \{p: p \in x\}$.

It can be proved that $\mathcal{R}$ is serial. Moreover, for all states x in W, $\mathcal{R}(x) \in \mathcal{N}(x)$ and $\emptyset \notin \mathcal{N}(x)$. Using a proof by induction on the complexity of the formula ϕ, one can show that for all states $x \in W$, $\phi \in x$ iff $\phi \in \bar{V}(x)$. As a result, if ϕ is a formula not derivable in LR, then $\neg\phi$ is LR-consistent and there is $x \in W$ such that $\neg\phi \in x$. Therefore, $\phi \notin x$ and $\phi \notin \bar{V}(x)$. It follows that ϕ is not valid in all frames.

Conversly, from the axioms and inference rules of LR, it is not possible to derive all the formulas of the following form:

- $\mathbf{R}\phi \wedge \mathbf{R}\psi \rightarrow \mathbf{R}(\phi \wedge \psi)$,
- $\mathbf{R}\phi \wedge \mathbf{P}\psi \rightarrow \mathbf{P}(\phi \wedge \psi)$,
- $\mathbf{P}\phi \wedge \mathbf{P}\psi \rightarrow \mathbf{P}(\phi \wedge \psi)$.

The cases of the second formula and the third formula can be simply explained by looking a the model given in Fig. 2 where, at state x, q is permitted/recommended, $\neg q$ is permitted and $q \wedge \neg q$ is not permitted. The case of the first formula is different. Although it is not derivable in LR, our intuition of the notion of recommendation could lead us to consider it as an additional axiom. Let LR^+ be the axiomatic system obtained from LR by adding the following formulas as axioms:

- $\mathbf{R}\phi \wedge \mathbf{R}\psi \rightarrow \mathbf{R}(\phi \wedge \psi)$.

We will say that a frame $\mathscr{F} = (W, \mathcal{R}, \mathcal{N})$ is $\cap$-stable iff for all states x in W, the set $\mathcal{N}(x)$ of all large subsets of $\mathcal{R}(x)$ is closed for the set-theoretical operation of intersection. Remark that the frame given in Fig. 2 is not $\cap$-closed.

It can be proved that:

Proposition 3. *All formulas derivable from the axioms and inference rules of LR^+ are valid in all $\cap$-stable frames.*

Reciprocally, by means of the canonical model construction mentioned above, on can show that:

Proposition 4. *All formulas valid in all ∩-stable frames are derivable from the axioms and inference rules of LR^+.*

Let us go further in our extension of our recommendation language. We can prove that from the axioms and the inference rules of LR^+, it is not possible to derive all the formulas of the following form:

- $\mathbf{O}(\phi \rightarrow \psi) \rightarrow (\mathbf{R}\phi \rightarrow \mathbf{R}\psi)$,
- $\mathbf{R}(\phi \wedge \psi) \rightarrow \mathbf{R}\phi \wedge \mathbf{R}\psi$.

Nevertheless, our intuition of recommendations lead us to accept such formulas:

- if ϕ implies ψ in all accessible, hence perfect, states, then one cannot recommend ϕ without recommending ψ,
- if ϕ and ψ are together recommended then they are separately recommended too.

This remark leads us to think that one should add to the axiomatic system LR^+, all formulas of the form $\mathbf{O}(\phi \rightarrow \psi) \rightarrow (\mathbf{R}\phi \rightarrow \mathbf{R}\psi)$ and all formulas of the form $\mathbf{R}(\phi \wedge \psi) \rightarrow \mathbf{R}\phi \wedge \mathbf{R}\psi$ considered above, thus obtaining the axiomatic system LR^{++}. We will say that a ∩-stable frame $\mathscr{F} = (W, \mathscr{R}, \mathscr{N})$ is filtered iff for all states x in W, the set $\mathscr{N}(x)$ of all large subsets of $\mathscr{R}(x)$ is closed upward, i.e.: for all subsets S, T of $\mathscr{R}(x)$, if S is in $\mathscr{N}(x)$ and $S \subseteq T$ then T is in $\mathscr{N}(x)$ too. It can be proved that

Proposition 5. *All formulas derivable from the axioms and inference rules of LR^{++} are valid in all filtered frames.*

Reciprocally, by means of the canonical model construction mentioned above, on can show that

Proposition 6. *All formulas valid in all filtered frames are derivable from the axioms and inference rules of LR^{++}.*

5 Using Our Formalism

5.1 Specification of the Security Policy

The axiomatic system defined in the last section, coupled with classical logic axioms could be used for several aims. In this section, two of the possible uses are explained: (1) query a given policy in order to know which rules apply to a given situation; and (2) Check the security policy consistency.

To achieve these tasks, it is first necessary to specify the operational rules, the security policy, and the security objectives. Operational rules are described by means of the propositional logic operators (non modal). For example, to specify that users play roles in their organizations, we can introduce the *play* predicate between the constant symbols: organizations, users and roles. An instance of this predicate could be for instance *Play(ToulouseUniversity, Bob, President)*.

Besides that, we suggest expressing security objectives by using modal operators. For example, the $\mathbf{R}$(*Customer, Read, notice*) security objective means that it is recommended that customers read the notice. Finally, we propose expressing security rules using modal formula with at least a non-modal clause (e.g., $f \to \mathbf{R}q$). It describes the link between the permissions, prohibitions, obligations, or recommendations and the state of the system. For example, the security rule: "'if the patient is minor, it is inadvisable that he/she read its medical file'" can be specified by: $Age(p) \prec 18 \to \mathbf{I}(p, read, MedicalFile(p))$. In this rule we have considered that p is a variable of type "'*patient*'"; Age (resp. $MedicalFile$) is a function that returns the age (resp. the medical file) of a certain patient).

5.2 Querying the Security Policy

Once we have specified the operational rules, the security policy, and the security objectives of the studied application, we can use our axiomatic to develop a tool which enables a user to query the security policy. For instance, let us assume that security administrator wants to know who is recommended to read a notice? This query is translated in the following logical formula: "$\exists n, Notice(n) \land \mathbf{R}(x, Read, n)$".

Note that there are two ways to program this formula in logical-based languages such as PROLOG. The first one lists the persons who are actually recommended to read a notice; while the second method answers by a formula which corresponds to a sufficient condition that satisfies the query. This second technique of query answering is called intentional answer in [30].

5.3 Checking the Security Policy Consistency

Different techniques can be used to check the security policy consistency, in particular, we can use:

- Axiom-based methods, called Frege-Hilbert methods. The idea is to derive new rules by applying the inference rules to the set of axioms until demonstrating the intended property. Note that it is difficult to mechanize this method since it is difficult to find the wanted property among all the possible deductions.
- Natural deduction methods: these techniques are closed to the reasoning used by mathematicians to demonstrate their theorems. In this kind of calculus, every derivation starts by some hypothesis and assumptions [31].

In our context, it is important to choose the method that (1) gives enough information about the reasons of success or failure while demonstrating a certain security property, (2) identifies the system state that is responsible (3) identifies some resident vulnerabilities in the system or a certain weakness in the security policy specification. This will greatly enhance the system security and rigorously help to refine the security objectives. For these reasons, we suggest using a constructive verification technique such as the "Tableau method" or its variant "Gentzen sequence calculus". In order to prove a certain formula ϕ, the main idea is to assume that $\neg\phi$ is true and to derive a contradiction by successively splitting up $\neg\phi$ in each of its derived sub-formulas, until obtaining a state satisfying a formula and its negation. Actually, in this method, we draw a graph where the initial node contains an initial secure state (e.g., a state where certain security objectives are true/satisfied). Then, we progressively apply some derivation rules (specific to this method). At each state we also apply one of the security rules (rules that specify how the system can, must or should evolve). The demonstration is ended when attending a non-secure state (a state where a contradiction is detected).

The "Tableau method" can also be used to detect conflicting situations, e.g., if, from a secure state, and by applying the security rules as well as the derivation rules, we reach a state where a certain user has the permission/obligation/recommendation and the prohibition to carry out a certain action on the same object); This problem comes to draw our graph and to look for nodes where one of the following formulas are true: $\mathbf{R}p \wedge \mathbf{F}q$ or $\mathbf{P}p \wedge \mathbf{F}q$ or $\mathbf{O}p \wedge \mathbf{F}q$ or $\mathbf{I}p \wedge \mathbf{F}q$ or $\mathbf{I}p \wedge \mathbf{R}q$ or $\mathbf{I}p \wedge \mathbf{O}q$.

6 Conclusion

Thanks to its ability to specify the concepts of obligation, permission and prohibition, Deontic logic is an attractive candidate for expressing security policies. Actually, this logic was first associated to epistemic logic and used by Glasgow and McEwen to specify confidentiality policies [28]. Bieber and Cuppens used it to model the causality, non-interference and non-deducibility security property [27]. Furthermore, Deontic logic was used in any kind of systems and applications such as databases [32]. We can thus assert that Deontic logic is well adapted to capture several security properties and modalities. However, none of the existing works have studied the recommendation and inadvisable access modalities, while these concepts are unavoidable in many current and emergent applications. Several regulations are in fact in the form of recommendations and directives, and these regulations should be reflected in security policies (in the specification as well as in the implementation phases). Modeling recommendations is thus a new challenge in the security policies and models field. In this paper, we have proposed a logical framework that covers the richness of these legislations and applications. In particular, we have enhanced Deontic logic by a new Recommendation Specification Language. Moreover, in order to be able to reason on the security policy and to derive new rules, we have suggested a new recommendation-based axiomatic. The latter can be combined by classical logic axioms to provide more general reasoning mechanisms. Now, we are integrating our language in a global access control model: OrBAC (Organization-Based Access Control) [18]. In fact, the latter is well adapted to several kinds of heterogeneous, multi-organizational and distributed systems, but it suffers from its incapacity to model and reason on recommendations. With the work presented in this paper, this weakness will be overcome. We also expect applying our work to a representative case study. Finally, we will also develop mechanisms to integrate the recommendation access modality in existing tools and languages such as Prolog.

References

1. Common Criteria for Information Technology Security Evaluation, Version 3.1 Revision 1, Part 1: Introduction and general model, CCMB-2006-09-001, 86 p. (September 2006)
2. Common Criteria for Information Technology Security Evaluation, Version 3.1 Revision 1, Part 2: Security functional components, CCMB-2006-09-002, 314 p. (September 2006)

3. Bettini, C., Jajodia, S., Wang et, X.S., Wijesekera, D.: Obligation Monitoring in Policy Management. In: International Workshop, Policies for Distributed Systems and Networks (Policy), Monterey, California, pp. 2–12. IEEE Computer Society Press, Los Alamitos (2002)
4. Demeanor, N., Delay, N., Lupus, E., Sloan, M.: The Ponder Policy Specification Language. In: International Workshop Policy, Bristol, UK, pp. 18–38. IEEE Computer Society Press, Los Alamitos (2001)
5. Ni, Q., Bertino, E., Lobo, J.: An Obligation model bridging access control policies and privacy policies. In: 13th ACM SACMAT, Estes Park, CO, USA, June 11-13 (2008)
6. Hilty, M., Pretschner, A., Basin, D., Schaefer, C., Walter, T.: A policy language for distributed usage control. In: Biskup, J., López, J. (eds.) ESORICS 2007. LNCS, vol. 4734, pp. 531–546. Springer, Heidelberg (2007)
7. Resolution A/RES/45/ General assembly of United Nations, Guidelines for the regulation of computerized personal data files (December 1990)
8. Recommendation of the Communication of Health Information in Hospitals, European Health Committee CDSP (92)8, Council of Europe, Strasbourg (June 1992)
9. Recommendations of the Council of Europe, R(97)5, On The Protection of Medical Data Banks, Council of Europe, Strasbourg (February 13, 1997)
10. Directive 95/46/EC of the European Parliament and of the Council of 24, On the protection of individuals with regard to the processing of personal data (October 1995)
11. European Council, Bangemann report recommendations to the EC (May 26, 1994)
12. International Risk Governance Council, Critical infrastructures at risk: Securing the European electric power system (2007)
13. North American Electric Reliability Council, Urgent action standard 1200 (2003)
14. Lampson, B.: Protection. In: 5th Princeton Symp. on Information Sciences and Systems (1971)
15. Harrison, M.A., Ruzzo, W.L., Ullman, J.D.: Protection in Operating Systems. Communication of the ACM 19(8), 461–471 (1976)
16. Bell, D.E., LaPadula, L.J.: Secure Computer Systems: Unified Exposition and Multics Interpretation, technical report, MTR 2997 Rev. 1, MITRE corp., Bedford, USA (1976)
17. Ferraiolo, D.F., Sandhu, R., Gavrila, S., Kuhn, D.R., Chandramouli, R.: A Proposed Standard for RBAC. ACM Tras. on Info. and System Security 4(3) (August 2001)
18. Abou El Kalam, A., Balbiani, P., Benferhat, S., Cuppens, F., Deswarte, Y., El-Baida, R., Miège, A., Saurel, C., Trouessin, G.: OrBAC: Organization-Based Access Control. In: 4th International Workshop Policy, Come, Italy, pp. 120–131. IEEE Computer Society Press, Los Alamitos (2003)
19. OASIS, eXtensible Access Control Markup Language TC v2.0, Normative XACML 2.0 documents, http://www.oasis-open.org/specs/index.php
20. Law 2002-303 related to the patient's rights and to the quality of healthcare systems, Article L. 1111-7 (March 2002)
21. W3C, W3C Recommendations, http://www.w3.org/TR
22. CISCO, Access Control Lists: Overview and Guidelines, http://www.cisco.com/en/US/docs/ios/11_3/security/configuration/guide/scacls.pdf
23. Computer Emergency Response Team, CERT alerts, http://www.cert.org
24. Bradner, S.: RFC2119: Key words for use in RFCs to Indicate Requirement Levels, IETF (March 1997)
25. Aqvist, L.: Next and Ought, alternative foundations for Von Wright's tense-logic, with an application to deontic logic. Logique & Analyse 9, 231–251 (1966)
26. Prior, A.: The paradoxes of derived obligation. Mind 63, 64–65 (1954)
27. Bieber, P., Cuppens, F.: A definition of secure dependencies using the logic of security. In: Computer Security Foundations Workshop IV. IEEE, Los Alamitos (1991)

28. Glasgow, J., MacEwan, G., Panagaden, P.: A logic for reasoning about security. ACM Transactions on Computer Science 10, 226–264 (1992)
29. Prakken, H., Sergot, M.: Dyadic deontic logic and contrary-to-duty obligations. In: Nute, D.N. (ed.) Defeasible Deontic Logic, Synthese Library, pp. 223–262. Kluwer, Dordrecht (1997)
30. Cholvy, L., Demolombe, R.: Querying a rule base. In: First International Conference on Expert Database Systems, Charleston (1986)
31. Fitting, M.: Basic Modal Logic. In: Gabbay, D.M., Hogger, C.J., Robinson, J.A. (eds.) Handbook of Logic in Artificial Intelligence and Logic Programming Logic Foundations, vol. 1(5), pp. 365–448. Oxford Science Publications (1993) ISBN 0-19-853745-X
32. Cuppens, F., Demolombe, R.: A Deontic Logic for Reasoning about Confidentiality. In: Brown, M., Camo, J. (eds.) Deontic Logic, Agency and Normative Sytems

On the Security Validation of Integrated Security Solutions[*]

Andreas Fuchs, Sigrid Gürgens, and Carsten Rudolph

Fraunhofer Institute for Secure Information Technology
{andreas.fuchs,sigrid.guergens,carsten.rudolph}@sit.fraunhofer.de

Abstract. Combining security solutions in order to achieve stronger (combined) security properties is not straightforward. This paper shows that security-preserving alphabetic language homomorphisms can be used to derive security results for combined security solutions. A relatively simple example of the combination of two different authentication properties (device authentication using a trusted platform module and user authentication using SSL) are integrated. Using security-preserving language homomorphisms it is shown that previously proposed combinations of solutions do not satisfy the desired integrated security properties. Finally, an improved integration of the two solutions is shown to satisfy the desired properties.

1 Introduction

Complex security properties can often not be realised by one single security mechanism in which case it is necessary to combine several mechanisms. This combination is usually far from trivial for several reasons. First, the complex security property is often different (stronger) than the union of the properties of the separate solutions. Furthermore, solutions need to be integrated in the correct way. This paper provides a relatively small example of two integrated security solutions where one intuitive approach does not satisfy the desired security properties. The security goal in this example is the combination of client authentication by using a secure channel, namely SSL, with the identification of the end-points of the channel based on TPM attestation. A formal approach based on formal languages and security-preserving alphabetic language homomorphisms is used to prove the security properties of the integration. Remarkably, this formal approach shows that two existing proposals for integrating TPM attestation with secure channel establishment [1,5] do not satisfy the desired combined security property.

Formal methods have been extensively studied and used for the security analysis of single security mechanisms like cryptographic protocols (see for example [13,12,9]). However, combinations of security solutions have mainly been studied

[*] Part of this work was accomplished within the project SERENITY 27587 funded by the European Commission.

in the context of additional attack possibilities derived from combining protocols [2,11] and refinement for security properties, in particular non-repudiation [10,14]. In contrast to these approaches, this paper shows a pragmatic way of applying formal methods to verify the security properties of integrated security solutions. This approach is based on an existing framework for security property specification [7,8]. This framework is briefly revisited in the following section before discussing the example of integrating SSL channels with TPM attestation.

2   The Underlying Framework for Security Property Specification

In this section we first give a very brief summary of the necessary concepts of formal languages to describe system behaviour and abstractions.

The behaviour B of a discrete system can be formally described by the set of its possible sequences of actions (traces). Therefore $B \subseteq \Sigma^*$ holds where Σ (called the alphabet) is the set of all actions of the system, Σ^* is the set of all finite sequences (called words) of elements of Σ, including the empty sequence denoted by ε, and subsets of Σ^* are called formal languages. Words can be composed: if u and v are words, then uv is also a word. For a word $x \in \Sigma^*$, we denote the set of actions of x by $alph(x)$. For more details on the theory of formal languages we refer the reader to [3].

Different formal models of the same application/system are partially ordered with respect to different levels of abstraction. Formally, abstractions are described by so called alphabetic language homomorphisms. These are mappings $h^* : \Sigma^* \longrightarrow \Sigma'^*$ with $h^*(xy) = h^*(x)h^*(y)$, $h^*(\varepsilon) = \varepsilon$ and $h^*(\Sigma) \subseteq \Sigma' \cup \{\varepsilon\}$ which implies $h^*(B) \subseteq (\Sigma')^*$. So they are uniquely defined by corresponding mappings $h : \Sigma \longrightarrow \Sigma' \cup \{\varepsilon\}$. In the following we denote both the mapping h and the homomorphism h^* by h.

We further extend the system specification by two components: *agents' initial knowledge* about the global system behaviour and *agents' view*. The initial knowledge $W_P \subseteq \Sigma^*$ of agent P about the system consists of all traces P initially considers possible, i.e. all traces that do not violate any of P's assumptions about the system. Every trace that is not explicitly forbidden can happen in the system. Further, in a running system P can learn from actions that have occurred. Satisfaction of security properties obviously also depends on what agents are able to learn. After a sequence of actions $\omega \in B$ has happened, every agent can use its *local view* of ω (denoted by λ) to determine the sequences of actions it considers to be possible. For a sequence of actions $\omega \in B$ and agent $P \in \mathbb{P}$ (where $\mathbb{P}$ denotes the set of all agents), $\lambda_P^{-1}(\lambda_P(\omega)) \subseteq \Sigma^*$ is the set of all sequences that look exactly the same from P's local view after ω has happened. Depending on its knowledge about the system B, underlying security mechanisms and system assumptions, P does not consider all sequences in $\lambda_P^{-1}(\lambda_P(\omega))$ possible. Thus it can use its knowledge to reduce this set: $\lambda_P^{-1}(\lambda_P(\omega)) \cap W_P$ describes all sequences of actions P considers to be possible when ω has happened.

Security properties can now be defined in terms of the agents' initial knowledge and local views. For more details we refer the reader to [7].

Our definition of authenticity (see [7]) uses the above described concepts and essentially states that a set of actions $\Gamma \subseteq \Sigma$ is authentic for agent P if in all sequences that P considers possible after a sequence of actions ω has happened, some time in the past an action of Γ must have happened.

Definition 1. *A set of actions $\Gamma \subseteq \Sigma$ is authentic for $P \in \mathbb{P}$ after a sequence of actions $\omega \in B$ with respect to W_P if $alph(x) \cap \Gamma \neq \emptyset$ for all $x \in \lambda_P^{-1}(\lambda_P(\omega)) \cap W_P$.*

The following definition (see again [7]), specifies sufficient conditions for a homomorphism to preserve authenticity.

Definition 2. *Let $h : \Sigma^* \to \Sigma'^*$ be an alphabetic language homomorphism and for $P \in \mathbb{P}$ let $\lambda_P : \Sigma^* \to \Sigma_P^*$ and $\lambda_P' : \Sigma'^* \to \Sigma_P'^*$ be the homomorphisms describing the local views of P on Σ and Σ', respectively. The language homomorphism h preserves authenticity on B if for each $P \in \mathbb{P}$ exists a mapping $h_P' : \lambda_P(B) \to \lambda_P'(B')$ with $\lambda_P' \circ h = h_P' \circ \lambda_P$ on B.*

$f \circ g$ denotes the composition of functions f and g, while Σ_P^* and $\Sigma_P'^*$ denote the images of the respective local views (the actual sets can only be determined for concrete local views).

Finally the next theorem provides the link between authenticity properties of systems on different levels of abstraction (see [7] for more details and for the proof of the theorem).

Theorem 1. *If $\Gamma' \subseteq \Sigma'$ is authentic for $P \in \mathbb{P}$ after $\omega' \in h(B)$ with respect to $W_P' \subseteq \Sigma'^*$, and if h preserves authenticity on B, then $\Gamma = h^{-1}(\Gamma') \cap \Sigma$ is authentic for $P \in \mathbb{P}$ after each $\omega \in h^{-1}(\omega') \cap B$ with respect to each W_P with $W_P \subseteq h^{-1}(W_P')$.*

3   Example: Integration of Two Security Solutions

3.1   The System Model

The system that we consider here consists of a server S, two clients C_1, C_2, two devices d_1, d_2, and an arbitrary number of channels ch_j, $j \in \mathbb{N}$. The devices and the server are connected via some kind of network and the clients may use any of these devices to send messages to the server. In this notion, the clients are human beings or applications, whilst the server and the entities denoted as devices are computer systems.

The system shall meet two security requirements: Messages of a client to the server shall be authentic for the server, and at the same time the server shall be able to identify the device the message was sent from. For each of these requirements there are standard solutions available.

3.1.1   User Authentication

The chosen scheme for user authentication is a simplified version of an authentic channel establishment as provided by SSL [4]. It is well-known that SSL with client certificate and signature can be used to provide authenticity of the client. Security analyses of SSL or of particular SSL implementations are not considered in this paper. We assume that SSL indeed establishes a secure authentic channel.

An abstract system can be modeled by introducing two actions: $ssl\text{-}init(C_i, ch_j(S))$ models the initiation of the SSL handshake with server S by one of the clients C_i on channel ch_j, and $ssl\text{-}rec(S, ch_j(C_i))$ models the completion of the SSL handshake by the server which establishes channel ch_j. Although the reduction of the SSL model to these two actions presents a considerable abstraction of the complex nature of the SSL session key establishment (e.g. we do not model the freshness of the channel) it is sufficient for our purposes.

This system provides the property that each time the server performs $ssl\text{-}rec$ for a channel $ch_j(C_i)$, the handshake initialisation $ssl\text{-}init(C_i, ch_j(S))$ by client C_i is authentic for the server as defined in Definition 1.

3.1.2   Device Identification

The solution that we choose for device identification is based on trusted computing technology as specified by the Trusted Computing Group [6]. The Trusted Platform Module (TPM) can be used to attest the integrity of software running on the platform it is integrated in. For this the software is measured (hashed) and the resulting value is stored in so-called Platform Configuration Registers (PCR) which are only accessible by the TPM. Then the TPM_Quote command instructs the TPM to calculate a signature over these PCR values. By associating the signature key with the TPM, the result of the TPM_Quote can be used to identify the platform. This description omits many details of the very complex process, for more information see [15].

A very abstract model of this solution uses three actions: Action $att\text{-}gen(d_k, quote(d_k))$ models the generation of $quote(d_k)$ (the signature on the PCR values) using device d_k, $att\text{-}send(d_k, S, quote(d_k))$ models the sending of the quote message to the server, and $att\text{-}rec(S, quote(d_k))$ models the reception of the quote message by the server. This system provides the property that each time the server performs $att\text{-}rec$ for a $quote(d_k)$ message, the generation of this message by device d_k is authentic for the server as defined in Definition 1.

3.2   Specification of the Abstract Integrated System

We will now model an idealized abstract system behaviour B that provides both user authenticity and device identification simultaneously by defining the following actions in Σ:

- $ssl\text{-}init(C_i, ch_j(S), d_k)$ models the initiation of the SSL handshake with server S by one of the clients C_i on channel ch_j using one of the devices d_k.
- $ssl\text{-}rec(S, ch_j(C_i, d_k))$ models the completion of the SSL handshake by the server which establishes channel ch_j. The parameters C_i and d_k of the channel

denote that server S considers the channel to be initiated by client C_i and that the end-point of the channel should be d_k.

The abstract system shall satisfy the property that every time the server completes an SSL handshake for a channel $ch_j(C_i, d_k)$, the channel was indeed initiated by client C_i using device d_k. This can be formalized as follows:

Property 1. $\forall \omega \in B$ *holds if* ssl-rec$(S, ch_j(C_i, d_k)) \in alph(\omega)$ *then* ssl-init$(C_i, ch_j(S), d_k)$ *is authentic for* S.

For the abstract model we assume the existence of a security mechanism that simultaneously authenticates client and device during establishment of a channel. Since for expressing this property we only need the view of server S, we define the assumptions for the system behaviour B in terms of the initial knowledge of the server:

$$B = \Sigma^* \setminus (W_S^1 \cup W_S^2 \cup W_S^3)$$

where W_S^1, W_S^2 and W_S^3 describe those sequences of actions that violate the properties we want the abstract system to provide:

$$W_S^1 = \bigcup_{j \in \mathbb{N}, i, k, l \in \{1,2\}} (\Sigma \setminus \{ssl\text{-}init(C_i, ch_j(S), d_k)\})^* \{ssl\text{-}rec(S, ch_j(C_i, d_l))\}^* \Sigma^*$$

describes that each handshake performed by the server on channel $ch_j(C_i, d_l)$ corresponds to a handshake initiation by the same client C_i on the same channel ch_j on some device d_k.

$$W_S^2 = \bigcup_{j \in \mathbb{N}, i, k, l, m \in \{1,2\}} \Sigma^* \{ssl\text{-}init(C_i, ch_j(S), d_k)\} \Sigma^* \{ssl\text{-}init(C_m, S, ch_j(S), d_l)\} \Sigma^*$$

describes that a channel can only be initiated once.

Finally, we assume that the server S recognizes the device on which the client started the handshake:

$$W_S^3 = \bigcup_{j \in \mathbb{N}, i, k, l \in \{1,2\}} (\Sigma \setminus \{ssl\text{-}init(C_i, ch_j(S), d_k)\})^* \{ssl\text{-}rec(S, ch_j(C_l, d_k))\}^* \Sigma^*$$

describes that each time the server performs a handshake that was presumably initiated on device d_k, some client indeed initiated the handshake on this device. In other words, the device that was used to initiate the handshake is authentic for the server.

It is easy to show that this system provides Property 1.

3.3 Specification of the Concrete Integrated System

3.3.1 A Naive Integration

The two mechanisms described in Sections 3.1.1 and 3.1.2 connect the client to a channel and the quote message to a device, respectively. By integrating these mechanisms one would expect to achieve a link between client, channel and device simultaneously. The most obvious approach of such an integration is to first start up an SSL-connection and then send the result of a TPM_Quote Attestation over that channel. In the following we will show that this approach does not satisfy the desired properties.

To this end we define a concrete system $\boldsymbol{B}$. It has the same participants C_1, C_2 and S, and uses the same channels $ch_j, j \in \mathbb{N}$, and devices d_1, d_2 as does the abstract system but uses a set of refined actions.

In the following, we use italic font for the abstract system and actions while using italic boldface font for the concrete system and actions.

Thus Σ contains the following actions:

- $\boldsymbol{ssl\text{-}init}(C_i, ch_j(C_i, S), d_k)$ As in the abstract system, this action models the initiation of the SSL handshake on channel ch_j by one of the clients C_i, using one of the devices. The channel has both endpoints as parameters.
- $\boldsymbol{ssl\text{-}rec}(S, ch_j(C_i, S))$ models the completion of the SSL handshake by the server which establishes channel $ch_j(C_i, S)$. Note that here S cannot tell to which device the end-point of the channel is connected. This information shall be provided in the subsequent attestation.
- $\boldsymbol{att\text{-}gen}(d_i, quote(d_k))$ This action models the generation of $quote(d_k)$ using device d_i.
- $\boldsymbol{att\text{-}send}(C_i, quote(d_k), ch_j(C_i, S))$ This action models the sending of the attestation message $quote(d_k)$ on channel $ch_j(C_i, S)$.
- $\boldsymbol{att\text{-}rec}(S, quote(d_k), ch_j(C_i, S))$ models the reception of the attestation message by the server on channel $ch_j(C_i, S)$.

For the refined system $\boldsymbol{B}$ we assume that SSL and TPM attestation are used to provide authenticity of the client and device identification, respectively. Thus, the system behaviour can be restricted through adequate assumptions representing the assumed properties for these solutions. Thus, we construct the system behaviour $\boldsymbol{B}$ based on the initial knowledge of the server S in the concrete system as $\boldsymbol{B} = \Sigma^* \setminus (\boldsymbol{W_S^1} \cup \boldsymbol{W_S^2} \cup \boldsymbol{W_S^3} \cup \boldsymbol{W_S^4} \cup \boldsymbol{W_S^5})$ where the $\boldsymbol{W_S^i}$ describe those sequences of actions that violate the properties we assume the concrete system to provide:

Assumption 1. *In analogy to the abstract system B we assume that the two SSL actions provide authenticity of the client to the server. It seems reasonable to assume that in combining the two solutions no SSL keying information is revealed by the TPM attestation process.*

$$\boldsymbol{W_S^1} = \bigcup_{j \in \mathbb{N}, i,k \in \{1,2\}} (\Sigma \setminus \{\boldsymbol{ssl\text{-}init}(C_i, ch_j(C_i, S), d_k)\})^* \{\boldsymbol{ssl\text{-}rec}(S, ch_j(C_i, S))\} \, \Sigma^*$$

Assumption 2. *For the two SSL actions we can also assume that a channel is only established once. This is justified by the fact that both communication parties involved in an SSL-communication influence the session secret and even if only one (the server S) uses a reliable random number generator, the session secret will be virtually unique to this communication session.*

$$W_S^2 = \bigcup_{j \in I\!N, i,k,l \in \{1,2\}} (\Sigma^* \{\boldsymbol{ssl\text{-}init}(C_i, ch_j(C_i, S), d_k)\} \; \Sigma^* \{\boldsymbol{ssl\text{-}init}(C_i, S, ch_j(C_i, S), d_l)\} \; \Sigma^*$$

Assumption 3. *By the nature of an SSL channel, if some message is received on it, there must be a respective send action on this channel. In analogy to Assumption 1 we further assume that this send action is authentic. Hence we assume that whenever the server receives an attestation message $quote(d_k)$ on channel $ch_j(C_i, S)$, the message must have been sent on this channel by the client C_i.*

$$W_S^3 = \bigcup_{j \in I\!N, i,k \in \{1,2\}} (\Sigma \setminus \{\boldsymbol{att\text{-}send}(C_i, quote(d_k), ch_j(C_i, S))\})^* \{\boldsymbol{att\text{-}rec}(S, quote(d_k), ch_j(C_i, S))\} \; \Sigma^*$$

Assumption 4. *We assume that the three attestation actions provide authenticity of the device for the server. Each time the server receives an attestation message $quote(d_k)$ on some channel $ch_j(C_i, S)$, in all sequences it considers possible indeed this device generated the message.*

$$W_S^4 = \bigcup_{j \in I\!N, i,k \in \{1,2\}} (\Sigma \setminus \{\boldsymbol{att\text{-}gen}(d_k, quote(d_k))\})^* \{\boldsymbol{att\text{-}rec}(S, quote(d_k), ch_j(C_i, S))\} \Sigma^*$$

Assumption 5. *SSL channels can only be used after a successful handshake. Thus, whenever a client sends the attestation message on channel $ch_j(C_i, S)$, the server has established this channel before.*

$$W_S^5 = \bigcup_{j \in I\!N, i,k \in \{1,2\}} (\Sigma \setminus \{\boldsymbol{ssl\text{-}rec}(S, ch_j(C_i, S))\})^* \{\boldsymbol{att\text{-}send}(C_i, quote(d_k), ch_j(C_i, S))\} \Sigma^*$$

4   Security Validation

In this section we will show that the concrete system defined in the previous section does not provide simultaneous authenticity of client and identification of device. We do this by formulating a proposition to Theorem 1 and trying to prove it using security preserving language homomorphisms as explained in Section 2.

Proposition 1. *For all $\omega \in \boldsymbol{B}$ with $\boldsymbol{att\text{-}rec}(S, quote(d_k), ch_j(C_i, S)) \in alph(\omega)$ holds that $\boldsymbol{ssl\text{-}init}(C_i, S, ch_j(C_i, S), d_k)$ is authentic for S after ω.*

In order to prove this proposition we need to find a language homomorphism that maps the concrete system $\boldsymbol{B}$ to the abstract system B and preserves authenticity. Then we can conclude on the authenticity properties that hold in the refined system.

4.1 Local Views and a Possible Homomorphism

Since we are interested in a security property concerning the server we only define its respective local views and disregard those of the clients. In a distributed system it is appropriate to assume that S can only see its own actions:

$$\lambda_{\mathbf{S}}(\mathbf{a}) = \begin{cases} a \text{ if } a \in \Sigma_{/\mathbf{S}} \\ \varepsilon \text{ else} \end{cases} \qquad \lambda_S(a) = \begin{cases} a \text{ if } a \in \Sigma_{/S} \\ \varepsilon \text{ else} \end{cases}$$

We now define homomorphism h to relate the two systems. In the concrete model, **att-rec** shall establish the binding of the channel to the device. Thus, this action is mapped to *ssl-rec* in the abstract system.

$$\begin{aligned}
h(\textbf{ssl-init}(C_i, ch_j(C_i, S), d_k)) &= ssl\text{-}init(C_i, ch_j(S), d_k) \\
h(\textbf{att-rec}(S, quote(d_k), ch_j(C_i, S))) &= ssl\text{-}rec(S, ch_j(C_i, d_k)) \\
h(\textbf{ssl-rec}(S, ch_j(C_i, S))) &= \varepsilon \\
h(\textbf{att-gen}(d_k, quote(d_k))) &= \varepsilon \\
h(\textbf{att-send}(C_i, quote(d_k), ch_j(C_i, S))) &= \varepsilon
\end{aligned}$$

4.2 Proof Attempt

According to Theorem 1, in order to prove that h preserves authenticity we need to find a homomorphism $h'_S : \lambda_{\mathbf{S}}(\boldsymbol{B}) \to \lambda_S(B)$ that is compliant both with h and the local views of the server in the abstract and concrete system, respectively. It is easy to see that the homomorphism defined in the following has this property:

$$\begin{aligned}
h'_S(\textbf{ssl-rec}(S, ch_j(C_i, S))) &= \varepsilon \\
h'_S(\textbf{att-rec}(S, quote(d_k), ch_j(C_i, S))) &= ssl\text{-}rec(S, ch_j(C_i, d_k))
\end{aligned}$$

So in order to be able to apply Theorem 1 we need to show that $h(\boldsymbol{B}) \subseteq B$.

Proof 1. *We show the reverse, namely that for $\omega \notin B$, i.e. for $\omega \in W_S^1 \cup W_S^2 \cup W_S^3$, it follows for all $x \in h^{-1}(\omega)$ that $x \notin \boldsymbol{B}$. For $\omega \in W_S^1$, the assertion can easily be shown using Assumptions 3, 5 and 1, for $\omega \in W_S^2$ the assertion follows from Assumption 2.*

*The interesting case is $\omega \in W_S^3$. Then ω contains ssl-rec$(S, ch_j(C_i, d_k))$ with no action ssl-init$(C_l, ch_j(S), d_k)$ before. For $x \in h^{-1}(\omega)$ it follows that x contains **att-rec**$(S, quote(d_k), ch_j(C_i, S))$. With Assumption 3 we can conclude that there is an action **att-send**$(C_i, quote(d_k), ch_j(C_i, S))$ before. Assumption 5 allows to conclude **ssl-rec**$(S, ch_j(C_i, S)) \in alph(x)$ and Assumption 1 leads to **ssl-init**$(C_i, ch_j(C_i, S), d_l) \in alph(x)$. Since h maps this action onto ssl-init$(C_i, ch_j(S), d_l)$ and $x \in h^{-1}(\omega)$ and $\omega \in W_S^3$, it follows $d_l \neq d_k$. In order to show $x \notin \boldsymbol{B}$ we need an assumption that refers to the devices being used in the actions. However, the only such assumption we have available is Assumption 4 which only allows to conclude that the generation of the message quote(d_k) indeed happened on device d_k. We cannot prove $x \notin \boldsymbol{B}$ because there is no link between **att-gen**$(d_k, quote(d_k))$ and the channel used in **att-send**$(C_i, quote(d_k), ch_j(C_i, S))$.*

Failing to show that the mapping defined in Section 4.1 indeed maps the concrete system $\boldsymbol{B}$ onto the abstract system B indicates that the concrete system might after all not provide the desired property.

4.3   Analysis of the Proof Attempt

Taking the failure of the proof as an input for a manual security evaluation indicates that the device establishing the handshake does not necessarily have to be the device that generates the quote message. The failed proof identifies a counter example: $ssl\text{-}init(C_i, ch_j(C_i, S), d_l)ssl\text{-}rec(S, ch_j(C_i, S))att\text{-}gen(d_k,$ $quote(d_k))$ $att\text{-}send(C_i, quote(d_k), ch_j(C_i, S))$ $att\text{-}rec(S, quote(d_k), ch_j(C_i, S))$ is one of the sequences of actions that h maps onto $\omega \notin B$ but that do not violate any of the assumptions for $\boldsymbol{B}$.

A possible attack scenario that exploits the missing link between the handshake initialization and the quoting device is the following: A company policy restricts access to its server to on-site or home offices, but disallows mobile access with laptops from trains or internet-cafes. A malicious client wants to connect to the server from e.g. a train. He uses SSL and e.g. a smart-card to authenticate himself. Then he establishes a connection to the home office PC, generates a quote message by this PC, and sends the quote message back to the server using the SSL channel. Even if the quote verification did not allow manual quote calls, it is still possible to use dns-spoofing for a man-in-the-middle attack and proceed similarly.

4.4   A Fixed Concrete System

In order to formally add the missing link between the device and the channel (in the next section we will discuss possible realizations) we add the channel to the quote message. We further assume that the channel contained in a quote message is always connected to the device that produced this message. Thus we obtain the following changes to the attestation actions:

- $att\text{-}gen(d_k, quote(d_k, ch_j(C_i, S)))$
- $att\text{-}send(C_i, quote(d_k.ch_j(C_i, S)), ch_j(C_i, S))$
- $att\text{-}rec(S, quote(d_k, ch_j(C_i, S)), ch_j(C_i, S))$

Assumption 6. *The channel that is contained in the quote message is initiated on the device that generates this message. Thus the sequences specified below can not be part of the concrete system:*

$$\boldsymbol{W}_{\mathsf{S}}^{6} = \bigcup_{j \in I\!\!N, i,k \in \{1,2\}} (\Sigma \setminus \{ssl\text{-}init(C_i, ch_j(C_i, S), d_k)\})^* \{att\text{-}gen(d_k, quote(d_k, ch_j(C_i, S)))\} \Sigma^*$$

Further assumptions regarding the chronology of $att\text{-}gen$ can be made but are not necessary for the proof.

Our fixed system $\boldsymbol{B}_{\mathsf{fix}}$ is now defined as

$$\boldsymbol{B}_{\mathsf{fix}} = \Sigma^* \setminus (\boldsymbol{W}_{\mathsf{S}}^{1} \cup \boldsymbol{W}_{\mathsf{S}}^{2} \cup \boldsymbol{W}_{\mathsf{S}}^{3} \cup \boldsymbol{W}_{\mathsf{S}}^{4} \cup \boldsymbol{W}_{\mathsf{S}}^{5} \cup \boldsymbol{W}_{\mathsf{S}}^{6})$$

Using these assumptions we can now prove that the concrete fixed system simultaneously provides client authentication and device identification. We use the homomorphism h_{fix} equivalent to the one used for the flawed system that maps $ssl\text{-}init(C_i, ch_j(C_i, S), d_k)$ onto $ssl\text{-}init(C_i, ch_j(S), d_k)$ and $att\text{-}rec(S, quote(d_k, ch_j(C_i, S)), ch_j(C_i, S))$ onto $ssl\text{-}rec(S, ch_j(C_i, d_k))$, and all other actions onto the empty word.

Clearly, also this homomorphism preserves authenticity. It remains to show that $h_{fix}(\boldsymbol{B}_{\text{fix}}) \subseteq B$. Again, we will show that for $\omega \notin B$, all $x \in h_{fix}^{-1}(\omega)$ are not elements of $\boldsymbol{B}_{\text{fix}}$.

Proof 2. *The cases $\omega \in W_S^1$ and $\omega \in W_S^2$ are analogous to the proof attempt presented in Section 4.2. The interesting case is the one were our first proof failed:*

Let $\omega \in W_S^3$. As in the previous proof, Assumptions 3, 5, and 1 imply the existence of a sequence $x \in h_{fix}^{-1}(\omega)$ with actions $ssl\text{-}init(C_i, ch_j(C_i, S), d_l)$, $ssl\text{-}rec(S, ch_j(C_i, S))$, $att\text{-}send(C_i, quote(d_k, ch_j(C_i, S)), ch_j(C_i, S))$, and $att\text{-}rec(S, quote(d_k, ch_j(C_i, S)), ch_j(C_i, S))$ in this order. Furthermore, from $att\text{-}rec(S, quote(d_k, ch_j(C_i, S)), ch_j(C_i, S)) \in alph(x)$ we can conclude, using Assumption 4, that $att\text{-}gen(d_k, quote(d_k, ch_j(C_i, S)))$ must have happened before, and Assumption 6 implies that $ssl\text{-}init(C_i, ch_j(C_i, S), d_k)$ must have happened before $att\text{-}gen(d_k, quote(d_k, ch_j(C_i, S)))$. Finally Assumption 2 implies $d_l = d_k$. By the definition of h_{fix} this implies $ssl\text{-}init(C_i, ch_j(S), d_k) \in \omega$, a contradiction to the assumption we started with. Hence one of the assumptions for the concrete system is violated and thus $x \notin \boldsymbol{B}_{\text{fix}}$.

The proof also shows that the quote message does not need to be sent on the SSL-Channel because the proof still holds with a respectively altered Assumption 4, as the link between the channel and the device results from the quote generation. However confidentiality concerns may imply to use the SSL channel nonetheless.

5 Practical Realisation of a Secure Integration

A possible realisation for the fixed system $\boldsymbol{B}_{\text{fix}}$ could be to reserve a PCR on the TPM for the sole purpose of authenticating the device's connections: Whenever an SSL connection is being established, the device would save the handshake messages into this PCR. The attested chain of integrity measurement values could prove that the platform will only extend the PCR by handshake messages for SSL sessions on this device. A local daemon on the platform could control the measurement of SSL session establishment on the platform.

Previously proposed approaches to construct a secure remote attestation fail to satisfy the non-obvious Assumption 6. In [5] a PCR dedicated to store the SSL client Public Key or Certificate and an additional Platform Property Certificate is proposed. This fails if the SSL private key is compromised and the client is tricked into providing a TPM_Quote. More importantly, it also fails if the client wants to pretend the use of a different device. In this case Assumption 6 is not justified since the client's certificate can very well be available on more than one device. The Network Interface Monitoring Agent (NIMA) introduced in [1] links the channel endpoint in terms of the IP-Address to the TPM_Quote by storing it in a PCR. This will also fail because a second platform could pretend to have the IP-Address of the attested platform.

6 Conclusions

In this paper we have shown that the combination of formal security protocol specifications with security-preserving language homomorphisms can indeed provide new insight into the properties of integrated security solutions. Although we used a very simplified model of the integration of TPM-based attestation with SSL security channels we were able to show that previously proposed integrations do not provide the desired security properties while a more sophisticated integration does. The example in this paper addresses only two very similar security properties. However, our framework allows to handle other important security properties such as different instantiations of confidentiality and non-repudiation.

Our method emphazises the importance of assumptions made on a particular system. While the assumptions used to prove the desired properties are reasonable with respect to the practical realisation of the integration we discussed, any further assumption for the trivial system that would allow a proof can not be argued.

Furthermore, the assumptions used in a proof can be the basis for design-time or run-time monitoring checks to verify their justification. This provides information about the applicability of an integrated security solution.

References

1. Choi, S., Han, J., Jun, S.: Improvement on TCG Attestation and Its Implication for DRM. In: Gervasi, O., Gavrilova, M.L. (eds.) ICCSA 2007, Part I. LNCS, vol. 4705, pp. 912–925. Springer, Heidelberg (2007)
2. Cremers, C.: Feasibility of multi-protocol attacks. In: Proc. of The First International Conference on Availability, Reliability and Security (ARES), pp. 287–294. IEEE Computer Society, Los Alamitos (2006)
3. Eilenberg, S.: Automata, Languages and Machines. Academic Press, London (1974)
4. Frier, A., Karlton, P., Kocher, P.: The SSL 3.0 Protocol. Netscape Communications Corp. (November 1996)
5. Goldman, K., Perez, R., Sailer, R.: Linking remote attestation to secure tunnel endpoints. In: STC 2006: Proceedings of the first ACM workshop on Scalable trusted computing, pp. 21–24. ACM, New York (2006)
6. Trusted Computing Group. TCG TPM Specification 1.2 revision 94 (2006), http://www.trustedcomputing.org
7. Gürgens, S., Ochsenschläger, P., Rudolph, C.: Authenticity and provability - A formal framework. In: Davida, G.I., Frankel, Y., Rees, O. (eds.) InfraSec 2002. LNCS, vol. 2437, pp. 227–245. Springer, Heidelberg (2002)
8. Gürgens, S., Ochsenschläger, P., Rudolph, C.: On a formal framework for security properties. International Computer Standards & Interface Journal (CSI), Special issue on formal methods, techniques and tools for secure and reliable applications 27(5), 457–466 (2005)
9. Gürgens, S., Rudolph, C., Scheuermann, D., Atts, M., Plaga, R.: Security evaluation of scenarios based on the tCG's TPM specification. In: Biskup, J., López, J. (eds.) ESORICS 2007. LNCS, vol. 4734, pp. 438–453. Springer, Heidelberg (2007)

10. Mantel, H.: Preserving Information Flow Properties under Refinement. In: IEEE Symposium on Security and Privacy, Oakland, pp. 78–91. IEEE Computer Science, Los Alamitos (2001)
11. Mathuria, A., Singh, A., Shravan, P.V., Kirtanka, R.: Some new multi-protocol attacks. In: ADCOM – Proceedings of the 15th International Conference on Advanced Computing and Communications, pp. 465–471. IEEE Computer Society, Los Alamitos (2007)
12. Meadows, C.: Analyzing the Needham-Schroeder Public Key Protocol: A Comparison of Two Approaches. In: Martella, G., Kurth, H., Montolivo, E., Bertino, E. (eds.) ESORICS 1996. LNCS, vol. 1146. Springer, Heidelberg (1996)
13. Paulson, L.C.: The inductive approach to verifying cryptographic protocols. Journal of Computer Security 6, 85–128 (1998)
14. Santen, T.: Preservation of probabilistic information flow under refinement. Information and Computation 206(2-4), 213–249 (2008)
15. Trusted Computing Group. TPM Main - Part 1 Design Principals, Specification Version 1.2, Level 2 Revision 103 (July 2007)

Verification of Security Policy Enforcement in Enterprise Systems*

Puneet Gupta and Scott D. Stoller

Computer Science Dept., Stony Brook University
{pgupta,stoller}@cs.stonybrook.edu

Abstract. Many security requirements for enterprise systems can be expressed in a natural way as high-level access control policies. A high-level policy may refer to abstract *information resources*, independent of where the information is stored; it controls both direct and indirect accesses to the information; it may refer to the context of a request, i.e., the request's path through the system; and its enforcement point and enforcement mechanism may be unspecified. Enforcement of a high-level policy may depend on the system architecture and the configurations of a variety of security mechanisms, such as firewalls, host login permissions, file permissions, DBMS access control, and application-specific security mechanisms. This paper presents a framework in which all of these can be conveniently and formally expressed, a method to verify that a high-level policy is enforced, and an algorithm to determine a trusted computing base for each resource.

1 Introduction

Many security requirements for enterprise systems can be expressed in a natural way as high-level access control policies. These policies may be high-level in multiple ways. First, a high-level policy may refer to abstract *information resources*, independent of where the information is stored. For example, consider the requirement that only employees in the registrar's office may access student transcripts. This should apply regardless of whether the transcripts are all stored in one DBMS, partitioned (e.g., by campus, college, or grad/undergrad) among multiple DBMSs, saved in backup files, etc. Second, a high-level policy controls both direct and *indirect* accesses to the information. For example, the above policy implies that other users cannot read transcripts by directly accessing them in a DBMS or by invoking operations of an application (possibly running with a different userid) that accesses the database and returns information from the transcripts. Third, a high-level policy may refer to the *context* of a request, i.e., the request's path through the system. For example, a policy might state that employees in the registrar's office are permitted to access student transcripts only via a web browser running on a host in the campus network and requesting the information from the Registrar Application Server. Note that this is analogous to the use of calling context (stack introspection) in the Java security model. Fourth, the policies may be *delocalized*, in the sense that the enforcement point and enforcement mechanism may be

---

* This work is supported in part by ONR under Grant N00014-07-1-0928 and NSF under Grants CNS-0831298, CNS-0627447, CCF-0613913, and CNS-0509230.

D. Gritzalis and J. Lopez (Eds.): SEC 2009, IFIP AICT 297, pp. 202–213, 2009.

unspecified. For example, if transcripts are stored in a DBMS, the above requirement might be enforced in the DBMS or an application that connects to the DBMS. With the latter approach, the system should be designed so that unauthorized users cannot circumvent that application and access the DB directly. This policy might also be enforced in part by the operating system (based on login permissions and file permissions on the relevant servers) and the network (blocking connections to the server from hosts on which unauthorized users have login permissions).

Each high-level policy is enforced by one or more security mechanisms in a system (perhaps involving DBMSs, middleware, operating systems, file systems, firewalls, etc.). Enforcement also depends on the system architecture, which affects the possible paths that requests can take through the system. We sometimes refer to the configurations of security mechanisms as *low-level policies*. Ensuring that the low-level policies, together with a given system architecture, correctly enforce given high-level policies is a challenging problem.

Since enforcement of the high-level policies that control access to an information resource might involve multiple hardware and software components in the system, a natural question during security analysis is to identify a *trusted computing base* (TCB) for each information resource. Note that the answer may depend on the low-level policies as well as the system architecture.

Security policies with one or more of the above "high-level" characteristics are natural during system design. The main contributions of this paper are (1) explicit identification of these characteristics of high-level policies, (2) a framework that allows *convenient* and *formal* specification of such high-level policies, modeling of low-level policies, and modeling of relevant aspects of system architecture, (3) a method for verifying that the low-level policies in a system correctly enforce ("implement") the high-level policies, and (4) an algorithm for computing a trusted computing base (TCB) for a component or information resource.

Although there is a sizable literature on formal specification and analysis of security policies, we are not aware of any previous work that explicitly deals with high-level policies with these characteristics. The interplay between system architecture and the policies has a significant impact on our framework. Frameworks for security policy specification and analysis generally ignore system architecture and request context (in the sense described above), except for specialized frameworks for network (e.g., firewall) policy analysis. Although our framework is broad and flexible enough to model relevant aspects of network security and operating system security, our focus is on application-level security policies.

We are implementing a policy development environment based on our framework and plan to evaluate it on case studies based on a university and a financial institution. Important directions for future work are to consider policy administration and trust management.

2   Related Work

Coordination of Policies in Distributed Systems. Firmato [BMNW99] is a higher-level language for specifying firewall policies. Firmato policies get translated into rule-sets for different models of firewalls, insulating administrators from the details of each model's configuration language. In addition, given the network topology, each firewall's policy can be specialized to contain only the rules relevant to traffic that may pass through it. Work on Firmato does not consider verification of firewall policies against overall network security requirements or analysis of how firewall policies interact with security policies of other components.

García-Alfaro, Cuppens, and Cuppens-Boulahia [GACCB06] define and give algorithms to detect several specific kinds of anomalies (inconsistencies and potential errors) in network security configuration, specifically, configuration of firewalls and network intrusion detection systems (NIDS). In contrast, our work is aimed at verification of general application-level security requirements, taking network security configuration into account but in less detail. Thus, the kinds of properties verified, and the analysis algorithms used, are quite different.

Ioannidis et al. [IBI+07] propose the concept of *virtual private services* (VPSs) to describe a service implemented by a collection of components whose security policies must be configured in a coordinated way to enforce an access control policy associated with the service. They express all access control policies in the same language, namely KeyNote [BFIr99], without distinguishing "high-level" and "low-level" policies. A policy for a VPS can be delocalized—in particular, its enforcement might involve multiple components—but is otherwise basically a low-level policy, in our terminology. They describe a system architecture for deploying and enforcing policies. They do not consider formal analysis, verification, or refinement of policies.

Bandara, Lupu, Moffett, and Russo [BLMR04] propose a formal methodology for policy refinement, based on event calculus [BLR03]. Since most policies today are developed in *ad hoc* ways, not using a formal refinement methodology, we focus instead on verification of given low-level policies against given higher-level policies (requirements). Also, their framework is completely generic; in order to use it for refinement of enterprise security policies, one would need to introduce relations and rules similar to those used in our framework to model system architecture and access control policies.

Sheyner, Haines, Jha, Lippmann, and Wing [SHJ+02] present a method to efficiently construct *attack graphs*, which represent attacks involving sequences of exploits of vulnerabilities in components of a system. Our work is largely complementary to attack graph analysis. Attack graphs are based primarily on vulnerabilities in components; access control policies and calling behavior are not considered, except when they affect a vulnerability. Also, attack graphs are generally used to find violations of system-level security requirements (e.g., who may login to a host), not application-level security policies.

3   Framework

Running Example. We use a student information system as a running example to illustrate our framework. Student information is classified as academic (transcript, etc.) or personal (SSN, citizenship, etc.). The system architecture is shown in Figure 1. Academic information and personal information are stored in separate databases. solar is a web-based university information system; for brevity, we model solar and the associated web server as a single component.

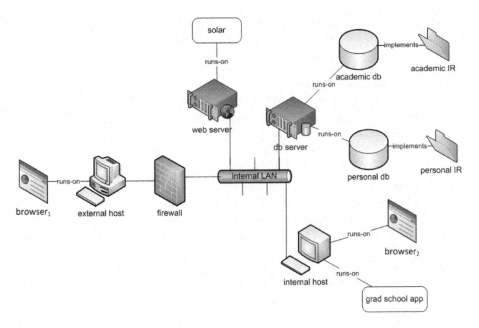

Fig. 1. Architecture of student information system. Edge labels specify the corresponding relation. The components connected on `internal LAN` are related to each other via `link` relation.

Information Resources. An *information resource*, abbreviated IR, represents a kind of information handled by the system. The relation `implements (C, I)` means that component C (partially or completely) implements IR I, i.e., C stores that kind of information. For example, the student information system contains two IRs, `academicIR` and `personalIR`, each implemented by a corresponding database (e.g., `implements (academicDB, academicIR)`). The distinction between an IR and the components that implement it is useful if the information in the IR is partitioned, replicated, archived, etc.

The information in an IR is assumed to be structured as a set of records, whose attributes (fields) and their types are specified in the definition of the IR. We refer to these as attributes of the IR, although they are actually attributes of the records in it. An attribute type can be a primitive data type (e.g., String) or an IR, denoting a reference to a record in another IR (recursive types are prohibited). For example, the attributes of `academicIR` and `studentIR` include an attribute `id` with type String, which identifies the student that the record is about. IRs have a straightforward API with operations for manipulating records. For example, the API includes an operation `readField` with arguments `record` (the record being accessed) and `field` (the field being accessed).

Components. A system is built from *components*, which may represent software (e.g., `solar`) or hardware (e.g., a host or firewall). Each component has attributes, accessed using the dot operator. For example, for a software component C, C.`host` is the host on which C runs. Attributes can also provide information about identity management, e.g., which authentication services and directory services are used by the component.

Each component has an API. For example, the API for the databases `academicDB` and `personalDB` is modeled (ignoring details of SQL) as containing functions like `readField`, `writeField`, `readRecord`, and `addRecord`. The API for `solar` contains `getTranscript`, `getSSN`, and `getCitizenship`. We model the browser as offering its user a single function, `request`, which non-deterministically sends some request to a web server (in this case, `solar`). For brevity, we consider only the above functions; other functions can be modeled and analyzed similarly.

Each component has a *low-level permit policy* that controls invocations of functions in the component's API and is enforced locally by the component. The language for low-level policies is described later in this section.

High-Level Policies. High-level policies are expressed in a simple rule-based language, which is an extension of Datalog with simple data structures that can be read, but not constructed or updated, by policy rules. A policy rule has the form $Q <- P_1, \ldots, P_n$ and means: Q holds if P_1 through P_n hold. Variables start with an uppercase letter, constants start with a lowercase letter, and string constants appear in single quotes. The rules define the relation `hPermit` ("high-level permit"). `hPermit(U, R, Op, C)` holds if the system should permit (allow) requests from user U to perform operation Op on resource R in context C. A *resource* is a component or IR. The rules may also define auxiliary relations. For convenience, the name and arguments of the operation are modeled as attributes of Op (this is just a modeling convention, not an assumption about the implementation); the operation name is stored in Op.`function`. The context C is a sequence of tuples (c, f)—where c is a component or IR, and f is a function in c's API—representing the call chain (or "path") by which the request propagated through the system. Figure 2 shows some high-level policies for the running example.

Call Map. A function in a component's API may call functions provided by other components. Such calls must be considered to determine whether the restrictions on indirect calls expressed by high-level policies are enforced. We introduce a function `callMap` that captures the possible calls made by each component function. For simplicity and efficiency, `callMap` provides, and our analysis tracks, only equalities involving function arguments. Such equalities are often needed to verify enforcement of high-level policies; for example, to verify enforcement of (P1) in Figure 2, the analysis must track equalities involving the `id` argument, which identifies the user whose record is being accessed. `callMap` represents all interactions between components, regardless of the actual communication mechanism.

Given a component C and a function F in its API, `callMap`(C, F) returns a set of tuples of the form $(calledBy, R, F', args)$, each describing a possible call made during execution of that function. The above tuple represents a call to function F' (the "target function") of the "target" resource (component or IR) R. *calledBy* is analogous to a setuid flag. If *calledBy*=`self`, the target resource sees the user executing the calling component C as the caller; if *calledBy*=`caller`, it sees the user that called F on C as the caller. *args* characterizes the possible arguments of the call to the target function. *args* is represented as a set of equalities of the form *attrib* = *val*, where *attrib* is an attribute name (recall that we model function arguments as attributes of an operation object), and *val* can be a constant, the name of an attribute (meaning that attribute *attrib*

```
% A Student can read any field in the records for himself or
% herself.
(P1) hPermit(User, Resource, Op, Context) <-
        Resource in {academicIR, personalIR},
        Op.function = readField, Op.record.id = User.id

% A Graduate School Clerk can read every student's transcript,
% if accessed through solar from (a browser running on) an
% internal host. Note: Context.head() is the first element of
% the context. internalHost(H) is an auxiliary predicate
% (definition elided) that holds if host H is part of the
% network.
(P2) hPermit(User, academicIR, Op, Context) <-
        Op.function = readField, Op.field = 'transcript',
        User.role = 'GradSchlClerk', Context.contains(solar),
        runs-on(Context.head(), H), internalHost(H)

% A registrar can read a student's personal information, if
% accessed from an internal host
(P3) hPermit(User, personalIR, Op, Context) <-
        Op.function = readRecord, User.role = 'Registrar',
        runs-on(Context.head(), H), internalHost(H)

% An administrative user can add new records to academicIR
(P4) hPermit(User, academicIR, Op, Context) <-
        Op.function = addRecord, User.role = 'admin'

% An administrative user can add new records to personalIR
(P5) hPermit(User, personalIR, Op, Context) <-
        Op.function = addRecord, User.role = 'admin'
```

Fig. 2. Illustrative high-level policy rules for the student information system

of the target call equals attribute *val* of the enclosing call to F), or newVar (meaning that a fresh variable will be used in the analysis to represent this value).

For example, callMap(solar, getTranscript) contains the tuple (self, academicDB, readField, {id=id, field='transcript'}). The values of callMap for solar's getSSN and getCitizenship functions are similar. callMap(browser₁, request) contains a tuple for every function of every other component, with newVar arguments, reflecting that browser₁ is untrusted and may make arbitrary calls.

When analyzing the security of a design, the callMap for each component is based on the component's behavior as described in the design. For an implemented system, callMap could be determined from the code. Determining it accurately might be difficult, but an over-approximation can safely be used when verifying enforcement of high-level policies. Over-approximations in callMap may cause false alarms, but in many cases, the low-level permit policy of the target component or an intervening component will block the spurious calls or nested calls they make, preventing false alarms.

If the analysis does raise false alarms, the corresponding call chains indicate exactly what assumptions about possible calls and their arguments are needed for enforcement of the high-level policies, and the `callMap`, permit policies, or system architecture can be refined accordingly.

Hosts and Firewalls. Each component has an attribute `type`. This attribute can have any value, but the values `host` and `firewall` have special significance. Hosts and firewalls are hardware components with network connections. Network connectivity is modeled by the relation `link(`C_1`, `C_2`)`, which means that the network may contain a path between C_1 and C_2 that does not pass through a host or firewall. This reflects the fact that we explicitly model hosts and firewalls but not routers. By taking all paths in the network topology into account in the `link` relation, we are making no assumptions about routing (or its security), although such assumptions could be used to restrict the `link` relation.

Hosts, like all components, have attributes, e.g., the set of users with accounts on the host. Since each software component must run on a host, we introduce a relation `runs-on(`C`, `H`)`, which means that component C may run on host H. Hosts provide various services, notably communication services, to components running on them. Host-based security mechanisms may limit the communication performed by a component, e.g., blocking connections with components on untrusted hosts. Firewalls provide a similar security mechanism, typically forwarding some messages and dropping others, based on the firewall's local policy. An obvious way to capture this is to model network security mechanisms as they are implemented (e.g., at the packet level). However, this level of detail would unnecessarily complicate the model and slow the analysis. We adopt a higher-level view, in which hosts and firewalls are modeled as forwarding (or dropping) inter-component function calls, rather than packets. We include relevant network-layer information, such as the source and destination network addresses, as attributes of the operation object Op representing the call. With this approach, the API of a host or firewall includes the operations (of other components) that it forwards; its low-level permit policy allows calls that it forwards and denies calls that it drops; and its `callMap` normally indicates that the call gets forwarded with unchanged arguments.

Low-Level Policies. Low-level policies for all components are represented in a common rule-based language. The actual configuration languages of the access control mechanisms get translated to this common language; this can be automated. Low-level policy rules have the same form as high-level policy rules. They define auxiliary relations (if desired) and the relation `permit(`U`, `R`, `Op`, `M`)`, where the user U, resource R, and operation Op are the same as for hPermit, and the mode M describes the communication mechanism through which the operation is invoked. The mode M enables us to model the fact that different functions may be offered through different interfaces or with different policies. To avoid irrelevant details and distinctions about communication mechanisms, we define modes that reflect how the communication mechanism relates to the system architecture. A mode M has an attribute `type` whose possible values are: `direct`, indicating that the function is called by a user directly executing/running the component; `local`, indicating that the function is called via some inter-process communication mechanism by another component on the same host; or `remote`, indicating that the function is called over the network via some communication mechanism. The mode M may have additional attributes, depending on its type. If $M.\text{type=local}$, $M.\text{requester}$ identifies the calling component. If $M.\text{type=remote}$, the attributes $M.\text{srcIP}$, $M.\text{srcPort}$, $M.\text{destIP}$, and $M.\text{destPort}$ represent the source IP address, source port, destination IP address, and destination port, respectively.

We could express low-level policies in an existing language for attribute-based access control, such as OrBAC [ABB$^+$03], which offers useful abstractions for structuring policies. Our language is simple but flexible and expressive: those abstractions can easily be represented in our language using auxiliary relations, and making them built-in would complicate our analysis algorithm without providing any additional leverage.

Figure 3 contains low-level policies for the student information system. `campusIPaddr` (*IPaddr*) is an auxiliary predicate that holds if the given IP address is part of the campus network.

4   Verification of Enforcement

This section sketches an algorithm for verifying that the low-level policies and system architecture together enforce the high-level policies. For simplicity, the algorithm assumes that the policies do not contain recursion. This restriction is satisfied by most policies and can easily be relaxed if necessary.

The default starting points for requests are all functions s_f of all components s_r that can be directly invoked . At each starting point, the arguments to the (top-level) function call and the identity of the user making the call are represented by variables. The algorithm computes all possible chains of functions call that can propagate from each starting point through the system, based on the system architecture and `callMap`. Note that these call chains, ignoring the arguments to each function, correspond to the "context" argument of `hPermit` in the high-level policy. If the call map contains cycles, the number of call chains may be infinite. If a possible call C would extend a call chain with a call that is the same, modulo renaming of variables introduced by `newVar`, as a call already in the call chain, then that call is not explored. To ensure this condition is sound, we include in the policy language only selected functions for accessing the context; currently, we include `head()` and `contains`(*expr*) (not, e.g., `length()`).

While constructing call chains, the algorithm accumulates constraints on the values of variables (the starting variables and variables introduced by `newVar`) that represent function arguments; the constraints express that the calls in the chain are permitted by the low-level policies of the components involved (including hosts and firewalls). Values of function arguments obtained from `callMap` are reflected in the formula as equality conjuncts; for example, if `callMap` indicates that a function call represented by `Op1` has CS as the value of the `dept` argument, `Op1.dept = CS` is conjoined to the formula. The constraint for a call is determined by matching the conclusions of the `permit` rules in the low-level policy of the component with the call, and, for each rule that matches, instantiating the variables in the rule based on the match and then backchaining to construct a first-order logic formula representing conditions under

```
firewall:
  permit(User, Resource, Op, Mode) <-
    Resource in {webServer, solar}, Mode.type = remote,
    Mode.destPort = 443

solar:
  permit(User, solar, Op, Mode) <-
    Op.function in {getTranscript, getSSN, getCitizenship},
    Op.recordId = User.id, Mode.type = remote
  permit(User, solar, Op, Mode) <-
    User.role = 'GradSchlClerk', Op.function = getTranscript,
    Mode.type = remote, campusIPaddr(Mode.srcIP)

webServer:
  permit(_, solar, _, _)

dbServer:
  permit(User, Resource, Op, Mode) <-
    Resource in {academicDB, personalDB}, Mode.type = remote,
    Mode.destPort = 8000

personalDB:
  permit(User, personalDB, Op, Mode) <-
    User.role = 'Registrar', Op.function = readRecord,
    Mode.type = remote, campusIPaddr(Mode.srcIP)
  permit(User, personalDB, Op, Mode) <-
    User.role = 'solar', Op.function = readField,
    Mode.type = remote
  permit(User, personalDB, Op, Mode) <-
    User.role = 'admin', Op.function = addRecord,
    Mode.type = direct

academicDB:
  permit(User, academicDB, Op, Mode) <-
    User.role = 'solar', Op.function = readField,
    Mode.type = remote
  permit(User, academicDB, Op, Mode) <-
    User.role = 'admin', Op.function = addRecord,
    Mode.type = direct
```

Fig. 3. Low-level policies for student information system

which the instantiated conclusion can be derived. Since we assume the policy rules
are not recursive, the backchaining always terminates. If the accumulated constraint
becomes unsatisfiable, the algorithm does not explore extensions of that call chain.

For each call chain S (including prefixes of longer call chains), the algorithm checks
whether the call chain is consistent with the high-level policy. Specifically, let Ψ_L be
the constraint computed for S, and let C be the context defined by S, i.e., $S[i]$ is a call
to function $first(C[i])$ of component $second(C[i])$, where $first$ and $second$ return the

indicated components of a tuple. Call chain S is consistent with the high-level policy if, for every instantiation of the variables that satisfies Ψ_L (in other words, S is feasible), the instantiated call $last(S)$ with context C is permitted by the high-level policy. To check this efficiently, we use backchaining to compute a first-order logic formula Ψ_H representing the conditions (including conditions on the context) under which the call $last(S)$ is permitted by the high-level policy, using a variable V to represent the call's context, and then we check whether the formula $(V = C) \wedge \Psi_L \wedge \neg \Psi_H$ is satisfiable. The satisfiability of this formula implies an inconsistency in the system. Our current prototype uses Yices (http://yices.csl.sri.com/) for this purpose. If the satisfiability check succeeds, the logic tool can provide an instantiation of the variables for which the formula is true; this instantiation of S is a counterexample that illustrates how the high-level policy can be violated.

The following example illustrates how our analysis works and how it can identify vulnerabilities. For this example, we modify the low-level policies in Figure 3 as follows: the rule for GradSchlClerk in solar's low-level policy is removed and replaced with the following rule in the low-level policy for academicDB:

```
permit(User, academicDB, Op, Mode) <-
    User.role = 'GradSchlClerk', Op.function = readField,
    Op.field = 'transcript', Mode.type = remote,
    campusIPaddr(Mode.srcIP)
```

Consider a call chain that propagates along the following path (i.e., context) C0: [(browser$_2$, request), (internalHost, request), (dbServer, readField), (academicDB, readField)]. The constraint associated with S is (note: when it is necessary to rename a variable in a rule during backchaining, in order to avoid name collisions, the algorithm appends the name of the component that the rule is for and/or a sequence number; variables characterizing the top-level call, such as User and Op in the formula below, never get renamed):

Ψ_L: Mode_academicDB.type = remote $\wedge$ Mode_academicDB.destPort =
    8000 $\wedge$ Op.function = readField $\wedge$ Op.field = 'transcript' $\wedge$
    User.role='GradSchlClerk' $\wedge$ campusIPaddr(Mode_academicDB.srcIP)

The last call in this chain is to function readField of component academicDB, which implements academicIR. The following constraint is computed for this function call from the high-level policy:

Ψ_H: Op.function = readField$\wedge$ Op.field = 'transcript' $\wedge$ User.role
    = 'GradSchlClerk' $\wedge$ Context.contains(solar) $\wedge$
    runs-on(Context.head(), H) $\wedge$ internalHost(H)

The formula (Context = C0 $\wedge$ Ψ_L) $\wedge$ $\neg\Psi_H$ is satisfiable; note that the conjunct Context.contains(solar) in Ψ_H is not satisfied when Context = C0. This shows that the modified low-level policy does not enforce the high-level policy. The significance of this violation depends on why the high-level policy requires that solar be in the context for these accesses. For example, solar might be responsible for logging accesses to student transcripts by grad school clerks, for compliance with student privacy regulations. Such an error might not be noticed during system execution, while our analysis exposes it during the design stage.

5 Trusted Computing Base

In general, a *trusted computing base* (TCB) consists of the hardware and software responsible for enforcing a security policy. We define a set T of components to be a TCB for resource (component or IR) r in system S (a system is defined by sets of components and IRs, with their attributes; `links`, `runs-on`, and `implements` relations; and low-level policies for each component) with high-level policy H if "correct" behavior by the components in T (i.e., behavior consistent with their low-level policy and `callMap`) is sufficient to ensure that all call chains that end at r are consistent with H. Recall that consistency of a call chain with a high-level policy is defined at the end of Section 4.

More formally, to check whether T is a TCB for enforcement of the high-level policy for r in system S with high-level policy H, we construct a variant $\text{relax}(S, \bar{T})$ of the system, where $\bar{T}$ (the complement of T) is the set of components of S not in T, and then use the method described in Section 4 to check whether call chains in that system that end at r are consistent with H. The variant $\text{relax}(S, \bar{T})$ is the same as system S except that, for every component C in $\bar{T}$, the low-level permit policy of C is replaced with the single rule `permit(User, Resource, Op, Mode) <- true`, and for every function F in C's API, `callMap`(C, F) returns the set containing all tuples of the form $(calledBy, R', F', args)$ such that $calledBy \in \{\text{self}, \text{caller}\}$, R' is a component or IR of S other than C, F' is a function in the API of R', and $args$ maps all parameters of F' to `newVar`.

Designers might want to specify conditions on the acceptable TCB for a resource—for example, that the TCB for a resource contains only components with specified administrators. Our TCB analysis provides a basis for checking such properties.

References

[ABB⁺03]   Abou El Kalam, A., El Baida, R., Balbiani, P., Benferhat, S., Cuppens, F., Deswarte, Y., Miège, A., Saurel, C., Trouessin, G.: Organization Based Access Control. In: 4th IEEE International Workshop on Policies for Distributed Systems and Networks (Policy 2003) (June 2003)

[BFIr99]   Blaze, M., Feigenbaum, J., Ioannidis, J., Ke romytis, A.D.: The KeyNote trust management system, version 2, IETF RFC 2704 (September 1999)

[BLMR04]   Bandara, A.K., Lupu, E., Moffett, J.D., Russo, A.: A goal-based approach to policy refinement. In: 5th IEEE Workshop on Policies for Distributed Systems and Networks (POLICY), pp. 229–239 (2004)

[BLR03]   Bandara, A.K., Lupu, E.C., Russo, A.: Using event calculus to formalise policy specification and analysis. In: Proc. 4th IEEE Workshop on Policies for Distributed Systems and Networks (Policy 2003) (2003)

[BMNW99]   Bartal, Y., Mayer, A.J., Nissim, K., Wool, A.: Firmato: A novel firewall management toolkit. In: IEEE Symposium on Security and Privacy, pp. 17–31 (1999)

[GACCB06]   Alfaro, J.G., Cuppens, F., Cuppens-Boulahia, N.: Analysis of policy anomalies
             on distributed network security setups. In: Gollmann, D., Meier, J., Sabelfeld,
             A. (eds.) ESORICS 2006. LNCS, vol. 4189, pp. 496–511. Springer, Heidelberg
             (2006)
[IBI+07]   Ioannidis, S., Bellovin, S.M., Ioannidis, J., Keromytis, A.D., Anagnostakis,
             K.G., Smith, J.M.: Virtual private services: Coordinated policy enforcement for
             distributed applications. International Journal of Network Security 4(1), 69–80
             (2007)
[SHJ+02]   Sheyner, O., Haines, J.W., Jha, S., Lippmann, R., Wing, J.M.: Automated genera-
             tion and analysis of attack graphs. In: IEEE Symposium on Security and Privacy,
             pp. 273–284 (2002)

Optimization of the Controlled Evaluation of Closed Relational Queries

Joachim Biskup, Jan-Hendrik Lochner, and Sebastian Sonntag

Fakultät für Informatik, Technische Universität Dortmund, D-44221 Dortmund, Germany
{biskup,lochner,sonntag}@ls6.cs.tu-dortmund.de

Abstract. For relational databases, controlled query evaluation is an effective inference control mechanism preserving confidentiality regarding a previously declared confidentiality policy. Implementations of controlled query evaluation usually lack efficiency due to costly theorem prover calls. Suitably constrained controlled query evaluation can be implemented efficiently, but is not flexible enough from the perspective of database users and security administrators. In this paper, we propose an optimized framework for controlled query evaluation in relational databases, being efficiently implementable on the one hand and relaxing the constraints of previous approaches on the other hand.

1 Introduction

Protection of sensible information is an important issue in modern database applications. The information to be protected has to be suitably declared by the "owner" of the information or a security administrator. In this context, it is important to differentiate between *data*, which is always explicitly represented in a database instance, and *information*, which can also be obtained by applying semantics to the data. E. g., the information that Smith has an account balance of $ 15,000 can be an explicit part of the instance of a bank database, or it can be inferred, e. g., by combining the facts "Smith has the account 12345" and "The account 12345 has a balance of $ 15,000". Consequently, it may not be sufficient to protect only data but possibly also unwanted information flows have to be avoided. Thus, mechanisms only regulating the access to data may not be adequate to enforce desired protection goals.

Among other approaches, controlled query evaluation (CQE) [4] is an effective method for protecting sensible information as declared by a confidentiality policy (hereafter called "policy" for short). This method checks whether the true answer to a query together with the a priori knowledge of the user enables the user to infer any information being protected by the policy and, if necessary, modifies the answer to the query, either by lying (i. e., returning the negated answer), or by refusal (i. e., returning no answer), or by a combination of both.

CQE is a highly flexible approach that guarantees preservation of confidentiality for logic-oriented information systems. Considering relational databases, CQE is also applicable in theory, but the underlying first-order logic of relational databases is undecidable in general. For employing CQE in practical applications it is therefore necessary to restrict the first-order logic used for expressing database queries and policies to a

D. Gritzalis and J. Lopez (Eds.): SEC 2009, IFIP AICT 297, pp. 214–225, 2009.

decidable fragment. Nevertheless, real database systems employing CQE would lack efficiency, because they had to rely on theorem prover calls which are known to be costly in general. These theorem prover calls result from the need of computing the inferences a database user can draw by means of his a priori knowledge about the database system and the answers to his queries. Avoiding theorem prover calls at all requires to substantially restrict the expressiveness of the query language and the policy language.

In this paper, we propose a framework that principally accepts every first-order logic sentence as a query (as long as decidability is guaranteed) but (as far as possible) eliminates costly theorem prover calls. More specifically, in Sect. 2, we briefly address approaches for the inference problem in relational databases in general and CQE in particular; in Sect. 3, we identify situations that allow for static inference control without theorem prover calls and propose flexible policy and query languages; in Sect. 4, we present SQL implementations of our static inference control; in Sect. 5, we develop an approach for an optimization framework based on the results of Sect. 3; in Sect. 6, we conclude and point out directions for future research.

2 Inference Control in Relational Databases

Security in relational databases in general and confidentiality in particular has been investigated from various perspectives. Early approaches, e. g. [16,18,22], focus on access control, which operates on the actual data and attaches access or classification information directly to this data.

Discretionary access control (DAC), whose general concept is described in popular textbooks on computer security, mainly suffers from the responsibility of the "data owner" or the security administrator to correctly assign access rights. Information disclosure by inferences cannot be controlled by DAC in general.

Mandatory access control (MAC) employs system-wide policies on classified data according to a security model; see, e. g., [20]. Among other approaches, multilevel secure databases, polyinstantiation, and various extensions have been proposed to enforce MAC; see, e. g., [13,17,18,19]. MAC is principally able to prevent unwanted information flows caused by sequences of read and write operations. Several authors propose entire frameworks, design processes, or comprehensive requirements analyses for secure database systems, e. g., [2,12]. A comprehensive overview of the inference problem in databases, the area of data mining, and Web-based applications can be found in the work of Farkas/Jajodia [15]. Further work on prevention of harmful inferences in databases has been published by Brodsky et al. [11] and Dawson et al. [14].

The first ideas of protecting information in databases according to security policies by giving lied answers or by refusing to answer at all arise from the work of Bonatti/Kraus/Subrahmanian [10] and Sicherman/de Jonge/van de Riet [21], respectively. These ideas are combined by Biskup/Bonatti to CQE, elaborated at first for logical databases [4,6,7] and extended for relational databases in [5]. Biskup/Embley/Lochner [8] propose a static form of CQE.

Beginning with some formal concepts, we now roughly sketch CQE in relational databases. A *relation schema* describes the structure of a relation in a relational database and is denoted by $\langle R, \mathcal{U}, \Sigma \rangle$ where R is the *relation symbol*, $\mathcal{U}$ is a finite set of *attributes*, and Σ is a finite set of *local semantic constraints*. We assume Σ to be a minimal cover (see [1]) of functional dependencies. An *instance* r of a relation schema is considered as the "contents" of the relation; from a (first-order-)logic-oriented perspective (see [1]), it is a finite Herbrand interpretation of the schema satisfying Σ and considering R as a predicate. With $\mu = R(c_1,\ldots,c_n)$ we denote a *tuple*; each c_i is element of an infinite set of constants *Const* and $n = |\mathscr{U}|$. Finally, $\models_M$ denotes the satisfaction relation between an interpretation and a formula, so if μ is element of r, we write $r \models_M \mu$. If $\mathscr{A}, \mathscr{B} \subseteq \mathscr{U}$ are attribute sets, r is said to satisfy the *functional dependency (fd)* $\mathscr{A} \to \mathscr{B}$ if any two tuples of r agreeing on the $\mathscr{A}$ values also agree on the $\mathscr{B}$ values. An attribute set $\mathscr{K}$ is a *key* of *RS* if $\Sigma \models \mathscr{K} \to \mathscr{U}$ and $\mathscr{K}$ is minimal with this property. *RS* is in *object normal form (ONF)* if it has a unique key and for each fd $\mathscr{A} \to \mathscr{B}$, logically implied by Σ and with $\mathscr{B} \not\subseteq \mathscr{A}$, $\mathscr{A}$ corresponds to this key or a superset of it [3].

Database queries are expressed in a suitable fragment of the relational calculus, meaning that each query must have a prenex normal form with prefix either $\forall^*$ or $\exists^*$; so, quantifiers may not be mixed. This condition guarantees that we do not leave the Bernays-Schönfinkel class of decidable first-order formulas [5]. Moreover, we concentrate on closed queries, i. e., we may not use free variables. The *ordinary evaluation* of a query Φ in an instance r is defined by $eval^*(\Phi)(r) := \text{if } r \models_M \Phi \text{ then } \Phi \text{ else } \neg\Phi$. *Controlled query evaluation (CQE)* deviates from this ordinary evaluation if any of the previously declared potential secrets is going to be disclosed by the database user. A *potential secret* Ψ is a sentence from the policy language. If $r \not\models_M \Psi$, the user may learn that Ψ is false in r; if, however, $r \models_M \Psi$, the user may not learn that Ψ is actually true. The (finite) set *pot_sec*, consisting of potential secrets, denotes a *confidentiality policy* being *known* to the user. The *a priori user knowledge* log_0 is assumed to comprise Σ and possibly further sentences being true in r. It is required that $log_0 \not\models \Psi$ for each $\Psi \in pot\_sec$ and $r \models_M log_0$ for the database instance r.

CQE for known potential secrets enforced by *(improved) refusal* is defined by $cqe(Q, log_0)(r, pot\_sec) := \langle (ans_1, log_1), (ans_2, log_2), \ldots \rangle$ for a query sequence $Q = \langle \Phi_1, \Phi_2, \ldots \rangle$. It uses a *censor function* to determine the returned answer ans_i (with mum denoting a refusal) and the current user knowledge log_i for each query, and preserves confidentiality in the sense of the following Def. 1 (see [6,7]).

$$censor(pot\_sec, log, \Phi) := \qquad\qquad\qquad\qquad\qquad\qquad\qquad (1)$$
$$(\text{exists } \Psi)(\Psi \in pot\_sec \text{ and } (log \cup \{\Phi\} \models \Psi \text{ or } log \cup \{\neg\Phi\} \models \Psi))$$
$$ans_i := \text{if } log_{i-1} \models eval^*(\Phi_i)(r) \text{ then } eval^*(\Phi_i)(r)$$
$$\text{else if } censor(pot\_sec, log_{i-1}, \Phi_i) \text{ then mum else } eval^*(\Phi_i)(r)$$
$$log_i := \text{if } censor(pot\_sec, log_{i-1}, \Phi_i) \text{ then } log_{i-1}$$
$$\text{else } log_{i-1} \cup \{eval^*(\Phi_i)(r)\}.$$

Definition 1 (Confidentiality preservation). *A CQE is* confidentiality preserving *for pot_sec if for every finite prefix Q' of a query sequence Q the following holds: For every $\Psi \in pot\_sec$, for every instance r_1, and for every a priori knowledge log_0 there exists an instance r_2 with $r_2 \models_M log_0$ and*

(1) $cqe(Q', log_0)(r_1, pot\_sec) = cqe(Q', log_0)(r_2, pot\_sec)$ and
(2) $eval^*(\Psi)(r_2) = \neg\Psi$.

A *CQE is* confidentiality preserving *if it is confidentiality preserving for all possible confidentiality policies.*

The above CQE definition is highly flexible, since it works for queries and secrets expressed in any compact logic with a suitably defined "model-of" operator. However, a general drawback of this approach is the (costly) computation of inferences each time the censor is invoked. The censor decision (1) can be reduced to a NEXPTIME complete satisfiability problem.

Biskup/Embley/Lochner [8] identify a parameter configuration allowing for simpler inference computations in form of pattern matching. Their approach roughly imposes the following restrictions to database schema, query language and policy language. The database schema has to be in ONF. The query language $\mathscr{L}_q$ is restricted to *existential-R-sentences*, i.e., closed formulas of the positive existential calculus [1] without logical connectives. Each query has the form $\Phi \equiv (\exists X_1) \ldots (\exists X_m) R(v_1, \ldots, v_n)$ with $v_i = X_j$ or $v_i \in Const$ and each X_i occurring exactly once in $v_1, \ldots, v_n$. The policy language $\mathscr{L}_{ps}$ is also restricted to existential-R-sentences; moreover, each potential secret Ψ must protect a *fact* of the schema, i.e., the constants in Ψ must instantiate the unique key and at most one additional attribute. E.g., a schema with $\mathscr{U} = \{A, B, C\}$ and $\Sigma = \{A \rightarrow BC\}$ has the *fact schemas* A, AB, and AC; thus, $(\exists X_B)(\exists X_C)R(c_A, X_B, X_C)$, $(\exists X_C)R(c_A, c_B, X_C)$, and $(\exists X_B)R(c_A, X_B, c_C)$ are proper potential secrets (with X_B, X_C being variables and $c_A, c_B, c_C, c_D \in Const$). These restrictions lead to the following *static* censor that is independent of the user log, which therefore needs not to be considered any longer.

$$censor_{stat}(pot\_sec, \Phi) := (\text{exists } \Psi)(\Psi \in pot\_sec \text{ and } \Phi \models \Psi) \tag{2}$$

We denote the CQE using $censor_{stat}$ by cqe_{stat}. In [8] it is proved that cqe_{stat} preserves confidentiality in the sense of Def. 1.

Biskup/Lochner [9] propose an algorithm with logarithmic runtime that can easily be adapted to cqe_{stat}. This algorithm performs a pattern matching between the query Φ and each potential secret Ψ. If and only if Φ and (at least one) Ψ agree on each constant in Ψ, $\Phi \models \Psi$ holds and mum is returned.

3   Optimizing Static Inference Control for Closed Queries

Unfortunately, we achieve the confidentiality preserving static inference control introduced in Sect. 2 only at the expense of the expressiveness of the underlying languages. The objective of this section is to identify relaxations of the restrictions while keeping up static inference control.

Inference control in relational databases in general and CQE in particular offer a variety of parameters. We confine ourselves to the following: Policies are supposed to consist only of potential secrets and to be known to database users. We believe that functional dependencies are the most important and prevalent type of (local) semantic constraints and therefore neglect other types of local semantic constraints, and global semantic constraints (like inclusion dependencies) as well. Thus, the relations of a database are independent of each other; so, for simplicity, we assume a database to consist of exactly one relation schema. We consider a single database user (besides the security administrator) and concentrate on the (improved) refusal method for enforcing policies. We assume languages $\mathscr{L}_q^{max}$ and $\mathscr{L}_{ps}^{max}$ as "upper bounds" for the query language and the policy language, respectively. Each element of $\mathscr{L}_q^{max}$ is a sentence of the form $\exists^* \varphi$ with $\exists^*$ being a sequence of existentially quantified variables and φ being a quantifier-free first-order formula, i. e., a Boolean combination of R-atoms. Each existentially quantified variable is supposed to occur only once in φ. Elements of $\mathscr{L}_{ps}^{max}$ may additionally contain free variables. Again, each free variable is supposed to occur only once in a formula from $\mathscr{L}_{ps}^{max}$.

For illustrating our investigations we hereafter refer to the following example.

Example 1. A (fictitious) group of banks maintains a common database for administrating information about the account holders. For each combination of bank and account number the account holder and the balance of the account are stored in the database. Let the schema of this database be given by $\langle bank\_db, \mathscr{U}, \Sigma \rangle$ with $\mathscr{U} = \{bank, acc\_no, acc\_holder, balance\}$ and $\Sigma = \{bank, acc\_no \rightarrow acc\_holder, balance\}$. Obviously, $bank\_db$ is in ONF with the key $\mathscr{K} = \{bank, acc\_no\}$. This yields the set of fact schemas $fs(bank\_db) = \{\{bank, acc\_no\}, \{bank, acc\_no, acc\_holder\}, \{bank, acc\_no, balance\}\}$. Consider this instance of $bank\_db$:

bank_db	bank	acc_no	acc_holder	balance
	Bank of Springfield	123654	Smith	$ 15,000
	Gotham City Bank	213456	Jones	$ 2,500
	Metropolis Financial Group	321645	Parker	$ 100
	Gotham City Bank	312564	Smith	$ 2,500
	Bank of Springfield	213456	Green	$ 15,000

Suppose that the group of banks outsources the statistical evaluation of their accounts to an external service provider. In doing so, certain information should be kept secret, e.g., the association between an account number and the corresponding account holder. Thus, a policy *pot_sec* is defined and enforced by a CQE.

3.1 The Query Language

In [8], the query language $\mathscr{L}_q$ ($\subseteq \mathscr{L}_q^{max}$) is introduced, which is restricted to existential-R-sentences. With this language it is possible to ask for (full) tuples or for subtuples (i. e., parts of tuples) only; thus we can express queries like

$\Phi_1 \equiv bank\_db$(Gotham City Bank, 213456, Jones, 2500) and
$\Phi_2 \equiv (\exists X_{acc})(\exists X_{bal})bank\_db$(Bank of Springfield, X_{acc}, Parker, X_{bal}).

Adding disjunction to $\mathscr{L}_q$ may cause problems as shown by the following example.

Example 2. Consider the following policy, meaning that the user may not learn that the Bank of Springfield maintains an account with the number 123654:

$pot\_sec = \{(\exists X_{hold})(\exists X_{bal})bank\_db$(Bank of Springfield, 123654, X_{hold}, X_{bal})$\}$.

The user with the a priori knowledge $log_0 = \emptyset$ now poses two queries using $\mathscr{L}_q$ enhanced with disjunction:

$$\Phi_1 \equiv (\exists X_{hold})(\exists X_{bal})bank\_db(\text{Bank of Springfield}, 123654, X_{hold}, X_{bal}) \vee$$
$$(\exists X_{bank})(\exists X_{acc})(\exists X_{bal})bank\_db(X_{bank}, X_{acc}, \text{Scott}, X_{bal})$$
$$\Phi_2 \equiv (\exists X_{bank})(\exists X_{acc})(\exists X_{bal})bank\_db(X_{bank}, X_{acc}, \text{Scott}, X_{bal})$$

The CQE with the censor (2) answers Φ_1 as well as Φ_2 correctly because neither of them directly implies the potential secret. However, since Φ_1 is true and Φ_2 is false in *bank_db*, the combination of both answers implies the secret.

The sketched problem is inherent to disjunctive queries: If $\Phi_1 \vee \ldots \vee \Phi_n$ is known to be true in an instance r and the formulas $\Phi_1, \ldots, \Phi_{n-1}$ are known to be false in r, then Φ_n must be true in r. Consequently, enhancements of $\mathscr{L}_q$ must prevent disjunctive structures in queries if static inference control is desired. We propose a query language $\mathscr{L}_q^{cn}$ by adding conjunction and negation such that disjunction cannot be simulated. This is achieved by restricting negation to existential-R-sentences.

Definition 2 (Query language with conjunction and negation). *The query language* $\mathscr{L}_q^{cn}$ $(\subseteq \mathscr{L}_q^{max})$ *is inductively defined as follows: (1) If $\Phi \in \mathscr{L}_q$ then $\Phi \in \mathscr{L}_q^{cn}$; (2) if $\Phi \in \mathscr{L}_q$ then $\neg\Phi \in \mathscr{L}_q^{cn}$; (3) if $\Phi_1, \Phi_2 \in \mathscr{L}_q^{cn}$ then $\Phi_1 \wedge \Phi_2 \in \mathscr{L}_q^{cn}$.*

An answer to a query from $\mathscr{L}_q^{cn}$ gives the user an "all or nothing" information: If each conjunct is true in the database instance, then the whole query is true; otherwise, the whole query is false. To provide a more differentiated answer in case the query is false, we suggest to consider a query $\Phi \equiv \Phi_1 \wedge \ldots \wedge \Phi_n$ from $\mathscr{L}_q^{cn}$ as a sequence $\langle \Phi_1, \ldots, \Phi_n \rangle$ of queries from $\mathscr{L}_q$. Thus, the answer to Φ is a sequence $\langle ans_1, \ldots, ans_n \rangle$. The resulting censor for queries from $\mathscr{L}_q^{cn}$ is denoted by $censor_{stat}^{cn}$.

Theorem 1. *The CQE induced by $censor_{stat}^{cn}$, hereafter called cqe_{stat}^{cn}, preserves confidentiality in the sense of Def. 1.*

3.2 The Policy Language

3.2.1 Revising the Definition of Fact Schemas

According to Sect. 2, the security administrator must restrict to facts when declaring a policy. Recall *fs(bank_db)* from Example 1: For protecting the association between an account number and the account holder, also the corresponding bank has to be protected.

In the following, we present an alternative definition of fact schemas leading to a greater flexibility in declaring policies while still guaranteeing confidentiality when these policies are enforced. This definition is driven by two ideas: It suffices to include a *subset* of the key into a fact schema; each *single* attribute suits as fact schema—whether or not it is a key attribute.

Definition 3 (Alternative fact schemas). *Let $\langle R, \mathscr{U}, \Sigma \rangle$ be a relation schema in ONF. The left-hand side of an fd $\sigma \in \Sigma$ is denoted by $lhs(\sigma)$. The alternative set of fact schemas of RS is then defined by*

$$fs_{alt}(RS) = \{A \mid A \in \mathscr{U}\} \cup \{\mathscr{A} \mid exists\ \sigma \in \Sigma : \mathscr{A} \subseteq lhs(\sigma)\} \cup$$
$$\{\mathscr{A}B \mid exists\ \sigma \in \Sigma\ such\ that\ \mathscr{A} \subseteq lhs(\sigma)\ and\ B \in \mathscr{U} \setminus lhs(\sigma)\}.$$

Theorem 2. *When exchanging the fact schema definition fs(RS) by $fs_{alt}(RS)$ from Def. 3, cqe_{stat} still preserves confidentiality in the sense of Def. 1.*

Reconsidering Example 1, we get the following set of alternative fact schemas:

$$fs_{alt}(bank\_db) = fs(bank\_db) \cup \{\{bank\}, \{acc\_no\}, \{acc\_holder\}, \{balance\},$$
$$\{bank, acc\_holder\}, \{bank, balance\}, \{acc\_no, acc\_holder\}, \{acc\_no, balance\}\}.$$

It is now possible to protect the association between an account number and the account holder without protecting the bank.

In general, for a relation schema in ONF with n attributes and a key of size k, the original facts definition yields $n - k + 1$ different fact schemas, whereas the alternative definition yields $2^k(n - k + 1) - 1$ different facts schemas.

3.2.2 Introducing Disjunction

Like the query language $\mathscr{L}_q$, also the policy language $\mathscr{L}_{ps}(\subseteq \mathscr{L}_{ps}^{max})$ in [8] is restricted to existential-R-sentences. Adding negation or conjunction to $\mathscr{L}_{ps}$ possibly enables the user to disclose secrets as illustrated by the following examples (which are based on Example 1). We thus propose a policy language by adding disjunction.

Example 3. Regarding negation, we consider the following policy and query:

$$pot\_sec = \{\neg(\exists X_{bal})bank\_db(\text{Bank of Springfield}, 213456, \text{Jones}, X_{bal})\}$$
$$\Phi \equiv (\exists X_{bal})bank\_db(\text{Bank of Springfield}, 213456, \text{Green}, X_{bal})$$

Obviously, Φ is answered correctly by cqe_{stat}. However, by employing the a priori knowledge Σ, the user knows that each instantiation of $(bank, acc\_no)$ is unique. The correct answer to Φ thereby implies the potential secret.

Example 4. Regarding conjunction, we consider the following policy and queries:

$$pot\_sec = \{\ (\exists X_{ah})(\exists X_{bal})bank\_db(\text{Bank of Springfield}, 123654, X_{ah}, X_{bal}) \wedge$$
$$(\exists X_{ah})(\exists X_{bal})bank\_db(\text{Gotham City Bank}, 312564, X_{ah}, X_{bal})\}$$
$$\Phi_1 \equiv (\exists X_{ah})(\exists X_{bal})bank\_db(\text{Bank of Springfield}, 123654, X_{ah}, X_{bal})$$
$$\Phi_2 \equiv (\exists X_{ah})(\exists X_{bal})bank\_db(\text{Gotham City Bank}, 312564, X_{ah}, X_{bal})$$

Obviously, cqe_{stat} answers both Φ_1 and Φ_2 correctly. However, combining both answers implies the potential secret.

Definition 4 (Disjunctive policy language). *The policy language $\mathscr{L}_{ps}^d (\subseteq \mathscr{L}_{ps}^{max})$ is inductively defined as follows: (1) If $\Psi \in \mathscr{L}_{ps}$ then $\Psi \in \mathscr{L}_{ps}^d$; (2) if $\Psi_1, \Psi_2 \in \mathscr{L}_{ps}^d$ then $\Psi_1 \vee \Psi_2 \in \mathscr{L}_{ps}^d$.*

Theorem 3. *The CQE emerging from cqe_{stat} by substituting $\mathscr{L}_{ps}$ with $\mathscr{L}_{ps}^d$, hereafter denoted with cqe_{stat}^d, preserves confidentiality in the sense of Def. 1.*

3.2.3 Introducing Free Variables

So far, elements of the policy language refer to tuples, subtuples, or disjunctions of (sub-)tuples. For practical purposes, this restriction might be unsatisfactory. Reconsider the schema from Example 1 and suppose a large instance of $bank\_db$. If the Bank of Springfield wants to keep the connections between account numbers and account holders confidential, the security administrator has to add formulas of the form $(\exists X_{bal})bank\_db(\text{Bank of Springfield}, N, H, X_{bal})$ to the policy for every single constant combination of account number N and account holder H actually occurring in $bank\_db$.

This is tedious and compromises the confidentiality: If the user knows that each *actually occurring* instantiation of a set of attributes is protected, he can simply determine these secrets from the policy (which is supposed to be public).

Protecting *every* constant combination of N and H (whether occurring in *bank_db* or not) requires to introduce free variables, since the underlying universe is supposed to be infinite. More specifically, we denote the policy language emerging from $\mathscr{L}_{ps}$ by introducing free variables with $\mathscr{L}_{ps}^f$. An element from $\mathscr{L}_{ps}^f$ is denoted by $\Psi(\vec{V})$ with $\vec{V} = (X_1, \ldots, X_l)$ being the vector of free variables occurring in $\Psi(\vec{V})$. A potential secret with free variables $\Psi(\vec{V}) \in \mathscr{L}_{ps}^f$ is expanded to the (infinite) set $ex(\Psi(\vec{V})) \subset \mathscr{L}_{ps}$ by substituting the free variables $\vec{V}$ with every possible constant combination. An element from $ex(\Psi(\vec{V}))$ is denoted by $\Psi(\vec{c})$ with $\vec{c}$ being a vector of constants. The expansion of a policy $pot\_sec \subset \mathscr{L}_{ps}^f$ is defined by $ex(pot\_sec) = \bigcup_{\Psi(\vec{V}) \in pot\_sec} ex(\Psi(\vec{V})) \subset \mathscr{L}_{ps}$. We now adapt the definition of the static censor (2) and the definition of confidentiality preservation to $\mathscr{L}_{ps}^f$:

$$censor_{stat}^f(pot\_sec, \Phi) := (\text{exists } \Psi(\vec{c}))(\Psi(\vec{c}) \in ex(pot\_sec) \text{ and } \Phi \models \Psi(\vec{c}))$$

Definition 5 (Confidentiality preservation for $\mathscr{L}_{ps}^f$). *This definition emerges from Def. 1 by replacing each Ψ with $\Psi(\vec{c})$ and $\Psi \in pot\_sec$ with $\Psi(\vec{c}) \in ex(pot\_sec)$.*

Theorem 4. *The CQE induced by $censor_{stat}^f$, hereafter called cqe_{stat}^f, preserves confidentiality in the sense of Def. 5.*

Unfortunately, $censor_{stat}^f$ has no straightforward algorithmic interpretation, since it has to check the elements of an infinite policy. We therefore propose an alternative censor, $censor_{stat}^{f,alt}$, which is defined in an algorithmic way and prove it equivalent to $censor_{stat}^f$. In the following, $\chi[A_i]$ denotes the instantiation of attribute A_i in the existential-R-sentence χ, e.g., if $\Psi(X_f) \equiv (\exists X_b)R(a, X_b, X_f)$, then $\Psi(X_f)[A_1] = a$, $\Psi(X_f)[A_2] = X_b$, and $\Psi(X_f)[A_3] = X_f$.

$$censor_{stat}^{f,alt}(pot\_sec, \Phi) := (\text{exists } \Psi(\vec{V}))(\Psi(\vec{V}) \in pot\_sec \text{ and for all } A \in \mathscr{U} :$$

$$\text{if } \Psi(\vec{V})[A] \in Const, \text{ then } \Phi[A] = \Psi(\vec{V})[A] \text{ and} \tag{3}$$

$$\text{if } \Psi(\vec{V})[A] \text{ is a free variable, then } \Phi[A] \in Const) \tag{4}$$

Lemma 1. *Let $\Phi \in \mathscr{L}_q$ be a query and $\Psi(\vec{V}) \in \mathscr{L}_{ps}^f$ a potential secret with free variables. Then, there exists a vector of constants $\vec{c}$ with $\Psi(\vec{c}) \in ex(\Psi(\vec{V}))$ such that $\Phi \models \Psi(\vec{c})$ if and only if for all attributes $A \in \mathscr{U}$ (3) and (4) hold.*

Theorem 5. *The CQE induced by $censor_{stat}^{f,alt}$, hereafter called $cqe_{stat}^{f,alt}$, preserves confidentiality in the sense of Def. 5.*

Finally, we justify that $\mathscr{L}_{ps}^d$ and $\mathscr{L}_{ps}^f$ are "compatible". Consider the policy language $\mathscr{L}_{ps}^{df}$ which is enhanced with disjunction *and* free variables. Following the proof of Theorem 3, under the given assumptions, static CQE is equivalent on $pot\_sec = \{\Psi_1, \ldots, \Psi_l\}$ and $pot\_sec' = \{\Psi_1 \vee \ldots \vee \Psi_l\}$ with $\Psi_i \in \mathscr{L}_{ps}$. The same argumentation can be applied if $\Psi_i \in \mathscr{L}_{ps}^f$. Thus, for each policy $pot\_sec \subset \mathscr{L}_{ps}^{df}$ we can break up each disjunctive secret into atomic secrets.

3.3 Limits of the Optimization

In Subsect. 3.1, we pointed out that using disjunction in queries can be harmful regarding confidentiality preservation. In particular, disjunctive structures can be interpreted as implicative structures, e. g., $\chi_1 \vee \chi_2 \equiv \neg\chi_1 \implies \chi_2$. If a purely static CQE is desired, disjunctive structures must be avoided in queries at all.

Regarding facts, Def. 3 requires each policy element to protect either a single attribute value or *at least* one key attribute value together with *at most* one non-key attribute value. The combination of two or more non-key attribute values could be disclosed with separate queries, each of which asking for one of the non-key attribute values in combination with the key value. E. g., consider a key $\mathcal{K}$ and two non-key attributes N_1 and N_2; if an element of the policy protects a value combination of $\mathcal{K} N_1 N_2$, then the user can first ask for the value combination $\mathcal{K} N_1$ and later for the value combination $\mathcal{K} N_2$. Considered separately, neither of the queries discloses a potential secret; however, exploiting the uniqueness property of the key leads to the disclosure of the value combination of $\mathcal{K} N_1 N_2$.

As demonstrated by Examples 3 and 4 in Subsect. 3.2, also the policy language cannot be enhanced arbitrarily. Negative potential secrets possibly enable the user to employ fds and conjunctive secrets can be disclosed "piece by piece". Thus, only disjunction can be added to the policy language without problems.

4 Implementing Static Inference Control in SQL

Implementations of static censors do not need external theorem provers but can utilize the functionality of the database management system. We assume that the potential secrets are encoded as tuples of a classification instance R_ps by replacing existentially quantified variables with the "new" symbol #. E. g., $\Psi \equiv (\exists X)R(a,X)$ is represented in R_ps by $R(a,\#)$. Let $\Phi \in \mathscr{L}_q$ be a query, $A\_1, \ldots, A\_l$ the attributes being instantiated by constants $a\_1, \ldots, a\_l$ in Φ, $B\_1, \ldots, B\_m$ the attributes being instantiated by existentially quantified variables in Φ, and $pot\_sec \subset \mathscr{L}_{ps}$ a policy. Elementary considerations indicate that $\Phi \models \Psi$ (as needed for $censor_{stat}$) holds for some $\Psi \in pot\_sec$ if and only if the following SQL statement yields a number greater than zero (adaptions for $censor_{stat}^{cn}$ and $censor_{stat}^{d}$ are straightforward):

```
SELECT COUNT(*) FROM R_ps
  WHERE (A_1 = 'a_1' OR A_1 ='#') AND (A_2 = 'a_2' OR A_2 ='#')
    AND ... AND (A_l = 'a_l' OR A_l = '#')
    AND (B_1 = '#') AND (B_2 = '#') AND ... AND (B_m = '#')
```

Considering $censor_{stat}^{f,alt}$, we encode free variables in R_ps by a "new" symbol $\sim$. E. g., $\Psi \equiv (\exists X_b)R(a,X_b,X_f)$ is represented in R_ps by $R(a,\#,\sim)$. Let Φ be defined as above, and $pot\_sec \subset \mathscr{L}_{ps}^f$ a policy. $\Phi \models \Psi'$ holds for some $\Psi' \in ex(pot\_sec)$ if and only if the following SQL statement yields a number greater than zero:

```
SELECT COUNT(*) FROM R_ps
  WHERE (A_1 = 'a_1' OR A_1 = '#' OR A_1 = '~')
    AND ... AND (A_l = 'a_l' OR A_l = '#' OR A_l = '~')
    AND (B_1 = '#') AND (B_2 = '#') AND ... AND (B_m = '#')
```

5 Towards an Optimized Inference Control System

We can put together the results of Sect. 3, i.e., substituting $\mathscr{L}_q$ with $\mathscr{L}_q^{cn}$ and $\mathscr{L}_{ps}$ with $\mathscr{L}_{ps}^{df}$, exchanging $fs(RS)$ by $fs_{alt}(RS)$, and sequencing conjunctions; the resulting CQE, denoted by cqe_{stat}^{opt}, preserves confidentiality in the sense of Def. 5.

Especially for a database user, the query language $\mathscr{L}_q^{cn}$ is still unsatisfactory. To improve the situation, we introduce an algorithm that principally accepts each query Φ from $\mathscr{L}_q^{max}$ but, if necessary, transforms Φ into a "stronger" query $\Phi_{cn} \in \mathscr{L}_q^{cn}$ with $\Phi_{cn} \models \Phi$ (but possibly $\Phi \not\models \Phi_{cn}$). Using this algorithm, we sketch an interactive system, providing expressive policy and query languages on the one hand, and (if possible) offering static inference control on the other hand. The idea to transform a "harmful" query into a "harmless" query is related to the concept of query modification, introduced by Stonebraker/Wong [22]. While query modification suitably appends a conjunct to each query, our approach rearranges the given syntactic structure of the query. Our algorithm expects a query $\Phi \in \mathscr{L}_q^{max}$, an a priori user knowledge log_0, an instance r, and a policy pot_sec as input. It works as follows:

(1) Convert Φ into prenex disjunctive normal form $\Phi_{PDNF} \equiv (\exists X_1)\ldots(\exists X_l)\ (\bigvee_{i=1}^{m} (\bigwedge_{j=1}^{n_i} \varphi_j))$, where φ_j denotes a (possibly negated) atomic formula.

(2) Rearrange Φ_{PDNF} into $\Phi_{DNF} \equiv \bigvee_{i=1}^{m}(\bigwedge_{j=1}^{n_i}(\exists X_{j_1})\ldots(\exists X_{j_l})\varphi_j)$, where X_{j_k} occurs in φ_j. This step is correct because of the assumption that each existentially quantified variable occurs only once in the formula.

(3) Transform Φ_{DNF} into $\Phi_{cn} := \bigwedge_{i=1}^{m}(\bigwedge_{j=1}^{n_i}(\exists X_{j_1})\ldots(\exists X_{j_l})\varphi_j)$. Note that $\Phi_{cn} \not\equiv \Phi$. However, it can easily be verified that $\Phi_{cn} \models \Phi_{DNF}$ and thus $\Phi_{cn} \models \Phi$.

(4) Return $cqe_{stat}^{cn}(\langle \Phi_{cn} \rangle, log_0)(r, pot\_sec)$.

An interactive inference control system now roughly proceeds in two phases. The database instance r is assumed to be set up in advance. Initially, the system starts in "static inference control mode" (SIC mode), which means that the static censors are used when answering user queries (analogously, in "dynamic inference control mode" (DIC mode), only the non-static censors are used).

Policy declaration phase: The security administrator declares $pot\_sec = \{\Psi_1, \ldots, \Psi_m\}$ with $\Psi_i \in \mathscr{L}_q^{max}$. If pot_sec contains a $\Psi_i \notin \mathscr{L}_{ps}^{df}$, a static inference control cannot be performed later on. For every such Ψ_i, the security administrator can choose between the following actions: a) withdraw Ψ_i; b) affirm Ψ_i; in this case, the system completely switches to DIC mode.

Query phase (usually performed repeatedly): A user sends a query $\Phi \in \mathscr{L}_q^{max}$ to the database. If the system is in DIC mode, Φ is answered. If the system is in SIC mode and $\Phi \notin \mathscr{L}_q^{cn}$, the user can choose between the following actions: a) withdraw Φ; b) affirm Φ; in this case, the system completely switches to DIC mode and Φ is answered; c) accept the rewrite suggestion Φ_{cn} (according to the above sketched algorithm); in this case, Φ_{cn} is answered instead of Φ.

6 Conclusion and Future Work

We investigated efficient inference control enforcing policies for closed queries in relational databases by identifying situations in which it is possible to apply static CQE and by presenting suitable SQL implementations. We proposed an interactive inference control system, issuing database users and security administrators with flexible languages for expressing queries and potential secrets. These languages have been enhanced compared to the static CQE in [8] while it is still possible to employ static censors guaranteeing feasible runtime.

However, our approach is not meant to be an exhaustive optimization of CQE in relational databases, but should be seen as a step in this direction. Further development could deal with global semantic constraints (such as inclusion dependencies), other types of local semantic constraints (such as multivalued dependencies), free variables in the query language to express open queries, and alternative CQE enforcement methods (lying and combined method; see [4]).

References

1. Abiteboul, S., Hull, R., Vianu, V.: Foundations of Databases. Addison-Wesley, Reading (1995)
2. Bertino, E., Sandhu, R.: Database security – concepts, approaches, and challenges. IEEE Trans. Dependable Sec. Comput. 2(1), 2–18 (2005)
3. Biskup, J.: Boyce-Codd normal form and object normal forms. Inf. Process. Lett. 32(1), 29–33 (1989)
4. Biskup, J., Bonatti, P.: Controlled query evaluation for enforcing confidentiality in complete information systems. Int. J. Inf. Sec. 3(1), 14–27 (2004)
5. Biskup, J., Bonatti, P.: Controlled query evaluation with open queries for a decidable relational submodel. Ann. Math. Artif. Intell. 50, 39–77 (2007)
6. Biskup, J., Bonatti, P.A.: Lying versus refusal for known potential secrets. Data Knowl. Eng. 38, 199–222 (2001)
7. Biskup, J., Bonatti, P.A.: Controlled query evaluation for known policies by combining lying and refusal. Ann. Math. Artif. Intell. 40, 37–62 (2004)
8. Biskup, J., Embley, D.W., Lochner, J.-H.: Reducing inference control to access control for normalized database schemas. Inf. Process. Lett. 106(1), 8–12 (2008)
9. Biskup, J., Lochner, J.-H.: Enforcing confidentiality in relational databases by reducing inference control to access control. In: Garay, J.A., Lenstra, A.K., Mambo, M., Peralta, R. (eds.) ISC 2007. LNCS, vol. 4779, pp. 407–422. Springer, Heidelberg (2007)
10. Bonatti, P., Kraus, S., Subrahmanian, V.S.: Foundations of secure deductive databases. IEEE Trans. Knowl. Data Eng. 7(3), 406–422 (1995)
11. Brodsky, A., Farkas, C., Jajodia, S.: Secure databases: constraints, inference channels, and monitoring disclosures. IEEE Trans. Knowl. Data Eng. 12(6), 900–919 (2000)
12. Byun, J.W., Bertino, E.: Micro-views, or on how to protect privacy while enhancing data usability—concepts and challenges. ACM SIGMOD Record 35(1), 9–13 (2006)
13. Cuppens, F., Gabillon, A.: Cover story management. Data Knowl. Eng. 37(2), 177–201 (2001)
14. Dawson, S., De Capitani di Vimercati, S., Samarati, P.: Specification and enforcement of classification and inference constraints. In: IEEE Symposium on Security and Privacy, pp. 181–195. IEEE Computer Society, Los Alamitos (1999)

15. Farkas, C., Jajodia, S.: The inference problem: a survey. SIGKDD Explorations 4(2), 6–11 (2002)
16. Griffiths, P.P., Wade, B.W.: An authorization mechanism for a relational database system. ACM Trans. Database Syst. 1(3), 242–255 (1976)
17. Jajodia, S., Sandhu, R.S.: Toward a multilevel secure relational data model. In: SIGMOD Conference, pp. 50–59. ACM, New York (1991)
18. Lunt, T.F., Denning, D.E., Schell, R.R., Heckman, M., Shockley, W.R.: The seaview security model. IEEE Trans. Software Eng. 16(6), 593–607 (1990)
19. Rjaibi, W., Bird, P.: A multi-purpose implementation of mandatory access control in relational database management systems. In: VLDB, pp. 1010–1020. ACM, New York (2004)
20. Sandhu, R.: Lattice-based access control models. Computer 26(11), 9–19 (1993)
21. Sicherman, G.L., de Jonge, W., van de Riet, R.P.: Answering queries without revealing secrets. ACM Trans. Database Syst. 8(1), 41–59 (1983)
22. Stonebraker, M., Wong, E.: Access control in a relational data base management system by query modification. In: ACM/CSC-ER, pp. 180–186. ACM, New York (1974)

Collaborative Privacy – A Community-Based Privacy Infrastructure

Jan Kolter[1], Thomas Kernchen[2], and Günther Pernul[1]

[1] Department of Information Systems, University of Regensburg,
D-93040 Regensburg, Germany
{jan.kolter,guenther.pernul}@wiwi.uni-regensburg.de
[2] Steria Mummert Consulting AG, Französische Str. 48, D-10117 Berlin, Germany
thomas.kernchen@steria-mummert.de

Abstract. The landscape of the World Wide Web with all its versatile services heavily relies on the disclosure of private user information. Service providers collecting more and more of these personal user data pose a growing privacy threat for users. Addressing user concerns privacy-enhancing technologies emerged. One goal of these technologies is to enable users to improve the control over their personal data. A famous representative is the PRIME project that aims for a holistic privacy-enhancing identity management system. However, approaches like the PRIME privacy architecture require service providers to change their server infrastructure and add specific privacy-enhancing components. In the near future, service providers are not expected to alter internal processes. In this paper, we introduce a collaborative privacy community that allows the open exchange of privacy-related information. We lay out the privacy community's functions and potentials within a user-centric, provider-independent privacy architecture that will help foster the usage and acceptance of privacy-enhancing technologies.

1 Introduction

Today's rich offer of services on the World Wide Web increasingly requires the release of personal user data, which poses a growing privacy threat to Internet users. Web site providers use these personal data to create and analyze profiles or to trigger personalized advertisements. At the worst, personal information is released or sold to third parties.

Motivated by users who needed technical means to protect their private data, privacy-enhancing technologies emerged [6,14]. A frequently discussed subject in this area is anonymity on network level. On application level, privacy-enhancing technologies aim for solutions that assist users in controlling and managing the disclosure of personal data. However, most approaches rely on the compliance of service providers who are required to reveal their data handling practices truthfully.

The goal of this paper is the introduction of a collaborative privacy community that facilitates a service-provider-independent privacy management. We propose a user-centric privacy architecture and show the functions and the potentials of an inherent collaborative privacy community. Finally, we present a prototypical implementation of our solution.

D. Gritzalis and J. Lopez (Eds.): SEC 2009, IFIP AICT 297, pp. 226–236, 2009.
© IFIP International Federation for Information Processing 2009

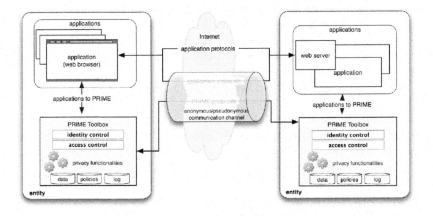

Fig. 1. High Level PRIME Architecture [18]

The remainder of this paper is structured as follows. After describing related work in Section 2, we present an overview as well as the components of a user-centric privacy architecture in Section 3. In Section 4 we introduce the content, functions and the implementation of our collaborative privacy community. Section 5 concludes the paper with an outlook on future work.

2   Related Work

The Platform for Privacy Preferences (P3P) [7] represents an early privacy-enhancing technology system. Offering a suitable policy language that allows service providers to express machine-readable privacy policies, P3P enables a privacy agent on user-side to indicate deviations from previously-specified privacy preferences.

Weaknesses of P3P have been subject to frequent discussions in the past [10,15]. As P3P assumes complete and truthful privacy policies, most service providers' hesitation to offer P3P privacy policies is a main reason for P3P's lagging acceptance.

Aiming to support users' ability to maintain their privacy, the European PRIME project[1] (Privacy and Identity Management for Europe) developed a privacy-enhancing identity management system, containing a privacy architecture with different design guidelines, protocols and prototypical scenarios [18].

The PRIME architecture (see Fig. 1) allows users to control the disclosure and the usage of their personal data [18,25]. A significant element of the architecture is the PRIME Toolbox, which needs to be installed both on client-side and on user-side. The PRIME Toolbox incorporates all necessary components for privacy-enhancing identity management and enables users to manage and use different digital identities with varying personal data.

A further element of the PRIME architecture is the PRIME Middleware that integrates all PRIME components and coordinates the communication between PRIME

---

[1] https://www.prime-project.eu/

interaction parties. The PRIME console serves as a graphical interface enabling users to set privacy-related preferences that are used to negotiate data handling practices with service providers. Furthermore, an overview of already disclosed data is provided. The architecture is capable of enforcing negotiated policies, utilizing the installed PRIME components of service providers.

In order to make use of the described PRIME functionality, both users and service providers need to install the PRIME Middleware and the PRIME Toolbox. From a user perspective the attractiveness of PRIME rises, if the majority of service providers adapt their service infrastructure. Hence, the success of PRIME highly relies on the service providers' willingness to integrate the described PRIME components into their applications.

3   User-Centric Privacy Architecture

In the last section we described existing privacy solutions that strongly rely on the compliance of service providers. From today's perspective it seems unlikely that service providers will fundamentally change their proven back-end services. Rising privacy threats of users will not convince service providers to adopt a comprehensive and complex privacy infrastructure. Furthermore, conflicting with their own interests, Web site providers will not contribute to the accuracy and quality of machine-readable privacy policies voluntarily.

Addressing these facts, we introduce a user-centric, provider-independent privacy architecture, employing a collaborative privacy community to share and exchange privacy-related information among Internet users. Unlike provider-dependent solutions our proposed architecture does not require service providers to set up additional components or functions. Accepting today's service landscape of the World Wide Web, we enable Internet users to control the disclosure and management of personal data.

In Fig. 2 we present an overview of our privacy architecture. Seeking means to make an informed decision about the disclosure of personal data, the user is supported by a browser plug-in, which serves as the user interface. The browser plug-in displays privacy-related information and functions, which are provided by three local privacy components. The Privacy Preference Generator component assists users in controlling future information flows of personal data. The Privacy Agent component helps users check and control actual information flows. Finally, the Data Disclosure Log provides an overview of past personal information flows. All local privacy components interact with a collaborative privacy community, which provides supplemental privacy-relevant information about service providers. The community is maintained cooperatively by all participating members.

In the following we shortly discuss the main functions of each local privacy component, before the collaborative privacy community is introduced in Section 4.

3.1   Local Privacy Components

Potential information flows reflect a system's potential to disclose information [17]. From a privacy perspective, modeling users' privacy preferences, which define future disclosures of personal data, is a critical challenge.

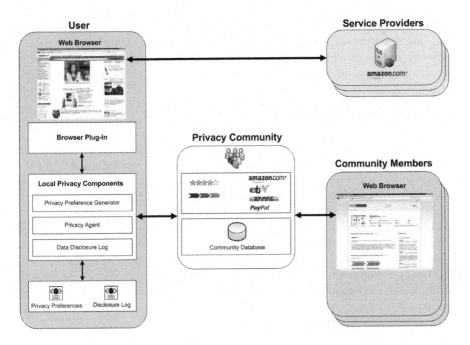

Fig. 2. Collaborative, Provider-independent Privacy Architecture

Our user-centric privacy architecture provides a user-friendly Privacy Preference Generator component. The resulting privacy preferences reflect users' willingness to release personal data under certain circumstances and serve as basis for underlying privacy tools. APPEL [9], a privacy preference language built for P3P, provides a language to represent rule-based privacy preferences.

In our architecture, we allow users to define privacy preferences individually for different Internet service types [4], guaranteeing more realistic and practical privacy preferences.

Privacy tools that protect actual information flows help users make an informed disclosure decision, when personal data is about to be released to a service provider.

The presented privacy architecture employs a Privacy Agent component that supervises data transactions. If available, the agent reads the privacy policy of a service provider and matches it with pre-defined privacy preferences. Doing so, the agent recommends a certain behavior to the user. The P3P specification [7] provides the necessary technical means for the representation of privacy policies. The XACML standard [21] allows a more fine-grained and flexible definition of policies [2]. An example for a P3P-compliant privacy agent is the Privacy Bird [8], a browser plug-in for the Microsoft Internet Explorer.

Finally, our privacy architecture provides a tool that keeps track of all personal data transactions. Such a disclosure log allows users to manage personal data once they have been transferred to a service provider [22,23]. A data transaction log bears the potential to present users a clear overview, which service provider stores what personal data at a certain time. This component requires both tracking functions that record and store data disclosures as well as usable interfaces that illustrate data transactions in an understandable way. Ideally, the disclosure log allows users to directly access, change or remove disclosed personal data stored by a service provider. Furthermore, a data disclosure log is capable of calculating potential linkabilities between data transactions.

4   Collaborative Privacy Community

Representing the central element of our presented privacy architecture, the collaborative privacy community facilitates the exchange of privacy-relevant information, ratings and experiences about service providers. These experiences involve, how personal data are used by certain service providers, and whether that usage is consistent with service providers' published privacy policies. These data represent a valuable, provider-independent information source for all three local privacy components, leading to a more informed disclosure behavior and enhanced privacy management of users.

The privacy community provides two access points. Internet users can browse a Wiki-like [19] Web front-end. Information about each service provider is grouped into articles, which can be viewed and edited by users. In addition, the privacy community provides a Web service interface, allowing local privacy components on user-side to directly access necessary information.

4.1   Content and Functions

Underscoring the advantages of a provider-independent privacy infrastructure, we present the following structural and functional characteristics of our introduced privacy community.

For each service provider the community stores and offers static information, the required amount of personal data for each offered process, third parties the service provider shares personal data with, a description and evaluation of current and past privacy policies, the adherence to the published privacy policies, as well as individual experiences and ratings of community users. Additionally, the privacy community facilitates the controlled exchange of privacy preferences among connected users.

4.1.1   Static Information about Service Providers

When accessing an unknown Web site without privacy-enhancing technologies, users generally have the option to trust a service provider's privacy statement at face value or to find information about the service provider's reputation. A survey [12] shows that many users do not look up reputational information, but rather judge service providers' trustworthiness by estimating the Web site's "Look and Feel", considering questionable factors.

As collecting information about a service provider is time-consuming, this behavior of especially inexperienced users is understandable. Addressing this fact, the privacy community gives users an overview of information about service providers, such as the server location, the service type and a short description of the service offer. That information is utilized by the local Privacy Agent component and displayed to the user on demand, enabling users to easily retrieve necessary data to judge the trustworthiness of service providers. The provider's service type enables the Privacy Agent to more accurately match privacy preferences of the user with a Web site's privacy policy. The local Data Disclosure Log component benefits from information, how to access and revoke personal information that have already been transferred to a service provider.

In particular, static information about a service provider in our privacy community include:

- The service provider's URL
- The location of the server
- The offered service type(s)
- Information how to change/revoke already transferred personal data
- Contact information
- A short textual description of the service provider
- Overall privacy rating

A URL is required to exactly identify each service provider. The server location clarifies jurisdictional matters, as different privacy laws apply in different countries. The offered service type(s) allow the application of more fine-tuned privacy preferences. As each service provider's service type (e.g. "Web Mail" or "Online Shopping") is accessible, privacy preferences can individually be defined and applied for each service type. Helping users exercise their rights to access and control already transferred data [11], the community provides information (e.g. a link or an e-mail address) how to change or remove these disclosed information. Exact contact information facilitates prosecution, if personal data are misused, or if users want to enforce their rights to revoke their personal data. Furthermore, a short description specifies the main characteristics of a service provider. Finally, an aggregated overall privacy rating shows a quick estimate of user ratings, which are explained below.

4.1.2   Required Amount of Personal Data

Our proposed privacy community enables users to know in advance, what personal information is needed to use a certain service in the World Wide Web.

Users generally understand the necessity to disclose, for example, their name, address and payment information for a product order at an online shop. If the service provider asks for additional information, such as the marital status, the date-of-birth or the annual salary, users tend to abort the process, if they feel uncomfortable releasing this excessive data. An online survey we conducted with 350 persons revealed that 77% of all test persons cancel registration and buying processes, if too many personal data are requested. Unfortunately, with today's technical means users are unable to determine at most Web sites, what personal information is necessary to use a specific service. To find out, users have to start the process of filling Web forms. In many cases the most privacy-sensitive information is requested on the last form page. If the user decides not to proceed, the frustrated user wasted valuable time and disclosed the already transferred information with no use.

The privacy community spares users from this negative experience and offers the amount of necessary data in advance. For each process a service provider offers the community stores all required personal data. In this context, a process refers to each separate action the service provider offers, such as "Buy" or "Subscribe to Newsletter". In addition, the community stores, when a process relies on the completion of a different process. The process "Buy" could, for instance, require the completion of the process "Registration". An automatic evaluation based on the service type assists users in evaluating the required amount of personal data a service provider requests.

As the amount of collected personal data represents a fundamental element of privacy policies, the local Privacy Agent can retrieve this information from the community and match it with individual privacy preferences, if no machine-readable privacy policy is available from the service provider.

4.1.3   Third Party Releases

The decision to disclose personal information to a service provider not only relies on the amount of data, but also on the service provider's data handling practices. Here, the release of user data to third parties is a considerably privacy-sensitive factor.

For each service provider the privacy community stores third parties the service provider shares personal data with. These parties could be affiliated companies or corporate networks. This information can be displayed to the user by the local Privacy Agent on demand. Again, information about third party releases can be utilized to replace a machine-readable privacy policy of the service provider.

4.1.4   Collecting and Explaining Privacy Policies

For many users the service provider's textual privacy policy is the only available information about data handling practices. Studies show, however, that privacy policies are not understandable to and are read by only a small fraction of Internet users [16,24]. A privacy community facilitates experienced users to write an understandable description of privacy policies. As privacy experts comprehend all aspects of a policy, they have the ability to paraphrase important elements of the privacy policy in a form that - compared to automatic privacy policy summaries [3,8] - is easy to understand.

Furthermore, as privacy policies change over time, the community keeps a history of privacy policies, containing both textual policies as well as machine-readable P3P policies, if available. This enables users to compare ex post, what privacy policy has been valid, when personal data have been disclosed to a service provider.

The privacy community also allows users to rate each stored privacy policy. A calculated privacy rank [1] supports inexperienced users to recognize and compare data handling practices of service providers.

4.1.5   Adherence to Privacy Policies

As a privacy-friendly privacy policy is no guarantee that a service provider will follow this expressed policy, our community enables users to rate the policy adherence of service providers. Based on their individual experiences users can evaluate, whether a service provider processes personal data as stated in a privacy policy. For example, if not expressed in the privacy policy, a personalized e-mail offering a product would justify a negative policy adherence rating of this service provider. Displayed by the local Privacy Agent, this information considerably influences users' decision to disclose personal data.

4.1.6   Sharing Privacy Preferences with Connected Users

In Section 3.1 we pointed out the purpose and usage of individual privacy preferences. The Privacy Preference Generator component allows the definition of these disclosure rules, which are in turn used by the Privacy Agent component to calculate disclosure recommendations. The quality of these recommendations strongly relies on the accuracy of the defined privacy preferences. Even though the Privacy Preference Generator component should alleviate this challenge by offering a usable and understandable user interface, building accurate privacy preferences is a critical task. This especially applies to inexperienced users, as they are not familiar with service providers' data handling practices and the privacy-related language used.

For these users the privacy community offers means to adopt privacy preferences from experienced users. Offering a social networking component [5], the privacy community allows users to upload and share privacy preferences with connected users. Privacy preferences of a trusted privacy expert represent valuable input for the local Privacy Agent of inexperienced users, resulting in improved disclosure recommendations.

4.2   User Management

The privacy community manages three different user roles. The basic user role is assigned to every user and allows the access of all information about service providers. Furthermore, it permits editing articles collaboratively. Basic users are able to create articles of new service providers. In order to prevent vandalism, the privacy community provides backup and archive functionality. An overview of all existing articles is available.

If users want to connect to other members of the privacy community, a simple registration is necessary. Registration only requires a username and a password. The community does not request any additional personal information. Registered users have the opportunity to upload their privacy preferences. Offering a social networking component, it is possible to look up and connect to friends who can share privacy preferences. We point out that this social networking component does not have the purpose of maintaining social contacts but only to exchange privacy experiences and privacy preferences. Users can self-assess their level of knowledge and experience in the area of privacy, helping inexperienced users to estimate the quality of their opinions and preferences.

Finally, users holding the administrator role define vocabularies of service providers' offered processes as well as personal data types. If necessary, administrators are able to block users/members.

4.3   Prototype

We implemented a prototype of our proposed privacy community. The Web front-end is available following this link[2].

4.3.1   Architecture

Figure 3 depicts the privacy community's architecture. As both the community's Web front-end and the local privacy components on user-side, access the community, we

___
[2] http://www-ifs.uni-regensburg.de/Privacy/Community

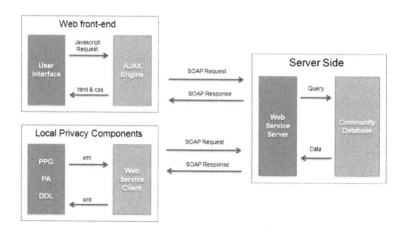

Fig. 3. Architecture of the Privacy Community

employ a service-oriented architecture (SOA) [20]. A SOA loosely couples client applications from the back-end and provides a high degree of interoperability. This enables a variety of clients to access the community database. Web services that provide a machine-readable WSDL definition encapsulate all information pieces of the community. Furthermore, the interaction via SOAP messages guarantees a consistent data exchange format.

For the Web front-end we utilize an Ajax-based [13] Web architecture, allowing asynchronous, interactive communication between the Web front-end and the community server. The client-side Ajax engine transforms JavaScript requests into SOAP requests, which are sent to the community server. The Web service server receives and processes requests querying the community database, before requested data are sent back to the client via SOAP. On client-side the Ajax engine transforms the SOAP messages to a user-friendly GUI, employing html and css. The local privacy components of our presented architecture - the Privacy Preference Generator (PPG), the Privacy Agent (PA) and the Data Disclosure Log (DDL) - directly access the Web service server via SOAP messages.

4.3.2   Implementation
For the Web front end we utilize the JavaScript framework Yahoo! UI Library[3] (YUI), which offers the necessary drag & drop and autocomplete functions as well as overlays and browser history handling.

The back-end employs NuSOAP[4], a PHP-based Web service server that provides the required functionality for our proposed solution. The Web service interface definitions can be accessed following this link[5].

For the sake of brevity the interested reader is referred to the hyperlink above for a detailed review of the front-end design.

---

[3] http://developer.yahoo.com/yui/

[4] http://sourceforge.net/projects/nusoap/

[5] http://www-ifs.uni-regensburg.de/Privacy/Community/server_side/soap_server.php

5   Conclusions

In this paper we present the concept and design of a collaborative privacy community. Marking a central element of our underlying user-centric privacy architecture, the privacy community allows a provider-independent exchange of privacy-relevant information and ratings about service providers. Moreover, our solution enables users to know in advance, what personal data is required for a specific service. Benefitting from the knowledge of experienced users, the privacy community facilitates a more informed decision about the disclosure and management of personal data. Provider independence as well as the collaborative character will contribute to a broader acceptance of privacy-enhancing technologies.

Future work will involve user tests as well as the integration of local privacy components.

References

1. Agrawal, R., Grosky, W.I., Fotouhi, F.: Ranking Privacy Policy. In: Proceedings of the 23rd International Conference on Data Engineering Workshops (ICDE 2007), pp. 192–197. IEEE Computer Society, Los Alamitos (2007)
2. Anderson, A.: The Relationship Between XACML and P3P Privacy Policies (November 2004),
   http://research.sun.com/projects/xacml/XACML_P3P_Relationship.html
3. Arshad, F.: Privacy Fox - A JavaScript-based P3P Agent for Mozilla Firefox. Technical report (2004)
4. Bergmann, M.: PRIME Internal Privacy Preference Survey About Privacy Concerns and Condidtions. Technische Universität Dresden, Technische Berichte, TUD-FI07-04-Mai- (May 2005)
5. Boyd, D.M., Ellison, N.B.: Social Network Sites: Definition, History, and Scholarship. Journal of Computer-Mediated Communication 13(1), 210–230 (2007)
6. Burkert, H.: Privacy-enhancing Technologies: Typology, Critique, Vision. In: Agre, P.E., Rotenberg, M. (eds.) Technology and Privacy: The New Landscape, pp. 125–142. MIT Press, Cambridge (1997)
7. Cranor, L., Dobbs, B., Egelman, S., Hogben, G., Humphrey, J., Langheinrich, M., Marchiori, M., Presler-Marshall, M., Reagle, J., Schunter, M., Stampley, D., Wenning, R.: The Platform for Privacy Preferences 1.1 (P3P1.1) Specification. W3C Working Group Note (November 2006)
8. Cranor, L., Guduru, P., Arjula, M.: User Interfaces for Privacy Agents. ACM Transactions on Computer-Human Interaction (TOCHI) 13(2), 135–178 (2006)
9. Cranor, L., Langheinrich, M., Marchiori, M.: A P3P Preference Exchange Language 1.0 (APPEL 1.0). W3C Working Draft (April 2002)
10. Electronic Privacy Information Center. Pretty Poor Privacy: An Assessment of P3P and Internet Privacy. Technical report (2000)
11. European Parliament. EU-Directive 95/46/EC. Official Journal of the European Communities No L 281 31 (October 1995)
12. Fogg, B.J., Marshall, J., Laraki, O., Osipovich, A., Varma, C., Fang, N., Paul, J., Rangnekar, A., Shon, J., Swani, P., Treinen, M.: What Makes Web Sites Credible?: A Report on a Large Quantitative Study. In: CHI 2001: Proceedings of the SIGCHI conference on Human Factors in Computing Systems, pp. 61–68. ACM, New York (2001)

13. J. J. Garrett. Ajax: A New Approach to Web Applications (February 2005), http://www.adaptivepath.com/ideas/essays/archives/000385.php
14. Goldberg, I., Wagner, D., Brewer, E.: Privacy-enhancing Technologies for the Internet. In: Proceedings of the 42nd IEEE Spring COMPCON. IEEE Computer Society Press, Los Alamitos (1997)
15. Hogben, G., Jackson, T., Wilikens, M.: A Fully Compliant Research Implementation of the P3P Standard for Privacy Protection: Experiences and Recommendations. In: Gollmann, D., Karjoth, G., Waidner, M. (eds.) ESORICS 2002. LNCS, vol. 2502, pp. 104–125. Springer, Heidelberg (2002)
16. Jensen, C., Potts, C., Jensen, C.: Privacy Practices of Internet Users: Self-reports versus Observed Behavior. International Journal of Human-Computer Studies 63(1-2), 203–227 (2005)
17. Lederer, S., Hong, I., Dey, K., Landay, A.: Personal Privacy through Understanding and Action: Five Pitfalls for Designers. Personal and Ubiquitous Computing 8(6), 440–454 (2004)
18. Leenes, R., Schallaböck, J., Hansen, M.: Privacy and Identity Management for Europe, PRIME white paper, version 3 (May 2008), https://www.prime-project.eu/prime_products/whitepaper/PRIME-Whitepaper-V3.pdf
19. Leuf, B., Cunningham, W.: The Wiki Way: Quick Collaboration on the Web. Addison-Wesley Longman, Amsterdam (2001)
20. MacKenzie, C.M., Laskey, K., McCabe, F., Brown, P.F., Metz, R.: Reference Model for Service Oriented Architecture 1.0. OASIS Standard (October 2006)
21. Moses, T.: eXtensible Access Control Markup Language (XACML) Version 2.0. OASIS Standard (February 2005)
22. Pettersson, J., Fischer-Hübner, S., Bergmann, M.: Outlining Data Track: Privacy-friendly Data Maintenance for End-users. In: Proceedings of the 15th International Conference on Informations Systems Development (ISD 2006). Springer Scientific Publishers, Heidelberg (2006)
23. Pettersson, J., Fischer-Hübner, S., Casassa Mont, M., Pearson, S.: How Ordinary Internet Users Can Have a Chance to Influence Privacy Policies. In: Proceedings of the 4th Nordic conference on Human-computer interaction (NordiCHI 2006), pp. 473–476. ACM Press, New York (2006)
24. Pollach, I.: What's Wrong With Online Privacy Policies? Commun. ACM 50(9), 103–108 (2007)
25. Sommer, D., Casassa Mont, M., Pearson, S.: PRIME Architecture version 3, Deliverable D14.2.d (July 2008), https://www.prime-project.eu/prime_products/reports/arch/pub_del_D14.2.d_ec_WP14.2_v3_Final.pdf

Security and Privacy Improvements for the Belgian eID Technology

Pieter Verhaeghe[1], Jorn Lapon[2], Bart De Decker[1], Vincent Naessens[2], and Kristof Verslype[1]

[1] Katholieke Universiteit Leuven, Department of Computer Science, Celestijnenlaan 200A, 3001 Heverlee, Belgium
`firstname.lastname@cs.kuleuven.be`
[2] Katholieke Hogeschool Sint-Lieven, Department of Industrial Engineering, Gebroeders Desmetstraat 1, 9000 Gent, Belgium
`firstname.lastname@kahosl.be`

Abstract. The Belgian Electronic Identity Card enables Belgian citizens to prove their identity digitally and to sign electronic documents. At the end of 2009, every Belgian citizen older than 12 years will have such an eID card. In the future, usage of the eID card may be mandatory. However, irresponsible use of the card may cause harm to individuals.

Currently, there exist some privacy and security problems related to the use of the eID card. This paper focuses on solutions to tackle these problems. A new authentication protocol is introduced to substantially reduce the risk of abusing the single sign-on authentication and privacy friendly identity files are proposed to improve the citizen's privacy.

1 Introduction

Belgium has introduced an electronic identity card [1,2] in 2002 as one of the first countries in Europe. The Belgian government aims at completing the roll-out by the end of 2009. At that time, each citizen will be the owner of an eID card. The card enables individuals to prove their identity digitally and to sign electronic documents. The Belgian eID card opens up new opportunities for the government, their citizens, service providers and application developers.

It is clear that many application developers benefit from this evolution. Today, integrating eID technology for authentication purposes is a real hot topic in Belgium. However, the usage of the eID card involves a few security and privacy hazards. Still, most citizens are unaware of these pitfalls, which is disturbing, since the usage of the card is highly encouraged both by the government and the industry.

This paper first explains the Belgian eID card technology in section 2 and outlines security and privacy hazards related to the usage of the card in section 3. Next, a new authenication protocol *auth* (using the eID card) is presented and privacy-friendly identity files are introduced in section 4 and evaluated in section 5. Finally, the paper draws conclusions and describes directions for future research.

2 Belgian eID Technology

This section gives an overview of the current Belgian eID technology. A more elaborate description can be found in [1,2].

D. Gritzalis and J. Lopez (Eds.): SEC 2009, IFIP AICT 297, pp. 237–247, 2009.

2.1   Contents of the Belgian eID Card

Private information such as the owner's name, birthdate and -place, address, digital picture and National Registration Number is stored in three separate files: an identity file, an address file and a picture file. The files are signed by the National Registration Bureau (NRB). The National Registration Number (NRN) is a unique nation-wide identification number that is assigned to each natural person.

Two key pairs are stored on the eID card. One key pair is used for authentication, the other is used is for signing. The (qualified) e-signatures are legally binding. The public keys are embedded in a certificate which also contains the NRN and the name of the card holder. The private keys are stored in a tamper-proof part of the chip and can only be activated (not *read*) with a PIN code. Authentication is single sign-on, i.e. the PIN code is only required for the first authentication. For signing, a PIN code is needed for each signature[3].

2.2   Belgian Public Key Infrastructure

The certificates on the eID card are part of a larger hierarchical infrastructure, the Belgian Public Key Infrastructure (be-PKI) [4]. The hierarchy is illustrated in figure 1. The citizen's signature and authentication certificates are issued by a *Citizen_CA* which is certified by the *Belgium_Root_CA*. Other governmental CAs such as the *Card_Admin_CA* and *Government_CA* also have certificates issued by the *Belgium_Root_CA*. The former can update the eID card. The latter certifies the National Registration Bureau (NRB) which signs the identity and address file and offers other services in the public sector. The *Belgium_Root_CA* has two certificates. The first is a self-signed certificate, that allows for offline validation of the signature and authentication certificates on the eID card. The second certificate is issued by GlobalSign. The latter is typically known to popular applications (such as browsers) and allows for the automatic validation of electronic signatures. The PKI provides Authority Revocation Lists (ARL) and Certificate Revocation Lists (CRL) [5] that keeps the serial numbers of the revoked certificates.

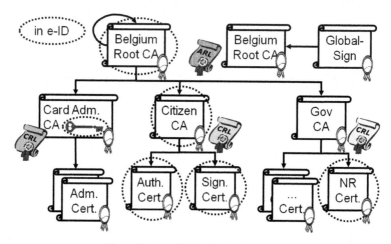

Fig. 1. Belgian Public Key Infrastructure

2.3 Official Middleware

The cryptographic functionalities in the Belgian eID card are accessed through middleware [6]. Applications typically interact with the card via a simple API [7] offered by this middleware. If a document needs to be signed, the middleware passes a hash of the document to the card. Similarly, a hash of the challenge is passed to the card for authentication purposes. When an application wants to authenticate or sign a document with the eID card, the middleware requests the user to enter his PIN code. The middleware can also verify the validity of the certificates (using CRL or OCSP). It is important to note that the use of the official middleware is not mandatory. Several alternatives, developed by different companies, are available.

3 Security and Privacy Hazards

This section elaborates on security and privacy hazards related to the usage of the eID card. Abuse of the single sign-on authentication mechanism and unrestricted release of the card holder's personal data are the major threats.

3.1 Single Sign-On Authentication

The card holder only needs to enter his PIN code for the first authentication. As long as the card is not removed from the reader, SK_{auth} remains activated. Hence, when the user browses to multiple sites that require eID authentication, authentication is performed transparently except for the first site. This implies that users are unaware that identity information (i.e. the authentication certificate) is transferred to these sites. Moreover, a trojan horse can secretly log in to these sites and collect or even modify the citizen's private data.

Some websites already use the eID card to set up a mutual authenticated HTTPS connection.

3.2 Unrestricted Release of Personal Data

The identity, address and picture files on the card are not PIN-protected. As soon as the eID card is inserted in a smart card reader, these three files can be read by any application.

Usually, the official middleware will intervene and request the user's consent to access these files. However, a program can directly access the card and collect these files. This is especially problematic when children use their eID card to login at a "secure" chat box. As the identity file can be copied to another smart card, identity theft is quite easy if authentication is not requested (e.g. to get access to the municipality's rubbish dump).

3.3 Other Threats

Since the certificates contain the NRN, all actions performed by the same citizen can be linked. The date of birth and gender of the individual can also easily be derived from the NRN.

Another threat is related to the default settings of the middleware. When the citizen inserts his eID card in the card reader, the authentication and signing certificates are stored in persistent memory by default. This behaviour can be disabled. However, some applications will fail to authenticate with the eID card (e.g. Internet Explorer).

A malicious application can easily deceive the user and let the eID card sign a different document than the one intended. The current user interface of the middleware does not show which document is actually signed.

A full list of threats can be found in a technical report [8].

4   Improving the Security and Privacy Properties of the eID Card

This section presents a number of improvements to increase the security of the eID technology and to make it more privacy friendly. Some solutions can be realised in software. However, it would be better to incorporate them in the card. Others require a modification of the card.

4.1   A New Authentication Protocol: Auth

Since single sign-on authentication can easily be abused by trojan horses, traditional client authentication (HTTPS) should be replaced by a new protocol.

4.1.1   Requirements

- The protocol should prevent trojan horses to authenticate secretly in the citizen's name and in addition require the user's consent for every authentication.
- The protocol should tackle man-in-the-middle attacks.
- The protocol should handle the authentication of sessions between a client and a web server. This makes it easy to integrate with web access.
- The protocol must be usable with every authentication mechanism that is based on a challenge and signature scheme. It should be compatible with all kinds of eID cards that allow for authentication based on a challenge-response protocol.
- The protocol only requires the presence of the eID card for a short time. After successful authentication, the card can be removed from the card reader.

4.1.2   Description and Implementation

Figure 2 shows the message flow of the *auth* protocol. First, the user browses to a web page containing an *auth*-URL. The URL has the following syntax:

```
auth://SPhost/path/auth-web-service#sessionID&types
```

A new HTTP session is started by the web server when this web page is requested. Each session has an unique number (*sessionID*). This number can be either stored in a cookie on the user side or can be propagated in the URL. When clicking on the *auth*-URL, the module in the middleware that handles the *auth* protocol is executed. The middleware will pop-up a warning window that shows the (domain) name of the other party, it will invite the user to select an authentication means from the list of supported

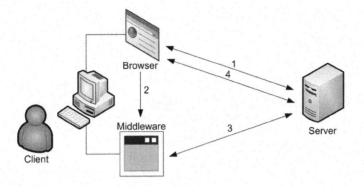

1. There exists an HTTP session between client and server.
2. User clicks on *auth* URL.
3. User authenticates to server and gives a reference of the HTTP session.
4. User can access private content in existing HTTP session.

Fig. 2. Connection flow of *auth* protocol

types (e.g. an eID card) and to give his consent for the authentication. Sometimes, the user will have to activate the authentication means by entering a PIN code or a password. The middleware module will set up a separate HTTPS connection with the web server and ask for a challenge. Validation of the server certificate is important when setting up this connection to prevent man-in-the-middle attacks. Next, extra information is appended to the challenge (the type of authentication means, the domain name of the SP, the *sessionID* and a *middleware_secret*) and the aggregate is signed with the authentication key. The *middleware_secret* is a secret message which is programmed in the middleware code and hidden through code obfuscation. The generated signature is sent together with the certificate chain of the used "authentication" keypair to the web server. The middleware module on the server verifies the signature and the certificate chain. Then the server needs to check the equality of the IP addresses used by the client in the browse-session and in the authentication session. If all the checks pass, the browse-session is converted into an authenticated session and the user can browse to private pages on the website. The session is active until the user logs out or the session times out. Table 1 contains a detailed description of the *auth* protocol. The pop-up message described in (1.b.12) can be avoided by including a Javascript program in the HTML-page with the *auth*-URL, which continuously polls for the termination of the *auth* protocol.

4.1.3 Modifying the Card

The *auth* protocol can be implemented by only adapting the current middleware. However, the security can be increased by having the card implement the *auth* protocol. Currently, the eID card receives a challenge from the middleware and signs it after the PIN is entered. If other parameters like *sessionID* and *SPhost* can also be sent to the card for authentication, the card can compose the message that has to be signed (like

Table 1. The *auth* protocol

<u>(1.a) Browse to login page</u>

(1) U → SP	:	HTTPS request
	:	Header: [GET /login.html — Host: *SPhost*]
(2) SP	:	startSession(*sessionID*; IP_{client}; *challenge*; $< now + timeout >$)
(3) U ← SP	:	HTTPS response
	:	Header: [Set-Cookie: session=*sessionID*; Expired=$< now + timeout >$; secure]
	:	Body: [HTML page with hyperlink to "auth://*SPhost*/auth.php#*sessionID&types*"]

<u>(1.b) Authentication over a new connection</u>

(1) U	:	Request user's consent with pop-up window
	:	[Do you want to authenticate with this authentication *type* to *SPhost*?]
(2) U	:	if(*user_input* === "yes"){select authentication means and activate it} else {abort}
(3) U → SP	:	HTTPS request
	:	Header: [POST /*path*/auth.php?session=*sessionID*&type=*typeID* — Host: *SPhost*]
	:	Body: ["getChallenge"]
(4) U ← SP	:	HTTPS response
	:	Body: [*challenge*]
(5) U	:	$signature = sign_{SK_{auth}}(< type \parallel challenge \parallel SPhost \parallel sessionID \parallel$
	:	$middleware\_secret >)$
(6) U → SP	:	HTTPS request
	:	Header: [POST /*path*/auth.php?session=*sessionID* — Host: *SPhost*]
	:	Body: [response=*signature*&authCertificate=$CertChain_{auth}$]
(7) SP	:	if(IP_{client} != lookupIP(*sessionID*)) abort
(8) SP	:	if(validateCertificate($CertChain_{auth}$) == false) abort
(9) SP	:	if(verify$_{PK_{auth}}$(*signature*; $< type \parallel challenge \parallel SPhost \parallel sessionID \parallel$
	:	$middleware\_secret >) ===$ false) abort
(10) SP	:	setSessionAuthenticated(*sessionID*; *signature*; $< now + timeout >$)
(11) U ← SP	:	HTTPS response
	:	Body: ["OK"]
(12) U	:	Show pop-up to user that authentication is performed successfully.

<u>(1.c) Browse to private content</u>

(1) U → SP	:	HTTPS request
	:	Header: [GET /private/index.html — Host: *SPhost* — Cookie: session=*sessionID*]
(2) SP	:	if(isAuthenticated(*sessionID*) === false) abort
(3) U ← SP	:	HTTPS response
	:	Header: [Set-Cookie: session= *sessionID*; Expired=$< now + timeout >$; secure]
	:	Body: [$<$ content of requested page $>$]

in 1.b.5). The *middleware_secret* can then be omitted, since the card will only sign when the user has given his consent (OK button or PIN code).

4.2   Privacy Friendly Identity Files

With the current eID card, it is only possible to disclose the entire identity, address and picture files. Otherwise, the server cannot check if the signature of the NRB on the identity file is valid. This section introduces more privacy friendly identity files (PFID-files). The concept allows for releasing only the necessary personal attributes.

4.2.1 Hashed Attributes

The PFID-file contains for each attribute the hash of its value. Hence, it is not possible to extract personal information out of the hash values without knowing the attribute value. To reduce brute-force or dictionary attacks, the hash function is randomized by adding an attribute specific random number to the plaintext value: hash($ATTRIBUTE \parallel rand_{ATTRIBUTE}$). The PFID-file is certified (signed) by the National Registration Bureau (NRB). To disclose certified personal attributes, the card releases the signed PFID-file together with the plaintext values and the attribute specific random numbers of these attributes: $ATTRIBUTE$, $rand_{ATTRIBUTE}$. The card should request the user's consent before releasing personal data. This consent could be given by entering a PIN code or pressing the OK button on a card reader with a separate PIN pad. The other party can verify the values by calculating the hashes and comparing them with the values in the PFID-file. Optionally, the user's consent could be overridden (no PIN code required) after proper authentication by privileged service providers. The latter can be useful for border control, police, emergency services, etc.

4.2.2 Encrypted Attributes

Some attributes can be encrypted in the identity file. Instead of just storing the National Registry Number (NRN) as attribute value, the NRN can be encrypted with a symmetric key only known by the government or by another trusted third party (TTP). The enciphered NRN serves as a unique pseudonym and can - in case of abuse - be deanonymized by that TTP during a legal investigation.

4.2.3 PFID-Files on eID Card

A PFID-file contains no personal information and does not need to be protected. However, in order to be sure that released personal attributes really belong to the card owner (and are not simply copied from another card), it is necessary to have that owner authenticate to the service provider. The service provider then needs to verify whether the PFID-file and the authentication certificate refer to the same holder and whether the certificate is still valid.

The attribute specific random number can be calculated from a master random number: $rand_{ATTRIBUTE}$ = hash($masterRandom \parallel ATTRIBUTE$); and can be calculated at runtime. Hence, the card only needs to store (1) the plaintext values of the personal attributes, (2) the master random number, (3) the signature of the NRB on the PFID-file and (4) the PIN-code for the user's consent. However, this requires that the card can calculate the hash at runtime. When no hash function is available, more storage is needed to store all the attribute hashes. To implement PFID-files, the API must be extended to pass the list of requested attributes to the card.

4.2.4 Multiple Domains

With only one PFID-file, multiple actions of the same citizen can easily be linked. To reduce linkability, multiple PFID files can be created and signed by the NRB. Each file is assigned to a domain and should only be used in that domain: e.g. "GOVERNMENT", "COMMERCIAL", "MEDICAL", etc. Linkability is then only possible within one domain. A similar technique is used in the German eID card[9]. That card also works with domains.

To build multiple PFID-files, the hash values must be different in order to prevent linkability. A unique domain is concatenated to the master random value and the attribute name to calculate the random value (see table 2):

$$rand_{(DOMAIN.ATTRIBUTE)} = hash(MasterRandom\|DOMAIN\|ATTRIBUTE)$$

For encrypted attributes, the domain name precedes the actual attribute value. Hence, the ciphertext is different for each domain. The ciphertext of the domain and the NRN can be considered as a domain specific pseudonym for the card holder.

Table 2. Overview of privacy friendly identity file

Attribute values	PFID-file for *DOMAIN*
Nym_{DOMAIN}	$encrypt_{K_{NRB}}(DOMAIN \| NRN)$
Name	$hash(Name \| rand_{(DOMAIN.Name)})$
Surname	$hash(Surname \| rand_{(DOMAIN.Surname)})$
Street	$hash(Street \| rand_{(DOMAIN.Street)})$
Zip code	$hash(Zip\ code \| rand_{(DOMAIN.ZipCode)})$
Municipality	$hash(Municipality \| rand_{(DOMAIN.Municipality)})$
Birth location	$hash(Birth\ location \| rand_{(DOMAIN.BirthLocation)})$
Birth date	$hash(Birth\ date \| rand_{(DOMAIN.BirthDate)})$
Hash photo	$hash(Hash\ photo \| rand_{(DOMAIN.Hashphoto)})$
...	...
	signature of the National Registration Bureau on the PFID-file for *DOMAIN*

To link PFID-files to card owners, different authentication certificates are necessary each referring to its own Nym_{DOMAIN}. Each certificate corresponds to its own keypair: $(SK_{auth_{DOMAIN}}, PK_{auth_{DOMAIN}})$. The only difference between the certificates is (1) the subject field, (2) the public key and hence (3) the signature of the certificate. The subject value is the domain pseudonym. Hence, each certificate can be linked to the corresponding PFID-file for each domain.

4.2.5 Storage Requirements

If only one PFID-file is used on the eID card, the additional storage space that is required compared to the current eID card is very small. An additional master random value needs to be stored.

When using multiple domains, more space is needed on the card. However, the extra space per domain is quite small. For each PFID-file, an extra Nym_{DOMAIN}, other encrypted attributes and the NRB's signature per PFID-file must be stored. Also, room for an extra authentication keypair and the signature on the domain specific authentication certificate must be provided.

4.2.6 Updating PFID-Files

Sometimes, the PFID-files need to be updated (e.g. if a citizen moves to a new address). This implies that the signatures of all PFID-files need to be updated. The NRB must build the new PFID-files by asking the master random value from the eID card. This is done after mutual authentication. This step is also needed with the current eID card to update the address file. As the NRN cannot be changed without replacing the eID card (because it is printed on it) the pseudonyms for the domains will be the same. Hence, the authentication certificates do not need to be updated.

4.3 Other Improvements

Currently, a citizen has to trust the middleware on his machine when using his eID card. To prevent that trojan horses mislead the citizen, smart card readers with a pinpad and LCD screen should be preferred to those without these features. The card can communicate via the LCD screen with the user (e.g. show hash value of the document to be signed, show the personal information that will be disclosed, etc.), the user is able to give his consent for or abort an operation, and PIN codes cannot be intercepted through key logging.

5 Evaluation

The *auth* protocol tackles the single sign-on problem by requesting user's consent before signing a challenge. However, with the current eID card, the PIN is only necessary for the first authentication. It would be better if future versions of the Belgian eID card no longer implement single sign-on. Moreover, to increase the security, the card should implement the *auth* protocol itself.

The *auth* protocol includes some countermeasures against man-in-the-middle attacks. The client checks the certificate chain of the server and will only trust certificates issued by a configured set of CAs. Moreover, *SPhost* must be included in the certificate of the server. Finally, the client side will only connect to the service provider with the DNS name *SPhost*.

An attacker could forward an *auth*-URL of his own browser session to another user and ask him to authenticate on his behalf. This authentication will only succeed if the external IP address (known to the server) of the victim is the same as that of the attacker (e.g. if they are behind the same proxy of NAT).

The implementation of the *auth* protocol can easily be integrated in every browser. Moreover, other types of authentication means (with other eID cards) are possible. The use of HTTPS as communication channel ensures that the authentication messages are protected against tampering and eavesdropping. In comparison with eID client authentication over HTTPS in a browser, the implementation of the *auth* protocol has its own trust policy for server certificates. Hence, the application can enforce that the certificate of the web server contains the DNS name. Otherwise, it aborts the authentication. In browsers, users can ignore this exception.

The *auth* protocol has as well advantages for the server side. In the current setting, a reverse proxy[10] is needed to implement the correct OCSP validation in the web server of the client's "authentication" certificate. Since most webmasters do not have access to the configuration files of the web server (e.g. shared hosting), they cannot use HTTPS with eID client authentication at this moment. Installing a web service and the middleware module is sufficient for the *auth* protocol to authenticate the client and does not require any configuration changes to the web server.

After a successful authentication with the *auth* protocol, the user can remove his eID card from the cardreader. This reduces the risk that trojan horses abuse the eID card.

The new PFID-files prevent that unauthorized applications have unrestricted access to the personal information stored on the eID card. Moreover, the user is no longer obliged to release all personal attribute values. The personal attributes of the identity and address file can be merged. Each domain has a separate PFID-file to prevent linkabilities between separate domains. However, linkabilities in the same domain are still possible. The PFID-files are signed by the National Registration Bureau. Hence, the server can easily check the integrity of the attribute values.

The PFID-files are not PIN protected. Copying the files from an eID card to another smart card is possible. Hence, the verifying party cannot be sure if the identity information on the eID card corresponds to that of the owner of the card. An authentication is necessary to be sure about the identity of the user. Using only identity files as a basis for access control to applications, buildings, etc. can imply a serious security threat.

The master random number is only stored on the card. The NRB only needs this value if new PFID-files must be updated. The NRB does not need to record this master random number for every citizen. This value can be retrieved from the card after proper authentication.

6   Conclusion and Future Work

The usage of the Belgian eID card implies some privacy and security hazards. The proposed solutions in this paper try to tackle the most important threats. However, these improvements cannot solve all the problems with the current eID card. Although it is quite easy to implement some of the proposed improvements in order to improve the security of the current eID card. To prevent abuse of the eID cards in the near future, the Belgian government should deploy a more secure and more privacy-friendly version of the eID card as soon as possible.

The main contribution of this paper is the *auth* protocol and the privacy friendly identity files. The *auth* protocol tackles single sign-on authentication and trojan horses at the client side. The PFID files only disclose the necessary personal information and reduce linkabilities.

As a first step, the paper proposes to implement the *auth* protocol in software. The next step would be a new eID card that implements PFID-files and the *auth* protocol itself.

Although the storage efficiency of PFID-files is good, the current eID card has not enough free storage available to accomodate several domains. Hence, a smart card with more persistent storage will be necessary.

The privacy of the card holder can even further be enhanced by using anonymous credentials.

Acknowledgement

This research is partially funded by the Interuniversity Attraction Poles Programme Belgian State, Belgian Science Policy and the Research Fund K.U.Leuven, the IWT-SBO project (ADAPID) "Advanced Applications for Electronic Identity Cards in Flanders" and the IWT-TeTra project (e-IDea) "Development of secure applications with the Belgian electronic identity card".

References

1. De Cock, D., Wolf, C., Preneel, B.: The Belgian Electronic Identity Card (Overview). In: Dittmann, J. (ed.) Sicherheit 2005: Sicherheit - Schutz und Zuverlässigkeit, Beiträge der 3rd Jahrestagung des Fachbereichs Sicherheit der Gesellschaft für Informatik e.v (GI), Magdeburg,DE. Lecture Notes in Informatics, vol. LNI P-77, pp. 298–301. Bonner Köllen Verlag, Magdeburg (2006)
2. De Cock, D., Wouters, K., Preneel, B.: Introduction to the Belgian EID Card. In: Katsikas, S.K., Gritzalis, S., López, J. (eds.) EuroPKI 2004. LNCS, vol. 3093, pp. 1–13. Springer, Heidelberg (2004)
3. Stern, M.: Belgian Electronic Identity Card content, 2nd edn. Zetes, CSC (2003)
4. Ramlot, G.: eID Hierarchy and Certificate Profiles, 3rd edn. Zetes, Certipost (2006)
5. Belgian certificate revocation list, http://status.eid.belgium.be/
6. Andries, P.: eID Middleware Architecture Document. Zetes, 1st edn. (2003)
7. Rommelaere, J.: Belgian Electronic Identity Card Middleware Programmers Guide, 1st edn. Zetes (2003)
8. De Decker, B., Naessens, V., Lapon, J., Verhaeghe, P.: Kritische beoordeling van het gebruik van de Belgische eID kaart. Report CW524 (2008)
9. Advanced security mechanisms for machine readable travel documents – extended access control (eac) and password authenticated connection establishment (pace). Technical Guideline TR-03110 (2008)
10. SSL Authentication Reverse Proxy, http://eid.belgium.be/nl/Achtergrondinfo/De_eID_technisch/

A Structured Security Assessment Methodology for Manufacturers of Critical Infrastructure Components

Thomas Brandstetter, Konstantin Knorr, and Ute Rosenbaum

Siemens AG, Corporate Technology, Information and Communications
Computer Emergency Response Team (CERT)
{Thomas.Brandstetter,Konstantin.Knorr,Ute.Rosenbaum}@siemens.com

Abstract. Protecting our critical infrastructures like energy generation and distribution, telecommunication, production and traffic against cyber attacks is one of the major challenges of the new millennium. However, as security is such a complex and multilayer topic often the necessary structured foundation is missing for a manufacturer to assess the current security level of a system. This paper introduces a methodology for structured security assessments which has been successfully applied during the development of several products for critical infrastructures. The methodology is described in detail and the lessons learnt are given from applying it to several systems during their development.

Keywords: Cyber Security, Security Assessment Methodology, Critical Infrastructure, NERC CIP, Security Assessment Plan, Risk Analysis.

1 Introduction

Manufacturers of critical infrastructure components (CIC) like control centers for energy generation or distribution are facing increasing security demands for their products from customers and regulatory bodies. The central questions to be answered are: How good does my product rank concerning security requirements and how secure is it in a real-world operation? The fundamental dilemma here is that the manufacturer is not operating the products and that an operational CIC typically comprises – besides the base product – additional components like networks, the corresponding processes and staff which is often unaware of IT security issues. Additionally, development budgets are tight. Therefore a manufacturer is highly interested in a cost-efficient methodology to assess and subsequently improve the security level of its products extrapolating the operational challenges.

This article describes a cyber security assessment methodology (SAM) which can be used during the development of CICs. The SAM is best effort based, pragmatic, cost-efficient, generic, flexible, and built on CIC industry standards. It has been successfully applied for several Siemens CICs.

What differentiates security assessments of CICs from the "classical" office environment? Though cyber and IT security are commonly used interchangeably, they have different mentalities. The term IT security was established in and for typical office IT. We however refer to CIC systems with utmost crucial value. Besides

D. Gritzalis and J. Lopez (Eds.): SEC 2009, IFIP AICT 297, pp. 248–258, 2009.
© IFIP International Federation for Information Processing 2009

terminology, there are also several significant technical deviations: In IT security it often is OK to shut something down to protect it (and take time to fix it), whereas CIC must stay up and running at all cost. For more information about the differences between "classical IT" and CICs see [5].

Over the last 8 years, a rapid and partly uncoordinated growth of cyber security publications can be observed. Both of the following sources [7] and [8] easily list more than 50 standards, guidelines, and regulations. To keep an overview it is important for a manufacturer to organize the publications according to the following categories:

- Who is the author? Industry bodies, customers / operators of CIC, regulatory bodies, laws, international standardization bodies?
- Technical publications vs. management
- Industry specific vs. general IT security standards
- Is the publication focusing on development or operation of the system

For example, the NERC CIP standard [6] is published by an industry regulatory body, rather management oriented, specific for the energy sector and focusing on the operation of CICs. Contrary, the procurement language [2] is published by a US information sharing center, rather technical, industry independent and focusing on the development of CICs. For an efficient and market-oriented SAM, a manufacturer must take current standardization and cyber security publications into account to determine subsequent SAM elements that suffice state-of-the-art cyber security requirements.

The remainder of the article has the following structure: After this introduction Section 2 presents SAM and its three major phases "Risk Analysis" (RA), "Theoretical Assessment" (TA) and "Practical Assessment" (PA). Examples will be given for illustration purposes. Finally, Section 3 gives conclusion, delineates SAM from related work, and discusses topics for future work.

2 Methodology

This section describes SAM and its individual phases in detail. Fig. 1 provides a high level overview.

1. Pre-assessment activities include preparation and signing of the project agreement which includes the definition of the detailed scope (CIC version and release), milestones, location of the assessment, time line, NDA, costs, staffing, liability, etc. For our assessments we follow the existing Siemens project process and corresponding tooling which provides a suitable framework for all these aspects.
2. The RA determines the individual risk level of the CIC and subsequently derives specific security measures for the CIC (cf. Section 2.1).
3. The TA assesses in how far security measures based on a standard (e.g. [2, 6]) are implemented for the CIC. This typically includes technical, organizational and process aspects. Subsequently security measures specific for the underlying document but unspecific for the CIC are derived (cf. Section 2.2).

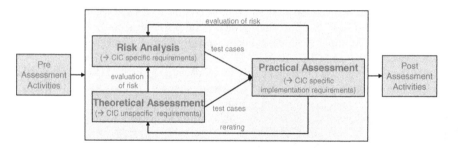

Fig. 1. SAM Overview: relations between the different components

4. During the PA practical tests – manually and with hacker tools – are done in a suitable test environment. By this the actual exploitability of the CIC can be proven (cf. Section 2.3).
5. Post assessment activities include the communication of the findings, final reporting, issuing of a SAM confirmation, help with fixing and track fixing of security holes, and help in defining requirements for future product releases.

2.1   Risk Assessment

The approach we follow for the risk assessment (RA) is based on ISO/IEC TR 13335-3:1998(E) and NIST's "Risk Management Guide for Information Technology Systems" [4] and is depicted in Fig. 2. As with all other SAM phases, security efforts are balanced with economical aspects. Therefore, the RA is conducted in the form of group workshops, typically in 1-3 days depending on the complexity of CIC. By relying on a broad spectrum of participants like product development, system test, service, sales & marketing, product management and engaging in a workshop discussion accompanied by introductory interviews of participants, the know-how existing in the staff of a CIC manufacturer is being brought in. As a product usually is not developed from scratch, these parties have comprehensive experience and knowledge that can be recycled and used to create a very efficient risk assessment process in terms of highly valuable outcome within a rather short amount of time. This process is guided by an experienced assessor who must provide both capabilities as a security expert but also as moderator.

The utmost goal of this process is to efficiently determine the adequate risks for a concrete CIC system. The output of this step also poses valuable input for the later practical assessment stage in determining attack goals.

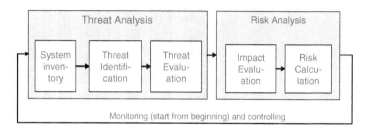

Fig. 2. Process and phases of a risk analysis

The output of a risk analysis is:

- List of critical assets: this list is the basis for the PA's SAP
- List of threats with corresponding likelihood and impact: Possibly new risks need to be added after the PA or the likelihood / impact of the threats need to be adjusted due to practical findings

2.2 Theoretical Assessment

For critical infrastructure systems (CICs) private and public operators and regulators perceived in the last years that security needs to be integrated into these systems and that a common approach ensures that enough security is realized within products and systems. This led to numerous standards and requirement documents that were published recently. For product management this is a challenge and an opportunity. They need to choose the right standards, assess their level of implementation and, based on the results, decide on further implementation steps. But many of these documents are a "pool" of agreed-upon security requirements contrasting the many customer specific requirements seen in many tenders. Therefore, in this section a method for assessing the level of implementation with regard to generic requirement documents is presented (see Fig. 3). The method has been applied using different standards for several products.

The principle assessment approach is to interview relevant persons based on a questionnaire derived from a standard and to evaluate the answers. Depending on the required assurance level, in addition to the interviews documentation is checked or the system itself is tested.

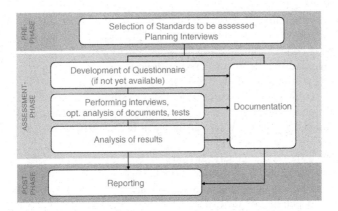

Fig. 3. Process and phases of a theoretical assessment

2.2.1 Requirement Documents

For each standard to be assessed, the requirements for the manufacturer need to be derived. Depending on the target group of the standard, the requirements may either be applied directly or need to be deducted in an intermediate step. As an example the aforementioned NERC CIP standard applies to operators of bulk electric systems. However for product manufacturers, requirements need to be derived. These requirements typically cover not only technical aspects, but also documentation requirements and organizational processes that are carried out by different departments – development, project groups, and support.

The requirements derivation is illustrated in an example. NERC CIP requires that the operator maintains logs of system events related to cyber security for 90 calendar days, and that these logs are reviewed regularly. Just asking if the product supports logging is not sufficient as most systems do support a basic form of logging already. Here, state-of-the-art logging technologies are asked for. Typical features are a possibility for central storage and comprehensible logging data that is stored for at least 90 days and protected against tampering. Also the review of the log data must be facilitated.

In contrast to NERC CIP, the German White Paper "Requirements for Secure Control and Telecommunication Systems" [1] as well as the US "Cyber Security Procurement Language for Control Systems" [2] summarize security principles that should be considered when designing and procuring control system products and are for use in tenders to specify the security requirements. Therefore, both documents are well suited as direct input for an assessment of the security level of a given product. All requirements can be checked directly, but, as the scope of the documents is broad, some requirements will not be applicable for a given product and need to be marked as not applicable during the assessment.

2.2.2 Questionnaire

For the theoretical assessments (TAs), a questionnaire per standard is used. The goal of the questionnaire is to provide a tool to make the degree of compliance measurable and to yield comparable results independent on the interviewer and the product. The questionnaires have a generic structure independent of the standard, with content structured according to the pattern of the underlying standard. For each requirement one or more corresponding questions are derived with predefined answers that can be selected, and a field where additional comments and descriptions shall be inserted, to make the answers comparable.

The challenge and the effort for deriving the questionnaire lie in content and formulation of the questions, as firstly questions have to be comprehensible and secondly the answers must allow easy benchmarking. The questionnaire itself and the functionality for evaluation of the answers are generated by a tool. As far as possible the questions are formulated in such a way that they can be answered with "Yes", "No", or "Not Applicable".

The experience shows that generic answers are not sufficient. For some requirements we specified "intermediate" answers out of our experience. One example is "Dependent on contract". It expresses that some requirements are not fulfilled by the standard product offering, but, depending on the contract, can be offered as additional feature.

For automatic evaluation, the answers are mapped to a value of a predefined range. These values are used to calculate the average compliance value per section and per chapter. "Not applicable" answers are not used for calculating the average. The question arises why we did not use numerical values for answering the questions right from the beginning and give an explanation how to use the numbers. We did this for some questionnaires but experienced drawbacks with regard to comparability and traceability. Different interviewers gave different values to the same answer, e.g. if something depends on the contract, one gave full points, as the requirement can be fulfilled; the other gave no point because the standard offering did not fulfill the requirement. Both interviewers have good reasons for their rating, but the results are quite different and cannot be compared. Also during one interview, for long question-naires, a bias can occur. At beginning the rating could be more strict whereas in the end be more "gentle". These effects are reduced by use of the predefined, named an-swers. In principle the mapping is nothing else as a user friendly explanation of each answer possibility.

2.2.3 Performing the Theoretical Assessment

Based on the questionnaire the TA is done within intensive workshops with product experts answering the questions, and experienced security experts independent from product development, who are doing the interviews and guide through the question-naire. Depending on the assessment goal different assessment depths are possible: (1) just documenting the oral statement of the interviewee(s), (2) additionally checking / studying the document or (3) doing practical test. The assessment depth can be varied on a per requirement or per section base, e.g. to focus on more important topics.

In practice we always used a compromise by doing spot tests for some topics and derived from the theoretical assessment topics for practical security assessments. This combination additionally assures that all intended security mechanisms are really im-plemented securely and thus raises the level of confidence.

The assessment could also be seen more comprehensive than an external audit. Here, documentation of the system and the processes are checked but also system functionality is reviewed. The scope of the checks is decided by the auditor and is limited by the defined timeframe.

2.2.4 Analysis of Results

The method and the underlying tool give an instant overview about the level of com-pliance for the different sections. The result of the theoretical assessment is the level of compliance with the requirements and the deviations identified. Fig. 4 shows the result of a sample NERC CIP compliance TA. For CIP 009, the assessed product had functions for backup, but no documented recovery concept.

The products we assessed are sold in different regions and markets, therefore typi-cally we checked against several standards. Some sections within different standards were covering the same topic; therefore consistency checks could easily be made.

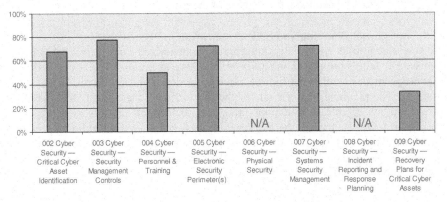

Fig. 4. Example of NERC CIP Compliance Assessment

2.3 Practical Assessment

In the next phase of the SAM, the resilience of the CIC against practical hacking-attacks is evaluated. This step is introduced in order to detect exploitable vulnerabilities and potential security flaws in a CIC, taking into account state-of-the-art hacking know-how and hacking tools. The results both from the RA and the TA are taken as input for actual attack patterns. This third step in the SAM complements the foregoing steps appropriately by verifying the actual implementation.

This is necessary because security requirements and design decisions have been made in earlier CIC development phases and flaws may have been introduced during the actual development phase. As with the whole SAM, the PA phase needs to be structured. We use the security assessment plan (SAP) process steps P1-P5 depicted in Fig. 5 for this purpose.

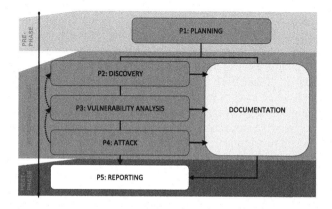

Fig. 5. Practical assessment process steps

Note that there are several options for the physical location of the PA. Typically vendors maintain test centers for the unit, module and system test. These test centers can be booked and prepared to perform the PA in house. Alternatively, operational sites can be used. In this case however special care must be taken concerning the definition of the SAP and the intrusiveness of the tests.

2.3.1 Pre-phase: Planning and SAP Preparation

The assessment tasks are initially collected and categorized from former SAM phases in phase P1. In this pre-phase, the assessor decides and evaluates the scope and depth of subsequent tasks, allowing him to control the depth and intrusiveness of the assessment. The planning phase is one of the most crucial ones, as all subsequent test cases in terms of intrusion attempt tasks are decided on here. This is necessary in order to match and tailor the assessment tasks to the overall requirements of the CIC, where certain test methods may be unsuitable, e.g. denial-of-service tests in productive environments. The actions are then arranged according to the structure of sections, modules and tasks. Fig. 6 gives an example on this task structure in a sample SAP.

ID	SECTION	MODULE	TASK	TOOL	ALT TOOL	CHECKLIST / LINK	STAGE	REM	E_SL
101	network	network surveying	system enumeration	ipconfig/ifconfig	ping		1	1	basic
102	network	network surveying	system identification	nmap	nessus	http://insecure.org/nm	1	1	basic
103	network	network surveying	information leaks	wireshark		http://www.wireshark.	1	1	bronze
104	network	port scanning	service enumeration	nessus	nmap	http://www.nessus.org	1	1	bronze
105	network	port scanning	service identification	nessus	nmap	http://www.nessus.org	1	1	bronze
106	network	port scanning	error checking	hping		http://www.hping.org/	2	1	silver
107	network	port scanning	protocol response verification	nmap	nessus	http://insecure.org/nm	2	1	silver
108	network	port scanning	packet level response verification	nmap	nessus	http://insecure.org/nm	2	1	silver
109	network	port scanning	distributed tcp/ip analysis	unicornscan		http://www.unicomsca	2	1	silver
110	network	perimeter review	security analysis (level 1)	cisecurity (rat)		http://www.cisecurity.	2	1	bronze
111	network	perimeter review	network security review	checklist		http://www.nsa.gov/sr	1	n/a	silver
113	network	perimeter review	switch security configuration	checklist		http://www.nsa.gov/sr	3	1	silver
114	network	perimeter review	router hardening test	cisco torch	ccsat	http://www.arhont.cor	3	1	silver
115	network	perimeter review	router security configuration	checklist		http://www.nsa.gov/sr	3	1	silver
116	network	perimeter review	firewall hardening test	ccsat	cisco torch	http://ccsat.sourcefor	3	1	silver
117	network	perimeter review	firewall security configuration	checklist		http://www.cisco.com	3	1	silver
118	network	perimeter review	IDS security analysis	manual checking			2	1	silver
119	network	perimeter review	trusted systems security analysis	manual checking			2	1	silver
121	network	DoS testing	DoS vulnerability analysis	manual checking			2	1	silver
122	network	DoS testing	DoS testing	datapool 3.3	DoS test suit	http://www2.packetstc	3	1	bronze
123	network	DoS testing	DoS testing	netcat		http://sourceforge.net	3	1	silver
124	network	DoS testing	DoS risk analysis	manual checking			2	n/a	silver
201	platform	windows/all	baseline security analysis	MBSA		http://www.microsoft.	2	0	basic
202	platform	windows/all	security analysis (level 1)	cisecurity (win)	cat4win	http://www.cisecurity.	2	0	bronze
203	platform	windows/all	security testing (level 1)	manual testing			3	0	bronze
204	platform	windows/all	security analysis (level 2)	GFI languard	?	http://www.gfi.com/la	2	0	silver
205	platform	windows/server 2003	security testing (level 2)	ms scw		http://www.microsoft.	3	1	silver
208	platform	unix/all	security analysis (level 1)	cisecurity (unix)	cat4nix	http://www.cisecurity.	2	0	bronze
209	platform	unix/all	security testing (level 1)	manual testing			3	0	bronze
210	platform	unix/all	security analysis (level 2)	cops	tiger, crack,	sftp.cerias.purdue	2	0	silver
211	platform	unix/all	security testing (level 2)	bastille		http://www.bastille-un	3	1	silver
214	platform	all	login credentials verification	john the ripper	manual check	http://www.openwall.	3	1	silver

Fig. 6. Sample SAP

2.3.2 Assessment Phase: Structured Execution of Attacks against the System

Once task planning has finished, the actual practical assessment phase starts. The discovery stage P2 includes information retrieval from the target and passive testing using analyzing tools and techniques. The vulnerability analysis stage P3 classifies vulnerabilities and weaknesses found. Besides the threat classification, this stage requires the tester to verify a threat, to identify associated risks and to document all significant findings for later reporting. The attack stage P4 involves active testing using invasive tools and techniques, trying to successfully gain access to the target or to crash a certain service or function. Strong dependencies exist between phases P2-P4, as newly gained findings are fed back into appropriate tasks.

Typical activities here include port and security scanning, service verification, account brute-forcing, utilization of commercial and self-developed protocol fuzzers, packet spoofing attempts, operating system and database hardening checks, patch level verification, denial-of-service attacks and web-application specific attacks like cross-site-request-forgery, sql injection and HTTP response splitting.

2.3.3 Post-assessment Phase: Reporting Phase

The reporting stage finally corresponds to the post assessment phase. A report documents all findings produced throughout the assessment phase and forms the base for potential workarounds or mitigation concepts; for an example see Fig. 7. The report also demonstrates and ensures that all sections chosen during the planning phase have actually been covered during the practical assessment phase and proves the scope of the PA phase.

2.4 Related Work and Delimitation

There are several approaches in the greater field of SAM that have been studied and evaluated for the purposes of application by a CIC manufacturer. The results are summarized here:

[F1]RSH service detected	
Criticality	HIGH
Vulnerability Location	The service was detected on port 514 TCP on the management server host.
Description	The host provides a remoteshell (RSH) daemon that allows operating system command execution with system privileges from remote without prior authentication. This is highly critical as it immediately gives a remote attacker full system access.
Prerequisites	An attacker with network access can immediately detect and connect to the rsh port.
Counter Measures	Remove the RSH service or replace it with its secure variant SSH.

Fig. 7. Sample finding of the PA

SAM vs. ISO 27002: While ISO 27002 is a management standard SAM is more on a technical level. SAM focuses on the ISO sections 7 and 8, requiring other sections like 1, 2, 3, and 4 as a basis. Other sections like 6 are entirely out-of-scope for SAM. The ISO risk assessment approach is a good way to map the potential exploitation of vulnerabilities identified by SAM to their financial impact.

SAM vs. OSSTMM: The hierarchical structure section / module / task and the process phases are shared between OSSTMM [3] and SAM. However, OSSTMM lacks SAM's RA and TA phases.

SAM vs. IEC/ISO 15408: SAM's scope and depth concept is similar to the common criteria[1]: (CC) approach, standardized in IEC/ISO 15408, but by far shorter and more pragmatic. CC defines the „Target of Evaluation" (scope) and "Evaluation Assurance Level" (EAL) (depth). Also, the mapping of specific tasks to certain inspection depths is shared between the two approaches.

CC provides a certification done by external bodies for external parties while SAM is mainly a manufacturer internal methodology. SAM helps the manufacturer to identify additionally relevant security measures for its CIC and is more oriented on practical aspects that are typically found in bids / tenders. Another difference is the typical size of corresponding projects – CC projects especially for higher EALs require a huge effort. Also CC is much more "paper / process" based than SAM which stresses the practical tests.

SAM can easily be "aligned" with other manufacturer-based certification programs like the one announced by the ISA Security Compliance Institute[2]

3 Conclusion

In this article a SAM for CICs was presented. The major advantages of the SAM are:
- Security level of the CIC can be measured & quantified. This provides an excellent input for subsequent security decisions e.g. on which security requirements to focus in future CIC versions.

---

[1] http://www.commoncriteriaportal.org/

[2] http://www.isa.org/Content/NavigationMenu/Technical_Information/ASCI/ISCI/ISCI.htm

- SAM has a broad basis as a practical and theoretical phase is included. Different techniques like interviews, document reviews and practical tests provide a broad insight into the security level of the CIC.
- SAM is flexible and generic since it can be adjusted to different CICs by using different cyber security standards as the basis and adopting the SAP to the CIC's needs, taking into account any concerns or restrictions.
- SAM is cost effective and has been successfully used for different CICs. Typically 1-3 assessors work for a few weeks on the SAM for a CIC.
- The theoretical assessments revealed missing technical features, but surprisingly also security deficiencies with regard to documentation and the processes along the complete product lifecycle, starting from the bidding process, where critical customer information needs to be protected to service during operation.

Over the last years many major IT manufacturers like Microsoft and SAP have started to tie their security activities to the product development process. Also SAM follows this approach. The different SAM phases can be done at different development milestones of the CIC. Risk Assessment (RA) should be done as early as possible (e.g. during plan / design). For Practical Assessment (PA) the product must be in a "testable" state, i.e. the required SW and HW modules must be available in a suitable test environment (e.g. during the "realization" phase). It should be noted that it is possible (but not recommended as important synergies get lost) to perform only selected parts of the entire SAM, e.g. (RA) + (PA) or (TA) + (PA).

The advantage of combining the three major SAM phases can finally be demonstrated by the catchy example patch management: Most cyber security standards ask for patch management and the corresponding processes and organization. With SAM, these requirements are checked via interviews and review of the corresponding documents in the TA. The actual patch level of the CIC and the implications of missing patches on CIC are tested in the PA. The risk of not applying required patches or late application of a patch is addressed in the RA.

SAM has been developed based on the experiences of security analysis of CICs and CIC security needs. It has been applied successfully to various CIC systems. As the method is generic, it could in principle be applied to other systems, e.g. standard office and IT systems. As a prerequisite, a set of relevant security standards for these systems need to be identified to be able to choose the most appropriate standards for the actual security analysis. Also, the practical assessment tools used need to be chosen in accordance with the new application fields.

References

1. Bundesverband der Energie- und Wasserwirtschaft: White Paper Requirements for Secure Control and Telecommunication Systems, Berlin (June 2008), http://www.bdew.de/bdew.nsf/id/A975B8333599F9B0C12574B400348E7A/$file/Whitepaper_Secure_Systems_Vedis_1.0final.pdf
2. Idaho National Laboratory: Cyber Security Procurement Language for Control Systems. Version 1.8 (February 2008), http://www.msisac.org/scada/
3. ISECOM: Open Source Software Testing Methodology (2007), http://www.isecom.org/osstmm/

4. National Institute of Standards and Technology Special Publication 800-30, Natl. Inst. Stand. Technol. Spec. Publ. 800-30, 54 pages (July 2002), http://csrc.nist.gov/publications/nistpubs/800-30/sp800-30.pdf
5. National Institute of Standards and Technology Special Publication 800-82 (FINAL PUBLIC DRAFT) Natl. Inst. Stand. Technol. Spec. Publ. 800-82, 156 pages (September 2008), http://csrc.nist.gov/publications/drafts/800-82/draft_sp800-82-fpd.pdf
6. North American Electric Reliability Council: Critical Infrastructure Protection (CIP), http://www.nerc.com/
7. US-CERT: Standards & References Web Site of the Control System Security Program of the US CERT, http://www.us-cert.gov/control_systems/csstandards.html
8. U.S. Department of Energy, Office of Electricity Delivery and Energy Reliability: National SCADA Test Bed, A Summary of Control System Security Standards Activities in the Energy Sector (October 2005), http://www.inl.gov/scada/publications/d/a_summary_of_control_system_security_standards_activities_in_the_energy_sector.pdf

Mining Stable Roles in RBAC

Alessandro Colantonio[1], Roberto Di Pietro[2], Alberto Ocello[3],
and Nino Vincenzo Verde[4]

[1] Engiweb Security, Roma, Italy
alessandro.colantonio@eng.it
and
Università di Roma Tre, Roma, Italy
colanton@mat.uniroma3.it
[2] Università di Roma Tre, Roma, Italy and
UNESCO Chair in Data Privacy, Tarragona, Spain
dipietro@{mat.uniroma3.it,urv.cat}
[3] Engiweb Security, Roma, Italy
alberto.ocello@eng.it
[4] Università di Roma Tre, Roma, Italy
nverde@mat.uniroma3.it

Abstract. In this paper we address the problem of generating a candidate role-set for an RBAC configuration that enjoys the following two key features: it minimizes the administration cost; and, it is a stable candidate role-set. To achieve these goals, we implement a three steps methodology: first, we associate a weight to roles; second, we identify and remove the user-permission assignments that cannot belong to a role that have a weight exceeding a given threshold; third, we restrict the problem of finding a candidate role-set for the given system configuration using only the user-permission assignments that have not been removed in the second step— that is, user-permission assignments that belong to roles with a weight exceeding the given threshold. We formally show—proof of our results are rooted in graph theory—that this methodology achieves the intended goals. Finally, we discuss practical applications of our approach to the role mining problem.

1 Introduction

Role-based access control (RBAC) [1] is a well known and recognized flexible security model for enterprise access control management. Central to the model is the *role* concept; a role is just a collection of access permissions, and users are assigned to roles based on duties to fulfil [9]. The main reason for the adoption of RBAC within many medium to large-size organizations is its simplicity. In particular, the RBAC model offers several benefits in terms of simplified access control administration, improved organizational productivity, and security policy enforcement. However, the overhead associated to role definition is often the main obstacle toward its adoption. Indeed, the first step in setting up an RBAC scheme is the role definition. To this aim, the *role engineering* discipline has been introduced. It refers to the set of methodologies and tools to define roles and to assign permissions to roles according to the actual needs of the company [5]. Existing role engineering approaches are usually classified in two categories: the *top-down* and the *bottom-up* approaches. The former carefully decomposes

D. Gritzalis and J. Lopez (Eds.): SEC 2009, IFIP AICT 297, pp. 259–269, 2009.
© IFIP International Federation for Information Processing 2009

the business processes into elementary components, identifying which system features are necessary to carry out specific tasks. The latter, based on the analysis of existing access controls permissions, elicits a set of roles that correctly describe the existing user-permission assignments. Since this approach can be easily automated, it has attracted many researchers. In the literature, bottom-up approaches are usually referred to as *role mining*.

A recently addressed problem is the analysis of the effort incurred by administrators when managing the set of roles elicited by role mining algorithms. To this aim, [2, 3] introduces the *administration cost function*. An *optimal candidate role-set* is a set of roles that correctly describes the existing permissions in such a way its administration cost is minimized. When new users, new permissions, or new user-permission assignments are added, there is the need to re-compute the optimal candidate role-set, that could lead to change the role-set in use. In particular, roles could be *unstable*, in the sense that the introduction of few users or few permissions could drastically change the optimal candidate role-set. Unstable roles could be difficult to be managed as they frequently change. Conversely, a role is *stable* if it is not greatly affected by the introduction of new users, new permissions or new user-permission assignments. That is why, when dealing with automated role mining algorithms, the stability of generated roles is a fundamental property that is worth investigating.

Contributions. The main contribution of this paper is to address the problem of finding a core of roles that is both stable and minimizes the cost function of the corresponding RBAC configuration. We model this problem with graphs, introducing a three-steps methodology that is able to prune user-permission assignments that lead to unstable roles. This way, we are able to build a core of roles which have the required characteristics. These results have been formally proven. In addition, relevant practical applications of the proposed methodology are shown.

Roadmap. The remainder of this paper is organized as follows: Section 2 offers an overview of previous approaches to the role mining problem. Section 3 sums up the concepts and the definitions used in this paper. In Section 4 the proposed model is discussed. Section 5 illustrates some of the possible applications of our approach. Finally, in Section 6 conclusions and some possible extensions of the work are presented.

2 Related Work

The term "role mining" was first introduced by Kuhlmann et al. [10] who applied existing data mining techniques to implement a bottom-up approach. They presented a clustering technique similar to the well known k-means clustering, which required a prior definition of the number of roles. In [13] it is described the first algorithm explicitly designed for role engineering, that is based on hierarchical clustering. Another approach to the role mining is explained by Vaidya et al. [17], that is based on the analysis of all possible intersections among permissions possessed by the users. Only recently researchers have started to formalize the role-set optimality concept, defining "interestingness" metric for roles [18, 11, 12]. Indeed, the importance of role completeness and role management efficiency resulting from the role engineering process has been evident from the earliest papers on the subject. However, the problem of identifying the role interestingness is only partially addressed.

Colantonio et al. [2, 3], introduced the administration cost concept, proposing a metric to evaluate "good" collection of roles, namely role-sets which are easily administrable. This approach makes it possible to easily mine administrable roles. Vaidya et al. [15, 16] also studied the problem of reducing the administration effort but, in this case, the cost is simply represented by the number of roles which cover all permissions possessed by the users. They defined this problem as the Basic Role Mining Problem (*basicRMP*). The authors proposed a branch and bound method, and then a greedy heuristic, to build a set of roles by including, at each step, the role that covers the largest possible set of previously uncovered user-permission assignments. They also demonstrated that *basicRMP* is NP-complete. As shown in [6], not only is the *basicRMP* problem equivalent to the minimum clique covering, but it can be reduced to many other NP-complete problems, like binary matrices factorization [14, 11] and tiling database [7] to cite a few.

Our approach is slightly different from the other ones. Though we preserve the existence of a general cost function, that is useful to identify the best possible roles, we also introduce a weight metric aimed at excluding the presence of unstable roles.

3   Background

In this section we introduce the fundamental concepts of the graph theory and some formal definitions of the RBAC standard that will be used later on.

Graphs Theory. A *graph* G is an ordered pair $G = \langle V, E \rangle$, where V is the set of vertices, and E is a set of unordered pairs of vertices. The endpoints of an edge $\langle v, w \rangle \in E(G)$ are the two vertices $v, w \in V(G)$. Given a subset S of $V(G)$, the subgraph *induced* by S is the graph whose vertex set is S, and whose edges are the members of $E(G)$ whose two endpoints are both in S. We denote with $G[S]$ the subgraph induced by S. A *bipartite graph* is a graph where the set of vertex can be partitioned into two subsets V_1 and V_2, such that for every edge $\langle v_1, v_2 \rangle \in E(G)$, $v_1 \in V_1$ and $v_2 \in V_2$.

A *clique* is a subset S of $V(G)$, such that the graph $G[S]$ is a complete graph, namely for every two vertices in S there exists an edge connecting the two. A *biclique* in a bipartite graph, also called *bipartite clique*, is a set of vertices $B_1 \subseteq V_1$ and $B_2 \subseteq V_2$, such that $\langle b_1, b_2 \rangle \in E$ for all $b_1 \in B_1$ and $b_2 \in B_2$. In the rest of the paper we will say that a set of vertices S induce a biclique in a graph G if $G[S]$ is a complete bipartite graph. In the same way, we will say that a set of edges induce a biclique if their endpoints induce a biclique. A *maximal* clique or biclique is a set of vertices, that induces a complete subgraph and is not a subset of the vertices of any larger complete subgraph.

A *clique cover* of G is a collection of cliques $C_1, \ldots, C_k$, such that for each edge $\langle u, v \rangle \in E$ there is some C_i that contains both u and v. A *minimum clique partition* (MCP) of a graph is the smallest collection of cliques such that each vertex is a member of exactly one of the cliques. It is a partition of the vertices into cliques. Similar to the clique cover, a *biclique cover* of G is a collection of biclique $B_1, \ldots, B_k$ such that for each edge $\langle u, v \rangle \in E$ there is some B_i that contains both u and v. We say that B_i covers $\langle u, v \rangle \in E$ if B_i contains both u and v. Thus, in a biclique cover, each edge of G is covered at least by one biclique. A *minimum biclique cover* (MBC) is the smallest collection of bicliques that covers the edges of a given bipartite graph.

Role-Based Access Control and Definitions. We now sum up the main concepts of the RBAC model [1] that will be used in the rest of the paper. In particular, the entities of interest are: *PERMS*, that is the set of access permissions; *USERS*, namely the set of all system users; *ROLES*, that is the set of all the roles; $UA \subseteq USERS \times ROLES$, that is the set of user-role assignments; $PA \subseteq PERMS \times ROLES$, that is the set of permission-role assignments. Given a role, the function assigned_users: $ROLES \rightarrow 2^{USERS}$ identifies all the assigned users, and the function assigned_perms: $ROLES \rightarrow 2^{PERMS}$ identifies all the assigned permissions. In addition to the RBAC standard entities, the set $UP \subseteq USERS \times PERMS$ identifies permission to user assignments. In an access control system it is represented by entities describing access rights (e.g., access control lists).

To formally describe the role mining problem we need other definitions:

Definition 1 (System Configuration). *Given an access control system, we refer to its* configuration *as the tuple* $\varphi = \langle USERS, PERMS, UP \rangle$, *that is the set of all existing users, permissions, and the corresponding relationships between them within the system.*

A system configuration represents the user authorization state before migrating to RBAC, or the authorizations derivable from the current RBAC implementation.

Definition 2 (RBAC State). *An RBAC state is a tuple* $\psi = \langle ROLES, UA, PA \rangle$, *namely an instance of all the sets characterizing the RBAC model.*

An RBAC state is used to obtain a system configuration. Indeed, the role engineering goal is to find the "best" state that correctly describes a given configuration. In particular we are interested in the following:

Definition 3 (Candidate Role-Set). *Given an access control system configuration* φ, *a* candidate role-set *is the RBAC state* ψ *that "covers" all possible combinations of permissions possessed by users according to* φ, *namely a set of roles whose union of permissions matches exactly with the permissions possessed by the user. Formally:* $\forall u \in USERS, \exists R \subseteq ROLES : \bigcup_{r \in R} assigned\_perms(r) = \{p \in PERMS \mid \langle u, p \rangle \in UP\}$.

Definition 4 (Cost Function). *Let* Φ, Ψ *be respectively the set of all possible system configurations and RBAC states. The* cost function *is defined as* cost: $\Phi \times \Psi \rightarrow \mathbb{R}^+$. *It represents an administration cost estimate for the state* ψ *used to obtain the configuration* φ.

The administration cost concept was first introduced in [2]. Leveraging the cost metric makes it possible to find candidate role-sets which lead to the lowest possible effort for the administration of the resulting RBAC state.

Definition 5 (Optimal Candidate Role-Set). *Given a configuration* φ, *an* optimal candidate role-set *is the corresponding configuration* ψ *that simultaneously represents a candidate role-set for* φ *and minimized the cost function* cost(φ, ψ).

The main goal of role mining algorithm is thus finding optimal candidate role-sets. Considering the users and the permissions associated with a role, we define a weight function.

Definition 6 (Role Weight). *Let r be a given role, P_r be a set of permissions and U_r be a set of users associated to r. We indicate with $w(r)$ the weight of r, where $w(r)$ is the function defined as*

$$w(r) = c_u|U_r| \oplus c_p|P_r|,$$

where the operator "$\oplus$" is associative with respect to multiplication, and c_u and c_p are real numbers.

The role weight concept can be used as an indicator of the stability of a role. If a role r has a limited weight, it could be unstable, in that if a new user or a new permission is introduced it could drastically change the configuration of the role. In this case, it could be better to manage this role in a simpler way, namely breaking down the role in many single-permission roles which are easier to manage. The main idea is thus identifying the user-permission assignments that can belong only to roles with a limited weight. We manage these assignments with single-permission roles, restricting the role mining problem to the remaining user-permission assignments only. In this way, the elicited roles are *representative* and *stable*. Representative in that they are used by several users, or they cover several permissions, or both. Stable because they are not greatly affected by the introduction within the system of new users or new permissions. Once a set of roles that minimize the cost function has been found, introducing a new user or permission may change the system equilibrium whenever roles with limited weight exist. In particular, a new RBAC state could be necessary in place of the current one. This translates in higher administration cost, which is something that RBAC administrators tend to avoid. So, roles with a consistent weight are preferable, since they are more stable and less affected by the modifications of the existing user-permission assignments.

Due to space limitation, proofs of lemmas and theorems are not reported in this paper, but they can be found in [4].

4   Problem Modeling

The configuration $\varphi = \langle USERS, PERMS, UP \rangle$ can be represented by a bipartite graph $G = \langle V, E \rangle$, where the vertex set V is partitioned into disjoint subsets $USERS$ and $PERMS$, and two vertices $u \in USERS$ and $p \in PERMS$ are connected by an edge if and only if $\langle u, p \rangle \in UP$. A biclique coverage of the graphs G univocally identifies a candidate role-set $\psi = \langle ROLES, UA, PA \rangle$ for the configuration φ [6]. Indeed, every biclique identifies a role, and the vertices of the biclique identify the users and the permission assigned to this role.

Starting from the graph G, it is possible to construct a new undirected unipartite graph G', where the edges of G become the vertices of G': two vertices in G' are connected by an edge if and only if the endpoints of the corresponding edges of G induce a biclique of G. Formally: $G' = \langle E, \{\langle e_1, e_2 \rangle \mid e_1, e_2 \text{ induce a biclique in } G\} \rangle$. That is, the vertices of a clique in G' correspond to a set of edges of G, where the endpoints induce a biclique in G. The edges covered by a biclique of G induce a clique in G'. Thus,

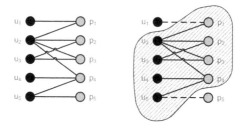

Fig. 1. An example of user-permission assignments and the subgraph to be considered

every biclique edge cover of G corresponds to a collection of cliques of G' such that their union contains all of the vertices of G'. From such a collection, a clique partition of G' can be obtained by removing any redundantly covered vertex from all but one of the cliques it belongs to. Similarly, any clique partition of G' corresponds to a biclique cover of G.

It is known that finding a clique partition of a graph $G = \langle V, E \rangle$ is equivalent to finding a coloring of its complement $\overline{G} = \langle V, (V \times V) \setminus E \rangle$ [6]. Thus, any coloring of $\overline{G'}$ identifies a candidate role-set of the given access control system configuration $\varphi = \langle USERS, PERMS, UP \rangle$, from which we have generated the graph G. Thus, finding a proper coloring for $\overline{G'}$ means finding a candidate role-set that covers all possible combinations of permissions possessed by users according to φ; namely, a set of roles such that the union of related permissions matches exactly with the permissions possessed by the users.

In this paper, we face the general problem of generating a candidate role-set that is stable and contextually minimizes the administration cost function. We split this problem in three steps:

1. Define a weight-based threshold.
2. Catch the user-permission assignments that do not belong to a role with a weight exceeding the given threshold.
3. Restrict the problem to find a set of roles that minimizes the administration cost function, including only the user-permission assignments that have not been identified in the second step.

In particular, we introduce a pruning operation on the vertices of $\overline{G'}$, that corresponds to identifying the user-permission assignments that can only belong to roles with a limited weight. These assignments are managed with single-permission roles, namely roles composed by only one permission. Using the pruning operation, we force the assignments to be assigned to roles with a higher weight. An example is shown in Figure 1: by creating single-permission roles for $u_1 p_1$, we are preventing the assignments $u_2 p_1$ for a role with a limited weight—composed by the users u_1 and u_2, and covering the permission p_1. The same happens for $u_5 p_5$ and $u_5 p_4$. Moreover, we will show that the portion of the graph that survives after the pruning operation is representable as a graph $\overline{G'}$ with a limited degree. Since the third step corresponds to coloring $\overline{G'}$, this property can be leveraged using many different coloring algorithms which make assumptions on the degree of the graph and available in the literature. The choice of which algorithm to use depends on the definition of the administration cost function.

4.1 Decomposition of the Bipartite Graph G

As seen in the previous section, any biclique coverage of G identifies a candidate role-set $\psi = \langle ROLES, UA, PA \rangle$ for the configuration φ. Moreover, any coloring of $\overline{G'}$ identifies a biclique coverage of G. If the graph G is not connected, it is possible to consider any connected component as a separate problem. Indeed, the union of the solutions of each component will be the solution of the original graph, as proved in the following lemma:

Lemma 1. *A biclique cannot exist across two or more disconnected components of a bipartite graph G.*

Since a biclique corresponds to a role, the previous lemma states that a role r, composed by a set of users U_r and a set of permissions P_r, cannot exist if all the users in U_r do not have all the permissions in P_r. If this is the case, we introduce some user-permission relations that are not in $\varphi = \langle USERS, PERMS, UP \rangle$. This lemma has an important implication, that is:

Theorem 1. *If G is disconnected, the union of the biclique coverage of each component of G is a biclique coverage of G. Moreover, if the biclique coverage of each component is optimal, their union will be an optimal biclique coverage for G.*

The main consequence of the theorem is that, if the graph G is disconnected, we can study each component independently. Therefore, we can use the union of the biclique coverage of the different components to build a biclique coverage of G. As we will see, we can use this result to limit the degree of $\overline{G'}$ when the bipartite graph G is disconnected.

4.2 Degree of $\overline{G'}$

In our model, the role mining problem corresponds to finding a proper coloring for the graph $\overline{G'}$. Indeed, this identifies a candidate role-set of the given access control system configuration. Depending on the cost function used, the optimal coloring could be different. For instance, if the cost function is defined as the total number of roles, the optimal coloring is the one which uses the minimum number of colors needed. However, if the cost function is more complex, the optimal coloring could be different. In this section we will analyze the degree of the graph $\overline{G'}$, highlighting what it represents and how this information can be used to simplify the role mining problem.

The graph $\overline{G'}$ is the graph composed by the same vertices of G', but $E(\overline{G'})$ is the complement of $E(G')$. The graph G' is built from the bipartite graph G, where each edge of G becomes a vertex of G', and two vertices of G' are connected by an edge if and only if the endpoints of the corresponding edges of G induce a biclique. Thus, a vertex $v \in G'$ univocally determines an edge $e \in G$. The degree of $v \in G'$ is the number of edges of G that induces a biclique together with e. Since $\overline{G'}$ is the complement of G', the degree of a vertex $v' \in \overline{G'}$ is the number of edges of G that do *not* induce a biclique together with the edge $e \in G$ identified by v'. According to the definition of the degree of a graph, the degree of $\overline{G'}$ is the maximum degree of its vertices. Formally, if e is an edge of the bipartite graph G, indicating with $b(e)$ the number of edges that do *not* induce biclique together with the edge e, then:

$$\Delta(\overline{G'}) = \max_{e \in E(G)} b(e).$$

To understand the meaning of the pruning operations we introduced, it is useful to describe the graphs in terms of RBAC semantic. A vertex of $\overline{G'}$ is a user-permission relation existing in the set UP. An edge in $\overline{G'}$ between two vertices v_1 and v_2 exists if the corresponding user-permission relations cannot be in the same role, because the user of v_1 does not have the permission in v_2, or the user of v_2 does not have the permission in v_1, or both. Thus, if a vertex of $\overline{G'}$ has a high degree, it means that this vertex cannot be colored using the same colors of a high number of other vertices; in other words, this user-permission relation cannot be in the same role together with a high number of other user-permission relations.

This consideration has an important aftermath: if a user-permission relation cannot be in the same role together with a high number of other user-permission relations, it will belong to a role with few user-permission relations, and we can estimate its maximal weight.

4.3   Pruning of the Given Access Control System Configuration

The main idea of our approach is pruning those user-permission relations which belong only to roles with a weight lower than a fixed threshold. If a role is composed only by few user-permission relations, its weight will be limited, and its administration cost could be acceptable even if we create for it a few single-permission roles. Moreover, when a change of the access control configuration happens, there is the need to recalculate the optimal candidate role-set. But a role with a limited weight is unstable, in the sense that the introduction of only one new user-permission assignment could drastically change the configuration of the role, according also to the specific cost function considered. Leveraging these observations, we will prune the given access control system configuration, creating single-permission roles for the pruned assignments and restricting the role mining to the rest of the assignments.

Suppose that for each $e \in E(G)$ there are at least d other edges, where the relative endpoints induce a biclique together with the endpoints of e. Every edge of G will not be in biclique with a maximum of $|E(G)| - d - 1$ other edges. That is:

Lemma 2. *If $\forall e \in E(G)$ there are at least d other edges, such that the endpoints of each one induce a biclique together with the endpoints of e, then:*

$$\Delta(\overline{G'}) \leq |E(G)| - d - 1$$

Thus, having chosen a suitable value for d, the idea is to prune the graph $\overline{G'}$ deleting the vertices that have a higher degree than $|E(G)| - d - 1$. Indeed, as it will be proven in the following Theorem 2, the user-permission assignments relative to these vertices will belong to roles with a limited weight, that could be administered using single-permission roles.

Theorem 2. *The pruning operation will prune only user-permission assignments that cannot belong to any role r, such that $w(r) > (d + 1)(c_U \oplus c_P)$.*

Note that the pruning operation of the vertices of $\overline{G'}$ can be executed directly on the edge of G: it corresponds to the pruning of the edges $e \in E(G)$ such that $b(e) \geq |E(G)| - d - 1$. The pruning on G, rather than on $\overline{G'}$, is more convenient, because in this way we have to work directly with a smaller graph $\overline{G'}$. Once we have a graph $\overline{G'}$, with a maximum degree of $\Delta(\overline{G'})$ we can use a coloring algorithm to find a candidate role-set for the access control system configuration from which we have built the graph G. Many coloring algorithms known in the literature make assumptions on the degree of the graph. Without our pruning operation, the degree of the graph $\overline{G'}$ could be high, up to $|E(G)| - 1$. This is the case when there exists a user-permission assignment that must be in a role alone. Note also that, when the graph G is disconnected in two or more components, any edge of one component is not in a biclique together with all the other edges belonging to different components. This involves a high degree for $\overline{G'}$, but for the argument given in Section 4.1 we can split the problem considering the different components distinctly, and then join the results of each component.

5   Applications of Our Approach to the Role Mining Problem

Having a bound for $\Delta(\overline{G'})$ makes it possible to use many known algorithms to color a graph. Indeed, finding a coloring for $\overline{G'}$ corresponds to finding a candidate role-set for the given access control system configuration. The choice of which algorithm to use depends on what we are interested in. For example, a company could be interested in obtaining only no more than a given number of roles, and to manage the others user-permission assignments with single-permission roles. This could happen when the company has just started a migration process to the RBAC model, and the administrators are not experts of role management. The *naive approach* presented in the following makes it possible to obtain no more than $\Delta + 1$ roles (without considering the single-permission roles). The the algorithm choice can also depend on the particular class of the obtained graph. For instance, if the given access control system configuration induces a dense graph G, it is possible to obtain Δ/k roles, where $k = O(\log \Delta)$, covering almost all the existent user-permission assignments. We will show how this is possible by adopting a *randomized approach* based on [8].

A Naive Approach. It is known that any graph with maximum degree Δ can be colored with $\Delta + 1$ colors by choosing an arbitrary ordering of the vertices and then coloring them one at time, labeling each vertex with a color not already used by any of its neighbors. In other words we can find $\Delta(\overline{G'}) + 1$ roles which cover all the user-permission assignments survived after the pruning. With the pruning operation, we are disregarding some user-permission assignments; this is the cost that we have to pay in order to have a Δ degree graph $\overline{G'}$. But the user-permission assignments that we are disregarding will belong to roles with a limited weight. So, it is better to create single-permission roles for those assignments.

The value $\Delta(\overline{G'}) + 1$ is not the optimum, it is only an upper bound for the chromatic number of $\overline{G'}$. If the coloring is optimal, namely if it uses the minimum number of colors needed, the candidate role-set found will be the smallest possible in cardinality. This problem is NP-hard and corresponds to *basicRMP*. If the degree of the graph is known, we can use many algorithms to approximate the solution.

A Randomized Approach. Using the randomized approach of [8] it is possible to generate Δ/k roles covering all the user-assignments which survive after the pruning, with $k = O(\log \Delta)$. This is a good result when minimizing the number of roles.

The hypothesis about which graph to color are basically two: it must be a Δ-regular graph, with $\Delta \gg \log n$, and it must have girths of length at least 4. The former is not a problem, because we can add some null nodes to the pruned graph $\overline{G'}$ and the relative edges obtaining a Δ-regular graph. The latter is more complex and we next discuss how to deal with this hypothesis. Every vertex of $\overline{G'}$ is a user-permission assignment in the given access control configuration; this means that it corresponds to an edge of G. Two vertices of $\overline{G'}$ are connected by an edge if the corresponding edges of G do not induce a biclique. Thus, a girth of length 3 in $\overline{G'}$ means that there are three edges of G, and every pair of this, does not induce a biclique. Having chosen two edges of G, let A be the event "these two edges induce a biclique" and let $\Pr(A) = p$. If $\overline{A}$ is the complement of A, then $\Pr(\overline{A}) = 1 - p$. Having chosen three edges, if B is the event "these three edges do not induce a biclique", $\Pr(B) = \Pr(\overline{A})^3$, indeed every unordered pair of the chosen triplet of edges must induce a biclique. Thus, $\Pr(B) = (1 - p)^3$. This is also the probability that, having chosen three vertices in $\overline{G'}$, they compose a girth of length 3. In other words, the probability to have a girth of length 3 in $\overline{G'}$, depends on the number of edges of the graph G. Therefore, it depends on how many user-permission assignments exist in the given access control configuration. Indeed, if the number of edges of G is close to the maximal number of edges, the probability p will be very high, and $\Pr(B)$ will be close to 0. However, suppose that $\overline{G'}$ is not completely free of girths of length 3, but there are only a few of such girths. We can still use the randomized approach by removing an appropriate edge for such girths, hence breaking these girths. Note that removing an edge from $\overline{G'}$ corresponds to forcing two edges of G, which do not induce a biclique, to induce a biclique. This means that with this operation we are adding some user-permission assignments not present in the given access control configuration. The roles obtained can then be sanitized by removing those users that do not have all the permissions of the role, and managing these users in other ways, i.e. creating some single-permission roles (which roles will not be numerous since we have shown that, in general, we will only obtain few girth of length 3).

6   Conclusions and Future Works

In this paper we have proposed a general method to elicit roles using a bottom-up role engineering approach, with the objective to limit the presence of unstable roles and to minimize the administration cost function. We have proposed a three steps methodology that, leveraging the graph modeling of this role mining problem, achieves the intended results supporting them with formal proofs. A further contribution is to show the applications of the proposed approach. Possible extensions of this work could address: refining the weight function including, for instance, access logs or business information; defining the optimal value of the pruning parameter d.

Acknowledgment

This work was partly supported by: The Spanish Ministry of Science and Education through projects TSI2007-65406-C03-01 "E-AEGIS" and CONSOLIDER CSD2007-00004 "ARES", and by the Government of Catalonia under grant 2005 SGR 00446.

References

1. American National Standards Institute (ANSI) and InterNational Committee for Information Technology Standards (INCITS): ANSI/INCITS 359-2004, Information Technology – Role Based Access Control (2004)
2. Colantonio, A., Di Pietro, R., Ocello, A.: A cost-driven approach to role engineering. In: Proceedings of the 23rd ACM Symposium on Applied Computing, SAC 2008, Fortaleza, Ceará, Brazil, vol. 3, pp. 2129–2136 (2008)
3. Colantonio, A., Di Pietro, R., Ocello, A.: Leveraging lattices to improve role mining. In: Proceedings of the IFIP TC 11 23rd International Information Security Conference, SEC 2008. IFIP International Federation for Information Processing, vol. 278, pp. 333–347. Springer, Heidelberg (2008)
4. Colantonio, A., Di Pietro, R., Ocello, A., Verde, N.V.: Mining stable roles in RBAC, TR 01-01-09. Tech. rep., Università degli Studi di Rome Tre (2009),
   http://www.dsi.uniroma1.it/~dipietro/TR01-01-09.pdf
5. Coyne, E.J.: Role engineering. In: RBAC 1995: Proceedings of the first ACM Workshop on Role-based access control, p. 4. ACM, New York (1996)
6. Ene, A., Horne, W., Milosavljevic, N., Rao, P., Schreiber, R., Tarjan, R.E.: Fast exact and heuristic methods for role minimization problems. In: Proceedings of the 13th ACM Symposium on Access Control Models and Technologies, SACMAT 2008, pp. 1–10 (2008)
7. Geerts, F., Goethals, B., Mielikäinen, T.: Tiling databases. In: Suzuki, E., Arikawa, S. (eds.) DS 2004. LNCS, vol. 3245, pp. 278–289. Springer, Heidelberg (2004)
8. Grable, D.A., Panconesi, A.: Fast distributed algorithms for brooks-vizing colorings. J. Algorithms 37(1), 85–120 (2000)
9. Jajodia, S., Samarati, P., Subrahmanian, V.S.: A logical language for expressing authorizations. In: SP 1997: Proceedings of the 1997 IEEE Symposium on Security and Privacy, p. 31. IEEE Computer Society, Washington (1997)
10. Kuhlmann, M., Shohat, D., Schimpf, G.: Role mining – revealing business roles for security administration using data mining technology. In: Proceedings of the 8th ACM Symposium on Access Control Models and Technologies, SACMAT 2003, Como, Italy, pp. 179–186 (2003)
11. Lu, H., Vaidya, J., Atluri, V.: Optimal boolean matrix decomposition: Application to role engineering. In: Proceedings of the 24th IEEE International Conferene on Data Engineering, ICDE 2008, pp. 297–306 (2008)
12. Rymon, R.: Method and apparatus for role grouping by shared resource utilization (2003); United States Patent Application 20030172161
13. Schlegelmilch, J., Steffens, U.: Role mining with ORCA. In: Proceedings of the 10th ACM Symposium on Access Control Models and Technologies, SACMAT 2005, pp. 168–176 (2005)
14. Siewert, D.J.: Biclique covers and partitions of bipartite graphs and digraphs and related matrix ranks of {0, 1} matrices. Ph.D. thesis, The University of Colorado at Denver (2000)
15. Vaidya, J., Atluri, V., Guo, Q.: The role mining problem: finding a minimal descriptive set of roles. In: Proceedings of the 12th ACM Symposium on Access Control Models and Technologies, SACMAT 2007, pp. 175–184 (2007)
16. Vaidya, J., Atluri, V., Guo, Q., Adam, N.: Migrating to optimal RBAC with minimal perturbation. In: Proceedings of the 13th ACM Symposium on Access Control Models and Technologies, SACMAT 2008, pp. 11–20 (2008)
17. Vaidya, J., Atluri, V., Warner, J.: RoleMiner: mining roles using subset enumeration. In: Proceedings of the 13th ACM Conference on Computer and Communications Security, pp. 144–153 (2006)
18. Zhang, D., Ramamohanarao, K., Ebringer, T.: Role engineering using graph optimisation. In: Proceedings of the 12th ACM Symposium on Access Control Models and Technologies, SACMAT 2007, pp. 139–144 (2007)

Privacy-Preserving Content-Based Publish/Subscribe Networks*

Abdullatif Shikfa, Melek Önen, and Refik Molva

EURECOM, France
{shikfa,onen,molva}@eurecom.fr

Abstract. Privacy and confidentiality are crucial issues in content-based publish/subscribe (CBPS) networks. We tackle the problem of end-user privacy in CBPS. This problem raises a challenging requirement for handling encrypted data for the purpose of routing based on protected content and encrypted subscription information. We suggest a solution based on a commutative multiple encryption scheme in order to allow brokers to operate in-network matching and content based routing without having access to the content of the packets. This is the first solution that avoids key sharing among end-users and targets an enhanced CBPS model where brokers can also be subscribers at the same time.

1 Introduction

Publish-subscribe paradigm allows for flexible and dynamic communication among a large number of participants. As opposed to classical messaging systems, in publish-subscribe, communicating parties are loosely coupled in that the source of the information does not need to know potential recipients of the information and the recipients do not need to know where the information originates from. In a content-based publish-subscribe system the forwarding of data segments between the sources and the recipients does not take into account the addresses of communicating parties but is performed based on the relationship between the content of each message and the interest of recipients. The recipients who inform the publish-subscribe system about the messages they are interested in through subscription messages are thus called subscribers. Publish-subscribe applications range from large scale content distribution applications such as stock-quote distribution to dynamic messaging between loosely-coupled parties in on-line social networks.

The flexibility of publish-subscribe comes on the other hand with a high cost in increased exposure in terms of data security and privacy. Apart from classical data security concerns such as the confidentiality and integrity of messages, the authentication of the source, access control and authorization of subscribers, publish-subscribe also raises new challenges inherent to the collapsed forwarding scheme that is the underpinning of publish-subscribe. In classical layered communication systems, the application layer information can be protected with various security mechanisms like encryption

---

* This work has been supported by the HAGGLE project, grant agreement number 027918, funded by the EC sixth framework program theme FP6-IST-2004-2.3.4 for Situated and Autonomic Communications. See http://www.haggleproject.org/ for further details.

D. Gritzalis and J. Lopez (Eds.): SEC 2009, IFIP AICT 297, pp. 270–282, 2009.

and message authentication without affecting the underlying data forwarding mechanisms implemented in the network layer. In case of publish-subscribe, protection of the content with similar security mechanisms would conflict with the forwarding functions since the latter rely on the very content that is being transmitted for their basic operations. Publish-subscribe therefore calls for new solutions to allow intermediate nodes to perform routing operations based on data protected with encryption and integrity mechanisms. The first requirement is for a secure forwarding mechanism that would achieve the look-up in forwarding tables using encrypted content as the search key. Furthermore, an important privacy requirement in content-based publish-subscribe is the confidentiality of the messages through which subscribers inform the network about their interests. Whilst encryption of these messages appears to be a suitable solution for subscriber privacy, such encryption operation raises an additional challenge for the forwarding mechanism. Hence not only the search key for the look-up mechanism but also the forwarding table itself would be based on encrypted data. Some existing security primitives such as keyword search with encrypted data or private information retrieval seem to partially meet the new requirements raised by secure and privacy preserving data forwarding in publish-subscribe but none of the existing security mechanisms actually address both the problem of secure look-up and the secure building of forwarding tables in a comprehensive manner.

In this paper, we suggest a set of security mechanisms that allow for privacy-preserving forwarding of encrypted content based on encrypted subscriber interest messages. The main advantages of this solution are that it achieves both data confidentiality from the point of view of the publishers and the privacy of the subscribers with respect to their interests in a potentially hostile model whereby the publishers, the subscribers and the intermediate nodes in charge of data forwarding do not trust one another. The solution relies on a scheme called multi-layer encryption that allows intermediate nodes to manage forwarding tables and to perform content forwarding using encrypted content and based on encrypted subscriber messages without ever accessing the cleartext version of those data. Our solution further avoids key sharing among end-users and targets an enhanced CBPS model where brokers can also be subscribers at the same time.

2   Reference Model and Problem Statement

2.1   Content-Based Publish/Subscribe (CBPS)

We consider a classical CBPS model as described in many papers like [5,19]. In this model the CBPS consists of:

- end-users divided in **publishers** which publish information in the form of event notifications, and **subscribers** which express their interests in a certain content in the form of subscription filters,
- the CBPS infrastructure composed of **brokers** (intermediate nodes) whose task is to disseminate notifications sent by publishers to the interested subscribers.

We assume that the CBPS infrastructure can be viewed, from the perspective of each publisher, as a tree whose root node is the publisher itself and whose leaf nodes are the subscribers (whether interested in the content published by the publisher or not). Based on this model, we only consider the case of a network with one publisher for the sake of simplicity.

Information contained in each event should fit within an event schema, and the subscription filters are predicates against this schema. Our model of subscription is equality filters with only one keyword and events are composed of two parts: one routable attribute and a second part which is the payload. The equality matching is the mostly used filtering function in the literature since it can be used as a basis to support range queries as introduced in [16]. Brokers use this matching operation between filters and routable attributes to route published content. If we take as an example the commonly used stock quote dissemination problem, a subscription filter could be $(price = 120)$ which would match an event like $(price = 120, [symbol = "STM", price = 120, volume = 1000])$.

In [5], authors show that content-based routing and in-network matching are vital for the performance and scalability of the CBPS system. To this extent, if two subscriptions match the same content, then only one of them should be propagated in the network. We thus define equivalence between filters as follows: we say that two filters f_1 and f_2 are equivalent if they match the same events.

As mentioned in the introduction, this paper focus on privacy issues in CBPS, hence we now describe our security assumptions to complete our reference model.

2.2 Threat Model and Security Assumptions

As in many papers (e.g. [19]), we assume a honest-but-curious model for the publishers, the subscribers and the brokers. Publishers, subscribers and brokers are computationally bounded and do not deviate from the designed protocol, but they may be interested in learning more than needed to correctly run the protocol to break subscriber privacy. A curious publisher may indeed be interested in knowing which subscribers are interested in the content it publishes. Subscribers may try to sneak on other subscribers to determine what their interest are or at least if they have some common interests. The same goes for curious brokers which may eavesdrop on the messages routed through them to discover their content.

However, all the nodes are honest and do not deviate from the designed protocol, meaning for instance that brokers correctly route the information they receive as indicated by the protocol, they do not drop packets or forward packets in a wrong way. Denial of service attacks are thus out of the scope of this paper. We also take into account malicious but passive nodes outside of the network, which can overhear communications and try to break end-users' privacy.

We now show the link between privacy and confidentiality issues and how the required confidentiality can be achieved through secure routing.

2.3 Privacy, Confidentiality and Secure Routing

In this paper, we focus on the problem of subscriber and publisher privacy. As pointed out in [13], privacy is expected to be a significant concern for acceptance of pervasive environments like CBPS systems. Privacy from the subscriber point of view refers to the fact that subscribers do not want any other nodes, be it brokers, publishers, other subscribers or even nodes outside the CBPS infrastructure, to spy on their interests and be able to profile them in any way. There are several ways of ensuring privacy; one of the classical approaches is to guarantee data confidentiality with cryptographic primitives.

Confidentiality in CBPS networks has first been analyzed in [20] where the authors identify three confidentiality issues. To ensure privacy only two are relevant:

- **Information confidentiality:** Can the infrastructure perform content-based routing, without the publishers trusting the infrastructure with the content? This confidentiality requirement may look paradoxical : content-based routing is indeed, by definition, based on evaluations of the content of notifications against subscription filters. The challenge is to be able to perform these evaluations on encrypted data without leaking information on the corresponding content or subscription filter. In the stock quotes example, this corresponds to be able to do content-based routing on an encrypted event where the brokers cannot discover in the event the value of the symbol, price or volume.

- **Subscription confidentiality:** Can subscribers obtain dynamic, content-based data without revealing their subscription filters to the publishers or to the infrastructure? This is the dual problem of information confidentiality. Here, subscribers do not want to reveal their interests either to brokers or publishers or other subscribers but they still want to receive the content they are interested in and only this one. So the challenge in this case is to match a content with an encrypted subscription without disclosing the subscription filter. In the stock quotes example, this requirement corresponds to the ability to find which events match which filter without accessing it in clear; it is a problem of secure function evaluation, where a broker has to evaluate a hidden function (the filter which was encrypted by the subscriber).

Information and subscriber confidentiality in CBPS call for new mechanisms to achieve secure routing of encrypted data with the capability of matching encrypted event notifications against encrypted subscription filters in order to ensure end-users privacy. Routing of encrypted data in CBPS involves two separate operations:

- **Building routing tables:** Brokers have to build routing tables using routing information -subscription filters- which is classically propagated upwards (from subscribers to publishers) by intermediate nodes to subsequently allow for the routing of content in a possibly optimized fashion. The challenge in our case is that subscription filters are encrypted, hence nodes have to build their routing tables with encrypted filters (to satisfy the subscription confidentiality constraint) and to aggregate theses encrypted routing information. Aggregation of routing tables' entries is not strictly a security concern but is nonetheless a strong requirement from the point of view of performance.

- **Look-up:** Once routing tables are built, nodes can forward data downwards (from publishers to subscribers) in an optimized way through the infrastructure. The challenge for brokers in the dissemination process is to be able to perform the look-up of encrypted data (to fulfill the information confidentiality requirement) in routing tables where entries include encrypted subscription filters.

CBPS privacy thus calls for a solution that achieves secure routing of encrypted data based on encrypted routing information. One naturally turns to searchable encryption and keyword search [4,18] that are cryptographic techniques most likely to meet the requirements of secure routing in CBPS. Unfortunately none of the existing searchable encryption and keyword schemes address both the secure forwarding and the table building requirement of CBPS. We tailor in this paper a dedicated solution to meet the specific requirements of CBPS.

3   Secure Routing with Multiple Layer Encryption

3.1   Multiple Layer Commutative Encryption (MLCE)

The basic idea behind our solution is to use a MLCE in order to meet the privacy requirements raised by CBPS systems. MLCE allows intermediate nodes in charge of routing secure traffic to perform secure transformations without having access to the data that is being transferred. This feature of MLCE lends itself very well to solving the problem of routing encrypted data as raised by CBPS. Multiple encryption was previously proposed in [9,11,14] in the context of multicast security and data aggregation. In multiple layer encryption data is encrypted several times with different keys. In the case where the encryption layers all use the same cryptosystem, and if this cryptosystem is commutative, then the layers can be added and removed in any order. An encryption mechanism $\mathcal{E}$ is commutative if, for any data d, any keys k_1, k_2 we have:

$$\mathcal{E}_{k_2}(\mathcal{E}_{k_1}(d)) = \mathcal{E}_{k_1}(\mathcal{E}_{k_2}(d)).$$

We propose to use multiple layer commutative encryption in order to ensure secure routing in CBPS applications where the publisher publishes encrypted events and the subscriber sends its encrypted subscription filter to the source over untrusted brokers. The idea is for the subscriber to encrypt its subscription filter with r layers corresponding to the $r \geq 2$ next hops, and for the publishers to do the same with their event notifications. Brokers en-route remove one encryption layer and add a new one without destroying the other layers so that the data is always protected by at least $r - 1$ layers of encryption. Thus brokers do not have access to data in cleartext. Still, this mechanism allows secure look-up as well as efficient and secure routing table building thanks to the commutativity of the layers. The number of layers r is a security parameter that has a performance impact, yet, for the sake of simplicity, we present our scheme only for the case $r = 2$ and discuss the choice of the parameter r in section 5.

To further introduce the solution, let us consider a minimalist example. In this example, we consider three nodes in line, namely a subscriber denoted by S, then a broker denoted by B and finally a publisher denoted by P. We denote by k_{ij} a key shared between node i and j. S encrypts its data x_S with $\mathcal{E}_{k_{SP}}(\mathcal{E}_{k_{SB}}(x_S))$ and so does P with its data x_P: $\mathcal{E}_{k_{SP}}(\mathcal{E}_{k_{BP}}(x_P))$. The broker now can remove the layers corresponding to k_{SB} and k_{BP} respectively to obtain $\mathcal{E}_{k_{SP}}(x_S)$ and $\mathcal{E}_{k_{SP}}(x_P)$. Hence, it cannot access the data directly but it is able to perform a matching operation for the secure look-up since x_S and x_P are encrypted under the same keys.

Therefore, given a commutative cryptosystem we are able to do secure routing and hence protect the privacy of publishers and subscribers. Yet, commutative cryptosystems are very rare, and although many security solutions assume the existence of a commutative cipher, few of them deal with a concrete commutative cryptosystem. We developed a scheme based on the Pohlig-Hellman cryptosystem, that we carefully adapted to our case in order to provide a complete and concrete solution. Privacy-preserving routing with MLCE is achieved through four security primitives that are detailed in the next section.

3.2 Security Primitives

To further refine the privacy-preserving routing using MLCE we identify four generic operations required for secure event dissemination as follows:

- **ENCRYPT_FILTER:** used by subscribers to generate encrypted subscription filters. On input a subscription filter and some keying material it outputs an encrypted version of the subscription filter.
- **ENCRYPT_NOTIFICATION:** used by the publisher to encrypt its notifications. On input an event notification and some keying material it outputs an encrypted version of the subscription filter.
- **SECURE_LOOK_UP:** allows a broker to decide whether an encrypted notification matches one of the encrypted subscriptions of its routing table. This primitive should only return the boolean result of the matching operation.
- **SECURE_TABLE_BUILDING:** allows the broker to build a routing table and to compare two encrypted subscriptions. If two subscriptions match the same content there is indeed no need to forward both of them to the broker's parent. The broker only needs to store both of them with the corresponding child in its routing table and it forwards one to its parent. As the previous primitive, this one should only return the boolean result of the matching operation, but it should not leak any additional information about the subscriptions. The aggregation is optional from a pure privacy point of view (it even induces additional difficulties) but it is vital from a performance point of view to comply with some content-based routing optimizations.

All brokers use the same general message processing, summarized in Table 1, to preserve MLCE and manage the security primitives at the same time. We now formally describe our solution in the next section.

4 Privacy and Confidentiality in the Hybrid Model

We propose a new solution based on the Pohlig-Hellman cryptosystem whereby subscribers do not need to share a unique and common key K with the publisher. This solution does not differentiate brokers from subscribers and therefore allows brokers to also act as subscribers by subscribing to events and sending their own subscription filters while performing the routing operation.

4.1 The Pohlig-Hellman Cryptosystem and Key Management

The Pohlig-Hellman cryptosystem [15] is defined as a tuple $(p, \mathcal{K}, \mathcal{E}, \mathcal{D})$ where:

- p is a large prime known by all nodes (it is a system parameter)
- $\mathcal{K}$ outputs a pair of keys (k_i, d_i) such that $k_i d_i \equiv (1 \bmod (p-1))$;

Table 1. Message processing at a broker. The broker is denoted by B, its grandparent by G, its grandchild by C, the encryption algorithm is $\mathcal{E}$ and the decryption one is $\mathcal{D}$. In the left column B receives an encrypted subscription filter SF and in the right column B receives an encrypted event notification EN.

Upwards: filter propagation	Downwards: event dissemination
Remove an encryption layer: $\mathcal{D}_{k_{BC}}(SF)$	Remove an encryption layer: $\mathcal{D}_{k_{BG}}(EN)$
Update the routing table RT_B: $SECURE\_TABLE\_BUILDING(RT_B, \mathcal{D}_{k_{BC}}(SF))$	Secure look-up: $SECURE\_LOOK\_UP(RT_B, \mathcal{D}_{k_{BG}}(EN))$
Add an encryption layer: $\mathcal{E}_{k_{BG}}(\mathcal{D}_{k_{BC}}(SF))$	Add an encryption layer: $\mathcal{E}_{k_{BC}}(\mathcal{D}_{k_{BG}}(EN))$
Forward the message upwards	Forward the message downwards

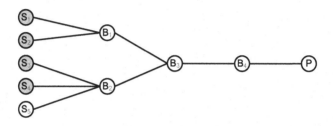

Fig. 1. Example of Publish/Subscribe network. This CBPS network has one publisher (P), four brokers (B_1 to B_4) and five subscribers (S_1 to S_5).

- $\mathcal{E}(p, k_i, x)$ returns $x^{k_i} \bmod p$;
- $\mathcal{D}(p, d_i, y)$ returns $y^{d_i} \bmod p$

Since $k_i d_i \equiv (1 \bmod (p-1))$, we have $x^{k_i d_i} \bmod n \equiv x \bmod n$.

The encryption operation is based on an exponentiation and is therefore inherently commutative. Indeed:

$$\mathcal{E}(p, k_i, \mathcal{E}(p, k_j, x)) = (x^{k_j k_i}) \bmod p = \mathcal{E}(p, k_j, \mathcal{E}(p, k_i, x))$$

Thanks to the commutative property of the Pohlig-Hellman cryptosystem, any broker is able to add and suppress encryption layers if it stores the corresponding keys. The addition and subtraction of a layer in this new hybrid model respectively correspond to a Pohlig-Hellman encryption and decryption operation. Since the security of this cryptosystem relies on the hardness of the Discrete Logarithm Problem the key k_i can be used to encrypt several different messages. Moreover, this cryptosystem is asymmetric in the sense that the encryption key differs from the decryption key. However, as opposed to classical asymmetric cryptosystems such as RSA [17], if a node knows one of the keys, it can automatically deduce the remaining key. Therefore there is no "public key"; all keys are secret and they are only revealed to authorized nodes. We therefore need a proper key distribution mechanism that is processed locally in a self-organized way. We do not address the key distribution issue in this paper and simply assume that each node N_i shares a Pohlig-Hellman key pair with each of its one or two hops neighbors, thanks to an appropriate key agreement scheme. In the example of Fig. 1, B_1 shares four pairs of keys $(k_{S_1B_1}, d_{S_1B_1})$, $(k_{S_2B_1}, d_{S_2B_1})$, $(k_{B_1B_3}, d_{B_1B_3})$ and $(k_{B_1B_4}, d_{B_1B_4})$ respectively with S_1, S_2, B_3 and B_4.

The Pohlig-Hellman cryptosystem being described, we formally define the four security primitives in the next sections.

4.2   Propagation of Subscription Filters and Building of Routing Tables

4.2.1   ENCRYPT_FILTER
ENCRYPT_FILTER used by subscriber S_i only requires the filter and two encryption keys $k_{S_iB_j}$ and $k_{S_iB_l}$ where B_j and B_l are respectively S_i's parent node and grandparent node. It outputs an encrypted filter SF_{S_i} computed as:

$$ENCRYPT\_FILTER(f, k_{S_iB_j}, k_{S_iB_l}) = \mathcal{E}(p, k_{S_iB_j}, \mathcal{E}(p, k_{S_iB_l}, f)) = f^{k_{S_iB_j}k_{S_iB_l}} \bmod p.$$

S_i then sends the message $[SF_{S_i} : S_i]$ to its parent node B_j.

4.2.2   SECURE_TABLE_BUILDING
Whenever an intermediate node B_j receives an encrypted filter $f^{k_{B_iB_j}k_{B_iB_l}} \bmod p$, it first removes one encryption layer with the use of $d_{B_iB_j}$ as follows:

$$\mathcal{D}(p, d_{B_iB_j}, f^{k_{B_iB_j}k_{B_iB_l}} \bmod p) = f^{k_{B_iB_l}} \bmod p$$

The *check − equivalence* operation is very simple, since B_j only checks in its routing table RT_j if there is an equality with some rows. There is no need for an additional information to use this operation. If there is an equality, then the destination in SF_{B_i} is added in the corresponding row and the message is not forwarded; otherwise, B_j creates a new row with SF_{B_i}, adds another encryption layer with the key $k_{B_jB_m}$ shared with its grand-parent node B_m and finally sends the following message to B_l: $f^{k_{B_iB_l}k_{B_jB_m}}$. Table 2 illustrates the previous mechanisms in the example of Fig. 1, where S_1 to S_4 subscribe to a filter f while S_5 subscribes to a different filter f'.

Table 2. Propagation of subscriptions phase. The left table corresponds to the routing table RT_3 of B_3 after the receipt of all subscribers' filters. B_3 needs to store two hops information for the content distribution phase and we observe that aggregation is performed also after two hops. The table on the right presents the whole propagation path of a filter f from S_1 to B_4.

R_{3-1}	$f^{k_{B_1B_4}} \to B_1(S_1), B_1(S_2)$
R_{3-2}	$f^{k_{B_2B_4}} \to B_2(S_3), B_2(S_4)$
R_{3-3}	$f'^{k_{B_2B_4}} \to B_2(S_5)$

S_1	f
$S_1 \to B_1$	$[f^{k_{S_1B_1}k_{S_1B_3}} \bmod p; S_1]$
B_1	$f^{k_{S_1 \cdot B_3}} \bmod p$
$B_1 \to B_3$	$[f^{k_{S_1B_3}k_{B_1B_4}} \bmod p; S_1]$
B_3	$f^{k_{B_1 \cdot B_4}} \bmod p$
$B_3 \to B_4$	$[f^{k_{B_1B_4}k_{B_3P}} \bmod p; B_1]$
B_4	$f^{k_{B_3 \cdot P}} \bmod p$

4.3   Content Distribution and Secure Look-Up

Symmetrically, the Publisher P first uses the $ENCRYPT\_NOTIFICATION$ to encrypt the event notification with the corresponding keys and forwards the packet to the next broker. Then, the broker, after removing one encryption layer, runs the $SECURE\_LOOKUP$ primitive and accordingly it adds another encryption layer and forwards the packet.

4.3.1   ENCRYPT_NOTIFICATION

$ENCRYPT\_NOTIFICATION$ that is used by a publisher P, takes the routable attribute ra in the event notification and two keys $k_{B_m P}$ and $k_{B_l P}$ that are respectively shared with its child node B_m and its grandchild node B_l. Moreover, P defines a payload encryption key k_P in order to encrypt the payload with a symmetric encryption algorithm. $ENCRYPT\_NOTIFICATION$ returns:

$$EN = ENCRYPT\_NOTIFICATION(ra, k_{B_m P}, k_{B_l P}, k_P, P) = [EN_1; EN_2; EN_3]$$
$$EN_1 = ra^{k_{B_m P} k_{B_l P}} \bmod p; EN_2 = k_P^{k_{B_m P} k_{B_l P}} \bmod p; EN_3 = \mathscr{F}_{k_P}(\mathscr{P})]$$

4.3.2   SECURE_LOOK_UP

When an intermediate node B_m receives the encrypted event notification $ra^{k_{B_m P} k_{B_l P}} \bmod p$ and the encryption payload encryption key $k_P^{k_{B_m P} k_{B_l P}} \bmod p$, it will first suppress a decryption layer with the use of $d_{B_m P}$ in order to obtain $EN_{1m} = ra^{k_{B_l P}} \bmod p$ and $k_P^{k_{B_l P}} \bmod p$. Given this partially decrypted routable attribute and the routing table RT_m, $SECURE\_LOOKUP(EN_{1m}, RT_m)$ returns the list of children nodes where the corresponding packet will be forwarded. The look-up in this case simply consist in an equality check between EN_{1m} and each of the rows of RT_m. Then, B_m adds a new encryption layer and forward the following packet to the correct destination:

$$[ra^{k_{B_l P} k_{B_m B_j}} \bmod p; k_P^{k_{B_l P} k_{B_m B_j}} \bmod p; \mathscr{F}_{k_P}(\mathscr{P})]$$

Only the encryption key k_P of the payload is modified at each node. The payload itself is never modified while being forwarded. An example of event propagation is presented in Table 3.

5   Analysis

In this section, we evaluate the security and the performance of the scheme. First, the proposed encryption mechanism with multiple encryption layers ensures confidentiality against honest-but-curious nodes. Bellare et al. have indeed shown in [2] that, if a cryptosystem is secure in the sense of indistinguishability, then the cryptosystem in the multi-user setting, where related messages are encrypted using different keys, is also secure. When a message is encrypted with two independent keys it is at least as secure as any individual encryption. Thus, the scheme is at least as secure as a one layer encryption. The latter is based on the discrete logarithm problem in a finite field of prime order which is believed to be hard when the exponent is unknown.

Table 3. Evolution of a message published by P on its path to a subscriber. This table only shows the path toward S_2 and we can observe how the information of RT_3 allows B_3 to properly forward the message in the direction of S_2.

Step	Event notification
P	$[f, k_P, \mathscr{P}]$
$P \to B_4$	$[f^{k_{B_3}p k_{B_4}P} \bmod p; k_P^{k_{B_3}p k_{B_4}P} \bmod p; \mathscr{F}_{k_P}(\mathscr{P})]$
B_4	$[f^{k_{B_3}P} \bmod p, k_P^{k_{B_3}P} \bmod p, \mathscr{F}_{k_P}(\mathscr{P})]$
$B_4 \to B_3$	$[f^{k_{B_3}p k_{B_1}B_4} \bmod p, k_P^{k_{B_3}p k_{B_1}B_4} \bmod p, \mathscr{F}_{k_P}(\mathscr{P})]$
B_3	$[f^{k_{B_1}B_4} \bmod p; k_P^{k_{B_1}B_4} \bmod p, \mathscr{F}_{k_P}(\mathscr{P})]$
$B_3 \to B_1$	$[f^{k_{B_1}B_4 k_{S_2}B_3} \bmod p, k_P^{k_{B1B4}k_{S_2}B_3} \bmod p, \mathscr{F}_{k_P}(\mathscr{P})]$
B_1	$[f^{k_{S_2}B_3} \bmod p, k_P^{k_{S_2}B_3} \bmod p, \mathscr{F}_{k_P}(\mathscr{P})]$
$B_1 \to S_2$	$[f^{k_{S_2}B_3 k_{S_2}B_1} \bmod p, k_P^{k_{S_2}B_3 k_{S_2}B_1} \bmod p, \mathscr{F}_{k_P}(\mathscr{P})]$
S_2	$[f, k_P, P]$

Furthermore, thanks to the use of multiple encryption layers, the confidentiality of messages relies on the use of keys belonging to different users. Messages are namely forwarded and continuously modified by the addition and removal of encryption layers but they remain unaccessible to brokers or eavesdroppers at all times. Even if two subscribers are subscribing with the same filter they are not able to tell so because each one encrypts it with different keys. Moreover, the protocol features a simple and secure aggregation operation, which consists of an equality test between two encrypted filters. Hence, our protocol preserves privacy through secure and efficient routing, which requires only a local key management. Finally, since there is no need for a shared secret between subscribers, brokers can act as subscribers while preserving the privacy of other subscribers.

Our protocol relies on the use of two encryption layers in order to simplify the description. However if two consecutive nodes, a node and its parent, collude and hence share their own keying material, they can decrypt their children nodes' subscriptions. Our scheme allows for a protection against collusion attacks by increasing the number of encryption layers as described in [11]. Therefore, the privacy of the scheme and its resistance to collusion attacks depends on the choice of the number of encryption layers denoted by r. The larger values for r imply a larger number of nodes to collude to break it. However, with large r, key storage per node becomes a burden and the key distribution overhead can have an impact on the performance of the protocol. Also aggregation occurs only after r hops so the larger the r the less efficient the aggregation mechanism. The choice of r is hence a trade-off that depends on the scenario and the topology of the network.

6 Related Work

Publish subscribe is a messaging paradigm that allows the creation of flexible and scalable distributed systems. SIENA ([5]) is an example of a popular CBPS system, but many others have been developed ([3,7]). Most of the efforts in this area concern pure networking issues, like performance or scalability.

Wang et al. [20] analyze the security issues and requirements that arise in CBPS systems. They mainly identify classical security problems (like authentication, integrity or confidentiality) and adapt them to the CBPS case. Yet, they do not provide concrete or specific solutions to these new problems.

Recently two interesting works concerning confidentiality in CBPS have been published. First, in [16], authors focus on notification and subscription confidentiality only. They define the confidentiality issues in a formal model and propose few solutions depending on the subscription and notification format. They assume that publishers and subscribers share a secret; this reduces the decoupling of CBPS. Furthermore, in their attacker model, only the brokers are honest-but-curious, the publishers and subscribers are assumed to be trustworthy. Hence, this scheme does not preserve subscribers' privacy against other curious subscribers or publishers. Second, in [19], authors propose a specific key management scheme and then a probabilistic multi-path event routing to prevent frequency inferring attacks. The main weakness of the scheme is the requirement for a KDC which is a centralized authority that is trusted not to be curious and decipher all the communication messages. Concerning content-based event routing, this scheme considers that events have some routable attributes which are tokenized in order to become pseudo-random chains and to prevent dictionary attacks. Like in [16], they adapt the protocol of Song et al. [18] but they do not motivate the use of this particular solution. Furthermore, their way of ensuring privacy is through multiple path routing thus affecting the performance, whereas we protect privacy by cryptographic means.

Finally, Opyrchal et al. deal with privacy in CBPS but from other perspectives. In [12] they focus on the confidentiality issue only on the last leg from end-point brokers to subscribers but they assume that brokers are completely trustworthy. And in [13] they focus on privacy policy management.

Private matching: The underpinning of the secure look-up and secure table building primitives is a matching operation using encrypted data. Private matching has been introduced for equality matches [1,10] and extended to more general settings [6,8]. Yet a careful study of the problem shows that there is a subtle but important difference between private matching and the requirements of our scheme. Private matching is indeed a two-party protocol between a client and a server where the client learns at the end the information that he shares with the server, whereas in our case the matching operation has to be performed by a third party which has no control over the data.

7   Conclusion

In this paper, we analyzed privacy issues in content-based publish/subscribe networks. In order to solve this problem with cryptographic tools, we analyzed the link between privacy and confidentiality and identified two confidentiality requirements, namely publisher and information confidentiality. This led us to the more general problem of routing encrypted events using encrypted subscription filters. This problem of secure routing requires two main primitives, namely **building of encrypted routing tables** with aggregation of encrypted filters and **secure look-up** of encrypted events with encrypted routing tables to disseminate the events efficiently. We then presented a solution to this problem based on multiple layers of Pohlig-Hellman encryptions. This is the first scheme which enables privacy-preserving routing with no shared secret between end-users, thanks to the commutativity of MLCE. Another key feature of this protocol is that it allows brokers to be subscribers at the same time while preserving privacy of all nodes which is appealing for peer-to-peer applications.

As future work, we intend to develop these schemes by improving their flexibility regarding the network topology and the subscription filter format. We would like indeed to extend subscription filters to encompass logical expressions.

References

1. Agrawal, R., Evfimievski, A.V., Srikant, R.: Information sharing across private databases. In: SIGMOD Conference, pp. 86–97 (2003)
2. Bellare, M., Boldyreva, A., Micali, S.: Public-key encryption in a multiuser setting: Security proofs and improvements. In: Preneel, B. (ed.) EUROCRYPT 2000. LNCS, vol. 1807, pp. 259–274. Springer, Heidelberg (2000)
3. Birman, K.P.: The process group approach to reliable distributed computing. Commun. ACM 36(12), 37–53 (1993)
4. Boneh, D., Di Crescenzo, G., Ostrovsky, R., Persiano, G.: Public key encryption with keyword search. In: Cachin, C., Camenisch, J.L. (eds.) EUROCRYPT 2004. LNCS, vol. 3027, pp. 506–522. Springer, Heidelberg (2004)
5. Carzaniga, A., Rosenblum, D.S., Wolf, A.L.: Design and evaluation of a wide-area event notification service. ACM Trans. Comput. Syst. 19(3), 332–383 (2001)
6. Chmielewski, L., Hoepman, J.-H.: Fuzzy private matching (extended abstract). In: ARES, pp. 327–334. IEEE Computer Society, Los Alamitos (2008)
7. Datta, A.K., Gradinariu, M., Raynal, M., Simon, G.: Anonymous publish/subscribe in p2p networks. In: IPDPS 2003: Proceedings of the 17th International Symposium on Parallel and Distributed Processing, Washington, DC, USA. IEEE Computer Society, Los Alamitos (2003)
8. Freedman, M.J., Nissim, K., Pinkas, B.: Efficient private matching and set intersection. In: Cachin, C., Camenisch, J.L. (eds.) EUROCRYPT 2004. LNCS, vol. 3027, pp. 1–19. Springer, Heidelberg (2004)
9. Goldschlag, D.M., Reed, M.G., Syverson, P.F.: Hiding routing information. In: Information Hiding, pp. 137–150. Springer, Heidelberg (1996)
10. Li, Y., Tygar, J., Hellerstein, J.M.: Private matching. IRB-TR-04-005 (February 2004)
11. Önen, M., Molva, R.: Secure data aggregation with multiple encryption. In: Langendoen, K.G., Voigt, T. (eds.) EWSN 2007. LNCS, vol. 4373, pp. 117–132. Springer, Heidelberg (2007)
12. Opyrchal, L., Prakash, A.: Secure distribution of events in content-based publish subscribe systems. In: SSYM 2001: Proceedings of the 10th conference on USENIX Security Symposium, Berkeley, CA, USA, pp. 21–21. USENIX Association (2001)
13. Opyrchal, L., Prakash, A., Agrawal, A.: Supporting privacy policies in a publish-subscribe substrate for pervasive environments. JNW, 17–26 (2007)
14. Pannetrat, A., Molva, R.: Multiple layer encryption for multicast groups. In: The proceedings of CMS 2002, Portoroz, Slovenia (September 2002)
15. Pohlig, S., Hellman, M.: An improved algorithm for computing logarithms over gf(p) and its cryptographic significance. IEEE Transactions on Information Theory 24(1), 106–110 (1978)

16. Raiciu, C., Rosenblum, D.S.: Enabling confidentiality in content-based publish/subscribe infrastructures. In: Securecomm and Workshops, 2006, 28 2006-September 1 2006, pp. 1–11 (2006)
17. Rivest, R.L., Shamir, A., Adleman, L.: A method for obtaining digital signatures and public-key cryptosystems. Communications of the ACM 21, 120–126 (1978)
18. Song, D.X., Wagner, D., Perrig, A.: Practical techniques for searches on encrypted data. In: Proceedings of the IEEE Symposium on Security and Privacy, pp. 44–55 (2000)
19. Srivatsa, M., Liu, L.: Secure event dissemination in publish-subscribe networks. In: ICDCS 2007: Proceedings of the 27th International Conference on Distributed Computing Systems, Washington, DC, USA, p. 22. IEEE Computer Society, Los Alamitos (2007)
20. Wang, C., Carzaniga, A., Evans, D., Wolf, A.: Security issues and requirements for internet-scale publish-subscribe systems. In: Proceedings of the 35th Annual Hawaii International Conference on System Sciences (HICSS 2002). IEEE Computer Society, Los Alamitos (2002)

Broadcast Encryption for Differently Privileged

Hongxia Jin[1] and Jeffery Lotspiech[2]

[1] IBM Almaden Research Center
San Jose, CA, 95120
jin@us.ibm.com
[2] Lotspiech.com, Henderson, Nevada
jeff@lotspiech.com

Abstract. Broadcast encryption is a primary technology that has been used for content protection. It enables a broadcaster to distribute content to a set of users so that only a privileged subset of users can access the content and another subset of revoked users cannot access the content. The main enabling block in a broadcast encryption scheme is the session key block, which each authorized user processes differently, but each gets the same valid session key. Currently all existing broadcast encryption schemes have assumed that the content and authorized users are equally privileged. There are emerging scenarios that demand protection for content with different privileges and for users with different privileges. In this paper we shall present a new broadcast encryption scheme that continues to employ single session key blocks but provides different privileged protections for different content and users. In particular we will expand the elegant subset-cover-based broadcast encryption scheme. We shall introduce a new concept called "security class" into the session key blocks. We use keys derived from a chain of one-way functions. Our approach is simple, efficient and secure.

1 Introduction

This paper is concerned with protection of copyrighted digital content. Piracy is becoming a more and more serious concern in the movie and music industries, since digital copies are perfect copies. Broadcast encryption is an important cryptographic key management approach, especially useful in content protection systems. It ensures content is distributed in a way that it is only accessible to a set of privileged (authorized) users and can exclude (revoke) another set of (compromised or non-compliant) users. In this paper, the devices that are used to decrypt and playback the content are interchangeably called devices or users. In a broadcast encryption system, each device is assigned a secret set of keys (called *device keys*). Another random chosen session key is indirectly used to encrypt the content. The content is usually video or music in a typical content protection system. The session key is also sometimes called the *media key*.

Device revocation is inherently tied to a broadcast encryption system. The fundamental enabling structure in a broadcast encryption for revocation is the session key block, or oftentimes called the media key blocks (MKB for short). It basically contains the media key encrypted by compliant device keys over and over. The MKB is distributed together with the encrypted content, for example, on the physical media.

D. Gritzalis and J. Lopez (Eds.): SEC 2009, IFIP AICT 297, pp. 283–293, 2009.

During playback time, a device will always process MKB first. If a device is compliant, it can use one of its device keys to decrypt the MKB and obtain the valid media key which ultimately allows decryption of the content. The revoking devices will decrypt the MKB and get garbage, thus they cannot decrypt the content. Those devices are therefore called revoked by the MKB.

Two popular practical broadcast-encryption-based systems are the Content Protection for Recordable Media (CPRM) system from IBM, Intel, Panasonic, and Toshiba, and the Advanced Access Content System (AACS) from Disney, IBM, Intel, Microsoft, Panasonic, Sony, Toshiba, and Warner Bros.

As one can imagine, a media key block is naturally associated with a piece of content. All devices that are authorized have equal privilege to access that content. However, some recent emerging use scenarios demand protection for content with different values and for devices with different privileges. For example, in case where a consumer might have a library of entertainment content in his home, and wants that library to be freely viewed by all the devices he owns. As one can imagine, in this case, not all the content being protected is equally valuable. For example, the user might have some movies in standard definition and some movies in high definition. From the point of view of the movies' creators, the high definition version is more valuable, and would have more serious economic consequences if the users were to make unlimited unauthorized copies. Likewise, not all devices are equally privileged. There is no reason, for example, why a standard definition television needs a set of keys that allows it to decrypt high definition video. Furthermore, it is even possible that a single piece of content might contain different material that are of different values. For example, a high definition movie may come with some "coming attractions". These materials are of less value than the high definition movie itself. Therefore it is highly desirable to design a broadcast encryption scheme to enable protection for content with different values on devices with different privileges.

Of course, in order to do that, one solution is to employ multiple MKBs, one for each class of content. For protecting a piece of content containing materials that are of different value, this solution implies the complication of having multiple MKBs associated with one piece of content. To make it even worse, this solution does not always work. As will be shown in Section 2, to provide content protection in the above-mentioned home network scenarios, the devices do need a common media key block for other reasons and therefore simply employing multiple MKBs is not a feasible solution.

The main contribution of this paper is to expand the single media key block in the traditional broadcast encryption scheme design so that it can be used to protect content with different privileges as well as enabling devices to have different privileges. To achieve this goal, we will introduce different security classes into the traditional media key blocks and make use of hierarchical keys derived from a chain of one-way functions.

In rest of paper, in Section 2, we will use the home network as a real use scenario to clarify the context of our work. We will show why it is infeasible to employ multiple MKBs to provide different levels of protection in this scenario. Then in Section 3, we will show our design of a broadcast encryption scheme having a single media key block but in which all content is not equally protected and all devices are not equally privileged. In Section 4, we will formalize our new broadcast encryption scheme and prove its security.

2   Background on Content Protection for Home Network

In this paper we are motivated by protecting content within a home network. In a home entertainment network, several devices with various capabilities (eg., content storage and rendering) inter-operate across the network. Within a home network, all authorized devices form a cluster. Within a single home network, content may be freely moved and copied from device to device, because it remains encrypted and bound to those devices in the cluster. No restrictions are imposed on the transmission mechanism, the physical location or even the ownership of devices. Broadcast encryption technology can be used for secure home network. Readers refer to ASCCT content protection protocol used in HANA consortium, High Definition AudioVideo Network Alliance [2].

In a home network, the notion of *compliance* is important: devices must follow an agreed-upon set of rules regarding copyrighted content. A device not playing by the rules, i.e. a circumvention or non-compliant device, will be revoked. The objective of a secure home network is for all nodes in the cluster to compute a common key, so that each can verify that the others are compliant. (Non-compliant devices would be revoked in the media key block and would be unable to calculate the common key.) Therefore a common media key block is essential to securely form the cluster. In fact, the media key block now needs to be associated with a set of devices, not a particular item of content.

Furthermore, a common media key block is needed to enable the devices to remain in synchronization when new media key blocks revoke newly discovered circumvention devices. A cluster contains not just a common media key block, but also other data files, in particular the list of the authorized devices in the cluster. This authorization list must be cryptographically "signed" by the common key(s) in the cluster. Obviously, if there is more than one key in use in the cluster, synchronizing the signing when the new media key block is delivered is much more complicated. Thus, having multiple media key blocks, although theoretically possible, would greatly complicate the synchronization process.

Currently the ASCCT content protection protocol [2] uses one single media key block for the reasons above and in the protocol all devices are equally privileged. In order to expand it to enable differently privileged protection, one has to design a new broadcast encryption scheme that continues to employ a single media key block.

3   Protection for Content and Users with Different Privileges

In our approach we introduce the concept of "security class" into the media key blocks, corresponding to the different privileges of the devices in the system. Our approach retains a single media key block, with its straightforward synchronization, while still allowing different classes of devices to learn different keys from the same media key block. These different keys will allow devices in different security classes to access content with different privileges. The different keys come from a hierarchy of keys derived from a one-way cryptographic chain function. The chain of one-way functions allow a high security class device not only to access the content in its corresponding privilege but also to calculate the keys needed to access low privileged content. More importantly this also allows an easy synchronization cryptographically with the lower security class devices. That is the essence of our approach.

3.1 Generating a Single MKB That Enables Differently Privileged Devices to Access Differently Privileged Content

In order to expand a single media key block in a current broadcast encryption scheme to support multiple privileged devices to access multiple privileged content, we will first need to take a look at a general broadcast encryption scheme at an abstract level. In a general broadcast encryption scheme, the devices are organized into overlapping subsets; each subset is associated with a device key. Each device belongs to many different subsets and knows the key for every subset it is a member of. In order to create a MKB that can enable all compliant devices and exclude all non-compliant devices, the license agency will first find a subset cover that "covers" all innocent devices and exclude all compromised devices. Every subset is associated with a key. The media key block comprises encryption of the media key with each of the keys associated with the chosen subsets in the subset cover. To construct a minimal size MKB, one wants to find the minimal subset cover.

More formally, let $\mathcal{D}$ be the set of devices and $\mathcal{K}$ be the set of device keys. Every device $d \in \mathcal{D}$ owns a subset of keys, denoted by $\mathcal{K}_d$. Similarly, associated with every key $k \in \mathcal{K}$ is a set of devices $\mathcal{D}_k = \{d \in \mathcal{D} : k \in \mathcal{K}_d\}$.

Suppose we want to broadcast some media M, which, for all intent and purposes, is a binary string. We would like to encrypt M in such a way that a set of legitimate devices $L \subseteq \mathcal{D}$ is able to decrypt and view the media. The first step is to encrypt M with some key Km, referred to as the *media key*. We will use the term *key* without a qualifier to refer to device keys. We then find a subset of device keys C such that all legitimate devices are *covered*. That is, C is chosen such that $\bigcap_{k \in C} \mathcal{D}_k = L$. Now, for every $k \in C$ we separately encrypt the media key, giving us $E_k(Km)$. Ultimately, the following items are broadcasted.

- The encrypted media: $E_{Km}(M)$
- The encrypted media key (MKB): $\langle E_{k_1}(Km), E_{k_2}(Km), \ldots, E_{k_{|C|}}(Km) \rangle$
- An index of the device keys used to encrypt the media key: $\langle 1, 2, \ldots, |C| \rangle$.

Every device $d \in L$ will own a key used in the MKB and every device $r \in \mathcal{D}/L$, referred to a *revoking device*, will own none. Hence, it cannot recover the content.

To expand the media key block so that it can enable differently privileged devices to access differently privileged content, we introduce a concept called device "security class" into the media key block. Each security class corresponds to a different privilege. Traditional broadcast encryption schemes view all compliant devices belonging to one same security class. Our goal is to design a broadcast encryption system in which the authorized (compliant) devices belong to different security classes.

To do that, in our approach when we organize the devices into subsets, we will group devices in the same security class into same subsets as much as possible. We will show how to construct a MKB from a simple tree-based broadcast encryption scheme as shown in Figure 1. As show in [7], in a tree-based broadcast encryption scheme, all devices are organized to be the leaves of a tree. Each node, including internal nodes, is associated with a key. Each device is assigned, as its device keys, all the keys associated with the nodes on the path from the root to the leaf where the device sits. We also arrange all devices with the same security class in the same subtree. For example, device

Simple Tree-based BE scheme

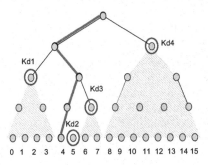

Fig. 1. A simple tree-based MKB

#0 to #3 belong to security class A. Device #4 to #7 belong to security class B. Device #8 to #15 belong to security class C.

In the example shown in Figure 1, device #4 is revoked. To distribute content that is accessible to every device except device #4, one needs to avoid encrypt media key Km using any key that device #4 knows, which is on the highlighted path in the figure. In order to construct a MKB, the first step is to find a subset cover C that covers all innocent devices. In this example, $C = \{K_{d1}, K_{d2}, K_{d3}, K_{d4}\}$. A traditional MKB contains

$$\langle E_{k_{d1}}(Km), E_{k_{d2}}(Km), E_{k_{d3}}(Km), E_{k_{d4}}(Km) \rangle.$$

For the example shown in Figure 1, in our approach, suppose there are three different security class devices in the system, each is authorized to play different classes of content. Suppose further class A content requires the least amount of security, class B content requires a higher level of security, and Class C requires the highest level of security. A device in security class A is configured to play only class A content. Devices in security class B is configured to play class A content and class B content. Devices in security class C is configured to play class A content, class B content and class C content C. For example, Class A content may be standard definition content, Class B may be high definition content, and Class C may be some premium content requiring even higher level of security than high-definition content.

In our approach, we will associate a common media key block (MKB) with a set of devices in different security classes so that they can access content with different privileges accordingly. This perfectly fits in the home network scenarios described earlier. A set of devices at one's home with different security classes form a cluster. Content with different privileges are allowed to move freely among all devices in the home cluster.

To construct a common MKB for a set of devices in different security classes, in our approach we will use multiple valid media keys, one for each security class. For the example above, there are three different media keys $Km1, Km2, Km3$ for the three different security class devices, $Km1$ for class A, $Km2$ for class B and $Km3$ for class C.

Furthermore, the valid media keys are not independently randomly chosen. In fact, only the media key for the highest security class is randomly chosen. The remaining media keys are derived from a chain of one-way function operations. In the above example, since $Km3$ is for the highest class C devices to access class C content, $Km3$ is randomly chosen. But $Km2 = f(Km3)$ and $Km1 = f(Km2)$ where $f()$ is a one-way function. Oftentimes we refer to the media key for the lowest security class simply as the *media key*, and we refer the media keys for the higher security classes as *media key precursors*. So $Km1$ is a media key, $Km2, Km3$ are media key precursors.

When constructing a common MKB in our approach, the different subset keys in the cover C will now encrypt different media keys instead of encrypting one same media key. In fact for the above example shown in Figure 1, in our approach the following items are broadcasted.

- The encrypted media: $E_{Km1}(M1)$, $E_{Km2}(M2)$, $E_{Km3}(M3)$.
- The encrypted media keys (common MKB): $\langle E_{k_{d1}}(Km1), E_{k_{d2}}(Km2), E_{k_{d3}}(Km2), E_{k_{d4}}(Km3)\rangle$.
- An index of the device keys used to encrypt the media keys

When a class A device extracts the common MKB and uses its device key to process the MKB, it will calculate a media key $Km1$ allowing decryption of only Class A content. When a class B device process the same MKB, it calculates a media key precursor $Km2$ which allows decryption of class B content. Class B devices also have the ability to process class A content. To do that, it will use the media key precursor $Km2$ and a one-way function to calculate a media key $Km1$ to decrypt class A content.

Similarly, when a class C device processes the common MKB, it will calculate a media key precursor $Km3$ which allows decryption of class C content. It may also decrypt class B content by calculating a media key precursor $Km2$ from the $Km3$ using the one-way function. This media key precursor $Km2$ may be used to decrypt class B content. Likewise, media player C may also process class A content by calculating a media key $Km1$ from the media key precursor $Km2$ using the one-way function. This media key $Km1$ may be used to decrypt class A content.

Our approach may utilize a variety of known one-way functions. For example, the following well-known one-way function, based on the Advanced Encryption Standard (AES) cipher, can be used:

$$r = AES\_D(k, d) \oplus d$$

where r is the result, k is a key, d is data, AES_D is AES decryption in electronic code book mode. This function is one-way in the following sense: from r, it is intractable to calculate either k or d, even if one of the values is known.

In our use, k would be a media key precursor and d would be a constant known to all devices. Note that d does not have to be a secret. It can be a published constant without hurting the security of our approach.

3.2 Protect Differently Privileged Materials within Content

In practice, media key is rarely directly used to encrypt content. There is often at least one level of indirection: the content is encrypted with a key, called *title key*; and then the title key is encrypted with the media key from the media key block. This encrypted title key is typically stored in a header associated with the content. As a result, for the example in Figure 1 the following items are actually broadcasted:

- The encrypted media and *title keys*: $E_{Km1}(Kt1)$, $E_{Km2}(Kt2)$, $E_{Km3}(Kt3)$; $E_{Kt1}(M1)$, $E_{Kt2}(M2)$, $E_{Kt3}(M3)$.
- The encrypted media keys (common MKB): $\langle E_{k_{d1}}(Km1), E_{k_{d2}}(Km2), E_{k_{d3}}(Km2),$ $E_{k_{d4}}(Km3)\rangle$.
- An index of the device keys used to encrypt the media keys

If a piece of content contains material that are of different value, it is also possible to use our approach to provide different privileged protection. Those materials with different privileges will be encrypted with different title keys. And the media keys for different security classes derived from the one-way chain can be used to encrypt the different title keys. For example, for a high definition movie that also contains lower valued "coming attractions", different title keys are used to encrypt the high definition movie content and the "coming attractions". One can use media key precursor to encrypt the title key for the high definition movie and use the media key to encrypt the title key for the "coming attractions".

As we can see, we have provided a general broadcast encryption system that employs a common media key block, while providing different levels of protection for different media and different devices, be it for different content with different privileges or for materials with different privileges within the same piece of content.

4   Formalization and Security Proof

Our scheme is expanded from a traditional single security class broadcast encryption scheme to multiple security classes. In our newly expanded scheme, the device key assignment can be exactly same as that in a traditional broadcast encryption scheme. In particular we expand the elegant state-of-art subset cover based NNL scheme [7] to enable multiple security classes. Our expanded scheme consists of the following algorithms:

1. *Setup*: Let $\mathscr{D}$ be the set of devices and $\mathscr{K}$ be the set of device keys. Every device $d \in \mathscr{D}$ is assigned a subset of keys, denoted by $\mathscr{K}_d$, based on subset cover NNL scheme key assignment. For device d, all the secret information including its device keys is denoted I_d.
2. *Subset cover*: Associated with every key $k \in \mathscr{K}$ is a set of users $\mathscr{D}_k = \{d \in \mathscr{D} : k \in \mathscr{K}_d\}$. Given a set of legitimate devices $L \subseteq \mathscr{D}$, find the subset cover of device keys C such that all legitimate devices are *covered*. That is, C is chosen such that $\bigcap_{k \in C} \mathscr{D}_k = L$.
3. *Encryption(M_j): encrypting a message belong to security class j*: Suppose there are s security classes. We will use s different media keys. $Km_{i+1} = f(Km_i)$. Suppose C contains m subsets which will be distributed among s security classes. There are m_j subsets in security class j and $\sum_{j=1}^{s} m_j = m$. Assume subsets $i_{j,1}, i_{j,2}, \cdots, i_{j,m_j}$ belong to security class j. Let $k_{j,1}, k_{j,2}, \cdots, k_{j,m_j}$ be their corresponding keys. Encrypt each content M_j with $E_{Km_j}(M_j)$ and put

$E_{k_{j,1}}(Km_j), E_{k_{j,2}}(Km_j), \cdots, E_{k_{j,m_j}}(Km_j)$ into MKB. The encryption methods $E(M)$ and $E(Km)$ can also be the same ones as those in NNL scheme.

4. *Decryption(j)*: For a device in security class j, use its device key $k_{j,i}$ to decrypt its corresponding part in MKB to get Km_j. Use Km_j to decrypt the encrypted content $E_{Km_j}(M_j)$ to get M_j.

Below is the general comparison. In a traditional broadcast encryption scheme the following items are actually broadcasted:

$$\langle E_{Km}(M), [E_{k_1}(Km), E_{k_2}(Km), \ldots, E_{k_{|C|}}(Km); 1, 2, \ldots, |C|] \rangle$$

In our s-security class broadcast encryption scheme we will distributes the s security class content messages containing the following items:

$$\begin{aligned}
\langle & E_{Km_1}(M_1), E_{Km_2}(M_2), \cdots, E_{Km_s}(M_s); \\
& [E_{k_{1,1}}(Km_1), E_{k_{1,2}}(Km_1), \cdots, E_{k_{1,m_1}}(Km_1), \\
& E_{k_{2,1}}(Km_2), E_{k_{2,2}}(Km_2), \cdots, E_{k_{2,m_2}}(Km_2), \\
& \cdots, \\
& E_{k_{s,1}}(Km_s), E_{k_{s,2}}(Km_s), \cdots, E_{k_{s,m_s}}(Km_s), \\
& i_{1,1}, i_{1,2}, \cdots, i_{1,m_1}, \\
& i_{2,1}, i_{2,2}, \cdots, i_{2,m_2}, \\
& \cdots, \\
& i_{s,1}, i_{s,2}, \cdots, i_{s,m_s},] \rangle
\end{aligned}$$

Our $E(M)$ and $E(Km)$ methods must satisfy the same property as those in NNL scheme. For example the method $E(Km)$ in our scheme has to be CCA-1 secure in the following sense: consider a feasible adversary $\mathcal{B}$ that for a random key Kd gets to adaptively choose polynomially many inputs and examine E_{Kd}'s encryption and similarly provide ciphertext and examine E_{Kd}'s decryption. Then $\mathcal{B}$ is faced with the following challenge: for a random plaintext message M, it gets back $E_{Kd}(M')$ where M' is either equal to M (or the 'real' case), or is equal to a totally random message (or the random case). The encryption method $E(Km)$ is CCA-1 secure if no polynomial adversary can distinguish these two cases with non-negligible advantage.

We used the same device key assignment in our expanded scheme in the setup step as NNL scheme, therefore our scheme shares the same *key indistinguishability* property. That is, for every subset S_i its associated key Kd_i is indistinguishable from a random key given all the information of all users that are not in S_i.

4.1   Definitions

Now we will prove the semantic security of our broadcast encryption revocation scheme. Intuitively, it more or less states that only the users in the designated security class and *its ancestors* can decrypt messages that are sent to that security class users, while no other users of the system can. The other users include the revoked users and the users in lower security class. By ancestor, we mean the users in a higher security class.

Formally we will define the first CCA-1 security of our broadcast encryption revocation scheme as follows:

Definition 1. *Consider an adversary $\mathscr{B}$ that gets to*

1. *Queries. Selects adaptively a set R of users and obtain I_u for all $u \in R$. By adaptively we mean that $\mathscr{B}$ may select messages $\mathscr{M}_1, \mathscr{M}_2, \cdots$ and revocation set $R_1, R_2, \cdots$. Each message can be divided into s smaller messages. In other words, $\mathscr{M}_i = \{m_{i1} \| m_{i2} \| \cdots \| m_{is}\}$). For each class j the center randomly choose a session key Km_j. $\mathscr{B}$ queries center with $< m_{ij}, j >$ and R_i for each $1 <= j <= s$. The center returns the encryption of each $m_{ij}, 1 <= j <= s$ with Km_j when the revoked set is R_i. Also $\mathscr{B}$ can create a ciphertext for a class j and see how any (non-corrupted) user in class j decrypts it. It then asks to corrupt a receiver u and obtains its I_u. This step is repeated $|R|$ times (for any $u \in R$).*
2. *Challenge. Choose a message $M = \{m_1 \| m_2 \| \cdots \| m_s\}$ as the challenge plaintext and a set R of revoked users that must include all the ones it corrupted (but may contain more). For each m_j, choose a random message Rm_j of similar length. For each j, ask the center to use security class j keys to encrypt message m_j or RM_j.*

$\mathscr{B}$ then receives all encrypted messages $M' = \{m_1', m_2', \cdots, m_s'\}$ with a revoked set R. For each j, it has to guess whether $m_j' = m_j$ or $m_j' = Rm_j$. We say a s-security class revocation scheme is secure if no polynomial adversary can distinguish between these two cases with non-negligible advantage.

4.2 The Security Theorem

It is not hard to imagine that the security of the s-security class revocation scheme depends on the traditional 1-security class revocation scheme which further depends on the device key indistinguishability. In the following, we state the security theorem and prove the s-security class revocation scheme has the same security strength as the 1-security class scheme under the same setup parameters.

Theorem 1. *Let $\mathscr{A}$ be an adversary that distinguishes ciphertexts defined in Definition 1 against our s-security class subset cover revocation scheme, and succeeds with probability δ in time τ. Then there exists an algorithm $\mathscr{B}$ which breaks the 1-security class subset cover revocation scheme with success probability $\delta' \approx \delta$ in time $\tau' = \tau$.*

Proof. The setup step is same for both schemes with same parameters. Suppose there is an adversary $\mathscr{A}$ against the s-security class subset-cover revocation scheme with success probability δ. Then we can construct an algorithm $\mathscr{B}$ that uses $\mathscr{A}$ as a subroutine to break the 1-security class subset-cover revocation scheme with a probability of $\delta' \approx \delta$.
  Consider an adversary $\mathscr{B}$ that gets to

1. *Queries.* Select adaptively a set R of users and obtain I_u for all $u \in R$. By adaptively we mean that $\mathscr{B}$ may select adaptively messages $\mathscr{M}_1, \mathscr{M}_2, \cdots$ and revocation set $R_1, R_2, \cdots$. $\mathscr{B}$ divides each message into s smaller messages. In other words, $\mathscr{M}_i = \{m_{i1} \| m_{i2} \| \cdots \| m_{is}\}$. $\mathscr{B}$ forwards a query with $\mathscr{M}_i$ and R_i to adversary $\mathscr{A}$. $\mathscr{A}$ randomly chooses a class $t, (1 <= t <= s)$ and asks the center to encrypt

each sub-message m_{ij} with class t key. The center returns the encryption of each $m_{ij}, 1 <= j <= s$ with security class t key Km_t when the revoked set is R_i. $\mathscr{A}$ aggregates the returned message together and forwards to $\mathscr{B}$. Adversary $\mathscr{B}$ can also create a ciphertext and forward it to $\mathscr{A}$ to see how any (non-corrupted) user in class t decrypts it. Whenever $\mathscr{B}$ decides to corrupt a user u, $\mathscr{A}$ asks I_u from the center and replies I_u to $\mathscr{B}$. The above step is repeated $|R|$ times (for any $u \in R$).

2. *Challenge.* $\mathscr{B}$ chooses a message $\mathscr{M} = \{m_1||m_2|| \cdots ||m_s\}$ as the challenge plaintext and a set R of revoked users that must include all the ones it corrupted in the query phase as well. Adversary $\mathscr{B}$ forwards the same challenge plain text with the same R to $\mathscr{A}$. Choose a random message Rm of similar length with M and divide into $Rm = \{Rm_1||Rm_2|| \cdots ||Rm_s\}$, each Rm_j is of similar length with m_j. Asks the center to use security class t key to encrypt message m_j or Rm_j.

$\mathscr{A}$ receives encrypted messages with the revoked set R and aggregate together $M' == \{m'_1, m'_2, \cdots, m'_s\}$ to return to adversary $\mathscr{B}$. Adversary $\mathscr{B}$ has to guess whether $m'_j = m_j$ or $m'_j = Rm_j$. $\mathscr{A}$ does the guess and forwards its answer back to $\mathscr{B}$. $\mathscr{B}$ will use $\mathscr{A}$'s answer as its answer.

If $\mathscr{A}$ succeeds with probability of δ in distinguishing the two cases, $\mathscr{B}$ succeeds with the same probability $\delta' \approx \delta$ and running time of algorithm $\mathscr{B}$ is same as that of $\mathscr{A}$'s.

The above theorem shows that revoked users cannot access the encrypted content sent to any authorized security class users. We believe it is also possible to show that, if media key $Km_i = f(Km_j)$ where $j < i$, then any non-revoked users in security class i cannot access content for security class j while the reverse is true. It is straightforward to see that this security relies on the intractability of the one-way function and the CCA-1 secure property of the encryption method $E(Km)$. More formally, an adversary cannot win the following game with non-negligible advantage.

Let $Km_1, \cdots, Km_s$ be the s media keys derived from the one-way function chain such that $Km_{j+1} = f(Km_j)$. Consider a feasible adversary $\mathscr{B}$ that

1. Selects j, $j \in [1, s]$, the adversary is allowed to access any key that is derivable from Km_j, but not Km_j and its ancestor.
2. *Queries*: Select any key Km_i where $j < i$, in other words, Km_i is derivable from Km_j. Adversary $\mathscr{B}$ gets to adaptively select polynomially many inputs and examine E_{Km_i}'s encryption and similarly provide ciphertext and examine E_{Km_i}'s decryption.
3. *challenge*: The adversary chooses a random plaintext message M, it gets back $E_{Km_i}(M')$ where M' is either equal to M (or the 'real' case), or is equal to a totally random message (or the random case). The adversary $\mathscr{B}$ cannot distinguish the two cases with non-negligible advantage.

5 Conclusion

In traditional broadcast encryption schemes every authorized user has equal privilege to access content. There is emerging need to enable differently privileged users to access differently privileged content. In this paper we have presented a new broadcast encryption scheme that can achieve this goal. In particular we have expanded the elegant subset-cover-based broadcast encryption scheme. We introduced a new concept called "security class" into the session key blocks. We use session keys derived from a chain of one-way functions. Each session key corresponds to one security class. This avoid using multiple session key blocks but still achieve our goal. Our approach is simple, flexible, efficient and secure.

References

1. http://www.aacsla.com/specifications
2. http://www.hanaalliance.org/
3. Fiat, A., Naor, M.: Broadcast encryption. In: Stinson, D.R. (ed.) CRYPTO 1993. LNCS, vol. 773, pp. 480–491. Springer, Heidelberg (1994)
4. Chor, B., Fiat, A., Naor, M.: Tracing traitors. In: Desmedt, Y.G. (ed.) CRYPTO 1994. LNCS, vol. 839, pp. 257–270. Springer, Heidelberg (1994)
5. Chor, B., Fiat, A., Naor, M., Pinkas, B.: Tracing traitors. IEEE Transactions on Information Theory 46, 893–910 (2000)
6. Naor, M., Pinkas, B.: Efficient trace and revoke schemes. In: Frankel, Y. (ed.) FC 2000. LNCS, vol. 1962, pp. 1–20. Springer, Heidelberg (2001)
7. Naor, D., Naor, M., Lotspiech, J.: Revocation and tracing schemes for stateless receivers. In: Kilian, J. (ed.) CRYPTO 2001. LNCS, vol. 2139, pp. 41–62. Springer, Heidelberg (2001)
8. Boneh, D., Waters, B.: A collusion resistant broadcast, trace and revoke system. ACM Communication and Computer Security (2006)
9. Fiat, A., Tassa, T.: Dynamic traitor tracing. In: Wiener, M. (ed.) CRYPTO 1999. LNCS, vol. 1666, pp. 354–371. Springer, Heidelberg (1999)
10. Safani-Naini, R., Wang, Y.: Sequential traitor tracing. In: Bellare, M. (ed.) CRYPTO 2000. LNCS, vol. 1880, pp. 316–332. Springer, Heidelberg (2000)
11. Jin, H., Lotspiech, J., Nusser, S.: Traitor tracing for prerecorded and recordable media. In: ACM DRM workshop (October 2004)
12. Jin, H., Lotspiech, J.: Renewable traitor tracing: A trace-revoke-trace system for anonymous attack. In: Biskup, J., López, J. (eds.) ESORICS 2007. LNCS, vol. 4734, pp. 563–577. Springer, Heidelberg (2007)
13. Jin, H., Lotspiech, J., Megiddo, N.: Efficient Coalition Detection in Traitor Tracing. In: IFIP 23rd Information Security conference, Milan, Italy, pp. 365–380.

Ontology-Based Secure XML Content Distribution

Mohammad Ashiqur Rahaman, Yves Roudier, Philip Miseldine, and Andreas Schaad

SAP Research, EURECOM
{mohammad.ashiqur.rahaman,
philip.miseldine,andreas.schaad}@sap.com,
{yves.roudier,mohammad.rahaman}@eurecom.fr

Abstract. This paper presents an ontology-driven secure XML content distribution scheme. This scheme first relies on a semantic access control model for XML documents that achieves three objectives: (1) representing flexible and evolvable policies, (2) providing a high-level mapping and interoperable interface to documents, and (3) automating the granting of fine-grained access rights by inferring on content semantics. A novel XML document parsing mechanism is defined to delegate document access control enforcement to a third party without leaking the document XML schema to it. The *Encrypted Breadth First Order Labels (EBOL)* encoding is used to bind semantic concepts with XML document nodes and to check the integrity of a document.

1 Introduction

The increasing standardization of XML processing (e.g. XML Schema, DTD, XSL) makes it possible for peer organizations to cooperate and to integrate their information systems through XML document production and exchanges. Documents are structured and modeled through XML schemas in peer organizations. Schemas may contain valuable and confidential information about resources, strategies, services, or information system structure closely tied to business processes which organizations do not want to expose. The data model may evolve due to changes in the organization, for instance after a merger; existing data exchanges with peers should however be maintained. We claim that, although data models may differ from one organization to another or vary with time, the semantics of document data units like subtrees or nodes might constitute a more stable and interoperable interface between organizations. Semantic Web languages like RDF [3] and OWL [2] make it possible to share an ontology describing a conceptual data model, independently from XML data structure yet that can be mapped to instances of XML schemas. We also claim that access control can be defined at the semantic level notably to achieve a simpler expression of policies with complex organization rules and constraints. First, expressing access rights over a single concept might result into granting authorizations to multiple XML documents or portions thereof. Second, and more importantly, authorizations on concepts might be automatically inferred from the expression of the right to access a related concept. Third and finally, as shown in related work like Rei [13], ontologies can formally describe an access control model by representing policy concepts as first-class objects. We contend that this feature is particularly suitable to inter-organizational document exchange systems, by making it

D. Gritzalis and J. Lopez (Eds.): SEC 2009, IFIP AICT 297, pp. 294–306, 2009.

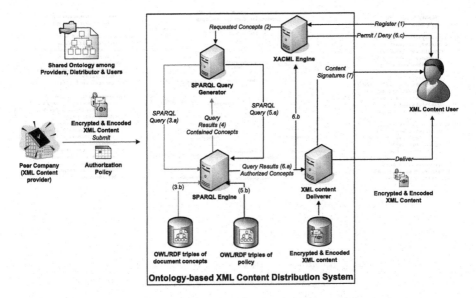

Fig. 1. The Ontology-based XML Content Distribution System. The numbered lines depict the sequence of operations upon a registration request.

possible to store incremental versions of access control policies, possibly timestamped in the same fashion as documents to which they apply, thereby easing user revocation.

This paper describes access control mechanisms addressing all three objectives: our solution integrates ontologies for describing and reasoning over documents and authorization policies, which we implement using SPARQL [4] together with XACML [11]. We assume a large scale system where documents have to be distributed to many users: scalability is an essential issue here, and the content providers can not serve content to a large number of users nor to authenticate each of them. Documents may be updated, even after they are initially released by their provider. We assume a third party which we term a distributor, takes care of the transient storage and of the distribution of documents. Its role is important since users may not be online when a document is sent around. Message oriented middleware (MOM) or publish/subscribe paradigms provide examples of middleware adapted to such tasks. Content providers and users may pertain to different organizations and even be competitors: not every document should thus be readable by any user (Fig 1).

2 Solution Overview

Semantic data model. A domain-specific ontology provides the common language to communicate the contents of an XML document. Fig 2 shows a semantic graph of concepts as it may be defined through such an ontology (e.g. work order, production and quality-inspection). It also illustrates how these concepts may be mapped to XML documents in a manufacturing production environment scenario. Two document providers are considered here, the production department and the quality inspection company. Conceptually, the metadata (e.g. ID, priority level (urgent, normal, escalated), issue

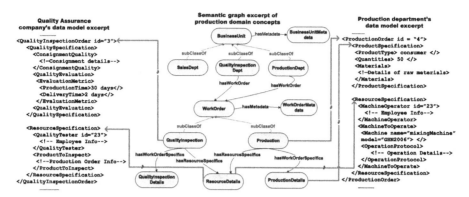

Fig. 2. A semantic graph of work order document concepts in a production domain. The 'Production' work order, 'QualityInspection' work order and 'ResourceDetails' concepts are mapped to the corresponding XML data model excerpts using a mapping relation. ∂.

date) for all work orders (production order, quality-inspection order) would be the same for all work orders. However, each work order contains specific details that will be taken into account by a specific business unit. For example, the quality inspection order would carry information regarding the specification of the product quality and the metrics to measure them.

Document encoding. Users and providers will not share all existing XML schemas, since these describe the provider's information system organization. Authorizations will be given to users to access contents related with particular semantics, as described through the concepts of an ontology. We assume the distributor is trusted by providers to host and to selectively deliver their contents to authorized users only. The distributor has access to the semantics of every node he receives from the provider. While it can decide whether to forward that node to a user, it should not know the structure of complete documents. On the other hand, an authorized user should clearly be able to read some content he receives. Such a secure exchange of documents can be achieved through the separate encryption of each document node with a secret that the provider and the consumer share. At the middleware level, a concept and the document portions to which it maps are encoded together by a content provider. The concepts described in that encoded document will be accessible by distributors. The document encoding will however hide the structure of the schema underlying the document and protect the content through encryption and integrity protection measures. Providers will define explicit access control rules and will also likely issue inference rules describing how to generate new access control rules. For instance, additional access rights might be granted on a subclass of a granted concept. Some inference rules might also describe constraints and prevent a single user from being granted two exclusive authorizations. The distributor enforces the authorization policy defined by the provider. XACML uses the notion of subjects, resources, and actions, to describe access control rules. In our setting, a user would be modeled as a subject, and ontological concepts as resources. Actions would largely consist in read, delete, and write, to describe the usage governing the mapped XML content.

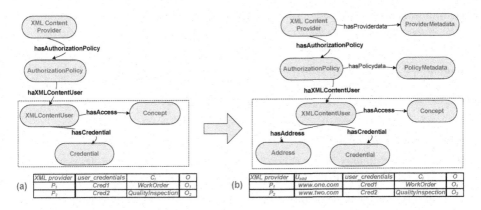

Fig. 3. The table represents the policy specification by the XML content providers. Policy ontology is maintained by the distributor. (a) Initial policy ontology.(b) Updated policy ontology.

Interaction Phases. We consider five basic phases in our document distribution system. In the first phase the provider sends encoded and encrypted XML content to the distributor using the *EBOL* technique detailed in Section 4 (Fig 1). Associated authorization policies might also be sent to the distributor which will enforce them on behalf of the provider. In a second phase, the user registers for some concepts with the distributor. The user has to provide valid credentials to access XML content mapped to the requested concept as discussed in Section 3. Credentials might for instance consist of certificates issued by some authority. Depending on the applicable authorization policy, the distributor then sends a set of *content signatures* (cf. Section 4) to the authorized users. The *content signature* describes the encoding, and serves as a mean to verify the XML content subsequently distributed. In a third phase, the distributor performs a selective delivery of relevant XML contents to registered users. It determines and extracts the authorized content out of the documents sent by one or multiple providers. This process is performed over the encoded and encrypted XML content. The user verifies the received XML content, both semantically and structurally, in a fourth phase using the *content signatures*. The fifth phase is the unregistration of a user. It may occur at user's request, or be forced by the distributor if the user credentials expired or if the provider's policy is changed. This final operation is outside the scope of this paper.

3   Authorization Policy

3.1   Ontology-Based Data Model

This section describes the ontology-based data model used to express flexible authorization policies. A concept C_i is an abstraction that can be communicated among peers. An ontology is a shared set of concepts in a domain. The ontology is defined primarily by the notions of *class*, *subclass*, and *properties* representing concepts and their relationships using OWL [2].

Definition 1. *Concept Containment: Let $\mathscr{C}$ be the collection of all concepts and C_i, C_j $\in \mathscr{C}$. If there is a subclass hierarchy from C_i to C_j denoted as $C_i \Rightarrow, ..., \Rightarrow C_j$ then C_i contains C_j and noted as $C_i \preceq C_j$.*

Example. Fig 2 shows a collection of concepts $\mathscr{C} = \{BusinessUnit, BusinessUnit Metadata,$ etc.$\}$ for a production hall. *WorkOrder* contains *QualityInspection* and *Production*, i.e. *WorkOrder* $\preceq$ *QualityInspection, WorkOrder* $\preceq$ *Production*.   □

3.2   Ontology-Based Authorization Policy

We describe an ontology-based authorization policy as a set of explicit rules constructed as follows ($[x+]$ is used to denote a non-empty set of elements of type x):

1. Rules take the general form $[user\_credentials, [C_i]+, \mathscr{O}]+$ stating that access over one or more concepts C_i is allowed to the user holding *user_credentials* provided $\mathscr{O}$ is true.
2. Expression $\mathscr{O}$ characterizes relationships and constraints verified by browsing the semantic graph (such as of Fig 2). This expression enables a provider to restrict eligible concepts of the ontology, and may be parameterized by *user_credentials* or elements of $[C_i]+$, as described in Section 5.

Fig. 3(a) shows an example of a policy specified by two XML content providers P_1 (i.e. Production department) and P_2 (i.e. Quality assurance company) of the Fig 2. $\mathscr{O}_1$ for the user with credential *Cred*1 is: if a user is allowed to access the concept *WorkOrder* then he is also allowed to access to all the contained concepts of *WorkOrder*. $\mathscr{O}_2$ for the user with credential *Cred*2 is: he is allowed to access the concept *QualityInspection* if he has access to the concept *ResourceDetails*. The distributor describes such policies of the providers and generates policy instances as an OWL triple (see Fig 1 and 3) using SPARQL. Any change in the policy such as adding an address parameter for request filtering or adding metadata about provider and policy (shown in Fig 3(b)) would introduce additional concepts and relationships among them. For example, P_2 may add a constraint, $\mathscr{O}_2$, expressing that the user is allowed to access *QualityInspection* if any other provider allows the user the same access right.

4   XML Parsing, Encoding and Encryption

Encoding requires parsing the XML document: we use a breadth-first order technique to parse the XML nodes level by level from root to the leaves and to encode structure and conceptual information on the fly (Fig 4). This section describes the mapping of concepts to XML data units and the parsing, encoding, and encryption method in detail.

4.1   Ontology Mapping to XML Structure

An XML document, d, identified by doc_{id} (e.g. URI, RDF) is a collection of parsed XML nodes and a document portion d_i is a subtree rooted at node i of d. A mapping defines relations (∂) from a concept and its sub-class hierarchical path to document portions d_i which is used to determine the XML content associated to concepts. Such a mapping is illustrated by the following example.

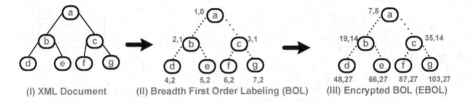

Fig. 4. (I) XML document tree. (II) BOL labeling. (III) Encrypted BOL labeling. Solid and dotted lines respectively depict explicit (I) and implicit (II,III) hierarchy representations and storage.

Example. In Fig 2, the concepts *ProductionDetails* and *ResourceDetails*, identified by the paths over the semantic graph *BusinessUnit.ProductionDept.hasWorkOrder. Workorder.Production.ProductionDetails* and *...Production.ResourceDetails* are mapped to the document portions rooted at <ProductSpecification> and <ResourceSpecification> of the production department's XML data model. In the quality assurance company's data model, the concepts *ResourceDetails* and *QualityInspection*, identified by the path expressions *...QualityInspection. ResourceDetails* and *...QualityInspection* are mapped to the document portions rooted at <ResourceSpecification> and <QualityInspectionOrder> respectively.   □

4.2   Encrypted Breadth-First Order Labels for XML Parsing

Once the mapping is done the provider parses the XML documents as follows: sibling nodes are stored into a FIFO queue and associated a BOL (an integer pair as defined below) capturing various structural relationships of the parsed XML node (i.e. parent-child, siblings, left/right child) with a minimal memory footprint.

Breadth First Order Labels (BOL): A *BOL* is a pair of integers associated to an XML node as it is parsed in breadth first order. The first integer in the pair is the order associated with a node whose left siblings and ancestors have already been parsed and thus have associated BOLs. The second integer is the depth of the node in the document which is increased by one as new depth level is reached. The BOL starts with (1,0) as illustrated in Fig. 4 (the example given is a binary tree, but BOLs can be defined on any type of tree)

Let a be the parent of two nodes $b,c \in d_i$. We denote its BOL as B_a. Let f_{order} and f_{level} be two functions operating on a BOL respectively returning the BOL order (first attribute of the BOL pair) and BOL depth (second attribute). Let us assume that b is the last child of a parsed and that c is to be parsed next. c will be associated a BOL with $f_{order}(B_c) = f_{order}(B_b) + 1$. $f_{level}(B_a)$ uniquely identifies the depth level of the node a in d. The order of the BOL exhibits the following structural properties:

1. $f_{order}(B_a)$ uniquely identifies node a in document d and the subtree d_a rooted at a.
2. Let $B^a_{Highest}$ be the largest BOL order of a parsed node in document portion d_a; then $B^a_{Highest} > f_{order}(B_z) > f_{order}(B_a)$, where $z \in d_a$.
3. $f_{order}(B_c) > f_{order}(B_b) > f_{order}(B_a)$.

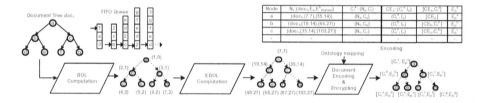

Fig. 5. Execution steps of the XML processing by document providers

The first property is used to identify and extract a specific document portion from a document. Combined with the depth level of a node, that property ensures that any unexpected move, copy or replace activity in the document is detected. The second property imposes an upper bound on the BOL of any queried node parsed in a document. In effect, it detects if a node is added or deleted and which one it is. The third property permits detecting any unintended swapping among the children in a received document portion (subtree).

A BOL is by definition plain text and thus may reveal important structure specific information (i.e. information leaking), such as number of nodes and thus the size of the document and even hierarchical relationship among the nodes to an adversary. Encryption over such BOL numbers protects this undesired information from leaking.

Encrypted BOL (EBOL): Let B_a be the BOL of an XML node a. Let f_e be an order preserving encryption function [5]. The EBOL of a, denoted as E_a is a pair of integers defined as : $(f_e(f_{order}(B_a)), f_e(f_{level}(B_a)))$. While $f_e(f_{order}(B_a))$ is performed for each node a, $f_e(f_{level}(B_a))$ is performed if a is the first node in a level.

The EBOL preserves exactly the same properties of BOL (see Fig 4). The EBOL order value hides the actual node number and its depth level as opposed to the BOL attributes and thus prevents information leaking.

4.3 Encoding Method

In the following, encoding elements are introduced to describe concepts that are mapped to data units (i.e. subtrees or nodes) as well as the properties of these data units and their encryption.

Node Identifier: Let x be a node in d_i. The node identifier of x denoted as N_x is a tuple formed by three elements $(doc_{id}, E_x, E^x_{Highest})$, where doc_{id} is the document identifier of d_i, E_x is the EBOL of x, $E^x_{Highest}$ is the highest EBOL in the document portion rooted at x. A node identifier is unique for all documents in the system. The depth included in E_x uniquely determines the node's level. E_x and $E^x_{Highest}$ together determine the parsed document portion. Finally, doc_{id} resolves appropriate XML nodes of the associated document with respect to the same concept.

Node Integrity: The node content consists of attributes, their values and text content inside the tag but not any descendants of the node. The node integrity code is a hash computed out of the concatenation of a node identifier and content, denoted as $I_x = H(N_x, Ct_x)$, where N_x is the node identifier, Ct_x is the content of x, and H is a one way collision resistant hash function.

Content Signature: Let C_i and x be a concept and an XML node respectively. The content signature, denoted as C_i^x, is a pair (N_x, C_i), where N_x is the node identifier of x and C_i is a concept mapped to x. The *content signature* incorporates semantic information such as conceptual and structural information attached to an XML nodes.

Content Encoding: An encoding information CE_x of a node x is $CE_x = (C_i^x, I_x)$, where C_i^x is the *content signature* and I_x is the node integrity respectively. Each XML node x is encoded as a pair $[CE_x, C_i^z]$, where CE_x is the encoding information of node x and C_i^z is the *content signature* of the parent node z of x. For the root node of a document the encoded node is $[CE_x]$.

Document Encryption: Each encoded node is encrypted using a key shared between the content provider and the content user. After encryption, an XML node x is represented as $[C_i^x, E_p^x]$, where C_i^x is the *content signature* of x and E_p^x is the encrypted value of the content encoding pair $[CE_x, C_i^z]$ of the node x.

Fig 5 depicts the encoding and encryption processing of XML nodes using EBOL described above.

5   Access Control Enforcement and Distribution

Semantic Access Control. The distributor maintains the shared OWL ontology describing the document concepts (Fig 2). It also maintains an OWL ontology describing the providers' authorization policies (Fig 1) so as to enforce access control through selective data distribution. Deciding on eligible concepts for a user as well as finding which access control rules apply requires reasoning on these ontologies. We suggest the use of SPARQL [4] as a way to implement such inference rules. A SPARQL query can be crafted to find concepts which a user can be implicitly granted access to starting from one concept to which the user is explicitly granted access. The result to such a query would for instance consist in a set of concepts related through a subclass relationship and that should equally be granted access according to the provider policy or to some domain-specific knowledge. SPARQL queries over the document concepts allow us to reason about the semantic graph patterns. SPARQL queries over the policy ontology can also be used to reason and evaluate the policies by dynamically computing the aggregated authorized concepts for a user. To this effect, the distributor would have to host an engine like Joseki [1] to interpret queries.

The distributor must host a XACML engine to evaluate a registration request for concepts and return a response (i.e. Permit/Deny) to the user. In case of a "Permit" it responds by sending the *content signatures* of the accessible concepts. (see Fig 1) Upon the receipt of a XACML request for a set of concepts (1), the service determines all the contained concepts of the requested concepts (by concept containment) to get all the candidate accessible concepts. The XACML engine forwards such a request to the SPARQL generator (2) to convert it into SPARQL queries (3.a) using the requested concepts over the shared ontology represented as OWL triples (3.b). For instance, a registration request for the concept *WorkOrder* from a user with credential *Cred1* is converted into the following SPARQL by the query generator:

```
PREFIX  po: <http://www.owl-ontologies.com/Ontology1223675912.owl#>
SELECT ?subClasses
WHERE { ?subClasses rdfs:subClassOf po:WorkOrder. }
```

The above SPARQL query returns all the subclass concepts of *WorkOrder* (4), i.e. *QualityInspection, Production*. If any of these result concepts also has subclass concepts then similar queries are performed recursively. To this end, multiple candidate concepts are determined while the initial request might only be for one concept. In case the user does not request for specific concepts then all the concepts in the ontology are candidate concepts to be evaluated further. In particular, a similar query should be performed starting from the most general concepts to determine all the concepts in the domain. In order to determine the authorized concepts for the requested user, the above query result (i.e. *QualityInspection, Production*) is then used into a further SPARQL query (5.a) which evaluates associated policy triples from all providers (5.b). The result of this query is the maximal set of aggregated concepts (possibly empty if none is permitted) that are accessible to the requester (6.a). The rule $\mathcal{O}_1$ of provider P_1 described at Section 3.2 allows the requester to access the subclass concepts. The following query is used to evaluate this rule:

```
PREFIX po: <http://www.owl-ontologies.com/Ontology1224765032.owl#>
SELECT   ?concept
WHERE{{?user po:hasCredential po:Cred1}{?user po:hasAccess ?concept.}}
```

The first WHERE clause determines the users with credential *Cred*1 and the second clause determines the accessible concepts for those users. If the result set contains the *QualityInspection* and *Production* concepts then the XACML engine returns a "Permit" response to the user (6.b,6.c). The XML content distributor in the system then extracts the *content signatures* of the authorized concepts by manipulating only the encrypted and encoded content for the requested user and sends those as a response to a successful registration (7). Otherwise, none of these concepts is accessible to the requester and the XACML engine simply denies access (6.c).

Selective XML Content Distribution. The XML content distributor sends the encrypted and encoded XML content to authorized users after identifying the appropriate XML content. This can be handled by two functions $auth\_list(U)$ and $distribution\_list(D)$. The former returns a maximal set of authorized concepts for a user U. The latter returns the set of concepts for which the mapped XML nodes are currently distributed by the distributor D. An encrypted XML content (i.e. $[C_i^x, E_p^x]$) for an authorized user contains node N_x, its content under encoding CE_x, and concept C_i in the *content signature*, i.e. C_i^x by definitions of Section 4.3. The selective delivery of XML content to an authorized user U proceeds as follows:

1. Separate allowed concepts: find all $C_i \in auth\_list(U) \in distribution\_list(D)$.
2. Determine allowed nodes: match concepts of $auth\_list(U)$ with encoded concepts in C_i^x
3. Extract associated encrypted and encoded XML nodes (i.e. $[C_i^x, E_p^x]$).
4. Finally, send user U the encoded and encrypted XML nodes extracted in step 2.

6   XML Content Verification

Upon receipt of encrypted and encoded XML nodes, an end user is able to perform a semantic verification followed by an EBOL-based verification. In the following, we use A_U to denote the list of *content signatures* and R_U the set of encrypted and encoded nodes received by the user U during registration and after delivery respectively. $\mathcal{N}_A$ and $\mathcal{N}_R$ denote the set of node identifiers in A_U and R_U respectively.

6.1   Semantic Verification

In order to detect any semantics-related authorization violation, the following verification steps must be performed.

1. (C-I) have all concepts been received?
2. (C-II) have all XML nodes from different documents been received?
3. (C-III) do the document nodes correspond to nodes mapped with a desired concept?

The user U verifies whether all the concepts of A_U it has access to are contained in R_U. The verification is as follows: $(\forall c \in A_U \exists r \in R_U \ni (N_R, C_i) = (N'_A, C'_i))$, where (N'_A, C'_i) is the *content signature*, if there is a concept in R_U with an identical concept, then all the authorized concepts have been received by U *(C-I verified)*.

U then verifies whether it has received all XML nodes from different documents. It checks a *belong-to* relation between all the document identifiers doc_{id} in the authorized node identifiers of A_U and the document identifiers doc'_{id} of the received node identifiers of R_U. This check is as follows: $(\forall n \in \mathcal{N}_A \exists r \in \mathcal{N}_R | (doc_{id} = doc'_{id}))$; i.e. for each node in $\mathcal{N}_A$, if there is an identical document identifier in $\mathcal{N}_R$, then all the nodes have been received by U *(C-II verified)*.

(C-III) can be verified by *C-I*. Let C_r be a received concept then a user verifies whether C_r belongs to A_U, that is $C_r \in A_U$. If this verification fails then the received concept C_r is not a desired one.

6.2   EBOL-Based Verification

After a successful semantic verification, a user U can verify the following EBOL-based integrity violations:

1. (S-I) has the node content been changed?
2. (S-II) has some XML nodes not been received?
3. (S-III) have some nodes been moved?
4. (S-IV) has the node order been changed?

U decrypts the received XML nodes in $\mathcal{N}_R$ and traverses each document portion rooted at $r \in \mathcal{N}_R$ in breadth first order. Let x be the current visiting node. After decrypting an encoded node x gives the following encoded node:

$$[x, C_i^x, [CE_x, C_i^z]] = [x, < N_x, C_i >, [[< N_x, C_i >, I_x], C_i^z]]$$

U takes N_x from the outer C_i^x and x's content, Ct_x, and then computes the local hash of x as $I'_x = H(N_x, Ct_x)$ which is then compared with I_x. If any mismatch is found, the node content has been changed *(S-I verified)*.

U further checks the *belong-to* relation between all node identifiers of A_U and the received node identifiers of R_U. This check is as follows: $(\forall a \in \mathcal{N}_A \exists r \in \mathcal{N}_R | (E_r, E^r_{Highest})$ $= (E'_a, E'^a_{Highest}))$; i.e. for each node in $\mathcal{N}_A$, if there is an identical node identifier in $\mathcal{N}_R$, then all the nodes have been received by U *(S-II verified)*.

The verification process continues as the value of the node identifier N_x in the outer C_i^x must match with the inner node identifier N_x in CE_x. If not, then an integrity violation is detected and the node x can be discarded immediately without knowing the precise violation. To be precise, the elements of outer N_x are compared with the corresponding elements of the inner one. (a) if $f_{order}(E_x) \neq f_{order}(E_x')$, where E_x' is in the inner N_x this means an order change is detected. (b) if $f_{level}(E_x) = f_{level}(E_x')$ then the depth level of x in outer N_x is compared with the depth level of the received node in the inner C_i^x. If they do not match then the node x is moved to another depth level *(S-III semi verified)*.

The success of previous element wise matching does not guarantee a full integrity check. The depth level of the outer N_x must be compared with the depth level of the parent z of x in the inner C_i^z. If the latter is not less than the former then the node x is moved *(S-III fully verified)*.

During the breadth-first order traversal for a current node x, an order of EBOL E_x smaller than that of any previously visited node detects to an integrity violation. No such detection ensures that no order change was performed in a set of received XML nodes *(S-IV verified)*.

7 Related Work

There has been remarkable progress in recent years regarding access control to XML data structures in a client/server paradigm [6,7,8,9,16,17,18]. In these approaches, the server enforces access control policies on a per request basis. Instead, our work focuses on delegating third parties the selective delivery of semantically equivalent content to authorized users independently of providers. The work of [14,15] focuses on the delivery of encrypted XML data: authorization policies are specified based on the XML hierarchical structure yet document parsing is in post order. Our approach is fundamentally different as policy specification is assumed to be on domain concepts and selective delivery is performed based on the semantics captured in concepts, not document structure. Moreover, the EBOL computation can be performed on the fly while parsing documents. Our previous work [20] focuses on enabling authorized users to exchange document portions using a group key based approach that allows users with similar interests to be independent of a central authority, although it does not address document semantics.

[12] and [19] propose an ontology based access control for XML documents having variant schemas and semantically related documents respectively. However, none of them considers issues related to dissemination of semantically related data or document integrity and confidentiality. [10] discusses two ways ontologies can make it possible to describe access control models, but in that case focusing on different features of RBAC models. Although this work aims at modelling access control in a generic manner using Semantic Web methods in much the same way as our work, it does not specifically address the protection of XML schemas defining the resources accessed nor the practical implementation of enforcement. [21] introduces a formal model for semantic access control and associated algorithms which can be used in conjunction with our mechanism to detect if two providers defined conflicting access control policies on documents they distribute.

8 Conclusion and Future Work

This paper described an ontology-based XML content distribution system. Our solution protects the confidentiality of the document content and structure to protect the information system structure from other organizations and its content from unauthorized users. Document nodes are tagged with their semantic description and also incorporate integrity protection measures. Access control enforcement relies on a middleware that makes use of the semantic tagging of each document node which our EBOL scheme renders readable even for parties which cannot decrypt nodes. Semantic tagging can be efficiently analyzed, even for large documents, because of the breadth-first order parsing scheme adopted.

Our solution also illustrates in what respect semantic access control makes document exchanges feasible across organizational boundaries while protecting the layout of an organization's information system. We described how access control enforcement might be implemented by combining a XACML engine with a SPARQL engine. The use of ontologies allows us not only to reason about document authorizations, but also on the access control model: alternative paradigms, like the separation of concerns, might be introduced as inference rules on the access control ontology. Future work will investigate the implementation of such evolvable policies with Semantic Web methods.

Acknowledgment. This work is partly sponsored by EU IST-2004-026650 project R4eGov. Thanks to Henrik, Lim, Smriti and Slim for their valuable comments.

References

1. Joseki - A SPARQL Server for Jena, http://www.joseki.org/
2. OWL Web Ontology Language Overview,
   http://www.w3.org/tr/owl-features/
3. Resource Description Framework (RDF), http://www.w3.org/rdf/
4. SPARQL Query Language for RDF,
   http://www.w3.org/tr/rdf-sparql-query/
5. Agrawal, R., Kiernan, J., Srikant, R., Xu, Y.: Order preserving encryption for numeric data. In: SIGMOD 2004: Proceedings of the 2004 ACM SIGMOD international conference on Management of data, pp. 563–574. ACM, New York (2004)
6. Lee, W.-C., Luo, B., Lee, D., Liu, P.: A flexible framework for architecting XML access control enforcement mechanisms. In: Jonker, W., Petković, M. (eds.) SDM 2004. LNCS, vol. 3178, pp. 133–147. Springer, Heidelberg (2004)
7. Damiani, E., di Vimercati, S.D.C., Paraboschi, S., Samarati, P.: Fine Grained Access Control for Soap E-services. In: WWW 2001: Proceedings of the 10th international conference on World Wide Web, pp. 504–513. ACM, New York (2001)
8. Damiani, E., di Vimercati, S.D.C., Paraboschi, S., Samarati, P.: A Fine-grained Access Control System for XML Documents. ACM Trans. Inf. Syst. Secur. 5(2), 169–202 (2002)
9. Fan, W., Chan, C.-Y., Garofalakis, M.: Secure XML Querying With Security Views. In: SIGMOD 2004: Proceedings of the 2004 ACM SIGMOD international conference on Management of data, pp. 587–598. ACM Press, New York (2004)
10. Finin, T., Joshi, A., Kagal, L., Niu, J., Sandhu, R., Winsborough, W., Thuraisingham, B.: Rowlbac: Representing Role Based Access Control in OWL. In: Proceedings of the 13th ACM Symposium on Access Control Models and Technologies (SACMAT 2008), Estes Park, CO, USA, pp. 73–82. ACM, New York (2008)
11. Godik, S., Moses, T.: eXtensible Access Control Markup Language (XACML), version 1.0, OASIS Standard (2003)

12. Jain, A., Wijesekera, D., Singhal, A., Thuraisingham, B.: Semantic-Aware Data Protection in Web Services. In: Proceedings of IEEE Workshop on Web Services Security held in Berkeley, CA (May 2006)
13. Kagal, L., Paolucci, M., Srinivasan, N., Denker, G., Finin, T., Sycara, K.: Authorization and privacy for semantic web services. IEEE Intelligent Systems 19(4), 50–56 (2004)
14. Kundu, A., Bertino, E.: A new model for secure dissemination of xml content. IEEE Transactions on Systems, Man, and Cybernetics, Part C: Applications and Reviews 38(3), 292–301 (2008)
15. Kundu, A., Elisa, B.: Secure Dissemination of XML Content Using Structure-based Routing. In: EDOC 2006: Proceedings of the 10th IEEE International Enterprise Distributed Object Computing Conference, Washington, DC, USA, pp. 153–164. IEEE Computer Society, Los Alamitos (2006)
16. Kuper, G., Massacci, F., Rassadko, N.: Generalized XML Security Views. In: SACMAT 2005: Proceedings of the tenth ACM symposium on Access control models and technologies, pp. 77–84. ACM Press, New York (2005)
17. Miklau, G., Suciu, D.: Controlling Access to Published Data Using Cryptography. In: VLDB, pp. 898–909 (2003)
18. Murata, M., Tozawa, A., Kudo, M., Hada, S.: XML Access Control Using Static Analysis. In: CCS 2003: Proceedings of the 10th ACM conference on Computer and communications security, pp. 73–84. ACM Press, New York (2003)
19. Parmar, V., Shi, H., Chen, S.-S.: XML Access Control for Semantically Related XML Documents. In: Proceedings of the 36th Annual Hawaii International Conference on System Sciences, p. 10 (January 2003)
20. Rahaman, M.A., Roudier, Y., Schaad, A.: Distributed Access Control for XML Document Centric Collaborations. In: EDOC 2008, 12th IEEE International Enterprise Distributed Object Computing Conference, Munich, Germany. IEEE Computer Society, Los Alamitos (2008)
21. Yagüe, M.I., del-mar Gallardo, M., Maña, A.: Semantic access control model: A formal specification. In: di Vimercati, S.d.C., Syverson, P.F., Gollmann, D. (eds.) ESORICS 2005. LNCS, vol. 3679, pp. 24–43. Springer, Heidelberg (2005)

NGBPA Next Generation BotNet Protocol Analysis

Felix S. Leder and Peter Martini

University of Bonn, Institute of Computer Science IV, Roemerstr. 164,
53117 Bonn, Germany
leder@cs.uni-bonn.de, martini@cs.uni-bonn.de

Abstract. The command & control (c&c) protocols of botnets are moving away from plaintext IRC communicationt towards encrypted and obfuscated protocols. In general, these protocols are proprietary. Therefore, standard network monitoring tools are not able to extract the commands from the collected traffic. However, if we want to monitor these new botnets, we need to know how their protocol decryption works.

In this paper we present a novel approach in malware analysis for locating the encryption and decryption functions in botnet programs. This information can be used to extract these functions for c&c protocols.

We illustrate the applicability of our approach by a sample from the *Kraken* botnet. Using our approach, we were able to identify the encryption routine within minutes. We then extracted the c&c protocol encryption and decryption. Both are presented in this paper.

1 Introduction

Botnets have been a major, growing threat in the Internet in the last years. Today, botnets are the source of more than 90% of all SPAM mails. They collect email addresses, passwords and sometimes even banking information. In addition, botnets have the ability to coordinate and conduct distributed denial of service attacks.

While the core functionality and behavior of malware is quite stable, obfuscation and polymorphic techniques[21] are used to circumvent signature detection. As a consequence, only behavioral analysis can be used to classify a given malware specimen.

The state-of-the-art method of classifying botnets is to run the bot in a monitored environment and analyze the behavior. The network traffic is a very reliable way to classify specimen to specific families. For commonly used protocols like IRC and HTTP, there is a wide range of automated analysis and monitoring tools[20,23]. These tools are very reliable for known protocols but fail for encrypted traffic.

Most botnets are sticking to traditional IRC communication [22] but more and more botnets are moving towards "stealthier" and robust communication. This includes P2P protocols as well as obfuscated and encrypted protocols[10,12]. In order to extract information from collected network data, the encryption and decryption has to be known and added to the monitoring tools.

The botnet software itself contains those encryption and decryption routines for the bot's communication with the control nodes. The recovery of encryption and decryption functionality from executables usually requires a lot of manual work and analysis.

D. Gritzalis and J. Lopez (Eds.): SEC 2009, IFIP AICT 297, pp. 307–317, 2009.
© IFIP International Federation for Information Processing 2009

In this paper, we present an approach that automates the localization of possible en- and decryption functions. This enables analysts to extract the functionality and create decryption add-ons for monitoring tools.

While traditional tools only scrutinize data leaving the malware, we correlate this information with details from inside the malware. For that, we determine the creation functions of I/O buffers, which are often close to the encryption functions or even include the functionality. A similar approach is used for input buffers and decryption routines.

Using our approach, we were able to find the encryption and decryption functions inside a *Kraken* botnet sample within minutes. We illustrate the applicability of our approach based on the Kraken sample. In addition, we release a *C* re-implementation of the encryption and decryption code extracted from the sample. This code can be used to monitor Kraken traffic.

The rest of the paper is structured as follows: Section 2 provides an overview of related work. Section 3 describes our approach in more detail. Section 4 shows the applicability of our approach based on this Kraken botnet sample and describes the extracted encryption and decryption routines. Implications of publishing our approach are discussed in section 5. Section 6 concludes and gives an overview of future work.

2   Related Work

Malware may be analyzed in two different ways: *Static analysis* and *dynamic analysis*.

Static analysis is performed on the binary without executing it. This is typically conducted by disassembling the binary and extracting information about data and control flow. This approach is usually faster than dynamic analysis [5]. Christodorescu et al. [8] have presented malware analysis techniques based on static analysis. A major drawback of static analysis is that the code analyzed may be different from the code executed. This is caused by packers [4,18], encryptors, polymorphism[21], or obfuscation techniques[16].

Dynamic analysis tools monitor the malware while it is running. Classical examples of dynamic analysis tools are debuggers. A series of dynamic analysis tools that monitor typical actions, like e.g. file, registry and network access, exist [9,11]. Some are based on API hooking and monitor malware from inside the system [24]. Others emulate a whole PC and monitor the malware behavior from outside [5,6]. Automated botnet monitoring systems, like e.g. [20,23], often rely on this kind of systems for extracting the c&c information.

These tools are designed for the mass-analysis of malware and obtain valuable information from malware using standard protocols. They fail for proprietary, encoded, and encrypted data if the decryption algorithms are not known. Typically, they only monitor the data leaving the malware, details from inside the malware are not taken into account.

Different debuggers are available [1,15,25], for scripting and flexible monitoring of Windows API calls. They can be used for locating the encryption and encoding functions of malware but require a lot of additional manual work. However, they are not able to automatically determine the data origin and correlations to I/O.

The approach closest to ours is the automated reverse engineering framework PaiMei [3]. It traces program execution and collects information at different trace points.

PaiMei is a generic framework. Data is collected about every function inside the application. It is left to the analyst to extract the necessary relations out of the lot of information collected.

3   Methodology

We have observed that the encryption and decryption functions are often close to the creation points of the buffers they use. From a software developer point of view, this is an intuitive behavior since the buffers are allocated only when they are needed.

In general, the encryption of data the last operation performed on the data, before it leaves the executable. The buffer passed to I/O interfaces is the one containing the result of the encryption process. The same holds for the decryption as displayed in figure 1. In order to receive (encrypted) data from an input interface, a buffer has to be created. The buffer is then passed to the input interface. It may pass an arbitrary number of management functions (c.f. section 3.2). The buffer is filled with encrypted data behind the input interface. After returning the buffer, it must be decrypted before data can be used.

We are monitoring the I/O interfaces, like e.g. *send()* or *recv()*. The buffer addresses detected at I/O interfaces allow us to automatically determine the buffer creation function inside the malware. As this creation point is close to the encryption or decryption function, it can be used as a starting point for deeper analysis and extraction of the cryption functions.

3.1   Assumptions

Our approach is based on some assumptions about the structure of the program. Of course, malware developers may adapt their programs to avoid meeting these assumptions. Implications are discussed in section 5.

We focus on the Windows operating system and x86 architectures because more than 95% of malware in-the-wild is developed for that platform[22].

Our most important assumption is that malware is using the standard I/O interfaces of the operating system (OS). This assumptions allows us to place monitoring points on these I/O interfaces. Malware authors, like authors of any other software, rely on the

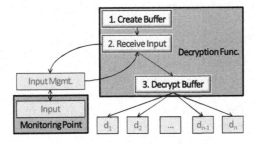

Fig. 1. Schematic flow of buffer creation and usage during the process of receiving encrypted data and decrypting the data. After the buffer is created, it is passed to the input routine. This returns the buffer filled with encrypted data. As a third step, the buffer is decrypted.

I/O functionality provided by the OS in order to be more independent from the system architecture. Malware with custom crafted file or network drivers would lack flexibility.

Additionally, we assume that buffers are created at the time they are needed. This reflects the intuitive behavior to allocate the buffer in the scope when it is required. It may be discarded after leaving their scope.

The encryption process is the last operation performed on the data before leaving the malware. Vice versa, the decryption process is the first operation performed on incoming data. We assume that the encryption functionality places its result in the output buffer and that this buffer is passed to the output interface. The same holds for the input buffer and decryption functionality.

A scenario, in which the encryption uses another buffer, which is later on copied into the output buffer, is not critical. In this case, the copy operation can be determined using other means, like e.g. copy signatures or using memory breakpoints. This allows for an iterative application of our approach.

3.2 Buffer Lifecycle

Buffers are used to transfer data in and out of the executable. Of course, there are different lifecycles for input and output operations. However, they show a similarity, which we exploit for finding the buffer origin.

Figure 1 shows the typical lifecycle of a buffer used for encrypted input. The buffer is created as part of the encryption initiation. It is then given to the input interface of the operating system. It may pass arbitrary management functions, which may perform error handling or add context information, like e.g. the socket descriptor. After the buffer has been filled with encoded data outside of the executable, it is returned. The buffer is then decrypted for extraction and usage of the original data.

Figure 2 displays the typical lifecycle of output buffers. In a first step, the buffer is created. It may be filled with the original, unencrypted data as an optional step. The buffer is then encrypted and the encryption result is passed to the output interface. Similar to the lifecycle of input data, it may pass arbitrary management functions for similar reasons.

Both lifecycles have in common that the buffer creation is preceding the I/O operations. We have observed that the buffer creation function is often close to the encryption functionality or may even include this functionality. In these cases, we can locate the cryption routines from the buffer creation point.

3.3 Monitoring Points

We are monitoring different I/O interfaces to gather information about buffer creation points and the context in which a buffer is used. The context includes information about data endpoints, like networking peers or files. The buffer creation functions and the context in which the buffer is used can automatically be determined when monitoring three different types of interfaces:

- Heap memory management functions
- I/O initialization
- I/O operations

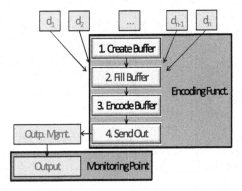

Fig. 2. Lifecycle of output buffers for encrypted data. After the buffer is created, it may be filled with unencrypted data chunks. The data is then encrypted and sent out to the output interface. It may pass management functions, before. When its scope ends, the buffer may be discarded.

Heap operations are monitored in order to detect the allocation of new buffers. The address and size of each allocated memory block is stored together with the function that initiated the allocation. This mapping is used to determine the creation point for heap buffers monitored in I/O operations.

The I/O initialization functions, like *connect()* or *OpenFile()*, are monitored to collect context information. The initialization functions provide information about the data endpoint, like filenames or IP addresses. Later, the collected information may be mapped to specific buffers. This eases the extraction of the desired functions for specific endpoints.

Monitoring points on the actual I/O interfaces, like *send()* or *ReadFile()*, are used to determine the actual buffer origin. Thus, they are essential for locating the cryption functions.

3.4 Determining the Buffer Origin

The primary goal of our approach is to find the creation point of buffers holding encrypted data. As we have observed, the creation point is often close to the encryption function for output buffers and respectively close to the decryption function for input buffers.

For this purpose, monitoring points are placed on relevant I/O interfaces. If a buffer is passed to a monitored I/O interface, three steps are performed:

1. Extraction of the buffer address
2. Mapping to type of memory
3. Mapping to function based on memory region

First, the buffer address is extracted from the call to the I/O interface. The location of the address depends on the calling convention of the interface but can be found at fixed positions. It is located either in registers or at fixed offsets on the call stack.

Based on the buffer address, a mapping to its memory region has to be performed because different methods have to be used for the mapping to a creation function. The

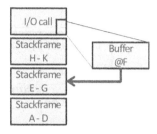

Fig. 3. A stack buffer passed to an I/O interface may be mapped to its creation function. The mapping is achieved by comparing the buffer address to the boundaries of different stack frames.

choice of the method depends on the memory region, which may be heap memory, stack memory, or global memory.

Figure 3 illustrates the mapping for buffers located on the stack. Each function on the stack has a dedicated stack frame. A stack frame is used for the return address, for call parameters as well as for local variables. Once the address of a stack buffer is known, the stack frame containing that address may be determined. The buffer is a local variable of the function that created this stackframe. The address of this function is the buffer creation point. In addition, the function address may be determined from the stackframe.

Heap buffers contain no information about the function that created them. In order to determine their creation function, we use monitoring points on heap management functions, like *RtlAllocateHeap()*. This way, we can create a mapping from the function using the heap management to the allocated memory space. If the address of the I/O buffer points to the heap, the list of mappings is examined for the space containing the buffer. As the heap memory is non-overlapping, the creation function can be determined and is unambiguous.

A creation function for global memory cannot be determined because it is created at program start. As it is constantly occupying memory and more difficult to manage, it is hardly ever used for I/O buffers.

4   Application - Extracting Kraken Encryption

We illustrate the applicability of our approach using a Kraken botnet sample: We were able to identify the encryption and decryption function within minutes. Based on this, we were able to recover the full cryption process for the proprietary Kraken command & control (c&c) protocol.

The Kraken Botnet is said to be the largest botnet in the world [19]. Estimations of the botnet size range from 185.000 to 600.000 zombie hosts worldwide.

Its main purpose is to spread SPAM mail. Single infected hosts have been observed transmitting as much as 500.000 junk mails. Besides that, it harvests the windows address book and local files for email addresses and can install additional malware.

The bots contain a list of dynamic DNS hostnames for contacting the botnet master [17]. They subsequently try to contact each hostname via UDP until a response is received. After a successful handshake, the bots use a proprietary, encrypted c&c protocol for data exchange.

For our evaluation, we have analyzed a Kraken sample from early 2008. It uses the Kraken protocol version 311. For manual verification of the results, we unpacked the sample[7].

For use in our NGBPA implementation, we have used the original, packed sample and placed monitoring points on networking functions like *sendto()* and *recvfrom()*. After having started the sample, we observed connection attempts to different SMTP servers for 20 seconds, which we intentionally dropped. 20 seconds later, the first encrypted buffer sent via UDP to port 447 was captured. This buffer - which was passed to *sendto()* - was located on the stack. The buffer was contained in the stack frame of function *sub_1A832C*. Not answering those requests, we could see similar requests to different hosts every 10 seconds. The buffer origin stayed the same for all of these.

```
.text:001A83CA mov  dword ptr [esp+80h+buf], eax
.text:001A83CE lea  eax, [esp+80h+buf] ; key1
.text:001A83D2 mov  [esp+80h+var_2C], edx ; key2
.text:001A83D6 mov  [esp+80h+var_28], ebx ; seed
.text:001A83DA mov  [esp+80h+var_24], 1 ; cmd 1
.text:001A83DF mov  [esp+80h+var_23], bl ; subcmd
.text:001A83E3 mov  [esp+80h+version], 137h ; vers.
.text:001A83EA mov  [esp+80h+var_20], ebx ; size
.text:001A83EE mov  [esp+80h+var_1C], ebx ; chksum

.text:001A83F2 call encryptHeader <----------

.text:001A83F7 call create_new_udp_sock
...
.text:001A8422 lea  eax, [esp+90h+buf]
.text:001A8426 push eax ; buf
...
.text:001A842B call ds:sendto   <-------------
```

Fig. 4. Kraken encryption origin

A closer look at the creation function revealed the code block shown in figure 4[1]. The excerpt shows, how different fields in the buffer are filled with keys, some seed, commands, protocol version, size, and a checksum. Looking at the two functions following this block, reveals suspicious mathematical operations in the first function (001A83F2) while the second (001A83F7) creates a UDP socket.

Having a candidate for the encryption, we loaded the binary in a debugger and placed a breakpoint on that function. Running the candidate functions shows that the buffer is modified. The result was the data sent out via UDP, afterwards. A manual investigation and a dissection from C. Pierce [17] verified this function to contain the encryption.

Based on these results, we were able to reconstruct the decryption and encryption functions used in the kraken botnet. A re-implementation in C can be found in the appendix. The protocol is shown in figure 5. The first three fields are two keys and a seed, which are used for encryption and decryption. The other fields are symmetrically encrypted before transmission. As the encryption is symmetric and keys are included in each payload, it is encryption by obfuscation but not secure in any way.

---

[1] The annotations and comments were added later.

Key 1	Key 2	Seed	Cmd	Sub.	Vers	Size	Cksum	Payl.
32	32	32	8	8	16	32	32	<size>
			Encrypted					

Fig. 5. The Kraken protocol. Shown is the protocol header including the number of bits for each field. Only the keys and seed are unencrypted.

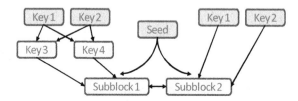

Fig. 6. The data dependencies of the Kraken encryption. Keys 3 and 4 are derived by bitshift operations of keys 1 and 2. Each block is divided into two subblocks. These are encrypted using the seed, two keys and the other subblock.

The two keys are derived from information about the host hardware. The derivation of the two keys together as well as of the checksum is described in more detail in [17]. We found the creation of the seed in the encryption function. It is different for each data packet. The seed is based on the processor tick count and computed by adding the 32 high-bits to the 32 low-bits.

Figure 6 illustrates the data dependency used in encryption and decryption. Details may be studied in our C re-implementation included in the appendix. As illustrated in figure 5, all fields except for the keys and seed are encrypted together with the c&c payload. The encryption algorithm can be applied in 8-byte-blocks or bytewise. The kraken sample studied uses block-encryption. The data is split into 8-byte-blocks, which are divided into two subblocks. Each subblock is used to encrypt the other in combination with the seed and the two keys. If the data size is not a multiple of 8 bytes, the last bytes are encrypted bytewise.

By spoofing UDP answers, we were able to locate the decryption function with our approach, too. The buffer for the *recvfrom()* call was created in the same function as the send buffer. Figure 7 shows the excerpt related to data reception. The decryption function is located right after the call to *recvfrom*

```
.text:001A8464 lea eax, [esp+90h+recvbuf]
.text:001A8468 push eax ; buf
...
.text:001A846D call ds:recvfrom    <---------------
...
.text:001A8478 lea esi, [esp+80h+recvbuf]

.text:001A847C call decryptHeader <--------------
```

Fig. 7. Kraken decryption origin

The keys and seed for the decryption are contained in the c&c protocol data. Thus, it is possible to decrypt all c&c traffic using the information transmitted over the network. Monitoring applications can make use of this to create their own decryption stub. A C re-implementation of the decryption is included in the appendix.

Identifying both encryption and decryption took us only a few minutes: Running the kraken botnet sample, our NGBPA tool took 20 seconds before the first packet was sent out, which immediately revealed the origin of the buffer. Around 5-10 minutes of manual investigation were needed afterwards to identify the encryption and decryption functions.

This example illustrates both the applicability and performance of our approach. The application of our approach to other malware samples, not mentioned here, showed a similar efficiency.

5   Discussion

Publishing our approach may invalidate it because malware authors may design new specimen specifically to not meet our assumptions. In this section, we discuss implications.

We assume that malware is using the OS for I/O. Our approach fails for custom I/O drivers directly accessing the hardware. However, for the malware author custom drivers increase development complexity and reduce flexibility.

Another assumption is that buffers are created at the time they are needed. Allocation long before is a rather unintuitive development strategy and complicates the design. The encryption can still be found using memory monitoring with breakpoints or emulator extension.

Other possibilities to break our approach are the use of global buffers or implementation of custom designed memory management functions. For malware authors, this complicates the software design and therefore maintainability, increases the risk for bugs, and may break modularity. This has an impact on the overall architecture and development efficiency. Since malware and especially botnet development is becoming more and more professional with a standard "testing and revision process" [12], it has to be efficient. It is questionable whether malware developers would take this step.

While malware authors probably stick with regular software design for reasons named before, our approach may be beneficial for a whole group of malware researchers. We therefore decided to publish even though there is a risk of limiting the lifespan of our approach this way.

6   Conclusions and Future Work

We were able to demonstrate the applicability of our approach. With a practical implementation, we were able to identify the encryption and decryption routines of the *Kraken* botnet within minutes. We were able to extract and re-implement the encryption and decryption logic, which is included in the appendix and can be integrated into botnet monitoring tools. We therefore conclude it to be a valuable component in the malware analysis toolchain.

One example is not enough to show a general usability. For that reason, our approach has to be evaluated with a representative set of malware samples. A major question in this context is how many samples from which sources are required to be representative for the malware in-the-wild.

In addition, an easy to configure interface to our implementation would be beneficial to speed up analysis. This includes the selection of typical I/O interfaces. Another future feature is the integration of additional buffer monitoring in case the considered malware violates our current assumptions.

References

1. Amini, P.: PyDbg - A pure Python win32 debugging abstraction class last visit (l.v.) (October 2008), http://pedram.redhive.com/PyDbg/
2. Amini, P.: Kraken Botnet Infiltration, Blog on DVLabs (April 2008), http://dvlabs.tippingpoint.com/blog/2008/04/28/kraken-botnet-infiltration
3. Amini, P.: PaiMei - Reverse Engineering Automization (October 2008), http://pedram.redhive.com/research/reverse_engineering_automation/
4. Archer and FEUERRADER, QuickUnpack, (August 2008), http://reversengineering.wordpress.com/2007/10/06/quick-unpack-v20-final/
5. Bayer, U., Kruegel, C., Kirda, E.: TTAnalyze: A Tool for Analyzing Malware. In: 15th Annual Conference of the European Institute for Computer Antivirus Research (EICAR) (2006)
6. Bellard, F.: QEMU, a Fast and Portable Dynamic Translator. In: USENIX Annual Technical Conference (2005)
7. Brulez, N.: Unpacking Storm Worm (August 2008), http://securitylabs.websense.com/content/Blogs/3127.aspx
8. Christodorescu, M., et al.: Semantics-aware malware detection. In: IEEE Symposium on Security and Privacy (2005)
9. Combs, G.: Wireshark - network protocol analyzer (October 2008), http://www.wireshark.org
10. Dittrich, D., Dietrich, S.: Command and control structures in malware. Usenix magazine 32(6) (December 2007)
11. Russinovich, R., Cogswell, B.: Windows Sysinterals (October 2008), http://technet.microsoft.com/en-us/sysinternals/default.aspx
12. Fisher, D.: Storm, Nugache lead dangerous new botnet barrage, Article (October 2008), http://searchsecurity.techtarget.com/news/article/0,289142,sid14_gci1286808,00.html
13. Hoglund, G., Butler, J.: Rootkits. Addison Wesley, Reading (2005)
14. Father, H.: Hooking Windows APITechnics of Hooking API Functions on Windows. Code-Breakers Journal 1(2) (2004)
15. Immunity Inc., Immunity Debugger, (October 2008), http://www.immunitysec.com/products-immdbg.shtml
16. Linn, C., Debray, S.: Obfuscation of executable code to improve resistance to static disassembly. In: Proceedings of the 10th ACM conference on Computer and communications security (2003)
17. Pierce, C.: Owning Kraken Zombies, a Detailed Dissection, Blog on DVLabs (October 2008), http://dvlabs.tippingpoint.com/blog/2008/04/28/owning-kraken-zombies
18. Royal, P., Halpin, M., Dagon, D., Edmonds, R., Lee, W.: PolyUnpack: Automating the Hidden-Code Extraction of Unpack-Executing Malware. In: ACSAC 2006: Proceedings of the 22nd Annual Computer Security Applications Conference on Annual Computer Security Applications Conference (2006)
19. Royal, P.: On the Kraken and Bobax Botnets, Whitepaper, Damball (April 2008)

20. Shadowserver Foundation, ShadowServer Homepage (October 2008), http://shadowserver.org
21. Szor, P.: The Art of Computer Virus Research and Defense. Addison-Wesley, Reading (2005)
22. Symantec Coorp. Symantec Internet Security Threat Report Volume XIII, Whitepaper (April 2008)
23. Wicherski, G.: botsnoopd - Sniffing on Botnets, Blog (October 2008), http://blog.oxff.net/2006/10/botsnoopd-sniffing-on-botnets.html
24. Willems, C., Holz, T., Freiling, F.: Toward Automated Dynamic Malware Analysis Using CWSandbox. In: IEEE Security & Privacy (2007)
25. Yuschuk, O.: OllyDbg Debugger (October 2008), http://www.ollydbg.de/

Appendix

C re-implementation of the Kraken protocol decryption function.

```
void decode(uint8_t* buffer, uint32_t buffer_size, uint32_t key1,
uint32_t key2,
            uint32_t seed, uint32_t blockwise_flag) {
  int i;
  uint32_t buffer_pos = 0;
  uint32_t keys[] = {key1, key2, (key2 >> 0x13) | (key1 << 0x0d),
                                 (key2 << 0x0d) | (key1 >> 0x13)};
  if (blockwise_flag) {
    while (buffer_size - buffer_pos >= 8) {
      uint32_t* data1 = (uint32_t*) &buffer[buffer_pos];
      uint32_t* data2 = (uint32_t*) &buffer[buffer_pos+4];
      uint32_t round_key = seed + seed;

      for (i=0; i<2; ++i) {
        *data2 -= (*data1 << 4) + keys[2] ^ (*data1 >> 5) + keys[3]    \
                  ^ (round_key + *data1);
        *data1 -= (*data2 << 4) + keys[0] ^ (*data2 >> 5) + keys[1]    \
                  ^ (round_key + *data2);
        round_key -= seed;
      }
      buffer_pos += 8;
    }
  } /* the rest is decrypted bytewise */
  buffer = &buffer[buffer_pos];
  buffer_size -= buffer_pos;
  for (i = 0; i < buffer_size; ++i) {
    uint8_t seedbyte = (seed >> 8 * (3 - i%4) ) & 0xff;
    buffer[i] ^= ((uint8_t*)keys)[i] + seedbyte;
  }
}
```

C re-implementation of the Kraken protocol encryption function.

```
void encode(uint8_t* buffer, uint32_t buffer_size, uint32_t key1,
uint32_t key2,
            uint32_t seed, uint32_t blockwise_flag) {
  int i;
  uint32_t buffer_pos = 0;
  uint32_t keys[] = {key1,key2,(key2 >> 0x13) | (key1 << 0x0d),
                               (key2 << 0x0d) | (key1 >> 0x13)};
  if (blockwise_flag) {
    while (buffer_size - buffer_pos >= 8) {
      uint32_t* data1 = (uint32_t*) &buffer[buffer_pos];
      uint32_t* data2 = (uint32_t*) &buffer[buffer_pos+4];
      uint32_t round_key = 0;

      for (i=0; i<2; ++i) {
        round_key += seed;

        *data1 += (*data2 << 4) + keys[0] ^ (*data2 >> 5) + keys[1] \
                  ^ (round_key + *data2);
        *data2 += (*data1 << 4) + keys[2] ^ (*data1 >> 5) + keys[3] \
                  ^ (round_key + *data1);
      }
      buffer_pos += 8;
    }
  } /* the rest is encrypted bytewise */
  buffer = &buffer[buffer_pos];
  buffer_size -= buffer_pos;
  for (i = 0; i < buffer_size; ++i) {
    uint8_t seedbyte = (seed >> 8 * (3 - i%4) ) & 0xff;
    buffer[i] ^= ((uint8_t*)keys)[i] + seedbyte;
  }
}
```

Non-repudiation Analysis with LySa[*]

Mayla Brusò and Agostino Cortesi

Computer Science Department, Ca' Foscari University, Italy
mabruso@dsi.unive.it, acortesi@dsi.unive.it

Abstract. This work introduces a formal analysis of the non-repudiation property for security protocols. Protocols are modelled in the process calculus LySa, using an extended syntax with annotations. Non-repudiation is verified using a Control Flow Analysis, following the same approach introduced by M. Buchholtz and H. Gao for authentication and freshness analyses.

The result is an analysis that can statically check the protocols to predict if they are secure during their execution and which can be fully automated.

1 Introduction

With the growth of Internet applications like e-shopping or e-voting, non-repudiation is becoming increasingly important, as a protocol property. Our aim is to provide a protocol analysis which checks this property to avoid that a protocol is used in malicious way. Among the existing techniques that perform the analysis of non-repudiation protocols, we may cite:

- The CSP (Communicating Sequential Processes) approach [12], [13]: it is an abstract language designed specifically for the description of communication patterns of concurrent system components that interact through message passing.
- The game approach [10]: it considers the execution of the protocol as a game, where each entity is a player; the protocols are designed finding a strategy, which has to defend an honest entity against all the possible strategies of malicious parties.
- The Zhou-Gollmann approach [16]: it uses *SVO Logic*, a modal logic that is composed by inference rules and axioms which are used to express beliefs that can be analysed by a judge to decide if the service provided the property.
- The inductive approach [1]: it uses an inductive model, a set of all the possible histories of the network that the protocol execution may produce; a history, called *trace*, is a list of network events, that can indicate the communication of a message or the annotation of information for future use.

We follow a different approach, the same as M. Buchholtz [5] and H. Gao [8], who show how some security properties can be analysed using the LySa [2] process calculus with annotations and a Control Flow Analysis (CFA) to detect flaws in the protocols. The main idea is to extend LySa with specific annotations, i.e. tags that identify part of the message for which the property has to hold and that uniquely assign principal and session identifiers to encryptions and decryptions.

---

[*] Work partially supported by PRIN 07 MUR Project 200793N42R SOFT.

D. Gritzalis and J. Lopez (Eds.): SEC 2009, IFIP AICT 297, pp. 318–329, 2009.

It is interesting to notice that the non-repudiation analysis that we propose easily fits into the CFA framework [11], yielding a suite of analyses that can be combined in various ways, with no major implementation overload.

The main differences between our proposal and the previously cited alternative approaches are the following: our analysis can check many protocols and can model scenarios with infinitely many principals while other approaches often are developed to analyse only a particular protocol and can model scenarios with finite principals.

The structure of the paper is the following: Section 2 is a quick overview of LYSA; Section 3 presents the CFA framework; Section 4 shows the new non-repudiation analysis, and its application to the protocols; Section 5 concludes.

2 LYSA

LYSA [2] is a process calculus in the π-calculus tradition that models security protocols on a global network. It incorporates pattern matching into the language constructs where values can become bound to variables. In LYSA all the communications take place directly on a global network and this corresponds to the scenario in which security protocols often operate, where channels are not considered.

2.1 Syntax and Semantics

An expression $E \in Expr$ may represent a name, a variable or an encryption. The set $Expr$ contains two disjointed subsets, $Name$ ranged over by n, which contains identifiers, nonces, keys, etc., and Var ranged over by x, which contains variables. The remaining expressions are symmetric and asymmetric encryptions of k-tuples of other expressions, defined as $\{E_1, \ldots, E_k\}_{E_0}$ and $\{| E_1, \ldots, E_k |\}_{E_0}$ respectively, where E_0 represents a symmetric or asymmetric key.

LYSA also allows to construct processes $P \in Proc$, which use the expressions explained above. Processes can have the following form:

- $\langle E_1, \ldots, E_k \rangle.P$: the process sends a k-tuple of values onto the global network; if the message reaches its destination, the process continues as P.
- $(E_1, \ldots, E_j; x_{j+1}, \ldots, x_k).P$: the process read a message and, if $E_1, \ldots, E_j$ are identical to the values expected, the remaining $k - j$ values are bound to the variables $x_{j+1}, \ldots, x_k$, and the process continues as P.
- decrypt E as $\{E_1, \ldots, E_j; x_{j+1}, \ldots, x_k\}_{E_0}$ in P: the process denotes the symmetric decryption and, if the encryption key is identical to E_0, then the process decrypts the k-tuple; if $E_1, \ldots, E_j$ are identical to the values expected, the remaining $k - j$ values are bound to the variables $x_{j+1}, \ldots, x_k$, and the process continues as P.
- decrypt E as $\{|E_1, \ldots, E_j; x_{j+1}, \ldots, x_k|\}_{E_0}$ in P: the process denotes the asymmetric decryption and it works like symmetric decryption except that E_0 and the key used to encrypt have to be a key pair m^+ and m^-.
- $(\nu\, n)P$: the process generates a new name n and it continues in P.
- $(\nu \pm m)P$: the process generates a new key pair, m^+ / m^-, and it continues in P.
- $P_1 \mid P_2$: the process denotes two processes running in parallel.

- !P: the process acts as an arbitrary number of processes P composed in parallel.
- 0: the process is the inactive or nil process that does nothing.

A binder introduces new names or variables which have scope in the rest of the process. Restriction, input and decryption constructs are binders of names, key pairs, and variables, which have scope in the subprocess P. Names and variables are called free whenever they are not bound by any binder; the functions $fn(P)$ and $fv(P)$ collect all the free names and variables in the process P, respectively. The bound variables are defined by the function $bv(P) \overset{def}{=} var(P) \setminus fv(P)$. All these functions are also defined on the terms.

Example 1. Let us see how to encode in LYSA the protocol defined by Cederquist, Corin and Dashti in [6].

$$
\begin{aligned}
A \rightarrow B: &\quad \{M\}_K, EOO_M &&\text{for } EOO_M = sig_A(B, TTP, H, \{|\,K, A\,|\}_{TTP}) \\
B \rightarrow A: &\quad EOR_M &&\text{for } EOR_M = sig_B(EOO_M) \\
A \rightarrow B: &\quad K \\
B \rightarrow A: &\quad EOR_K &&\text{for } EOR_K = sig_B(A, H, K)
\end{aligned}
$$

where $H = h(\{M\}_K)$ and h is a hash function. The encoding is the following:

let $X \subseteq S$ in $(\nu_{\pm i \in X} AK_i)(\nu \pm TTP)($
  $|_{i \in X}|_{j \in X}$ $!(\nu SK_{ij})(\nu H_{ij})(\nu M_{ij})$
   $\langle \{M_{ij}\}_{SK_{ij}}, \{|I_j, TTP, H_{ij}, \{|SK_{ij}, I_i|\}|\}\rangle.(:xEORM_{ij}).$
   decrypt $xEORM_{ij}$ as $\{|\{|I_j, TTP, H_{ij}, \{|SK_{ij}, I_i|\}|\}|\}$ in
   $\langle SK_{ij}\rangle.(:xEORK_{ij}).$decrypt $xEORK_{ij}$ as $\{|I_i, H_{ij}, SK_{ij};\}$ in 0
  $|_{i \in X}|_{j \in X}$ $!(:xEnMsg_{ij}, xEOOM_{ij}).$
   decrypt $xEOOM_{ij}$ as $\{|I_j, TTP; xH_{ij}, xTTP|\}$ in
   $\langle\{|xEOOM_{ij}|\}\rangle.(:xSK_{ij}).$
   decrypt $xEnMsg_{ij}$ as $\{xMsg_{ij}\}_{xSK_{ij}}$ in $\langle\{|I_i, xH_{ij}, xSK_{ij}|\}\rangle.0)$

LYSA provides a reduction semantics that describes the evolution of a process step-by-step, using a *reduction relation* between two processes, written $P \rightarrow P'$. If the reduction relation holds then P can evolve in P' using the rules depicted in Table 1.

The structural congruence between two processes, written $P \equiv P'$, means that P is equal to P' except for syntactic aspects, but this does not interfere with the way they

Table 1. Semantics of LYSA calculus

(Com)	$\dfrac{\bigwedge_{i=1}^{j} V_i = V'_i}{\langle V_1 \ldots V_k\rangle.P \mid (V'_1 \ldots V'_j; x_{j+1} \ldots x_k).P' \rightarrow_{\mathscr{R}} P \mid P'[V_{j+1}/x_{j+1} \ldots V_k/x_k]}$
(Dec)	$\dfrac{\bigwedge_{i=1}^{j} V_i = V'_i}{\text{decrypt } \{V_1 \ldots V_k\}_{V_0} \text{ as } \{V'_1 \ldots V'_j; x_{j+1} \ldots x_k\}_{V'_0} \text{ in } P \rightarrow_{\mathscr{R}} P[V_{j+1}/x_{j+1} \ldots V_k/x_k]}$
(ADec)	$\dfrac{\bigwedge_{i=1}^{j} V_i = V'_i}{\text{decrypt } \{|V_1 \ldots V_k|\}_{m^+} \text{ as } \{|V'_1 \ldots V'_j; x_{j+1} \ldots x_k|\}_{m^-} \text{ in } P \rightarrow_{\mathscr{R}} P[V_{j+1}/x_{j+1} \ldots V_k/x_k]}$
(ASig)	$\dfrac{\bigwedge_{i=1}^{j} V_i = V'_i}{\text{decrypt } \{|V_1 \ldots V_k|\}_{m^-} \text{ as } \{|V'_1 \ldots V'_j; x_{j+1} \ldots x_k|\}_{m^+} \text{ in } P \rightarrow_{\mathscr{R}} P[V_{j+1}/x_{j+1} \ldots V_k/x_k]}$
(New)	$\dfrac{P \rightarrow_{\mathscr{R}} P'}{(\nu n)P \rightarrow_{\mathscr{R}} (\nu n)P'}$ (ANew) $\dfrac{P \rightarrow_{\mathscr{R}} P'}{(\nu \pm m)P \rightarrow_{\mathscr{R}} (\nu \pm m)P'}$
(Par)	$\dfrac{P_1 \rightarrow_{\mathscr{R}} P'_1}{P_1 \mid P_2 \rightarrow_{\mathscr{R}} P'_1 \mid P_2}$ (Congr) $\dfrac{P \equiv P' \wedge P' \rightarrow_{\mathscr{R}} P'' \wedge P'' \equiv P'''}{P \rightarrow_{\mathscr{R}} P'''}$

Table 2. Instantiation relation $MP \to_{\mathscr{S}} P$

(ILet)	$\dfrac{MP[X \mapsto S'] \to_{\mathscr{S}} P}{\text{let } X \subseteq S \text{ in } MP \to_{\mathscr{S}} P}$ if $S' \subseteq_{fin} S$
(IIPar)	$\dfrac{MP[i \mapsto a_1] \to_{\mathscr{S}} P_1 \dots MP[i \mapsto a_k] \to_{\mathscr{S}} P_k}{\mid_{i \in \{a_1,\dots,a_k\}} MP \to_{\mathscr{S}} P_1 \mid \dots \mid P_k}$
(IINew)	$\dfrac{MP \to_{\mathscr{S}} P}{(\nu_{\bar{i} \in \{\overline{a_1}\dots\overline{a_k}\}} n_{\overline{ai}}) MP \to_{\mathscr{S}} (\nu\, n_{\overline{aa_1}}) \dots (\nu\, n_{\overline{aa_k}}) P}$
(IIANew)	$\dfrac{MP \to_{\mathscr{S}} P}{(\nu_{\pm \bar{i} \in \{\overline{a_1}\dots\overline{a_k}\}} m_{\overline{ai}}) MP \to_{\mathscr{S}} (\nu \pm m_{\overline{aa_1}}) \dots (\nu\, m_{\overline{aa_k}}) P}$
(IOut)	$\dfrac{MP \to_{\mathscr{S}} P}{\langle ME_1, \dots, ME_k \rangle.MP \to_{\mathscr{S}} \langle ME_1, \dots, ME_k \rangle.P}$
(IInp)	$\dfrac{MP \to_{\mathscr{S}} P}{(ME_1, \dots, ME_j; mx_{j+1}, \dots, mx_k).MP \to_{\mathscr{S}} (ME_1, \dots, ME_j; mx_{j+1}, \dots, mx_k).P}$
(IDec)	$\dfrac{MP \to_{\mathscr{S}} P}{\text{decrypt } ME \text{ as } \{ME_1, \dots, ME_j; mx_{j+1}, \dots, mx_k\}_{ME_0} \text{ in } MP \to_{\mathscr{S}}}$ $\text{decrypt } ME \text{ as } \{ME_1, \dots, ME_j; mx_{j+1}, \dots, mx_k\}_{ME_0} \text{ in } P$
(IADec)	$\dfrac{MP \to_{\mathscr{S}} P}{\text{decrypt } ME \text{ as } \{\mid ME_1, \dots, ME_j; mx_{j+1}, \dots, mx_k \mid\}_{ME_0} \text{ in } MP \to_{\mathscr{S}}}$ $\text{decrypt } ME \text{ as } \{\mid ME_1, \dots, ME_j; mx_{j+1}, \dots, mx_k \mid\}_{ME_0} \text{ in } P$
(INew)	$\dfrac{MP \to_{\mathscr{S}} P}{(\nu\, n_{\overline{a}}) MP \to_{\mathscr{S}} (\nu\, n_{\overline{a}}) P}$
(IRep)	$\dfrac{MP \to_{\mathscr{S}} P}{!MP \to_{\mathscr{S}} !P}$
(INil)	$0 \to_{\mathscr{S}} 0$

And to the right:

(IANew)	$\dfrac{MP \to_{\mathscr{S}} P}{(\nu \pm m_{\overline{a}}) MP \to_{\mathscr{S}} (\nu \pm m_{\overline{a}}) P}$
(IPar)	$\dfrac{MP_1 \to_{\mathscr{S}} P_1 \quad MP_2 \to_{\mathscr{S}} P_2}{MP_1 \mid MP_2 \to_{\mathscr{S}} P_1 \mid P_2}$

evolve. We refer to [2] [4] for a detailed description of the semantics. Notice that a substitution $P[n_1 \mapsto n_2]$ substitutes all the free occurrences of n_1 in P for n_2. Finally, we define values $V \in Val$, which are used in the reduction as expressions without variables $x \in Var$:

$$V ::= n \mid m^+ \mid m^- \mid \{V_1, \dots, V_k\}_{V_0} \mid \{\mid V_1, \dots, V_k \mid\}_{V_0} \tag{1}$$

A *reference monitor* is used to force additional requirements at each step before allowing it to be executed. A *substitution function* is used in the reduction rules, written $P[V/x]$, to substitute a variable x for a value V in the process P.

2.2 Meta Level Calculus

The meta level describes different scenarios in which many principals execute a protocol at the same time, simply running several copies of the processes. The syntax of the meta level is identical to the syntax seen so far, except that each name and each variable are renamed using indexes. Four new processes are introduced to model these scenarios, which use a countable indexing set S to include a set of variables X and $\bar{i}$, as shorthand for $i_1, \dots, i_k$ (a sequence of indexes); the processes are the following:

- $\mid_{i \in S} MP$: the process describes the parallel composition of instances of the process MP where the index i is an element in the set S.
- let $X \subseteq S$ in MP: the process declares a set identifier X which has some values of the index set S in the process MP; the set X can be infinite.
- $(\nu_{\bar{i} \in \bar{S}} n_{\overline{ai}}) MP$, $(\nu_{\pm \bar{i} \in \bar{S}} m_{\overline{ai}}) MP$: the processes describe the restriction of all the names $n_{\overline{ai}}$ and all the key pairs $m_{\overline{ai}}^+$ and $m_{\overline{ai}}^-$ respectively; $\overline{a}$ is a prefix of the index that can be empty.

In this syntax, the process let $X \subseteq S$ in MP is a binder of X, while the process $|_{i \in S} MP$ is a binder of i and the indexed restrictions are binders of names and key pairs.

An instantiation relation, written $MP \rightarrow_{\mathscr{I}} P$, is introduced to describe that a process P is an instance of a meta level process MP, as depicted in Table 2.

3   Control Flow Analysis

In this section we introduce our Control Flow Analysis (CFA) as an extension of [11]. The aim of the CFA is to collect information about the behavior of a process and to store them in some data structures $\mathscr{A}$, called analysis components. To be finite, static analysis is forced to compute approximations rather than exact answers. Therefore the analysis can give false positives but it has to preserve soundness.

We will use Flow Logic settings [11][3] for the specifications and the proofs. It is a formalism for specifying static analysis and it focuses on the relationship between an analysis estimate and the process to be analysed, formally $\mathscr{A} \vDash P$.

Table 3. Analysis of terms and processes

(AN)	$\rho \vDash n : \vartheta$ iff $\lfloor n \rfloor \in \vartheta$

(AN) $\rho \vDash n : \vartheta$ iff $\lfloor n \rfloor \in \vartheta$ (ANp) $\rho \vDash m^{+} : \vartheta$ iff $\lfloor m^{+} \rfloor \in \vartheta$

(ANm) $\rho \vDash m^{-} : \vartheta$ iff $\lfloor m^{-} \rfloor \in \vartheta$ (AVar) $\rho \vDash x : \vartheta$ iff $\rho(\lfloor x \rfloor) \subseteq \vartheta$

(AEnc) $\rho \vDash \{E_1, \ldots, E_k\}_{E_0} : \vartheta$ iff $\bigwedge_{i=0}^{k} \rho \vDash E_i : \vartheta_i \wedge \forall U_0, \ldots, U_k : \bigwedge_{i=0}^{k} U_i \in \vartheta_i \Rightarrow \{U_1, \ldots, U_k\}_{U_0} \in \vartheta$

(AAEnc) $\rho \vDash \{|E_1, \ldots, E_k|\}_{E_0} : \vartheta$ iff $\bigwedge_{i=0}^{k} \rho \vDash E_i : \vartheta_i \wedge \forall U_0, \ldots, U_k : \bigwedge_{i=0}^{k} U_i \in \vartheta_i$
$\Rightarrow \{|U_1, \ldots, U_k|\}_{U_0} \in \vartheta$

(AOut) $\rho, \kappa \vDash \langle E_1, \ldots, E_k \rangle.P$ iff $\bigwedge_{i=1}^{k} \rho \vDash E_i : \vartheta_i \wedge \forall U_1, \ldots, U_k : \bigwedge_{i=1}^{k} U_i \in \vartheta_i$
$\Rightarrow (\langle U_1, \ldots, U_k \rangle \in \kappa \wedge \rho, \kappa \vDash P)$

(AInp) $\rho, \kappa \vDash (E_1, \ldots, E_j; x_{j+1}, \ldots, x_k).P$ iff $\bigwedge_{i=1}^{j} \rho \vDash E_i : \vartheta_i \wedge \forall \langle U_1, \ldots, U_k \rangle \in \kappa :$
$\bigwedge_{i=1}^{j} U_i \in \vartheta_i$
$\Rightarrow \left(\bigwedge_{i=j+1}^{k} U_i \in \rho(\lfloor x_i \rfloor) \wedge \rho, \kappa \vDash P \right)$

(ASDec) $\rho, \kappa \vDash$ decrypt E as $\{E_1, \ldots, E_j; x_{j+1}, \ldots, x_k\}_{E_0}$ in P iff $\rho \vDash E : \vartheta \wedge \bigwedge_{i=0}^{j} \rho \vDash E_i : \vartheta_i \wedge$
$\forall \{U_1, \ldots, U_k\}_{U_0} \in \vartheta \wedge \bigwedge_{i=0}^{j} U_i \in \vartheta_i \Rightarrow (\bigwedge_{i=j+1}^{k} U_i \in \rho(\lfloor x_i \rfloor) \wedge \rho, \kappa \vDash P)$

(AADec) $\rho, \kappa \vDash$ decrypt E as $\{|E_1, \ldots, E_j; x_{j+1}, \ldots, x_k|\}_{E_0}$ in P iff $\rho \vDash E : \vartheta \wedge \bigwedge_{i=0}^{j} \rho \vDash E_i : \vartheta_i \wedge$
$\forall \{|U_1, \ldots, U_k|\}_{U_0} \in \vartheta : \forall U_0' \in \vartheta_0 : \forall (m^+, m^-) : (U_0, U_0') = (\lfloor m^- \rfloor, \lfloor m^+ \rfloor) \wedge$
$\bigwedge_{i=1}^{j} U_i \in \vartheta_i \Rightarrow \left(\bigwedge_{i=j+1}^{k} U_i \in \rho(\lfloor x_i \rfloor) \wedge \rho, \kappa \vDash P \right)$

(AASig) $\rho, \kappa \vDash$ decrypt E as $\{|E_1, \ldots, E_j; x_{j+1}, \ldots, x_k|\}_{E_0}$ in P iff $\rho \vDash E : \vartheta \wedge \bigwedge_{i=0}^{j} \rho \vDash E_i : \vartheta_i \wedge$
$\forall \{|U_1, \ldots, U_k|\}_{U_0} \in \vartheta : \forall U_0' \in \vartheta_0 : \forall (m^+, m^-) : (U_0, U_0') = (\lfloor m^+ \rfloor, \lfloor m^- \rfloor) \wedge$
$\bigwedge_{i=1}^{j} U_i \in \vartheta_i \Rightarrow \left(\bigwedge_{i=j+1}^{k} U_i \in \rho(\lfloor x_i \rfloor) \wedge \rho, \kappa \vDash P \right)$

(ANew) $\rho, \kappa \vDash (\nu n)P$ iff $\rho, \kappa \vDash P$ (AANew) $\rho, \kappa \vDash (\nu \pm m)P$ iff $\rho, \kappa \vDash P$

(APar) $\rho, \kappa \vDash P_1 | P_2$ iff $\rho, \kappa \vDash P_1 \wedge \rho, \kappa \vDash P_2$ (ARep) $\rho, \kappa \vDash !P$ iff $\rho, \kappa \vDash P$

(ANil) $\rho, \kappa \vDash 0$ iff *true*

CFA abstracts the executions and represents only some aspects of the behavior of a process which can also be infinite. We will prove the correctness of the analysis by showing that the analysis components $\mathscr{A}$ are such that the property they represent also holds when the process evolves.

Formally:

$$\mathscr{A} \models P \wedge P \rightarrow P' \Rightarrow \mathscr{A} \models P' \tag{2}$$

The Flow Logic specifications use the verbose format "$\mathscr{A} \models P$ iff a logic formula $\mathscr{F}$ holds" or the succinct format "$\mathscr{A} \models P : A'$ iff a logic formula $\mathscr{F}$ holds", i.e. they record information about a process globally or locally, respectively.

The analysis components record canonical values from the set $\lfloor Val \rfloor$ ranged over by U to represent values generated by the same restriction. The component $\kappa \in \mathscr{P}(\lfloor Val \rfloor^*)$ collects the tuples of canonical values corresponding to the values communicated in the global network while $\rho : \lfloor Var \rfloor \rightarrow \mathscr{P}(\lfloor Val \rfloor)$ records the canonical values corresponding to the values that variables may become bound. A predicate $\rho, \kappa \models P$ says that ρ and κ are valid analysis results describing the behavior of P. To analyse the expressions it is used the form $\rho \models E : \vartheta$ to describe a set of canonical values $\vartheta \in \mathscr{P}(\lfloor Val \rfloor)$ that the expression E may evaluate.

The analysis of terms and processes is described in Table 3. The rules (AN), (ANp) and (ANm) say that names may evaluate to themselves iff the canonical names are in ϑ. The rule (AVar) says that variables may evaluate to the values described by ρ for the corresponding canonical variable. The rules (AEnc) and (AAEnc) use the analysis predicate recursively to evaluate all the subexpressions in the encryption and they require ϑ to contain all the encrypted values that can be formed combining the values that subexpressions may evaluate to. The rule (AOut) says that the expressions are evaluated and it is required that all the combinations of the values found by this evaluation are recorded in κ. The rule (AInp) says that the first j expressions in the input construct are evaluated to be the sets ϑ_i for $i = 1, \ldots, j$; if the pattern match with the values in κ is successful, the remaining values of the k-tuple is recorded in ρ as possible binding of the variables and the continuation process is analysed. The rule (ASDec), (AADec) and (AASig) evaluate the expression E into the set ϑ and the first j expressions in the decryption constructs are evaluated to be the sets ϑ_i for $i = 1, \ldots, j$; if the pattern match with the values in κ is successful, the remaining values of the k-tuple is recorded in ρ as possible binding of the variables and the continuation process is analysed. Notice that the original syntax [5] [8] uses only the rule (AADec) to define both asymmetric decryption and signature while we introduce here two rules imposing an order in the choice of the keys to make our analysis more efficient. The rule (ANew), (AANew), (APar) and (ARep) require that the subprocesses are analysed. The rule (ANil) deals with the trivial case.

Whenever the requirements hold, the continuation process is analysed.

The analysis is also defined for the meta level as an extension of the analysis seen so far and it takes the form

$$\rho, \kappa \models_\Gamma M \tag{3}$$

where $\Gamma : SetID \cup \mathscr{P}(Index_{fin}) \rightarrow \mathscr{P}(Index_{fin})$ is a mapping from set identifiers to finite sets of indexes.

Table 4. The meta level analysis $\rho, \kappa \vDash_\Gamma M$: meta level constructs

(MLet)	$\rho, \kappa \vDash_\Gamma \text{let } X \subseteq S \text{ in } M$	iff $\rho, \kappa \vDash_{\Gamma[X \mapsto S']} M$ where $S' \subseteq_{fin} \Gamma(S)$ and $\lfloor S' \rfloor = \lfloor \Gamma(S) \rfloor$
(MIPar)	$\rho, \kappa \vDash_\Gamma \mid_{i \in S} M$	iff $\bigwedge_{a \in \Gamma(S)} \rho, \kappa \vDash_\Gamma M[i \mapsto a]$
(MINew)	$\rho, \kappa \vDash_\Gamma (\nu_{i \in \tilde{S}} n_{\overline{ai}}) M$	iff $\rho, \kappa \vDash_\Gamma M$
(MIANew)	$\rho, \kappa \vDash_\Gamma (\nu_{\pm i \in \tilde{S}} m_{\overline{ai}}) M$	iff $\rho, \kappa \vDash_\Gamma M$

Table 5. The attacker's capabilities

(1) The attacker may learn by eavesdropping

$$\bigwedge_{k \in \mathscr{A}_\kappa} \forall \langle V_1, \ldots, V_k \rangle \in \kappa : \bigwedge_{i=1}^k V_i \in \rho(z_\bullet)$$

(2) The attacker may learn by decrypting messages with keys already known

$$\bigwedge_{k \in \mathscr{A}_{Enc}} \forall \{V_1, \ldots, V_k\}_{V_0} \in \rho(z_\bullet) : V_0 \in \rho(z_\bullet) \Rightarrow \bigwedge_{i=1}^k V_i \in \rho(z_\bullet)$$

$$\bigwedge_{k \in \mathscr{A}_{Enc}} \forall \{|V_1, \ldots, V_k|\}_{m^+} \in \rho(z_\bullet) : m^- \in \rho(z_\bullet) \Rightarrow \bigwedge_{i=1}^k V_i \in \rho(z_\bullet)$$

$$\bigwedge_{k \in \mathscr{A}_{Enc}} \forall \{|V_1, \ldots, V_k|\}_{m^-} \in \rho(z_\bullet) : m^+ \in \rho(z_\bullet) \Rightarrow \bigwedge_{i=1}^k V_i \in \rho(z_\bullet)$$

(3) The attacker may construct new encryptions using the keys known

$$\bigwedge_{k \in \mathscr{A}_{Enc}} \forall V_0, \ldots, V_k : \bigwedge_{i=0}^k V_i \in \rho(z_\bullet) \Rightarrow \{V_1, \ldots, V_k\}_{V_0} \in \rho(z_\bullet)$$

$$\bigwedge_{k \in \mathscr{A}_{Enc}} \forall m^+, V_1, \ldots, V_k : m^+ \in \rho(z_\bullet) \wedge \bigwedge_{i=1}^k V_i \in \rho(z_\bullet) \Rightarrow \{|V_1, \ldots, V_k|\}_{m^+} \in \rho(z_\bullet)$$

$$\bigwedge_{k \in \mathscr{A}_{Enc}} \forall m^-, V_1, \ldots, V_k : m^- \in \rho(z_\bullet) \wedge \bigwedge_{i=1}^k V_i \in \rho(z_\bullet) \Rightarrow \{|V_1, \ldots, V_k|\}_{m^-} \in \rho(z_\bullet)$$

(4) The attacker may actively forge new communications

$$\bigwedge_{k \in \mathscr{A}_\kappa} \forall V_1, \ldots, V_k : \bigwedge_{i=1}^k V_i \in \rho(z_\bullet) \Rightarrow \langle V_1, \ldots, V_k \rangle \in \kappa$$

(5) The attacker initially has some knowledge

$$\{n_\bullet, m_\bullet^\pm\} \cup \mathscr{N}_f \subseteq \rho(z_\bullet)$$

The meta level analysis is defined in Table 4 for the new constructs. The rule (MLet) updates Γ with the mapping $X \mapsto S'$, where S' is required to be finite and it has the same canonical names as the set S. The rule (MIPar) expresses that the analysis holds for all the processes where the index i is substituted by all the elements in $\Gamma(S)$. The rules (MINew) and (MIANew) ignore the restriction operators.

3.1   The Attacker

The attacker is unique and runs its protocol $P_\bullet$ following the Dolev-Yao formula $\mathscr{F}_{RM}^{DY}$ [7] shown in Table 5, which explains its powers. We write $P_{sys} \mid P_\bullet$ to show that an arbitrary attacker controls the whole network while principals exchange messages using the protocol. A protocol process P_{sys} has type whenever it is close, all its free names are in $\mathscr{N}_f$, all the arities of the sent or received messages are in $\mathscr{A}_\kappa$ and all the arities of the encrypted or decrypted messages are in $\mathscr{A}_{Enc}$. These three sets are finite, like $\mathscr{N}_c$ and $\mathscr{X}_c$, used to collect all the names and all the variables respectively in the process P_{sys}. The attacker uses a new name, $n_\bullet \notin \mathscr{N}_c$, and a new variable, $z_\bullet \notin \mathscr{X}_c$, which do not overlap the names and the variables used by the legitimate principals. It is again considered a process with finitely many canonical names and variables. A formula $\mathscr{F}_{RM}^{DY}$ of the type $(\mathscr{N}_f, \mathscr{A}_\kappa, \mathscr{A}_{Enc})$, which is capable of characterizing the potential effect of all the attackers $P_\bullet$ of the type $(\mathscr{N}_f, \mathscr{A}_\kappa, \mathscr{A}_{Enc})$, is defined as the conjunction of the components in Table 5.

4 Non-repudiation Analysis

Non-repudiation guarantees that the principals exchanging messages cannot falsely deny having sent or received the messages. This is done using evidences [9] that allow to decide unquestionably in favor of the fair principal whenever there is a dispute. In particular, non-repudiation of origin provides the recipient with proof of origin while non-repudiation of receipt provides the originator with proof of receipt. Evidences [15] should have verifiable origin, integrity and validity.

The syntax of the process calculus LYSA has to be extended to guarantee, given a protocol, the non-repudiation property, i.e. authentication (only the sender of the message can create it), integrity and freshness. This is done using electronic signatures and unique identifiers for users and sessions. To this aim, we introduce two sets, used in the body of the messages to collect information that will be useful to perform the analysis: *ID*, where $id \in ID$ is a unique identifier for a principal, and *NR*, where $nr \in NR$ says that non-repudiation property is required for that part of the message nr. To include these sets in our analysis, a redefinition of the syntax is required, and this is done by applying a function called $\mathscr{G}$ to the processes of the protocol analysed, that acts recursively on the subprocesses and redefines subterms using another function, called $\mathscr{F}$ (see Table 6). In the new syntax *id*s are attached whenever an asymmetric key appears and a session identifier u is attached to each encryption and decryption; parallel composition and replication are modified to assign different *id*s to different processes. The rule

Table 6. Functions $\mathscr{F}$ and $\mathscr{G}$

$\mathscr{F} : E \times ID \to \varepsilon$

- $\mathscr{F}(n, id) = n$ - $\mathscr{F}(x, id) = x$
- $\mathscr{F}(m^+, id) = [m^+]_{id}$ - $\mathscr{F}(m^-, id) = [m^-]_{id}$
- $\mathscr{F}(\{E_1, \ldots, E_k\}_{E_0}, id) = \{\mathscr{F}(E_1, id), \ldots, \mathscr{F}(E_k, id)\}_{\mathscr{F}(E_0, id)}$
- $\mathscr{F}(\{| E_1, \ldots, E_k |\}_{E_0}, id) = \{| \mathscr{F}(E_1, id), \ldots, \mathscr{F}(E_k, id) |\}_{\mathscr{F}(E_0, id)}^u$

$\mathscr{G} : P \times ID \to \mathscr{P}$

- $\mathscr{G}(\langle E_1, \ldots, E_k \rangle. \mathscr{P}, id) = \langle \mathscr{F}(E_1, id), \ldots, \mathscr{F}(E_k, id) \rangle. \mathscr{G}(P, id)$
- $\mathscr{G}((E_1, \ldots, E_j; x_{j+1}, \ldots, x_k). P, id) = (\mathscr{F}(E_1, id), \ldots, \mathscr{F}(E_j, id); x_{j+1}, \ldots, x_k). \mathscr{G}(P, id)$
- $\mathscr{G}(\text{decrypt } E \text{ as } \{E_1, \ldots, E_j; x_{j+1}, \ldots, x_k\}_{E_0} \text{ in } P, id) =$
  decrypt $\mathscr{F}(E, id)$ as $\{\mathscr{F}(E_1, id), \ldots, \mathscr{F}(E_j, id); x_{j+1}, \ldots, x_k\}_{\mathscr{F}(E_0, id)}$ in $\mathscr{G}(P, id)$
- $\mathscr{G}(\text{decrypt } E \text{ as } \{| E_1, \ldots, E_j; x_{j+1}, \ldots, x_k |\}_{E_0}^u \text{ in } P, id) =$
  decrypt $\mathscr{F}(E, id)$ as $\{| \mathscr{F}(E_1, id), \ldots, \mathscr{F}(E_j, id); x_{j+1}, \ldots, x_k |\}_{\mathscr{F}(E_0, id)}^u$ in $\mathscr{G}(P, id)$
- $\mathscr{G}((v\, n)P, id) = (v\, n)\mathscr{G}(P, id)$ - $\mathscr{G}((v \pm m)P, id) = (v \pm [m]_{id})\mathscr{G}(P, id)$
- $\mathscr{G}(P \mid Q, id) = \mathscr{G}(P, id) \mid \mathscr{G}(Q, id')$ - $\mathscr{G}(!P, id) = [!P]_{id}$
- $\mathscr{G}(0, id) = 0$

$!P \equiv P \mid !P$ has to be removed because the structural equivalence does not hold in this case. The replication process evolves in $\mathscr{G}(P, id) \mid \mathscr{G}(!P, id')$, where id' is a unique user identifier by the replication rule. Finally, we have to add the following annotations to the signatures:

- [from id] is associated to encryption and it means that the recipient expects a message from id.
- [check NR] is associated to decryption and it means that for all the elements of the set NR, non-repudiation property must be guaranteed. It is interesting to notice that the elements in the set NR can specify a part of the message, not necessarily the whole message, according to the definition of non-repudiation.

The syntax of asymmetric encryption becomes $\{|\varepsilon_1, \ldots, \varepsilon_k|\}_{\varepsilon_0}^{u}$ [from id] while the syntax of asymmetric decryption becomes decrypt ε as $\{|\varepsilon_1, \ldots, \varepsilon_j; x_{j+1}, \ldots, x_k|\}_{\varepsilon_0}^{u}$ [check NR] in $\mathscr{P}$.

Notice that the annotation [from id] and the label u have a different role in the analysis. The first says that the principal who encrypted the message must be the same specified in the label associated to the private key used, while the second expresses that the message has to belong to a precise session.

To guarantee the dynamic property, the values have to be redefined into $NVal$:

$$NV ::= n \mid [m^+]_{id} \mid [m^-]_{id} \mid \{NV_1, \ldots, NV_k\}_{NV_0} \mid \{|NV_1, \ldots, NV_k|\}_{NV_0}^{u} [\text{from } id] \quad (4)$$

The reference monitor semantics $P \rightarrow_{RM} P'$ defines RM as

$$RM(id, id', u, u', \{NV_1, \ldots, NV_n\}, NR)$$
$$= (id = id' \wedge u = u' \wedge \forall nr \in NR : nr \in \{NV_1, \ldots, NV_n\})$$

where $\{NV_1, \ldots, NV_n\}$ is a set of redefined values for non-repudiation analysis. The main difference between the standard and the redefined semantics is expressed by the rule used to verify a signature, which ensures that the non-repudiation property holds for the elements specified by the annotations:

$$\frac{\bigwedge_{i=1}^{j} NV_i = NV_i' \wedge RM(id, id', u, u', \{NV_{j+1}, \ldots, NV_k\}, NR)}{\text{decrypt } \{|NV_1, \ldots, NV_k|\}_{[m^-]_{id}}^{u} [\text{from } id'] \text{ as } \{|NV_1', \ldots, NV_j'; x_{j+1}, \ldots, x_k|\}_{[m^+]_{id}}^{u'}}$$
$$[\text{check } NR] \text{ in } \mathscr{P} \rightarrow_{RM} \mathscr{P}[NV_{j+1}/x_{j+1}, \ldots, NV_k/x_k]$$

Definition 1 (Dynamic Non-Repudiation). *A process* $\mathscr{P}$ *ensures dynamic non-repudiation property if for all the executions* $\mathscr{P} \rightarrow^* \mathscr{P}' \rightarrow_{RM} \mathscr{P}''$ *then* $id = id'$ *and* $u = u'$ *and* $\forall nr \in NR : nr \in \{NV_1, \ldots, NV_k\}$ *when* $\mathscr{P}' \rightarrow_{RM} \mathscr{P}''$ *is derived using* *(ASig) on the asymmetric decryption construct.*

Definition 1 says that an extended process $\mathscr{P}$ ensures non-repudiation property if there is no violation in any of its execution.

4.1 Static Property

A component $\psi \subseteq \mathscr{P}(NR)$ will collect all the labels nr such that the non-repudiation property for the element nr is possibly violated. The $\propto$ operator is introduced to ignore the extension of the syntax. The non-repudiation property has to be checked whenever a signature is verified, therefore the rule (ASig) becomes the following:

$$\rho, \kappa, \psi \vDash \text{decrypt } \varepsilon \text{ as } \{| \varepsilon_1, \ldots, \varepsilon_j; x_{j+1}, \ldots, x_k |\}_{\varepsilon_0}^{u'} [\text{check } NR] \text{ in } \mathscr{P}$$

$$\text{iff } \rho \vDash \varepsilon : \vartheta \wedge \bigwedge_{i=0}^{j} \rho \vDash \varepsilon_i : \vartheta_i \wedge \forall \{| NV_1, \ldots, NV_k |\}_{NV_0}^{u} [\text{from } \lfloor id \rfloor] \propto \vartheta :$$

$$\forall NV_0' \propto \vartheta_0 : \forall m^+, m^-, id, id' : (NV_0, NV_0') = ([\lfloor m^+ \rfloor]_{id'}, [\lfloor m^- \rfloor]_{id'})$$

$$\wedge \bigwedge_{i=1}^{j} NV_i \propto \vartheta_i \Rightarrow (\bigwedge_{i=j+1}^{k} NV_i \in \rho(\lfloor x_i \rfloor) \wedge \rho, \kappa, \psi \vDash \mathscr{P} \wedge \forall nr \in NR :$$

$$(id \neq id' \vee u \neq u' \vee nr \notin \{NV_{j+1}, \ldots, NV_k\}) \Rightarrow \lfloor nr \rfloor \in \psi).$$

To prove the correctness of our analysis we must prove that it respects the extended operational semantics of LYSA, i.e. if $\rho, \kappa, \psi \vDash \mathscr{P}$ then the triple (ρ, κ, ψ) is a valid estimate for all the states passed through in a computation of $\mathscr{P}$. Furthermore, we prove that when ψ is empty, then the reference monitor is useless.

Theorem 1 (Correctness of the non-repudiation analysis). *If* $\rho, \kappa, \psi \vDash \mathscr{P}$ *and* $\psi = \emptyset$ *then* $\mathscr{P}$ *ensures* static non-repudiation.

The proof of this theorem, as well as the proof of the next ones, can be found in [4].

4.2   The Attacker

In the setup of $\mathscr{P} \mid \mathscr{P}_\bullet$, the attacker process $\mathscr{P}_\bullet$ has to be annotated with the extended syntax. We will use a unique label $u_\bullet$ to indicate the session and a unique label $id_\bullet$ to indicate the encryption place used by the attacker. The Dolev-Yao condition has to be redefined to be used for the non-repudiation analysis.

The main enhancement with the usual LYSA attacker can be seen in rule (3.): whenever the attacker is able to generate an encrypted message with a known key, the receiver checks the id of the sender, and, in case the latter does not correspond to the intended one, the component ψ becomes non empty, as a signal of a non-repudiation violation:

$$\bigwedge_{k \in \mathscr{A}_{Enc}} \forall [m^-]_{id}, NV_1, \ldots, NV_k : [m^-]_{id} \in \rho(z_\bullet) \wedge \bigwedge_{i=1}^{k} NV_i \in \rho(z_\bullet)$$

$$\Rightarrow \{| NV_1, \ldots, NV_k |\}_{[m^-]_{id_\bullet}}^{u_\bullet} \in \rho(z_\bullet) \wedge \forall \text{ decrypt } \{| NV_1', \ldots, NV_k' |\}_{[m^-]_{id_\bullet}}^{u_\bullet} [\text{from } id'] \text{ as}$$

$$\{| NV_1'', \ldots, NV_j''; x_{j+1}, \ldots, x_k |\}_{[m^+]_{id''}}^{u''} [\text{check } NR] \text{ in } \mathscr{P} :$$

$$\forall nr \in NR \, ((id' \neq id_\bullet \vee u'' \neq u_\bullet \vee nr \notin \{NV_{j+1}', \ldots, NV_k'\}) \Rightarrow \lfloor nr \rfloor \in \psi)$$

Theorem 2 (Correctness of Dolev-Yao Condition). *If* (ρ, κ, ψ) *satisfies* $\mathscr{F}_{RM}^{DY}$ *of type* $(\mathscr{N}_f, \mathscr{A}_\kappa, \mathscr{A}_{Enc})$ *then* $\rho, \kappa, \psi \vDash \overline{Q}$ *for all attackers Q of extended type* $(\{z_\bullet\}, \mathscr{N}_f \cup \{n_\bullet\}, \mathscr{A}_\kappa, \mathscr{A}_{Enc})$.

The theorem says that the redefined Dolev-Yao condition holds.

Theorem 3. *If* $\mathscr{P}$ *guarantees static non-repudiation then* $\mathscr{P}$ *guarantees dynamic non-repudiation.*

Example 2. **Protocol 1.** The encoding with annotations of the protocol by Cederquist, Corin, and Dashti introduced in Example 1 becomes:

$$\text{let } X \subseteq S \text{ in } (\nu_{\pm i \in X} [AK_i]_{I_i})(\nu \pm TTP)($$

$$|_{i \in X} |_{j \in X} \quad !(\nu SK_{ij})(\nu H_{ij})(\nu M_{ij})\langle \{M_{ij}\}_{SK_{ij}}, \{| EOO_M |\}_{[AK_i^-]_{I_i}}^{u_{ij}} [\text{from } I_i] \rangle.$$

$$(;xEORM_{ij}).\text{decrypt } xEORM_{ij} \text{ as } \{| \{| EOO_M |\}_{[AK_i^-]_{I_i}}^{u_{ij}} [\text{from } I_i] |\}_{[AK_j^+]_{I_j}}^{u_{ij}}$$

$$[\text{check } \{|EOO_M|\}] \text{ in } \langle SK_{ij} \rangle.$$
$$(;xEORK_{ij}).\text{decrypt } xEORK_{ij} \text{ as } \{|I_i, H_{ij}, SK_{ij};|\}^{u_{ij}}_{[AK_j^+]_{I_j}} [\text{check } H_{ij}, SK_{ij}] \text{ in } 0$$
$$|_{i \in X}|_{j \in X} \quad !(;xEnMsg_{ij}, xEOOM_{ij}).$$
$$\text{decrypt } xEOOM_{ij} \text{ as } \{|I_j, TTP; xH_{ij}, xTTP|\}^{u_{ij}}_{[AK_i^+]_{I_i}} [\text{check } xH_{ij}] \text{ in}$$
$$\langle \{|xEOOM_{ij}|\}^{u_{ij}}_{[AK_j^-]_{I_j}} [\text{from } I_j] \rangle.(;xSK_{ij}).$$
$$\text{decrypt } xEnMsg_{ij} \text{ as } \{xMsg_{ij}\}_{xSK_{ij}} \text{ in } \langle \{|I_i, xH_{ij}, xSK_{ij}|\} \rangle.0)$$

where $EOO_M = I_j, TTP, H_{ij}, \{|SK_{ij}, I_i|\}^{u_{ij}}_{[TTP^+]_{TTP}} [\text{from } \emptyset]$

Protocol 2 (Zhou-Gollmann [14]):

$$A \rightarrow B: \quad f_{NRO}, B, L, C, NRO$$
$$B \rightarrow A: \quad f_{NRR}, A, L, NRR$$
$$A \rightarrow TTP: \quad f_{SUB}, B, L, K, sub\_K$$
$$B \leftrightarrow TTP: \quad f_{CON}, A, B, L, K, con\_K$$
$$A \leftrightarrow TTP: \quad f_{CON}, A, B, L, K, con\_K$$

The result of the analysis of Protocol 1 shows that a possible flaw may arise. In fact, it does not use labels to identify the session, and this is why our analysis says that this protocol does not guarantee non-repudiation property. However the protocol is correct, because of an implicit additional assumption on the uniqueness of the keys, which prevents from replay attacks. On the other side, Protocol 2 passes the analysis and this guarantees that it is secure with respect to non-repudiation.

5   Conclusions and Future Works

This paper extends the work by M. Buchholtz and H. Gao who defined a suite of analyses for security protocols, namely authentication, confidentiality, freshness, simple and complex type flaws. The annotations we introduce allow to express non-repudiation also for part of the message: this allow to tune the analysis focussing on relevant components. It results that the CFA framework developed for the process calculus LYSA can be extended to security properties by identifying suitable annotations, thus re-using most of the theoretical work.

References

1. Bella, G., Paulson, L.C.: Mechanical proofs about a non-repudiation protocol. In: Boulton, R.J., Jackson, P.B. (eds.) TPHOLs 2001. LNCS, vol. 2152, pp. 91–104. Springer, Heidelberg (2001)
2. Bodei, C., Buchholtz, M., Degano, P., Nielson, F., Nielson, H.R.: Static validation of security protocols. Journal of Computer Security, 347–390 (2005)
3. Braghin, C., Cortesi, A., Focardi, R.: Information flow security in boundary ambients. Inf. Comput. 206(2-4), 460–489 (2008)
4. Brusò, M., Cortesi, A.: Non-repudiation analysis using LYSA with annotations. CS Tech. Report, Univ. Ca Foscari. Tech. rep. (2008),
http://www.unive.it/nqcontent.cfm?a_id=5144#rapporti08
5. Buchholtz, M., Lyngby, K.: Automated analysis of security in networking systems. Ph. d. thesis proposal, Tech. rep. (2004), http://www.imm.dtu.dk/~mib/thesis

6. Cederquist, Corin, Dashti: On the quest for impartiality: Design and analysis of a fair non-repudiation protocol. In: ICIS 2005. LNCS. Springer, Heidelberg (2005)
7. Dolev, D., Yao, A.C.: On the security of public key protocols. Tech. rep., Stanford, CA (1981)
8. Gao, H.: Analysis Of Protocols By Annotations. Ph. D. Thesis, Informatics and Mathematical Modelling, Technical University of Denmark (2008)
9. Gollmann, D.: Computer security. John Wiley & Sons, Inc., New York (1999)
10. Kremer, S., Raskin, J.F.: A game-based verification of non-repudiation and fair exchange protocols. Journal of Computer Security, 551–565 (2001)
11. Nielson, F., Nielson, H.R., Hankin, C.: Principles of Program Analysis. Springer, New York (1999)
12. Schneider, S.: Formal analysis of a non-repudiation protocol. In: 11th IEEE Computer Security Foundations Workshop, p. 54 (1998)
13. Schneider, S., Holloway, R.: Security properties and csp. In: IEEE Symp. Security and Privacy, pp. 174–187. IEEE Computer Society Press, Los Alamitos (1996)
14. Zhou, J., Gollmann, D.: A fair non-repudiation protocol. IEEE Computer Society Press, Los Alamitos (1996)
15. Zhou, J., Gollmann, D.: Evidence and non-repudiation. J. Netw. Comput. Appl. 20(3), 267–281 (1997), http://dx.doi.org/10.1006/jnca.1997.0056
16. Zhou, J., Gollmann, D.: Towards verification of non-repudiation protocols. In: Proceedings of International Refinement Workshop and Formal Methods Pacific. Springer, Heidelberg (1998)

A Provably Secure Secret Handshake with Dynamic Controlled Matching*

Alessandro Sorniotti and Refik Molva

SAP Research and Institut Eurécom
`firstname.lastname@eurecom.fr`

Abstract. A Secret Handshake is a protocol that allows two users to mutually verify one another's properties, and in case of simultaneous matching, to share a key used to secure subsequent communications. In this paper, we present the first Secret Handshake scheme that allows dynamic matching of properties under stringent security requirements: in particular, the right to prove and to verify is strictly under the control of an authority. This work merges characteristics of Secret Handshake with features peculiar to Secure Matchmaking.

1 Introduction

Parties cooperating in hostile networked environments often need to establish an initial trust. Trust establishment can be very delicate when it involves the exchange of sensitive information, such as affiliation to a secret society or to an intelligence agency. Two mechanisms, *Secret Handshakes* and *Secure Matchmaking*, have tackled this problem, coming up with solutions for secure initial exchange between mistrusting principals. The relevance of this problem as a research topic is evidenced by the number of recent publications on the subject [1,10,11,15,16].

A *Secret Handshake*, first introduced by Balfanz et al. in [3], is a mechanism devised for two users to simultaneously prove to each other possession of a *property*, for instance membership to a certain group. The ability to prove and verify is strictly controlled by a certification authority, that issues *property credentials* and *matching references* respectively allowing to prove to another user, and to verify another user's, possession of a property. Users are not able to perform a successful handshake without the appropriate credentials and matching references; in addition protocol exchanges are often untraceable and anonymous. Most of the Secret Handshake schemes available in the literature only allow for the matching of own group membership.

Matchmaking protocols, presented first in [2], solve the same problem in a slightly different setting: users express "wishes" about the property expected from the other communicating party, and the communication is established only if both users' wishes are mutually matched. The main difference from Secret Handshakes, is the ability of

---

* This work has been partially supported by the SOCIALNETS project, grant agreement number 217141, funded by the EC seventh framework programme theme FP7-ICT-2007-8.2 for Pervasive Adaptation (see http://www.social-nets.eu/ for further details), by the Seventh Framework Programme IST Project TAS^3, grant agreement number 216287, and by the Sixth Framework Programme IST Project WASP, contract number IST-034963.

D. Gritzalis and J. Lopez (Eds.): SEC 2009, IFIP AICT 297, pp. 330–341, 2009.
© IFIP International Federation for Information Processing 2009

a Matchmaking user to set credential and matching reference, thus freely choosing the properties object of the match.

Recently, Ateniese et al. presented in [1] a scheme that allows Secret Handshake with dynamic matching, allowing to verify the presence of properties different from the user's own. This scheme is somewhat in between Secret Handshakes and Secure Matchmaking protocols. It inherits from secret handshake the need for credentials issued by an authority; however, the choice of the property to be verified in the other party is left at the discretion of the verifying user, as in Secure Matchmaking.

In this paper, we present the first Secret Handshake scheme with *dynamic controlled matching*: users are required to possess credentials and matching references issued by a trusted certification authority in order to be able to prove and to verify possession of a given property. Therefore the certification authority retains the control over who can prove what and who can disclose which credentials. However verification is dynamic, in that it is not restricted to own property, as opposed to [3,7,13,16,17].

This new scheme is of clear practical use. For instance, it fulfills the requirements identified by the EU Project R4EGov [9]. In one of the project's use cases, EU justice forces cooperate with one another in order to solve cross-boundary criminal cases. EU regulations define official processes that must imperatively be followed by operating officers: in particular, these processes mandate which institutions must cooperate upon each particular case. During such collaboration, for instance, a member of France's *Ministère de la Défense* must cooperate with a member of the *Bundesnachrichtendienst*, Germany's intelligence service, to investigate on an alleged internal scandal. The two officers may need to meet secretly, and authenticate themselves on-the-fly. Both are definitely reluctant to disclose their affiliation and purpose to anybody but the intended recipient.

It is evident that they cannot use matchmaking or plain secret handshake: the former does not offer any certification on the exchanged properties, the latter only allows matching within the same organization. Handshakes with dynamic matching too fall short of providing a suitable solution for the problem. The freedom of matching any property gives too much liberty to the officials, who must instead strictly abide by EU regulations that mandate which institution must cooperate on a case-by-case basis. Indeed, these officials are acting on behalf of the State and of the people: they must follow rules and ought not make personal choices.

To this end, we propose a novel cryptographic scheme, called SecureMatching, that allows *an authorized prover* to convince *an authorized verifier* that she owns a property (such as group membership). Our work thus addresses requirements that are not met by existing Secret Handshake and Matchmaking protocols, by combining the mandatory control of a third party over credentials and matching references – akin to Secret Handshakes – with the dynamic matching features of Matchmaking. In Section 4 we show, by means of reductionist proofs, that this primitive is secure under the random oracle model, under the assumption that the Bilinear Decisional Diffie-Hellman (BDDH) problem is hard. Finally, we show how to use SecureMatching to build a full-fledged Secret Handshake scheme with dynamic controlled matching.

2   Related Work

Secret Handshakes are first introduced in 2003 by Balfanz et al. [3] as mechanisms designed to prove group membership, and share a secret key, between two fellow group members. The purpose of these protocols is – as pointed out in [16] – to model in a cryptographic protocol the folklore of real handshakes between members of exclusive societies, or guilds.

Since this early work, many papers have further investigated the subject, considerably advancing the state of the art. New schemes have been introduced, achieving for instance reusable credentials (the possibility to generate multiple protocol exchanges out of a single credential with no loss in untraceability) and dynamic matchings (the ability to verify membership for groups different from one's own). Castelluccia et al. in [7] introduce the concept of CA-Oblivious encryption and show how to build a Secret Handshake scheme from such a primitive. Users are equipped with credentials and matching references (in this particular case embodied by a public key and a trapdoor) that allow them to pass off as a group member and to detect one. In [13], Meadows introduces a scheme that is similar to Secret Handshakes, despite the fact that the security requirements are slightly different – for instance, untraceability is not considered. In [10], Hoepman presents a protocol, based on a modified Diffie-Hellman key exchange, to test for shared group membership, allowing users to be a member of multiple groups. In [16], Vergnaud presents a secret handshake scheme based on RSA. In [17], Xu and Yung present the first secret handshake scheme that achieves unlinkability with reusable credentials: previous schemes had to rely upon multiple one-time credentials being issued by the certification authority. However, the presented scheme only offers a weaker anonymity. In [11], Jarecki, Kim and Tsudik introduce the concept of affiliation-hiding authenticated key exchange, very similar to group-membership secret handshakes; the authors study the security of their scheme under an interesting perspective, allowing the attacker to schedule protocol instances in an arbitrary way, thus including MITM attacks and the like. However their scheme is not suitable in our context, since it only allows to verify own group membership and does not consider untraceability of protocol exchanges.

A closely related topic is secure Matchmaking, introduced by Baldwin and Gramlich in [2]. In [18], Zhang and Needham propose a protocol for on-line matchmaking, based on an on-line database service available to all users. In [15], Shin and Gligor present a new matchmaking protocol based on password-authenticated key exchanges [5].

In [1], Ateniese et al. present the first Secret Handshake protocol that allows for matching of properties different from the user's own. Property credentials are issued by a certificate authority. However, the authors study the protocol in the Matchmaking setting, where the matching reference is a low entropy keyword that can be set at each user's discretion.

A related topic is represented by oblivious signature-based envelopes (OSBEs), introduced by Li et al. in [12]; using OSBE, a sender can send an envelope to a receiver, with the assurance that the receiver will only be able to open it if he holds the signature on an agreed-upon message. Nasserian and Tsudik in [14] argue – albeit with no proofs – that two symmetric instances of OSBE may yield a Secret Handshake. The scheme we introduce in Section 3.2 shares some similarities with OSBE, although some substantial differences are present: OSBE does not consider unlinkability and anonymity, as it requires the explicit agreement on a signature beforehand.

3 The Scheme

In this Section we introduce SecureMatching, a novel cryptographic scheme that allows a user to convince a verifier that she owns a given property. We afterward leverage on this building block to create a Secret Handshake protocol used to secure the mutual exchange of property credentials and to share a common key in case of mutual successful verification of properties.

3.1 Preliminaries

We assume that the system includes users from a set of users $\mathcal{U}$. Each user can possess properties drawn from a set of properties $\mathcal{P}$. Given a security parameter k, let $(\mathbb{G}_1, +)$ and $(\mathbb{G}_2, *)$ be two groups of order q for some large prime q, where the bit-size of q is determined by the security parameter k. Our scheme uses a computable, non-degenerate bilinear map $\hat{e} : \mathbb{G}_1 \times \mathbb{G}_1 \to \mathbb{G}_2$ for which the *Computational Diffie-Hellman Problem (CDH)* problem is assumed to be hard. Modified Weil or Tate pairings on supersingular elliptic curves are examples of such maps. We recall that a bilinear pairing satisfies the following three properties:

- Bilinear: for $P, Q \in \mathbb{G}_1$ and for $a, b \in \mathbb{Z}_q^*$, $\hat{e}(aP, bQ) = \hat{e}(P, Q)^{ab}$
- Non-degenerate: $\hat{e}(P, P) \neq 1$ is a generator of $\mathbb{G}_2$
- Computable: an efficient algorithm exists to compute $\hat{e}(P, Q)$ for all $P, Q \in \mathbb{G}_1$

We also introduce a one-way hash function $H : \mathcal{P} \to \mathbb{G}_1$. A suitable implementation is the MapToPoint function introduced in [6].

3.2 SecureMatching

SecureMatching is a prover-verifier protocol wherein a prover can convince a verifier that she owns a property. Provers receive credentials for a given property, allowing them to convince a verifier that they possess that property. Verifiers in turn receive matching references for a given property, which allow them to detect possession of that property after the protocol exchange.

Let $P \in \mathbb{G}_1$ be a random generator of $\mathbb{G}_1$. Let $r, s, t, v \in \mathbb{Z}_q^*$ be random values. We set $\tilde{P} \leftarrow rP$, $S \leftarrow sP$, $T \leftarrow tP$ and $V \leftarrow vrP$. The system public parameters are $\{q, P, \tilde{P}, S, T, V, \hat{e}, \mathbb{G}_1, \mathbb{G}_2, H\}$. The system secret parameters are the values r, s, t and v.

When a user $u \in \mathcal{U}$ joins the system, a secret value $x_u \xleftarrow{R} \mathbb{Z}_q^*$ is drawn. Then, the value $X_u = x_u s^{-1} rP$ is issued to u through a secure channel; this value is kept secret by the user. Users receive their credentials and matching references through these algorithms, run by a certification authority:

$$A \longrightarrow B \; n_A P, n_A \tilde{P}$$
$$A \longleftarrow B \; n_B P, n_B \tilde{P}, r_{1B}(cred_{P2} + r_{3B}P), r_{2B}(n_A \tilde{P}), r_{1B}r_{2B}S, r_{1B}r_{2B}T$$
$$A \longrightarrow B \; r_{1A}(cred_{P1} + r_{3A}P), r_{2A}(n_B \tilde{P}), r_{1A}r_{2A}S, r_{1A}r_{2A}T$$

Fig. 1. Using SecureMatching to build a Secret Handshake

- Certify is executed by the certification entity upon a user's request. The certification entity verifies that the supplicant user $u \in \mathcal{U}$ possesses the property $p \in \mathcal{P}$ she will later claim to have during the protocol execution; after a successful check, the certification entity issues to u the appropriate credential $cred_p = vH(p)$. The user verifies that $\hat{e}(cred_p, \tilde{P}) = \hat{e}(H(p), V)$. If the verification succeeds, she accepts the credential; otherwise she aborts;
- Grant is executed by the certification entity upon a user's request. First of all the certification entity verifies that – according to the policies of the system – the user u is entitled to verify that another user possesses property $p \in \mathcal{P}$. If the checking is successful, the certification entity issues the appropriate matching reference $match_{u,p} = t^{-1}r(cred_p + x_u P)$, where x_u is the secret value associated with user u; the user verifies that

$$\hat{e}(match_{u,p}, T) = \hat{e}(H(p), V) \cdot \hat{e}(X_u, S)$$

If the verification is not successful, she aborts;

Let A be a prover and B a verifier. A has $cred_{p_A}$ to prove possession of property p_A; B holds $match_{B,p_B}$ to detect property p_B. The protocol proceeds as follows:

1. B picks $n \xleftarrow{R} \mathbb{Z}_q^*$, and sends $N_1 = nP$ and $N_2 = n\tilde{P}$ to A;
2. A checks whether $\hat{e}(N_1, \tilde{P}) = \hat{e}(N_2, P)$; if so, she picks $r_1, r_2 \xleftarrow{R} \mathbb{Z}_q^*$ and sends to B the tuple $disguisedCred_{p_A} = < r_1 cred_{p_A}, r_2 N_2, r_1 r_2 S, r_1 r_2 T >$;
3. B checks whether

$$K = \frac{\hat{e}(r_1 cred_{p_A}, r_2 N_2)^{n^{-1}} \cdot \hat{e}(r_1 r_2 S, X_B)}{\hat{e}(r_1 r_2 T, match_{B,p_B})} \tag{1}$$

equals to one; if so, B concludes that A possesses property p_B (or similarly that p_A and p_B are the same). X_B is the secret value associated to B.

3.3   From SecureMatching to Secret Handshake

In order to use SecureMatching to perform secret handshakes, we need two additional characteristics: (i) the capability of establishing a session key out of the protocol exchange and (ii) the assurance that the key is mutually established only if SecureMatching is successful at both sides. If the key is successfully shared by both users, each of them is certain that the other possesses the expected property as defined by the local matching reference. Note that the properties verified by both users need not be identical.

Let us assume two users, Alice and Bob, want to perform a Secret Handshake and share a key if the Handshake is successful. Alice owns the tuple $(cred_{P1}, match_{A,P2}, X_A)$ and Bob owns $(cred_{P2}, match_{B,P1}, X_B)$. Alice and Bob can draw four random values each, $r_{1A}, r_{2A}, r_{3A}, n_A$ for Alice and $r_{1B}, r_{2B}, r_{3B}, n_B$ for Bob. Then – as we can see in Figure 1 – each performs the steps of SecureMatching, with the only exception that Alice sends $r_{1A}(cred_{P1} + r_{3A}P)$ instead of sending $r_{1A}cred_{P1}$. The same applies to Bob, who sends $r_{1B}(cred_{P3} + r_{3B}P)$.

The addition of a random value to the credential, prevents Alice and Bob from checking whether K, as defined in Equation 1, equals to one in case of successful matching. Indeed, $K_{Bob} = \hat{e}(P,P)^{r_{1A}r_{2A}r_{3A}r}$;[1] similarly, $K_{Alice} = \hat{e}(P,P)^{r_{1B}r_{2B}r_{3B}r}$.

However, Alice can compute the values $K' = (K_{Alice})^{r_{1A}r_{2A}r_{3A}}$ and Bob can compute $K'' = (K_{Bob})^{r_{1B}r_{2B}r_{3B}}$, and – in case of successful simultaneous matching – $K' = K''$. This value can be subsequently used to derive a secret key, shared between Alice and Bob only if the matching is successful.

4 Security Analysis

The security requirements of the SecureMatching protocol can be effectively resumed as follows. With the focus on properties, an attacker can perform three different types of actions: *linking*, *knowing* and *forging*. Linking refers to the ability of an attacker to recognize a common property in two separate instances of the protocol, without the appropriate matching references. Knowing refers to the unfeasibility of a verifier to detect a prover's property without the appropriate matching reference. Finally, forging refers to the unfeasibility of a prover to convince a verifier that she possesses a given property without the appropriate property credential. In the rest of this section we introduce three games, Trace, Detect and Impersonate, that capture the essence of the attacks mentioned above, and we show the impossibility of these attacks. Similar proofs can be shown for the Secret Handshake of Section 3.3, which simply consists of two symmetric instances of SecureMatching. We do not show them here due to space restrictions.

Notice that we prove the security of our scheme in the exact same setting as the one chosen in the closest state-of-the-art paper by Ateniese et al. [1], which in turn is similar to the one chosen by Balfanz et al. in [3]. To estimate the success probability of the attacker, we can use the same technique used by Balfanz et al. in [3]; we therefore omit the detailed probability estimation here. Before proceeding further, we state the well-known BDDH problem:

Definition 1 (*Bilinear Decisional Diffie-Hellman* **Problem**). *We say that the Bilinear Decisional Diffie-Hellman Problem (BDDH) is hard if, for all probabilistic, polynomial-time algorithms B,*

$$\mathsf{AdvBDDH}_B := Pr[B(P, aP, bP, cP, xP) = \top \ if \ x = abc] - \tfrac{1}{2}$$

is negligible in the security parameter.

This probability is taken over random choice of $P \in \mathbb{G}_1$, a, b, c and $x \in \mathbb{Z}_q^*$. This problem has been extensively used in the literature, for instance in [8]. The security proofs for the

---

[1] By K_{Bob} we mean the value K computed by Bob; the same applies to K_{Alice}.

scheme follow from the hardness of the BDDH problem in the random oracle model, as introduced by Bellare and Rogaway in [4], whereby the hash function H is considered a truly random oracle.

4.1 Untraceability

Consider an adversary A whose goal is – given any two disguised credentials – to trace them to having been generated from the same credential, so as to prove possession of the same property. The attacker cannot decide whether there is a property that both credentials can be matched to.

A can receive valid credentials and matching references of his choice and can engage in SecureMatching protocol execution with legitimate users. A is then challenged as follows: she is given $disguisedCred_1$ and $disguisedCred_2$, for which she has not received a matching reference, and she returns true if she can decide that a property $p \in \mathscr{P}$ exists, to which both credentials can be matched to. This implies that $K = 1$ for both credentials with matching references in the set $S_{match,p} = \{match_{u_i,p} : u_i \in \mathscr{U}\}$. We call this game Trace.

Lemma 1. *If an adversary A has a non-null advantage*

$$\mathsf{AdvTrace}_A := Pr[A \text{ wins the game } \mathsf{Trace}]$$

then a probabilistic, polynomial time algorithm B can create an environment where it uses A's advantage to solve any given instance of the Bilinear Decisional Diffie-Hellman problem (BDDH).

Proof. We define B as follows. B is given an instance (P, aP, bP, cP, xP) of the BDDH problem and wishes to use A to decide if $x = abc$. The algorithm B simulates an environment in which A operates, using A's advantage in the game Trace to help compute the solution to the BDDH problem. In particular, B acts as an oracle for H.

Setup. Here is a description of how the algorithm B works. B picks $s, t, v \xleftarrow{R} \mathbb{Z}_q^*$, sets $\tilde{P} \leftarrow (bP)$, $S \leftarrow sP$, $T \leftarrow tP$ and $V \leftarrow v(bP)$. She then publishes the public parameter according to the rules of the protocol.

Queries. At first, A queries B for an arbitrary number of tuples $< H(p_i)$, $cred_{p_i}$, X_{u_i} and $match_{u_i,p_i} >$ for any given pairs $(u_i, p_i) \in \mathscr{U} \times \mathscr{P}$. The queries can be adaptive. B answers as follows: if u_i has never been queried before, B picks $x_{u_i} \xleftarrow{R} \mathbb{Z}_q^*$ and stores the pair (u_i, x_{u_i}) in a table. If p_i has never been queried before, B picks $h_i \xleftarrow{R} \mathbb{Z}_q^*$, storing the pair (p_i, h_i) in a table.

Then, B looks up in the table for the values h_i and x_{u_i}, and answers: $H(p_i) = h_i P$, $cred_{p_i} = vh_i P$, $X_{u_i} = x_{u_i} s^{-1}(bP)$ and $match_{u_i,p_i} = t^{-1}(vh_i + x_{u_i})(bP)$. A can check that both $\hat{e}(cred_{p_i}, P) = \hat{e}(H(p_i), V)$ and $\hat{e}(T, match_{u_i,p_i}) = \hat{e}(H(p_i), V) \cdot \hat{e}(X_{u_i}, S)$ hold.

Challenge. At the end of this phase, A inputs two nonce pairs $N_1 = n_1 P, N_1' = n_1 \tilde{P}$ and $N_2 = n_2 P, N_2' = n_2 \tilde{P}$ according to the specification of the protocol. B then produces two hidden credentials constructed as follows:

$$\begin{cases} disguisedCred_1 =< r_1 v(aP), r_2 N_1', r_1 r_2 S, r_1 r_2 T > \\ disguisedCred_2 =< v(xP), r_3 N_2, r_3 s(cP), r_3 t(cP) > \end{cases}$$

where r_1, r_2, r_3 are random values $\in \mathbb{Z}_q^*$. Then, A outputs her decision.

Analysis of A's answer. It is straightforward to verify that, if A wins the game, B can give the same answer to solve the BDDH problem. Indeed, if A wins the game, she is able to decide if $\exists \alpha \in \mathbb{Z}_q^*$ such that

$$\begin{cases} r_1 r_2 vab + r_1 r_2 bx_{u1} = r_1 r_2 b(x_{u1} + v\alpha) \\ r_3 vx + r_3 cbx_{u2} = r_3 cb(x_{u2} + v\alpha) \end{cases} \tag{2}$$

are both verified for any user $u1, u2 \in \mathcal{U}$. Since this system of equations is by definition valid for any value of x_{u1} and x_{u2}, we can rewrite 2 as

$$\begin{cases} r_1 r_2 vab = r_1 r_2 bv\alpha \\ r_3 vx = r_3 cbv\alpha \end{cases} \tag{3}$$

and solve the first equation as $\alpha = a$. If A wins the game and decides that the two disguised credentials can be matched to the same property, then we can solve the second equation as $x = abc$, which is the positive answer to BDDH. Conversely, $x \neq abc$, which is the negative answer to BDDH. $\square$

4.2   Detector Resistance

Consider an adversary A whose goal is to verify presence of a property of his choice without owning the corresponding matching reference. At first, A queries the system for an arbitrary number of tuples $< H(p_i), cred_{p_i}, X_{u_i}$ and $match_{u_i,p_i} >$ for any given pairs $(u_i, p_i) \in \mathcal{U} \times \mathcal{P}$. She is free to engage in the SecureMatching protocol execution with legitimate users.

A then choses a property $p_* \in \mathcal{P}$, not yet queried in the previous phase, which will be the object of the challenge. She receives $H(p_*)$ and $cred_{p_*}$. Finally she receives a disguised credential. She is then challenged to tell whether K, as defined in Equation 1, equals to one for any matching reference in the set $S_{match,p_*} = \{match_{u_i,p_*} : u_i \in \mathcal{U}\}$ for the property $p_* \in \mathcal{P}$ object of the challenge. A clearly does not posses any of the matching references in S_{match,p_*}. We call this game Detect.

Lemma 2. *If an adversary A has a non-null advantage*

$$\mathsf{AdvDetect}_A := Pr[A \text{ wins the game } \mathsf{Detect}]$$

then a probabilistic, polynomial time algorithm B can create an environment where it uses A's advantage to solve any given instance of the Bilinear Decisional Diffie-Hellman problem (BDDH).

Proof. We define B as follows. B is given an instance (P, aP, bP, cP, xP) of the BDDH problem and wishes to use A to decide if $x = abc$. The algorithm B simulates an environment in which A operates, using A's advantage in the game Detect to help compute the solution to the BDDH problem. In particular, B will run for A an oracle for the hash function H.

Setup. Here is a high-level description of how the algorithm B will work. B picks $s, t, v \xleftarrow{R} \mathbb{Z}_q^*$ and sets $\tilde{P} \leftarrow (bP), S \leftarrow sP, T \leftarrow tP$ and $V \leftarrow v(bP)$. She then publishes the public parameter according to the rules of the protocol.

Queries. At first, A queries B for an arbitrary number of tuples $< H(p_i), cred_{p_i}, X_{u_i}$ and $match_{u_i, p_i} >$ for any given pairs $(u_i, p_i) \in \mathcal{U} \times \mathcal{P}$. The queries can be adaptive. B answers as follows: if u_i has never been queried before, B picks $x_{u_i} \xleftarrow{R} \mathbb{Z}_q^*$ and stores the pair (u_i, x_{u_i}) in a table. If p_i has never been queried before, B picks $h_i \xleftarrow{R} \mathbb{Z}_q^*$, storing the pair (p_i, h_i) in a table.

Then, B looks up in the table for the values h_i and x_{u_i}, and answers: $H(p_i) = h_i P$, $cred_{p_i} = v h_i P$, $X_{u_i} = x_{u_i} s^{-1}(bP)$ and $match_{u_i, p_i} = t^{-1}(v h_i + x_{u_i})(bP)$. A can check that both $\hat{e}(cred_{p_i}, \tilde{P}) = \hat{e}(H(p_i), V)$ and $\hat{e}(T, match_{u_i, p_i}) = \hat{e}(H(p_i), V) \cdot \hat{e}(X_{u_i}, S)$ hold.

Challenge. A then chooses the property $p_* \in \mathcal{P}$ which is object of the challenge among the ones not queried in the previous phase. She then queries B for $H(p_*)$ and $cred_{p_*}$. B's response is $H(p_*) = (aP)$ and $cred_{p_*} = v(aP)$. A can check that $\hat{e}(cred_{p_*}, P) = \hat{e}(H(p_*), V)$ holds.

Then A sends to B a pair of nonces $N_1 = nP, n_2 = n\tilde{P}$ according to the specifications of the protocol. B answers by sending the disguised credential

$$disguisedCred = < v(xR), r_1 N_1, r_1 s(cR), r_1 t(cR) > \tag{4}$$

Analysis of A's answer. Let's assume $x = abc$. For every user $u_* \in \mathcal{U}$, we can then write

$$K = \frac{\hat{e}(v(abcR), r_1 nP)^{n^{-1}} \cdot \hat{e}(r_1 s(cR), X_{u_*})}{\hat{e}(r_1 t(cR), t^{-1}(cred_{p_*} + x_{u_*})(bP))} = 1 \tag{5}$$

which implies a successful matching for the disguised credential of Expression 4. Indeed

$$r_1 vx + r_1 bc x_{u_*} - r_1 c(vab + x_{u_*}b) = 0 \tag{6}$$

is satisfied $\forall x_{u_*} \in \mathbb{Z}_q^*$ if and only if $x = abc$.

Therefore, if A wins the game and is able to match the disguised credential, thus detecting property p_*, B can give the same answer to the BDDH. $\square$

4.3   Impersonation Resistance

An adversary A has as its goal to impersonate a user owning a given credential, which she does not dispose of. At first, A queries the system for an arbitrary number of tuples $< H(p_i), cred_{p_i}, X_{u_i}$ and $match_{u_i, p_i} >$ for any given pairs $(u_i, p_i) \in \mathcal{U} \times \mathcal{P}$. She is free to engage in SecureMatching protocol execution with legitimate users.

A then choses a property $p_* \in \mathcal{P}$, not yet queried in the previous phase, which will be the object of the challenge. A queries the system for many matching references for property p_* and users $u_j \in \mathcal{U}$ of his choice. A is then challenged in the following way: she receives a nonce value, and she has to produce a valid handshake message, able to convince a user $u_* \in \mathcal{U}$, among the ones not queried before, with a valid matching reference for property p_*, that she owns the credential $cred_{p_*}$. We call this game Impersonate.[2]

Lemma 3. *If an adversary A has a non-null advantage*

$$\text{AdvImpersonate}_A := Pr[A \text{ wins the game Impersonate}]$$

then a probabilistic, polynomial time algorithm B can create an environment where it uses A's advantage to solve a given instance of the Bilinear Decisional Diffie-Hellman Problem (BDDH).

Proof. We define B as follows. B is given an instance (P, aP, bP, cP, xP) of the BDDH problem and wishes to use A to decide if $x = abc$. The algorithm B simulates an environment in which A operates: B will in particular act as an oracle for H.

Setup. B picks random values r, s, t and $v \in \mathbb{Z}_q^*$ and sets $\tilde{P} = rP$, $S = sP$, $T = t(bP)$ and $V = vr(bP)$. She then publishes the public parameter according to the rules of the protocol.

Queries. At first, A queries B for an arbitrary number of tuples $< H(p_i)$, $cred_{p_i}$, X_{u_i} and $match_{u_i, p_i} >$ for any given pairs $(u_i, p_i) \in \mathcal{U} \times \mathcal{P}$. The queries can be adaptive. B answers as follows: if u_i has never been queried before, B picks $x_{u_i} \xleftarrow{R} \mathbb{Z}_q^*$ and stores the pair (u_i, x_{u_i}) in a table. If p_i has never been queried before, B picks $h_i \xleftarrow{R} \mathbb{Z}_q^*$, storing the pair (p_i, h_i) in a table.

Then, B looks up in the table for the values h_i and x_{u_i}, and answers: $H(p_i) = h_i P$, $cred_{p_i} = v h_i (bP)$, $X_{u_i} = x_{u_i} rs^{-1}(bP)$ and $match_{u_i, p_i} = t^{-1} r(v h_i P + x_{u_i} P)$. A can check that both $\hat{e}(cred_{p_i}, \tilde{P}) = \hat{e}(H(p_i), V)$ and $\hat{e}(T, match_{u_i, p_i}) = \hat{e}(H(p_i), V) \cdot \hat{e}(X_{u_i}, S)$ hold.

A then chooses the property $p_* \in \mathcal{P}$ which is object of the challenge among the ones not queried in the previous phase. She then queries B for $H(p_*)$. B's response is aP. A choses many users $u_j \in \mathcal{U}$ of her choice and asks B for $match_{u_j, p_*}$. After picking the values x_{u_j} as in the previous phase, B's response is $match_{u_j, p_*} = t^{-1} r(v(aP) + x_{u_j} P)$ along with $X_{u_j} = x_{u_j} rs^{-1}(bP)$. A can easily check that it is a valid matching reference by verifying that the equivalence $\hat{e}(T, match_{u_j, p_*}) = \hat{e}(H(p_*), V) \cdot \hat{e}(X_{u_j}, S)$ holds.

Challenge. After this phase, B sends to A nonces $cP, r(cP)$ according to the protocol, and challenges A to produce $disguisedCred_{p_*}$ for which K of Equation 1 equals to one with matching reference $match_{u_*, p_*}$ and X_{u_*} of a user $u_* \in \mathcal{U}$ not queried in the previous phase.

A answers the challenge with $(A, B, C, D) \in \mathbb{G}_1^4$, and wins the game if K equals to one, which implies $\hat{e}(A, B)^{c^{-1}} \cdot \hat{e}(X_{u_*}, C) = \hat{e}(D, match_{u_*, p_*})$.

---

[2] Notice that this game does not prevent an attacker from stealing legitimate users' credentials and claiming to possess their properties. This is common to many Secret Handshakes schemes in the literature, for instance [1]. We could require credentials to be stored on password-protected, tamper resistant hardware; an algorithmic solution however would require an efficient revocation method, which we do not investigate here and leave as a major item for future work.

Analysis of A's response. Let us write $A = \alpha P$, $B = \beta P$, $C = \gamma P$ and $D = \delta P$. Let us assume that A wins the game; then we can write

$$\alpha\beta c^{-1} + \gamma s^{-1} r x_{u_*} b = \delta(t^{-1} rva + t^{-1} r x_{u_*}) \tag{7}$$

If A wins the game, she should be able to convince a user u_* that she owns the credentials for property p_*. B can choose any value for x_{u_*}, since user u_* has never been object of queries before, and this value is unknown to A. Consequently, $\alpha\beta c^{-1}$ and $\delta t^{-1} rva$ must be independent of x_{u_*}. We can then rewrite Equation 7 as

$$\begin{cases} \alpha\beta c^{-1} = \delta t^{-1} rva \\ \gamma s^{-1} r x_{u_*} b = \delta t^{-1} r x_{u_*} \end{cases} \tag{8}$$

Solving the second equation as $\delta = \gamma s^{-1} tb$ and substituting the resulting expression of δ in the first, yields $\alpha\beta = \gamma s^{-1} rvabc$. Therefore if A wins the game, B can decide whether $x = abc$ based on the outcome of $\hat{e}(A,B)^{sr^{-1}v^{-1}} = \hat{e}(C,xP)$. □

5   Conclusion and Future Work

In this paper we have proposed a prover-verifier protocol and a two-party Secret Handshake protocol using bilinear pairings. Our work studies the problem of Secret Handshakes under new requirements, different than the ones considered before in the state of the art, thus completing the landscape of available techniques in the field. As future work, we intend to extend the protocol, allowing the certification authority to revoke credentials formerly issued, in order to cope with compromised users and we intend to study the security of the protocol in the more complete setting suggested in [11].

References

1. Ateniese, G., Blanton, M., Kirsch, J.: Secret handshakes with dynamic and fuzzy matching. In: Network and Distributed System Security Symposuim, pp. 159–177. The Internet Society, 02 2007. CERIAS TR 2007-24 (2007)
2. Baldwin, R.W., Gramlich, W.C.: Cryptographic protocol for trustable match making. In: IEEE Symposium on Security and Privacy (1985)
3. Balfanz, D., Durfee, G., Shankar, N., Smetters, D.K., Staddon, J., Wong, H.-C.: Secret handshakes from pairing-based key agreements. In: IEEE Symposium on Security and Privacy, pp. 180–196 (2003)
4. Bellare, M., Rogaway, P.: Random oracles are practical: A paradigm for designing efficient protocols. In: ACM Conference on Computer and Communications Security (1993)
5. Bellovin, S., Merritt, M.: Encrypted key exchange: password-based protocols secure against dictionary attacks. In: IEEE Computer Society Symposium on Research in Security and Privacy, pp. 72–84 (May 1992)
6. Boneh, D., Franklin, M.: Identity-based encryption from the weil pairing. SIAM J. Comput. 32(3), 586–615 (2003)
7. Castelluccia, C., Jarecki, S., Tsudik, G.: Secret handshakes from CA-oblivious encryption. In: Lee, P.J. (ed.) ASIACRYPT 2004. LNCS, vol. 3329, pp. 293–307. Springer, Heidelberg (2004)

8. Chabanne, H., Phan, D.H., Pointcheval, D.: Public traceability in traitor tracing schemes. In: Cramer, R. (ed.) EUROCRYPT 2005. LNCS, vol. 3494, pp. 542–558. Springer, Heidelberg (2005)
9. Europol and Eurojust and Thomas Van Cangh and Abdelkrim Boujraf. Wp3-cs2: The Eurojust-Europol Case Study (2007), http://www.r4egov.eu/resources
10. Hoepman, J.-H.: Private handshakes. In: Stajano, F., Meadows, C., Capkun, S., Moore, T. (eds.) ESAS 2007. LNCS, vol. 4572, pp. 31–42. Springer, Heidelberg (2007)
11. Jarecki, S., Kim, J., Tsudik, G.: Beyond secret handshakes: Affiliation-hiding authenticated key exchange. In: Malkin, T.G. (ed.) CT-RSA 2008. LNCS, vol. 4964, pp. 352–369. Springer, Heidelberg (2008)
12. Li, N., Du, W., Boneh, D.: Oblivious signature-based envelope. In: Proceedings of the 22nd ACM Symposium on Principles of Distributed Computing (PODC 2003), pp. 182–189. ACM Press, New York (2003)
13. Meadows, C.: A more efficient cryptographic matchmaking protocol for use in the absence of a continuously available third party. sp 0, 134 (1986)
14. Nasserian, S., Tsudik, G.: Revisiting oblivious signature-based envelopes. In: Di Crescenzo, G., Rubin, A. (eds.) FC 2006. LNCS, vol. 4107, pp. 221–235. Springer, Heidelberg (2006)
15. Shin, J.S., Gligor, V.D.: A new privacy-enhanced matchmaking protocol. In: Network and Distributed System Security Symposuim. The Internet Society (February 2007)
16. Vergnaud, D.: RSA-based secret handshakes. In: Ytrehus, Ø. (ed.) WCC 2005. LNCS, vol. 3969, pp. 252–274. Springer, Heidelberg (2006)
17. Xu, S., Yung, M.: k-anonymous secret handshakes with reusable credentials. In: CCS 2004: Proceedings of the 11th ACM conference on Computer and communications security (2004)
18. Zhang, K., Needham, R.: A private matchmaking protocol (2001)

Towards a Theory of White-Box Security

Amir Herzberg[1], Haya Shulman[1], Amitabh Saxena[2], and Bruno Crispo[3]

[1] Bar Ilan, Ramat-Gan, 52900, Israel
amir.herzberg@gmail.com, haya.shulman@gmail.com
[2] International University in Germany, Bruchsal 76646, Germany
saxena.amitabh@gmail.com
[3] University of Trento, Italy
crispo@disi.unitn.it

Abstract. *Program hardening* for secure execution in remote untrusted environment is an important yet elusive goal of security, with numerous attempts and efforts of the research community to produce secure solutions. Obfuscation is the prevailing practical technique employed to tackle this issue. Unfortunately, no provably secure obfuscation techniques currently exist. Moreover, *Barak et. al.*, showed that not all programs can be obfuscated. Theoretical research exhibits provably secure albeit inefficient constructions, e.g. using tools from encrypted domain.

We present a rigorous approach to software execution in remote environment based on a new white box primitive, the White Box Remote Program Execution (WBRPE), whose security specifications include confidentiality and integrity of both the local and the remote hosts. *WBRPE* can be used for many applications, e.g. grid computing, digital rights management, mobile agents.

We then present a construction of a specific program such that if there exists a secure *WBRPE* for that program, then there is a secure *WBRPE* for *any* program, reducing its security to the underlying *WBRPE* primitive. The security of *WBRPE* construction is established by reduction among two white box primitives and it introduces new techniques of programs manipulation.

1 Introduction

Ensuring secure execution of programs in remote untrusted environment is of high theoretical and practical importance and is required for a wide range of applications, e.g., digital rights management (DRM), grid computing, private information retrieval, mobile agents, network gaming, Voice over IP (VoIP). In remote program execution a program leaves the site of the originator and is transferred to the remote host for execution, defining a *white-box security* model. In particular, the originator loses all control over its software, which is completely exposed to the executing environment, and the entity controlling the execution environment obtains full access to the program, and can observe and manipulate the execution, code and data. This is in contrast to traditional cryptography, which assumes a trusted platform, i.e., a *black-box*, on which secrets, e.g., secret keys, can be stored. In black-box security all the computations are performed on a trusted platform, and the secret keys never leave its boundaries. More importantly, attackers obtain a black-box access to the cryptographic implementation and can only

D. Gritzalis and J. Lopez (Eds.): SEC 2009, IFIP AICT 297, pp. 342–352, 2009.

observe an input/output behaviour, but cannot access the code or data, or observe the execution inside the platform.

In hardware based approach, an additional hardware that constitutes a secure trusted platform, is supplied, e.g., a smartcard or a trusted third party in [1], on which the secret data can be stored and the computations involving it performed. Hardware based approach produces solutions in *black box security* model, in which an attacker cannot access and observe the internals of the hardware, e.g. secret keys inside it, and can only control the input/output behaviour of the system.

Although applications that employ hardware benefit from high security promises, there are disadvantages, such as high cost, vulnerability to side channel attacks, unreliability and inflexibility of the hardware. In addition the security completely depends on the trust relationship with the additional hardware, thus making it inapplicable to many useful scenarios. Furthermore, in practice hardware alone is often not enough, since even hardware based solutions rely on software to accomplish the overall security. Therefore in order to enable a variety of practical applications secure software white-box techniques should be provided.

In addition to practical importance, understanding the level of security that can be attained by employing software only techniques is intriguing on its own, especially due to prevailing belief that it is difficult to provide a reasonable level of security by employing software only approach, let alone a level of security comparable to the one in black box security. In this work, we present a new basic candidate white-box security building block, the *White-Box Remote Program Execution (WBRPE)* for remote program execution in hostile environment, along with definitions and game-based security specifications. We present a construction based on *WBRPE* scheme, and establish its security by reduction.

It is important to identify weakest possible primitives for white-box security, e.g., by failed cryptanalysis, which could serve as basic building blocks for provably secure protocols and schemes. More specifically, the security of the scheme would be reduced to the security of the building block that underlies the construction. This is similar in nature to traditional cryptography where few basic, simple building blocks are employed in constructions of cryptographic schemes and primitives.

Security of protocols is established by reduction to the basic building blocks. The motivation is that the cryptanalysis proven standard should be simple and basic, so that it is easy to test its security and the security of the overall construction that uses it. We propose the *WBRPE* as a candidate white-box security building block, which could be employed to develop and analyse well-defined white-box security constructions. Existing practical primitives are proprietary, and their security relies on vague assumptions.

The *WBRPE*, in Figure 1, is comprised of two phases, the generation phase, run by offline trusted third party, and the protocol execution phase, between the local and the remote hosts. The trusted party generates the parameters of the scheme, i.e. the keys which are sent to local host, and the *OVM*, which is transfered to the remote host. The *OVM* emulates a trusted platform, and executes the input programs supplied by the local host in a secure manner. The local host uses the keys to harden programs which it sends to remote host for execution. The *OVM* receives the hardened program, and possibly an input of the remote host. It has the corresponding keys to unharden and execute the program, and then harden the result of the computation. The remote host returns the hardened result to the local host. We require that the local host learns only the result of the computation, while the remote host learns nothing at all.

1.1 Existing Works

Obfuscation. Is a candidate building block for white box security, which received substantial attention from theoreticians and practitioners. An obfuscator $\mathcal{O}$ is an efficient compiler that transforms a program P into a hardened program $\mathcal{O}(P)$, which pertains the functionality of the original program but is equivalent to black-box access to P, i.e. should be hard to analyse and to reverse engineer.

Obfuscation is the prevailing practical approach to software hardening, and was also investigated by theoreticians. However in both theory and practice, obfuscation exhibited insufficient results. The impossibility result by [2] states that there does not exist a general obfuscator for any program. Although there are some positive results, e.g. [6], these are restricted and do not suffice for practical applications. In addition, experts in practical obfuscation, e.g. [10], cannot say whether obfuscators can protect even simple programs, e.g. to hide intermediate state of programs.

White-Box Cryptography. (A special case of obfuscation) aims at protecting secret data embedded inside software implementations of cryptographic algorithms, by integrating a secret key in the cryptographic algorithms, thus preventing from attacker, which controls the execution environment, and may be a legitimate user, from extracting the keys for use on a different platform.

A number of cryptographic implementations have appeared for symmetric key ciphers such as [15] and [11], that have claimed to be secure in a white-box model. More specifically, the white box AES in [9], and the white-box DES in [8]. So far, proposed white box cryptography solutions were subsequently broken [4,13,16]. The *WBRPE* scheme that we present can be seen as an extension of white-box cryptography.

Mobile Code Cryptography. It is possible to employ theoretical tools from two party computation protocols, to produce provably secure white-box security schemes. The central approaches used to tackle two party computation scenario are secure function evaluation, computing with encrypted data, and encrypted function. One of the earliest techniques for two party computation, due to [17], is via encrypted circuit construction and evaluation. A solution to mobile code, for computing all polynomial time functions efficiently, based on encrypted circuit evaluation, is presented in [5] using tools from two-party computation. However, their solution only provides for privacy of one of the inputs, but not both. As a result if the input of one participant is a program, it may expose the input of the other participant, e.g. if the program is computing an identity function. In [14] they construct a practical implementation of two party-secure function evaluation, thus showing a practical feasibility of encrypted circuits evaluation approach.

1.2 White Box Remote Program Execution (WBRPE)

In this work, we propose the *White Box Remote Program Execution (WBRPE)* scheme, as a candidate white-box security building block. *WBRPE* can be employed to facilitate a variety of applications, see Section 1.4.

In *Remote Program Execution*, programs are sent by a *local host* (a.k.a. the originator) for execution on a *remote host*, and possibly use some data available to the *remote
host*. The local and the remote hosts may be with conflicting interests, therefore the
security issues need to be dealt with. In particular, these include confidentiality and
integrity of input programs supplied by the local host and confidentiality of inputs provided by the remote host. The *WBRPE* should satisfy confidentiality and integrity, employing software only techniques without assuming secure hardware, i.e. trusted third
party or smartcards. The *WBRPE* scheme is composed of three efficient procedures,
generation, hardening and unhardening, see Figure 1:

- The generation procedure produces a hardening key *hk*, and a program, which we
  call the *obfuscated virtual machine (OVM)*.
- The hardening key *hk* is used by the hardening procedure to harden, e.g. encrypt
  and/ or authenticate, the input programs.
- The obfuscated virtual machine *OVM* receives a hardened input program along with
  input from the remote host. It decodes the hardened program, e.g. decrypts and/ or
  validates it, and returns the encoded result, e.g., encrypted and/or authenticated, of
  the program applied to the inputs.
- The unhardening procedure unhardens, e.g. decrypts and validates the result received from the remote host.

1.3   White Box RPE for ALL Programs

The negative result by Barak *et al.* [2], shows that an obfuscator for all programs does
not exist, however this result does not imply that there cannot be alternative hardening
schemes which would work for any program. In particular, is there a *WBRPE* for all
programs? To address this question we present a specific program, denoted *UP* (for

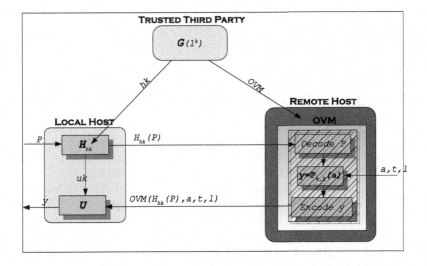

Fig. 1. *WBRPE* scheme

universal program), with parameter K (key). Given a *WBRPE* scheme that works for the family of universal programs $\{UP_K\}$, we present a *'Universal'* WBRPE scheme that works for any program, i.e. provides the security specifications of *WBRPE* for *any* input program.

1.4 Applications of WBRPE

Following are some potential applications of *WBRPE*:

- Mobile agent, that traverses the Web, searching and purchasing goods on behalf of its owner. The agent may include secret data, e.g., secret signing/decryption keys, credit card number, and therefore needs to be protected from a possibly hostile execution platform or from other agents, which e.g., may try to learn the secret information of the agent, or modify its execution.
- In grid computing a large number of users (nodes) donate their idle CPU cycles to perform computation on behalf of the local host. *WBRPE* can ensure that the confidentiality and integrity of the program and input data are not violated.
- In P2P systems, e.g., for VoIP systems (such as Skype), the client code contains secrets (e.g., cryptographic keys and proprietary protocols) that, if leaked to the remote host, would e.g., allow users to make free calls.
- Protection of intellectual property, e.g, music and programs.
- Typically applications based on the setting of online database, e.g. the model of Private Information Retrieval in [7], involve two parties, a server which holds the database and a client who wishes to query the database. The privacy and the integrity of both the local and the remote hosts should be provided. *WBRPE* can be applied directly to map the security requirements of applications based on online databases. In *WBRPE* scheme, the client is the local host and the server is the remote host. The input supplied by the client is a query, and the remote input of the server is a database, and the client wishes to compute the result of its query on the database. The privacy and the integrity of both inputs of the client and the server are preserved, since the server cannot observe the queries submitted by the client, further since the database is queried inside the *OVM* the server cannot observe the process of the computation.

2   White-Box RPE Definitions

A *WBRPE* scheme W is comprised of three efficient algorithms, (G,H,U) for generation, hardening and unhardening, respectively. The generation procedure G generates the obfuscated virtual machine *OVM* and the hardening key hk. The hardening procedure applied on some input program, computes the hardened program, e.g. encryption and/ or authentication of the original program, and produces two outputs, the hardened program and a one time unhardening key. The remote host passes the hardened program, along with the remote input a to the *OVM* for execution. The *OVM* has the required keys, and can therefore extract and evaluate the program P on remote input a, and returns the (hardened) output $P(a)$. The local host, upon receipt the hardened output, applies the unhardening procedure with the unhardening key, to obtain the final result of the computation.

Given a Turing machine $P \in \mathbb{TM}$, where $\mathbb{TM}$ is a set of all Turing machines, let $P(a)$ denote a value of the computation of P on a. We introduce a time parameter, to hide the time that it takes each program to execute, and the length parameter to hide the length of the result. Let $P_{t,l}(a) = P_t(a)[1...l]$ denote an l bit value of the t step computation of P on input a. The definition follows.

Definition 1 (WBRPE). *A White Box RPE (WBRPE) scheme W for programs family* $\{P_k\}_{k \in \mathbb{N}}$ *consists of a tuple* $W = \langle G, H, U \rangle$ *of PPT algorithms s.t. for all* $(hk, OVM) \xleftarrow{R}$ $G(1^k), a \in \{0,1\}^*, P \in \mathbb{TM}, OVM \in PPT, t, l \in \mathbb{N}$ *and* $(c, uk) \leftarrow H_{hk}(P)$, *holds:* $P_{t,l}(a) = U_{uk}(OVM(c, a, t, l))$.

2.1 Indistinguishability of the Local Inputs Specification

The first security specification we consider is to hide the contents of the input programs from the remote host. To ensure local inputs privacy we employ a variation of the indistinguishability experiment for encryption schemes [12]. We specify the indistinguishability definition w.r.t. a PPT algorithm $A = (A_1, A_2)$, denoting by HO the hardening oracle which the algorithm A obtains access to, during the indistinguishability experiment. The experiment is described in detail in Figure 1, we now give an informal definition. As its first step the experiment generates the keys and the obfuscated virtual machine. Next it invokes the adversarial algorithm with an OVM in an input, and provides it with an oracle access to the hardening functionality for its hardening queries. Each application of the hardening procedure generates a hardened program and a one time unhardening key. Eventually the adversary outputs two programs of equal size. The experiment tosses a bit b and one of the programs is subsequently hardened. During the second phase the adversary keeps an oracle access to HO, obtains the hardened challenge program and has to distinguish. If the adversary guesses correctly, the experiment returns 1, i.e., the adversary won, and otherwise returns 0, the adversary lost.

In the sequel we introduce a flag $\varphi \in \{PK, SK\}$, and when $\varphi = PK$ we refer to an asymmetric *WBRPE*, while $\varphi = SK$ denotes a symmetric *WBRPE*. When $\varphi = PK$ the adversary receives the public hardening key hk in an input and can harden the programs by itself.

Definition 2 (Indistinguishability). *Let* $W = (G, H, U)$ *be a* WBRPE *scheme and let* $A = (A_1, A_2)$ *be a pair of PPT algorithms. For* $k \in \mathbb{N}, r \in \{0,1\}^*$ *we define the advantage of the adversary A in the* W B-IND-CPA *experiment as follows:*

$$Adv_{W,A}^{WB\text{-}IND\text{-}CPA\text{-}\varphi}(k) = 2 * \Pr[Exp_{W,A}^{WB\text{-}IND\text{-}CPA\text{-}\varphi}(k) = 1] - 1$$

Where the probabilities are taken over G, H and A. The experiment $\mathbf{Exp}_{W,A}^{WB\text{-}IND\text{-}CPA\text{-}\varphi}(k)$ is defined in Experiment 1. A *WBRPE* scheme W is $WB\text{-}IND\text{-}CPA\text{-}\varphi$ secure if the advantage function $\mathbf{Adv}_{W,A}^{WB\text{-}IND\text{-}CPA\text{-}\varphi}(\cdot)$ is negligible over all PPT adversarial algorithms A. In private key *WBRPE* there is a secret shared key hk between the OVM and the local host. This hk key is employed by the local host to harden programs and by the

OVM to subsequently unharden them for execution. This implies that there is a unique OVM for every local host. In public key $WBRPE$ the hardening key hk is public, which the attacking algorithm obtains in an input, and there is a corresponding unhardening key embedded inside the OVM. Namely, everyone can harden programs and send to OVM for execution, and only the OVM can unharden the programs, which implies the asymmetry. The obvious advantage of the asymmetric $WBRPE$ is in its flexibility, i.e. new hosts can join the system without any effort, e.g. a marketplace scenario where everyone can work with one central remote host and the same OVM.

Experiment 1. The indistinguishability $\mathbf{Exp}_{W.A}^{WB\text{-}IND\text{-}CPA\text{-}\varphi}(k)$ and unforgeability $\mathbf{Exp}_{W.A}^{WB\text{-}UNF\text{-}\varphi}(k)$ experiments. Where HO is a hardening oracle that the algorithm A obtains access to during the course of the experiments.

$\mathbf{Exp}_{W.A}^{WB\text{-}IND\text{-}CPA\text{-}\varphi}(k)$

   $\langle hk, OVM \rangle \leftarrow G(1^k)$
   $(P_0, P_1, s) \leftarrow A_1^{HO_{hk}(\cdot, \varphi)}(1^k, OVM, hk)$
   $b \in \{0,1\}^k$
   $(c_b, uk_b) \leftarrow H_{hk}(P_b)$
   $b' \leftarrow A_2^{HO_{hk}(\cdot, \varphi)}(c_b, s)$
   if $((b = b') \wedge (|P_0| = |P_1|))$ {return 1}
   return 0

$HO_{hk}(P, \varphi)$
   if $(\varphi = PK)$ {return (hk)}
   return $(H_{hk}(P))$

$\mathbf{Exp}_{W.A}^{WB\text{-}UNF\text{-}\varphi}(k)$

   $\langle hk, OVM \rangle \leftarrow G(1^k)$
   $(P, s) \leftarrow A_1^{HO_{hk}(\cdot, \varphi)}(1^k, OVM)$
   $(c, uk) \leftarrow H_{hk}(P)$
   $(\omega, t) \leftarrow A_2^{HO_{hk}(\cdot, \varphi)}(c, s)$
   $y \leftarrow U_{uk}(\omega)$
   if $(y = \bot)$ {return 0}
   if $(\forall a \in \{0,1\}^*, y \neq P_{t.|y|}(a))$ {
      return 1
   }
   return 0

2.2 Unforgeability Specification

In some scenarios, e.g. shopping mobile agent, a remote host may try to change the result of the programs sent by the originator, e.g. such that instead of looking for the best offer the agent purchases the most expensive item. Our goal is to circumvent adversarial attempts to forge the result output by the scheme. This is captured by the unforgeability specification, based on unforgeability experiment which we present below. The unforgeability experiment applies the generation procedure and obtains hardening key hk, and OVM. It then invokes the adversary with oracle access to hardening functionality, and with the OVM as input. Eventually, the adversary outputs the forgery, i.e. the hardened result of the computation, denoted ω, an input program P, and the unhardening key uk. The experiment applies the unhardening procedure U on ω, P and t, and obtains the result of the computation y. If y is valid, then the experiment checks if it is a forgery for any t and a, and if yes, returns 1, i.e. the adversary successfully generated a forgery, otherwise returns 0, the adversary failed.

In the asymmetric $WBRPE$ everyone can harden programs for execution. After recovering the result by applying the unhardening procedure, we cannot know what input program was hardened to generate the result, and the forgery in this case means that the output is not a result of the computation of the input program on any remote input. Since the adversary has the public hardening key hk, it can harden programs by itself. The trivial solution to this issue is to supply the program to the local host as part of the unhardening key uk. Local host would then compare the program returned to the program supplied as part of uk. However in case of a security specification which requires to keep the input program secret from other remote recipients in this solution we expose the input program, and thus cannot achieve programs privacy from remote recipients. Therefore in asymmetric *WBRPE* a forgery is a generation of a valid result ω such that there does not exist a program P, which could result in $y \leftarrow U_{uk}(\omega)$ on any remote input a, i.e. $\forall a \; y \neq P_{t,|y|}(a)$.

In the symmetric *WBRPE*, the adversary obtains an oracle access to the hardening procedure. If the adversary did not query the hardening oracle on the program for which the result was generated, then the adversary wins the experiment. The experiment keeps a vector $Q[..]$, with queried programs and the respective unhardening keys output along with the hardening upon each query. In this type of forgery, the legitimate party never queried the hardening oracle with a program for which the result was generated. Instead, the adversary replaces the authentic hardened program with some other program (replay or a forgery).

Definition 3 (Unforgeability). *Let $W = (G, H, U)$ be a WBRPE scheme and let A be a PPT algorithm. For $k \in \mathbb{N}$, $\varphi \in \{PK, SK\}$ we define the advantage of the adversary A in the unforgeability experiment as follows:*

$$Adv_{W,A}^{WB\text{-}UNF\text{-}\varphi}(k) = \Pr[Exp_{W,A}^{WB\text{-}UNF\text{-}\varphi}(k) = 1]$$

Where $\mathbf{Exp}_{W,A}^{WB\text{-}UNF\text{-}\varphi}(k)$ and the hardening oracle are defined in Experiment 1. A *WBRPE* scheme W is $WB\text{-}UNF\text{-}\varphi$ secure, if the advantage $\mathbf{Adv}_{W,A}^{WB\text{-}UNF\text{-}\varphi}(\cdot)$ is a negligible function for all PPT adversarial algorithms A.

3   Universal WBRPE

In this section we show that if there exists a *WBRPE* scheme that satisfies the security specifications for a *specific* family of universal programs, UP then there exists a *Universal WBRPE* scheme that satisfies the security specifications for every program. More specifically, we present the construction of the *Universal WBRPE* scheme given a *WBRPE* scheme for a specific universal program UP in Figure 2.

3.1   The Universal Program UP

Let $\Pi = (G_{AE}, AE, VD)$ be a scheme, that performs encryption and authentication, see [3], and decryption and validation of inputs. The universal program UP_K (in Figure 2) is a Turing machine, that is created and instantiated with a secret key K, by the hardening procedure H. When invoked by the obfuscated virtual machine OVM, the universal program UP_K reads a' off the input tape, and parses it to obtain

Algorithm 2. The *Universal WBRPE* scheme $W' = (G', H'.U')$, where *createOVM* and *createUP* are macros, each generating a string that encodes a program (*OVM'* and *UP* respectively)

```
                                          G'(1^k)
                                            (hk,OVM)←G(1^k)
                                            OVM' ← createOVM(OVM,k)
                                            return ⟨hk,OVM'⟩

U'_uk'(ω)                                 createOVM'(OVM)
     y ← U_uk'(ω)                            return |read (c,a,t,1)
     return y                                  (c_UP,c_P) ← c
                                               a' ← (a,t,1,c_P)
                                               t'=p(t)+3
                                               1'=1+|P|+|t|+|K|
H'_hk(P)                                       return OVM(c_UP,a',t',1')|
K←G_AE(1^k)
     c_P ← AE_K(P)
     UP_K ← createUP(K)                   createUP(K)
     (c_UP,uk) ← H_hk(UP_K)                  return |read a'
     c ← ⟨c_UP,c_P⟩                            (a,t,1,c_P) ← a'
     uk' ← ⟨uk,K,P⟩                            P ← VD_K(c_P)
     return (c,uk')                            y ← P_t,1(a)
                                               return y|
```

(a,t,l,c_P), i.e. the remote input, the number of steps of program's execution, the length of the output and the encrypted program. UP decrypts and validates c_P using the key K. The UP then runs P on a for t steps and truncates the output y' to l bits. Finally, UP writes $y' = ⟨y,P,t,K⟩$ on the output tape and halts. The parameters (P,t,K) are output to allow the unhardening procedure U' to verify that the result of the computation is authentic. The output y' of UP is encoded, i.e. encrypted and/ or authenticated, by the OVM (the encoded value returned by the OVM is denoted $ω$).

The macro *createUP*, in Figure 2, given a secret key K, generates and returns the Turing machine UP_K, represented as a string. The secret key K, is instantiated during the generation and is concatenated to the constant parts of the string.

3.2   The Generation Procedure

The generation procedure G' of the *Universal WBRPE* scheme W' applies G of the specific *WBRPE* W and obtains the the hardening key hk, and the OVM. It applies the *createOVM'* function on the OVM of the specific *WBRPE* scheme to generate the OVM' of the *Universal WBRPE* scheme W' and returns the tuple $⟨hk,OVM'⟩$. See Figure 2. The *createOVM'* function generates the OVM' Turing machine encoded in a string. The OVM' reads (c,a,t,l) of the input tape and generates an input for the OVM Turing machine. The OVM decodes c_{UP} and runs the universal program on input a', for t' steps and writes an l' bit output on its output tape, where t' comprised of the number of steps performed by UP, the number of steps the input program P is executed and of the number of steps it takes the virtual machine to execute P, i.e. bounded by some polynomial $p(\cdot)$ in t. The output length l' is the length of UP's output, which is the tuple $⟨y,P,t,K⟩$.

3.3   The Hardening Procedure

The input to the hardening procedure H' of the *Universal WBRPE* scheme W' is a program P supplied by the local host. The universal hardening procedure first applies the generation procedure of the authenticated encryption scheme, e.g. in [3], obtains the secret key K and then encrypts the input program P using K, which results in c_P. Next, it generates the universal program, given the secret key K, and hardens it using H to obtain the pair c_{UP} and uk, subsequently returning the ordered pairs $\langle c_{UP}, c_P \rangle$ and $\langle uk, K \rangle$. Details in Figure 2.

We employ authenticated encryption in order to prevent forgery of the input programs, and to ensure that the input program P of the *Universal WBRPE* was not modified on transit, and replaced with some other input program P'.

3.4   The Unhardening Procedure

The unhardening procedure receives an ω and optional $[P,t]$ in an input, and applies the unhardening procedure U of the specific *WBRPE* scheme W on ω. Obtains the tuple $(y, \tilde{P}, \tilde{t}, \tilde{K})$. It then checks if the P,t parameters were supplied, if not it simply returns y, otherwise the validation of the input is also performed. U' verifies that the pair (P,t) supplied by the adversarial algorithm and the pair $(\tilde{P}, \tilde{t})$ output from the universal program UP_K are identical, and that the secret key K from uk equals to the secret key $\tilde{K}$ from the output of UP. This is critical in order to verify that the result of the computation is authentic and not a forgery. If the result is authentic, U is applied on the universal program UP_K, t' and ω, such that UP_K and t' are generated from the input parameters supplied to U'. These steps are performed in order to validate the result ω, i.e. that it is an authentic computation the universal program after a t' steps execution. The universal unhardening procedure returns y as its output. See the details of the implementation in Algorithm 2.

Theorem 1. *Let* $\phi \in \{WB\text{-}IND\text{-}CPA\text{-}\varphi, (WB\text{-}UNF\text{-}\varphi \ \& \ WB\text{-}IND\text{-}CPA)\}$ *and let* $\Pi = (G_{AE}, AE, VD)$ *is an IND-CPA secure authenticated encryption scheme. If* $W = (G, H, U)$ *is a* ϕ *secure* WBRPE *scheme for the universal program* UP, *then* $W' = Univ(W)$ *is a* ϕ *secure* WBRPE *scheme for every program.*

We prove the theorem for each value of ϕ, in full version of the paper.

Acknowledgements. We thank Yoram Ofek, Jasvir Nagra, and Christian S. Collberg for useful discussions and helpful comments. This work was supported by funds from the European Commission (contract N 021186-2 for the RE-TRUST project). Part of this research was supported by the NATO Collaborative Linkage Grant n. 982332.

References

1. Algesheimer, J., Cachin, C., Camenisch, J., Karjoth, G.: Cryptographic security for mobile code. In: SP 2001: Proceedings of the 2001 IEEE Symposium on Security and Privacy, p. 2. IEEE Computer Society, Washington (2001)

2. Barak, B., Goldreich, O., Impagliazzo, R., Rudich, S., Sahai, A., Vadhan, S., Yang, K.: On the (Im)possibility of obfuscating programs. In: Kilian, J. (ed.) CRYPTO 2001. LNCS, vol. 2139, p. 1. Springer, Heidelberg (2001)
3. Bellare, C., Pointcheval, D., Rogaway, P.: Authenticated Encryption: Relations among notions and analysis of the generic composition paradigm (2000)
4. Billet, O., Gilbert, H., Ech-Chatbi, C.: Cryptanalysis of a white box AES implementation. In: Handschuh, H., Hasan, M.A. (eds.) SAC 2004. LNCS, vol. 3357, pp. 227–240. Springer, Heidelberg (2004)
5. Cachin, C., Camenisch, J., Kilian, J., Muller, J.: One-round secure computation and secure autonomous mobile agents. In: Welzl, E., Montanari, U., Rolim, J.D.P. (eds.) ICALP 2000. LNCS, vol. 1853, pp. 512–523. Springer, Heidelberg (2000), citeseer.ist.psu.edu/article/cachin00oneround.html
6. Canetti, R.: Towards Realizing Random Oracles: Hash Functions that Hide All Partial Information. LNCS, pp. 455–469. Springer, Heidelberg (1997)
7. Chor, B., Goldreich, O., Kushilevitz, E., Sudan, M.: Private Information Retrieval. Journal of the ACM 45(6), 965–982 (1998)
8. Chow, S., Eisen, P.A., Johnson, H., van Oorschot, P.C.: A white-box DES implementation for DRM applications. In: Feigenbaum, J. (ed.) DRM 2002. LNCS, vol. 2696, pp. 1–15. Springer, Heidelberg (2003)
9. Chow, S., Eisen, P.A., Johnson, H., van Oorschot, P.C.: White-box cryptography and an AES implementation. In: Nyberg, K., Heys, H.M. (eds.) SAC 2002. LNCS, vol. 2595, pp. 250–270. Springer, Heidelberg (2003)
10. Collberg, C., Thomborson, C.: Watermarking, tamper-proofing, and obfuscation-tools for software protection. IEEE Transactions on Software Engineering 28(8), 735–746 (2002)
11. Daemen, J., Rijmen, V.: The Design of Rijndael: AES–the Advanced Encryption Standard. Springer, Heidelberg (2002)
12. Goldreich, O.: Foundations of Cryptography. Basic Applications, vol. 2. Cambridge University Press, Cambridge (2004)
13. Goubin, L., Masereel, J., Quisquater, M.: Cryptanalysis of a white box AES implementation. In: Handschuh, H., Hasan, M.A. (eds.) SAC 2004. LNCS, vol. 3357, pp. 227–240. Springer, Heidelberg (2004)
14. Malkhi, D., Nisan, N., Pinkas, B., Sella, Y.: Fairplay: a secure two-party computation system. In: Proceedings of the 13th USENIX Security Symposium, pp. 287–302 (2004)
15. United States. National Bureau of Standards: Data Encryption Standard, Federal Information Processing Standards publication, vol. 46. U.S. National Bureau of Standards, pub-NBS:adr (1977)
16. Wyseur, B., Michiels, W., Gorissen, P., Preneel, B.: Cryptanalysis of White-Box DES Implementations with Arbitrary External Encodings. In: Adams, C., Miri, A., Wiener, M. (eds.) SAC 2007. LNCS, vol. 4876, pp. 264–277. Springer, Heidelberg (2007)
17. Yao, A.C.: Protocols for secure computations. In: Proc. 23rd IEEE Symp. on Foundations of Comp. Science, pp. 160–164. IEEE, Chicago (1982)

On a Taxonomy of Delegation

Quan Pham, Jason Reid, Adrian McCullagh, and Ed Dawson

Information Security Institute, Queensland University of Technology, Brisbane, QLD, Australia
{q.pham,jf.reid,a.mccullagh,e.dawson}@isi.qut.edu.au

Abstract. Delegation, from a technical point of view, is widely considered as a potential approach in addressing the problem of providing dynamic access control decisions in activities with a high level of collaboration, either within a single security domain or across multiple security domains. Although delegation continues to attract significant attention from the research community, presently, there is no published work that presents a taxonomy of delegation concepts and models. This paper intends to address this gap.

1 Introduction

Traditionally, delegation may be used as a term for describing how duties and the required authority propagate through an organisation. In technical settings, often the term *delegation* is used to describe how an entity passes some specific capabilities on to another entity. However, delegation in technical settings is an ill-defined concept. Currently, there is no single study that provides a comprehensive taxonomy of delegation concepts and models. Thus, there is a need for a taxonomy which acts as a conceptual framework to help researchers position their research. This paper proposes a set of taxonomic criteria which can then be used to analyse a range of delegation proposals and models. This paper also investigates a number of delegation approaches from various perspectives such as actors, credentials, attributes, protocols, etc. to characterise each approach.

In this paper, for purposes of precision and clarity, we adopt the terminology used in the XACML specification. *Attributes* will be used to describe the following information: group, role and other information which can be ascribed to a particular entity. The entity that performs a delegation is referred to as a *delegator* and the entity that receives a delegation is referred to as a *delegatee*. An attribute will be said to be *delegatable* if it can be successfully granted from one entity to another.

The rest of the paper is organised as follows. Section 2 presents a taxonomy for delegation support in information systems. Section 3 discusses some notable works and their characteristics in the field and maps them with the characteristics described in the taxonomy. Section 4 discusses notable characteristics of these approaches and future trends in development of the delegation concept. Section 5 concludes the paper.

2 A Taxonomy

This paper is concerned with the implementation of the delegation concept in technical settings. This paper considers delegation as *a proxy process in which one entity grants/*

D. Gritzalis and J. Lopez (Eds.): SEC 2009, IFIP AICT 297, pp. 353–363, 2009.

Table 1. Characteristics of Delegation

Characteristic	Factor
Motivation	- Lack of Authorisation - Lack of or Conflicted Policies
Delegation Boundary	- Within a security domain - Across multiple security domains
Who requests delegation?	- User - System Authority
Who delegates?	- User (Ad-hoc) - System Authority (Administrative)
Relationship of the parties	- Direct - Indirect
What to delegate?	- Capability - Responsibility
How much to delegate?	- Partial - Total
How long to delegate?	- Temporal - Permanent
How to delegate?	- Transfer - Grant
Authority Pre-Approval	- Yes - No (Optimistic Delegation)
Type of Credential	- X.509 - SAML Assertion - Generic Token
Key Scheme	- Symmetric Key - Asymmetric Key
Where delegation happens?	- User Level (Application) - System Level
Where is delegation honoured?	- Access Decision Point - An additional authority for delegation

allocates the necessary attributes to another entity to enable the receiver to be able to perform certain responsibilities or capabilities while meeting certain obligations and constraints (e.g. with respect to duration, frequency etc.). A delegation process usually includes a mechanism to revoke the delegated attributes (revocation). This section discusses in detail each dimension of the taxonomy which are summarised in Table 1.

Motivation. Depending on the type of the operational environment, there may be different factors motivating delegation between the entities. From a technical point of view, these include:

- *Lack of authorisation* An entity does not have sufficient authorisation to perform certain actions over certain resources to complete a task.
- *Lack of or conflicted policies* Policies required to achieve a certain goal may conflict and the entity involved with the activities may need to delegate the tasks to another entity which is not affected by the conflicted policies.

Delegation Boundary. The delegation can happen *within a single security domain*, or *across multiple security domains*. Delegation within a single security domain is the simplest case and is relatively easy to manage because of the centralised storage of policies and credentials. Until recently, most proposals restrict their scope to delegation within a single security domain. As the issues of security for collaborative environments have emerged, the concept of delegation needs to be considered from a new angle: delegation across multiple security domains, e.g. an entity from one system can delegate to another entity on another system. Cross domain delegation can bring flexibility to collaborative activities and can meet the needs of such dynamic environments [10]. However, cross domain delegation must cope with the complexity in building delegation protocols and exchanging/validating delegation tokens due to the potential inconsistency of security approaches by different systems.

Who requests delegation? As the motivations discussed above can happen with both normal users and the system authority, delegation can be requested by either a *user* or a *system authority*. Delegation requested by users is common. Consider for example, when a CEO employs a company secretary, he will want to allocate certain duties to the company secretary, for example, preparing the annual financial report. In a sense, this is the allocation of responsibility (a granting process) from the CEO to the company secretary. In contrast, delegation from the system authority is considered as a special case. The delegation of system authority is fixed and to some extent, well pre-defined by the organisation's policies and procedures. In this type of delegation, the system authority actually does not request the delegation for itself; in fact, it requests the delegation on behalf of the delegator and the delegatee.

Who delegates? (Who is the delegator?) The delegator can be a *user (ad-hoc)*, or *system authority (administrative)*. Schaad argued that user ad-hoc delegation and administrative delegation can be differentiated based on three factors [11]: the representation of the authority to delegate, the specific relation of the delegator to the delegated attributes, and the duration of the delegation (how long the delegated attributes can last?).

Administrative delegation is the basic form of delegation in which an administrator or system authority assigns attributes and privileges to enable users to conduct certain tasks. This process typically happens when a user joins a security domain. The delegator, in this case, represents the authority of the system (system administration). In user delegation, the delegator is a normal user. So the delegator represents the authority of the user only. This is the case in which a user grants or transfers the whole or a subset of his/her attributes to other users. As the user is the delegator, the user must possess the ability to utilise the attributes to be able to perform delegation. This type of delegation is typically short-lived and intended for a specific purpose [6, 11].

Relationship of the parties in the delegation process. The relationship between the delegator and the delegatee can be considered as either *direct delegation* or *indirect delegation (sub-delegation)*. Direct delegation is defined as the delegation in which the delegator directly sends the delegation assertion to the delegatee. In contrast, indirect delegation is performed with the involvement of one or many intermediate parties which can forward the delegation assertion from the delegator to the delegatee. This type of delegation is sometimes called sub-delegation. Indirect delegation is mainly performed to achieve a *multi-step delegation*. Indirect delegation is especially important in the context of cross domain delegation when the delegation token traverses various security domains.

What to delegate? What to delegate is the main and the most controversial topic in the field. The object of the delegation process is a key aspect on which proposed models differ. The following three main cases are evident in published proposals:

- *Case 1*: The delegatee takes on attributes of another entity (the delegator) via an unforgeable token which has the capability to perform the task.
- *Case 2*: The delegatee is assigned some attributes that the authority will evaluate in the context of a set of applicable policies. The difference to Case 1 is that the delegated attributes are considered as new attributes of the delegatee while in Case 1, the delegated attributes are treated as if they are from the delegator.
- *Case 3*: The delegatee is assigned new responsibilities as part of the delegation commitment between the involved parties or part of the constraints set by the applicable policies. It is very often that the attribute that represents new responsibility is "role". This case, however, more precisely reflects the social nature of the delegation concept.

To stimulate the above cases, at the abstract level, there are two trends:

- *Delegation of Capability*: Case 1 and Case 2 represent a type of delegation of capability as the delegation will enable new capability in the delegatee. In this paper, the term *capability* is used in the sense which it is defined in POSIX Draft 1003.1e/2c as simply a representation of the ability to perform a specified task.
- *Delegation of Responsibility (Case 3)*: It is a form of transferring tasks as well as obligations/conditions or commitments which are associated and covered by certain responsibilities from one entity to another [1, 7].

In general, delegation of capability is technically well defined. This type of delegation is defined to cope with the demand for a high level of granularity and is appropriate for environments which require a high level of flexibility. However, delegation of responsibility is considered as a broader concept compared to delegation of capability. From the responsibility perspective, the process is defined via the responsibility to transfer or grant and it is assumed that necessary attributes or rules to complete the duties will be transferred or granted upon completing the process. The associated obligations/conditions or commitments are considered as part of the delegation process.

How much to delegate? In general, depending on the needs of the delegator and delegatee, the delegation can be *partial* or *total delegation*. Partial delegation can be achieved by delegating just a specific subset of capabilities/responsibilities. On the other hand, total delegation can be achieved by delegating the whole set of capabilities/responsibilities associated with certain attributes. Total delegation is the extreme case. In fact, the concepts of partial and total delegation are quite relative.

How long to delegate? Delegation can be *temporal* or *permanent*. Temporal delegation is a time-constrained delegation of which the validity period is set by either the delegator or the system authority. On the other hand, permanent delegation is a type of delegation which does not need a specified expiry time. The delegation and revocation process is triggered by a specified event. This type of delegation can be considered as relatively permanent. Permanent delegation is usually associated with administrative delegation due to the nature of the relationship of the delegator and the delegatee and the organisation's policies. In ad-hoc delegation, permanent delegation is rare and is usually considered as a failure of the system to reflect a change in circumstances.

How to delegate? From the operational perspective, delegation may be classified into two categories: *grant delegation* or *transfer delegation* [6]. In grant delegation, a successful delegation operation allows a delegated attribute to be available to both the delegator and delegatee. So after a grant delegation, both delegatee and delegator will share some common attributes. Grant delegation makes the availability of attributes increase monotonically with delegations [6]. Grant delegation is primarily concerned with allowing the delegatee to use the delegated attributes. On the other hand, in transfer delegation, besides allowing the delegatee to use the delegated attributes, the mechanism must be able to prevent the use of the delegated attributes by the delegator.

Authority Pre-Approval. Delegation can be *pre-approved* or *optimistic*. At the time a delegator receives a delegation request, it does not necessarily know in advance whether a particular set of delegated attributes will be useable by the delegatee, since it may not have a complete understanding of the current security context of the delegatee, the current set of attributes of the delegatee, and the policies of the delegatee's systems, etc. To avoid making a delegation that will not be honoured, the delegator could contact the relevant authorisation authorities to ask "if I delegate these attributes to user X from domain Y, will they be honoured?" But asking this question in advance for each delegation transaction is inefficient as the authorisation authority will then need to evaluate the request twice - once for the pre-approval and once for the actual execution by the delegatee. Therefore, in optimistic delegation, the delegator agrees to conduct the delegation transaction on the basis of its best knowledge of the constraints and conditions for the delegation transaction, for example, the policies of its systems, the attributes, etc. It does not guarantee that the delegatee will be able to successfully use this attribute for service invocation.

Type of Credential. In general, there are three forms of credentials which are commonly used to bear delegation information: *X.509*, *SAML assertion*, and *generic token*. The generic token is a signed statement that includes the public keys of the delegator and the delegatee, the involved attributes and a timestamp. Over time, the delegation credential has become more sophisticated. Currently, most proposals use the SAML assertion and more popularly X.509-based attribute certificate (such as in the PRIMA [9] and PERMIS [4] systems) as the means to bear the delegation credential. It is worthy to note that the generic form of delegation token above can be only useful in a single delegation transaction. For a multi-step delegation with the involvement of multiple intermediate entities, it is essential to employ a more complex form of delegation token via a different combination of multiple delegation tokens.

Key Scheme. In general, keys play an important role in securing the exchanged delegated attributes between the delegator and the delegatee. Keys are primarily used to encrypt and sign the delegation tokens. Currently, due to the increasingly popular and well standardised PKI with X.509 certificate, asymmetric key scheme seems to be the default option for constructing delegation protocols. However, Varadharajan suggests that both *symmetric key* and *asymmetric key* schemes can be used either separately or in combination in a hybrid form to support the delegation process [12, 13]. The symmetric key approach is somewhat similar to the asymmetric key approach, in that the underlying principle of signing or encrypting the delegation token is the same. However, in this case, the secret key used to encrypt or sign the delegation token is assumed to be shared between the delegator and the delegatee and issued by a trusted third party which can be the system authority.

Where delegation happens? The delegation can happen at multiple levels: *system level* and *user/application level*. At the system level, the delegation is classic in the sense that the delegation is pre-defined in a concise manner. This type of delegation is often limited to a set of well studied scenarios. In the system level, delegation usually happens as part of the supported access control model, for example, adding a user to a group in UNIX. Delegation at this level is considered as part of the access control infrastructure but there is a lack of flexibility to cope with unconventional scenarios, especially in collaborating activities with external parties. This is where delegation at the user level can make a difference. Delegation at the user or application level is usually ad-hoc in nature and is necessary to address the flexibility of the access control system. At the user or application level, people may need to accommodate not only different technical standards but also different workflows, business processes and frameworks. In this context, delegation is an essential element in business processes which require a high level of collaboration. In general, workflows control the execution of business processes in an organisation at the technical or information system level [1, 3].

Where is delegation honoured? In general, any access control system is centred around the following two functions: access decision function and access enforcing function. Commonly, they are also known as Policy Decision Point (PDP) and Policy Enforcement Point (PEP) respectively. Therefore, when a request is associated with a delegation, the validation process can be conducted at: *Policy Decision Point (PDP)* with the partial contribution of the PEP or *an additional authority* which governs for delegation transactions.

In theory, it is safe to consider the PEP as part of the delegation validation process. This is because the PEP is the authority who receives the request from the user (the requestor). From this point of view, the PEP is the one who is responsible for receiving the credentials from users and passing them to the PDP for decision making. On the other hand, the PDP is responsible for evaluating the policy (also taking into account the credentials provided by users/subject). Most delegation-supporting access control models consider the validation process as an additional function of the PDP.

The second approach is to use an additional authority such as the Credential Validation Service [5] or the Delegation Authority [8] to govern the delegation function. For example, the Credential Validation Service could be incorporated into the XACML model. In fact, the PDP is still responsible for decision making. However, in this approach, the PEP is not the authority to collect and transfer the delegation credential to the PDP for decision making. This role now belongs to the new delegation authority.

In the context of XACML, the delegation authority could also act as a replacement of the Policy Information Point (PIP). The advantage of this approach is that systems with existing access control models do not need to change. The only change is to provide an interface to call and respond to the delegation authority. In the design of Chadwick et al., the Credential Validation Service could be either an additional component to be called by the PEP or the PIP [5].

3   Some Approaches to Delegation Problem and Classifications

In this section, the taxonomy criteria are utilised to compare some notable delegation approaches. For brevity, this paper does not discuss in detail each approach, but instead gives a brief discussion about the notable features and characteristics of each approach based on the taxonomy dimensions presented in Table 2.

Varadharajan, Allen and Black's work in 1991 discussed in detail how a protocol for delegation should be structured [13]. Based on the taxonomy, it can be said that the

Table 2. Comparison of some notable delegation approaches using the taxonomy's characteristics

Characteristics	Varadharajan, Allen & Black's Model	PBDM Family	Atluri and Warner's Model	Gomi et al.'s Model	Chadwick's Model
Motivation	Lack of authorisation	Lack of authorisation	Lack of authorisation and conflicted policies	Lack of authorisation	Lack of authorisation and conflicted policies
Delegation Boundary	Within a single domain	Within a single domain	Within and cross security domains	Within and cross security domains	Within and cross security domains
Who requests delegation?	User	User or System authority	Mainly focus on User level	User	User
Who delegates?	User	User or System authority	User	User	User
Relationship of the parties	Both direct and indirect	Both direct and indirect	Both direct and indirect	Both direct and indirect	Direct. Indirect delegation is not clearly discussed.
What to delegate?	Capability or Responsibility	Capability and Responsibility	Capability and Responsibility	Capability and Responsibility	Capability and Responsibility
How much to delegate?	Partial or Total	Partial or Total	Partial or Total	Partial or Total	Partial delegation is not specified
How long to delegate?	Temporal or Permanent	Temporal or Permanent	Temporal or Permanent	Temporal or Permanent	Temporal or Permanent
How to delegate?	Grant	Grant	Grant or Transfer	Grant	Grant
Authority Pre-Approval	Yes	Not specified	Not specified	Yes	Partially discussed
Type of Credential	Generic Token	Not specified but can be any	Not specified but can be any	X.509, SAML or Generic token	X.509, SAML or Generic token
Key Scheme	Symmetric or Asymmetric	Not specified but can either	Not specified but can either	Symmetric or Asymmetric	Symmetric or Asymmetric
Where delegation happens?	User level	Both but mainly target the System level	User level	User level	User level
Where delegation is honoured?	Not specified	Not specified	A central authority based on RBAC	An additional component called *Delegation Authority*	An additional component called *Credential Validation Service*

model of Varadharajan, Allen and Black is specifically designed to support *both key schemes*. From delegation perspective, the work, via the delegation of privilege, does not clearly explain the objective of the delegation process (*capability or responsibility*). It also fails to explicitly discuss *the relationship of delegator and delegatee*. While the protocol has the potential to extend to cover *cross domain transactions*, it does not cover this issue in detail.

Zhang, Oh and Sandhu presented a new permission-based delegation model (PBDM) in 2003 [15]. This model fully supports user to *user, temporal, partial and multi-step delegation*. This model is later extended and presented in three variants called PBDM0, PBDM1 and PBDM2. The PDBM family can support *multi-step delegation*, but they neither support constraints in delegation, nor *delegation across multiple security domains* [6]. In this model, both types of *grant and transfer delegation* are supported. The PBDM family can be considered as an extension of the RBDM [2] and RDM [14] models.

In 2005, in an effort to address constraint issues in delegation, Atluri and Warner [1] studied delegation in the workflow context and introduced a conditional delegation model. This is an interesting delegation approach as it investigates the problem of delegation with an *ad-hoc nature*. This is also one of the first models that details how delegation should be handled at the *user level* and *how/where the delegation should be honoured*. This model is one of the pioneers in the field that address the issue of delegation in the workflow context. However, similar to previous models, this work also fails to discuss *the relationships* between the delegator, the delegatee and the service provider.

Gomi et al. presented a basic framework to conduct *grant delegation* and revocation of access privileges *across security domains*. The model of Gomi et al. [8] requires the delegator to request the delegation assertion via *an additional authority called Delegation Authority (DA)*. This model lacks the capability to check for constraints and resolve conflicts between delegated privileges and between the delegated privileges with the involved policies. Therefore, it can cause problems in *indirect delegation which happens across multiple security domains*. The issue of *authority pre-approval* in the delegation process is partially discussed via the appearance of the delegation authority.

As part of efforts to develop PERMIS, Chadwick et al. proposed a mechanism based on the XACML conceptual and data flow models to address the issue of dynamic delegation of authority which involves the issuing of credentials from one user to another (*user delegation*) [5]. They proposed a new conceptual entity called the *Credential Validation Service*, to work alongside the PDP in making authorisation decisions. The model does not support *indirect delegation* well. Similarly to Gomi et al.'s work, this model, via the Credential Validation Service, partially discusses the issue of *authority pre-approval* but does not explicitly describe how delegation can happen without the pre-approval.

4   Discussion

To date, most delegation models have been centralised and based on the RBAC model. Delegation of capabilities seems to be a major concern of most models, except for some recent delegation models for workflow such as the works of Atluri and Warner, Gomi et al. and Chadwick et al. Most models have problems with partial and user (ad-hoc) delegation. It is also worth noting that, until 2004, most published works regarding delegation focused primarily on delegation between entities within a single security domain. More recently, there has been a trend toward increasing focus on cross domain issues. It can be seen that most recently developed models such as Atluri and Warner, Gomi et al., Chadwick et al., etc. are purposefully designed to support cross domain delegation.

Cross domain delegation is designed to achieve flexibility to meet the demand of collaborative activities. However, it is much more complicated to implement and enforce constraints over the ad-hoc delegation in cross domain models (Chadwick et al. vs. Varadharajan, Allen and Black). In addition to the same issues of classic delegation (within a single domain), the complexity of protocol and policy is a paramount issue. Such complexity requires a very well designed protocol and a high level of agreement between systems. To achieve cross domain delegation, the involved authority must also take into account the distribution of applicable policies across various security domains. For example, if the delegatee, the delegator and the service provider reside on three different security domains, all policy sets of these three domains must be considered and fed to the authority in charge of the delegation process for any decision making. This process is quite simple in single-domain delegation as there is only one single authority to handle the storage of credentials and feed them to the access decision authority. However, in addition to the distribution of policy, credential and delegation information are also distributed in cross domain delegation. The typical scenario is that the delegator and its local authority store and maintain part of the delegation information related to the delegator while the delegatee and the authority of the delegatee's domain store and maintain the rest. It is important to note that the main characteristics of delegation, such as delegation boundary, where delegation happens and where delegation is honoured, have a significant impact on making design decisions. This is because these factors are vital to form the backbone for a flexible and scalable cross domain delegation solution.

Together with the current trend in supporting cross domain collaborating activities, it is also important to note that there is an increasing demand in providing context-aware information to accommodate constraints and commitments for the delegation process. As current role-based approaches use the relationship of user-role-permission to impose constraints, it is difficult to present the additional context information to the access decision authority. Thus, there is a demand for a more expressive approach than the current role-based mechanisms. This is the reason why recent approaches such as Chadwick et al. (using XACML) or Gomi et al. (using SAML), etc. have adopted the policy language-based approach. With well defined languages such as XACML, SAML, etc., these models show that they can better address the issue of constraints. Even though policy language-based communication is exposed to high overhead and may result in low performance, this may be the only feasible approach to address the needs of highly collaborative activities across multiple security domains where constraints and context-awareness are critical. Depending on the level of application of a policy language-based approach, each model achieves a different level of expressiveness. The positive effects of applying the policy language-based approach can be seen clearly in Chadwick et al.'s model against the classic role-based approach in PBDM or RBDM family. However, application of a policy language is not the sole factor that determines the usefulness of a model because there are other factors that affect the final outcomes such as how the language is implemented, to what extent the language is implemented, the power of the language itself, etc.

5 Conclusion

This paper discussed the concept of delegation via a number of dimensions and presented a taxonomy of delegation concepts in the context of information systems and applied it to several delegation proposals. The taxonomy can be used to understand the major focus of a particular delegation approach by observing the characteristics involved. The taxonomy can help raise awareness of various design settings and potential implications on existing access control infrastructures.

Therefore, it can be said that this study is significant for several reasons. First of all, with the emerging demands in federating multiple enterprise systems together to achieve complex and collaborative activities, delegation is becoming a common approach to provide dynamic and flexible access control decisions. Secondly, delegation is considered a comparatively new research area and requires more input from the academic and industrial community and, although recent research has addressed the problems, several issues still remain to be investigated and resolved. Therefore, this research should provide system designers a clear picture about the characteristics of different types of delegation approaches and the involved actors so that they can choose the type of delegation that best satisfies their requirements. Thirdly, as collaboration environments require a great level of interoperability, knowledge of characteristics and protocols of different types of delegation could vastly improve the integration process.

Finally, as the main focus of this paper is delegation approaches which can be used in secured task distribution in workflow or secure ad-hoc collaboration, currently, this paper does not cover the complete set of delegation approaches with the ad-hoc nature that can be applied highly dynamic and ad-hoc transaction such as secure task distribution in workflow or secure collaboration. Therefore, as the future work, some other aspects of delegation will be considered such as the rubric of trust management, logic-based and cryptographic approaches.

Acknowledgements. The research is kindly funded by the Smart Services CRC, the Information Queensland, Queensland State Government, Australia and the Australian Research Council - Project *DP0773706*. This paper has been abridged due to space constraints. The full version of the paper can be found in the technical report at QUT ePrints - http://eprints.qut.edu.au/17213/.

References

1. Atluri, V., Warner, J.: Supporting conditional delegation in secure workflow management systems. In: Proceedings of the 10th ACM symposium on Access control models and technologies (SACMAT 2005), Stockholm, Sweden, pp. 49–58 (2005)
2. Barka, E., Sandhu, R.: Role-Based Delegation Model - Hierarchical Roles (RBDM1). In: Proceedings of the 20th Annual Computer Security Applications Conference (ACSAC 2004), pp. 396–404 (2004)

3. Botha, R.A., Eloff, J.H.P.: A framework for access control in workflow systems. Information Management & Computer Security 9(3), 126–133 (2001)
4. Chadwick, D.W., Otenko, A.: The PERMIS X.509 Role Based Privilege Management Infrastructure. In: Proceedings of the 7th ACM symposium on Access control models and technologies, Monterey, California, USA, pp. 135–140 (2002)
5. Chadwick, D.W., Otenko, S., Nguyen, T.A.: Adding support to XACML for dynamic delegation of authority in multiple domains. In: Leitold, H., Markatos, E.P. (eds.) CMS 2006. LNCS, vol. 4237, pp. 67–86. Springer, Heidelberg (2006)
6. Crampton, J., Khambhammettu, H.: Delegation in role-based access control. In: Gollmann, D., Meier, J., Sabelfeld, A. (eds.) ESORICS 2006. LNCS, vol. 4189, pp. 174–191. Springer, Heidelberg (2006)
7. Crispo, B.: Delegation of responsibility. In: Christianson, B., Crispo, B., Harbison, W.S., Roe, M. (eds.) Security Protocols 1998. LNCS, vol. 1550, p. 626. Springer, Heidelberg (1999)
8. Gomi, H., Hatakeyama, M., Hosono, S., Fujita, S.: A delegation framework for federated identity management. In: Proceedings of the ACM Workshop on Digital Identity Management, pp. 94–103 (2005)
9. Lorch, M., Adams, D., Kafura, D., Koneni, M., Rathi, A., Shah, S.: The PRIMA System for Privilege Management, Authorization and Enforcement in Grid Environments. In: Proceedings of the 4th International Workshop on Grid Computing - Grid 2003, Phoenix, AR, USA (2003)
10. Pham, Q., McCullagh, A., Dawson, E.: Consistency of user attribute in federated systems. In: Lambrinoudakis, C., Pernul, G., Tjoa, A.M. (eds.) TrustBus. LNCS, vol. 4657, pp. 165–177. Springer, Heidelberg (2007)
11. Schaad, A.: A Framework for Organisational Control Principles. PhD Thesis, The University of York, York, England (2003)
12. Varadharajan, V.: Authentication in mobile distributed environment. In: Proceedings of the 7th IEE European Conference on Mobile and Personal Communications, pp. 173–188 (1993)
13. Varadharajan, V., Allen, P., Black, S.: An analysis of the proxy problem in distributed systems. In: Proceedings of the 1991 IEEE Symposium on Research in Security and Privacy, Oakland, CA, USA, pp. 255–275 (1991)
14. Zhang, L., Ahn, G.L., Chu, B.T.: A rule-based framework for role based delegation. In: Proceedings of the 6th ACM symposium on Access control models and technologies, Chantilly, VA, USA, pp. 153–162 (2001)
15. Zhang, X., Oh, S., Sandhu, R.: PBDM: a flexible delegation model in RBAC. In: Proceedings of the 8th ACM symposium on Access control models and technologies, Como, Italy, pp. 149–157 (2003)

Efficient Key Management for Enforcing Access Control in Outsourced Scenarios

Carlo Blundo[1], Stelvio Cimato[2], Sabrina De Capitani di Vimercati[2],
Alfredo De Santis[1], Sara Foresti[2], Stefano Paraboschi[3], and Pierangela Samarati[2]

[1] Università di Salerno, 84084 Fisciano - Italy
{carblu,ads}@dia.unisa.it
[2] Università di Milano, 26013 Crema - Italy
{cimato,decapita,foresti,samarati}@dti.unimi.it
[3] Università di Bergamo, 24044 Dalmine - Italy
parabosc@unibg.it

Abstract. Data outsourcing is emerging today as a successful paradigm allowing individuals and organizations to exploit external servers for storing and distributing data. While trusted to properly manage the data, external servers are often not authorized to read them, therefore requiring data to be encrypted. In such a context, the application of an access control policy requires different data to be encrypted with different keys so to allow the external server to directly enforce access control and support selective dissemination and access.

The problem therefore emerges of designing solutions for the efficient management of the encryption policy enforcing access control, with the goal of minimizing the number of keys to be maintained by the system and distributed to users. Since such a problem is NP-hard, we propose a heuristic approach to its solution based on a key derivation graph exploiting the relationships among user groups. We experimentally evaluate the performance of our heuristic solution, comparing it with previous approaches.

1 Introduction

Data outsourcing has become increasingly popular in recent years. The main advantage of data outsourcing is that it promises higher availability and more effective disaster protection than in-house operations. However, since data owners physically release their information to external servers that are not under their control, data confidentiality and even integrity may be put at risk. As a matter of fact, sensitive data (or data that can be exploited for linking with sensitive data) are stored on external servers. Besides protecting such data from attackers and unauthorized users, there is the need to protect the privacy of the data from the so called *honest-but-curious* servers: the server to whom data are outsourced, while trustworthy to properly manage the data, may not be trusted by the data owner to read their content. The problem of protecting data when outsourcing them to an external honest-but-curious server has emerged to the attention of researchers very recently. Existing proposals (e.g., [4, 8, 13]) in the data outsourcing area typically resort to store the data in encrypted form, while associating with the encrypted data additional indexing information that is used by the external DBMS to select the data to be returned in response to a query. Also, existing works typically assume

D. Gritzalis and J. Lopez (Eds.): SEC 2009, IFIP AICT 297, pp. 364–375, 2009.

that the data owner is a single organization that encrypts the data with a single key and that all users have complete visibility of the whole database. Such approaches clearly are limiting in today's scenarios, where remotely stored data may need to be accessible in a selective way, that is, different users may be authorized to access different views of the data.

There is therefore an increasing interest in the definition of security solutions that allow the enforcement of access control policies on outsourced data. A promising solution in this direction consists in integrating access control and encryption. Combining cryptography with access control essentially requires that resources should be encrypted differently depending on the access authorizations holding on them, so to allow their decryption only to authorized users [5, 6]. The application of this approach in data outsourcing scenarios allows owners: *1)* to encrypt data, according to an encryption policy regulated by authorizations, *2)* outsource the data to the external servers, and *3)* distribute to users the proper encryption keys. Proper encryption and key distribution automatically ensure obedience of the access control policy, while not requiring the data owner to maintain control on the data storage and on accesses to the data. In the literature, there are different proposals exploiting encryption for access control [5, 6, 10]. In [5], the authors address the problem of access control enforcement in the database outsourcing context, by exploiting selective encryption and hierarchical key assignment schemes on trees. Since a crucial aspect for the success of such a solution is the efficacy, efficiency, and scalability of the key management and distribution activities, the authors propose an algorithm that minimizes the number of secret keys in users' key rings. In [6], the authors address the problem of policy updates. Here, two layers of encryption are imposed on data: the inner layer is imposed by the owner for providing initial protection, the outer layer is imposed by the server to reflect policy modifications (i.e., grant/revoke of authorizations). In [10], the authors introduce a framework for enforcing access control on published XML documents by using different cryptographic keys over different portions of the XML tree and by introducing special metadata nodes in the structure.

In this paper we propose a novel heuristic approach minimizing the number of keys to be maintained by the system and distributed to users. Consistently with other proposals in the literature [5,6], we base our solution on *key derivation* exploiting a *key derivation graph* that allows users to derive new keys by combining other keys and public tokens. As we will show, compared with previous proposals, our heuristics prove efficient and effective in the computation of a key derivation graph.

2   Basic Concepts

We assume that the data owner defines a discretionary access control policy to regulate access to the distributed resources. Consistently with other approaches for data outsourcing, we assume access by users to the outsourced resources to be read-only. Given a set $\mathscr{U}$ of users and a set $\mathscr{R}$ of resources, an *authorization policy* over $\mathscr{U}$ and $\mathscr{R}$ is a set of pairs $\langle u, r \rangle$, where $u \in \mathscr{U}$ and $r \in \mathscr{R}$, meaning that user u can access resource r. An authorization policy can be modeled via an *access matrix* $\mathscr{A}$, with a row for each user $u \in \mathscr{U}$, a column for each resource $r \in \mathscr{R}$, and $\mathscr{A}[u, r]$ set to 1 (0, resp.) if u has (does

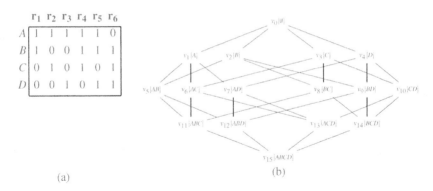

Fig. 1. An example of access matrix (a) and of user graph over $\mathcal{U}=\{A,B,C,D\}$ (b)

not have, resp.) authorization to access r. Given an access matrix $\mathcal{A}$, $acl(r)$ denotes the *access control list* of r (i.e., the set of users that can access r), and $cap(u)$ denotes the *capability list* of u (i.e., the set of resources that u can access). Figure 1(a) illustrates an example of access matrix with four users (A, B, C, D) and six resources ($r_1, \ldots, r_6$), where, for example, $acl(r_2)=\{A,C\}$ and $cap(C)=\{r_2,r_4,r_6\}$.

In the data outsourcing scenario, the enforcement of the authorization policy cannot be delegated to the remote server, which is trusted neither for accessing data content nor for enforcing the authorization policy. Consequently, the data owner has to be involved in the access control enforcement. To avoid the owner's involvement in managing access and enforcing authorizations, recently *selective encryption* techniques have been proposed [5, 6, 10]. Selective encryption means that the *encryption policy* (i.e., which data are encrypted with which key) is dictated by the authorizations to be enforced on the data. The basic idea is to use different keys for encrypting data and to release to each user the set of keys necessary to decrypt all and only the resources the user is authorized to access. For efficiency reasons, selective encryption is realized through symmetric keys.

A straightforward solution for implementing selective encryption associates a key with each resource r and communicates to each user u the keys used to encrypt the resources in $cap(u)$. It is easy to see that this solution, while correctly enforcing the authorization policy, is too expensive to manage, due to the high number of keys each user has to keep. Indeed, any user $u \in \mathcal{U}$ would need to hold as many keys as the number of resources she is authorized to access.

To avoid users having to store and manage a huge number of (secret) keys, consistently with other proposals in the literature [5, 6], we exploit a *key derivation method* that allows the derivation of a key starting from another key and some public information [1, 2, 3, 9, 11, 7]. In our scenario, the derivation relationship between keys can be represented through a graph with a vertex v for each possible set of users and an edge (v_i, v_j) for all pairs of vertices such that the set of users represented by v_i is a subset of the set of users represented by v_j. In the following, we use $v.acl$ to denote the set of users represented by vertex v and $v.key$ to denote the key associated with v. Formally, a user graph is defined as follows.

Definition 1 (User Graph). *Given a set $\mathcal{U}$ of users, a user graph over $\mathcal{U}$, denoted $G_{\mathcal{U}}$, is a graph $\langle V_{\mathcal{U}}, E_{\mathcal{U}} \rangle$, where $V_{\mathcal{U}} = P(\mathcal{U})$ is the power set of $\mathcal{U}$, and $E_{\mathcal{U}} = \{(v_i, v_j) \mid v_i.acl \subset v_j.acl\}$.*

As an example, consider the set of users $\mathcal{U} = \{A,B,C,D\}$. Figure 1(b) reports the user graph, where, for each vertex v_i, the users in the square brackets represent $v_i.acl$ and, for clearness of the picture, edges that are implied by other edges (relationships between sets differing for more than one user) are not reported.

By exploiting the user graph defined above, the authorization policy can be enforced: *i)* by encrypting each resource with the key of the vertex corresponding to its access control list (e.g., resource r_4 should be encrypted with $v_{11}.key$ since $acl(r_4)=v_{11}.acl= \{A,B,C\}$), and *ii)* by assigning to each user the key associated with the vertex representing the user in the graph. Since edges represent the possible key derivations, each user u, starting from her own key, can directly compute the keys of all vertices v such that $u \in v.acl$. It is easy to see that this approach to design the encryption policy *correctly enforces* the authorization policy represented by matrix $\mathcal{A}$, meaning that each user u can only derive the keys for decrypting the resources she is authorized to access. For instance, with reference to the user graph in Fig. 1(b), user A knows the key associated with vertex v_1 from which she can derive, following the edges outgoing from v_1, the set of keys of vertices $v_5, v_6, v_7, v_{11}, v_{12}, v_{13}$, and v_{15}.

3   Problem Formulation

The key derivation methods working on trees are in general more convenient and simpler than those working on DAGs and require a lower amount of publicly available information. Indeed, given two keys k_i and k_j in $\mathcal{K}$, where $\mathcal{K}$ is the set of symmetric encryption keys in the system, such that k_j can be directly derived from k_i, then $k_j = h(k_i, l_j)$, where l_j is a publicly available label associated with k_j and h is a deterministic cryptographic function. We then transform, according with the proposal in [5], the user graph $G_{\mathcal{U}}$ in a *user tree*, denoted T, enforcing the authorization policy in $\mathcal{A}$. Since each resource r is encrypted with the key associated with the vertex representing $acl(r)$, the user tree must include the set, denoted $\mathcal{M}$, of all vertices, called *material vertices*, representing acl values and the empty set of users (i.e., $\mathcal{M} = \{v \in V_{\mathcal{U}} \mid v.acl = \emptyset \vee \exists\, r \in \mathcal{R}$ with $v.acl = acl(r)\}$), as formally defined in the following.

Definition 2 (User tree). *Let $\mathcal{A}$ be an access matrix over a set $\mathcal{U}$ of users and a set $\mathcal{R}$ of resources, and $G_{\mathcal{U}} = \langle V_{\mathcal{U}}, E_{\mathcal{U}} \rangle$ be the user graph over $\mathcal{U}$. A user tree, denoted T, is a tree $T = \langle V, E \rangle$, subgraph of $G_{\mathcal{U}}$, rooted at vertex v_0, with $v_0.acl = \emptyset$, where $\mathcal{M} \subseteq V \subseteq V_{\mathcal{U}}$, and $E \subseteq E_{\mathcal{U}}$.*

In other words, a user tree is a tree, rooted at the vertex representing the empty user group $\emptyset$, subgraph of $G_{\mathcal{U}}$, and spanning all vertices in $\mathcal{M}$.

To grant the correct enforcement of the authorization policy, each user u has a key ring, denoted $key\_ring_T(u)$, containing all the keys necessary to derive the keys of all vertices v such that $u \in v.acl$. The key ring of each user u must then include the keys associated with all vertices v such that $u \in v.acl$ and $u \notin v_p.acl$, where v_p is the parent

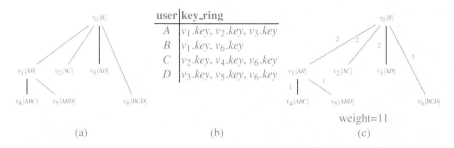

Fig. 2. A user tree (a), the corresponding key rings (b), and its weighted version (c)

of v. If $u \in v_p.acl$, u must already have access to the key in v_p and must be able to derive $v.key$ through the key of v_p, which she knows either by derivation or by direct communication.

Clearly, given a set of users and an authorization policy $\mathscr{A}$, more user trees may exist. Among all possible user trees, we are interested in determining a *minimum user tree*, correctly enforcing a given authorization policy and minimizing the number of keys in users' key rings.

Definition 3 (Minimum user tree). *Let $\mathscr{A}$ be an access matrix and T be a user tree correctly enforcing $\mathscr{A}$. T is* minimum *with respect to $\mathscr{A}$ iff $\nexists T'$ such that T' correctly enforces $\mathscr{A}$ and* $\sum_{u \in \mathscr{U}} |key\_ring_{T'}(u)| < \sum_{u \in \mathscr{U}} |key\_ring_T(u)|.$

Figure 2(a) illustrates an example of user tree and Fig. 2(b) reports the corresponding user key rings.

We observe that the keys in the key ring could be managed with the use of *tokens*, public pieces of information that allow the reconstruction of a secret from another one [2,3]. The minimality of the user tree implies a minimization in the number of tokens, making the approach presented in this paper applicable to scenarios using tokens.

Given an access matrix $\mathscr{A}$, different minimum user trees may exist and our goal is to compute one of them, as stated by the following problem definition.

Problem 1. Let $\mathscr{A}$ be an access matrix. Determine a minimum user tree T.

Since Problem 1 is NP-hard, in [5] we proposed a heuristic algorithm working as follows: *1)* the algorithm initially computes the closure of $\mathscr{M}$ with respect to the intersection operator; *2)* the algorithm selects, for each vertex, a parent choosing first the vertices representing larger sets of users, and then material vertices; finally *3)* the algorithm prunes non necessary vertices.

4   Minimum Spanning Tree Heuristics

Our solution is based on a reformulation of Problem 1 in terms of a weight minimization problem. We start by introducing the concept of weight in association with a user tree.

Definition 4 (Weight function). *Let* $T = \langle V, E \rangle$ *be a user tree.*

- $w\colon E \to \mathbb{N}$ *is a weight function such that* $\forall (v_i, v_j) \in E,\ w(v_i, v_j) = |v_j.acl \setminus v_i.acl|$
- $\texttt{weight}(T) = \displaystyle\sum_{(v_i, v_j) \in E} w(v_i, v_j).$

According to this definition, the weight $w(v_i, v_j)$ of edge (v_i, v_j) in E is the number of users in $v_j.acl \setminus v_i.acl$. The weight $\texttt{weight}(T)$ of user tree T is then defined as the sum of the weights of its edges. Problem 1 can be reformulated as the problem of finding a *minimum weight* user tree. In fact, the presence of an edge $(v_i, v_j) \in E$ implies that users in $v_i.acl$ should know both keys $v_i.key$ and $v_j.key$ while users in $v_j.acl \setminus v_i.acl$ need only to know $v_j.key$. It is then sufficient to include key $v_i.key$ in the key rings of all users in $v_i.acl$, since $v_j.key$ can be derived from $v_i.key$, and to include key $v_j.key$ in the key rings of users in $v_j.acl \setminus v_i.acl$. This is equivalent to say that $w(v_i, v_j)$ corresponds to the number of users whose key ring must include key $v_j.key$. Generalizing, it is immediate to conclude that $\texttt{weight}(T)$ is equal to the sum of the total number of keys stored in users' key rings (i.e., $\texttt{weight}(T) = \sum_{u \in \mathcal{U}} |key\_ring_T(u)|$).

The problem of computing a user tree with minimum weight is NP-hard since the Vertex Cover problem can be reduced to it (for space reason, we do not report the proof of this reduction). We therefore propose a heuristic algorithm for solving such a problem that consists first in computing a minimum spanning tree (MST) over a graph $G = \langle V, E', w \rangle$, with $V = \mathcal{U}$, $E' = \{(v_i, v_j) \mid v_i, v_j \in V \wedge v_i.acl \subset v_j.acl\}$, and w the weight function defined in Definition 4, rooted at v_0. It is immediate to see that the MST over G is a user tree whose weight can be further reduced with the addition of vertices obtained from the intersection of at least two vertices already in the MST. The insertion of a new vertex v as a parent of at least two vertices, say v_i and v_j, can reduce the weight of the tree since the key ring of users in $v.acl$ should only include $v.key$ instead of both $v_i.key$ and $v_j.key$.

The basic idea behind our approach is that for each internal vertex v of the minimum spanning tree (i.e., for each vertex with at least one child) and for each pair $\langle v_i, v_j \rangle$ of children of v, we first compute the set U of users in $v_i.acl$ and $v_j.acl$, that is, $U = v_i.acl \cap v_j.acl$. If $U \neq v.acl$, we then evaluate if the insertion in T of vertex v_k representing U can reduce $\texttt{weight}(T)$. Among all possible pairs of children of v, we then choose the pair $\langle v_i, v_j \rangle$ such that, when v_k is possibly inserted in the tree (or it becomes the parent of at least one of two vertices v_i and v_j), we obtain the highest reduction in the weight of the tree. Such a weight reduction, formally defined by function $weight\_red\colon V \times V \times V \to \mathbb{N}$, depends on whether v_k exists in T or it needs to be inserted. The following three cases, represented in Fig. 3, may occur.

Case 1. $v_k = v_i$ (or $v_k = v_j$), that is, one of the two children represents a subset of the users represented by the other child. The user tree can be updated by removing the edge connecting vertex v with v_j (v_i, resp.) and by inserting the edge connecting v_i with v_j (v_j with v_i, resp.). As a consequence, the weight of the tree is reduced by $w(v, v_j) - w(v_i, v_j)$, which is equal to $|v_i.acl| - |v.acl|$.

Case 2. $v_k \in V$ and $v_k \neq v_i$ and $v_k \neq v_j$, that is, there is a vertex in the tree representing U. The user tree can be updated by removing the edges connecting vertex v with both

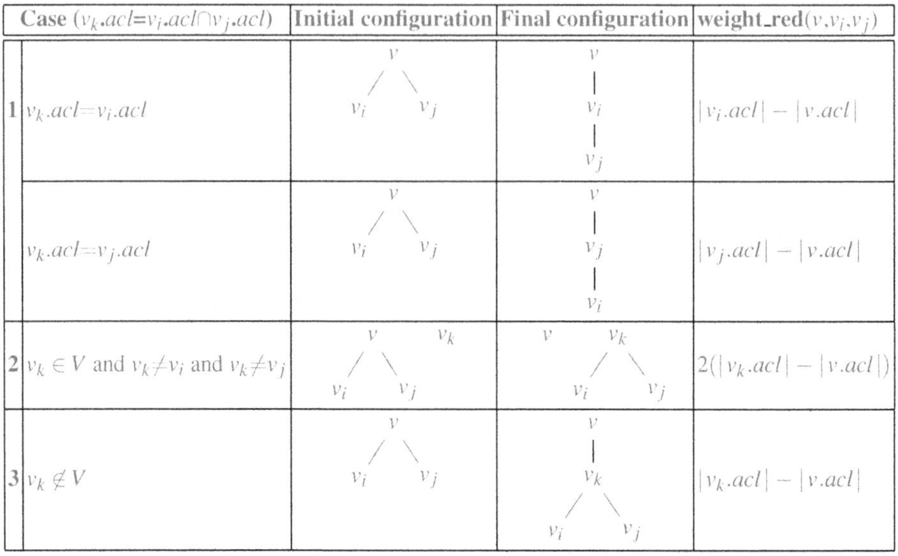

Case ($v_k.acl=v_i.acl\cap v_j.acl$)	Initial configuration	Final configuration	weight_red(v,v_i,v_j)
1 $v_k.acl=v_i.acl$	v with children v_i, v_j	$v - v_i - v_j$	$|v_i.acl| - |v.acl|$
$v_k.acl=v_j.acl$	v with children v_i, v_j	$v - v_j - v_i$	$|v_j.acl| - |v.acl|$
2 $v_k \in V$ and $v_k \neq v_i$ and $v_k \neq v_j$	v, v_k with children v_i, v_j	v, v_k with children v_i, v_j	$2(|v_k.acl| - |v.acl|)$
3 $v_k \notin V$	v with children v_i, v_j	$v - v_k$ with children v_i, v_j	$|v_k.acl| - |v.acl|$

Fig. 3. Possible updates to the user tree

v_i and v_j, and by inserting two new edges, connecting v_k with v_i and v_j, respectively. As a consequence, the weight of the tree is reduced by $w(v,v_i) + w(v,v_j) - (w(v_k,v_i) + w(v_k,v_j))$, which is equal to $2(|v_k.acl| - |v.acl|)$.

Case 3. $v_k \notin V$, that is, there is no vertex representing U in the tree.[1] The user tree can be updated by: creating a new vertex v_k with $v_k.acl=U$; removing the edges connecting v with both v_i and v_j; and inserting three new edges connecting respectively: *1)* v with v_k, *2)* v_k with v_i, and *3)* v_k with v_j. As a consequence, the weight of the tree is reduced by $w(v,v_i) + w(v,v_j) - (w(v,v_k) + w(v_k,v_i) + w(v_k,v_j))$, which is equal to $|v_k.acl| - |v.acl|$.

As an example, consider the weighted user tree in Fig. 2(c) and suppose to compute the intersection between the pairs of children of the root vertex v_0. In this case, all possible intersections correspond to singleton sets of users that are not already represented in the tree and therefore each intersection requires the addition of a new vertex in the tree as child of v_0 and parent of the considered pair of children.

Formally, for each internal vertex v of the minimum spanning tree $ST = \langle V,E \rangle$, we first compute the set CC_v of pairs of *candidate children* as follows: $CC_v = \{\langle v_i,v_j \rangle \mid (v,v_i), (v,v_j) \in E \land v_i.acl \cap v_j.acl \neq v.acl\}$. Among all possible pairs in CC_v, we then choose a pair $\langle v_i,v_j \rangle$ that maximizes *weight_red*. Note that different pairs of vertices in CC_v may provide the same maximum weight reduction. In this case, different preference criteria may be applied for choosing a pair, thus obtaining different heuristics. In particular, we propose the following three criteria:

---

[1] Note that this is the only case that can occur if both v_i and v_j belong to $\mathscr{U}$, since T is initially obtained as a minimum spanning tree over G.

INPUT
set $\mathscr{U}$ of users
set $\mathscr{R}$ of resources
access matrix $\mathscr{A}$
criterion (I_{max}, I_{min}, or I_{rnd}) to adopt
 	
OUTPUT
user tree $T = \langle V, E \rangle$
 	
MAIN
$V := \emptyset$
$E := \emptyset$
/* **Phase 1**: select material vertices */
$Acl_{\mathscr{A}} := \{acl(r) \mid r \in \mathscr{R}\} \cup \{\emptyset\}$
for each $acl \in Acl_{\mathscr{A}}$ **do**
   create vertex v
   $v.acl := acl$
   $V := V \cup \{v\}$
/* **Phase 2**: compute a minimum spanning tree */
$E' := \{(v_i, v_j) \mid v_i, v_j \in V \wedge v_i.acl \subset v_j.acl\}$
let w be a weight function such that
$\forall (v_i, v_j) \in E', w(v_i, v_j) = \lvert v_j.acl \setminus v_i.acl \rvert$
$G := (V, E', w)$
let v_0 be the vertex in V with $v_0.acl = \emptyset$
$T := \textbf{Minimum\_Spanning\_Tree}(G, v_0)$
/* **Phase 3**: insert non-material vertices */
$T := \textbf{Factorize\_Internal\_Vertices}(T, \text{criterion})$
return(T)
	FACTORIZE_INTERNAL_VERTICES(ST, $criterion$)
	let ST be $\langle V, E \rangle$
	for each $v \in \{v_i \mid v_i \in V \wedge \exists (v_i, v_j) \in E\}$ **do**
	  $CC_v := \{\langle v_i, v_j \rangle \mid (v, v_i), (v, v_j) \in E \wedge v_i.acl \cap v_j.acl \neq v.acl\}$
	  $max\_red := \textbf{max}\{weight\_red(v, v_i, v_j) \mid \langle v_i, v_j \rangle \in CC_v\}$
	  while $CC_v \neq \emptyset$ **do**
	    $MC_v := \{\langle v_i, v_j \rangle \mid \langle v_i, v_j \rangle \in CC_v \wedge weight\_red(v, v_i, v_j) = max\_red\}$
	    case $criterion$ **of**
	     I_{rnd}: choose $\langle v_i, v_j \rangle \in MC_v$ randomly
	     I_{max}: choose $\langle v_i, v_j \rangle \in MC_v$: $\lvert v_i.acl \rvert + \lvert v_j.acl \rvert$ is maximum
	     I_{min}: choose $\langle v_i, v_j \rangle \in MC_v$: $\lvert v_i.acl \rvert + \lvert v_j.acl \rvert$ is minimum
	    $U := v_i.acl \cap v_j.acl$
	    find $v_k \in V$: $v_k.acl = U$
	    case v_k **of**
	     /* case 1 */
	     $= v_i$: $E := E \setminus \{(v, v_j)\} \cup \{(v_i, v_j)\}$
	     $= v_j$: $E := E \setminus \{(v, v_i)\} \cup \{(v_j, v_i)\}$
	     /* case 2 */
	     $\neq v_i \wedge \neq v_j$: $E := E \setminus \{(v, v_i), (v, v_j)\} \cup \{(v_k, v_i), (v_k, v_j)\}$
	     /* case 3 */
	     UNDEF: create a vertex v_k
	            $v_k.acl := U$
	            $V := V \cup \{v_k\}$
	            $E := E \setminus \{(v, v_i), (v, v_j)\} \cup \{(v, v_k), (v_k, v_i), (v_k, v_j)\}$
	    $CC_v := \{\langle v_i, v_j \rangle \mid (v, v_i), (v, v_j) \in E \wedge v_i.acl \cap v_j.acl \neq v.acl\}$
	    $max\_red := \textbf{max}\{weight\_red(v, v_i, v_j) \mid \langle v_i, v_j \rangle \in CC_v\}$
	return(ST)

Fig. 4. Heuristic algorithm for computing a minimal user tree

- I_{rnd}: at random;
- I_{max}: in such a way that $\lvert v_i.acl \rvert + \lvert v_j.acl \rvert$ is maximum, ties are broken randomly;
- I_{min}: in such a way that $\lvert v_i.acl \rvert + \lvert v_j.acl \rvert$ is minimum, ties are broken randomly.

Any of these three preference criteria can be used to compute an approximation of the minimum user tree.

Figure 4 illustrates our algorithm that, given an authorization policy represented through an access matrix $\mathscr{A}$, creates a user tree correctly enforcing the policy. The algorithm creates the set V of material vertices and builds a graph G, where the set of vertices coincides with the set V of material vertices and the set E' of edges includes an edge (v_i, v_j) for each pair of vertices $v_i, v_j \in V$ such that $v_i.acl \subset v_j.acl$. The algorithm then calls function **Minimum_Spanning_Tree**[2] on G and vertex v_0, with $v_0.acl = \emptyset$, and returns a minimum spanning tree of G rooted at v_0. On such a minimum spanning tree, the algorithm calls function **Factorize_Internal_Vertices**. Function **Factorize_Internal_Vertices** takes a minimum spanning tree ST and a selection criterion as input and returns a minimal user tree. For each internal vertex v in ST (first **for** loop in the function), the function first computes the set CC_v of pairs of candidate children of v and determines the maximum reduction max_red of the weight of the tree that any of these pairs can cause. At each iteration of the **while** loop, the function selects, according to the given criterion, a pair $\langle v_i, v_j \rangle$ in CC_v such that $weight\_red(v, v_i, v_j)$ is

---

[2] This function may correspond to any algorithm commonly used for computing a minimum spanning tree. Our implementation is based on Prim's algorithm.

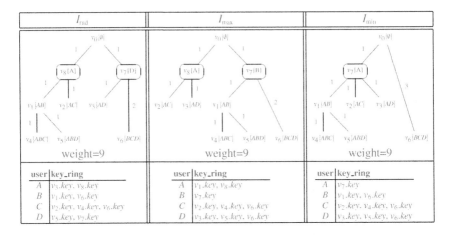

Fig. 5. User trees and key rings computed by our heuristics over the MST of Fig. 2(c)

equal to *max_red*. The tree is then updated as illustrated in Fig. 3. Then, both CC_v and *max_red* are re-evaluated on the basis of the new topology of the tree. Note that CC_v does not need to be recomputed at each iteration of the **while** loop, since it can be simply updated by removing the pairs involving v_i and/or v_j and possibly adding the pairs resulting from the new vertex v_k. The process is repeated until CC_v becomes empty. The function terminates when all internal vertices have been evaluated (i.e., when the **for** loop has iterated on all internal vertices). As an example, consider the authorization policy $\mathscr{A}$ in Fig. 1(a). The table in Fig. 5 is composed of three columns, one for each of the preference criteria defined for our heuristic (i.e., I_{rnd}, I_{max}, and I_{min}). Each column represents the user tree and the user key rings computed by our heuristic, following one of the three preference criteria. Note that the vertices inserted by the algorithm are circled in Fig. 5, to distinguish material from non-material vertices.

5   Experimental Results

A correct evaluation of the performance of the proposed heuristics is requested to provide the system designer with a valid set of tools she can use for the selection of the right strategy to implement a given authorization policy. In large scale access control systems, where the number of users and resources is large, the time needed to set the right key assignment scheme can be considerably large. So, the analysis we provide can help the designer to select the right trade-off between the quality of the solution returned by the selected heuristic and the amount of time invested on obtaining such a result. The heuristics have then been implemented by using Scilab [12] Version 4-1 on Windows XP operating system on a computer equipped with Centrino 1,7 Mhz CPU. We ran the experiments on randomly generated access matrices, considering different numbers of users and resources in the system.

A first set of experiments, whose results are reported in Fig. 6, has been devoted to compare the quality of the solutions returned by the different heuristics. For a fixed

Number of resources	5 users				6 users				10 users			
	I_{tot}	I_{min}	I_{max}	I_{rnd}	I_{tot}	I_{min}	I_{max}	I_{rnd}	I_{tot}	I_{min}	I_{max}	I_{rnd}
5	937	932	924	927	865	863	830	834	828	802	692	709
10	879	872	849	849	778	693	648	657	709	633	219	269
15	947	946	936	936	735	720	637	634	729	685	168	205
20	987	983	979	982	780	751	671	685	717	626	118	120
25	1000	998	998	998	781	763	705	714	694	598	90	131
30	1000	1000	1000	1000	846	835	808	815	626	543	77	131
35					891	886	853	858	554	484	64	104
40					943	940	924	928	570	538	59	85
45					981	978	966	973	501	488	57	68
50					993	992	989	991	501	478	55	67

Fig. 6. Number of times that our heuristics are better than the heuristic in [5]

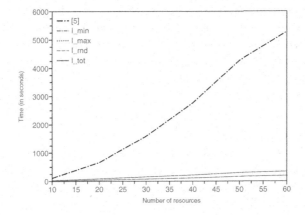

Fig. 7. Execution time (in seconds) for the heuristics for 10 users (1000 runs)

number of users and resources, we generated 1000 access matrices for each trial and applied to the resulting access matrix the heuristic proposed in [5] and our heuristics, considering all the possible choices (i.e., I_{min}, I_{max}, or I_{rnd}) for the selection of a candidate pair among the pairs maximizing the *weight_red* function. Columns I_{min}, I_{max}, and I_{rnd} list the number of times the selected heuristic computes a user tree better than the user tree obtained by running the heuristic in [5], meaning that the total number of keys, in the key rings of the users, computed by our heuristic is less than or equal to the total number of keys in the key rings of the users obtained with the heuristic in [5]. Column I_{tot} lists the number of times that any of our heuristics returns a better solution than one returned by the heuristic in [5]. Note that while the I_{min} heuristic returns a better solution in most of the cases, there are cases where I_{max} or I_{rnd} perform better. On the basis of the data reported in Fig. 6, it is possible to observe the good behavior of our heuristics in the sense that they compute a solution that, in many cases, is better than the one returned by the heuristic in [5].

Figure 7 reports the sum of the execution times for all the considered instances. Note that the lines representing the I_{max}, I_{min}, and I_{rnd} heuristics are overlapping. For each instance (i.e., each randomly generated access matrix), the execution time is composed of the time for the construction of the graph G (see Sect. 4), the time for the construction of the minimum spanning tree on G, and the time for the execution of the selected heuristic. As shown in the figure, our heuristics are very efficient compared with the heuristic in [5]. Considering that in many cases, such heuristics return a better solution than the one computed by the heuristic in [5], we can conclude that they represent a good trade-off between quality and execution time. Also, since our heuristics are fast to execute, after graph G and the corresponding minimum spanning tree have been generated, it should be also possible to execute all our heuristics to select the best of the three returned results (without need of generating the graph and the MST again).

6 Conclusions

There is an emerging trend towards scenarios where resource management is outsourced to an external service providing storage capabilities and high-bandwidth distribution channels. In this context, selective dissemination of data requires enforcing measures to protect the resource confidentiality from both unauthorized users as well as honest-but-curious servers. Current solutions provide protection by exploiting encryption in conjunction with proper indexing capabilities, and by exploiting selective encryption for access control enforcement. In this paper we proposed a heuristic algorithm for building a key derivation graph that minimizes the total number of keys to be distributed to users in the system. The experimental results obtained by the implementation of the algorithm prove its efficiency with respect to previous solutions.

Acknowledgements. This work was supported in part by the EU, within the 7FP project, under grant agreement 216483 "PrimeLife" and by the Italian MIUR, within PRIN 2006, under project 2006099978 "Basi di dati crittografate".

References

1. Akl, S., Taylor, P.: Cryptographic solution to a problem of access control in a hierarchy. ACM Transactions on Computer System 1(3), 239–248 (1983)
2. Atallah, M.J., Frikken, K.B., Blanton, M.: Dynamic and efficient key management for access hierarchies. In: Proc. of the ACM CCS 2005, Alexandria, VA (2005)
3. Ateniese, G., De Santis, A., Ferrara, A.L., Masucci, B.: Provably-secure time-bound hierarchical key assignment schemes. In: Proc. of ACM CCS 2006, Alexandria, VA (2006)
4. Ceselli, A., Damiani, E., De Capitani di Vimercati, S., Jajodia, S., Paraboschi, S., Samarati, P.: Modeling and assessing inference exposure in encrypted databases. ACM TISSEC 8(1), 119–152 (2005)
5. Damiani, E., De Capitani di Vimercati, S., Foresti, S., Jajodia, S., Paraboschi, S., Samarati, P.: Selective data encryption in outsourced dynamic environments. In: Proc. of VODCA 2006, Bertinoro, Italy (2006)
6. De Capitani di Vimercati, S., Foresti, S., Jajodia, S., Paraboschi, S., Samarati, P.: Over-encryption: Management of access control evolution on outsourced data. In: Proc. of VLDB 2007, Vienna, Austria (2007)
7. De Santis, A., Ferrara, A.L., Masucci, B.: Cryptographic key assignment schemes for any access control policy. Information Processing Letters 92(4), 199–205 (2004)
8. Hacigümüs, H., Iyer, B., Mehrotra, S., Li, C.: Executing SQL over encrypted data in the database-service-provider model. In: Proc. of SIGMOD 2002, Madison, WI (2002)

9. MacKinnon, S., Taylor, P., Meijer, H., Akl, S.: An optimal algorithm for assigning cryptographic keys to control access in a hierarchy. IEEE TC 34(9), 797–802 (1985)
10. Miklau, G., Suciu, D.: Controlling access to published data using cryptography. In: Proc. of VLDB 2003, Berlin, Germany (2003)
11. Sandhu, R.S.: Cryptographic implementation of a tree hierarchy for access control. Information Processing Letters 27(2), 95–98 (1988)
12. Scilab Consortium: Scilab, the open source platform for numerical computation, V. 4-1, http://www.scilab.org
13. Wang, H., Lakshmanan, L.V.S.: Efficient secure query evaluation over encrypted XML databases. In: Proc. of VLDB 2006, Seoul, Korea (2006)

A Probabilistic Bound on the Basic Role Mining Problem and Its Applications

Alessandro Colantonio[1], Roberto Di Pietro[2], Alberto Ocello[3], and Nino Vincenzo Verde[4]

[1] Engiweb Security, Roma, Italy
and Università di Roma Tre, Roma, Italy
alessandro.colantonio@eng.it,
colanton@mat.uniroma3.it
[2] Università di Roma Tre, Roma, Italy and UNESCO Chair in Data Privacy, Tarragona, Spain
dipietro@{mat.uniroma3.it,urv.cat}
[3] Engiweb Security, Roma, Italy
alberto.ocello@eng.it
[4] Università di Roma Tre, Roma, Italy
nverde@mat.uniroma3.it

Abstract. The aim of this paper is to describe a new probabilistic approach to the role engineering process for RBAC. We address the issue of minimizing the number of roles, problem known in literature as the Basic Role Mining Problem (*basicRMP*). We leverage the equivalence of the above issue with the vertex coloring problem. Our main result is to prove that the minimum number of roles is sharply concentrated around its expected value. A further contribution is to show how this result can be applied as a stop condition when striving to find out an approximation for the *basicRMP*. The proposal can be also used to decide whether it is advisable to undertake the efforts to renew a RBAC state. Both these applications can result in a substantial saving of resources. A thorough analysis using advanced probabilistic tools supports our results. Finally, further relevant research directions are highlighted.

1 Introduction

An *access control model* is an abstract representation of security technology, providing a high-level logical view to describe all peculiarities and behaviors of an access control system. The *Role-Based Access Control* (RBAC, [1]) is certainly the most widespread access control model proposed in the literature for medium to large-size organizations. The simplicity of this model is one of the main reasons for its adoption: a role is just a collection of privileges, while users are assigned to roles based on duties to fulfil [10].

The migration to RBAC introduces several benefits, such as simplified system administration, enhanced organizational productivity, reduction in new employee downtime, enhanced system security and integrity, simplified regulatory compliance, and enhanced security policy enforcement [6]. To maximize all these advantages, the model must be customized to describe the organizational roles and functions [3]. However, this migration process often has a high economic impact. To optimize the customization, the *role*

D. Gritzalis and J. Lopez (Eds.): SEC 2009, IFIP AICT 297, pp. 376–386, 2009.

engineering discipline has been introduced. It can be defined as the set of methodologies and tools to define roles and to assign permissions to roles according to the actual needs of the company [5].

To date, various role engineering approaches have been proposed in order to address this problem. They are usually classified in literature as: *top-down* and *bottom-up*. The former carefully decomposes business processes into elementary components, identifying which system features are necessary to carry out specific tasks. This approach is mainly manual, as it requires a high level analysis of the business. The bottom-up class searches legacy access control systems to find *de facto* roles embedded in existing permissions. This process can be automated resorting to data mining techniques, thus leading to what is usually referred to as *role mining*.

Since the bottom-up approach can be automated, it has attracted a lot of interest from researchers who proposed new data mining techniques particularly designed for role engineering purposes. Various role mining approaches can be found in the literature [17, 3, 20, 18, 19, 22, 7, 12, 16]. A problem partially addressed in these works is the "interestingness" of roles. Indeed, the importance of role completeness and role management efficiency resulting from the role engineering process has been evident from the earliest papers on the subject. However, only recently have researchers started to formalize the role-set optimality concept. One possible optimization approach is minimizing the total number of roles [18, 7, 12]. Yet, the identification of the role-set that describes the access control configuration with the minimum number of roles is an NP-complete problem [18]. Thus, all of the aforementioned papers just offer an approximation of the optimal solution in order to address the complexity of the problem. However, since none of them quantify the introduced approximations, it is not possible to estimate the quality of the proposed role mining algorithm outcomes.

Contributions. In this paper we provide a probabilistic method to optimize the number of roles needed to cover all the existing user-permission assignments. The method leverages a known reduction of the role number minimization problem to the chromatic number of a graph. The main contribution of this work is to prove that the optimal role number is sharply concentrated around its expected value. We further show how this result can be used as a *stop condition* when striving to find an approximation of the optimum for any role mining algorithm. The corresponding rational is that if a result is close to the optimum, and the effort required to discover a better result is high, it might be appropriate to accept the current result.

Roadmap. This paper is organized as follows: Section 2 reports relevant related works. Section 3 summarizes the main concepts used in the rest of the paper; namely, a formal description of the RBAC model, some probabilistic tools, and a brief review of graph theory. In Section 4 the role minimization problem is formally described. Section 5 provides the main theoretical result and discusses some practical applications of this result. Finally, Section 6 presents some concluding remarks and further research directions.

2   Related Work

Kuhlmann et al. [11] first introduced the term "role mining", trying to apply existing data mining techniques (i.e., clustering similar to k-means) to implement a bottom-up approach. The first algorithm explicitly designed for role engineering is described in [17], applying hierarchical clustering on permissions. Another example of a role mining algorithm is provided by Vaidya et al. [20]; they applied subset enumeration techniques to generate a set of candidate roles, computing all possible intersections among permissions possessed by users.

The work of Colantonio et al. [3,4] represents the first attempt to discover roles with business meanings. The authors define a metric for evaluating good collections of roles that can be used to minimize the number of candidate roles. Vaidya et al. [18, 19] also studied the problem of finding the minimum number of roles covering all permissions possessed by the users, calling it the basic *Role Mining Problem* (*basicRMP*). They also demonstrated that such a problem is NP-complete. Ene et al. [7] offer yet another alternative model to minimize the number of candidate roles. In particular, they reduced the problem to the well-known minimum clique partition problem or, equivalently, to the minimum biclique covering. Actually, not only is the role number minimization equivalent to the clique covering, but it has been reduced to many other NP problems, like binary matrices factorization [12] and tiling database [9] to cite a few. These reductions make it possible to apply fast graph reduction algorithms to exactly identify the optimal solution for some realistic data set—however, the general problem is still NP-complete.

Recently, Frank et al. [8] proposed a probabilistic model for RBAC. They defined a framework that expresses user-permission relationships in a general way, specifying the related probability. Through this probability it is possible to elicit the role-user and role-permission assignments which then make the corresponding direct user-permission assignments more likely. The authors also presented a sampling algorithm that can be used to infer their model parameters. The algorithm converges asymptotically to the optimal value; the approach described in this paper can be used to offer a stop condition for the quest to the optimum.

3   Background

In this section we review all the notions used in rest of the paper, namely the RBAC entities, some probabilistic tools, and some graph theory concepts.

3.1   Role-Based Access Control

The RBAC entities of interest are:

- *PERMS*, the set of access permissions;
- *USERS*, the set of all system users;
- *ROLES*, the set of all roles, namely permission combinations.
- $UA \subseteq USERS \times ROLES$, the set of user-role assignments; given a role, the function assigned_users: $ROLES \rightarrow 2^{USERS}$ identifies all the assigned users.
- $PA \subseteq PERMS \times ROLES$, the set of permission-role assignments; given a role, the function assigned_perms: $ROLES \rightarrow 2^{PERMS}$ identifies all the assigned perms.

In addition to the RBAC standard entities, the set $UP \subseteq USERS \times PERMS$ identifies permission to user assignments. In an access control system it is represented by entities describing access rights (e.g., access control lists).

3.2   Martingales and Azuma-Hoeffding Inequality

We shall now present some definitions and theorems that provide the mathematical basis we will further discuss later on in this paper. In particular, we introduce: martingales, Doob martingales, and the Azuma-Hoeffding inequality. These are well known tools for the analysis of randomized algorithms [15, 21].

Definition 1 (Martingale). *A sequence of random variables* $Z_0, Z_1, \ldots, Z_n$ *is a martingale with respect to the sequence* $X_0, X_1, \ldots, X_n$ *if for all* $n \geq 0$, *the following conditions hold:*

- Z_n *is function of* $X_0, X_1, \ldots, X_n$,
- $\mathbb{E}[|Z_n|] \leq \infty$,
- $\mathbb{E}[Z_{n+1} \mid X_0, \ldots, X_n] = Z_n$,

where the operator $\mathbb{E}[\cdot]$ *indicates the expected value of a random variable. A sequence of random variables* $Z_0, Z_1, \ldots$ *is called* martingale *when it is a martingale with respect to himself. That is* $\mathbb{E}[|Z_n|] \leq \infty$ *and* $\mathbb{E}[Z_{n+1} \mid Z_0, \ldots, Z_n] = Z_n$.

Definition 2 (Doob Martingale). *A* Doob martingale *refers to a martingale constructed using the following general approach. Let* $X_0, X_1, \ldots, X_n$ *be a sequence of random variables, and let* Y *be a random variable with* $\mathbb{E}[|Y|] < \infty$. *(Generally* Y, *will depend on* $X_0, X_1, \ldots, X_n$.) *Then*

$$Z_i = \mathbb{E}[Y \mid X_0, \ldots, X_i], \quad i = 0, 1, \ldots, n,$$

gives a martingale with respect to $X_0, X_1, \ldots, X_n$.

The previous construction assures that the resulting sequence $Z_0, Z_1, \ldots, Z_n$ is always a martingale.

A useful property of the martingales that we will use in this paper is the Azuma-Hoeffding inequality [15]:

Theorem 1 (Azuma-Hoeffding inequality). *Let* $X_0, \ldots, X_n$ *be a martingale s.t.*

$$B_k \leq X_k - X_{k-1} \leq B_k + d_k,$$

for some constants d_k *and for some random variables* B_k *that may be functions of* $X_0, X_1, \ldots, X_{k-1}$. *Then, for all* $t \geq 0$ *and any* $\lambda > 0$,

$$\Pr(|X_t - X_0| \geq \lambda) \leq 2 \exp\left(\frac{-2\lambda^2}{\sum_{k=1}^{t} d_k^2}\right). \tag{1}$$

The Azuma-Hoeffding inequality applied to the Doob martingale gives the so called *Method of Bounded Differences* (MOBD) [14].

3.3   Graphs Modeling

This section describes some graph related concepts that will be used to generate our model. A *graph* G is an ordered pair $G = \langle V, E \rangle$, where V is the set of vertices, and E

is a set of unordered pairs of vertices. We say that $v, w \in V$ are *endpoints* of the edge $\langle v, w \rangle \in E$. Given a subset S of the vertices $V(G)$, then the subgraph *induced* by S is the graph where the set of vertices is S, and the edges are the members of $E(G)$ such that the corresponding endpoints are both in S. We denote with $G[S]$ the subgraph induced by S. A *bipartite graph* is a graph where the set of vertex can be partitioned into two subsets V_1 and V_2 such that $\forall \langle v_1, v_2 \rangle \in E(G), v_1 \in V_1, v_2 \in V_2$.

A *clique* is a subset S of vertices in G, such that the subgraph induced by S is a complete graph, namely for every two vertices in S there exists an edge connecting the two. A *biclique* in a bipartite graph, also called *bipartite clique*, is a set of vertices $B_1 \subseteq V_1$ and $B_2 \subseteq V_2$ such that $\langle b_1, b_2 \rangle \in E$ for all $b_1 \in B_1$ and $b_2 \in B_2$. In other words, if G is a bipartite graph, a set S of vertices $V(G)$ is a biclique if and only if the subgraph induced by S is a complete bipartite graph. In this case we will say that the vertices of S induce a biclique in G. A *maximal* clique or biclique is a set of vertices that induces a complete subgraph, and that is not a subset of the vertices of any larger complete subgraph.

A *clique cover* of G is a collection of cliques $C_1, \ldots, C_k$, such that for each edge $\langle u, v \rangle \in E$ there is some C_i that contains both u and v. A *minimum clique partition* (MCP) of a graph is a smallest by cardinality collection of cliques such that each vertex is a member of exactly one of the cliques; it is a partition of the vertices into cliques. Similar to the clique cover, a *biclique cover* of G is a collection of biclique $B_1, \ldots, B_k$ such that for each edge $\langle u, v \rangle \in E$ there is some B_i that contains both u and v. We say that B_i covers $\langle u, v \rangle$ if B_i contains both u and v. Thus, in a biclique cover, each edge of G is covered at least by one biclique. A *minimum biclique cover* (MBC) is the smallest collection of bicliques that covers the edges of a given bipartite graph, or in other words, is a biclique cover of minimum cardinality.

4   Problem Modelling

4.1   Definitions

The following definitions are required to formally describe the problem:

Definition 3 (System Configuration). *Given an access control system, we refer to its configuration as the tuple* $\varphi = \langle USERS, PERMS, UP \rangle$, *that is the set of all existing users, permissions, and the corresponding relationships between them.*

A system configuration represents the user authorization state before migrating to RBAC, or the authorizations derivable from the current RBAC implementation—in this case, the user-permission relationships may be derived as:

$$UP = \{ \langle u, p \rangle \mid \exists r \in ROLES : u \in \text{assigned\_users}(r) \ \wedge \ p \in \text{assigned\_perms}(r) \}$$

Definition 4 (RBAC State). *An RBAC state is a tuple* $\psi = \langle ROLES, UA, PA \rangle$, *namely an instance of all the sets characterizing the RBAC model.*

An RBAC state is used to obtain a system configuration. Indeed, the role engineering goal is to find the "best" state that correctly describes a given configuration. In particular, we are interested in finding the following kind of states:

Definition 5 (Candidate Role-Set). *Given an access control system configuration* φ, *a* candidate role-set *is the RBAC state* ψ *that "covers" all possible combinations of permissions possessed by users according to* φ, *namely a set of roles such that the union of related permissions exactly matches with the permissions possessed by the user. Formally*

$$\forall u \in USERS, \exists R \subseteq ROLES : \bigcup_{r \in R} \text{assigned\_perms}(r) = \{p \in PERMS \mid \langle u, p \rangle \in UP\}.$$

Definition 6 (Cost Function). *Let* Φ, Ψ *be respectively the set of all possible system configurations and RBAC states. We refer to the* cost function cost *as*

$$\text{cost}: \Phi \times \Psi \to \mathbb{R}^+$$

where $\mathbb{R}^+$ *indicates positive real numbers including 0; it represents an administration cost estimate for the state* ψ *used to obtain the configuration* φ.

The administration cost concept was first introduced in [3]. Leveraging the cost metric enables to find candidate role-sets with the lowest effort to administer them.

Definition 7 (Optimal Candidate Role-Set). *Given a configuration* φ, *an* optimal candidate role-set *is the corresponding configuration* ψ *that simultaneously represents a candidate role-set for* φ *and minimized the cost function* $\text{cost}(\varphi, \psi)$.

The main goal related to mining roles is to find optimal candidate role-sets. In the next section we focus on optimizing a particular cost function. Let *cost* indicate the number of needed roles. The role mining objective then becomes to find a candidate role-set that has the minimum number of roles for a given system configuration. This is exactly the *basicRMP*. We will show that this problem is equivalent to that of finding the chromatic number of a given graph. Using this problem equivalence, we will identify a useful property on the concentration of the optimal candidate role-sets. This allows us to provide a stop condition for any iterative role mining algorithm that approximates the minimum number of roles.

4.2 The Proposed Model

Given the configuration $\varphi = \langle USERS, PERMS, UP \rangle$ we can build a bipartite graph $G = \langle V, E \rangle$, where the vertex set V is partitioned into the two disjoint subset *USERS* and *PERMS*, and where E is a set of pairs $\langle u, p \rangle$ such that $u \in USERS$ and $p \in PERMS$. Two vertices u and p are connected if and only if $\langle u, p \rangle \in UP$.

A biclique coverage of the graph G identifies a unique candidate role-set for the configuration φ [7], that is $\psi = \langle ROLES, UA, PA \rangle$. Indeed, every biclique identifies a role, and the vertices of the biclique identify the users and the permission assigned to this role. Let the function *cost* return the number of roles, that is:

$$\text{cost}(\varphi, \psi) = |ROLES| \tag{2}$$

In this case, minimizing the cost function is equivalent to finding a candidate role-set that minimizes the number of roles. This corresponds to *basicRMP*. Let $\mathscr{B}$ a biclique coverage of a graph G, we define the function *cost'* as:

$$\text{cost}'(\mathscr{B}) = \text{cost}(\varphi, \psi)$$

where ψ is the state $\langle UA, PA, ROLES \rangle$ that can be deduced by the biclique coverage $\mathscr{B}$ of G, and G is the bipartite graph built from the configuration φ that is uniquely identified by $\langle USERS, PERMS, UP \rangle$. In this model, the problem of finding an optimal candidate role-set can be equivalently expressed as finding a biclique coverage for a given bipartite graph G that minimizes the number of required bicliques. This is exactly the *minimum biclique coverage* (MBC) problem. In the following we first recall both the reduction of the MBC problem to the *minimum clique partition* (MCP) problem [7] and the reduction of MCP to the chromatic number problem.

From the graph G, it is possible to construct a new undirected unipartite graph G' where the edges of G become the vertices of G': two vertices in G' are connected by an edge if and only if the endpoints of the corresponding edges of G induce a biclique in G. Formally:

$$G' = \langle E, \{\langle e_1, e_2 \rangle \mid e_1, e_2 \text{ induce a biclique in } G\} \rangle$$

The vertices of a (maximal) clique in G' correspond to a set of edges of G, where the endpoints induce a (maximal) biclique in G. The edges covered by a (maximal) biclique of G induce a (maximal) clique in G'. Thus, every biclique edge cover of G corresponds to a collection of cliques of G' such that their union contains all of the vertices of G'. From such a collection, a clique partition of G' can be obtained by removing any redundantly covered vertex from all but one of the cliques to which it belongs to. Similarly, any clique partition of G' corresponds to a biclique cover of G. Thus, the size of a minimum biclique coverage of a bipartite graph G is equal to the size of a minimum clique partition of G'.

Finding a clique partition of a graph $G = \langle V, E \rangle$ is equivalent to finding a coloring of its complement $\overline{G} = \langle V, (V \times V) \setminus E \rangle$. This implies that the biclique cover number of a bipartite graph G corresponds to the chromatic number of $\overline{G'}$ [7].

5   A Concentration Result for Optimal Candidate Role-Sets

Using the model described in the previous section, we will prove that the cost of an optimal candidate role-set ψ for a given system configuration φ is tightly concentrated around its expected value. We will use the concept of martingales and the Azuma-Hoeffding inequality to obtain a concentration result for the chromatic number of a graph G [14, 15]. Since finding the chromatic number is equivalent to both MCP and MBP, we can conclude that the minimum number of roles required to cover the user-permission relationships in a given configuration is tightly concentrated around its expected value.

Let G be an undirected unipartite graph, and $\chi(G)$ its chromatic number.

Theorem 2. *Given a graph G with n vertices, the following equation holds:*

$$\Pr(|\chi(G) - \mathbb{E}[\chi(G)]| \geq \lambda) \leq 2 \exp\left(\frac{-2\lambda^2}{n}\right) \tag{3}$$

Proof. We fix an arbitrary numbering of the vertices from 1 to n. Let G_i be the subgraph of G induced by the set of vertices $1, \ldots, i$. Let $Z_0 = \mathbb{E}[\chi(G)]$ and $Z_i = \mathbb{E}[\chi(G) \mid G_1, \ldots, G_i]$. Since adding a new vertex to the graph requires no more than one new color, the gap between Z_i and Z_{i-1} is at most 1. This allows us to apply the Azuma-Hoeffding inequality, that is Equation 1 where $d_k = 1$.

Note that this result holds even without knowing $\mathbb{E}[\chi(G)]$. Informally, Theorem 2 states that the chromatic number of a graph G is sharply concentrated around its expected value. Since finding the chromatic number of a graph is equivalent to MCP, and MCP is equivalent to MBC, this result holds also for MBC. Translating these concepts in terms of RBAC entities, this means that the cost of an optimal candidate role-set of any configuration φ with $|UP| = n$ is sharply concentrated around its expected value according to Equation 3, where $\chi(G)$ is equal to the minimum number of required roles. It is important to note that n represents the number of vertices in the coloring problem but, according to the proposed model, it is also the number of edges in MBP; that is, the user-permission assignments of the system configuration.

Figure 1(a) shows the plot of the Equation 3 for n varying between 1 and 500,000, and λ less than 1,500. It is possible to see that for $n = 500,000$ it is sufficient to choose $\lambda = 900$ to assure that $\Pr(|\chi(G) - \mathbb{E}[\chi(G)]| \geq \lambda) \leq 0.1$. In the same way, choosing $\lambda = 600$, then $\Pr(|\chi(G) - \mathbb{E}[\chi(G)]| \geq \lambda)$ is less than 0.5. Figure 1(b) shows the values for λ and n to have the left part of the inequality in Equation 3 to hold with probability less than 0.5, 0.3, and 0.1 respectively.

Setting $\lambda = \sqrt{n \log n}$, Equation 3 can be expressed as:

$$\Pr(|\chi(G) - \mathbb{E}[\chi(G)]| \geq \sqrt{n \log n}) \leq \frac{2}{n^2} \qquad (4)$$

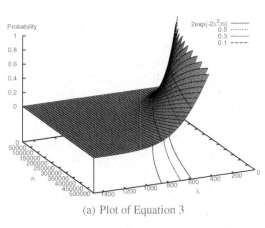

(a) Plot of Equation 3

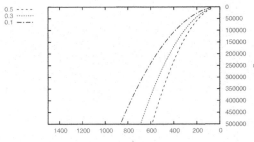

(b) Highlight of some λ values for Figure 1(a)

Fig. 1. Relationship between the parameters λ, n and the resulting probability

That is, the probability that our approach differ from the optimum more than $\sqrt{n \log n}$ is less than $2/n^2$. This probability becomes quickly negligible as n increases. To support the viability of the result, note that in a large organization there are usually thousands user-permission assignments.

5.1 Applications of the Bound

Assuming that we can estimate an approximation $\tilde{\mathbb{E}}[\chi(G)]$ for $\mathbb{E}[\chi(G)]$ such that $|\tilde{\mathbb{E}}[\chi(G)] - \mathbb{E}[\chi(G)]| \leq \varepsilon$ for any $\varepsilon > 0$, Theorem 2 can be used as a *stop condition* when striving to find an approximation of the optimum for any role mining algorithm. Indeed, suppose that we have a probabilistic algorithm that provides an approximation of $\chi(G)$, and suppose that its output is $\tilde{\chi}(G)$. Since we know $\tilde{\mathbb{E}}[\chi(G)]$, we can use this value to evaluate whether the output is acceptable and therefore decide to stop the iterations procedure. Indeed, we have that:

$$\Pr(|\chi(G) - \tilde{\mathbb{E}}(\chi(G))| \geq \lambda + \varepsilon) \leq 2\exp\left(\frac{-2\lambda^2}{n}\right).$$

This is because

$$\Pr(|\chi(G) - \tilde{\mathbb{E}}(\chi(G))| \geq \lambda + \varepsilon) \leq \Pr(|\chi(G) - \mathbb{E}(\chi(G))| \geq \lambda)$$

and, because of Theorem 2, this probability is less than or equal to $2\exp\left(-2\lambda^2/n\right)$. Thus, if $|\tilde{\chi}(G) - \tilde{\mathbb{E}}[\chi(G)]| \leq \lambda + \varepsilon$ holds, then we can stop the iteration, otherwise we have to reiterate the algorithm until it outputs an acceptable value.

For a direct application of this result, we can consider a system configuration with $|UP| = x$. If $\lambda = y$, the probability that $|\chi(G) - \mathbb{E}[\chi(G)]| \leq y$ is greater than $2\exp\left(-2y^2/x\right)$. We do not know $\mathbb{E}[\chi(G)]$, but since $|\tilde{\mathbb{E}}[\chi(G)] - \mathbb{E}[\chi(G)]| \leq \varepsilon$ we can conclude that $|\chi(G) - \tilde{\mathbb{E}}[\chi(G)]| < y + \varepsilon$ with probability at least $2\exp\left(-2y^2/x\right)$. For instance, we have considered the real case of a large size company, with 500,000 user-permissions assignments. With $\lambda = 1,200$ and $\varepsilon = 100$, the probability that $|\chi(G) - \tilde{\mathbb{E}}[\chi(G)]| < \lambda + \varepsilon$ is at least 99.36%. This means that, if $\tilde{\mathbb{E}}[\chi(G)] = 24,000$, with the above probability the optimum is between 22,700 and 25,300. If a probabilistic role mining algorithm outputs a value $\tilde{\chi}(G)$ that is estimated quite from this range, then it is appropriate to reiterate the process in order to find a better result. Conversely, let us assume that the algorithm outputs a value within the given range. We know that the identified solution differs, from the optimum, by at most $2(\lambda + \varepsilon)$, with probability at least 99.36%. Thus, one can assess whether it is appropriate to continue investing resources in the effort to find a better solution, or to simply accept the provided solution. This choice can depend on many factors, such as the computational cost of the algorithm, the economic cost due to a new analysis, and the error that we are prone to accept, to name a few.

There is also another possible application for this bound. Assume that a company is assessing whether to renew its RBAC state, just because it is several years old [19]. By means of the proposed bound, the company can establish whether it is the case to invest money and resources in this process. Indeed, if the cost of the RBAC state in use is between $\tilde{\mathbb{E}}[\chi(G)] - \lambda - \varepsilon$ and $\tilde{\mathbb{E}}[\chi(G)] + \lambda + \varepsilon$, the best option would be not to renew it because the possible improvement is likely to be marginal. Moreover, changing the RBAC state requires a huge effort for the administrators, since they need to get used to the new configuration. In our proposal it is quite easy to assess if a renewal is needed. This indication can lead to important time and money saving.

Note that in our hypothesis, we assume that the value of $\tilde{\mathbb{E}}[\chi(G)]$ is known. Currently, not many researchers have addressed this specific issue in reference to a generic graph, whereas plenty of results have been provided for Random Graphs. In particular, it has been proven [13, 2] that for $G \in G_{n,p}$:

$$\mathbb{E}[\chi(G)] \sim \frac{n}{2\log_{\frac{1}{1-p}} n}$$

We are presently striving to apply a slight modification of the same probabilistic techniques used in this paper, to derive a similar bound for the class of graphs used in our model.

6   Conclusions and Future Works

In this paper we proved that the optimal administration cost for RBAC, when striving to minimize the number of roles, is sharply concentrated around its expected value. The result has been achieved by adopting a model reduction and advanced probabilistic tools. Further, we have shown how to apply this result to deal with practical issues in administering RBAC; that is, how it can be used as a stop condition in the quest for the optimum.

This paper also highlights a few research directions. First, a challenge that we are currently addressing is to derive an estimate of the expected optimal number of roles ($\mathbb{E}[\chi(G)]$) from a generic system configuration. Another research path is applying both the exposed reduction and the probabilistic tools to obtain similar bounds while simultaneously minimizing more parameters.

Acknowledgment

This work was partly supported by: The Spanish Ministry of Science and Education through projects TSI2007-65406-C03-01 "E-AEGIS" and CONSOLIDER CSD2007-00004 "ARES", and by the Government of Catalonia under grant 2005 SGR 00446.

References

1. American National Standards Institute (ANSI) and InterNational Committee for Information Technology Standards (INCITS): ANSI/INCITS 359-2004, Information Technology – Role Based Access Control (2004)
2. Bollobás, B.: The chromatic number of random graphs. Combinatorica 8(1), 49–55 (1988)
3. Colantonio, A., Di Pietro, R., Ocello, A.: A cost-driven approach to role engineering. In: Proceedings of the 23rd ACM Symposium on Applied Computing, SAC 2008, Fortaleza, Ceará, Brazil, vol. 3, pp. 2129–2136 (2008)

4. Colantonio, A., Di Pietro, R., Ocello, A.: Leveraging lattices to improve role mining. In: Proceedings of the IFIP TC 11 23rd International Information Security Conference, SEC 2008. IFIP International Federation for Information Processing, vol. 278, pp. 333–347. Springer, Heidelberg (2008)
5. Coyne, E.J.: Role engineering. In: RBAC 1995: Proceedings of the first ACM Workshop on Role-based access control, Gaithersburg, Maryland, United States, p. 4. ACM, New York (1996)
6. Coyne, E.J., Davis, J.M.: Role Engineering for Enterprise Security Management. Artech House (2007)
7. Ene, A., Horne, W., Milosavljevic, N., Rao, P., Schreiber, R., Tarjan, R.E.: Fast exact and heuristic methods for role minimization problems. In: Proceedings of the 13th ACM Symposium on Access Control Models and Technologies, SACMAT 2008, pp. 1–10 (2008)
8. Frank, M., Basin, D., Buhmann, J.M.: A class of probabilistic models for role engineering. In: Proceedings of the 15th ACM Conference on Computer and Communications Security, CCS 2008, pp. 299–310 (2008)
9. Geerts, F., Goethals, B., Mielikäinen, T.: Tiling databases. In: Suzuki, E., Arikawa, S. (eds.) DS 2004. LNCS, vol. 3245, pp. 278–289. Springer, Heidelberg (2004)
10. Jajodia, S., Samarati, P., Subrahmanian, V.S.: A logical language for expressing authorizations. In: SP 1997: Proceedings of the 1997 IEEE Symposium on Security and Privacy, p. 31. IEEE Computer Society, Los Alamitos (1997)
11. Kuhlmann, M., Shohat, D., Schimpf, G.: Role mining – revealing business roles for security administration using data mining technology. In: Proceedings of the 8th ACM Symposium on Access Control Models and Technologies, SACMAT 2003, pp. 179–186 (2003)
12. Lu, H., Vaidya, J., Atluri, V.: Optimal boolean matrix decomposition: Application to role engineering. In: Proceedings of the 24th IEEE International Conferene on Data Engineering, ICDE 2008, pp. 297–306 (2008)
13. Łuczak, T.: The chromatic number of random graphs. Combinatorica 11(1), 45–54 (1991)
14. McDiarmid, C.J.H.: On the method of bounded differences. In: Siemons, J. (ed.) Surveys in Combinatorics: Invited Papers at the 12th British Combinatorial Conference. London Mathematical Society Lecture Notes Series, vol. 141, pp. 148–188. Cambridge University Press, Cambridge (1989)
15. Mitzenmacher, M., Upfal, E.: Probability and Computing: Randomized Algorithms and Probabilistic Analysis. Cambridge University Press, New York (2005)
16. Rymon, R.: Method and apparatus for role grouping by shared resource utilization. United States Patent Application 20030172161 (2003)
17. Schlegelmilch, J., Steffens, U.: Role mining with ORCA. In: Proceedings of the 10th ACM Symposium on Access Control Models and Technologies, SACMAT 2005, pp. 168–176 (2005)
18. Vaidya, J., Atluri, V., Guo, Q.: The role mining problem: finding a minimal descriptive set of roles. In: Proceedings of the 12th ACM Symposium on Access Control Models and Technologies, SACMAT 2007, pp. 175–184 (2007)
19. Vaidya, J., Atluri, V., Guo, Q., Adam, N.: Migrating to optimal RBAC with minimal perturbation. In: Proceedings of the 13th ACM Symposium on Access Control Models and Technologies, SACMAT 2008, pp. 11–20 (2008)
20. Vaidya, J., Atluri, V., Warner, J.: RoleMiner: mining roles using subset enumeration. In: Proceedings of the 13th ACM Conference on Computer and Communications Security, pp. 144–153 (2006)
21. Williams, D.: Probability with Martingales. Cambridge University Press, Cambridge (1991)
22. Zhang, D., Ramamohanarao, K., Ebringer, T.: Role engineering using graph optimisation. In: Proceedings of the 12th ACM Symposium on Access Control Models and Technologies, SACMAT 2007, pp. 139–144 (2007)

Automating Access Control Logics in Simple Type Theory with LEO-II*

Christoph Benzmüller

International University in Germany, Bruchsal, Germany
c.benzmueller@googlemail.com

Abstract. Garg and Abadi recently proved that prominent access control logics can be translated in a sound and complete way into modal logic S4. We have previously outlined how normal multimodal logics, including monomodal logics K and S4, can be embedded in simple type theory and we have demonstrated that the higher-order theorem prover LEO-II can automate reasoning in and about them. In this paper we combine these results and describe a sound (and complete) embedding of different access control logics in simple type theory. Employing this framework we show that the off the shelf theorem prover LEO-II can be applied to automate reasoning in and about prominent access control logics.

1 Introduction

The provision of effective and reliable control mechanisms for accessing resources is an important issue in many areas. In computer systems, for example, it is important to effectively control the access to personalized or security critical files.

A prominent and successful approach to implement access control relies on logic based ideas and tools. Abadi's article [2] provides a brief overview on the frameworks and systems that have been developed under this approach. Garg and Abadi recently showed that several prominent access control logics can be translated into modal logic S4 [18]. They proved that this translation is sound and complete.

We have previously shown [10] how multimodal logics can be elegantly embedded in simple type theory (*STT*) [15,5]. We have also demonstrated that proof problems in and about multimodal logics can be effectively automated with the higher-order theorem prover LEO-II [12].

In this paper we combine the above results and show that different access control logics can be embedded in *STT*, which has a well understood syntax and semantics [22,4,3,9].

The expressiveness of *STT* furthermore enables the encoding of the entire translation from access control logic input syntax to *STT* in *STT* itself, thus making it as transparent as possible. Our embedding furthermore demonstrates that prominent access control logics as well as prominent multimodal logics can be considered and treated as natural fragments of *STT*.

Using our embedding, reasoning in and about access control logic can be automated in the higher-order theorem prover LEO-II. Since LEO-II generates proof objects, the

---

* This work was supported by EU grant PIIF-GA-2008-219982 (THFTPTP).

D. Gritzalis and J. Lopez (Eds.): SEC 2009, IFIP AICT 297, pp. 387–398, 2009.

entire translation and reasoning process is in principle accessible for independent proof checking.

This paper is structured as follows: Section 2 reviews background knowledge and Section 3 outlines the translation of access control logics into modal logic S4 as proposed by Garg and Abadi [18]. Section 4 restricts the general embedding of multimodal logics into *STT* [10] to an embedding of monomodal logics K and S4 into *STT* and proves its soundness. These results are combined in Section 5 in order to obtain a sound (and complete) embedding of access control logics into *STT*. Moreover, we present some first empirical evaluation of the approach with the higher-order automated theorem prover LEO-II. Section 6 concludes the paper.

2   Preliminaries

We assume familiarity with the syntax and semantics and of multimodal logics and simple type theory and only briefly review the most important notions.

The multimodal logic language *ML* is defined by

$$s,t ::= p \mid \neg s \mid s \vee t \mid \Box_r s$$

where p denotes atomic primitives and r denotes accessibility relations (distinct from p). Other logical connectives can be defined from the chosen ones in the usual way.

A Kripke frame for *ML* is a pair $\langle W, (R_r)_{r \in I := \{1,...,n\}} \rangle$, where W is a non-empty set (called possible worlds), and the R_r are binary relations on W (called accessibility relations). A Kripke model for *ML* is a triple $\langle W, (R_r)_{r \in I}, \models \rangle$, where $\langle W, (R_r)_{r \in I} \rangle$ is a Kripke frame, and $\models$ is a satisfaction relation between nodes of W and formulas of *ML* satisfying: $w \models \neg s$ if and only if $w \not\models s$, $w \models s \vee t$ if and only if $w \models s$ or $w \models t$, $w \models \Box_r s$ if and only if for all u with $R_r(w, u)$ holds $u \models s$. The satisfaction relation $\models$ is uniquely determined by its value on the atomic primitives p. A formula s is valid in a Kripke model $\langle W, (R_r)_{r \in I}, \models \rangle$, if $w \models s$ for all $w \in W$. s is valid in a Kripke frame $\langle W, (R_r)_{r \in I} \rangle$ if it is valid in $\langle W, (R_r)_{r \in I}, \models \rangle$ for all possible $\models$. If s is valid for all possible Kripke frames $\langle W, (R_r)_{r \in I} \rangle$, then s is called valid and we write $\models^K s$. s is called S4-valid (we write $\models^{S4} s$) if it is valid in all reflexive, transitive Kripke frames $\langle W, (R_r)_{r \in I} \rangle$, that is, Kripke frames with only reflexive and transitive relations R_r.

Classical higher-order logic or simple type theory *STT* [5,15] is a formalism built on top of the simply typed λ-calculus. The set $\mathscr{T}$ of simple types is usually freely generated from a set of basic types $\{o, \iota\}$ (where o denotes the type of Booleans) using the function type constructor $\rightarrow$.

The simple type theory language *STT* is defined by ($\alpha, \beta, o \in \mathscr{T}$):

$$s,t ::=$$
$$p_\alpha \mid X_\alpha \mid (\lambda X_\alpha \bullet s_\beta)_{\alpha \rightarrow \beta} \mid (s_{\alpha \rightarrow \beta}\, t_\alpha)_\beta \mid (\neg_{o \rightarrow o}\, s_o)_o \mid (s_o \vee_{o \rightarrow o \rightarrow o} t_o)_o \mid (\Pi_{(\alpha \rightarrow o) \rightarrow o}\, s_{\alpha \rightarrow o})_o$$

p_α denotes typed constants and X_α typed variables (distinct from p_α). Complex typed terms are constructed via abstraction and application. Our logical connectives of choice are $\neg_{o \rightarrow o}$, $\vee_{o \rightarrow o \rightarrow o}$ and $\Pi_{(\alpha \rightarrow o) \rightarrow o}$ (for each type α). From these connectives, other logical connectives, such as $\Rightarrow$, $\wedge$, $\bot$, and $\top$, can be defined in the usual way. We often use binder notation $\forall X_\alpha \boldsymbol{.} s$ and $\exists X_\alpha \boldsymbol{.} t$ for $(\Pi_{(\alpha \to o) \to o}(\lambda X_\alpha \boldsymbol{.} s_o))$ and $\neg(\Pi_{(\alpha \to o) \to o}(\lambda X_\alpha \boldsymbol{.} \neg t_o))$. We denote substitution of a term s_α for a variable X_α in a term t_β by $[s/X]t$. Since we consider α-conversion implicitly, we assume the bound variables of B avoid variable capture. Two common relations on terms are given by β-reduction and η-reduction. A β-redex $(\lambda X.s)t$ β-reduces to $[t/X]s$. An η-redex $(\lambda X.sX)$ where variable X is not free in s, η-reduces to s. We write $s =_\beta t$ to mean s can be converted to t by a series of β-reductions and expansions. Similarly, $s =_{\beta\eta} t$ means s can be converted to t using both β and η.

Semantics of *STT* is well understood and thoroughly documented in the literature [9,3,4,22]; our summary below is adapted from Andrews [6].

A frame is a collection $\{D_\alpha\}_{\alpha \in \mathscr{T}}$ of nonempty domains (sets) D_α, such that $D_o = \{T, F\}$ (where T represents truth and F represents falsehood). The $D_{\alpha \to \beta}$ are collections of functions mapping D_α into D_β. The members of D_ι are called individuals. An interpretation is a tuple $\langle \{D_\alpha\}_{\alpha \in \mathscr{T}}, I \rangle$ where function I maps each typed constant c_α to an appropriate element of D_α, which is called the denotation of c_α (the denotations of $\neg$, $\vee$ and Π are always chosen as intended). A variable assignment ϕ maps variables X_α to elements in D_α. An interpretation $\langle \{D_\alpha\}_{\alpha \in \mathscr{T}}, I \rangle$ is a Henkin model (general model) if and only if there is a binary function $\mathscr{V}$ such that $\mathscr{V}_\phi s_\alpha \in D_\alpha$ for each variable assignment ϕ and term $s_\alpha \in L$, and the following conditions are satisfied for all ϕ and all $s, t \in L$: (a) $\mathscr{V}_\phi X_\alpha = \phi X_\alpha$, (b) $\mathscr{V}_\phi p_\alpha = I p_\alpha$, (c) $\mathscr{V}_\phi(s_{\alpha \to \beta} t_\alpha) = (\mathscr{V}_\phi s_{\alpha \to \beta})(\mathscr{V}_\phi t_\alpha)$, and (d) $\mathscr{V}_\phi(\lambda X_\alpha \boldsymbol{.} s_\beta)$ is that function from D_α into D_β whose value for each argument $z \in D_\alpha$ is $\mathscr{V}_{[z/X_\alpha], \phi} s_\beta$, where $[z/X_\alpha], \phi$ is that variable assignment such that $([z/X_\alpha], \phi)X_\alpha = z$ and $([z/X_\alpha], \phi)Y_\beta = \phi Y_\beta$ if $Y_\beta \neq X_\alpha$.[1]

If an interpretation $\langle \{D_\alpha\}_{\alpha \in \mathscr{T}}, I \rangle$ is a Henkin model, the function $\mathscr{V}_\phi$ is uniquely determined. An interpretation $\langle \{D_\alpha\}_{\alpha \in \mathscr{T}}, I \rangle$ is a standard model if and only if for all α and β, $D_{\alpha \to \beta}$ is the set of all functions from D_α into D_β. Each standard model is also a Henkin model.

We say that formula $A \in L$ is valid in a model $\langle \{D_\alpha\}_{\alpha \in \mathscr{T}}, I \rangle$ if an only if $\mathscr{V}_\phi A = T$ for every variable assignment ϕ. A model for a set of formulas H is a model in which each formula of H is valid.

A formula A is Henkin-valid (standard-valid) if and only if A is valid in every Henkin (standard) model. Clearly each formula which is Henkin-valid is also standard-valid, but the converse of this statement is false. We write $\models^{STT} A$ if A is Henkin-valid and we write $\Gamma \models^{STT} A$ if A is valid in all Henkin models in which all formulas of Γ are valid.

3   Translating Access Control Logic to Modal Logic

The access control logic *ICL* studied by Garg and Abadi [18] is defined by

$$s ::= p \mid s_1 \wedge s_2 \mid s_1 \vee s_2 \mid s_1 \supset s_2 \mid \perp \mid \top \mid A \text{ says } s$$

p denotes atomic propositions, $\wedge$, $\vee$, $\supset$, $\perp$ and $\top$ denote the standard logical connectives, and A denotes principals, which are atomic and distinct from the atomic propositions p. Expressions of the form A says s, intuitively mean that A asserts (or

---

[1] Since $I\neg$, $I\vee$, and $I\Pi$ are always chosen as intended, we have $\mathscr{V}_\phi(\neg s) = T$ iff $\mathscr{V}_\phi s = F$, $\mathscr{V}_\phi(s \vee t) = T$ iff $\mathscr{V}_\phi s = T$ or $\mathscr{V}_\phi t = T$, and $\mathscr{V}_\phi(\forall X_\alpha \boldsymbol{.} s_o) = \mathscr{V}_\phi(\Pi^\alpha(\lambda X_\alpha \boldsymbol{.} s_o)) = T$ iff for all $z \in D_\alpha$ we have $\mathscr{V}_{[z/X_\alpha], \phi} s_o = T$. Moreover, we have $\mathscr{V}_\phi s = \mathscr{V}_\phi t$ whenever $s =_{\beta\eta} t$.

supports) s. *ICL* inherits all inference rules of intuitionistic propositional logic. The logical connective says satisfies the following axioms:

$$\vdash s \supset (A \text{ says } s) \qquad \text{(unit)}$$
$$\vdash (A \text{ says } (s \supset t)) \supset (A \text{ says } s) \supset (A \text{ says } t) \quad \text{(cuc)}$$
$$\vdash (A \text{ says } A \text{ says } s) \supset (A \text{ says } s) \qquad \text{(idem)}$$

Example 1 (from [18]). We consider a file-access scenario with an administrating principal admin, a user Bob, one file file1, and the following policy:

1. If admin says that file1 should be deleted, then this must be the case.
2. admin trusts Bob to decide whether file1 should be deleted.
3. Bob wants to delete file1.

This policy can be encoded in *ICL* as follows:

$$\text{(admin says deletefile1)} \supset \text{deletefile1} \qquad (1.1)$$
$$\text{admin says ((Bob says deletefile1)} \supset \text{deletefile1)} \qquad (1.2)$$
$$\text{Bob says deletefile1} \qquad (1.3)$$

The question whether file1 should be deleted in this situation corresponds to proving deletefile (1.4), which follows from (1.1)-(1.3), (unit), and (cuc).

Garg and Abadi [18] propose the following mapping $\lceil . \rceil$ of *ICL* formulas into modal logic S4 formulas (similar to Gödels translation from intuitionistic logic to S4 [19] and by providing a mapping for the additional connective says).

$$\lceil p \rceil = \Box p$$
$$\lceil s \wedge t \rceil = \lceil s \rceil \wedge \lceil t \rceil \qquad\qquad \lceil \top \rceil = \top$$
$$\lceil s \vee t \rceil = \lceil s \rceil \vee \lceil t \rceil \qquad\qquad \lceil \bot \rceil = \bot$$
$$\lceil s \supset t \rceil = \Box (\lceil s \rceil \supset \lceil t \rceil) \qquad \lceil A \text{ says } s \rceil = \Box(A \vee \lceil s \rceil)$$

Logic $ICL^{\Rightarrow}$ extends *ICL* by a *speaks-for* operator (represented by $\Longrightarrow$) which satisfies the following axioms:

$$\vdash A \Longrightarrow A \qquad \text{(refl)}$$
$$\vdash (A \Longrightarrow B) \supset (B \Longrightarrow C) \supset (A \Longrightarrow C) \qquad \text{(trans)}$$
$$\vdash (A \Longrightarrow B) \supset (A \text{ says } s) \supset (B \text{ says } s) \quad \text{(speaking-for)}$$
$$\vdash (B \text{ says } (A \Longrightarrow B)) \supset (A \Longrightarrow B) \qquad \text{(handoff)}$$

The use of the new $\Longrightarrow$ operator is illustrated by the following modification of Example 1.

Example 2 (from [18]). Bob delegates his authority to delete file1 to Alice (see (2.3)), who now wants to delete file1.

$$\text{(admin says deletefile1)} \supset \text{deletefile1} \qquad (2.1)$$
$$\text{admin says ((Bob says deletefile1)} \supset \text{deletefile1)} \qquad (2.2)$$
$$\text{Bob says Alice} \Longrightarrow \text{Bob} \qquad (2.3)$$
$$\text{Alice says deletefile1} \qquad (2.4)$$

Using these facts and (handoff) and (speaking-for) one can prove deletefile (2.5)

The translation of $ICL^{\Rightarrow}$ into S4 extends the translation from ICL to S4 by

$$\lceil A \Longrightarrow B \rceil = \Box(A \supset B)$$

Logic ICL^B differs from ICL by allowing that principals may contain Boolean connectives (a denotes atomic principals distinct from atomic propositions):

$$A, B ::= a \mid A \wedge B \mid A \vee B \mid A \supset B \mid \perp \mid \top$$

ICL^B satisfies the following additional axioms:

$$\vdash (\perp \text{ says } s) \supset s \qquad\qquad\qquad\qquad (\text{trust})$$
$$\text{If } A \equiv \top \text{ then} \vdash A \text{ says } \perp \qquad\qquad\qquad (\text{untrust})$$
$$\vdash ((A \supset B) \text{ says } s) \supset (A \text{ says } s) \supset (B \text{ says } s) \quad (\text{cuc'})$$

Abadi and Garg show that the speaks-for operator from $ICL^{\Rightarrow}$ is definable in ICL^B. The use of ICL^B is illustrated by the following modification of Example 1.

Example 3 (from [18]). admin is trusted on deletefile1 and its consequences (3.1). (3.2) says that admin further delegates this authority to Bob.

$$(\text{admin says } \perp) \supset \text{deletefile1} \qquad\qquad\qquad\qquad (3.1)$$
$$\text{admin says } ((\text{Bob} \supset \text{admin}) \text{ says deletefile1}) \qquad\qquad (3.2)$$
$$\text{Bob says deletefile1} \qquad\qquad\qquad\qquad\qquad\qquad (3.3)$$

Using these facts and the available axioms one can again prove deletefile (3.4).

The translation of ICL^B into S4 is the same as the translation from ICL to S4. However, the mapping $\lceil A \text{ says } s \rceil = \Box(A \vee \lceil s \rceil)$ now guarantees that Boolean principal expressions A are mapped one-to-one to Boolean expressions in S4.

Garg and Abadi prove their translations sound and complete:

Theorem 1 (Soundness and Completeness). $\vdash s$ *in ICL (resp. $ICL^{\Rightarrow}$ and ICL^B) if and only if* $\vdash \lceil s \rceil$ *in S4.*

Proof. See Theorem 1 (resp. Theorem 2 and Theorem 3) og Garg and Abadi [18].

4   Embedding Modal Logic in Simple Type Theory

Embeddings of modal logics into higher-order logic have not yet been widely studied, although multimodal logic can be regarded as a natural fragment of *STT*. Gallin [16] appears to mention the idea first. He presents an embedding of modal logic into a 2-sorted type theory. This idea is picked up by Gamut [17] and a related embedding has recently been studied by Hardt and Smolka [20]. Carpenter [14] proposes to use lifted connectives, an idea that is also underlying the embeddings presented by Merz [24], Brown [13], Harrison [21, Chap. 20], and Kaminski and Smolka [23].

In our previous work [10] we pick up and extend the embedding of multimodal logics into *STT* as studied by Brown [13]. The starting point is a characterization of multimodal logic formulas as particular λ-terms in *STT*. A distinctive characteristic of the encoding is that the definiens of the $\Box_R$ operator λ-abstracts over the accessibility relation R. As we have shown this supports the formulation of meta properties of encoded multimodal logics such as the correspondence between certain axioms and properties of the accessibility relation R. And some of these meta properties can be efficiently automated within our higher-order theorem prover LEO-II.

The general idea of this encoding is very simple: Choose base type ι and let this type denote the set of all possible worlds. Certain formulas of type $\iota \to o$ then correspond to multimodal logic expressions, whereas the modal operators $\neg$, $\lor$, and $\Box_r$ itself become λ-terms of type $(\iota \to o) \to (\iota \to o)$, $(\iota \to o) \to (\iota \to o) \to (\iota \to o)$, and $(\iota \to \iota \to o) \to (\iota \to o) \to (\iota \to o)$ respectively.

The mapping $\lfloor . \rfloor$ translates formulas of multimodal logic *ML* into terms of type $\iota \to o$ in *STT*:

$$\lfloor p \rfloor = p_{\iota \to o} \qquad\qquad |p| = p_{\iota \to o}$$
$$\lfloor r \rfloor = r_{\iota \to \iota \to o} \qquad\qquad |r| = r_{\iota \to \iota \to o}$$
$$\lfloor \neg s \rfloor = \lambda X_\iota \cdot \neg (\lfloor s \rfloor X) \qquad |\neg| = \lambda A_{\iota \to o} \cdot \lambda X_\iota \cdot \neg (AX)$$
$$\lfloor s \lor t \rfloor = \lambda X_\iota \cdot (\lfloor s \rfloor X) \lor (\lfloor t \rfloor X) \qquad |\lor| = \lambda A_{\iota \to o} \cdot \lambda B_{\iota \to o} \cdot \lambda X_\iota \cdot (AX) \lor (BX)$$
$$\lfloor \Box_r s \rfloor = \lambda X_\iota \cdot \forall Y_\iota \cdot (\lfloor r \rfloor X Y) \Rightarrow (\lfloor s \rfloor Y) \qquad |\Box| = \lambda R_{\iota \to \iota \to o} \cdot \lambda A_{\iota \to o} \cdot$$
$$\lambda X_\iota \cdot \forall Y_\iota \cdot (RXY) \Rightarrow (AY)$$

The expressiveness of *STT* (in particular the use of λ-abstraction and $\beta\eta$-conversion) allows us to replace mapping $\lfloor . \rfloor$ by mapping $|.|$ which works locally and is not recursive.[2]

It is easy to check that this local mapping works as intended. For example,

$$|\Box_r p \lor \Box_r q)| := |\lor| (|\Box| |r| |p|)(|\Box| |r| |q|) =_{\beta\eta} \lfloor \Box_r p \lor \Box_r q)\rfloor$$

Further local definitions for other multimodal logic operators can be introduced this way. For example, $|\supset| = \lambda A_{\iota \to o} \cdot \lambda B_{\iota \to o} \cdot \lambda X_\iota \cdot (AX) \Rightarrow (BX)$, $|\bot| = \lambda A_{\iota \to o} \cdot \bot$, $|\top| = \lambda A_{\iota \to o} \cdot \top$, and $|\land| = \lambda A_{\iota \to o} \cdot \lambda B_{\iota \to o} \cdot \lambda X_\iota \cdot (AX) \land (BX)$.

A notion of validity for the λ-terms (of type $\iota \to o$) which we obtain via definition expansion is still missing: We want $A_{\iota \to o}$ to be valid if and only if for all possible worlds w_ι we have $(A_{\iota \to o} w_\iota)$, that is, $w \in A$. This notion of validity is again introduced as a local definition:

$$|\text{Mval}| := \lambda A_{\iota \to o} \cdot \forall W_\iota \cdot A W$

---

[2] Note that the encoding of the modal operators $\Box_r$ is chosen to explicitly depend on an accessibility relation r of type $\iota \to \iota \to o$ given as first argument to it. Hence, we basically introduce a generic framework for modeling multimodal logics. This idea is due to Brown and it is this aspect where the encoding differs from the LTL encoding of Harrison. The latter chooses the interpreted type *num* of numerals and then uses the predefined relation $\leq$ over numerals as fixed accessibility relation in the definitions of $\Box$ and $\Diamond$. By making the dependency of $\Box_r$ and $\Diamond_r$ on the accessibility relation r explicit, we cannot only formalize but also automatically prove some meta properties of multimodal logics as we have previously demonstrated [10].

Garg and Abadi's translation of access control into modal logic as presented in Section 3 is monomodal and does not require different $\Box_r$-operators. Thus, for the purpose of this paper we restrict the outlined general embedding of multimodal logics into STT to an embedding of monomodal logic into STT. Hence, for the remainder of the paper we assume that ML provides exactly one $\Box_r$-operator, that is, a single relation constant r.

We next study soundness of this embedding. Our soundness proof below employs the following mapping of Kripke frames into Henkin models.

Definition 1 (Henkin model M^K for Kripke Model K). *Given a Kripke model $K = \langle W, (R_r), \models \rangle$. Henkin model $M^K = \langle \{D_\alpha\}_{\alpha \in \mathcal{T}}, I \rangle$ for K is defined as follows: We choose the set of individuals D_ι as the set of worlds W and we choose the $D_{\alpha \to \beta}$ as the set of all functions from D_α to D_β. Let $p^1, \dots, p^m$ for $m \geq 1$ be the atomic primitives occuring in modal language ML. Remember that $\Box_r$ is the only box operator of ML. Note that $|p^j| = p^j_{\iota \to o}$ and $|r| = r_{\iota \to \iota \to o}$. Thus, for $1 \leq i \leq m$ we choose $I p^j_{\iota \to o} \in D_{\iota \to o}$ such that $(I p^j_{\iota \to o})(w) = T$ for all $w \in D_\iota$ with $w \models p^j$ in Kripke model K and $(I p^j_{\iota \to o})(w) = F$ otherwise. Similarly, we choose $I r_{\iota \to \iota \to o} \in D_{\iota \to \iota \to o}$ such that $(I r_{\iota \to \iota \to o})(w, w') = T$ if $R_r(w, w')$ in Kripke model K and $(I r_{\iota \to \iota \to o})(w, w') = F$ otherwise. Clearly, if R_r is reflexive and transitive then, by construction, $I r_{\iota \to \iota \to o}$ is so as well. It is easy to check that $M^K = \langle \{D_\alpha\}_{\alpha \in \mathcal{T}}, I \rangle$ is a Henkin model. In fact it is a standard model since the function spaces are full.*

Lemma 1. *Let $M^K = \langle \{D_\alpha\}_{\alpha \in \mathcal{T}}, I \rangle$ be a Henkin model for Kripke model $K = \langle W, (R_i)_{i \in I}, \models \rangle$. For all $q \in L$, $w \in W$ and variable assignments ϕ the following are equivalent: (i) $w \models q$, (ii) $\mathcal{V}_{[w/Z_\iota], \phi}(\lfloor q \rfloor Z) = T$, and (iii) $\mathcal{V}_{[w/Z_\iota], \phi}(\lfloor q \rfloor Z) = T$.*

Proof. We prove (i) if and only if (ii) by induction on the structure of q. Let $q = p$ for some atomic primitive $p \in L$. By construction of M^K, we have $\mathcal{V}_{[w/Z_\iota], \phi}(\lfloor p \rfloor Z) = \mathcal{V}_{[w/Z_\iota], \phi}(p_{\iota \to o} Z) = (I p_{\iota \to o})(w) = T$ if and only if $w \models p$. Let $p = \neg s$. We have $w \models \neg s$ if and only $w \not\models s$. By induction we get $\mathcal{V}_{[w/Z_\iota], \phi}(\lfloor s \rfloor Z) = F$ and hence $\mathcal{V}_{[w/Z_\iota], \phi} \neg(\lfloor s \rfloor Z) =_{\beta\eta} \mathcal{V}_{[w/Z_\iota], \phi}(\lfloor \neg s \rfloor Z) = T$. Case $p = (s \vee t)$ is similar. Let $q = \Box_r s$. We have $w \models \Box_r s$ if and only if for all u with $R_r(w, u)$ we have $u \models s$. By induction, for all u with $R_r(w, u)$ we have $\mathcal{V}_{[u/V_\iota], \phi}(\lfloor s \rfloor V) = T$. Hence, $\mathcal{V}_{[u/V_\iota], [w/Z_\iota], \phi}((\lfloor r \rfloor Z V) \Rightarrow (\lfloor s \rfloor V)) = T$ and $\mathcal{V}_{[w/Z_\iota], \phi}(\forall Y_\iota \bullet ((\lfloor r \rfloor Z Y) \Rightarrow (\lfloor s \rfloor Y))) =_{\beta\eta} \mathcal{V}_{[w/Z_\iota], \phi}(\lfloor \Box_r s \rfloor Z) = T$.

We leave it to the reader to prove (ii) if and only if (iii).

We now prove soundness of the embedding of normal monomodal logics K and $S4$ into STT. In the case of $S4$ we add axioms that correspond to modal logic axioms T (reflexivity) and 4 (transitivity).[3] Here we call these axiom R and T.

Theorem 2 (Soundness of the Embedding of K and $S4$ into STT). *Let $s \in ML$ be a monomodal logic proposition.*

1. *If $\models^{STT} |Mval\ s|$ then $\models^K s$.*
2. *If $\{R, T\} \models^{STT} |Mval\ s|$ then $\models^{S4} s$, where R and T are shorthands for $\forall X_{\iota \to o} \bullet |Mval\ \Box_r X \supset X|$ and $\forall X_{\iota \to o} \bullet |Mval\ \Box_r X \supset \Box_r \Box_r X|$ respectively.*

---

[3] Note that $T = (\Box_r s \supset s)$ and $4 = (\Box_r s \supset \Box_r \Box_r s)$ are actually axiom schemata in modal logic. As we show here, their counterparts in STT actually become proper axioms.

394 C. Benzmüller

Proof

(1) The proof is by contraposition. For this, assume $\not\models^K s$, that is, there is a Kripke model $K = \langle W, (R_r), \models \rangle$ with $w \not\models s$ for some $w \in W$. By Lemma 1, for arbitrary ϕ we have $\mathcal{V}_{[w/W_\iota].\phi}(\lfloor s \rfloor W) = F$ in Henkin model M^K for K. Thus, $\mathcal{V}_\phi(\forall W_\iota.(\lfloor s \rfloor W) = \mathcal{V}_\phi \lfloor \text{Mval}\, s \rfloor = F$. Hence, $\not\models^{STT} \lfloor \text{Mval}\, s \rfloor$.

(2) The proof is by contraposition. From $\not\models^{S4} s$ we get by Lemma 1 that $\lfloor \text{Mval}\, s \rfloor$ is not valid in Henkin model $M^K = \langle \{D_\alpha\}_{\alpha \in \mathcal{T}}, I \rangle$ for Kripke model $K = \langle W, (R_r) \rangle$. R_r in K is reflexive and transitive, hence, the relation $(Ir) \in D_{\iota \to \iota \to o}$ is so as well. We leave it to the reader to verify that axioms R and T are valid in M^K. Hence, $\{R, T\} \not\models^{STT} \lfloor \text{Mval}\, s \rfloor$.

Reasoning problems in modal logics K and $S4$ can thus be considered as reasoning problems in *STT*. Hence, any off the shelf theorem prover that is sound for *STT*, such as our LEO-II, can be applied to them. For example, $\models^{STT} \lfloor \text{Mval}\, \Box_r \top \rfloor$, $\models^{STT} \lfloor \text{Mval}\, \Box_r a \supset \Box_r a \rfloor$, and $\models^{STT} \lfloor \text{Mval}\, \Diamond_r(a \supset b) \vee (\Box_r a \supset \Box_r b) \rfloor$ are automatically proved by LEO-II in 0.024 seconds, 0.026 seconds, and 0.035 seconds respectively. All experiments with LEO-II reported in this paper were conducted with LEO-II version v0.98 [4] on a notebook computer with a Intel Pentium 1.60GHz processor with 1GB memory running Linux.

More impressive example problems illustrating LEO-II's performance for reasoning in and *about* multimodal logic can be found in our previous work [10]. Amongst these problems is also the equivalence between axioms $\Box_r s \supset s$ and $\Box_r s \supset \Box_r \Box_r s$ and the reflexivity and transitivity properties of the accessibility relation r:

Example 4. $\models^{STT} (R \wedge T) \Leftrightarrow (\text{refl}\, r \wedge \text{trans}\, r)$ where R and T are the abbreviations as introduced in Theorem 2 and refl and trans abbreviations for $\lambda R_{\iota \to \iota \to o}.\forall X_\iota. R X X$ and $\lambda R_{\iota \to \iota \to o}.\forall X_\iota.\forall Y_\iota.\forall Z_\iota. R X Y \wedge R Y Z \Rightarrow R X Z$. LEO-II can solve this modal logic meta-level problem in 2.329 seconds.

5 Embedding Access Control Logic in Simple Type Theory

We combine the results from Sections 3 and 4 and obtain the following mapping $\|\cdot\|$ from access control logic *ICL* into *STT*:

$$\|p\| = \lfloor \Box_r p \rfloor = \lambda X_\iota.\forall Y_\iota. r_{\iota \to \iota \to o} X Y \Rightarrow p_{\iota \to o} Y$$
$$\|A\| = \lfloor A \rfloor = a_{\iota \to o} \ (\text{distinct from the } p_{\iota \to o})$$
$$\|\wedge\| = \lambda S.\lambda T.\lfloor S \wedge T \rfloor = \lambda S_{\iota \to o}.\lambda T_{\iota \to o}.\lambda X_\iota. S X \wedge T X$$
$$\|\vee\| = \lambda S.\lambda T.\lfloor S \vee T \rfloor = \lambda S_{\iota \to o}.\lambda T_{\iota \to o}.\lambda X_\iota. S X \vee T X$$
$$\|\supset\| = \lambda S.\lambda T.\lfloor \Box_r(S \supset T) \rfloor$$
$$= \lambda S_{\iota \to o}.\lambda T_{\iota \to o}.\lambda X_\iota.\forall Y_\iota. r_{\iota \to \iota \to o} X Y \Rightarrow (S Y \Rightarrow T Y)$$
$$\|\top\| = \lfloor \top \rfloor = \lambda S_{\iota \to o}. \top$$
$$\|\bot\| = \lfloor \bot \rfloor = \lambda S_{\iota \to o}. \bot$$
$$\|\text{says}\| = \lambda A.\lambda S.\lfloor \Box_r(A \vee S) \rfloor$$
$$= \lambda A_{\iota \to o}.\lambda S_{\iota \to o}.\lambda X_\iota.\forall Y_\iota. r_{\iota \to \iota \to o} X Y \Rightarrow (A Y \vee S Y)$$

---

[4] LEO-II is available from http://www.ags.uni-sb.de/~leo/.

Table 1. Performance of LEO-II when applied to problems in access control logic *ICL*

Name	Problem	LEO (s)
unit	$\{R,T\} \models^{STT} \|\texttt{ICLval}\, s \supset (A \text{ says } s)\|$	0.031
cuc	$\{R,T\} \models^{STT} \|\texttt{ICLval}\, (A \text{ says } (s \supset t)) \supset (A \text{ says } s) \supset (A \text{ says } t)\|$	0.083
idem	$\{R,T\} \models^{STT} \|\texttt{ICLval}\, (A \text{ says } A \text{ says } s) \supset (A \text{ says } s)\|$	0.037
Ex1	$\{R,T, \|\texttt{ICLval}\, (1.1)\|, \dots, \|\texttt{ICLval}\, (1.3)\|\} \models^{STT} \|\texttt{ICLval}\, (1.4)\|$	3.494
unit^K	$\models^{STT} \|\texttt{ICLval}\, s \supset (A \text{ says } s)\|$	–
cuc^K	$\models^{STT} \|\texttt{ICLval}\, (A \text{ says } (s \supset t)) \supset (A \text{ says } s) \supset (A \text{ says } t)\|$	–
idem^K	$\models^{STT} \|\texttt{ICLval}\, (A \text{ says } A \text{ says } s) \supset (A \text{ says } s)\|$	–
Ex1^K	$\{\|\texttt{ICLval}\, (1.1)\|, \dots, \|\texttt{ICLval}\, (1.3)\|\} \models^{STT} \|\texttt{ICLval}\, (1.4)\|$	–

It is easy to verify that this mapping works as intended. For example:

$$\|\text{admin says } \bot\| := \|\text{says}\| \|\text{admin}\| \|\bot\|$$
$$=_{\beta\eta} \lambda X_\iota . \forall Y_\iota . r_{\iota \to \iota \to o} X Y \Rightarrow (\text{admin}_{\iota \to o} Y \vee \bot)$$
$$=_{\beta\eta} |\Box_r(\text{admin} \vee \bot)| =_{\beta\eta} \lfloor \Box_r(\text{admin} \vee \bot) \rfloor$$
$$= \lfloor \lceil \text{admin says } \bot \rceil \rfloor$$

We extend this mapping to logic $ICL^{\Rightarrow}$ by adding a clause for the speaks-for connective $\Longrightarrow$:

$$\| \Longrightarrow \| = \lambda A. \lambda B. |\Box_r(A \supset B)| = \lambda A_{\iota \to o}. \lambda B_{\iota \to o}. \lambda X_\iota . \forall Y_\iota . r_{\iota \to \iota \to o} X Y \Rightarrow (A Y \Rightarrow B Y)$$

For the translation of ICL^B we simply allow that the ICL connectives can be applied to principals. Our mapping $\|.\|$ needs not to be modified and is applicable as is.

The notion of validity for the terms we obtain after translations is chosen identical to before

$$\|\texttt{ICLval}\| = \lambda A_{\iota \to o}. |\text{Mval}\, A| = \lambda A_{\iota \to o}. \forall W_\iota . A W$$

Theorem 3 (Soundness of the Embeddings of *ICL*, *ICL*$^{\Rightarrow}$, and *ICL*^{B} in *STT*). *Let* $s \in ICL$ *(resp.* $s \in ICL^{\Rightarrow}$, $s \in ICL^B$*) and let R and T be as before. If* $\{R,T\} \models^{STT}$ $\|\texttt{ICLval}\, s\|$ *then* $\vdash s$ *in access control logic ICL (resp.* $ICL^{\Rightarrow}$, ICL^B*).*

Proof. If $\{R,T\} \models^{STT} \|\texttt{ICLval}\, s\|$ then $\models^{S4} s$ by Theorem 2 since $\|\texttt{ICLval}\, s\| = |\text{Mval}\, s|$. This implies that $\vdash \lceil s \rceil$ for the sound and complete Hilbert System for S4 studied by Garg and Abadi [18].[5] By Theorem 1 we conclude that $\vdash s$ in access control logic *ICL* (resp. $ICL^{\Rightarrow}$, ICL^B).

Completeness of our embeddings of *ICL*, $ICL^{\Rightarrow}$, and ICL^B into *STT* can be shown by similar means [8]. This also implies soundness and completeness for the entailed embedding of intuitionistic logic into *STT*.

We can thus safely exploit our framework to map problems formulated in control logics *ICL*, $ICL^{\Rightarrow}$, or ICL^B to problems in *STT* and we can apply the off the shelf

---

[5] See Theorem 8 of Garg and Abadi [18] which is only given in the full version of the paper available from http://www.cs.cmu.edu/~dg/publications.html.

Table 2. Performance of LEO-II when applied to problems in access control logic $ICL^{\Rightarrow}$

Name	Problem	LEO (s)
refl	$\{R,T\} \models^{STT} \|ICLval\, A \Longrightarrow A\|$	0.052
trans	$\{R,T\} \models^{STT} \|ICLval\, (A \Longrightarrow B) \supset (B \Longrightarrow C) \supset (A \Longrightarrow C)\|$	0.105
sp.-for	$\{R,T\} \models^{STT} \|ICLval\, (A \Longrightarrow B) \supset (A\, says\, s) \supset (B\, says\, s)\|$	0.062
handoff	$\{R,T\} \models^{STT} \|ICLval\, (B\, says\, (A \Longrightarrow B)) \supset (A \Longrightarrow B)\|$	0.036
Ex2	$\{R,T,\|ICLval\,(2.1)\|,\ldots,\|ICLval\,(2.4)\|\} \models^{STT} \|ICLval\,(2.5)\|$	0.698
refl^K	$\models^{STT} \|ICLval\, A \Longrightarrow A\|$	0.031
trans^K	$\models^{STT} \|ICLval\, (A \Longrightarrow B) \supset (B \Longrightarrow C) \supset (A \Longrightarrow C)\|$	–
sp.-for^K	$\models^{STT} \|ICLval\, (A \Longrightarrow B) \supset (A\, says\, s) \supset (B\, says\, s)\|$	–
handoff^K	$\models^{STT} \|ICLval\, (B\, says\, (A \Longrightarrow B)) \supset (A \Longrightarrow B)\|$	–
Ex2^K	$\{\|ICLval\,(2.1)\|,\ldots,\|ICLval\,(2.4)\|\} \models^{STT} \|ICLval\,(2.5)\|$	–

Table 3. Performance of LEO-II when applied to problems in access control logic ICL^B

Name	Problem	LEO (s)
trust	$\{R,T\} \models^{STT} \|ICLval\, (\bot\, says\, s) \supset s\|$	0.049
untrust	$\{R,T,\|ICLval\, A \equiv T\|\} \models^{STT} \|ICLval\, A\, says\, \bot\|$	0.053
cuc'	$\{R,T\} \models^{STT} \|ICLval\, ((A \supset B)\, says\, s) \supset (A\, says\, s) \supset (B\, says\, s)\|$	0.131
Ex3	$\{R,T,\|ICLval\,(3.1)\|,\ldots,\|ICLval\,(3.3)\|\} \models^{STT} \|ICLval\,(3.4)\|$	0.076
trust^K	$\models^{STT} \|ICLval\, (\bot\, says\, s) \supset s\|$	–
untrust^K	$\{\|ICLval\, A \equiv T\|\} \models^{STT} \|ICLval\, A\, says\, \bot\|$	0.041
cuc'^{K}	$\models^{STT} \|ICLval\, ((A \supset B)\, says\, s) \supset (A\, says\, s) \supset (B\, says\, s)\|$	–
Ex3^K	$\{\|ICLval\,(3.1)\|,\ldots,\|ICLval\,(3.3)\|\} \models^{STT} \|ICLval\,(3.4)\|$	–

higher-order theorem prover LEO-II (which itself cooperates with the first-order theorem prover E [25]) to solve them. Times are given in seconds.

Table 1 shows that LEO-II can effectively prove that the axioms unit, cuc and idem hold as expected in our embedding of *ICL* in *STT*. This provides additional evidence for the correctness of our approach. Example 1 can also be quickly solved by LEO-II. Problems unit^K, cuc^K, idem^K, and Ex1^K modify their counterparts by omitting the axioms R and T. Thus, they essentially test whether these problems can already be proven via a mapping to modal logic K instead of $S4$. LEO-II answers this questions positively for the cases of cuc^K, and Ex1^K.

Tables 2 and 3 extend this experiment to the other access control logics, axioms and examples presented in Section 3.

In a separate technical report [8] we present the concrete encoding or our embedding together with the problems unit, cuc, idem, and Ex1 in the new TPTP THF syntax [11], which is also the input syntax of LEO-II.

6   Conclusion and Future Work

We have outlined a framework for the automation of reasoning in and about different access control logics in simple type theory. Using our framework off the shelf higher-order theorem provers and proof assistants can be applied for the purpose. Our embedding of access control logics in simple type theory and a selection of example problems have been encoded in the new TPTP THF syntax and our higher-order theorem prover LEO-II has been applied to them yielding promising initial results. Our problem encodings have been submitted to the higher-order TPTP library [1] under development in the EU project THFTPTP and are available there for comparison and competition with other TPTP compliant theorem provers such as TPS [7].

Recent experiments have shown that the scalability of our approach for reasoning within access control logics still poses a challenge to LEO-II. However, more promising is the application of LEO-II to meta-properties of access control logics analogous to Example 4 and its use for the exploration of new access control logics.

Acknowledgments. Catalin Hritcu inspired this work and pointed to the paper by Garg and Abadi. Chad Brown, Larry Paulson, and Claus-Peter Wirth detected some problems and typos in an earlier version of this paper. Also Deepak Garg provided very valuable feedback to this work.

References

1. The TPTP THF library, http://www.tptp.org
2. Abadi, M.: Logic in access control. In: 18th IEEE Symposium on Logic in Computer Science, Ottawa, Canada, Proceedings, 22-25 June 2003. IEEE Computer Society, Los Alamitos (2003)
3. Andrews, P.B.: General models and extensionality. J. of Symbolic Logic 37, 395–397 (1972)
4. Andrews, P.B.: General models, descriptions, and choice in type theory. J. of Symbolic Logic 37, 385–394 (1972)
5. Andrews, P.B.: An Introduction to Mathematical Logic and Type Theory: To Truth Through Proof, 2nd edn. Kluwer Academic Publishers, Dordrecht (2002)
6. Andrews, P.B.: Church's type theory. In: Zalta, E.N. (ed.) The Stanford Encyclopedia of Philosophy (2008), http://plato.stanford.edu/archives/fall2008/entries/type-theory-church/
7. Andrews, P.B., Brown, C.E.: Tps: A hybrid automatic-interactive system for developing proofs. J. Applied Logic 4(4), 367–395 (2006)
8. Benzmüller, C.: Automating access control logics in simple type theory with LEO-II. SEKI Technical Report SR-2008-01, FB Informatik, U. des Saarlandes, Germany (2008)
9. Benzmüller, C., Brown, C.E., Kohlhase, M.: Higher order semantics and extensionality. J. of Symbolic Logic 69, 1027–1088 (2004)
10. Benzmüller, C., Paulson, L.: Festschrift in honour of Peter B. Andrews on his 70th birthday. In: Exploring Properties of Normal Multimodal Logics in Simple Type Theory with LEO-II. IFCoLog, Studies in Logic and the Foundations of Mathematics (2009)
11. Benzmüller, C., Rabe, F., Sutcliffe, G.: The core TPTP language for classical higher-order logic. In: Armando, A., Baumgartner, P., Dowek, G. (eds.) IJCAR 2008. LNCS, vol. 5195 (LNAI), pp. 491–506. Springer, Heidelberg (2008)
12. Benzmüller, C., Theiss, F., Paulson, L., Fietzke, A.: LEO-II - A cooperative automatic theorem prover for classical higher-order logic (System description). In: Armando, A., Baumgartner, P., Dowek, G. (eds.) IJCAR 2008. LNCS (LNAI), vol. 5195, pp. 162–170. Springer, Heidelberg (2008)

13. Brown, C.E.: Encoding hybrid logic in higher-order logic. Unpublished slides from an invited talk presented at Loria Nancy, France (April 2005), http://mathgate.info/cebrown/papers/hybrid-hol.pdf
14. Carpenter, B.: Type-logical semantics. MIT Press, Cambridge (1998)
15. Church, A.: A Formulation of the Simple Theory of Types. J. of Symbolic Logic 5, 56–68 (1940)
16. Gallin, D.: Intensional and Higher-Order Modal Logic. North-Holland Mathematics Studies, vol. 19. North-Holland, Amsterdam (1975)
17. Gamut, L.T.F.: Logic, Language, and Meaning. Intensional Logic and Logical Grammar, vol. II. The University of Chicago Press (1991)
18. Garg, D., Abadi, M.: A modal deconstruction of access control logics. In: Amadio, R. (ed.) FOSSACS 2008. LNCS, vol. 4962, pp. 216–230. Springer, Heidelberg (2008)
19. Gödel, K.: Eine interpretation des intuitionistischen aussagenkalküls. Ergebnisse eines Mathematischen Kolloquiums 8, 39–40 (1933)
20. Hardt, M., Smolka, G.: Higher-order syntax and saturation algorithms for hybrid logic. Electr. Notes Theor. Comput. Sci. 174(6), 15–27 (2007)
21. Harrison, J.: HOL Light Tutorial (for version 2.20). Intel JF1-13 (September 2006), http://www.cl.cam.ac.uk/~jrh13/hol-light/tutorial_220.pdf
22. Henkin, L.: Completeness in the theory of types. J. of Symbolic Logic 15, 81–91 (1950)
23. Kaminski, M., Smolka, G.: Terminating tableaux for hybrid logic with the difference modality and converse. In: Armando, A., Baumgartner, P., Dowek, G. (eds.) IJCAR 2008. LNCS (LNAI), vol. 5195, pp. 210–225. Springer, Heidelberg (2008)
24. Merz, S.: Yet another encoding of TLA in isabelle (1999), http://www.loria.fr/~merz/projects/isabelle-tla/doc/design.ps.gz
25. Schulz, S.: E – A Brainiac Theorem Prover. Journal of AI Communications 15(2/3), 111–126 (2002)

In Law We Trust? Trusted Computing and Legal Responsibility for Internet Security

Yianna Danidou[1] and Burkhard Schafer[2]

[1] Computer Science Department, Americanos College, 2 & 3 Omirou Avenue, P.O. Box 22425, 1521 Nicosia, Cyprus, and PhD candidate, School of Law, University of Edinburgh
yianna.danidou@ac.ac.cy
[2] SCRIPT, School of Law, University of Edinburgh, Old College Edinburgh, EH8 9YL
B.Schafer@ed.ac.uk

Abstract. This paper analyses potential legal responses and consequences to the anticipated roll out of Trusted Computing (TC). It is argued that TC constitutes such a dramatic shift in power away from users to the software providers, that it is necessary for the legal system to respond. A possible response is to mirror the shift in power by a shift in legal responsibility, creating new legal liabilities and duties for software companies as the new guardians of internet security.

1 Introduction

Trusted Computing (TC), a project commenced by an industry organization known as the Trusted Computing Group (TCG), was set up to achieve higher levels of security for the information technology infrastructure. It was driven by the recognition that it is insufficient to rely on users taking the necessary precautions, such as regularly updated firewalls and anti-virus systems themselves. The notion of *'trust'* as used in this paper is not the sociological concept, but was taken from the field of trusted systems, that is systems that can be relied upon to perform certain security policies. Nonetheless, the outcome ultimately would be to allow the user to "blindly trust" his computer again, without a constant need for self-monitoring. Prevention of Denial of Service (DoS) attacks, the performance of access control and monitoring and the achievement of scalability are just some of the numerous technical challenges that the current distributed systems need to overcome. A trusted environment must fulfil three basic conditions: protected capabilities; integrity measurement and integrity reporting, all creating and ensuring platform trust [4].

TCG is an alliance of promoters like AMD, Hewlett-Packard (HP), IBM, Intel Corporation, Microsoft, Sun Microsystems Incorporation and of contributors like Nokia, Fujitsu-Siemens Computers, Philips, Vodafone and many more. The project was targeted to allow the computer user to trust his own computer and for "others" to trust that specific computer [15]. In a more intuitive way, as Ross Anderson [2] noted,

> TC provides a computing platform on which you cannot tamper with the application software, and where these applications can communicate securely with their authors and with each other.

D. Gritzalis and J. Lopez (Eds.): SEC 2009, IFIP AICT 297, pp. 399–409, 2009.

A preliminary literature survey suggests that while computer scientists seem primarily concerned with the technical feasibility of implementing TC, legal academics have tended to concentrate on content control and privacy issues [1,2,3,5,6,9,11,16,17,19,20,25,27]. Neither group appears to be overly concerned with an analysis of the implications of the imposition of legal liability for failure within such a system, or potential responsibility for wider social and legal concerns to which they may give rise. If greater legal responsibility is placed upon hardware/software providers, this may have a significant impact upon the speed and scope of system roll-out, and may leave the system vulnerable to threats from market pressures. This paper will analyse how law and regulatory responses to TC can on the one hand address some of the widespread public concern about the technology, while on the other hand can create both incentives and disincentives for TC developers to take a greater share of the burden to secure the information infrastructure from malicious attacks.

2   The TC Environment: Protecting the IT Infrastructure

Attacks on computing infrastructure safety is an increasingly safety critical matter, as a large and vital number of system procedures depend on it. The weak spot in the defence against DoS attacks - an obvious technical challenge - is unsophisticated customers who forget updating their software. As software providers can increasingly take on this task on behalf of the end-user, there is increased pressure on big software companies to take on more of the responsibility for internet safety [8]. Consequently, software and hardware industries try to find ways to create more secure systems - like TC. The importance of the security of the information infrastructure has, belatedly, also been recognised by governments worldwide. In the UK, the House of Lords Select Committee on Science and Technology submitted in 2007 a comprehensive report on personal internet security [13], which identified not only a long list of current dangers, but also the key stakeholders and their respective responsibility for internet security. They conclude that:

> The current emphasis of Government and policy-makers upon end-user responsibility for security bears little relation either to the capabilities of many individuals or to the changing nature of the technology and the risk. It is time for Government to develop a more holistic understanding of the distributed responsibility for personal Internet security. This may well require reduced adherence to the "end-to-end principle", in such a way as to reflect the reality of the mass market in Internet services.

However, in its 2007 report, the House of Lords did not ask for a change in the attribution of legal liability to software vendors. In its follow-up report in 2008 [12], a much more aggressive stance towards the role of vendor liability was taken, and the Government was urged to raise the potential for substantive changes in the legal liability of software vendors for the safety of the internet both in the EU and internationally. With similar considerations also taking place elsewhere, the solution promoted by the TC community can also be seen as an attempt to pre-empt potential legislative imposition of liability - if industry is seen playing its part, governments may be more reluctant to impose new statutory burdens[1].

This paper proposes a new look at the interaction between internet security, trusted computing and legal liability. It is argued that even if technical solutions to internet security will decrease the pressure on governments to introduce new liability legislation, the shift of power and control away from the user to software providers will also change the legal landscape of liability and the attribution of legal responsibility, with or without new legislative initiatives.

TC is often seen as a threat to privacy, understood in its more common meaning as a political concept. It gives multinational companies access to information we would prefer to keep private. But following the analysis of reliance liability by Collins [7], it is argued that TC is intimately linked to a rather different understanding of privacy, one that software companies may well want to preserve. Privacy in the field of contract law is linked to, but different from, the political concept of privacy. Classical contract law embodied a notion of *'privacy' (or privity)* of contract[2]. This concept restricted heavily possible liabilities arising from contractual relations to the parties of the contract. More specifically, it meant two related things: - one that a contract is private between parties and the other that the individual does not owe legal obligations to associates. However, modern contract law recognises increasingly systematic exceptions to this principle. In particular, as Collins notes, *'reliance liability'* has increasingly been accepted as a conceptual foundation of both tort and contract law. In practical terms, this means that liability can be imposed between persons outside a contractual nexus if one of them relied reasonably on the performance of the other party. A typical example is the possible legal recognition of the interests of an employer who hired a person on recommendation of a third party. While there is no contractual relation between employer and recommender, legal systems are increasingly willing to conceptualise this relation as *quasi-contractual* and protect through the imposition of liability the reasonable expectation or reliance of the employer in the correctness of the recommendation. We will examine whether TC's services can be understood in analogy to such a recommendation, whether as a result reliance liability should ensue, if TC promoters are aware of this possibility and whether they tend to take any action about the liability issue in general.

While delictual (reliance) liability is a paradigmatic example of the rebalancing between power and responsibility discussed in this paper, there are other possibilities on the horizon that are just as troublesome: at present, enforcement of internet law, both private and criminal, rest on the ability to create reliable and authentic (digital) evidence. The "Trojan defence", a claim that a third party had access to a suspect's machine, is a notable threat to this precondition of enforceable internet law. However, TC would grant a much larger number of people remotely accessing people's computers, potentially invalidating any evidence secured from the machine. Can the state impose the right type of standards on the TC providers, and enforce compliance, to counter this

---

[1] Parallel developments to this strategy can be found elsewhere, e.g. in the response of gun manufacturers to the thread of state imposed liability for misuse of guns by unauthorised users, by exploring the use of biometric devices that make this type of misuse impossible.

[2] For a comparative analysis see [23].

threat? Will on the substantive law side the fact that TC providers routinely gather data about illicit activities on customer's computers carry also a legal obligation to act on this knowledge?

3 The TC Controversy

The proponents of TC suggest that TC promises to provide four crucial advantages: reliability, security, privacy and business integrity. Together these guarantee a system that will be available when in need, that will resist any attack once protecting the system itself and the data, that will give the demanded privacy to the user and finally that provides to businesses the ability to interact effectively with their customers. Also, TC could provide protection from viruses due to the fact that a check will be applied to all files trying to "enter" the system. New applications will be structured to achieve protection while this means that TC could be used to restrict access to everything from music files to pornography to writings that criticize political leaders. As our last, and for the time being fictitious, example shows, this approach is not without controversy. Content-owning businesses may wish to prevent end-users from doing particular things with files e.g. ripping copyright music files; and employers may wish to control employees' ability to access and/or distribute information across corporate networks, and so support this functionality. However, individuals are likely to have significant concerns about the effect of such technical solutions on their rights for privacy and freedom of speech. This may well lead possible buyers to refuse the purchase of TC systems [2].

There is also a significant risk in such a scenario of the promotion of anti-competitive behavior. The personal computing market already faces competitive failures caused by the domination of "Wintel"; adding TC, where 'non-trusted' computers and applications can be frozen out, and unauthorized files can be barred or deleted, without significant safeguards, may only make things worse [10,22].

Given the foregoing, it is unsurprising that TC has given rise to a number of controversies between its proponents and opponents. This is due to the fact that the aim of TCG will provide more trustworthiness from the point of view of software vendors and the content industry, but there is a real danger that it will be perceived as less trustworthy by the users, despite an objective increase in security. There are two reasons for this. First, because of the perception of constant surveillance by software providers, that generates a persistent feeling of exposure. Second, because research into risk and risk perception shows that risks are perceived comparatively more serious when people do not feel in control. Even though statistically speaking air travel is more secure than driving a car, the lack of control that an air passenger experiences increases also the perception of being at risk. Similarly, TC requires the user to trust a third party, a "pilot". Consequently opponents say that cryptographic systems do not offer enough security for the computer and thus for the user, but instead provide vendors and technology companies with the freedom to make *"decisions about data and application that typically have been left to users"* [26]. Proponents state that the implementation and application of technologies that provide TC will increase users' trust in their ability to protect their systems from malicious code and guard their data from theft.

Some harsh critics have emerged, who will not be easily won over. Richard Stallman, founder of the Free Software Foundation and creator of the well-known GPL open source license, is one such opponent to TC. He declares that "treacherous computing", as he brands TC, will allow content providers, together with computer companies to make the computers obey them, instead of the users. In other words, the *"computer will stop functioning as a general-purpose computer"* and *"every operation may require explicit permission"* [24]. Even when one does not buy this specific conspiracy theory, it does bring one of the problems with TC to the point: it signifies a dramatic shift in power away from the user towards the software providers, a shift to which the law ought to react by also shifting liability and more general legal responsibility.

Table 1. Brief overview of the TC controversy

Proponents	Opponents
TC will provide:	Concerns on:
<ul><li>reliability</li><li>security</li><li>privacy</li><li>business integrity</li><li>protection</li><li>more trustworthiness</li><li>increment of user's trust for protection</li></ul>	<ul><li>invasion of privacy</li><li>breach of security</li><li>freedom of speech</li><li>non-trusted applications can be frozen out and unauthorized files can be remotely deleted</li><li>less trustworthiness due to:<ul><li>– constant surveillance by TC providers</li><li>– lack of user control</li></ul></li><li>user restrictions</li><li>loss of anonymity</li><li>mandatory use of TC technology to grant communication</li></ul>

4 Critisism of TC

A number of problems will arise from the adoption of TC technology. The foremost problems as stated by the opponents of TC are that sharing of content will be much more difficult due to the fact that TC will be used for what they term "Digital Restrictions Management", so that videos, music and other multimedia can be played only on a specified computer. Secondly, Digital Rights Management (DRM) will be used for email and documents, leading to documents and emails that will disappear, or will not be readable on certain computers. Restrictions in downloading and installing all types of software unless permitted by the TC technology may also cause problems. Critics also suggest that TC might threaten Open Source Software (OSS) development, as both OSS operating systems and applications may fail to be recognized as trustworthy by TC systems, which will then refuse to run them. In addition, programs that use TC when installed will be able to continually download new authorization rules through the Internet and impose those rules automatically. In such circumstances it is claimed, that computers may apply the new instructions downloaded, without notification, to such a degree that a user will no longer be able to fully interact with their computer [2,24].

Y. Danidou and B. Schafer

It is almost inevitable that TC will cause problems of incompatibility with legacy systems, both hardware and software. As a result, users (home or business) may find themselves at risk of "forced upgrades" and lost data from old applications e.g. applications whose serial numbers have been removed from support schedules or blacklisted. For businesses the impact will also be on the economical area. The cost of any swapping between products plus the cost of training the employees for proper use of the new products will be extravagant [2]. Although this paper does not focus on this aspect of TC, this clearly has the potential to raise competition law issues - particularly where existing near-monopoly players such as Microsoft and Intel are involved [22].

Remote Censorship is another "feature" that TC can provide. Applications that delete pirated music or other non-authenticated files via remote-control are possible. Anderson's "traitor tracing" applications that report files that are not authenticated in order to report the user and then remotely delete the files, are about to be applied in business models [2].

Interoperation with other products will be achieved only where the vendor wants it to be applied. Vendors have a very good reason as to why they would want the latter to happen: because then all buyers will purchase the same product from the same company - so that they can interoperate with each other - and therefore there will be a network effect. In such a market, the leading company may choose not to interoperate with other companies and thus locking all other companies outside this network and all the users inside it [10].

Opponents of TC have not been unaware of these implications, and some have claimed that the reason for Intel investing in TC was a *"defensive play"* [2]. By increasing market size, enlargement of the company will be achieved. Anderson points out that *"They were determined that the pc will be the hub of the future home network"* and that Microsoft's motivation was the economic enlargement by the cost created by switching software to any similar competitive products [2].

As a result of the short overview on the aforementioned issues, it is foreseeable that power is taken away from the user - i.e. user restrictions, loss of anonymity, mandatory use of the TC technology to grant communication with other networks and personal computers. Then again, the paper argues that this must be controlled and rebalanced by increasing the legal liability and responsibility of the TC providers for the favor of the user.

Summarizing the above-mentioned study concerning the critisim that has emerged from TC:

- Difficult sharing of content due to DRM
- Documents and email can be remotely deleted or unreadable
- Downloading and installing software restrictions
- Might constist a thread to OSS development
- User interaction problems
- Incompatibility with legacy systems
- High cost for swapping between products and employees' training
- Competition law
- Remote cencorship
- Interoperation with other products

5   Law Addressing These Ethical Concerns

TC is characterised by a dramatic shift of power and control away from the human user to the software itself; power that is ultimately exercised by software providers. The overall argument we present in this paper, is that with such great powers, great responsibility will have to come (legally regulated). Governments (and citizens) will ultimately accede to this power shift, and the resulting dangers to values such as personal privacy and autonomy, only if there is a corresponding increase of responsibility on the side of the software provider.

5.1   Imposing 'Reliance Liability'

As an example of this rebalancing of power and responsibility, the paper aims to argue that the nature of TC lends itself to the imposition of reliance liability at some point in the future. TC becomes a guaranteed seal of approval on which third parties will increasingly rely. To the extend that TC providers anticipate this development at all, an insurance based solution seems likely to have the potential to further increase the digital divide.

We argue that TC has the potential to change radically the way we think about internet governance. It will shift the balance of power totally to commercial entities, more specifically to the members of the TCG. One argument of the paper is that the legal analysis of this shift has so far been very limited, and where it took place at all, has been highly selective. We also argue that the discussion so far has not taken account of the fact that a power shift of this magnitude will (or should) also result in a shift of responsibility, and ultimately liability, to the commercial entities. After describing such a theory of *'legal responsibility in an age of trusted computing'*, issues such as DRM and copyright will have to be revisited.

It is suggested that a possible outcome of greater legal responsibility, created either through the use of express warranties, or through implied terms imposed by the courts, is an increase in the cost of TC, as hardware and software producers seek to reduce their financial exposure via insurance. This in turn raises questions about the cost/benefit of TC systems to end-users, and whether the use of such systems would further exacerbate the 'digital divide' amongst end-users. The uncertainty about 'digital divide' issues is increased by the fact that in the literature, different players in the TC environment appear to have different end-user groups in mind. HP seems to be aiming TC at corporate users, whilst other companies such as Microsoft, with its Palladium initiative, seems to have wider aims. Will potential liability play as large, or perhaps a larger part in *determining the viability* of TC as copyright and privacy issues?

Liability for faulty software is an area of considerable legal controversy, not least because it remains unclear in UK law whether software is to be treated as a good, a service, or something else. The distinction is important because it determines the nature and scope of liability that can be implied into a contract, and also to some extent what can be legitimately excluded by contract. TC further complicates the issue because a failure in such a system may be hardware or software related. Hardware is clearly a good [3] - if software is deemed to be a service or sui generis in nature, this suggests that different components of the TC concept might be held to different standards.

In a TC world, my computer can "trust" other computers that identify themselves as "Trusted Computing", and in turn is trusted by them. If the system fails, two possible scenarios occur:

1. I behave less conscientiously, relying on the TC protection, and my economic interests are damaged (by downloading e.g. malware). This is primarily a contractual issue between me and the TC provider. However, a dimension of complexity is added by the fact that without TC, my computer may not be any longer functional as an internet enabled device (as other machines will not talk to it). This "must have" aspect of TC means that the scope to exclude contractually liability by the TC provider may well be limited under good faith rules.
2. Someone else, relying on my computer's certificate, downloads harmful software from me. Does this third party have any claims against *my* TC provider, given that he acted in reasonable reliance on the TC certificate?

It has been suggested in the past that it would be useful to apply pressure to software vendors to improve software security and to ensure that the software provides the security it should provide, and that if this is not the case, then purchasers should be able to sue the software vendors for any kind of harm caused by the use of their products. However, while the House of Lords report [13] does indeed suggest that this type of liability can play a role to incentivize software producers to develop more secure applications, so far there is no attempt made to attribute liability to software producers if they deliver software that is "designed unsafe". TC software would by design be more secure, but also "warrant" this security explicitly. Potentially therefore, the law could create a counterproductive incentive structure: Software that is by design (relatively) unsafe might avoid liability for damage caused by malicious software, but the comparatively more secure TC could be held liable because its security is contractually and explicitly guaranteed.

Chandler [5] analyses two approaches where the law could intervene in the software development process to provide the standards that the end-user demands. The first approach is the use of regulations or laws to overcome market failures (i.e. where the market fails to put pressure on manufacturers to produce more secure software, such as in a monopoly situation) by mandating minimum security standards. The second approach is *"to impose liability for negligently-designed software"* [5] an approach that presents some advantages for example:

> software intended for use in conditions where design flaws may lead to substantial losses may be treated differently from software that does not present high risks. [5]

Chandler [5] notes that applying a negligence standard to software security might be a way forward, but specifically warns that taking that path might cause the software industry to take measures that while improving security could have other, less desirable implications (loss of consumer freedom and the implications for competition). She also clarifies (in the context of DDoS attacks) that, currently, purchasers may find it difficult to sue vendors for liability for damage caused by their product's failure. Firstly, license terms disclaiming or limiting liability may affect possible lawsuits. Secondly, users may face counterclaims of contributory negligence if they did not maintain properly their security by patches or virus scanning.

5.2 Imposing the Duty to Preserve Evidence

The literature review indicates that TC providers can identify computer crimes [2,21] that fall under the UK Computer Misuse Act. This can be easily done through the tamper-resistant security chip that will be contained in the trusted computing platform. Trustworthiness verification will be performed from the operating system before execution from the client [18].

Moreover, Professor Zittrain speaking in images, has stated that the TC:

...will employ digital gatekeepers that act like the bouncers outside a nightclub, ensuring that only software that looks or behaves a certain way is allowed in. The result will be more reliable computing – and more control over the machine by the manufacturer or operating system maker, which essentially gives the bouncer her guest list. [28]

Given that the TC providers will have the control over the client machine, and will know about computer crime, this brings up the questions whether they should be responsible to mention this crime to the authorities and in addition whether they are responsible to ensure that any data recovered during an investigation of a customer's TC are not tarnished. From the above statement of [28] it is clear that the TC providers, will have the control over the machines, and they will be able to access the machines in any possible way. This raises a lot of issues, like privacy and the owner's reference on "Trojan defense".

Pleading the "Trojan defense" has and will continue to be a legal issue, as long as there is lack in tracking and tracing cyber-attacks as Lipson stated .

The lack of proven techniques for effectively and consistently tracking sophisticated cyber-attacks to their source (and rarely to the individuals or entities responsible) severely diminishes any deterrent effect. Perpetrators feel free to act with nearly total anonymity. [14]

This makes things worse, as with the TC platform, the group of people accessing the PC widens considerably to potentially any individuals within a TC organization that can legally or maliciously get access to the relevant control interfaces. Thus, the possibility and the danger for malicious intrusions will be larger and the legal tracking route will be more complicated.

Conversely, when a TC provider spots illicit software on its customer's computer, it might make them under some legal regimes complicit in the crime. From this point an issue arises; what is the legal obligation of the TC organization? There are in fact, two possible answers: either the TC provider informs the user and arrange the matter discreetly and unofficially, or the TC provider can report the illegal material.

6 Conclusions

The security of the communication infrastructure has belatedly gained by governments the interest that it deserves. In addition to the protection of safety critical infrastructure, consumers too need to be confident in internet security to allow digital economies to flourish. The House of Lords Report rightly criticized the UK government for over-emphasizing the responsibility of individual computer users. However, its main recommendation is a more prominent role of the state. TC offers an alternative, where security is not entrusted to the user, nor enforced by state sanctions, but embedded into the very fabric of the internet.

However, this would entail a dramatic *shift of power* away from consumers and state regulatory bodies to the software providers, a shift that has been described as unacceptable by many commentators. The argument that has been developed in this paper stated that such a shift can be justifiable, but only if it is accompanied by an equivalent shift in legal responsibility. With software providers taking on a role previously deemed to be the prerogative of the state (i.e. protection of crucial infrastructure), the user-TC relation needs to come closer to the citizen-state relation. Users will only accept TC as a technology that in fact infringes their autonomy if they can rely on robust legal safeguards if things go wrong. Imposing reliance liability is as we argued one well-established legal mechanism to address this power/responsibility shift that worked well in other fields of economic activity. But since it makes TC providers liable in tort for the proper functioning of user's computers also outside the contractual nexus (and hence outside their control) it may well increase the costs and decrease the incentives for TC development. Similarly, we argued that other legal duties previously associated with the state, such as the robust preservation of evidence in criminal proceedings and crime investigation more generally, may have in parts to be transferred to TC providers. So far, our research indicates that awareness of these possible developments in the TC community is low. They need to be raised to ensure that the costs, benefits and dangers can be properly quantified.

References

1. Anderson, R.: Cryptography and Competition Policy Issues with Trusted Computing. In: Proc. of the twenty-second annual symposium on Principles of distributed computing (PODC 2003), pp. 3–10. ACM, Boston (2003)
2. Anderson, R.: Trusted Computing Frequently Asked Questions /TCG / LaGrande / NGSCB / Longhorn / Palladium / TCPA - Version 1.1 (2003) (Cited October 2, 2008), http://www.cl.cam.ac.uk/~rja14/tcpa-faq.html
3. Bradgate, R.: Beyond the Millennium - The Legal Issues: Sale of Goods Issues and The Millennium Bug. JILT 1999(2) (1999) (Cited October 2, 2008), http://www2.warwick.ac.uk/fac/soc/law/elj/jilt/1999_2/bradgate/
4. Burmester, M., Mulholland, J.: The advent of trusted computing: implications for digital forensics. In: Proc. of the 2006 ACM symposium on Applied computing, pp. 283–287. ACM, Dijon (2006)
5. Chandler, J.A.: Security in Cyberspace: Combating Distributed Denial of Service Attacks. UOLTJ 1(1-2), 231–261 (2003)
6. Charlesworth, A.J.: DRM: the Straw to Break the Back of Procrustean Approaches to Copyright? In: Grosheide, F.W., Brinkhof, J.J. (eds.) Intellectual Property 2004, Articles on Crossing Borders between traditional and actual, pp. 405–422. Intersertia, Belgium (2005)
7. Collins, H.: The Decline of Privacy in Private Law. J. Law Soc. 14(1), 91–103 (1987)

8. Edwards, L.: Dawn of the Death of Distributed Denial of Service: How to Kill Zombies. Cardozo AELJ 24(1), 23–62 (2006)
9. Erickson, J.S.: Fair use DRM and Trusted Computing. Commun. ACM 46(4), 34–39 (2003)
10. Felten, E.: Understanding Trusted Computing - Will Its Benefits Outweigh Its Drawbacks? IEEE Security and Privacy 1(3), 60–62 (2003)
11. Hilley, S.: Trusted computing - path to security or road to servitude? Network Security 2004(8), 12–15 (2004)
12. House of Lords Publications. Science and Technology - Fourth Report, Session 2007-08. House of Lords (2008) (Cited December 10, 2008), http://www.publications.parliament.uk/pa/ld200708/ldselect/ldsctech/131/131.pdf
13. House of Lords Publications. Science and Technology - Fifth Report, Session 2006-07. House of Lords (2007) (Cited October 13, 2008), http://www.publications.parliament.uk/pa/ld200607/ldselect/ldsctech/165/16502.htm
14. Lipson, H.F.: Tracking and Tracing Cyber-Attacks: Technical Challenges and Global Policy Issues. In: University, C.M. (ed.) CERT Coordination Center, Special Report, CMU/SEI-2002-SR-009:49 (2002)
15. von Lohmann, F.: Meditations on Trusted Computing. In: Electronic Frontier Foundation, Whitepapers (2004) (Cited January 10, 2009), http://www.eff.org/wp/meditations-trusted-computing
16. Pearson, S.: Trusted Computing: Strengths, Weaknesses and Further Opportunities for Enhancing Privacy. In: Herrmann, P., Issarny, V., Shiu, S.C.K. (eds.) iTrust 2005. LNCS, vol. 3477, pp. 305–320. Springer, Heidelberg (2005)
17. Reid, J., Nieto, J.M.G., Dawson, E., et al.: Privacy and Trusted Computing. In: Proc. of the 14th International Workshop on Database and Expert Systems Applications (DEXA 2003), pp. 383–388 (2003)
18. Richardson, R.: Eighth Annual 2003 CSI/FBI Computer Crime and Security Survey. In: Computer Security Institute (2003) (Cited October 20, 2008), http://www.gocsi.com
19. Roemer, R.: Locking Down Loose Bits: Trusted Computing Digital Rights Management and the Fight for Copyright Control on Your Computer. UCLA J. of Law & Technology 8 (2003) (accessed October 20, 2008), http://www.lawtechjournal.com/articles/2003/08_040223_roemer.php
20. Samuelson, P.: DRM {and, or vs.} the Law. Commun. ACM 46(4), 41–45 (2003)
21. Schell, R., Michael, F.: Platform security: What is lacking? Information Security Technical Report 5(1), 26–41 (2000)
22. Schoen, S.: Compatibility, competition, and control in Trusted computing environments. Information Security Technical Report 10(2), 105–119 (2005)
23. Snijders, H.J.: Privacy of Contract. In: Studies - Oxford Institute of European and Comparative Law. Hart 2007(5), 105–116 (2007)
24. Stallman, R.: Can you trust your computer? In: NewsForge - The Online Newspaper for Linux and OpenSource (2002) (Cited October 15, 2008), http://www.gnu.org/philosophy/can-you-trust.html
25. Turner, M., Budgen, D., Brereton, P.: Turning software into a service. Computer 36(10), 38–44 (2003)
26. Vaughan-Nichols, J.S.: How Trustworthy is Trusted Computing? Computer 36(3), 18–20 (2003)
27. Woodford, C.: Trusted Computing or Big Brother? Putting the Rights back in Digital Rights Management. U Colo L Rev. (75), 253–300 (2004)
28. Zittrain, J.L.: Taming the Consumer's Computer. In: The New York Times (2002) (Cited October 15, 2008), http://query.nytimes.com/gst/fullpage.html?res=990DEED81130F932A25750C0A9649C8B63

Persona: Network Layer Anonymity and Accountability for Next Generation Internet

Yannis Mallios[1], Sudeep Modi[1], Aditya Agarwala[2], and Christina Johns[2]

[1] Carnegie Mellon University, Information Networking Institute, Pittsburgh PA, USA
imallios@andrew.cmu.edu, sdmodi@andrew.cmu.edu
[2] Carnegie Mellon University, Dept. of Electrical and Computer Eng., Pittsburgh PA, USA
adityaag@andrew.cmu.edu, cjohns@andrew.cmu.edu

Abstract. Individual privacy has become a major concern, due to the intrusive nature of the services and websites that collect increasing amounts of private information. One of the notions that can lead towards privacy protection is that of anonymity. Unfortunately, anonymity can also be maliciously exploited by attackers to hide their actions and identity. Thus some sort of accountability is also required. The current Internet has failed to provide both properties, as anonymity techniques are difficult to fully deploy and thus are easily attacked, while the Internet provides limited level of accountability. The Next Generation Internet (NGI) provides us with the opportunity to examine how these conflicting properties could be efficiently applied and thus protect users' privacy while holding malicious users accountable. In this paper we present the design of a scheme, called Persona that can provide anonymity and accountability in the network layer of NGI. More specifically, our design requirements are to combine these two conflicting desires in a stateless manner within routers. Persona allows users to choose different levels of anonymity, while it allows the discovery of malicious nodes.

1 Introduction

Advances in Information and Communication Technologies (ICT) that make data collection and processing fast and efficient, have brought privacy protection to the spotlight. For that reason several anonymity mechanisms have been proposed and implemented [1]. Most of these mechanisms rely on providing anonymity in the higher network layers, like the application or transport layer, while for efficiency and usability reasons they use weaker mechanisms for anonymity protection (e.g. no use of dummy traffic). This however can introduce greater threats to anonymity. For example TOR [2], one of the most popular anonymizing networks, has been proven vulnerable to several attacks that could degrade the level of anonymity provided [3,4].

The disadvantage of making use of the application layer to provide anonymity is that applications are not necessarily bound to using the anonymity service. It is possible to circumvent the anonymizing procedures by directly making use of the functionality of the lower layers. For example, a javascript or flash file embedded in an html page could initiate another connection to a third party server without using the anonymizing application, which could reveal the user's IP address. Thus, it is important to apply

D. Gritzalis and J. Lopez (Eds.): SEC 2009, IFIP AICT 297, pp. 410–420, 2009.

anonymizing procedures at the lowest networking layer possible, so as to avoid application bypasses and lower layer attacks. However, due to the structure of today's Internet, there is no straightforward implementation. For that reason, Next Generation Internet (NGI) can be used as a point of reference and infrastructure, so as to design and explore an efficient and effective anonymity solution. Despite the need for privacy and anonymity, there is also a need for some sort of accountability not only for security purposes but also for purposes such as billing, management, measurement, etc [5].

In this paper we present a solution that incorporates both privacy and accountability in the network layer, in the context of NGI. We introduce Persona, a scheme that describes the design of a network layer which provides routing and addressing services in a manner which ensures that packets are routed and delivered with the highest level of anonymity between the communicating parties. Finally, if required, Persona can be used to reveal anonymity in an appropriate manner, thereby providing the right degree of accountability as required. We must mention that in this paper we decided to focus our design requirements on combining the conflicting desires of anonymity and accountability in the network layer. However, anonymity could be also applied as an overlay in a higher networking layer, as used today. Answering the question whether anonymity techniques should be applied in the network layer, or in an overlay in a higher networking layer, is out of the scope of this paper. Our work is inspired by research like Accountable Internet Protocol [6], and SIFF [7], at least in the context of discussion about NGI. More specifically, we do not refer to the NGI as the means of a new radical design proposal for the internet; rather we try to improve the current network layer, by adding the components necessary to meet the requirements of both anonymity and accountability. It is for these changes that we refer to NGI.

In this paper we make two major contributions. First, we introduce a novel approach to provide anonymity in the network layer. This paper is the first one, to our knowledge, that provides anonymity per packet, rather than per session, and in stateless manner in the routers. Second, we discuss how this approach is applicable to the NGI and we show how our novel approach provides accountability in case of misbehaving nodes. The paper is organized as follows. In section 2 we provide definitions of the relevant terms, and we elaborate on our assumptions, the attacker model and the attacks that our scheme defends against. In Section 3 we present the design and functionality of Persona, while in section 4 we discuss the evaluation of our scheme in terms of anonymity, efficiency and applicability. In section 5 we discuss some related work and finally, in section 6 we present some ideas for further research.

2   Definitions, Assumptions and Attacker Model

Anonymity is a concept that has received wide research attention, due its ability to protect privacy. For that reason a precise set of formal definitions has been proposed for the concepts of anonymity and its relevant terms [8]. In this context, anonymity of a subject is defined as the property by which the subject is not identifiable within a set of subjects, the anonymity set [8]. Since most communications are a bi-directional, anonymity is often distinguished to sender and receiver anonymity. Sender anonymity is achieved when it is not possible to identify the sender within a set of possible subjects that sent the message. Similarly receiver anonymity is achieved when it is not possible to identify the receiver of the message within a set of possible receivers [8]. Another important term relevant to anonymity is pseudonymity which is defined as the use of pseudonyms as IDs. Pseudonyms refer to identifiers of a subject other than one of the subject's real names [8]. An advantage of pseudonymity over the previous terms is that accountability for misbehavior can be enforced. Accountability can be defined as the state of a subject being held responsible for a certain action taken by that subject. It is easy to see that if a subject is held accountable for a particular action, that subject is no longer anonymous.

Our proposed architecture is described within the context of some assumptions. The first set of assumptions is with regards to the network infrastructure. Specifically, we assume that ISPs will not have any legacy systems or routers. All links between the sender and receiver are assumed to go through new hardware that supports our solution. As far as the hardware infrastructure is concerned we make the following assumptions. First, we assume routers that have the computational power to perform encryption and decryption with symmetric keys in hardware. Additionally we assume that routers will come equipped with a Trusted Platform Module (TPM). A TPM is a microcontroller that stores keys, passwords and digital certificates [9]. This is a safe assumption considering most new desktops and laptops already come equipped with these. Finally, we assume that TPM units are actually as secure and tamper resistant as they are claimed to be. We do not try and define a secure TPM protocol but assume the ones defined are secure and work as described [9]. It must be mentioned that the assumption for hardware capabilities of encryption and decryption, is a weak assumption; the architecture would still be effective without this assumption, and its efficiency would be decreased by only a small factor as we analyze later.

Finally, to define a valid solution, assumptions need to be made on the capabilities of the attacker. In our scheme we assume a rather strong attacker model as defined in [10]. Following this attacker model, several attacks on anonymity protocols have been proposed, with traffic analysis attacks being considered the most potent ones. In this context, the attacks, against which we provide anonymity guarantees, are Brute Force Attacks, Communication Pattern Attacks, Timing Attacks and Packet Counting Attacks [11].

3   Persona

As mentioned in section 2 anonymity and accountability are the two conflicting notions. However, pseudonymity enables users to hide their true identity, until some event is triggered by which a third party can reveal it. In this paper we focus on providing sender anonymity and accountability by exploiting the notion of pseudonymity. Persona is structured around the following concept. While a packet is being routed through the network and towards the destination, we obfuscate the source address (in each hop) to provide anonymity (through pseudonymity). Additionally, we want the ability to trace back the origin of the packet, for accountability and routing replies. These two properties can be achieved through symmetric cryptography. More specifically, in the "forward path" encryption helps obfuscate the source address, while in the "trace-back path" decryption helps reveal the original path. It can be seen that the approach used for packet replies is also used for accountability. The only difference is the context in which the traceback functionality is provided. For this reason, we focus on describing the technical details of tracing back packets, as accountability has several additional policy related issues that are out of the scope of this paper. However, we do provide a description on how accountability can be achieved, using our scheme.

3.1   First Hop Communication

Today, when a user registers with an ISP, it is common for the ISP to provide the user with a router in order to connect to the ISP and the Internet. As mentioned in the previous section, we assume that routers come installed with a TPM. Embedded within the TPM are symmetric keys that the router shares with the ISP. The ISP also has routers that use TPMs, to ensure trusted and secure software execution, attestation, and key storage.

When the user first connects to the network through his router, the keys in the TPMs are used to encrypt the information exchanged between the ISP and the user. This includes 1) the addresses of the routers that the user can contact as "first hop" from an ISP perspective (i.e. the routers that will eventually provide the anonymizing service), and 2) the shared keys between these routers and the user. After the "handshake", each user connected to the ISP follows a traffic sending pattern in order to exchange information in a secure and anonymous way. First the TPM of the user's router pseudorandomly chooses one of the newly received trusted routers to forward the packet. Thus, each packet will be forwarded to the Internet through a different router. In the case of a node compromise the attacker only has a probabilistic opportunity of identifying the sender. The second pattern that each user follows is that all packets sent are of same length. This length can be ISP specific, and can be established through the initial TPM handshake. This way traffic analysis attacks are prohibited and the attacker cannot correlate between messages' sizes. Next, the users of the ISP continuously send packets, by using dummy traffic whenever the user has no data to send. Thus, timing attacks and traffic pattern analysis are also difficult to achieve. This means that the link capacity between the users and the ISP will be always completely utilized. It has been shown that dummy traffic is the only way to protect against timing attacks [4]. Our model makes weaker and more efficient assumptions than previous proposed ones (like mix nets [12]), since the only part of the network that will utilize its maximum capacity at all times will be the connection between the user and the ISP. In conclusion, by requiring the usage of dummy traffic only in the first hop of the communication, we strike a balance between strong anonymity guarantees and efficiency (i.e. realistic use of dummy traffic). Finally, the receiver's address is encrypted using the shared key between the TPM of the user's router and the TPM of the ISP's router.

For the rest of the paper we assume that the receiver's address is sent in clear text after the first hop (i.e. the ISP of the sender). If a receiver's key is known (either public or shared), the router (i.e. the network layer) can also encrypt the payload, so as to provide confidentiality to the upper layers, especially if the higher level applications do not use encryption.

3.2   Persona Network Operation

As mentioned in the introduction, our approach introduces the concept of per packet anonymity. In order to achieve this, the packets need to be uniquely identifiable, at least for a given time interval, in order to avoid collisions. For that reason, the user (sender) has a Sequence Number (SN) which is incremented for each packet sent. We identify each packet by two unique fields. The first is the sender's IP, which will be unique in the Internet, and the second is the SN. If the SN is 128 bits long each user can send 2^{128} distinct packets before there is a duplicate packet in the network.

After the user has created a packet following the principles described in the previous section, she forwards the packet to the ISP. The main goal of the ISP is to hide the source identity of the packet. Each router holds a secret key that it can use for encryption. Using that key and a symmetric encryption function, the router maps the source IP address of the sender, to another randomly selected IP address from the range that its ISP holds. After the IP address has been changed the packet is forwarded to the Internet, according to the routing tables that the router has. This way the ISP shuffles the address of each packet and the attacker cannot determine the user that actually sent each packet. Finally the ISP routers batch the packets to be sent before actually forwarding them to the network. The communication and messages exchanged between the user and the router are as follows[1]:

User		Router	
User		**Router**	
U:	$E_{KUR}(\text{destination}) \Rightarrow Q$	R:	$E_{KR}(IP_1 \parallel SN_1) \Rightarrow (IP_x \parallel SN_x)$
U=>R: $(IP_1 \parallel SN_1) \parallel \text{Address}_R \parallel Q \parallel \text{payload}$		R:	$D_{KUR}(Q) \Rightarrow \text{destination}$
		R=>Internet: $(IP_x \parallel SN_x) \parallel \text{destination} \parallel \text{payload}$	

Fig. 1. Message exchanged between User and Router

where KUR is the key shared by the user and the specific router, $Address_R$ is the IP address of the router, and destination is the IP address of the recipient. This operation will be done by each router until the packet reaches the destination as shown in Figure 2 (IPv4 addresses are used due to familiarity reasons with addressing).

It is easily understood that if sender anonymity is to be achieved, the receiver will not know how to reply to the packet. The reason is that there is no tunnel established, and thus there is a need to keep some state in order to return the reply to the sender. However by using the above scheme, packets can be routed to the original sender even if no state is kept. To better illustrate this, we will use an example. Let us assume that

---

[1] The semantics of the equations of the network operations are the following: The left column is used to denote the parties that take place in a given operation. If there is a single party, for example "a" then the right column is the action performed locally by that party. If there is a statement of the format "$a \Rightarrow b$", then this means that a sends to b, the message that exists in the right column. The right column denotes either actions or message contents. $E_k(m) \Rightarrow q$, denotes encryption of m under key k and q as the result of the encryption. $D_k(q) \Rightarrow m$, means decrypt q using key k and get m as the result of the decryption. If the right column is a message, then the symbol $\parallel$ is used to denote concatenation of the information that are included in the packet.

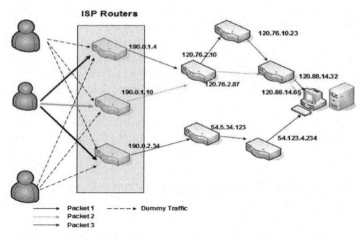

Fig. 2. Example of Persona Routing

after the first packet was forwarded to the Internet as explained above. Table 1 in Figure 3 depicts the operations that will take place in the last 2 hops (i.e. the router immediately before the receiver, and the receiver itself; the sequence of hops is $R_{n-1} => R_n =>$ *Receiver*). Now, the receiver has to create a packet that will have as destination the duple $(IP_d || SN_d)$ and forward it to Rn in order to send a reply, following the steps depicted in Table 2 in Figure 3.

$R_{n-1} => R_n:$ $(IP_i || SN_i) ||$ destination $||$ payload
$R_n:$ $E (IP_i || SN_i)_{KRn} => (IP_d || SN_d)$
$R_n => $Receiver: $(IP_d || SN_d) ||$ destination $||$ payload

Table 1

Receiver $=> R_n:$ $IP_{Receiver} || (IP_d || SN_d) ||$ payload
$R_n:$ $D (IP_d || SN_d)_{KRn} => (IP_i || SN_i)$
$R_n => R_{n-1}:$ $IP_{Receiver} || (IP_i || SN_i) ||$ payload
...
$R_1 => R:$ $IP_{Receiver} || (IP_x || SN_x) ||$ payload
$R:$ $D (IP_x || SN_x)_{KR} => (IP_1 || SN_1)$
$R:$ $E (IP_{Receiver})_{KUR} => W$
$R => U:$ $W || (IP_1 || SN_1) ||$ payload
$U:$ $D (W)_{KUR} => IP_{Receiver}$

Table 2

Fig. 3. Process of Routing Back Replies to Sender

Using this scheme, packets can be routed backwards, without the need for the routers to keep any state. The only distinction that needs to be made by the routers is whether the packet is being sent "forward" or "backwards", so as to know whether to encrypt or decrypt. This can be done by an identifier, for example a single bit, which would be set by the receiver before sending his reply.

Given the size of the Internet in terms of hosts, routers and packets being sent, we use the SN in each packet to minimize the possibility of collision in an intermediate router (no packet is the same in the network since there are 10^{128} unique packets per address). If no SN was used, a router could end up assigning the same output IP address to two different incoming packets due to its limited IP address range. For example, if a router has an input of 2^{10} distinct IPs, an output range of 2^{10} distinct IPs and a SN of 128 bits then there must be 2^{138} packets (128 bits of SN and 10 bits of IP range) sent before there is a possibility of collision of two different packets, with different sources. Thus by using SN it can be ensured that there will be no collision until the SN space is exhausted[2]. One assumption that we made was that each router has the same size of input and output IP ranges. However this might not always be the case. Let us assume that a given router R has some IP range that it can use in order to map outgoing IP addresses (denoted as "/x" output, where x is essentially the number of bits the router can manipulate), while it receives input from other routers that also have some IP range (denoted as "/y" input). It is expected that a lot of routers in the Internet will have a smaller output space than input space, and thus our router R will need y-x additional bits in order to perform one-to-one mapping. In order to include these additional bits to the packet, we use piggybacking.

Having explained the operation of the routers, we now discuss in detail the structure of the packets that our scheme uses. As mentioned previously, our protocol ensures collision free operation until the SN space is exhausted, after which each router changes its key. For this solution to be effective, the router needs to add some information in each packet, about the key it used for changing the IP address of the particular packet. The information that needs to be stored in each packet in order to make our protocol more efficient includes: 1) Sequence Number, 2) index of Router's secret key, 3) size of input space of addresses, 4) size of output space of addresses[3], and 5) the level of anonymity required. The level of anonymity is an optional variable that could be used to route the message through paths that provide better anonymity, but have more latency. Essentially all this information could be piggybacked in the packet. Thus all that needs to be added in the IP header will be the indexing of this information.

3.3 Persona Accountability

In the previous sections we discussed how our scheme operates in terms of routing and anonymity preservation. In this section we are going to describe how our scheme ensures accountability. As mentioned in the beginning of section 3, the operational principles of accountability are structured around backwards routing. Thus we will describe

---

[2] It must be mentioned that although there are 64 bits for addressing, not all of them are available to a particular router. If that was the case, and every router was assigning output (pseudo) addresses, based on all 64 bits, then it would be really difficult to keep track of the routing of packets (i.e. routing tables). Thus in order not to modify the routing tables, and yet allow Persona to fully operate, we assume that each router will only output addresses that he has been assigned: this means that each router will be able to manipulate only a number of bits (that correspond to its IP range), and not all the 64 available ones. This is depicted in the example where we assume a 10 bit manipulation.

[3] The input and output space, are the /x and /y that the router used during the encryption of the message. In a dynamic environment like the Internet, relationships between ASes and IPSs might change, and thus x and y are not expected to remain static, and thus the router needs to know what were the variables used for encryption at a particular time.

the context in which backwards routing can be used for accountability. We will classify accountability into two categories; short term and long term. By short term accountability we refer to the accountability about attacks that are "currently" taking place like DoS attacks, DDoS attacks, network scanning, etc, which essentially require the identification of the attacker as soon as possible. For better illustrating Persona's accountability operations, we assume that there exist other mechanisms that deal with IP spoofing. In short term accountability, ISPs can cooperate in order to identify and stop malicious attackers. For example, let as assume that a DoS attack takes place against a specific IP address (e.g. webserver). The router that forwards the packets to that IP address, can backtrace the routers from which it received the packets by decrypting the IPs reported by the webserver. Then it can contact these routers, reporting that a DoS attack takes place. If this procedure is applied recursively backwards, the originator of the attack can be found, and if the routers cooperate (i.e. routers can query other routers for packet throttling and the recipients of the requests indeed apply that throttling), the attack can be mitigated.

Long term accountability refers to examples like fraud detection, were the attacker is found after days or moths of investigation or forensics. In that case, the routers could be queried for past key usage, and since they keep a table of all keys used in the past in the corresponding table, the attacker could be easily tracked down (if memory constraints are placed on the table, past keys can always be stored on external backup media).

4 Persona Evaluation

In this section we are going to describe how our scheme defends against the attacks mentioned in section 2 and provide an efficiency analysis of Persona. Persona resists anonymity attacks as follows. 1) Brute Force Attack: In this attack, the attacker follows the life of every single packet that enters the network. Persona, by encrypting the packet during the first hop (possibly adding some nonce to each packet), and the subsequent source IP change, renders this attack useless. The user is at least provided with k anonymity where k is the number of active senders of ISP. 2) Communication Pattern Attacks: In this scenario the attacker monitors the two ends of a communication channel and tries to correlate entering and exiting packets. This attack is thwarted fairly well with the dummy traffic introduced in our solution. The use of dummy traffic and change of source IP address prevents the attacker from knowing which entering packet corresponds to the exiting packet. The best the strongest attacker can do is to deduce the originating ISP. The attacker still cannot determine which of the ISP's customers sent the packet. 3) Timing Attacks: Here, the attacker can deduce the origination of a packet based on the amount of time it took to reach the destination. In our scheme the ISP batches the messages and thus it is difficult for the attacker to identify which client of the ISP actually sent the message. Additionally, if more routers implement batching, the level of anonymity achieved is greater. Finally, even if the packets follow the same route, the attacker will not be able to apply timing attacks. This is because the source address will be changing for each packet and the attacker will not be able to tell if there are multiple senders sending to a single receiver. Thus she will not be able to deduce the identity of the senders or even the number of senders. 4) Packet Counting

Attacks: The attacker can connect unusual bursts of outgoing traffic with unusual bursts of incoming traffic. Since our model uses dummy traffic and same packet size there are no bursts of traffic to identify.

Our solution incorporates most of the suggested countermeasures proposed in mix-nets, namely encryption, same packet size, batching and dummy traffic [11]. These countermeasures are applied at minimum to the first hop, between the user and the ISP. Thus at minimum, each user will have a level of k-anonymity, where k is the number of active users connected to the ISP at a particular moment. This makes our scheme resilient to additional attacks that are defeated with these countermeasures, whilst the level of anonymity our scheme provides, increases with the number of routers that actually implement the abovementioned properties.

In order to provide the abovementioned anonymity guarantees and functionality, Persona requires a lot of cryptographic operations to take place in each router and for each packet. We know that for symmetric encryption there can be approximately 10^7 operations per second in 1 GHz processor if done in hardware. Let us assume that users are using a line speed of 100Mbps, and that an average IPv6 packet size is used (i.e. 20000 bytes without Ethernet limitations). Each user will be sending, and each router will be receiving, 10^3 packets per user, and thus, given that it can calculate 10^7 operations per second, 10^4 users per router per second can be accommodated. For the first router that belongs to the ISP, multiple routers can be used, both for increase anonymity and better efficiency. The only bottleneck would be top level routers. These routers already have to forward packets at line speed, so there is a tradeoff between the anonymity and the efficiency that NGI will offer. In that case the optional bits for level of anonymity discussed in the previous section could be used.

Finally it has to be mentioned that we approached the problem of anonymity and accountability from a network layer's perspective. That is we did not take into account the above protocols, and we only defined the services that are going to be provided to them. However, one question that might be of importance is how our protocol can assist and support connection oriented services (e.g. TCP). In that case we see two possible solutions. The first one is the redesign of the transport layer so as not to use IP addresses as point of reference for keeping sessions' state. The second solution would be to have a handshake between the sender and the server, so as the sender is granted with a session identifier that he can use for session identification. This identifier can be encrypted alongside with the payload, so as to avoid traffic analysis based on its identification in the various packets.

5   Related Work

Currently, most of the techniques used for anonymity make use of the concept of mix networks introduced by Chaum [12]. Mix networks, are networks composed of mix servers which batch a set of messages encrypted by their corresponding public keys. They then decrypt these messages and send them out in a rearranged order such that an external observer cannot tell which outgoing messages correspond to incoming messages. Babel [13], Mixmaster [14], Mixminion [15] and Onion routing [16] are some of the most important systems based on mix networks. A common aspect of all the solutions mentioned above is that none of these systems have accountability as one of their main goals, as Persona does. In addition, in Persona the sender does not need to know the path that the packet will follow, as done in Onion Routing for example. Moreover Persona does not encrypt the packet in an "onion style" with the public keys of the routers which has additional efficiency advantages.

Two systems that make use of pseudonymity in the network to achieve anonymity are Freedom [17] and Tarzan [18]. Both these techniques are similar, in the sense that the user connects to a node anonymously. This node then sends the packet to the destination but changes the source address of the packet by assigning it a pseudonym. Once a packet is sent the receiver sends a reply addressed to the pseudonym. The node that had performed the network address translation while sending maps the pseudonym to the original address and sends the reply to the sender using the anonymous channel. The two approaches differ in the way a user connects to the node doing the network address translation. However, in both cases the sender requires information about the path between itself and the exit node performing the NAT. Our approach differs from these approaches in three ways. Firstly, we do not need to keep any state in the nodes to translate the IP addresses back to the original address. This saves a lot of memory and the time to look up the translations in memory. Secondly, we do the translation per packet and not per session. This increases the Unlinkability between the sender and receiver as each packet is routed independently giving the attacker little information. Thirdly, in our scheme the sender does not need to set up the path every time before sending a packet. This path is preconfigured when the router is installed. Not having to set up the path avoids wasting time.

6 Conclusions and Further Research

This paper has presented Persona, a scheme that incorporates anonymity and accountability in the network layer of the Next Generation Internet. We have proposed a novel approach by which each packet is provided with anonymity, thus achieving stronger properties from previous solutions. Additionally we adopted proven solutions from previous research on anonymity techniques, so as to ensure a maximum level of anonymity, at minimum within the ISP of a client. Finally, we described how our scheme can be used for achieving accountability, in cases of malicious and misbehaving users. Continuing our effort, we examine how we can optimize our solution and provide additional types of anonymity (e.g. recipient anonymity). Additionally we examine how our scheme can be applied to the current Internet. Finally we are planning to do simulations so as to identify the tradeoffs of our approach in terms of current IP deployment and existing anonymity techniques.

Acknowledgements. The authors would wish to thank Professor Adrian Perrig for his support, guidance and constructive suggestions, and the anonymous reviewers for their helpful comments. We greatfully acknowledge support for this research by CyLab at Carnegie Mellon under grant DAAD19-02-1-0389 from the Army Research Office. The views and conclusions contained here are those of the authors and should not be interpreted as necessarily representing the official policies or endorsements, either express or implied, of ARO, CMU, or the U.S. Government or any of its agencies.

References

1. Danezis, G., Diaz, C.: A Survey of Anonymous Communication Channels. Microsoft Research technical report MSR-TR-2008-35 (January 2008)
2. Dingledine, R., Mathewson, N., Syverson, P.: Tor: The Second-Generation Onion Router. In: The Proceedings of the 13th USENIX Security Symposium (August 2004)
3. Murdoch, S.J., Danezis, G.: Low-cost traffic analysis of Tor. In: Proceedings of the 2005 IEEE Symposium on Security and Privacy (May 2005)
4. Murdoch, S.J.: Covert channel vulnerabilities in anonymity systems. Technical report, University of Cambridge (August 2007)
5. Bellovin, S.M., Clark, D.D., Perrig, A., Song, D.: A Clean-Slate Design for the Next-Generation Secure Internet. In: NSF Workshop on a clean-slate design for the next-generation secure Internet (2005)
6. Andersen, D.G., Balakrishnan, H., Feamster, N., Koponen, T., Moon, D., Shenker, S.: Accountable Internet Protocol (AIP). SIGCOMM Comput. Commun. Rev. Journal 38(4), 339–350 (2008)
7. Yaar, A., Perrig, A., Song, D.: SIFF: A Stateless Internet Flow Filter to Mitigate DDoS Flooding Attacks. In: Proceedings of the IEEE Symposium on Security and Privacy (May 2004)
8. Pfitzmann, A., Hansen, M.: Anonymity, Unlinkability, Undetectability, Unobservability, Pseudonymity, and Identity Management A Consolidated Proposal for Terminology, Version v0.31 (2008)
9. McCune, J.M., Parno, B., Perrig, A., Reiter, M.K., Seshadri, A.: Minimal TCB code execution (Extended abstract). In: Proceedings of the 2007 IEEE Symposium on Security and Privacy (May 2007)
10. Diaz, C.: Anonymity Metrics Revisited. In: Dolev, S., Ostrovsky, R., Pfitzmann, A. (eds.) Anonymous Communication and its Applications (2006)
11. Raymond, J.F.: Traffic Analysis: Protocols, Attacks, Design Issues, and Open Problems. In: Federrath, H. (ed.) Designing Privacy Enhancing Technologies. LNCS, vol. 2009, pp. 10–29. Springer, Heidelberg (2001)
12. Chaum, D.: Untraceable electronic mail, return addresses, and digital pseudonyms. Communications of the Association for Computing Machinery 24(2), 84–88 (1981)
13. Gulcu, C., Tsudik, G.: Mixing E-mail with Babel. In: Network and Distributed Security Symposium - NDSS 1996. IEEE, Los Alamitos (1996)
14. Mller, U., Cottrell, L.: Mixmaster Protocol - Version 2. Unfinished draft (January 2000)
15. Danezis, G., Dingledine, R., Mathewson, N.: Mixminion: Design of a Type III Anonymous Remailer Protocol. In: The Proceedings of the 2003 IEEE Symposium on Security and Privacy, pp. 2–15 (May 2003)
16. Syverson, P.F., Goldschlag, D.M., Reed, M.G.: Anonymous connections and onion routing. In: IEEE Symposium on Security and Privacy, Oakland, California, pp. 44–54 (1997)
17. Boucher, P., Shostack, A., Goldberg, I.: Freedom Systems 2.0 Architecture, Zero Knowledge Systems, Inc. White Paper (December 2000)
18. Freedman, M.J., Morris, R.: Tarzan: A Peer-to-Peer Anonymizing Network Layer. In: The Proceedings of the 9th ACM Conference on Computer and Communications Security (CCS 2002), Washington, DC (November 2002)

Jason: A Scalable Reputation System
for the Semantic Web

Sandra Steinbrecher[1], Stephan Groß[1], and Markus Meichau[2]

[1] Technische Universität Dresden, Fakultät Informatik, D-01062 Dresden, Germany
steinbrecher@acm.org, stephan.gross@tu-dresden.de
[2] Max-Planck-Gesellschaft, Amalienstraße 33, D-80799 München, Germany
meichau@mpdl.mpg.de

Abstract. The recent development of the Internet, especially the expanding use
of social software and dynamic content generation commonly termed as Web 2.0
enables users to find information about almost every possible topic on the Web.
On the downside, it becomes more and more difficult to decide which information can be trusted in. In this paper we propose the enhancement of Web 2.0 by
a scalable and secure cross-platform reputation system that takes into account a
user's social network. Our proposed solution *Jason* is based on standard methods of the semantic web and does not need a central entity. It enables the fast
and flexible evaluation of arbitrary content on the World Wide Web. In contrast
to many other reputation systems it provides mechanisms to ensure the authenticity of web content, thus, enabling the user to explicitly choose information
published by trusted authors.

Keywords: Trust management, reputation system, secure semantic web, identity
management, privacy-preserving data management, secure information
integration.

1 Introduction

Internet users have increasing possibilities not only to consume but also to publish information. Numerous wikis, weblogs, communities and other platforms collect and publish information users generate. The most popular example used by many users when
they would have consulted an encyclopedia 20 or even 10 years ago is Wikipedia[1]. The
English version contains more than 2.6 million articles at the beginning of 2009. While
printing a dictionary is expensive and the review process of articles is usually long, generating web content is cheap and easy. It needs neither technical nor other specialised
know-how from the authors. This leads to the drawback that the quality of information
on the Internet is very difficult to estimate.

Information on the Internet changes frequently. Controversial topics might be
changed often by different editors who wage a so-called "edit war". For this reason
once-established trust in information might not be continuously given. To help users in
estimating the quality of arbitrary objects reputation systems have been designed and
established that collect the opinions others announced about its quality.

---

[1] http://www.wikipedia.org/

D. Gritzalis and J. Lopez (Eds.): SEC 2009, IFIP AICT 297, pp. 421–431, 2009.
© IFIP International Federation for Information Processing 2009

However, most users do not only collect information from one website or community but make use of various sources of information on the Internet. There is the need for a cross-platform reputation system independent from one single provider that allows to compare information from different sources.

In this paper we present our scalable and secure cross-platform reputation system *Jason* that was built utilizing methods and techniques of the semantic web like the Resource Description Framework (RDF) [8]. Every rating is annotated to a content as meta information. The collected ratings form the content's reputation.

In contrast to many papers we neither propose a certain algorithm for calculating a reputation nor we define a specific set of possible reputations or ratings. Instead, we allow every user to assign his own meaning to a certain rating and spread this interpretation within his social network. Every user evaluating this rating might either use the interpretation of the rating presented by his social network or he creates his own based on his experience with the rater, the content rated and/or the author. As long as an author is not part of a rater's social network he is usually not able to distinguish between positive and negative ratings of this rater. Thus, he will hopefully publish all ratings along with the content.

The remainder of this paper is structured as follows. In section 2 we outline our application scenario and its requirements. Section 3 presents the design of our system. The results of validating it by means of a prototype implementation are given in section 4. Finally, we come up with some concluding remarks and an outlook on future work.

2   Scenario

2.1   Terminology

Reputation assigned to web content can help the content's users, i. e. the readers, to estimate its truth or usefulness. Therefore, users who are already able to estimate the content can become raters and make use of a **rating algorithm** to give a rating to the content. The reputation of the content is then calculated from these ratings with the help of a **reputation algorithm**. There exist countless models to design rating and reputation algorithms [5].

The **propagation of reputation and ratings** of a content needs some kind of reputation network. A reputation network is a social network that can be modelled as a graph with its vertices describing the members of the network and the directed edges between them representing the information flow when propagating ratings from one user to another.

Raters usually give subjective ratings that are influenced by their personal estimation of the truth or usefulness of the content. Thus, for the **evaluation of a content's reputation** users have not only to trust in the rater's honesty but also need some means to map the rater's subjective rating to their own view. Hence a trust network overlaying the reputation network is needed. The vertices of the trust network are once again the users. However, the directed edges in the trust network describe the trust a user has in a rating he receives from another member of the network. We do not further elaborate the numerous existing trust models to implement trust in a social network. Instead, we demand that both the sources and the context of some rated information (including all those who created, stored, evaluated and propagated reputation) are weighted according to the trustworthiness they have for the evaluator of a reputation. An example for such a technical trust model that makes use of interpersonal context-specific trust is developed in [1]. Unfortunately, this model is by far too complex for practical applications with a large number of users.

After their creation reputation and ratings have to be stored somewhere. The **storage of reputation and ratings** might either be distributed on user devices in the reputation network, centrally stored at specific reputation servers or decentrally stored with the content itself. All reputation stored can only be evaluated by a user of the reputation system if there is an information flow in the reputation network towards him.

2.2 Requirements

As outlined above there are five components of a reputation system:

- **rating algorithm** of the content rater,
- **reputation algorithm**,
- **propagation of reputation and ratings**,
- **storage of ratings and reputation**, and
- **evaluation of a content's reputation** by the content user.

To find design options for these components one has to consider several security requirements. Our solution follows a multilateral secure approach [10] to respect all stakeholder's security requirements. Together, these requirements form a subset of the generic security requirements of a reputation system stated in [3]:

Availability of reputation. As a functional requirement, each user of the reputation system wants to access reputations to estimate the quality of web content.

Integrity of web content and ratings. Users want web content and ratings to be preserved from manipulations, both in propagation and in storage.

Accountability of authors and raters. Users want a content's authors and raters to be accountable for the web content they provided respectively rated.

Completeness of reputation. Users want the aggregated reputation to consider all ratings given. During the storage and propagation of reputation it should not be possible for the entities involved to omit certain ratings.

Pseudonymity of raters and authors. Users want to rate and provide web content under a pseudonym to not necessarily allow others to link this rating to their real name. In the real world there are also authors who write under a pseudonym and many services in the Internet also allow the use of pseudonyms instead of real names following EC Directive 95/46 [4].

Unlinkability of ratings and web content. Users want to rate and provide different web content without being linkable. Otherwise behaviour profiles of pseudonyms (e.g. time and frequency of web site visits, valuation of and interest in specific items) could be built. If the pseudonym can be linked to a real name the profile can be related to this real name as well.

Anonymity of users. Users want to evaluate reputation anonymously to prevent others from building personal behaviour profiles of their possible interests.

Confidentiality of ratings. Although a reputation system's functional requirement is to collect and provide information about a reputation object, raters might prefer to provide only a subset of their ratings to a specific group of other users while keeping it confidential to all others.

3 System Design

In the following we outline a multilateral secure system design using existing technologies. It was designed with special emphasis on the scalability for large user sets. As in real life it considers the already established trust relationships in a user's social network. In addition to the basic components of a reputation system identified in section 2 we introduce a public key infrastructure and privacy-enhancing identity management as further elements for realising multilateral security.

3.1 System Components

3.1.1 Public Key Infrastructure (PKI)

Web content can be identified in the Web 2.0 by its URI (Universal Resource Identifier). A web content's URI represents a globally unique description of its address and name. However, it does not give any information about recent changes or substitutions of the content behind this URI. To ensure the **integrity of web content and ratings** our system needs to establish a public key infrastructure for digital signatures in the reputation network. By utilizing the PKI an author can sign his content as well as a rater can sign his rating whereas the signatures can be verified by any member of the reputation network. To improve the efficiency for large content (e. g., multimedia data) we apply a cryptographically secure hash function on the content and only sign the resulting value. The combination of URI and signature can then be used as a unique identifier of unmodified web content.

3.1.2 Privacy-Enhancing Identity Management

The public keys of our PKI must not be linked to real names but only to pseudonyms to enable **pseudonymity of raters and authors**. If **accountability of raters and authors** should be given an identity provider is needed who is either able to reveal a pseudonym's corresponding real name or to pay a fee for misuse deposited by the pseudonym's owner in advance. **Unlinkability of web content and ratings** can be reached by using unlinkable pseudonyms and respecting unlinkable public keys. A user-controlled privacy-enhancing identity management system (PE-IMS) [2] can assist a user in separating different pseudonyms' contexts. Unfortunately, prototype implementations like PRIME[2] currently do not assist Web 2.0 technologies. First systems exploring also this field of research are only expected to be developed, e. g. PrimeLife[3]. For this reason our design is open for interoperability with identity management but

---

[2] Privacy and Identity Management for Europe (http://www.prime-project.eu/), funded by the European Union in the 6. Framework Programm, March 2004 - May 2008.

[3] Privacy and Identity Management in Europe for Life, funded by the European Union in the 7. Framework Program, starting March 2008.

currently does not implement it. Following [12] we propose to use different keys for every context and role a user is involved in. For the role this means separating authors and raters. For the context this means separating roughly the topic discussed in the web content authored or rated, e.g., separating Linux expertise and Roman history expertise. This makes different web content of the same author unlinkable to each other. The same holds for the rater who rated different contexts.

3.1.3 Rating Algorithm

Our approach aims at giving the user the largest possible flexibility in defining his subjective set of possible ratings. This holds both for the concrete values as for the size of the set. The user u with a pseudonym p_u is free to define his finite rating set $R_{p_u} = \{r_1, r_2, \ldots, r_n\}$. Every rating r_i within the rating set represents a degree of usefulness or truthfulness content might have for him. A possible example for such a rating set might be school marks or just the distinction between good and bad.

To achieve **unlinkability of a user's different possible ratings** every element of the rating set R_{p_u} is mapped to a different public key by

$$f_{p_u} : \{r_1, r_2, \ldots, r_n\} \rightarrow \{pk_{r_1}, pk_{r_2}, \ldots, pk_{r_n}\}$$

So we have a two-level pseudonym instantiation. The principle of separating context and role by different pseudonyms is dealt with on the first level by a PE-IMS. On the second level for the rating algorithm different ratings are made unlinkable by choosing different public keys. This needs an appropriate PKI and typically also identity providers for installing these public keys to guarantee accountability of the users. These two levels are illustrated in figure 1.

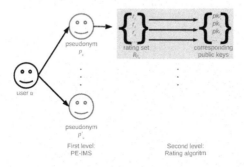

Fig. 1. Relation of a user's pseudonyms, rating sets and public keys

The ratings given in the system are not publicly known. A rater might inform his friends in the reputation network to which rating a public key corresponds (grey part in figure 1). In other words, he reveals a partial view of the function f. These friends may of course re-distribute this correspondence to others in the reputation network. Furthermore, users in the reputation network can recognize recurring public keys themselves and are free to map them to their own ratings. However, **confidentiality of ratings** against unauthorized users is still given in a weak sense.

3.1.4   Reputation Storage and Propagation

We choose to store every rating given to a content as meta data together with the web content itself. Therefore, the reputation of a content is given by the set of ratings available as meta data with the content. This should guarantee the best possible **availability of reputation**. The **integrity of web content and ratings** is secured by digital signatures of their author resp. rater as outlined above. Web content can be made accessible anonymously by an anonymising service. If web content and/or reputation information should be paid for an anonymous payment system is needed. This reaches **anonymity of users**.

The author and provider of web content is usually not aware which ratings he actually received from raters and how these ratings are evaluated as reputation of his web content by other users. This will hopefully encourage authors not to omit single ratings given but to attach all ratings to the semantic information of their web contents. This should enhance **completeness of reputation**. Another concept would be to assume that users only recommend web content and give only positive ratings as it is suggested in [13]. However, this approach does not allow the distinction between missing and bad reputation making the reputation system less expressive.

3.1.5   Reputation Algorithm and Evaluation of a Content's Reputation

If a user v wants to evaluate the reputation of a content he has to define a reputation algorithm for calculating the reputation from the ratings available as meta data of the content. Let R_v be the set of reputations a content might have for v. Let further K_{pk} be the set of public keys known in a reputation network. A single user evaluating a content's reputation usually knows only a subset of the corresponding public keys of the signatures provided for the content in question.

Now let $(pk_1, \ldots, pk_n) \in K_{pk}^*$ be the tuple of public keys with which a content was signed and that are known to the user evaluating the content. Then the user v has to define a reputation algorithm in the form of a function

$$\mathrm{rep}_v : K_{pk}^* \to R_v$$

that maps the tuple of signatures to a reputation. The reputation the tuple of ratings is mapped to might correspond to a rating he would have given himself under a pseudonym p_v but it needs not.

We abstract here from the concrete reputation algorithm. It should respect the trust values assigned to the information flow in the trust network. These might be individual trust values that are adapted frequently. It might also consider the mapping functions f_{p_u} between public keys and ratings other users in the reputation network told him. One possibility for the reputation algorithm is the generation of trust trees from the relations between users as in TrustNet [11] or EigenTrust [6].

3.2   System Composition

Our system tries to reach best possible integration into the existing Web 2.0 paradigm without loss of flexibility by relying only on well-founded and platform independent technologies. In other words, it does not require essentially more than a common web

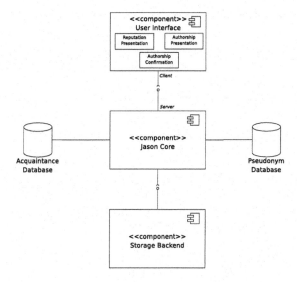

Fig. 2. Jason's basic system architecture

browser and a cross-platform application software. In the following we describe the basic components of our system architecture depicted in figure 2.

The *Jason core component* represents the heart and brain of our system. It is responsible for all security sensitive and performance critical operations. This includes both the generation of ratings and the adoption of authorship. For the publication of newly generated ratings, authorship statements or other public data it relies on a *storage back end* that forms the necessary interface with the content provisioning platform, e.g. a web site or community platform. As a user-centric component it also takes care of managing the user's pseudonyms and his acquaintance. The necessary data for these tasks is stored in the *pseudonym* and the *acquaintance database* respectively. Finally, the core component provides a message based interface for the implementation of a graphical user interface nearby a given reputation object. We define at least three such GUIs: one to display the actual rating of a reputation object (*reputation presentation*), one to state its author (*author presentation*) and one to integrate the authorship takeover process into the underlying content provisioning platform (*authorship confirmation*). By decoupling the user interface from the core functionality we aim at enabling concurrency, thus minimizing latency times.

4   Validation

We validated our proposed system architecture by a first prototype implementation based on the Java Runtime Environment 1.5. The Java Security API is used to realise the necessary cryptographic primitives, i.e. cryptographic hash functions and digital signatures. The usability of our prototype was evaluated in a limited field trial.

4.1   Prototype Implementation

Our prototype implementation realises the generic system architecture presented in the previous section. The core component is implemented by a Java application to be locally run at the user's device. On startup, the user has the choice to generate a new pseudonym or to login with an already created one. For each pseudonym one has to define at least a specific rating set and a password to secure the corresponding sensitive data like private keys. As the reputation function in our current implementation is based on the statistical average of all given ratings the user must also map each element of the rating set to a base metric, thus, allowing for ratio measurement. Corresponding configurations must be added for each new acquaintance to define the mapping between his ratings and the personal preferences. The acquaintance as well as the pseudonym database are realized by RDF/XML files that are secured by the already mentioned password. The definition of a rating set element shown in listing 1 presents an exemplary part of such an RDF/XML structure. Line 1 declares the identifier of the element whereas in line 2 the corresponding numerical value of the base metric is defined. Line 5 binds a specific public key to the element in question, thus enabling the interpretation of a rating. Finally, line 6 links the element to a friend's rating set element.

```
1   <rdf:Description rdf:ID="good">
        <jason:numValue>2</jason:numValue>
3   <jason:statedBy>
        <rdf:Alt>
5           <rdf:li >http://jason.nourl.xxx/pk_good.rdf.xml</rdf:li >
            <rdf:li >Alice#Acceptable</rdf:li>
7       </rdf:Alt>
    </jason:statedBy>
9   </rdf:Description>
```

Listing 1. Exemplary RDF representation of a rating set element

To minimize user interferences *Jason's* prototype core implementation does also provide a FTP/SFTP-Backend to automatically publish any user specific public data on a configurable web server.

The representation of the reputation information as well as the authorship statement is realised by two Java Script applets *ReputationApplet.jar* and *AuthorIndicationApplet.jar* respectively. Listing 2 summarizes the essential code fragment to include those applets in web content. Line 1–6 handle the annotation of web content with reputation information whereas line 7–12 describe the inclusion of authorship information. Line 2 and 8 define the content in question, line 3 and 9 point to the RDF document in which the ratings and authorship statements are collected, whereas line 4 and 10 provide a link to the storage back end at the content provisioning platform, i.e. the web server. In our prototype this is realised by a simple PHP-based CGI script.

4.2   Experiences with the Prototype

We tested our prototype on three different platforms, namely MAC OS X 10.4, MS Windows XP Pro and Ubuntu Linux, without any severe problems. The tests were conducted by several test persons. Time-consuming cryptographic operations (like signing or hashing content) are done while the user already performs other actions and by

```
1  <APPLET archive="ReputationApplet.jar" code="ReputationApplet" width=150 height=36>
      <PARAM NAME="content" VALUE="http://en.wikipedia.org/wiki/Jason">
3     <PARAM NAME="RDF" VALUE="http://jason.nourl.xxx/StdFile.rdf.xml">
      <PARAM NAME="replyTo" VALUE="http://jason.nourl.xxx/jason_upload.php">
5     Your browser does not support Java, so nothing is displayed.
   </APPLET>
7  <APPLET archive="AuthorIndicationApplet.jar" code="AuthorIndicationApplet" width=150 height=20>
      <PARAM NAME="content" VALUE="http://en.wikipedia.org/wiki/Jason">
9     <PARAM NAME="RDF" VALUE="http://jason.nourl.xxx/StdFile.rdf.xml">
      <PARAM NAME="replyTo" VALUE="http://jason.nourl.xxx/jason_upload.php">
11    Your browser does not support Java, so nothing is displayed.
   </APPLET>
```

Listing 2. Integrating Jason in a web page

caching values already loaded at the user side and only loading the differences. Unfortunately, the delay at reputation system startup cannot be eliminated because this time is needed to initialise the system in a way that the other actions become less consuming (e.g., loading keys and trust values).

4.3   Fulfilment of Security Requirements

The system design fulfills the security requirements of a reputation system as listed in section 2.2 in the sense of multilateral security:

Availability of reputation. The availability of a content's reputation for a content user v depends on several factors:

- Other users need to be willing to rate this content.
- The public key of a rater needs to be available for a content user.
- The content user needs to use this public key in a function rep_v to map a set of public keys the content was signed with to a reputation.

In social networks information spreading characteristicly depends on several factors. This also holds for the public keys to be distributed. Actually, to establish an information flow it must exist a path from the rater to the content user to communicate the necessary public keys. Every possible vertice on such a path propagates the public key with a certain probability. Additionally, there is a probability that the node itself checked whether he agrees to a function value $rep_v(pk)$ he received and that he sends a (possibly updated) function to other nodes. Due to the observation in social networks that neighbours more likely seem to have the same attributes/attitudes [7] the agreement of a neighbour to a function seems to be more important than a simple forward. There exists both research on information spreading in models of social networks that usually make assumptions on uniformly distributed probabilities in certain areas of a social network depending on its structure and on the evaluation of actual information spreading in existing social networks like the one built by GPG keys [14] or Flickr [9].

Integrity of web content and ratings. The integrity of data is based on the cryptographic security of the digital signatures and hash functions used.

Accountability of authors and raters. The PE-IMS and its identity providers guarantee the accountability of the users making pseudonymous signatures.

Completeness of reputation. For information distribution the same holds as already outlined for the availability of ratings.

Pseudonymity of raters and authors. The PE-IMS allows users to choose their pseudonyms appropriately to separate contexts and roles.

Unlinkability of ratings and web content. The pseudonyms used for making ratings are bound to the different possible ratings and are not re-used as an author.

Anonymity of users. Visiting a website and evaluating a reputation anonymously can be realised on the communication layer by an anonymising service.

Confidentiality of ratings. The confidentiality of ratings is a contradicting requirement to the availability of reputation and rating. In our system this means that for a given public key pk a user v's corresponding function value $rep_v(pk)$ is confidential to unauthorised users. This means there should not exist any path in the network that forwards v's function value in an accountable way to unauthorised users. Unauthorised users might know a set of possible function values but they should not know to which function value the public key is mapped to for v.

5   Conclusion and Future Work

We developed a scalable and secure cross-platform reputation system and demonstrated its usability for the average Internet user who evaluated our prototype implementation. Our system is based on open and standardised data formats (RDF/XML). In future work we will extend our system that both authors and raters can collect reputation. Future user testing will be done by offering templates as sets of possible ratings to enhance both usability and privacy. Furthermore, we intent to integrate our system with evolving user-controlled PE-IMS instead of a separate program.

Acknowledgements. The research leading to these results has received funding from the European Communitys Sixth and Seventh Framework Programme (FP6/2002-2006 resp. FP7/2007-2013) for the projects FIDIS, PRIME and PrimeLife. The information in this document is provided as is, and no guarantee or warranty is given that the information is fit for any particular purpose. The PrimeLife consortium members shall have no liability for damages of any kind including without limitation direct, special, indirect, or consequential damages that may result from the use of these materials subject to any liability which is mandatory due to applicable law.

References

[1] Abdul-Rahman, A., Hailes, S.: Supporting trust in virtual communities. In: HICSS 2000: Proceedings of the 33rd Hawaii Intern. Conference on System Sciences, vol. 6. IEEE Computer Society, Los Alamitos (2007)

[2] Clauß, S., Pfitzmann, A., Hansen, M., Herreweghen, E.V.: Privacy-enhancing identity management. The IPTS Report 67, 8–16 (2002)

[3] ENISA, Position paper. reputation-based systems: a security analysis (2007) (last visited 07/01/09), http://www.enisa.europa.eu/doc/pdf/deliverable/enisa_pp_reputation_based_system.pdf

[4] European Parliament, Directive 95/46 EC. Official Journal L281, 23/11/1995, 31–50 (1995)

[5] Jøsang, A., Ismail, R., Boyd, C.: A survey of trust and reputation systems for online service provision. Decision Support Systems 43(2), 618–644 (2007)

[6] Kamvar, S., Schlosser, M., Garcia-Molina, H.: The Eigentrust algorithm for reputation management in P2P networks. In: WWW 2003: Proc. of the 12th Intern. Conf. on World Wide Web, pp. 640–651. ACM Press, New York (2003)

[7] Lazarsfeld, P., Merton, R.: Friendship as a Social Process: A Substantive and Methodological Analysis. In: Berger, M., Abel, T., Page, C. (eds.) Freedom and Control in Modern Society, pp. 18–66. Van Nostrand, New York (1954)

[8] Manola, F., Miller, E.: RDF Primer. W3C Recommendation, W3C (last visited 07/01/09) (2004), http://www.w3.org/TR/rdf-primer/, http://www.w3.org/TR/rdf-primer/

[9] Mislove, A., Marcon, M., Gummadi, K.P., Druschel, P., Bhattacharjee, B.: Measurement and analysis of online social networks. In: IMC 2007: Proc. of the 7th ACM SIGCOMM Conf. on Internet Measurement, pp. 29–42. ACM, New York, USA (2007)

[10] Pfitzmann, A.: Technologies for multilateral security. In: Müller, G., Rannenberg, K. (eds.) Multilateral Security for Global Communication, pp. 85–91. Addison-Wesley, Reading (1999)

[11] Schillo, M., Funk, P., Rovatsos, M.: Using trust for detecting deceitful agents in artificial societies. Applied Artificial Intelligence 14(8), 825–848 (2000)

[12] Steinbrecher, S.: Design options for privacy-respecting reputation systems within centralised internet communities. In: Proceedings of IFIP Sec 2006, 21st IFIP International Information Security Conference: Security and Privacy in Dynamic Environments. IFIP, vol. 201, pp. 123–134. Springer, Heidelberg (2006)

[13] Voss, M., Heinemann, A., Mühlhäuser, M.: A Privacy Preserving Reputation System for Mobile Information Dissemination Networks. In: First Intern. Conf. on Security and Privacy for Emerging Areas in Communications Networks (SECURECOMM 2005), pp. 171–181. IEEE, Los Alamitos (2005)

[14] Warren, R.H., Wilkinson, D.F., Warnecke, M.: Empirical Analysis of a Dynamic Social Network Built from PGP Keyrings. In: Airoldi, E.M., Blei, D.M., Fienberg, S.E., Goldenberg, A., Xing, E.P., Zheng, A.X. (eds.) ICML 2006. LNCS, vol. 4503, pp. 158–171. Springer, Heidelberg (2007)

Which Web Browsers Process SSL Certificates in a Standardized Way?

Ahmad Samer Wazan[1], Romain Laborde[1], David W. Chadwick[2], François Barrere[1],
and AbdelMalek Benzekri[1]

[1] IRIT Laboratory
[2] University of Kent
{wazan,laborde,barrere,benzekri}@irit.fr
d.w.chadwick@kent.ac.uk

Abstract. SSL is the primary technology used to secure web communications. Before setting up an SSL connection, web browsers have to validate the SSL certificate of the web server in order to ensure that users access the expected web site. We have tested the handling of the main fields in SSL certificates and found that web browsers do not process them in a homogenous way. An SSL certificate can be accepted by some web browsers whereas a message reporting an error can be delivered to users by other web browsers for the same certificate. This diversity of behavior might cause users to believe that SSL certificates are unreliable or error prone, which might lead them to consider that SSL certificates are useless. In this paper, we highlight these different behaviors and we explain the reasons for them which can be either a violation of the standards or ambiguity in the standards themselves. We give our opinion of which it is in our analysis.

1 Introduction

The technology used for securing web-based applications is mainly SSL (Secure Socket Layer) [8] or its equivalent standard TLS (Transport Layer security) [9]. SSL relies on X.509 certificates, called here SSL certificates, to provide the confidentiality, authentication, and integrity services for web-based applications.

X.509 certificates are digital identity cards that bind a public key to an entity's name. The entity can be a person, mobile phone, server or any other type of machine. Certificates are issued by Certification Authorities and the X.509v3 standard [6] defines the syntax of these certificates and the semantics of their various fields. Some of the fields are mandatory and some are optional extensions. RFC 5280 [2] refines X.509 for use on the Internet. The Certification Authority (CA) represents the heart of a public key infrastructure (PKI).

Before using a certificate, the relying party[1] (RP) must check whether the certificate is valid or not. The validation process is a complicated task and a multi-risk operation [4]. In the web, executing the validation process by the relying party for each

---

[1] The entity that relies on the data in the certificate before making its decisions.

D. Gritzalis and J. Lopez (Eds.): SEC 2009, IFIP AICT 297, pp. 432–442, 2009.
© IFIP International Federation for Information Processing 2009

SSL connection is impractical for human users. So web browsers execute this process automatically on behalf of them. This implies that web browsers have to be trusted by the users, and consequently, that they should all behave in the same way when processing the same SSL certificate. Web browsers are supposed to conform to the public key standards in order to handle certificates in a uniform way and they should be as transparent as possible from the user's point of view. The experiments presented in this article show that this is not true. Two web browsers might give two different responses for the same certificate. And they often ask complex questions of the user (e.g., "The servers' certificate chain is incomplete, and the signer(s) are not registered. Accept?"). The origin of the differences of behavior is due to either violations of the standards by the browser manufacturers or ambiguity of the standards themselves which leads to multiple interpretations. We give our opinion of which it is in our analysis.

We have tested the latest versions of three popular web browsers (Internet Explorer 7, FireFox 3 and Opera 9.5). The results we obtained have been analyzed to understand the origins of the problems. We have also evaluated the next generation of SSL certificates called Extended Validation certificates (EV certificate) [5] to see if they solve the problems or not. When the cause of inconsistent behavior is the ambiguity of the standards, we propose explicit corrections to the standard to clarify this.

The rest of this paper is structured as follows. Section 2 exposes and analyses the results of tests executed on the three web browsers, and shows why the behaviors of the web browsers are heterogeneous. We also propose remedies to the problems of heterogeneous behavior. In section 3, we discuss the exact role of the relying party. Finally, in section 4 we conclude our study.

2 Analysis of Web Browsers' Behavior

In this section, we provide the results of our tests with Internet Explorer 7 (IE7), Firefox 3 (FF3) and Opera 9.5(OP9) when they validate SSL certificates containing various standard fields. We focus our tests on the fields related to the subject, the key usage and the certificate status. Our approach is to understand the exact meaning applied to these fields by web browsers in web secured communications, by testing their responses when they are confronted with specific test values. The results are analyzed by comparing them to the expected behaviors described in the X.509 standards [6][2]. However, the latter are sometimes ambiguous which may explain the diversity of the browsers' behavior in some cases.

During our experiments, we found three possible responses when web browsers handle SSL certificates, denoted as follows:

- A: accept the certificate without any intervention by the user,
- W: inform the user about the existence of a problem by showing a warning message and asking him/her to take a decision,
- R: refuse the certificate and prohibit the access to the web server without any intervention by the user.

2.1 SSL Certificate Subject

The SSL certificate subject represents the web server. The identity of the server may be either a Fully Qualified Domain Name (FQDN) or an IP address or both. FQDNs and IP addresses are different types of name (called name forms in the standards). A web server could hold many FQDNs that all point to the same IP address, e.g. as in virtual hosting.

2.1.1 What Do the Standards State about the Subject?

The X.509 standard [6] states that the subject field identifies the entity associated with the public-key found in the subject public key field. An entity could have one or more alternative names, of different types (or forms), held in the subjectAltName extension. According to the X.509 standard, an implementation which supports this extension is not required to process all the name types. If the extension is flagged critical, at least one of the name types that is present must be recognized and processed, otherwise the certificate must be considered invalid.

RFC 5280 states that the subject name may be carried in the subject field and/or the subjectAltName extension. If the subject naming information is present only in the subjectAltName extension, then the subject name should be empty and the subjectAltName extension must be critical. According to this statement an SSL certificate can hold multiple names in a combination of the Subject field (CN component) and the Subject Alternative Name (SubjectAltName) extension. These names must all refer to the same entity, although a browser need not recognize all the different name types.

2.1.2 Test and Results

The identity of a server could be represented by a FQDN value or by an IP address or both. We have performed experiments to test certificates holding the two types of name separately as well as both types together.

In the first set of experiments, we tested how the browsers reacted when the certificate contains zero, one or more FQDN names. We configured our web server to respond to requests sent to either www.server1.com or www.server2.com. As the names could be mentioned in either or both of the Subject Name - Common Name (SCN) and SubjectAltName - DNS Name (SAN-DNS) fields, we have tested the following different combinations of names in our web server certificate:

1. SCN=www.server1.com, SAN-DNS=www.server2.com
2. SCN=null, SAN-DNS=www.server2.com
3. SCN=www.server1.com, no SAN-DNS field
4. SCN=null, no SAN-DNS field
5. SCN=null, SAN-DNS = www.server1.com and www.server2.com.

For each combination, we recorded the reaction of each web browser when accessing www.server1.com and www.server2.com (Table 1). We also state whether the certificate is Valid (V) or Invalid (I) according to the X.509 standards. Because we obtained the same results when the SubjectAltName extension was marked critical or not, we haven't indicated this in Table 1.

Table 1. Multiple FQDN Server Identities

Values in fields By address	IE7		FF3		OP9		X.509	
	S1	S2	S1	S2	S1	S2	S1	S2
i) SCN=S1, SAN-DNS=S2	W	A	W	A	A	A	?	V
ii) SCN=Null, SAN-DNS=S2	W	A	W	A	W	A	I	V
iii) SCN=S1, no SAN-DNS	A	W	A	W	A	W	V	I
iv) SCN=Null, no SAN-DNS	W	W	W	W	W	W	I	I
v) SCN=Null, SAN-DNS=S1,S2	A	A	A	A	A	A	V	V

Where: **S1** = www.server1.com, **S2**= www.server2.com

Table 2. IP Address Server and/or FQDN Identities

Values in fields Accessed by	IE7		FF3		OP9		X.509	
	S1	@IP	S1	@IP	S1	@IP	S1	@IP
i) SAN-IP=192.168.0.6	W	W	W	A	W	W	I	V
ii) SAN-DNS=S1, SAN-IP=192.168.0.6	A	W	A	A	A	W	V	V
iii) SAN-DNS=S1, no SAN-IP	A	W	A	W	A	W	V	I
iv) SAN-DNS=null, SAN-IP=192.168.0.6	W	W	W	A	W	W	I	V

Where: **S1** = www.server1.com, **@IP**=192.168.0.6

In the second set of experiments, we tested how the browsers react when an IP address only, or an IP address and a FQDN, or a FDQN only, are used to identify a web server running at an IP address (with or without the DNS name S1). In all cases the SCN field was null. We obtained the same results when the subjectAltName was marked critical or not, so we have not shown these results in Table 2.

2.1.3 Analysis of the Results

An X.509 certificate binds an identity (the identity of a web server is either a FQDN name or an IP address) to a public key. When the identity of the server is null (Table 1 iv) the browser cannot authenticate the server, so the SSL certificate is invalid. Whether a browser should immediately refuse an invalid certificate (R) or ask the user what to do (W) is partly a usability issue and partly a security issue. But it is not a standard's issue. The standards will only give guidance on whether a certificate is invalid or not, but will not advise a relying party what to do with it. From a security perspective, if the browser cannot authenticate the web server, the certificate should be rejected (R). From a usability perspective the user could be given a choice (W), although in practice most users simply click OK to all the pop up windows so invalid certificates end up being accepted. RFC 5280 mandates that the IP address if present must contain either four (for IPv4) or sixteen (for IPv6) octets, and that the FQDN if present must not be null. So the Table 1 iv) certificate is clearly invalid. But none of the browsers reject it. Instead they ask the user what to do.

If, the standards are not clear about a certificate's validity, this can lead to web browser implementers holding different interpretations of this. FQDNs should be held in the SAN-DNS extension since this is designed to hold DNS names. However they may also be stored in the common name of the subject distinguished name field (SCN). But what if they are stored in both? [2] states "if the only subject identity included in the certificate is an alternative name form then the subject distinguished name MUST be empty (an empty sequence), and the subjectAltName extension MUST be present." In Table 1, certificate i) appears to violate this rule. But nowhere does the standard explicitly state that such a certificate is invalid; and anyway one can argue that this certificate actually contains two name forms: a subject distinguished name and a SAN DNS name. So this probably explains why IE7 and FF3 treat it as invalid, whilst OP9 treats it as valid. This is why we show a ? in Table 1 i). We have raised the ambiguity of the X.509 standard with ISO/ITU-T and a defect report has been raised and accepted.

[2] says that web browsers must "recognize" the SAN extension, but only that "all parts of the subject alternative name MUST be verified by the CA". This does not place any requirements on the web browser to do likewise. Similarly [6] states "An implementation is not required to be able to process all name forms". So browsers do not have to support SAN-IP, and in fact, IE7 and OP9 do not, so they do not recognise the IP name of the server. FF3 on the other hand does support the IP name form and so does recognise the server's name. This accounts for the different results of Table 2 i), ii) and iv). Whilst all three browsers are still conformant to the standard, they give different results, and a user is not likely to know that this is because the IP name form is not supported by IE7 and OP9.

2.1.4 Do EV Certificates Solve the Problem?

According to the guidelines of the EV certificate, the domain name field can contain one or more host domain name(s) owned or controlled by the subject and be associated with Subject's server. But it doesn't clarify the situation when the identities are held in the CN component and/or in the SAN extension. Also the support of the IP option is not required in this type of certificate. So unfortunately the support for EV certificates will not solve the problems we have identified above.

2.2 Key Usage, Extended Key Usage

Key usage and extended key usage are used to determine the purpose of the public key contained in the certificate. An SSL server certificate could have a key usage extension or not. The standards [2][6] don't constrain the authorities to issue SSL certificates with key usage extensions.

2.2.1 What Do the Standards State about the Key Usage and Extended Key Usage Extensions?

The X.509 standard [6] states that if either the extended key usage or key usage extensions are recognized by the relying party then the certificate must be used just for one of the purposes indicated in the certificate. The key usage and the extended key usage must be treated separately but they must have consistent values. If there is no purpose consistent with both fields, then the certificate shall not be used for any purpose [6].

RFC 5280 states that the key usage extension, when it appears, should be a critical extension. For an SSL certificate, RFC 5280 recommends that the key usage, when it is defined, should have the value of "digital signature, key encipherment and/or key agreement" and the consistent value of the extended key usage should be "Server Authentication".

The RFC 5280 [2] doesn't restrict any combination of values. The appropriate values for the Key usage extension for particular algorithms are specified in RFC 3279 [7], and other RFCs [2]. For the RSA algorithm, any combination of digitalSignature, nonRepudiation, keyEncipherment and dataEncipherment may be present in the key usage extension [7].

2.2.2 Tests and Results

Technically, the RSA algorithm needs the keyEncipherment value for enciphering the secret keys. Any other value is not needed for the RSA algorithm.

In this experiment, we tested how the web browsers reacted when they validated a certificate which conveyed an RSA public key and had a key usage value different from "keyEncipherment". The same results were obtained when the key usage was

Table 3. Key Usage Test

	IE7	FF3	OP9	X.509
KU=KA and EKU absent				I
KU=DE and EKU absent	A	W	R	I
KU=DE, KA and EKU absent				I
KU=KA and EKU=SA				I
KU=DE and EKU=SA	A	W	R	I
KU=DE, KA and EKU=SA				I
KU=KE and EKU absent				V
KU=KE,DE and EKU absent				V
KU=KE,KA and EKU absent	A	A	A	V
KU=KE,DE,KA and EKU absent				V
KU=KE and EKU=SA				V
KU=KE, DE and EKU=SA				V
KU=KE,KA and EKU=SA	A	A	A	V
KU=KE, DE, KA and EKU=SA				V
KU absent and EKU=CA	R	A	R	I
KU=KE and EKU=CA	R	A	R	I

Where: **KU:** Key Usage extension. **EKU:** Extended Key Usage extension
DE: dataEncipherment, **KE:** keyEncipherment, **KA:** keyAgreement, **CA:** ClientAuth,
SA: ServerAuth

critical or not, which is correct. We chose wrong values "keyAgreement" and "dataEncipherment" and the correct value "keyEncipherment" as test values for the key usage extension. The final column indicates whether the certificate is valid or invalid according to the standards.

2.2.3 Analysis of Results

Here, the diversity of the web browsers' behaviors is due to violations of the standards when the key usage and/or the extended key usage extension contain wrong values. Certain certificates which should have been treated as invalid were treated as acceptable by IE7 and FF3. OP9 behaved correctly in all the tests and rejected invalid certificates (without asking the user, who is not likely to know anyway). Specifically, IE7 accepted certificates when the key usage had wrong values of data encryption or key agreement instead of key encipherment, and FF3 when the extended key usage had the wrong value of client authentication instead of server authentication. Although not shown in the table, the previous version of Firefox 2 behaves correctly and blocks these accesses. We are not convinced that FF3's behavior in the first six test cases, by asking the user if they wish to use a certificate with an unsuitable key usage value by adding an exception is very helpful, since this will invariably result in an invalid certificate being accepted.

2.2.4 Do EV Certificates Solve the Problem?

The guidelines of the extended validation certificate add new requirements about the presence of the key usage extension for the root certificate and the sub root certificate. For subscriber certificates, EV certificates should follow RFC 5280, so no new requirements are introduced here.

2.3 Revocation

The primary objective of revocation is to remove a non valid certificate from circulation as quickly as possible. This is usually done by asking the relying party to check the certificate's status before accepting it.

Certification authorities can revoke a certificate by either publishing its serial number in a Certificate Revocation List (CRL) that can be downloaded from a repository, or by running a specialized server that can be accessed by the Online Certificate Status Protocol (OCSP) [1]. CrlDistributionPoints *(CDP)* and AuthorityInfoAccess (AIA) extensions are used to hold the CRL and the OCSP indicators respectively in a certificate.

In general, most of the relying parties agreements [e.g. 3] state that relying parties are responsible for taking the risk of using revoked certificates. As a result, relying parties must be aware of the certificate's status before using it in a transaction.

2.3.1 What Do the Standards State about the CRL Distribution Points and Authority Info Access Extensions?

The X.509 standard states that the CDP extension can be, at the option of the certificate issuer, critical or not; but it recommends it to be non-critical for interoperability reasons. When it is a critical extension, the certificate-using systems shall not use the certificate without first retrieving and checking the certificate against the downloaded

CRL [6]. However, when the extension is not critical the certificate-using systems can use the certificate only if the revocation checking is not required by a local policy or it is accomplished by other means [6].

According to RFC 5280, the CDP and AIA extensions should be non-critical extensions, but it recommends supporting these extensions by the authorities and applications [2].

2.3.2 Tests and Results

In the first experiment, we show what are the supported approaches in each web browser and if it is automatically configured or not (Table 4).

Table 4. Supported Approaches

	IE7	FF3	OP9
CRL checking	Automatic	Manual	Automatic
OCSP checking	Automatic	Manual	Automatic

Where: Automatic means that the browser checks the certificate status automatically, and , Manual means that the browser needs to be configured in order to check the certificate status, but once configured checking can be automatic.

In the second experiment (Table 5), we show the reaction of web browsers when the OCSP server is down and checking is automatic.

Table 5. OCSP Server is Down

	IE7	FF2	FF3	OP9
OCSP server is down	A	R	A/R configurable	A

In the third experiment (Table 6), we test the reaction of web browsers when they encounter a certificate signed by an unknown authority.

Table 6. Unknown Authority

Not trusted authority	IE7	FF3	OP9
	W	W	W

Table 7. Certificate is on CRL

	IE7	FF3	OP9
CRL retrieved	R	R	R
CRL not retrieved	A	A	A and degrade

In the fourth experiment (Table 7) we test what happens when we put the certificate serial number on a CRL which is pointed to from a CDP extension, when the CRL can and cannot be retrieved by the browser.

2.3.3 Analysis of Results

The heterogeneity of revocation processes comes from the different implementation efforts by the web browser manufacturers.

Maintaining a revocation service (either CRLs or OCSP) is a requirement for CAs. The standards [2][6] also recommend, but do not mandate, that relying parties ensure that the certificates are not revoked before they rely on them.. However, when the AIA and CDP extensions are present and understood, the relying parties are required to process them. X.509 states about the CDP extension "a certificate-using system shall not use the certificate without first retrieving and checking a CRL from one of the nominated distribution points" Therefore browsers should not ignore these extensions and they should fetch the revocation information and check it before accepting a certificate.

There is some ambiguity over what should happen when a CA says it maintains an OCSP service but does not. RFC 2560 [1] states "the OCSP client suspends acceptance of the certificate in question until the responder provides a response" and "In the event such a connection cannot be obtained, certificate-using systems could implement CRL processing logic as a fall-back position". Thus in the second experiment (Table 5), the responses provided by IE7 and OP9 are not compliant to the standard. Only FF2 and FF3 reject the certificate, although the latest version allows users to configure the browser to accept them. If the browsers cannot fetch the CRL information, then Table 7 shows that none of the browsers are fully conformant as none of them block access, although OP9 removes the padlock icon and asks the user not to send sensitive information.

We conclude that the implementation of the verification mechanisms by the web browsers is weak to say the least, and may allow a relying party to use a revoked certificate without being aware of this:

- Not all web browsers support the automatic verification of certificate status (Table 4)
- When an OCSP server is down the behavior of the browsers is generally not safe (Table 5).
- FF3 updates the CRL list according to the *next update* field of the CRL list. But in reality, nothing prevents a CA from publishing an updated CRL list before the time indicated in this field.
- The relying party may establish a SSL connection with a site without verifying its certificate status and without authenticating the server (Table 6).
- If CRLs are not available the browsers will continue to use the certificate even though they may have been revoked (Table 7).

2.3.4 What Do EV Certificates Say about the Problem?

The guidelines of the EV certificate ask the root authorities to maintain an online 24x7 repository mechanism whereby Internet browsers can automatically check online the current status of all certificates. Conforming CAs must issue a certificate with either the CDP extension or the AIA extension. However, the guidelines prohibit the CAs from marking these extensions as critical. S

3 Discussion

Sometimes the web browser informs the user of an error in the certificate and asks him/her to take a decision to accept or refuse a connection with the web server, whilst other times the web browser just prohibits the user from accessing the web server or makes the connection immediately even though the certificate is (potentially) invalid. Why are there these conflicting behaviors? Which is the best one? The standards don't answer these questions as they only consider whether a certificate is valid or not. The relying party must make the decision [6] what to do next, but the relying party is sometimes the browser acting on behalf of the user, and sometimes it is the user himself.

Certificate processing should be divided into 2 steps: the validation process (VP) and the decision process (DP). The VP consists of validating the information in a certificate. Most of this processing requires a computer system (e.g. checking a digital signature), some of it requires a human being (e.g. deciding which CA to trust). When the VP process is finished, the DP can choose to accept or not the server's certificate and then make a secure connection, an insecure connection or no connection at all with the server. The latter decision can be based on the certificate's validity and other information (such as failure to get revocation information). However, today, if the browser decides the certificate is valid, it automatically makes the connection without asking the user to decide. If the browser decides the certificate is invalid, then it may decide to send a warning message to the user, and let the user performs the DP, or it may prohibit the user from accessing the web server, and perform the DP itself on behalf of the user. Worse still, occasionally the browser makes the connection automatically using a certificate which it incorrectly decided was valid, without telling the user about this, so that it is opening the user up to potential harm.

If the browser manufacturers had considered the role of the relying party (RP) as two sub-roles, one for the DP and the second for the VP, their behavior could have been more consistent. If a human user performs the DP role and the browser performs the VP role, then the browser cannot either refuse to make a connection or automatically make a connection. The downside of this is that users may get bored with making these decisions and hence always make the connection regardless. If however the browser performs both roles (DP and VP), then the three sets of responses that we see today are possible, and not all browsers will behave in the same way.

4 Conclusions

Which web browser processes SSL certificates in a standardized way? Our experiments have shown that each browser has some non-conformant features. Although the browser implementations were mostly compliant with the standards, occasionally the standards were ambiguous and subject to multiple interpretations which may explain some of the conflicting browser behaviors. Our study was based on an experimental approach to identifying the non-standard behavior and clarifying the ambiguities in the standards.

The solution to these problems is twofold. Firstly, promoting and clarifying the standards, and secondly, ensuring the web browsers are compliant to these standards. A third approach may be to let the users decide when and if to connect to a web server after the browser informs them of the status of a certificate. Our experiments have led to a defect report on the X.509 standard that has been balloted and accepted. Also our studies show the need for acceptance testing tools to ensure the conformity of web browsers to the standards.

References

1. Myers, M., Ankney, R., Malpani, A., Galperin, S., Adams, C.: X.509 Internet Public Key Infrastructure: Online Certificate Status Protocol – OCSP, RFC 2560 (1999)
2. Cooper, NIST, Santesson, Microsoft, Farrell, Trinity College Dublin, Boeyen, Entrust, Housley, Vigil Security, Polk: Internet X.509 Public Key Infrastructure Certificate and Certificate Revocation List (CRL) Profile, RFC 5280 (May 2008)
3. THAWTE Certification Practice Statement,
   http://www.thawte.com/en/guides/pdf/Thawte_CPS_2_1.pdf
4. Berbecaru, D., Antonio, L., Marius, M.: On the Complexity of Public-Key Certificate Validation. In: Davida, G.I., Frankel, Y. (eds.) ISC 2001. LNCS, vol. 2200, p. 183. Springer, Heidelberg (2001)
5. CA/Browser forum guidelines for the issuance and management of extended validation certificates, http://www.cabforum.org/EV_Certificate_Guidelines.pdf
6. ITU-T Recommendation X.509 | ISO/IEC 9594-8: Information Technology—Open Systems Interconnection-The Directory: Public-Key and Attribute Certificate Frameworks
7. Polk, W., Housley, R., Bassham, L.: Algorithms and Identifiers for the Internet X.509 Public Key Infrastructure Certificate and Certificate Revocation List (CRL) Profile; RFC 3279 (April 2002)
8. Freier, A., Karlton, P., Kocher, P.: The SSL Protocol Version 3.0,
   http://wp.netscape.com/eng/ssl3/draft302.txt
9. Dierks, T., Rescorla, E.: The Transport Layer Security (TLS) Protocol Version 1.2. RFC 5246, IETF (August 2008)

Author Index

Abou El Kalam, Anas   176
Agarwala, Aditya   410

Balbiani, Philippe   176
Barrere, François   432
Benzekri, AbdelMalek   432
Benzmüller, Christoph   387
Biskup, Joachim   214
Blasco, Jorge   132
Blundo, Carlo   364
Brandstetter, Thomas   248
Brusò, Mayla   318

Chadwick, David W.   432
Cimato, Stelvio   364
Clarke, Nathan   1
Colantonio, Alessandro   259, 376
Cortesi, Agostino   318
Cotrina, Josep   87
Crispo, Bruno   342

Danidou, Yianna   399
Dawson, Ed   353
De Capitani di Vimercati, Sabrina   364
De Decker, Bart   237
De Santis, Alfredo   364
Di Pietro, Roberto   259, 376
Domingo, Neus   87

Farley, Ryan   39
Fernandez, Marcel   87
Foresti, Sara   364
Fuchs, Andreas   190
Fukushima, Kazuhide   119
Furnell, Steven   1

Garcia-Alfaro, Joaquin   164
Gritzalis, Dimitris   25
Groß, Stephan   421
Gueron, Shay   143
Gunter, Carl A.   119
Gupta, Puneet   202
Gürgens, Sigrid   190

Hernandez-Castro, Julio C.   132
Herzberg, Amir   13, 342

Iyer, Ravishankar   63

Jin, Hongxia   283
Johns, Christina   410

Kalbarczyk, Zbigniew   63
Karatzouni, Sevasti   1
Kernchen, Thomas   226
Kiyomoto, Shinsaku   119
Knorr, Konstantin   248
Kolter, Jan   226
Kostmajer, Gerald Stefan   76
Kuntze, Nicolai   152

Laborde, Romain   432
Lapon, Jorn   237
Leder, Felix S.   307
Leicher, Andreas   152
Leitold, Herbert   109
Lochner, Jan-Hendrik   214
Lotspiech, Jeffery   283

Mallios, Yannis   410
Martini, Peter   307
McCullagh, Adrian   353
Meichau, Markus   421
Miseldine, Philip   294
Modi, Sudeep   410
Molva, Refik   270, 330

Naessens, Vincent   237
Nakka, Nithin   63
Navarro-Arribas, Guillermo   164
Neyron, Pierre   51
Nussbaum, Lucas   51

Ocello, Alberto   259, 376
Önen, Melek   270
Orellana-Quiros, Miguel A.   132

Paraboschi, Stefano   364
Pattabiraman, Karthik   63
Pernul, Günther   226
Pham, Quan   353
Posch, Reinhard   109

Rahaman, Mohammad Ashiqur   294
Reid, Jason   353
Ribagorda, Arturo   132
Richard, Olivier   51
Rosenbaum, Ute   248
Rössler, Thomas   109
Roudier, Yves   294
Rudolph, Carsten   190

Samarati, Pierangela   364
Saxena, Amitabh   342
Schaad, Andreas   294
Schafer, Burkhard   399
Schmidt, Andreas U.   152
Seifert, Jean-Pierre   143
Shikfa, Abdullatif   270
Shin, Wook   119
Shulman, Haya   342
Sonntag, Sebastian   214
Soriano, Miguel   87
Sorniotti, Alessandro   330

Soupionis, Yannis   25
Steinbrecher, Sandra   421
Stögner, Herbert   76
Stoller, Scott D.   202

Tanaka, Toshiaki   119
Tapiador, Juan M.E.   132
Tountas, George   25

Uhl, Andreas   76

Verde, Nino Vincenzo   259, 376
Verhaeghe, Pieter   237
Verslype, Kristof   237

Wang, Xinyuan   39
Wazan, Ahmad Samer   432

Yao, Li   98

Zhang, Ning   98